Lecture Notes in Computer Science   6825

Commenced Publication in 1973
Founding and Former Series Editors:
Gerhard Goos, Juris Hartmanis, and Jan van Leeuwen

Pietro Liò   Giuseppe Nicosia
Thomas Stibor (Eds.)

Artificial
Immune Systems

10th International Conference, ICARIS 2011
Cambridge, UK, July 18-21, 2011
Proceedings

 Springer

Volume Editors

Pietro Liò
University of Cambridge, Computer Laboratory, William Gates Building
15 JJ Thomson Avenue, Cambridge CB3 0FD, UK
E-mail: pl219@cam.ac.uk

Giuseppe Nicosia
University of Catania, Department of Mathematics and Computer Science
Viale A. Doria, 6, 95125 Catania, Italy
E-mail: nicosia@dmi.unict.it

Thomas Stibor
Technische Universität München, Fakultät für Informatik
Boltzmannstraße 3, 85748 Garching, Germany
E-mail: thomas.stibor@in.tum.de

ISSN 0302-9743   e-ISSN 1611-3349
ISBN 978-3-642-22370-9   e-ISBN 978-3-642-22371-6
DOI 10.1007/978-3-642-22371-6
Springer Heidelberg Dordrecht London New York

Library of Congress Control Number: 2011931422

CR Subject Classification (1998): I.6, I.2, J.3, F.1, F.2, I.5

LNCS Sublibrary: SL 1 – Theoretical Computer Science and General Issues

Typesetting: Camera-ready by author, data conversion by Scientific Publishing Services, Chennai, India

Printed on acid-free paper

Springer is part of Springer Science+Business Media (www.springer.com)

Preface

The subject of artificial immune systems (AIS) is a maturing area of research that bridges the disciplines of immunology, computer science, and engineering. The scope of AIS ranges from modelling and simulation of the immune system through to immune-inspired algorithms and engineering solutions. In recent years, algorithms inspired by theoretical immunology have been applied to a wide variety of domains, including machine learning, computer security, fault tolerance, bioinformatics, data mining, optimization, and synthetic biology. Increasingly, theoretical insight into aspects of artificial and real immune systems has been sought through mathematical and computational modelling and analysis. This vigorous field of research investigates how immunology can assist our technology, and along the way is beginning to help biologists understand their unique problems.

AIS researchers are now forming their own community and identity. The International Conference on Artificial Immune Systems is proud to be the premier conference in the area. As its organizers, we were honored to have such a variety of innovative and original scientific papers presented this year.

ICARIS 2011 was the tenth international conference dedicated entirely to the field of AIS. It was held in the UK, at the prestigious University of Cambridge, during July 18–21, 2011.

With respect to the previous editions, ICARIS 2011 had some new and exciting features. For this edition we organized and managed two distinct Programme Committees: *Programme Committee for Computational Immunology and Immunoinformatics* and *Programme Committee for Immunological Computation, Immune-Inspired Engineering, Immune-Inspired Metaheuristics*, comprising 117 Programme Committee members and 12 external reviewers.

There were five plenary lectures by Arup Chakraborty, MIT, USA; Jonathan Jones, Sainsbury Laboratory, UK; Andrew Phillips, Microsoft Research Cambridge, UK; Rino Rappuoli, Novartis, Italy; and Jon Timmis, University of York, UK. Moreover, the Organizing Committee devoted several special sessions to the topic of "Immunoinformatics and Computational Immunology." Immunoinformatics is a new discipline that aims to apply computer science techniques to molecules, cells, and organs of the immune system and to use bioinformatics and systems biology tools for a better understanding of the immune functions.

We had more submissions than ever this year, and each manuscript was independently reviewed by at least four members of the Programme Committee in a blind review process. In these proceedings there are 36 papers written by leading scientists in the field, from 38 different countries in 5 continents, describing an impressive array of ideas, technologies, algorithms, methods, and applications for AIS.

We could not have organized this conference without these researchers, so we thank them all for coming. We also could not have organized ICARIS without the excellent work of all of the Programme Committee members, stream leaders, Publicity Chairs, and Organizing Committee members.

We would like to express our appreciation to the keynote and tutorial speakers who accepted our invitation, and to all authors who submitted research papers to ICARIS 2011.

July 2011

Pietro Liò
Giuseppe Nicosia
Thomas Stibor

Organization

ICARIS 2011 Committees

Conference Chairs

Pietro Liò   University of Cambridge, UK
Giuseppe Nicosia   University of Catania, Italy
Thomas Stibor   Technische Universität München, Germany

Stream Leaders

Immunoinformatics   Giuseppe Nicosia, University of Catania, Italy
Theory   Andy Hone, University of Kent, UK
Applications   Jon Timmis, University of York, UK

Publicity Chairs

Giuseppe Narzisi   New York University, USA
Mario Pavone   University of Catania, Italy
Giovanni Stracquadanio   Johns Hopkins University, USA

Organizing Committee

Claudio Angione   University of Catania, Italy
Piero Conca   University of York, UK
Jole Costanza   University of Catania, Italy
Anil Sorathiya   University of Cambridge, UK
Renato Umeton   MIT, USA
Luca Zammataro   University of Milan, Italy

Steering Committee

Peter Bentley   University College London, UK
Hugues Bersini   IRIDA, Belgium
Leandro de Castro   Mackenzie University, Brazil
Stephanie Forrest   University of New Mexico, USA
Emma Hart   Napier University, UK
Christian Jacob   University of Calgary, Canada
Doheon Lee   KAIST, Korea
Mark Neal   University of Wales, Aberystwyth, UK
Giuseppe Nicosia   University of Catania, Italy
Jon Timmis (Chair)   University of York, UK

Programme Committee for Immunoinformatics and Computational Immunology Stream

Colin C. Anderson	University of Alberta, Canada
Becca Asquith	Imperial College London, UK
Sergio Baranzini	University of California San Francisco, USA
Catherine Beauchemin	Ryerson University, Canada
Gennady Bocharov	Russian Academy of Sciences, Russia
Julie Magarian Blander	Mount Sinai School of Medicine, USA
Ulisses M. Braga-Neto	Texas A&M University, USA
Salvador E. Caoili	University of the Philippines Manila, Philippines
Gastone Castellani	University of Bologna, Italy
Franco Celada	New York University, USA
Chang-Zheng Chen	Stanford University, USA
Cliburn Chan	Duke University, USA
Tong Joo Chuan	Institute for Infocomm Research, Singapore
Hilary Clark	Genentech - Roche Group, USA
Francesco Colucci	University of Cambridge, UK
Anne DeGroot	University of Rhode Island, USA
David S. DeLuca	Dana-Farber Cancer Institute, Harvard University, USA
Omer Dushek	University of Oxford, UK
Darren Flower	Aston University, UK
Bruno Andre Gaeta	University of New South Wales, Australia
Fernand Hayot	Mount Sinai School of Medicine, USA
Yongqun He	University of Michigan, USA
Uri Hershberg	University of Drexel, USA
John Iacomini	Harvard Medical School, Harvard University, USA
Mikhail Ivanchenko	University of Nizhniy Novgorod, Russia
Can Kesmir	Utrecht University, The Netherlands
Koichi S. Kobayashi	Harvard Medical School, Harvard University, USA
Klaus Ley	La Jolla Institute for Allergy & Immunology, USA
Fabio Luciani	University of New South Wales, Australia
Terry Lybrand	Vanderbilt University, USA
Yoram Louzoun	Bar Ilan University, Israel
Shev MacNamara	University of Oxford, UK
Ernesto Marques	University of Pittsburgh, USA
Steven Marsh	University College London, UK
Andrew Martin	University College London, UK
Piero Mastroeni	University of Cambridge, UK
Polly Matzinger	NIH, USA
Satoru Miyano	University of Tokyo, Japan
Carmen Molina-Paris	University of Leeds, UK
Simon Moon	Imperial College London, UK
German Nudelman	Mount Sinai School of Medicine, USA

Dimitri Perrin	Osaka University, Japan
Bjoern Peters	La Jolla Institute for Allergy & Immunology, USA
Nikolai Petrovskyv	Flinders University, Australia
Philippe Pierre	Centre d'Immunologie, University of Marseille, France
G.P.S. Raghava	Institute of Microbial Technology, India
Shoba Ranganathan	Macquarie University, Australia
Timothy Ravasi	University of California, San Diego, USA
Pedro A. Reche	Universidad Complutense de Madrid, Spain
Christian Schönbach	Kyushu Institute of Technology, Japan
Alessandro Sette	La Jolla Institute for Allergy & Immunology, USA
Johannes Sollner	Emergentec Biodevelopment GmbH, Austria
Derek Smith	University of Cambridge, UK
Daron Standley	Osaka University, Japan
Stefan Stevanovic	University of Tübingen, Germany
Stephen Taylor	University of Oxford, UK
Rajat Varma	NIH, USA
Elena Vigorito	Babraham Institute and University of Cambridge, UK
Gur Yaari	Yale University, USA
Luca Zammataro	University of Milan, Italy
Guanglan Zhang	Dana-Farber Cancer Institute, Harvard University, USA

Programme Committee for Immunological Computation, Immune-Inspired Engineering, Immune-Inspired Metaheuristics Stream

Uwe Aickelin	Nottingham University, UK
Paul Andrews	University of York, UK
Bruno Apolloni	University of Milan, Italy
Roberto Battiti	University of Trento, Italy
Peter Bentley	University College London, UK
Tadeusz Burczynski	Cracow University of Technology, Poland
Carlos Coello Coello	CINVESTAV-IPN, Mexico
Piero Conca	University of York, UK
Ernesto Costa	University of Coimbra, Portugal
Paulo J. Costa Branco	Universidade Tecnica de Lisboa, Portugal
Vincenzo Cutello	University of Catania, Italy
Dipankar Dasgupta	University of Memphis, USA
Leandro de Castro	Mackenzie University, Brazil
Matteo De Felice	University of Rome "Roma Tre", Italy
Benjamin Doerr	Max-Planck-Institut für Informatik, Germany
Marco Dorigo	Université Libre de Bruxelles, Belgium

Fernando Esponda	University of New Mexico, USA
Stephanie Forrest	University of New Mexico, USA
Simon Garrett	Aispire Ltd., UK
Masoud Ghaffari	GE Aviation, USA
Maoguo Gong	Xidian University, China
Julie Greensmith	University of Nottingham, UK
Walter Gutjahr	University of Vienna, Austria
Emma Hart	Napier University, UK
Andy Hone	University of Kent, UK
Christian Jacob	University of Calgary, Canada
Thomas Jansen	University College Cork, Ireland
Licheng Jiao	Xidian University, China
Colin Johnson	University of Kent, UK
Natalio Krasnogor	University of Nottingham, UK
Henry Lau	University of Hong Kong, China
Doheon Lee	KAIST, Korea
Jiming Liu	Hong Kong Baptist University, Hong Kong
Chris McEwan	Napier University, UK
Giuseppe Narzisi	New York University, USA
Frank Neumann	Max-Planck-Institut für Informatik, Germany
Mark Neal	University of Wales, Aberystwyth, UK
Peter Oliveto	University of Birmingham, UK
Elisa Pappalardo	University of Catania, Italy and University of Florida, USA
Mario Pavone	University of Catania, Italy
Richard E. Overill	King's College London, UK
Andrea Roli	University of Bologna, Italy
Peter Ross	Napier University, UK
Sven Schaust	G.W. Leibniz Universität Hannover, Germany
Susan Stepney	University of York, UK
Giovanni Stracquadanio	John Hopkins University, USA
Dirk Sudholt	University of Birmingham, UK
Alexander Tarakanov	St. Petersburg Institute, Russia
Johannes Textor	University of Lübeck, Germany
Jon Timmis	University of York, UK
Andy Tyrrell	University of York, UK
Renato Umeton	MIT, USA
Fernando J. Von Zuben	State University of Campinas, Brazil
Stefan Voss	University of Hamburg, Germany
Carsten Witt	Technical University of Denmark, Denmark
Christine Zarges	Technical University of Dortmund, Germany

Keynote and Tutorial Speakers

Arup Chakraborty	MIT, USA
Jonathan Jones	Sainsbury Laboratory, UK
Andrew Phillips	Microsoft Research Cambridge, UK
Rino Rappuoli	Novartis, Italy
Jon Timmis	University of York, UK

Sponsoring Institutions

University of Cambridge, Computer Laboratory, UK
Tao Science Research Center, Italy

Table of Contents

Part II: Theory of Immunological Computation

Part III: Applied Immunological Computation

The Value of Inflammatory Signals in Adaptive Immune Responses

Soumya Banerjee[1], Drew Levin[1], Melanie Moses[1], Frederick Koster[2], and Stephanie Forrest[1]

[1] Department of Computer Science, University of New Mexico, USA
[2] Department of Pathology, University of New Mexico, USA

Abstract. Cells of the immune system search among billions of healthy cells to find and neutralize a small number of infected cells before pathogens replicate to sufficient numbers to cause disease or death. The immune system uses information signals to accomplish this search quickly. Ordinary differential equations and spatially explicit agent-based models are used to quantify how capillary inflammation decreases the time it takes for cytotoxic T lymphocytes to find and kill infected cells. We find that the inflammation signal localized in a small region of infected tissue dramatically reduces search times, suggesting that these signals play an important role in the immune response, especially in larger animals.

1 Introduction

Rapid search is crucial for an effective immune response: Immune system cells must find, identify and neutralize pathogens before those pathogens replicate in sufficient numbers to cause disease or death. The adaptive immune system has a small number of pathogen-specific cells that must search for and neutralize a small number of initially localized pathogens in a very large tissue space. We investigate how inflammatory signals accelerate this search.

The adaptive immune response must conduct two "searches" to neutralize pathogens. First, recirculating antigen-specific T and B cell precursors must interact with antigen-loaded dendritic cells, and the architecture of the lymph node facilitates this interaction [1,2,3]. The second search is T cells activated in the lymph node efficiently finding and neutralizing infected cells in tissue with the help of inflammatory signals. In this paper we analyze these two searches in response to influenza infection in the lung.

CTLs are activated within the infected site LN and are released into the bloodstream where they travel through a branching network of arteries until they reach a capillary in the lung. Capillaries in infected regions of the lung are permeated by an inflammatory signal which causes CTLs to exit the capillary and enter the lung tissue, where a chemokine gradient guides the CTL to infected cells. When CTLs recognize the antigen displayed on the surface of infected cells, they neutralize those cells. The information represented by the inflammatory signals is local, and occurs in an initially small region of the lung

P. Liò, G. Nicosia, and T. Stibor (Eds.): ICARIS 2011, LNCS 6825, pp. 1–14, 2011.

surface, possibly as small as a few mm^2 in a 100 m^2 surface area in a human lung
[17]. We ask how much the local inflammatory signal reduces the time for CTLs
to find the site of infection and eradicate the influenza pathogen. Without an
inflammation signal indicating which capillaries are near infected tissue, CTLs
would have to exit capillaries in random locations and begin a slow random walk
(at speeds measured in microns per minute) through the large area of lung tissue
to search for the site of infection. With the inflammatory signal, CTLs can exit
the relatively fast flow of the circulatory network only when they are in close
proximity to infected cells.

In this paper we describe two sets of models. The first (null) model predicts
how long it would take for CTLs to find infected cells by searching via a random
walk through the entire lung tissue. The second set of models are simplified
representations of how inflammatory signals guide CTL search in real immune
systems. This second set of models is parametrized from experimental data.
By comparing predictions of the null model to the more realistic model with
inflammation, we estimate how much the inflammatory signal reduces the time
for CTLs to find and eradicate influenza.

We use ordinary differential equation (ODE) and agent-based models (ABM)
to quantify the value of the inflammatory signal, measured as the decrease in
the time it takes for CTLs to both find and eradicate virus from the lung. The
ABM incorporates the spatial aspect of virus spread and CTL mediated killing
of infected cells, and the ODE model can scale up to realistic cell population
sizes. In both cases, we first model an immune response without inflammatory
signals where CTLs exit to tissue at the first capillary they encounter and search
by random walks until they find a chemokine gradient that guides them to
the infected cells. Second, we model an immune response with inflammatory
signals where CTLs exit to tissue only when the capillary has an inflammatory
signal. If there is no signal, CTLs recirculate through the cardiovascular network
until they find an inflamed capillary. We suggest that localized signals like the
inflammatory signal are enormously important to immune function. Here we
take a first step toward quantifying the value of that signal in terms of time
required to get T cells to sites of infection and to control influenza infection. This
has important consequences for understanding the role of information signals in
immune systems more generally, and also the role that local information signals
can play in other complex biological systems [11,12] and in artificial immune
systems where decentralized search requires effective use of local signals to solve
computational problems [2,3].

The remainder of the paper reviews relevant features of the immune system (Section 2), outlines our hypotheses (Section 2), and describes the models
(Sections 4 and 5). Section 4 presents the ODE model and compares its predictions to empirical data. Section 5 uses the ABM to verify some of the ODE
predictions and produce more realisitic spatially explicit simulations, including
pathogen spread during the CTL search. We conclude by quantifying how much
inflammatory signals improve immune response in these models.

2 A Review of the Relevant Immunology

This study characterizes how a key type of adaptive immune cells (cytotoxic T lymphocytes, also called $CD8^+$ T cells or CTLs) [6] search for and neutralize a common respiratory tract pathogen (influenza) in the principal target organ, the lung (Fig. 1). Among the many immune cells and molecules involved in providing defense against influenza [14], there is a complex set of interactions to guide CTLs to the site of infection and to produce chemokines and other information signals to help contain the infection. We simplify the array of chemokines with a single signal that causes inflammation and attracts CTLs to site of infection.

Infection begins when influenza virus is inhaled into the lung. It enters epithelial cells lining the airways and the air sacs (alveoli) of the lung. Epithelial cells initiate the first line of innate immune defense through the activation of interferon and the secretion of chemokines to attract inflammatory cells such as macrophages [10]. Inflammation increases local blood flow to the infected region and amplifies the chemokine signal. To initiate the adaptive immune response, resident lung dendritic cells capture virus and carry it to the draining lymph nodes (LN). LNs provide a dense tissue in which T and B lymphocytes and antigen-loaded dendritic cells encounter each other efficiently. Antigen-specific CTLs are activated within the LN, undergo cell division, and leave the LN to enter the blood circulation. We focus on the response of cytotoxic T lymphocytes (CTLs) because recovery from influenza pneumonia in wildtype mice has been shown to require neutralization of infected cells by CTLs [8].

The cardiovascular network in the lung follows the fractal branching of the airways.The branching arterioles end in a capillary network which nourishes the airsacs (alveoli) of the lung. The capillary density in mouse lung is approximately $5000/cm^2$ (estimated from [17]). The surface area of a mouse lung is approximately $100 cm^2$ giving 500,000 capillaries in the mouse lung. Capillary density decreases as $M^{-1/4}$ where M is organism body mass [18,17] and since humans are 10,000 times larger than mice, the capillary density in a human lung is $500/cm^2$. The surface area of a human lung is approximately $100m^2$ and hence the number of capillaries in a human lung is approximately $5 \cdot 10^8$.

The CTL flow through the arterial network without any signal to guide them to the tiny fraction of capillaries near the initial infection. If an activated CTL reaches an inflamed capillary, it exits the capillary into lung interstitial tissue. The tissue surrounding inflamed capillaries also contains a chemokine gradient which the CTL follows to locate infected epithelial cells and reduce viral replication. The chemotactic signals are composed of cytokines and chemokines which provide a region of attraction larger than that provided by antigen and infected cells. If an activated CTL reaches an uninflamed capillary, it may wander short distances through the capillary network. If it still does not encounter an inflammatory signal, it recirculates through the blood and eventually returns to another capillary in the lung. The recirculation time for mice is 6 seconds and 60 seconds for humans [13].

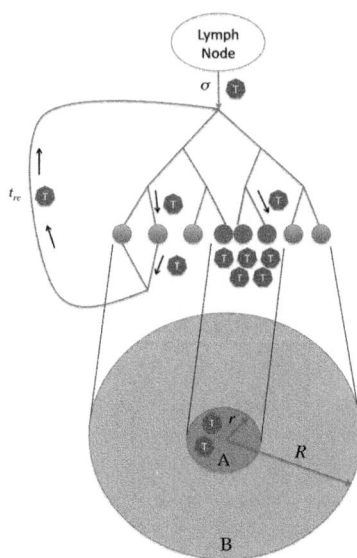

Fig. 1. A region (A of radius r) of infected tissue, chemokines and inflammatory signals, surrounded by region B which does not have any infected cells, inflammation or chemokines. CTLs (green hexagons) leave the LN at rate σ and travel through the branching arteries to capillaries. If capillaries are inflamed (in region A) CTLs exit capillaries and search for infected cells (small red circles) in lung tissue. If the capillaries are not inflamed (in region B) the CTLs recirculate.

3   Goals and Hypotheses

Inflammatory signals and chemotactic gradients are examples of signals that serve to guide search processes in the adaptive immune system. We hypothesize that these and other signals enable the activated immune cells to find and neutralize pathogens more quickly than in the absence of such signals. More specifically, we aim to quantify the benefit provided by the inflammation in the capillaries, which allows circulating CTLs to know that they have reached a site of infection.

We examine a hypothetical immune response without inflammatory signals (CTLs searching for infected tissue by randomly walking through lung tissue) and a more realistic immune response with inflammatory signals (CTLs recirculate through the arterial network until the presence of inflammation signals them to exit near infected tissue). We study how long it takes for the first CTL to find the infected region, how quickly CTLs accumulate in infected tissue, and how many epithelial cells become infected in a specified time period. We quantify the value of the information signal as the ratio of these values with inflammatory signal to those values without the signal. We use ODE and ABM to estimate the value of the inflammation signal. The ODE can model large numbers of cells, so we use ODEs to compare the value of the inflammatory signal in mice and humans. We then use an agent based model to investigate the dynamics of infection growth and spatial interactions between cells in the mouse.

4   Ordinary Differential Equation Model

In this section we analyze how quickly CTLs arrive at the site of infection with and without an inflamation signal using an ODE model. We represent the region of infection as a circular area (region A) of radius r of tissue expressing a general chemotactic signal. This region is surrounded by a region of uninfected tissue (a concentric circle of radius R (region B)) without inflammation or chemokines.

Any activated CTLs that flow to capillaries in region A will have an inflammatory signal that causes the CTL to exit the capillary and a chemokine gradient that will direct those CTLs to infected cells. In contrast, CTLs that arrive in the lung via capillaries in region B will have no inflammatory signal and no chemokines to guide them to the infected cells in region A. We assume that CTLs that exit into tissue do not go back into circulation.

There are several simplifying assumptions in the ODE model. It ignores viral replication and assumes that the infected region A is a fixed size. It also ignores the movement of CTLs inside capillaries, and instead assumes that CTLs either immediately sense inflammation and exit into tissue or immediately recirculate. The model also ignores CTL death in the lung.

The dynamics of the system are represented by coupled ODEs. We parameterize the ODEs to consider two cases. In the first case, CTLs search for virus using only the random walk (null model). In the second case, CTLs in region A receive an inflammation signal that allows them to exit and follow the chemotactic gradient, while CTLs in region B continue to recirculate through the lymph system until they find an inflamed capillary in region A as in Fig. 1.

4.1   ODE Model 1: CTL Search without an Inflammation Signal

In this scenario there is no signal to direct CTLs to an infected region, therefore CTLs always exit into tissue as soon as they reach a capillary. The capillaries are assumed to be uniformly distributed througout the lung, and a single activated lymph node is assumed to produce activated CTLS at a fixed rate of σ CTLs per hour. The infection is in a region of constant radius r, and the lung surface is a circle of radius R. The time taken for CTLs to circulate through the lymph system is denoted by t_{rc}. The combined system is represented by the following differential equations:

$$\frac{dN_c}{dt} = \sigma - \frac{N_c}{t_{rc}} \tag{1}$$

$$\frac{dN_w}{dt} = \frac{(R^2 - r^2) \cdot N_c}{R^2 \cdot t_{rc}} - \frac{D \cdot N_w}{\pi((2/3(R-r)+r)^2 - r^2)} \tag{2}$$

$$\frac{dN_f}{dt} = \frac{r^2 \cdot N_c}{R^2 \cdot t_{rc}} + \frac{D \cdot N_w}{\pi((2/3(R-r)+r)^2 - r^2)} \tag{3}$$

Equation (1) describes the change in the number of recirculating activated CTLs in the cardiovascular system (N_c) due to the rate of production of new CTLs in the LN (σ) and time it takes CTLs to travel to the capilaries (t_{rc}). Since the relevant time step in this setting is the minimum time taken for CTLs to complete one circuit through the arterial and venous circulation system (the recirculation time t_{rc}) and is different from the simulation time step (dt), all rate constants are divided by t_{rc}.

Equation (2) describes the change in the number of CTLs (N_w) that are doing a random walk in tissue and searching for infected cells. The change in N_w is due to the rate at which CTLs exit into region B from circulation (a fraction of $\frac{N_c}{t_{rc}}$) and the rate at which these searching CTLs find region A. The fraction of circulating CTLs that enter capillaries in region B is given by the relative area of region B ($\frac{R^2-r^2}{R^2}$). The rate at which CTLs find region A is calculated as follows: an average CTL in region B will be at a distance 2/3 from the periphery of region A (obtained by integrating over all CTLs at each distance in region B). The mean area that this CTL will cover before reaching region A is given by the quantity $\pi((2/3(R-r)+r)^2 - r^2)$, and the mean time in which this area is covered is this quantity divided by the diffusion constant for random walk (D), again adjusted for the recirculation time. The reciprocal of this time gives the rate at which a single CTL enters region A. To complete the analysis we multiply this quantity by the number of searching CTLs. Finally, Equation (3) describes the change in the number of CTLs (N_f) that have found infected cells (in region A). This is composed of the searching CTLs from Equation (2) that find the infected region and the fraction of the recirculating CTLs from Equation (1) that enter capillaries in region A (represented by the area of region A relative to the total lung area). We use the model to study the arrival of CTLs at the site of infection, first in the mouse lung and then in the human lung.

In order to numerically integrate Equations (1)-(3) we first estimate the diffusion rate of CTLs. Since we are not aware of any published values for diffusion rates of activated CTLs within tissue, we used measured mean square displacements of T cells within the LN [4]. Following Beauchemin et al. [4], the equation relating mean square displacement of a random walking particle in two dimensions at time t is given by $\mid m \mid= \sqrt{4Dt}\frac{\Gamma(\frac{3}{2})}{\Gamma(\frac{1}{2})}$ where $\mid m \mid$ is the mean square displacement, D is the diffusion constant and Γ is the gamma function. We estimated D as $56(\mu m)^2/h$ in the LN [4], and we use this value to characterize the random walk in lung tissue.

We estimate the parameter σ from experimental data (detailed in the next section) as 864 activated CTLs per hour, and the time to recirculate (t_{rc}) is 6 seconds [5]. The area of infection has a radius (r) of 1 mm (personal observation for seasonal strains in mice) and the total lung surface is represented by a circle with a radius of 10 cm (R) [17].

The model shows that there is a steady state of approximately 2 circulating activated CTL. So few CTLs are in circulation because they exit the LN approximately 1 every 4 seconds and spend only 6 seconds in blood before immediately exiting the blood to search in the lung. We numerically simulated the ODE system and found that the time for the first CTL to reach the site of infection (region A) is approximately 12 hours post activation in the LN (Fig. 2, Panel A). Approximately 10 CTLs find the infected region at day 5 post activation.

Next we use ODE Model 1 to predict how quickly CTLs arrive at the infected site in a human. Human body mass is approximately 10,000 times larger than a mouse. Human lungs are a corresponding 10,000 times greater area, so R becomes 10 meters [17]. We assume that the initial area of infection r remains the same 1mm^2. CTL recirculation time (t_{rc}) increases to 60 seconds [5].

In order to calculate the rate of CTL production from LN (σ) we scale the (σ) estimated for mice by a factor of $M^{3/7}$ following [3]. This scaling assumes that LNs in larger animals are larger and have more high endothelial venules to release activated CTLs at a faster rate. From this we estimate σ as approximately 45000 CTLs per hour. Numerically simulating the ODE system, we predict the time for a CTL to find an infected cell in a human lung as approximately 90 days, which is much longer than the actual time taken to resolve influenza infections (approximately 10 days) [8].

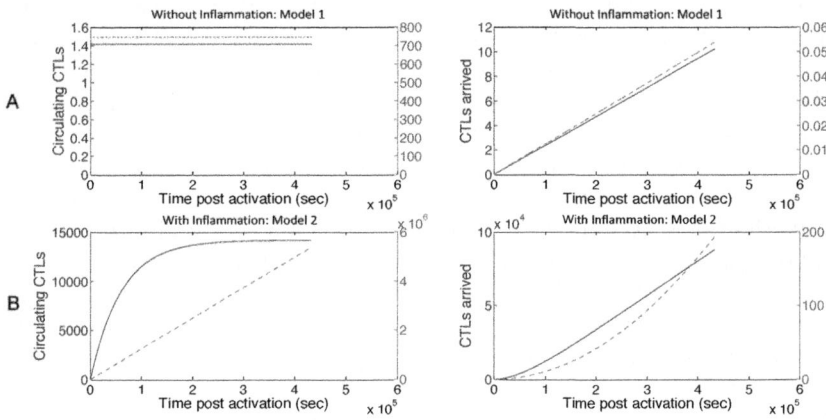

Fig. 2. Row A: The number of circulating CTLs (N_c) and CTLs that have arrived at the site of infection(N_f) vs. time post activation of the first CTL in LN for CTLs %walking searching without an inflammatory signal (ODE Model 1) for mice (blue, left axis) and humans (green dotted, right axis). The number of recirculating CTLs reaches a steady state because once they enter the lung they never recirculate. Row B: N_c and N_f vs. time post activation for CTLs circulating in the presence of inflammatory signals (ODE Model 2 fit to experimental data) for mice (blue, left axis) and humans (green dotted, right axis). Note the difference in y-axis scale between the two rows.

4.2   ODE Model 2: CTL Search with an Inflammatory Signal

Here we model an immune response with inflammatory signals. CTLs exit capillaries and enter lung tissue only when there is an inflammatory signal in the capillary. All other parameters are identical to ODE Model 1. The system is represented by the following differential equations:

$$\frac{dN_c}{dt} = \sigma - \frac{r^2 \cdot N_c}{R^2 \cdot t_{rc}} \tag{4}$$

$$\frac{dN_f}{dt} = \frac{r^2 \cdot N_c}{R^2 \cdot t_{rc}} \tag{5}$$

Equation (4) describes the change in the number of circulating activated CTLs circulating in the cardiovascular system (N_c). (N_c) changes due to the addition of new CTLs from the LN at rate (σ), and the loss of CTLs from circulation that exit capillaries expressing inflammatory signals and enter infected tissue (region A). Equation (5) describes the increase in the number of CTLs that find infected cells. This is the same as the loss term from the pool of recirculating CTLs from Equation (4).

We fit Model 2 to experimental numbers of CTLs in lung at various time points post infection for influenza in mice [8]. The fitting procedure found free parameters that minimized the mean squared error between the model and the data. We only considered data up to the peak of CTL activation and did not consider the decline of CTLs after the infection is cleared.

Model 2 (Equations 4 and 5) was solved numerically using Berkeley Madonna [7]. The curve fitter option in Berkeley Madonna (Runge-Kutta 4, step size = 0.0004 sec) was used to establish the best-fit parameter estimates. The curve-fitting method uses nonlinear least-squares regression that minimizes the sum of the squared residuals between the experimental and predicted values of N_f.

Next we compared model output for mice and humans. For mice, we fixed r to 1 mm, R to 10 cm, and the recirculation time (t_{rc}) to 6 seconds. We then estimated the LN rate of output of CTLs (σ). The best fit estimate for σ was approximately 864 activated CTLs per hour. Model output is shown in Fig. 2 Panel B (a list of all ODE model parameters is given in Table 1). Numerically simulating the ODE system, we estimated the time taken for the first CTL to reach infected tissue to be approximately 15 minutes (Fig. 2 Panel B). Approximately 80000 CTLs find the infected region at day 5 post activation. We modeled CTL search in the human lung using the same values as in ODE Model 1 ($R = 10$ meters, $t_{rc} = 60$ seconds and $\sigma = 45000$ CTLs per hour) and numerically simulated the ODE system. The predicted time for an activated CTL to discover an infected cell in a human lung is approximately 8 hours, and the number of CTLs that reach the lung by 5 days post activation in the LN is approximately 190.

In summary, the presence of an inflammatory signal and a chemokine gradient around infected cells results in a earlier first discovery of infection by activated CTLs in both mice and humans. In mice, the first CTL with inflammation arrives in 15 minutes compared to 12 hours without it, a 48-fold speedup. The inflammation signal reduces search time in humans more than in mice: The first CTL with inflammation arrives in 8 hours compared to 90 days without it, a nearly 270-fold speedup.

Table 1. The parameters used in the ODE and ABM for mice with a short description of their role and default value ([§] measured in human cell lines)

Description	Value	Source
Release rate of activated CTLs (σ)	864/h	Fit to data in [8]
CTL recirculation time (t_{rc})	6 s	[13]
CTL diffusion coefficient (D)	$56(\mu m)^2/h$	Calculated from [4]
Radius of lung area (R)	10cm	[17]
Radius of circle lung infected area (r)	0.1cm	Personal observation
Length of cubic ABM simulation compartment	$2000\mu m$	Model parameter
Time between infection and secretion [§]	10.5h	[9]
Duration of productive infection [§]	17.15h	[9]
ABM virus secretion rate [§]	2.6 $virions/h$	[9]
ABM CTL sensing radius	$10\mu m$	Model parameter
ABM Epithelial cell diameter	$10\mu m$	Model parameter
ABM CTL diameter	$4\mu m$	Model parameter

Fig. 3. A snapshot of the CyCells ABM in action. The epithelial cell layer is made up of healthy cells (dark red), infected incubating cells (green), virus expressing cells (blue), and dead cells (yellow). The area of lighter red surrounding the infection shows that free virus particles (semi-transparent white) are present. T-cells (pink) are seen swarming over locations with high virus concentration.

5   Agent Based Model

The ABM extends the earlier results to consider spatial and stochastic effects of CTL migration and recirculation, also incorporating infection spread and CTL mediated killing of infected cells. The CyCells [16,15] modeling tool explicitly represents healthy cells, infected cells, and CTLs, and represents cytokines, chemokines, and virus as concentrations. We model the release of virions from infected cells, diffusion of chemokines and inflamatory signals, and chemotaxis of CTLs up a chemokine gradient. A screenshot of the graphical representation is shown in Fig. 3.

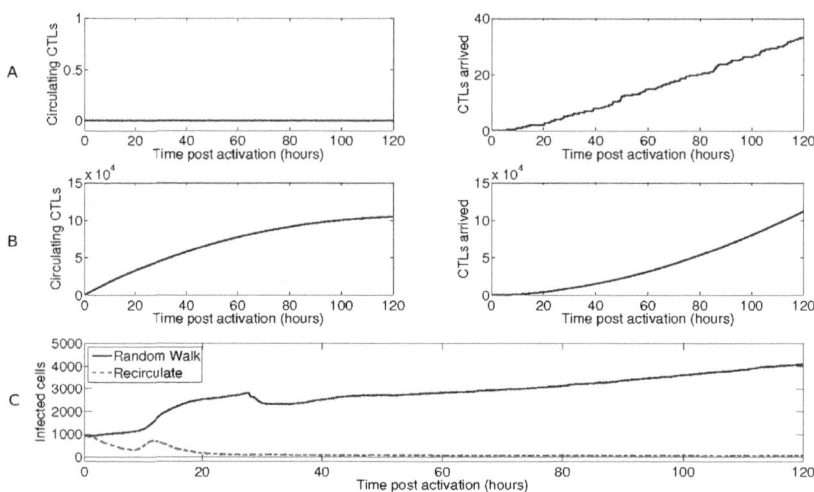

Fig. 4. Panel A: Plot of the number of recirculating CTLs (N_c) and CTLs that have found infected cells (N_f) vs. time post activation for CTLs only walking randomly (ABM 1). Panel B: Plot of N_c and N_f vs. time for CTLs only recirculating (ABM 2). Panel C: Plot of the number of infected cells over time for ABM 1 and ABM 2. The population bumps in Panel C during the first day post activation are an artifact of the model initialization scheme and do not affect the final results.

5.1   ABM Model 1: Dynamics without Inflammation

We start by modelling a $2mm$ by $2mm$ grid with an area of infection that represents five days of growth in the absence of a secondary immune response. After five days, specific CTLs become activated and enter the grid at a random location at $\sigma = 864/hour$, scaled down to adjust for the $4mm^2$ subset of the $10cm \times 10cm$ area of the mouse lung. In ABM Model 1, there is no inflammatory signal, so CTLs that enter the grid immediately exit the capillary and begin a random walk through lung tissue. Infected cells produce virions which then infect healthy cells. Virus infected cells are differentiated into two populations: infected cells that are incubating but not secreting virus, and expressing cells that are actively producing new virions. The parameters describing rate of infection of healthy cells are taken from a previous study [9] (summarized in Table 1). Our primary results comparing system dynamics with and without inflammation signals do not depend on these parameters.

The time taken for the first CTL to detect an infected cell is 90 minutes. 33 CTLs find the infection five days post activation (Fig. 4 Panel A). There are 4,077 infected cells five days post activation.

5.2 ABM Model 2: Dynamics with Inflammation and CTL Recirculation

Next we study an immune response with inflammatory signals. We simulated an influenza infection using the same parameters as ABM 1, but allowed CTLs to recirculate until they encountered an inflammation signal. We evaluate the value of the inflammatory signal by comparing the results of ABM 1 and ABM 2.

The time taken for the first CTL to find an infected cell is 3.3 minutes. The number of CTLs which find infected cells in 5 days is 111,572 compared to 33 in ABM 1 (Fig. 4 Panel C). The number of infected cells remaining in the simulation is much lower for ABM 2 (46.7) compared to ABM 1 (4,077). Hence the value of the inflammation signal is a reduction in the number of infected cells at day 5 (from approximately 4,077 without an inflammatory signal to approximately 47 with the signal).

Table 2. The effect of inflammation on the time taken by CTLs to first detect infection, the number of CTLs that arrive in the infected region by day 5 post activation and the number of infected cells in the simulated lung tissue by day 5 post activation. ABM means and standard deviations are from three independent runs of each ABM.

Mice		Without Inflammation	With Inflammation	Benefit of Inflammation
Time to first detection	ODE	12 hr	15 min	48
	ABM	90 min ± 31.3 min	3.3 min ± 1.9 min	27
Arrived CTLs	ODE	10	80,000	8,000
	ABM	33 ± 4.6	111,572 ± 1,536	3,380
Infected cells	ODE	-	-	-
	ABM	4,077 ± 518	46.7 ± 4.7	87

Humans		Without Inflammation	With Inflammation	Benefit of Inflammation
Time to first detection	ODE	90 days	8 hr	270
Arrived CTLs [§]	ODE	0.05	190	3,800
Infected Cells [§]	ODE	-	-	-

6 Discussion

6.1 Summary of Results

In this study we used ODE and ABM models to quantify how much inflammation of infected tissue improves the adaptive immune response. This is measured in terms of three different values: how much the inflammatory signal speeds up the arrival of the first CTL at the site of infection; how much the inflammatory signal increases the number of CTLs that find the site of infection five days after CTL activation; and how much the inflammatory signal decreases the number of infected cells at five days after CTL activation. We used ODE and ABM models to quantify these improvements in mice and the results are summarized in Table 2. The speed up for the first CTL to arrive in the infected region in a mouse is tens of times faster in both the ODE and ABM models. The number of CTLs that reach the infected region by day five post activation is thousands of times faster in both models. The ABM includes CTL mediated killing of infected cells and predicts that with an inflammatory signal, the number of infected cells at day five is 87 times lower.

We scaled up the ODE model to make the same predictions for the human lung which is 10,000 times larger than the mouse lung. The ODE models predict that with an inflammatory signal the speed up in arrival of the first CTL humans is 270 times faster and 3800 times more CTL arrive at the site of infection at day five. Thus, the inflammatory signal improves the CTL search much more in the human than in the mouse.

6.2   Caveats and Limitations

We have made many simplifying assumptions in our models. We have ignored death of activated CTLs. We have assumed that LNs produce activated CTLs at a constant rate. We have ignored the time that activated CTLs spend in transit through a capillary network before going back into circulation if there is no inflammation. Because our interest is in the effect of a single signal (the inflammation signal the causes CTL to exit circulation and enter lung tissue near the site of infection), we ignore a vast array of signaling mechanisms and complex interactions between innate and adaptive immune system cells.

However, our assumptions and simplifications do not affect our primary conclusions about the relative speed of CTL search with and without an inflammatory signal. For example including a death rate of activated CTLs would give us a slightly higher estimate of the rate at which LNs release activated CTLs (σ) which would decrease search times with and without an inflammatory signal. Incorporation of a time dependent rate (σ) would give us more accurate production rates, but, again, this would change search times with and without an inflammatory signal in similar ways. Our conclusions that inflammation greatly speeds up CTL search in the lung depends primarily on two assumptions: first the relative speed of the random walk of CTL in the lung vs the speed of circulation, and second, the initial size of the infected region and its rate of growth.

6.3   Conclusions

Together, the ODE and ABM allow us to quantify the value of an information signal in biologically relevant terms. The local inflammation signal in the capillary allows search to be faster because it allows CTLs to recirculate when they arrive in capillaries in uninflamed regions of the lung. Because the lung surface area is so large, and CTL that have exited capillaries move so slowly relative to circulating CTL, this information signal drastically changes the ability of CTL to search the lung quickly. It allows CTL to effectively search the large surface area of the lung in the relatively fast flow of the blood circulatory system, and to exit only very near the site of infection. Further, because the human lung is 10,000 times larger than the mouse lung, the search for an initially small site of infection is much more difficult. This work shows that the effect of the local inflammatory signal is much larger in the search for influenza in the human lung vs the mouse lung. This suggests that the role of inflammation, chemokines and other immune signals may be different in humans and mice. Understanding these differences is important because so much knowledge of immunology and vaccine design depends on experimental work in mouse models.

The implications of this work extend beyond CTL search for influenza in the lung. An effective immune response often requires finding rare localized sites of infection. Models can make important contributions to our understanding of immune function by explaining how the multitude of immune signaling mechanisms improve such search processes.

By understanding the role of information signals in the immune system we can build models that allow us to understand how immune systems form distributed information exchange networks to search, adapt and respond to infections. Without central control, the interactions among millions of communicating components enable immune systems to search and respond to complex, dynamic landscapes effectively. We hypothesize that ant colonies, immune systems and other complex biological systems use common informational strategies to allocate components effectively to tasks and direct their search in space [11].

Our approach may be useful for developing decentralized search in Artificial Immune Systems [2,3]. We anticipate that a quantitative characterization of information flow and its effect on performance will help us understand why systems of different sizes and in different environments use different information, organizational structures and strategies to accomplish similar tasks.

Acknowledgements

We thank Neal Holtschulte for suggesting the use of ODEs to model recirculation. This work is supported by grants from the National Institute of Health (NIH RR018754), DARPA (P-1070-113237) and National Science Foundation (NSF EF 1038682).

References

1. Banerjee, S., Moses, M.E.: A hybrid agent based and differential equation model of body size effects on pathogen replication and immune system response. In: Andrews, P.S., Timmis, J., Owens, N.D.L., Aickelin, U., Hart, E., Hone, A., Tyrrell, A.M. (eds.) ICARIS 2009. LNCS, vol. 5666, pp. 14–18. Springer, Heidelberg (2009)
2. Banerjee, S., Moses, M.: Modular RADAR: An immune system inspired search and response strategy for distributed systems. In: Hart, E., McEwan, C., Timmis, J., Hone, A. (eds.) ICARIS 2010. LNCS, vol. 6209, pp. 116–129. Springer, Heidelberg (2010)
3. Banerjee, S., Moses, M.: Scale Invariance of Immune System Response Rates and Times: Perspectives on Immune System Architecture and Implications for Artificial Immune Systems. Swarm Intelligence 4(4), 301–318 (2010)
4. Beauchemin, C., Dixit, N., Perelson, A.: Characterizing T Cell Movement within Lymph Nodes in the Absence of Antigen. The Journal of Immunology 178, 5505–5512 (2007)
5. Calder, W.: Size, Function and Life History. Dover Publications, New York (1984)

6. La Gruta, N., Doherty, P.: Influenza Virology Current Topics. In: chap. Quantitative and qualitative characterization of the CD8+ T cell response to influenza virus infection. Caister Academic Press (2006)
7. Macey, R.I., Oster, G.: Berkeley Madonna, version 8.0. Tech. rep. University of California, Berkeley, California (2001)
8. Miao, H., Hollenbaugh, J., Zand, M., Holden, W., Mosmann, T.R., Perelson, A., Wu, H., Topham, D.: Quantifying the Early Immune Response and Adaptive Immune Response Kinetics in Mice Infected with Influenza A Virus. Journal of Virology 84(13), 6687–6698 (2010)
9. Mitchell, H., et al.: Higher replication efficiency of 2009 (h1n1) pandemic influenza than seasonal and avian strains: kinetics from epithelial cell culture and computational modeling. Journal of Virology, JVI, 01722–10 (2010)
10. Moser, B., Loetscher, P.: Lymphocyte Traffic Control by Chemokines. Nature Immunology 2, 123–128 (2001)
11. Moses, M., Banerjee, S.: Biologically Inspired Design Principles for Scalable, Robust, Adaptive, Decentralized Search and Automated Response (RADAR). In: IEEE Symposium Series in Computational Intelligence, (SSCI) (2011)
12. Paz, T., Letendre, K., Burnside, W., Fricke, G., Moses, M.: How Ants Turn Information into Food. In: IEEE Symposium Series in Computational Intelligence, (SSCI) (2011)
13. Peters, R.: The ecological implications of body size. Cambridge University Press, Cambridge (1983)
14. Saenz, R., et al.: Dynamics of Influenza Virus Infection and Pathology. Journal of Virology 84(8), 3974–3983 (2010)
15. Warrender, C.: CyCells (Open source software) (2003), http://sourceforge.net/projects/cycells
16. Warrender, C.: Modeling intercellular interactions in the peripheral immune system. Ph.D. thesis, University of New Mexico (2004)
17. Weibel, E.R.: Scaling of structural and functional variables in the respiratory system. Annual Review of Physiology 49, 147–159 (1987)
18. West, G., Brown, J., Enquist, B.: A general model for the origin of allometric scaling laws in biology. Science 276(5309), 122–126 (1997)

Large Scale Agent-Based Modeling of the Humoral and Cellular Immune Response

Giovanni Stracquadanio[1], Renato Umeton[2], Jole Costanza[3], Viviana Annibali[4],
Rosella Mechelli[4], Mario Pavone[3], Luca Zammataro[5], and Giuseppe Nicosia[3]

[1] Department of Biomedical Engineering
Johns Hopkins University
217 Clark Hall, Baltimore, MD 21218, USA
stracquadanio@jhu.edu
[2] Department of Biological Engineering
Massachusetts Institute of Technology
77 Massachusetts Avenue, Cambridge, MA 02139, USA
umeton@mit.edu
[3] Department of Mathematics and Computer Science
University of Catania
Viale A. Doria 6, 95125, Catania, Italy
{costanza,mpavone,nicosia}@dmi.unict.it
[4] Neurology and Centre for Experimental Neurological Therapies (CENTERS),
S. Andrea Hospital Site, Sapienza University of Rome
Via di Grottarossa 1035, 00189, Roma, Italy
{viviana.annibali,rosella.mechelli}@uniroma1.it
[5] Humanitas, University of Milan
Via Manzoni 56, 20089, Rozzano, Milan, Italy
luca.zammataro@humanitasresearch.it

Abstract. The Immune System is, together with Central Nervous
System, one of the most important and complex unit of our organism.
Despite great advances in recent years that shed light on its understanding and in the unraveling of key mechanisms behind its functions, there
are still many areas of the Immune System that remain object of active research. The development of in-silico models, bridged with proper
biological considerations, have recently improved the understanding of
important complex systems [1,2]. In this paper, after introducing major
role players and principal functions of the mammalian Immune System,
we present two computational approaches to its modeling; i.e., two in-
silico Immune Systems. (i) A large-scale model, with a complexity of
representation of $10^6 - 10^8$ cells (e.g., APC, T, B and Plasma cells) and
molecules (e.g., immunocomplexes), is here presented, and its evolution
in time is shown to be mimicking an important region of a real immune response. (ii) Additionally, a viral infection model, stochastic and
light-weight, is here presented as well: its seamless design from biological
considerations, its modularity and its fast simulation times are strength
points when compared to (i). Finally we report, with the intent of moving towards the virtual lymph note, a cost-benefits comparison among
Immune System models presented in this paper.

P. Liò, G. Nicosia, and T. Stibor (Eds.): ICARIS 2011, LNCS 6825, pp. 15–29, 2011.
© Springer-Verlag Berlin Heidelberg 2011

1   Introduction

The theory of clonal selection, formalized by Nobel Laureate F. M. Burnet (1959, whose foundation are in common with D. Talmage's idea (1957) of a cellular selection as the basis of the immune response), suggests that among all possible cells, B and T lymphocytes, with different receptors circulating in the host organism, only those who are actually able to recognize the antigen will start to proliferate by duplication (cloning). Hence, when a B cell is activated by binding an antigen, it produces many clones, in a process called clonal expansion. The resulting cells can undergo somatic hypermutation, and then they can give rise to offspring B cells with mutated receptors. During the immune activity, antigens compete with these new B cells, with their parents and with other clones. The higher the affinity of a B cell to bind to available antigens, the more likely it will clone. This results in a Darwinian process of variation and selection, called affinity maturation. By increasing the size of those cell populations through clonal expansion, and through the production of cells with longer lifetime expectation, and then establishing a defense over time (immune memory), the immune system (IS) assures the organism a higher specific responsiveness to recognized antigenic attacks. In particular, on recognition, memory lymphocytes are produced. Plasma B cells, deriving from stimulated B lymphocytes, are in charge of the production of antibodies targeting the antigen. This mechanism is usually observed in population of lymphocytes in two subsequent antigenic infections. More in detail, the first exposition to the antigen triggers the primary response; in this phase the antigen is recognized and the memory is developed. During the second response, that occurs when the same antigen is found again, as a result of the stimulation of the cells already specialized and present as memory cells, a rapid and more abundant production of antibodies is observed. The secondary response can be elicited from any antigen, which is similar, although not necessarily identical, to the original one, which established the memory. This is known as cross-reactivity.

In this article we present two new computational models capable of capturing fundamental aspects of the IS, at two different complexity levels. A high-complex model, large scale agent-based, that embeds all of the entities and all of the interaction detailed above; thanks to this computational model we have successfully reproduced many IS processes and behaviors. In a second, low-complexity model, we show how a stochastic model based on Gillespie algorithm, captures major behaviors of the IS during a viral infection, even if we are borderline with the definition of "well-mixed" solution. The paper is structured as follows: next Section (S2) details the high-complexity agent-based model; it spans from the introduction of role-playing entities in the model, to real simulations and discussion. Section 3 details the low-complexity IS model; there, after the introduction of process algebra concepts adopted, it is presented a viral infection model based on π-calculus. Conclusions (S4) end the paper and give a cost-benefit comparison of the two models in order to pave the way for the *whole lymph node simulation.*

2   Agent-Based Modeling

Research on the IS dynamics, in the last two decades, has produced several mathematical and computational models. Different approaches include differential equation based models [3,4,5], cellular automata models [6,7], classifier systems [8], genetic algorithms [9], network/computational models [10,11,12] and agent-based models [13,14,15,16], which seem to be the best suited abstraction to handle the great complexity of IS reality.

The first model here presented is based on the deterministic agent-based paradigm; the high-complexity of this model comes from the fact that it can be considered a *large scale* model and it is extremely realistic; indeed, there are totally $10^6 - 10^8$ cells (e.g., APC, T, B and Plasma cells) and molecules (e.g., immunocomplexes) involved in this model: all of the major role-players of the IS are embedded and represented in our model. It is worth remarking the centrality of the scale problem, as choosing a proper model scale have recently allowed for important improvements in the IS simulation [17,18,19,20]. Much like the nervous system, the IS performs pattern recognition tasks and, additionally, it retains memory of the antigens to which it has been exposed. To detect an antigen, the IS activates a particular recognition process that involves many role-players. An overall view of IS role-players includes: antigens (Ag), B lymphocytes (B), plasma B cells (PLB), antigen presenting cells (APC), T helper lymphocytes (Th), immunocomplexes (IC) and antibodies (Ab). The Ag is the target of the immune response. Th and B lymphocytes are responsible for the discrimination of the self-nonself, while PLBs produce antibodies able to label the Ags to be taken by the APCs, which represent the wide class of macrophages. Their function is to present the phagocytised antigens to T helper cells for activation. The ICs are Ab–Ag ties ready to be phagocytised by the macrophages. All of the role-playing entities here described are encoded in our model: each agent has a type (i.e.: Ag, B, PLB, etc.) and those typical features that characterize the type (e.g., the Ag has a unique code, or bit string, that will determine whether there will be a bind with a complementary entity); each agent belongs to a population (e.g., the Ags, Bs, etc.) whose size is plotted in order to quantify group presence, affinity driven interactions, mutations, clonal selection and all of the processes detailed above.

2.1   Immuno Responses

The IS mounts two different responses against pathogenic entities: the humoral response, mediated by antibodies, and the cellular one, mediated by cells. Along with the aforementioned entities, the IS includes the T killer cells, the Epithelial cells or generic virus-target cells, and various lymphokines. These components are necessary to activate the cellular response. One can, from an abstract point of view, envision two types of precise interaction rules: specific interactions, that occur when an entity binds to another by means of receptors; and, non-specific interactions, that occur when two entities interact without any specific recognition process. Only a specific subset of mature lymphocytes will respond to a

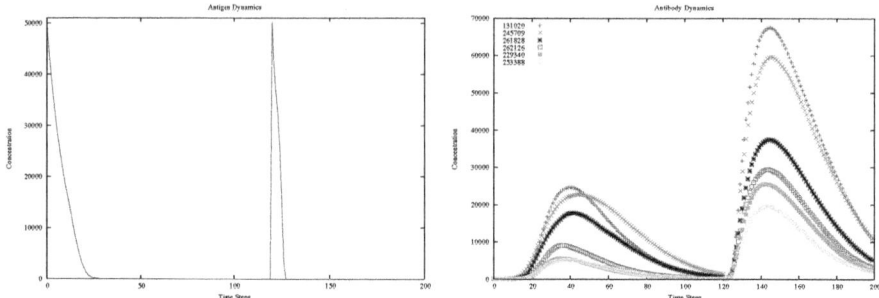

Fig. 1. Immunization - Antigen and Antibody dynamics. Injections of antigens at time steps 0 and 120.

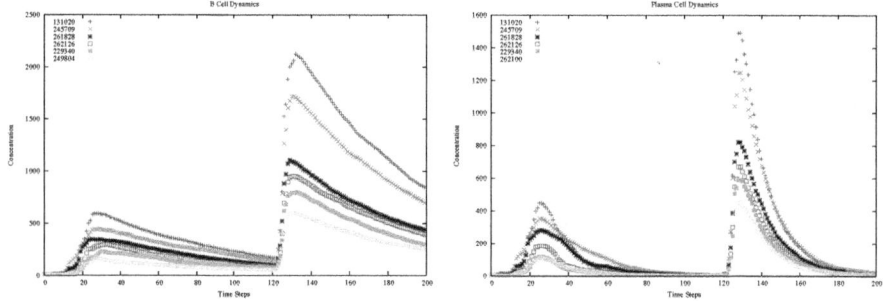

Fig. 2. Immunization - B Cell and Plasma cell dynamics

given Ag, specifically those bearing the receptors that will bind the Ag. Binding usually occurs on a small patch on the Ag (receptor or antigenic determinant or epitope), and the antigen-binding sites on T cell receptors and antibodies (paratopes or idiotypes). Thus, immune recognition of Ags comes from the specific binding of antigen-to-antigen receptors on B and T cells. Hence, the immune response derives its specificity from the fact that Ags select the clones. A non-active B or T cell that has never responded to an Ag before is called virgin or naive. When a naive, mature lymphocyte bearing receptors of the appropriate affinity, binds an Ag (in combination with other signals, usually cytokines), it responds by: proliferating, i.e., cloning itself and, in turn, expanding the population of cells bearing those receptors; the produced clones will differentiate into effector cells that will produce an appropriate response (antibody production for a B cell; cytotoxic responses or help responses for a T cell), and memory cells that will be ready (somewhat like the naive cell) to encounter the Ag in the future and respond in the same way (but this time with many more cells).

Switching from theory right to simulations, we present the results of our agent-based encoding with 18 bits; its representation capability is of the order of 10^6 cells/molecules. Fig. 1 shows time track of antigen, and antibody population

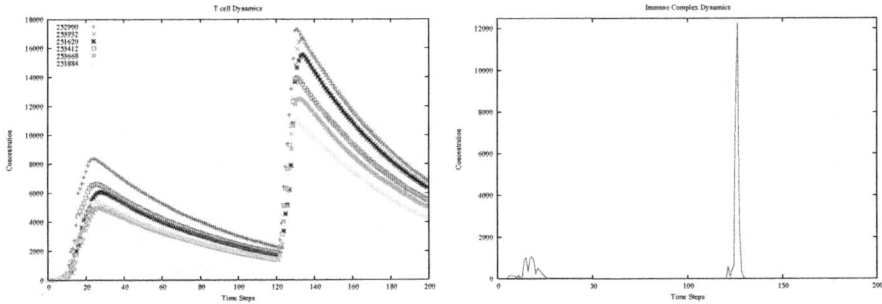

Fig. 3. Immunization - T cell and Immunocomplexes dynamics

of a system injected with the antigen at time steps 0 and 120. Figure 2 shows primary and secondary immune responses of B lymphocyte and Plasma cell population. Figure 3 reports T cell population and Immunocomplexes. We have three main immune response types to a given antigen: immune response by T killer (cytotoxic) lymphocyte; by T helper lymphocyte; and, by B lymphocyte. In Figure 2, we can see the immune response performed by lymphocytes of class B: the free Ag selects a B lymphocyte, whose receptors match its own. These two entities bind together. A B lymphocyte, which has -internalized- and transformed the Ag, shows on its surface fragments of Ags bound to a protein coded by MHC molecule of class II. The mature T helper lymphocyte can, now, bind to the complex antigen-protein, visible on the B lymphocyte. Such a binding frees the interleukin IL2, which in turn allows the B lymphocyte to clone and differentiate. The cellular cloning goes on as long as the B lymphocytes are stimulated by T helper lymphocytes. Mature PLBs free their receptors, Abs, which bind free Ags, creating ICs. In turn, they will be phagocytised by APCs (the "garbage collectors" of the IS). Other mature B lymphocytes stay in the system as B memory cells. Lastly, the IS comprises the hypermutation phenomena observed during the immune responses: the DNA portion coding for Abs is subjected to mutation during the proliferation of the B lymphocytes. This gives the IS the ability to generate diversity. We should underline that, even if the knowledge on the various mechanisms of the immune system is quite advanced, the relative importance of its components with respect to each specific task is not deeply understood.

2.2   Cross-Reactivity and Epithelial Cell Signaling

Now we show the molecular and cellular population dynamics correlated with two further events involved in the clonal selection principle: cross-reactivity and epithelial cell signaling. Cell concentrations give us a clear picture of the learning and immunization processes that occurred during immune responses. To do this, we need some recollection about a model extended by our agent-based model: the Celada-Seiden model [7]; the manner is a robust computational model based

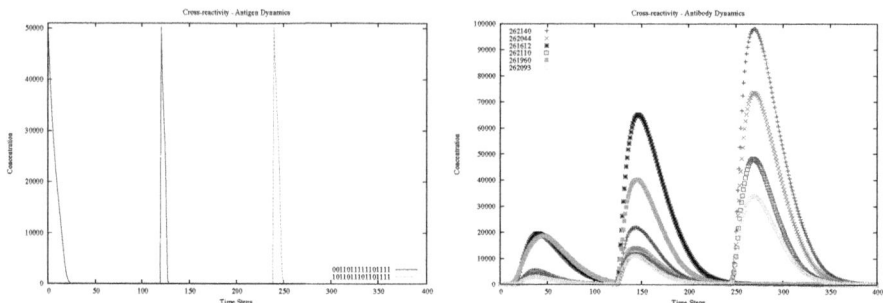

Fig. 4. Cross-Reactivity, Antigen and Antibody dynamics

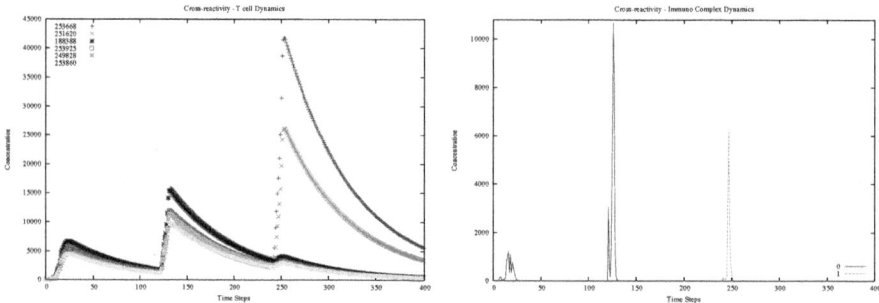

Fig. 5. Cross-Reactivity, T cell and Immunocomplexes dynamics

on the cellular automata paradigm that has been validated with in vitro and in vivo experiments. In particular, it has been shown that Celada-Seiden model can reproduce real phenomena of the immune response. The model includes the following seven entities: Ags, B cells, PLB, APC, T-helper cells, IC, and Ab. The chemical interactions between receptors (the bindings) are mimicked as stochastic events. The probability that two receptors interact is determined by a bit-to-bit matching over the bit strings representing them. Every cell can be in one of the allowed states (e.g., a B cell can be Active, Internalized, Exposing, Stimulated or Memory according to whether it has bound an antigen or not, if it expose the MHC/peptide complex, if it duplicates or if it is considered a memory B cell) and successful interactions between two entities produce a cell-state-change. The cellular automata of the Celada-Seiden's model has an underlying regular, hexagonal, two-dimensional lattice. Each site incorporates many entities, which interact in loci and diffuse to adjacent sites and then move randomly. Every site of the automaton includes a large number of bit strings accounting for the definition of the various entities and for their states (i.e., both receptors and cell-states). In our agent-based simulation, initially there are neither PLBs nor Abs, nor ICs in the Host, given a specific class of antigens. The plot of Fig. 4 (left plot) shows the three injections of antigens. In the first two injections,

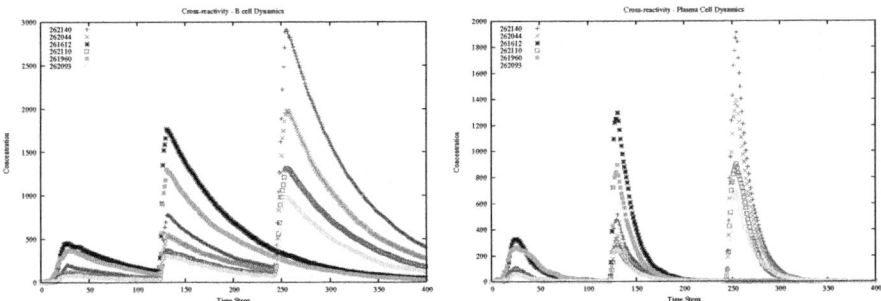

Fig. 6. Cross-Reactivity, B Cell and Plasma cell dynamics

we insert the same antigen, namely the binary string (0011011111101111). The third time we inject a - mutated - antigen (two bits underwent a simulated flip mutation), namely the binary string (1011011101101111). It is of note how the cross-reactivity, observed in nature is here reproduced: Fig. 4 (right plot), Fig. 5 and Fig. 6 present the dynamics of cell populations under control, presenting important similarities with real immunological responses.

Moving towards larger and then more complex (but closer to the reality) systems, we have enriched our IS simulation scenario: we indeed simulated a 20 bit encoded IS. With such an encoding, we have been able to simulate more than 10^8 cells and molecules. We have simulated such an environment for 400 time steps. Fig. 7(a) presents those Ags introduced in the system, while Fig. 7(b) shows the Interferon response released by lymphocytes, a countermeasure that the IS has dynamically adopted. It is of note how the Interferon response is triggered rightly after the introduction of Ags, with a diversified intensity. Such intensity variation is motivated by the primary and secondary responses and cross-reactivity reaction.

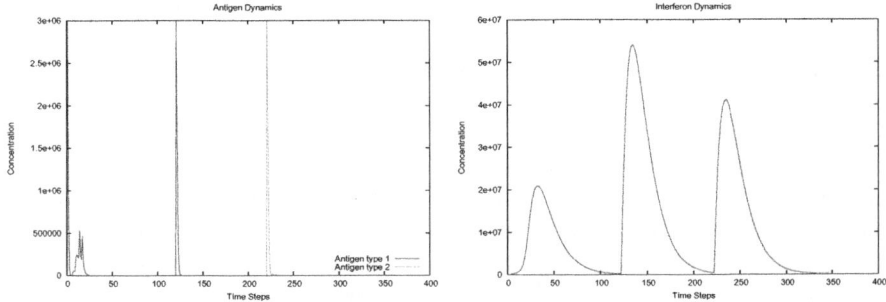

Fig. 7. (a) Antigen Dynamics, as observed after its introduction in the 20 bits simulation environment. (b) Interferon response, dynamically triggered after the Ag detection.

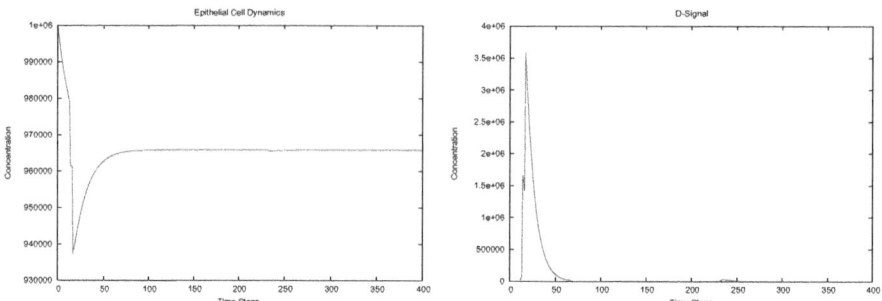

Fig. 8. (a) Epithelial cells in the IS; the change in time of this cell population is a key component in the natural IS. (b) D-signal propagated by epithelial cells to warn other IS components thought a signaling mechanism.

In Fig. 8(a) it is presented how the number of epithelial cells changes in time: these cells are part of our natural IS. It has been validated that these cells represent not only a mechanical barrier in our IS, but they are also enabled to communicate the infection through an ad-hoc signal as described in [21,22]; in fact a "warning signal", namely the *D-signal* is used to propagate the information that something uncommon is taking place. Fig. 8(b) presents the D-signal in object, as observed within this 20 bit simulation.

3 Modeling and Simulation by Stochastic π-Calculus

Biological entities, such as proteins or cells, are social entities (i.e., they act as an organized group), and life depends on their interactions. We can then reduce a biological system to a network of entities interacting among each others in a particular way, i.e., a way in which each elementary process is coded and controlled. The stochastic π-calculus has been recently used to model and simulate a range of biological systems; in particular, stochastic-based models [23] and more in general statistics-based models [24], have recently improved our understanding of key components of the immune system. In this section we want to show the new features of this approach, the pros and cons, and finally the results obtained in simulating HBV infections.

In recent years, there has been considerable research on designing programming languages for complex parallel computational tasks. Interestingly, some of this research is also applicable to biological systems, which are typically highly complex and massively parallel systems. In particular, a mathematical programming language known as the stochastic π-calculus [25] has been recently used to model and simulate many biological systems. One of the main benefits of this calculus is its ability to model large systems incrementally, by composing simpler models of subsystems in an intuitive way (i.e., modularity). Such *in silico* experiments can be used to formulate testable hypotheses on the behavior of biological systems, as a guide to future experiments *in vivo*. Currently available simulators for the stochastic π-calculus are implemented based on standard theory of chemical kinetics, using an adaptation of the Gillespie algorithm [26]. There has already been substantial research on efficient implementation techniques for variants of the π-calculus, in the context of programming languages for parallel computer systems. However, this research does not take into account some specific properties of biological systems, which differ from most computer systems in fundamental ways. A key difference is that biological systems are often composed of large numbers of processes with identical (or equivalent) behavior, such as thousands of proteins of the same type. Another difference is that the scope (the environment where the interaction can actually take place) of private interaction channels is often limited to a relatively small number of processes, usually to represent the formation of complexes. In general *two fundamental intuitions* are shared by all of these proposals: 1. *molecules* (individual biological agents, in general) can be abstracted as *processes*; 2. molecular *interactions* can be modeled as *communications*. Here we introduce SPiM [27], the calculus simulator used in our experiments, and our simulation of infection, i.e., the HBV virus, based on the Perelson's model [28].

3.1 SPiM

Proceeding from the concept that molecules are represented as processes and interactions are communications, we can see that the syntax of processes and environments in SPiM is a subset of the syntax of the stochastic π-calculus (SPi) with the additional constraint that each choice of action is defined separately in the environment. Stochastic behavior is incorporated into the system by associating to each channel x its corresponding interaction rate given by $\rho(x)$, and by associating each delay τ_r with a corresponding rate r. Each rate characterizes an exponential distribution, such that the probability of a reaction with rate r occurring within the time t is given by $F(t) = 1 - e^{-rt}$. The average duration of the reaction is given by the mean $1/r$ of this distribution. A machine term V consists of a set of private channels Z, a store S and a heap H. The heap keeps track of the number of copies of identical species, while the store records the activity of all the reactions in the heap. The system is executed according to the reduction rules of the stochastic π-machine [25]. The rules rely on a construction operator $V \oplus P$, which adds a machine process P to a machine term V (cf. Table 1 for detail).

For the calculus dialect implemented by SPiM, Phillips et al. proved a formal equivalence between an ad-hoc graphical notation and a SPiM program [29]. This is very interesting because people without programming background can formalize a complete and correct model in π-calculus without knowing SPiM: for instance, biologists can detail a biological system using this graphical notation and, SPiM is particularly suited to simulate a complete biological system without building a full mathematical model of the interactions. Together with good features there are also some drawbacks; in particular, SPiM is suitable when all rates are known, and they do not change at running time: this is a very strict hypothesis, because many biological systems have entities that change their rate of interaction at running time or in some particular situations. E.g., in the

Table 1. Syntax of processes and environments in SPiM. The syntax is a normal form for the stochastic π-calculus, in which each choice of actions can only occur at the top level of a definition. For convenience, C is used to denote a restricted choice νnM and D is used to denote the body of a definition. For each definition of the form $X(m) = D$ it is assumed that $fn(D) \subset m$.

P,Q ::=	0	Null	E::=		Empty
	X(n)	Instance		E,X(m)=P	Process
	P — Q	Parallel		E,X(m)=νnM	Choice
	νxP	Restriction			
			π::=	?x(m)	Input
M::=	0	Null		!x(n)	Output
	$\pi.P + M$	Action		τ_r	Delay

immune system, the rate of interaction, the affinity, between B-cell and Antigen can change over the time because a B-cell can undergo hypermutations and then altering its receptor and so its affinity with the Antigen [30].

3.2   Modeling HBV Infection with SPiM

Here we present a stochastic pi-calculus model of infection caused by hepatitis B virus (HBV). The simulation is based on the basic model of virus infection proposed in [28]. The choice of the Perelson model is justified by the fact that this model was tested in vivo and found a broad consensus where HBV is concerned [31]. The model considers a set of cells susceptible to infection (i.e., target cells), T which, through interactions with a virus V, become infected. Infected cells I are assumed to produce new virus particles at a constant average rate p and to die at rate δ, per cell. The average lifespan of a productively infected cell is $1/\delta$, and so if an infected cell produces a total of N virions during its lifetime, the average rate of virus production per cell, $p = N\delta$. Newly produced virus particles, V, can either infect new cells or be cleared from the Host at rate c per virion. HBV infection was modeled with these Ordinary Differential Equations (ODE):

$$dT/dt = s - dT - \beta VT \tag{1}$$
$$dI/dt = \beta VT - \delta I \tag{2}$$
$$dV/dt = pI - cV \tag{3}$$

Target cells become infected at a rate taken proportional to both the virions concentration and the uninfected cell concentration (βVT); while infected cells (I) are produced at the same rate (βVT) and it is assumed that they are depleted at rate δ per cell. Finally, it is assumed that free virions are produced at a constant rate, p, per cell and cleared at constant rate, c. We have simulated an HBV infection with a high number of virions in blood; we have set virions at 20% of target cells as we used a population of 5×10^3 target cells and 10^3 virions. This ratio corresponds to the scenario in which the infection is growing,

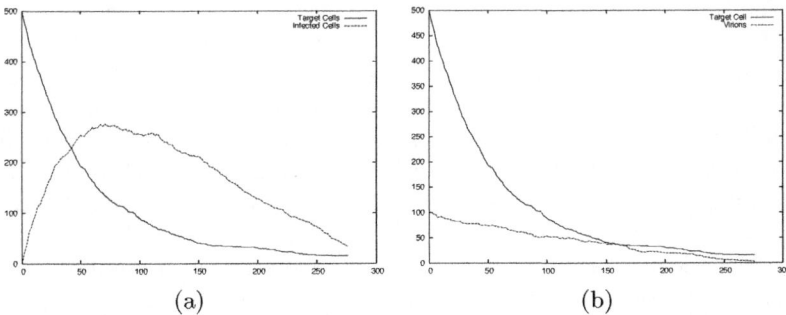

Fig. 9. Simulation of HBV infection using a stochastic π-calculus model. In (a), we report the variation over time (x-axis) of the number of target and infected cells (y-axis); in (b), we present the variation over time (x-axis) of the number of target cells and virions (y-axis).

rapidly, possibly degenerating in a chronic status. We have set the infection rate at a relatively low rate, but from the analysis of the plot in Fig. 9, we can see that the number of virions is big enough to kill target cells. Moreover, infected cells rapidly grow with respect to healthy ones; it is clear that after a first phase where initial virions infect target cells, thanks to the growth of infected cells, the growth in terms of number of virions comes along. This observation is confirmed by Perelson studies, where, after an initial steady state, virions grow proportionally to the number of infected cells. As in Perelson model, the immune system response is implicitly considered by setting the rate of death for virions and infected cells; although there is an *in-vivo* assessment of this model, in general, fine-grained simulation should take into account several other boundary conditions, like cell type and pharmacological treatment.

4   Conclusions

In this paper we have given a broad understanding of the Immune System and we have presented two models for its simulation (i.e., a large-scale agent-based model, and a simpler stochastic one), each model has been introduced together with its strength key points, and with its pertinence context. It is worth mentioning in our conclusions, which are the *modeling factors* that have to be taken into account in the choice of a modeling approach for the IS. If the choice is between a more complex agent-based model versus a stochastic simpler model, there are three factors that play a major role in the modeling outcome: (i) simulation time, (ii) model precision and accuracy, and (iii) model applicability. Where simulation time is concerned, stochastic models have surely to be preferred; in fact, models here outlined base their evolution process on the evaluation of a stochastic function; e.g., the Gillespie algorithm used in SPiM, guarantees light binaries and execution times in the order of *seconds* on a desktop computer for a small model, such as the one we presented on HBV. As far as agent-based models are concerned, execution times are generally larger of at least one order of magnitude, moving towards *minutes* and, according to the number of molecules involved in the simulations, maybe towards *hours*. It is also interesting how, for agent-based and cellular automata models, there is a direct mapping (through an opportune scaling factor) between simulated time steps and real-world timing; the latter, can provide interesting insights about the reliability of an IS simulation and its biological plausibility (e.g., a model where humoral immune response is seen within the same day of the infection has to be preferred when compared to another model where the same response can be observed only after a simulation time that corresponds to one year in real-world timing). The second factor that has to be considered in the modeling is the precision and the accuracy: if stochastic models provide faster answers, with agent-based models we can track the behavior of the single cell/molecule involved in the system and then we have a significantly higher precision in the model controlling. This means, for instance, that we can operate single element alterations at run-time (e.g., an unexpected mutation), without the need of hard-coding this event in our model specification (as one has to do in π-calculus and in process algebra in general). Moreover, in agent-based models, we can tune affinity and the equivalent of reaction rate constants at run-time. Finally, we can track the behavior of a family of agents involved in the system and then study how different cell populations interact one versus the other. These interesting features of agent-based models, come with a price, that is the longer execution time discussed above. The last factor here discussed, is the model applicability and its pertinence: with this argument we want to highlight the fact that not all the modeling approaches can be really extended towards the perfect virtual simulation that has a 1:1 mapping with reality. With respect to this, it is worth noting that when the spatial characteristic of the IS has to be simulated, stochastic models based on the Gillespie algorithm loose one of their theoretical axes, that is the fact that all of the molecules in the simulation are in a "well-mixed" context. Recent extensions of the Gillespie algorithm have been proposed to account for the spatial information [32]; in an example in which there are areas where Antigens are the majority and the immune response begins, then there are regions where almost nothing happens, and finally there are other regions where naive lymphocytes are the majority, it seems clear that the spatial information has an important role.

In conclusion, where SPiM based modeling of the IS is concerned, its features are definitely preferable when either *light computation* or system *modularity* are more important than *model precision and accuracy* and when the spatial aspect of the system does not play an important role. Finally, moving towards *the virtual lymph node*, agent-based models, and in particular the 20 bit model here presented, seems a valuable approach for the simulation of this (very)large scale system, made of a number of cells/molecules in the order of 10^8, that can interact among eachothers in a spatially aware context where different regions are devoted to different functions. In the following we give some insights about possible applications of such a system. *Biological transferability and applicability of a very-large scale system are important and wide; where prevention therapies* are concerned, a verified computational model could be employed in the development of new *vaccines*. The idea would be to perform a simulation on a number of new molecules (e.g., molecule $[A]$ and molecule $[B]$) and study how they interact with the Host, i.e.: $f(new_{molecule})$ and among eachothers, as the effect could be additive ($f([A]+[B]) = f([A]) + f([B])$), neutral, i.e.: molecules designed for a competing aim ignore eachothers resulting in $f([A]+[B]) = f([A]) = f([B])$, or even disruptive. With a verified IS computational model, we could even study time-series of the simulated response – a practical application would be (i) to modulate vaccine injection schedule in order to have and enhanced immunization; (ii) drug resistance could be studied in terms of time-series as well. To move towards such beautiful scenarios, we are currently considering the conversion of the Binary epitope into a realistic one, built on top of the amino acid alphabet; with respect to the latter point we are investigating an alternative epitope library employing an accepted framework [33] for the (i) *Single-* and (ii) *Multi-Objective* modeling approach aimed at a design of the antibody complementary determining regions that is (iii) extended with the notion of functional *Robustness* [34] at the epitope binding task.

References

1. Stracquadanio, G., Umeton, R., Papini, A., Liò, P., Nicosia, G.: Analysis and optimization of c3 photosynthetic carbon metabolism. In: Rigoutsos, I., Floudas, C.A. (eds.) Proceedings of BIBE 2010, 10th IEEE International Conference on Bioinformatics and Bioengineering, May 31 - June 3, pp. 44–51. IEEE Computer Society Press, USA (2010)

2. Umeton, R., Stracquadanio, G., Sorathiya, A., Papini, A., Liò, P., Nicosia, G.: Design of robust metabolic pathways. In: DAC 2011 - Proceedings of the 48th Design Automation Conference, June 5-10, ACM, San Francisco (2011)

3. Perelson, A.S.: Immune network theory. Immunol. Rev. 110, 5–36 (1989)

4. Perelson, A., Weisbuch, G.: Theoretical and experimental insights into immunology. Springer, Heidelberg (1992)

5. Bersini, H., Varela, F.: Hints for adaptive problem solving Gleaned from Immune networks. Parallel Problem Solving from Nature, 343–354 (1991)

6. Stauffer, D., Pandey, R.: Immunologically motivated simulation of cellular automata. Computers in Physics 6(4), 404 (1992)

7. Seiden, P., Celada, F.: A model for simulating cognate recognition and response in the immune system*. Journal of theoretical biology 158(3), 329–357 (1992)

8. Farmer, J., Packard, N., Perelson, A.: The Immune System, Adaptation & Learning. Physica D 22, 187–204 (1986)

9. Forrest, S., Javornik, B., Smith, R.E., Perelson, A.S.: Using genetic algorithms to explore pattern recognition in the immune system. Evolutionary computation 1(3), 191–211 (1993)

10. Kim, P.S., Levy, D., Lee, P.P.: Modeling and Simulation of the Immune System as a Self-Regulating Network. Methods in Enzymology, 79–109 (2009)

11. Castiglione, F., Mannella, G., Motta, S., Nicosia, G.: A network of cellular automata for the simulation of the immune system. International Journal of Modern Physics C (IJMPC) 10(4), 677–686 (1999)
12. Rapin, N., Lund, O., Bernaschi, M., Castiglione, F.: Computational immunology meets bioinformatics: the use of prediction tools for molecular binding in the simulation of the immune system. PLoS One 5(4), 9862 (2010)
13. Bailey, A.M., Thorne, B.C., Peirce, S.M.: Multi-cell agent-based simulation of the microvasculature to study the dynamics of circulating inflammatory cell trafficking. Ann. Biomed. Eng. 35(6), 916–936 (2007)
14. Bogle, G., Dunbar, P.R.: Agent-based simulation of t-cell activation and proliferation within a lymph node. Immunol Cell Biol 88(2), 172–179 (2010)
15. Bauer, A.L., Beauchemin, C., Perelson, A.S.: Agent-based modeling of host-pathogen systems: the successes and challenges. Information sciences 179(10), 1379–1389 (2009)
16. An, G., Mi, Q., Dutta-Moscato, J., Vodovotz, Y.: Agent-based models in translational systems biology. Wiley Interdisciplinary Reviews: Systems Biology and Medicine 1(2), 159–171 (2009)
17. Mitha, F., Lucas, T.A., Feng, F., Kepler, T.B., Chan, C.: The multiscale systems immunology project: software for cell-based immunological simulation. Source Code Biol. Med. 3, 6 (2008)
18. Beyer, T., Meyer-Hermann, M.: Multiscale modeling of cell mechanics and tissue organization. IEEE Eng. Med. Biol. Mag. 28(2), 38–45 (2009)
19. Nudelman, G., Weigert, M., Louzoun, Y.: In-silico cell surface modeling reveals mechanism for initial steps of b-cell receptor signal transduction. Mol. Immunol. 46(15), 3141–3150 (2009)
20. Perrin, D., Ruskin, H.J., Crane, M.: Model refinement through high-performance computing: an agent-based hiv example. Immunome Res 6(1), 3 (2010)
21. Janeway, C., Travers, P., Walport, M., Capra, J.: Immunobiology: The Immune System in Health and Disease (1996)
22. Eckmann, L., Kagnoff, M.F., Fierer, J.: Intestinal epithelial cells as watchdogs for the natural immune system. Trends Microbiol. 3(3), 118–120 (1995)
23. Chao, D.L., Davenport, M.P., Forrest, S., Perelson, A.S.: Stochastic stage-structured modeling of the adaptive immune system. In: Proc. IEEE Comput. Soc. Bioinform. Conf., vol. 2, pp. 124–131 (2003)
24. Chakraborty, A., Košmrlj, A.: Statistical Mechanical Concepts in Immunology. Annual Review of Physical Chemistry 61, 283–303 (2010)
25. Priami, C.: Stochastic pi-calculus. Comput. J. 38(7), 578–589 (1995)
26. Gillespie, D.T.: A general method for numerically simulating the stochastic time evolution of coupled chemical reactions. J. Comput. Phys. 22, 403 (1976)
27. Phillips, A., Cardelli, L.: A correct abstract machine for the stochastic pi-calculus. Concurrent Models in Molecular Biology (August 2004)
28. Perelson, A.S., Neumann, A.U., Markowitz, M., Leonard, J.M., Ho, D.D.: Hiv-1 dynamics in vivo: virion clearance rate, infected cell life-span, and viral generation time. Science 271(5255), 1582–1586 (1996)
29. Phillips, A., Cardelli, L., Castagna, G.: A graphical representation for biological processes in the stochastic pi-calculus. Transactions in Computational Systems Biology 4230, 123–152 (2006)
30. Priami, C., Quaglia, P.: Beta binders for biological interactions. In: Danos, V., Schachter, V. (eds.) CMSB 2004. LNCS (LNBI), vol. 3082, pp. 20–33. Springer, Heidelberg (2005)

31. Perelson, A.S.: Modelling viral and immune system dynamics. Nature Reviews Immunology 2(1), 28–36 (2002)
32. Isaacson, S.A., Peskin, C.S.: Incorporating diffusion in complex geometries into stochastic chemical kinetics simulations. SIAM Journal on Scientific Computing 28(1), 47–74 (2007)
33. Cutello, V., Narzisi, G., Nicosia, G.: A multi-objective evolutionary approach to the protein structure prediction problem. J. R. Soc. Interface 3(6), 139–151 (2006)
34. Stracquadanio, G., Nicosia, G.: Computational energy-based redesign of robust proteins. Computers and Chemical Engineering 35(3), 464–473 (2011)

Logic-Based Representation of Connectivity Routes in the Immune System

Pierre Grenon and Bernard de Bono

European Bioinformatics Institute, UK
{pgrenon,bdb}@ebi.ac.uk

Abstract. This work is part of a general treatment of physiological phenomena grounded on connectivity between anatomical compartments. As
a number of immune-related mechanisms may be formally described in
terms of white cell movement across body compartments, this paper is
concerned with the representation of routes of connectivity in the immune system, focusing on its lymphatic part. The approach relies on ontologies and their expression in a logic-based language supporting spatial
knowledge representation and reasoning. The paper discusses informally,
and provides elements of formalisation for, a core ontology of the immune system. This ontology is designed to support the representation of
topological aspects of immune phenomena at the levels of systems and
subsystems of connected tissues, organs, and conduits. The result is a
theory i) grounding the representation of immune-related mechanisms
on spatial relationships between immunological sites and ii) allowing to
infer affordances that relations between sites create for agents.

The present contribution is part of work concerned with the logic-based knowledge representation of physiological processes as they unfold in relation to
anatomical structures. We address here the representation of connectivity routes
throughout the system of body fluid circulation (blood, tissue fluid and lymph)
that is relevant to immunology. This is to form the basis of a framework for the
representation of connectivity for transportation processes within the immune
system. This framework could be applied, for example, to the modelling of the
compartmental transitions of (i) antigen presenting cells from bone marrow to
any tissue fluid compartment involved in inflammation, as well as (ii) their interaction with lymphocytes in lymph nodes and subsequent antibody production.
In this paper, we present the most elementary components needed in order to
achieve such a representation: the topological aspects of the immune system as
a system of moving objects. Such a representation bears three distinguishable
aspects which can be regarded as belonging to three levels of work even if these
are not without overlap. These levels are:

1. Ontology, in the form of a formal theory (of the immune system)
2. Knowledge, in the form of a repository of relevant factual knowledge
3. Integration and application, in the form of a context relying on the above
   two levels and integrating ontologies and knowledge from related domains.

P. Liò, G. Nicosia, and T. Stibor (Eds.): ICARIS 2011, LNCS 6825, pp. 30–43, 2011.
© Springer-Verlag Berlin Heidelberg 2011

In the next section, we present our methodological approach and its logically separate, but operationally interdependent, levels. Section 2 focuses on the core ontology of the immune system and, in particular, its topological dimension. In section 3, we overview the propotype implementation, knowledge acquisition and integration and application aspects of our work.

1   Approach

Ontology.   Ontology [1], as we regard it, is an approach to the representation of reality that involves the identification of the different *kinds* of entities, together with the varied sorts of *relations* there are between them, in a given domain. Thus an ontology of the immune system is a theoretical product that intends to sustain an account of that domain of reality. Such a domain is delineated by those parts of the body that are involved in the functioning and dysfunctioning of the immune system. Of course, the immune system is a complex system made of many different kinds of entities, of different biological scales, and of a large variety of phenomena that involve the body and, sometimes, its environment. Therefore, in order to do justice to the immune system domain, an *extensive* ontological treatment has to involve varied connected biomedical domains. Related domains, from closest to more peripheral, include virtually most of anatomy, physiology, and pathology, but also cell and molecular biology, microbiology, pharmacology and many clinical domains. A *core* ontology of the immune system, in contrast, will focus on the particular and specific aspects, entities, and phenomena that characterise the domain as such.

In the present paper, we are primarily concerned with only a portion of the core ontology of the immune system: the minimum portion of a core ontology of the immune system that is required to articulate accounts of that system's main topological aspects. In its more diminutive expression, this portion ought to be reduced to the topology of lymphoid tissues and lymphatic vessels at the scale at which translocation of immune agents occurs within the body. But of course, such a restriction is extremely drastic and this is not least because such translocations occur, inter alia, outside of lymphoid tissues and lymphatic vessels. Therefore our account, while narrowly focused, ought to be understood as part of a broader, more extensive account. This broader account involves a general treatment of body fluid circulation, in particular, of cardiovascular circulation. In the present paper we will assume a treatment of cardiovascular circulation which we leave for discussion elsewhere [2].

Knowledge.   An ontology provides a theory of a domain. It may be used, in particular, to classify entities in that domain. But these entities have to be described in terms of ground facts that represent the kinds under which entities fall, the properties they have, and the relations in which they enter—both specific facts about particular instances and generic facts akin to the expression of laws and other patterns.

The epistemic part of our work is concerned with instances of categories such as, for example, the category of *lymphatic vessel*. Its goal is to establish the reservoir of facts that describe such instances; for example, that the thoracic duct connects to the left subclavian vein. In our context, this means establishing a number of facts about the body and, in combination with our focus on the core ontology of the immune system, about those peculiar parts of the body which are specifically or particularly involved in the working of the immune system:

- facts about agents and their relations to locations in the immune system such as, for example, that lymphocytes can be found in lymph nodes
- facts about immunological processes and their relations to locations in the immune system such as, for example, that the maturation of T-lymphocytes occurs in the thymus
- facts about lymphoid tissue connectivity such as, for example, that the tonsil is supplied with blood by the tonsillar branch of the facial artery or that the spleen is drained of blood by the splenic vein
- facts of connections between lymphatic vessels and nodes such as, for example, that the left subclavian lymphatic chain is directly connected to and supplies the thoracic duct
- facts about tissue connections to the lymphatic system (and blood vessels for the cardiovascular system) such as, for example, that the lateral diaphragmatic lymphatic chain drains the right lobe of the liver.

Integration and Application. Our work on the ontology of the immune system is directed towards the human immune system. It is first concerned with the representation of the adult mature immune system. We are looking for a basis for representing logically and reasoning upon such representation of immune phenomena. The approach can be extended in further directions, also to build more complex, detailed representations by way of connection to relevant domains. It is our aim to do so in order to enable the application of our work in biomedical domains. There are a number of ontologies covering, to various degrees of breadth, depth and sophistication, biomedical knowledge domains. These include anatomy, physiology, clinical, with distinctions according scales, such as organs levels or cellular levels (see for example the repositories of the OBO Foundry [3] or the BioPortal [4]). The main motivation for relating to relevant publicly available ontologies or controlled vocabularies in the biomedical domain is that such integration can contribute to a priming step of the knowledge acquisition process (acquiring knowledge, for example, anatomical from the FMA [5] and cellular from CellType [6]). Another motivation is to expand the applicabilty of our representation of immune processes, for example, in combination with disease related ontologies, in the context of pathological mechanisms. Finally, we see our work as part of a plateform contributing greater access to and integration of terminological and ontological resources.

2   Ontology

The scope of the immune system ontology has two immediate dimensions: i) structural and ii) processual. The first one is concerned primarily with structures which, at different scales, partake in immune processes. The second one is concerned with processes and corresponds to an account of immune phenomena in terms of physiological (and pathological) processes. There is also a more fundamental topological dimension. This is because processes occur within or between structures (as locations or delimiters of locations) and involve additional structures (as agents or patients). They do so within a network of connected (anatomical) structures that can be navigated, inter alia, by immunological agents. Here lies the core of the immune system ontology which, as a primary requirement, needs to be able to account for the theater of all immune phenomena.

Our ontological treatment involves two main categories of entity: spatial or material objects and processes associated with a number of basic relations (parthood and location in particular). As these categories are very general, we assume a treatment of these along the lines of the Basic Formal Ontology (BFO) [7].

Substantial: structures (cells, tissues, vessels ...)

Processual: spatial and physiological processes

parts: between a whole and its parts

involves: between a processual and a substantial

occurs-in: location of a processual in a substantial

occupies: location of a substantial in a substantial

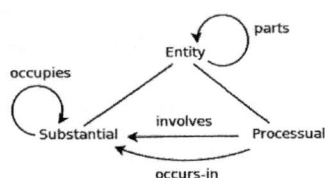

Fig. 1. Main categories from BFO and some general relations. We use *Substantial* as a predicate applied to structures and parts of the body and *Processual* applied to processes of various kinds. We use relations to link, for examples, entities with their parts, processes with their participants, and processuals and substantials with their (substantial) locations. While primitive relations of location tie entities to their *exact* location, we allow a standard generalisation whereby location relations also link to sites containing exact locations as parts [8].

The structural dimension of the immune system ontology involves primarily the selection and representation of the most relevant elements of human anatomy at a number of scales, particularly at the levels of organs, tissues and cells. The most important organs are of course the primary and secondary lymphoid organs. At this level too we include the entirety of the lymphatic system. At the cellular level, among the numerous relevant types of cell, the most salient for us is that of leucocytes. At the processual level, we primarily focus on the basic processes taking place within the immune system and involving these structures.

2.1   Structural Primer

The immune system contains three main kinds of structural elements (Figure 2):

1. immunological biological agents, among which cells, antigens and antibodies
2. lymphoid tissues and organs, whether encapuslated (for example, the thymus) or non-encapsulated (for example, MALT).
3. vascular elements, including lymphatic vessels and nodes to which we limit our discussion.

An important part of an extensive ontology of the immune system is to account for the structure, development, and functions of these parts, but here we ignore these aspects. For our present purpose, an important delineation that occurs already at the structural level comes from the systemic view underlying an account of the immune phenomena. It is a delineation between three systemic levels standing in partonomic relations. From more general to more specific, these are the i) immune, ii) lymphoid, and iii) lymphatic systems (Figure 2-a).

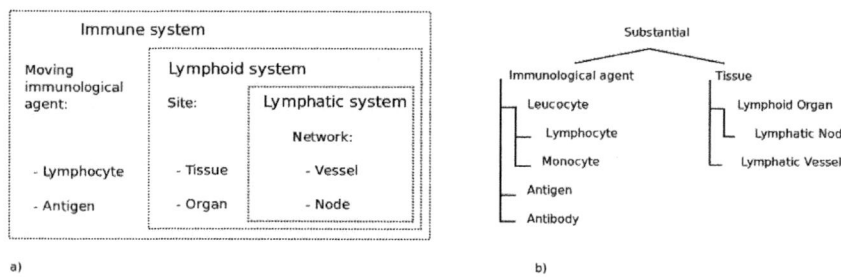

a)   b)

Fig. 2. Structures. a) Intrinsic components of the immune system as a system of moving biological objects. Such objects, in particular immunological agents, move in and between sites, passing through, inter alia, specific lymphatic routes (parts of the lymphatic network). b) Taxonomy of these components under the category of *Substantial*.

The immune system as a whole is characterised by being composed of sites and biological agents (Figure 2-b). The latter are i) produced in some sites (for example, B-lymphocytes in the bone marrow) or by some agents (for example, antibodies by B-lymphocytes) and ii) can circulate within the body. If biological agents are the entities that circulate, sites are what mark out the relevant locations for circulation. Our focus here is on sites as landmarks delineating anatomical connections circulated by biological agents at a large scale in the body. The most obvious result of such delineation is the network of connected lymphatic vessels and nodes (in fact, a two-component network leading to the right lymphatic and thoracic ducts). These constitute the lymphatic system proper. But the lymphatic system is only part of a more general partition of the body which is particularly relevant to the immune system and the circulation of biological agents. That part, which we call here the 'lymphoid system' adds to the lymphatic system a number of scattered organs and tissues such as the thymus, marrow of bones, MALT, white pulp of spleen, parts of the intestine.

In general, connections between components of the lymphoid system are mediated partly through portions of the cardiovascular system (blood circulation) proper and partly through barrier-controlled connectivity between tissue fluid regions and the lymphatic system (Figure 3). Such systems of tissues represent in their own right important high-level aggregate structures and are recognised as such by our ontology whose goal is to account for their parts and the articulations between them.

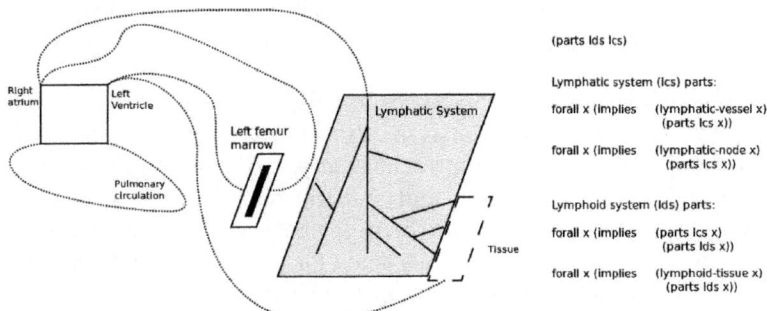

Fig. 3. Lymphatic and lymphoid systems. a) The lymphatic system forms a (dual) topologically self-connected tile in a partition of the body, while the lymphoid system represents scattered tiles (including, in particular, the lymphatic system itself and the marrow of the left femur). b) Partonomy of these systems regarded as designated individuals (*lcs* stands for the lympahtic system and *lds* for the lymphoid one).

2.2   Processual Primer

Processes are entities in their own right, which involve other entities (their participants) and occur in various sites. For example, the process of activation of a lymphocyte in a lymph node involves, inter alia, that lymphocyte and occurs in that lymph node. Processes correspond to various kinds of changes (qualitative, locational or substantial as when an entity comes into being [9]). Two main kinds of processes are significant for our purpose: translocation processes of agents and production (and maturation) of agents.

Production/Maturation. Leucocytes have an history. They are derived through various processes from stem cells in the marrow where some achieve maturation (B-lymphocytes and monocytes) while other migrate to mature in different parts of the body (T-lymphocytes in the thymus). The treatment of the various kinds of differentiation and related intercellular activities of leucocytes (development, education, activity, and so on) is outside the scope of the present paper. Formally, such a treatment could rely, in particular, on *transformation* and *derivation* relations such as found in the Relational Ontology [10]. Moreover, our treatment of production and maturation is not concerned with the structure of leucocytes, rather with the locational (in which kinds of site they occur) and topological (how are the relevant sites connected) aspects of these processes in relation to the lymphoid and lymphatic systems.

   For our purpose, a production process can simply be defined as a process whereby an entity is produced, including cases of creation and development. It is characterised by a relation, *object-produced*, between the process and the entity produced (a substantial)—a specialisation of the *involvement* relation [11]. Every production process has at least one product. We can then define the site of production of a substantial as that site in which its production process occurs. Similar strategies apply to other specific kinds of process, including maturation.

forall x (implies (production x) (exists y (object-produced x y)))
production-site x y $\equiv_{def}$ exists p (and (object-produced p x) (occurs-in p y))

Translocation. Translocation processes are the basis for the circulation of leu-cocytes (and other immune agents) in the immune system. This is the most significant kind of process in the present context. Although perhaps at different levels of granularities, production and maturation involve translocations of in-strumental entities contributing to them or can even require that a process of translocation occurs prior to them (so that, for example, a cell produced in the marrow may reach its maturation site in the thymus).

Here we do not attempt to find a strict formal definition nor a minimal vocab-ulary for the general category of translocation processes but we are interested in characterising such processes in relation to a number of entities: the entity mov-ing (*translocated-object*), the locations from and to which it moves (*from-location* and *to-location*), and the location through which it moves (*translocation-site*). As an approximation, we regard a translocation site as the site in which the translocation process occurs (representing the entire translocation path of the moving object). Every translocation process has at least a translocated object, a location from where it starts and one where it ends:

forall x (implies (translocation x)
                (exists uvw (and (translocated-object x u)
                (from-location x v) (to-location x w)))))

Translocation occurs through sites which are generally filled with a medium (typically a fluid) which, according to BFO, is also part of that site. We consider two basic types of translocation processes which all happen in body fluids:

1. *Advection*: a translocation process whereby an entity is moved in a fluid medium as a result of the movement of the fluid medium itself:
2. *Diffusion*: a translocation process whereby an entity moves in a fluid medium without that movement resulting from the movement of the medium itself.

We do not provide formal definitions for these basic kinds of process as they are pervasive in the body and their detailed treatment is general. Also, we leave aside kinds of process which may be seen as related to these; for example, secretion as facilitated diffusion. We can, however, consider a composite kind of translocation, *convection*, whose instances combine advection and diffusion.

2.3 Topological Primer

Our treatment of the topological dimension results from the overview above. It is primarily intended to support the representation of movements within the immune system of cellular and subcellular objects such as, for example, lympho-cytes and cytokines. Therefore, it requires an account of location and transloca-tion along a number of routes. In its strictest guise, here, the account is primarily concerned with navigation in the lymphatic system. As the lymphatic system is not closed, there are two additional elements that have to be taken into account:

i) the production of mature lymphocytes in primary lymphoid organs; ii) the collection of fluid from tissues by the lymphatic system and its advection into the cardiovascular system. We will focus on this second element.

Regionalisation of processes. The regionalisation of processes is a distinction with respect to the sites in which processes occur in their relationships to the structural decomposition of the immune system illustrated by Figure 2-a. The distinction generates different levels of systemic connectivity. Transregional translocation involves exiting and entering distinct systems, possibly via the crossing of barriers (consider Figure 3-a and the route taken from tissue fluid to the marrow and back). We identify three main process regionalisations:

1. *Lymphatic processes.* Such processes occur within the lymphatic system (in the formal definition below, *occurs-in* should be interpreted as exact location). They are regionally among the most specific immune process (occurring in a designated material part of it). For example, a cell navigating the lymphatic tree from the draining lymphatic vessels of the kidney area to the thoracic duct.

lymphatic-p x $\equiv_{def}$ forall y (implies (occurs-in x y) (parts lcs y))

2. *Lymphoid processes.* Such processes may occur partly in the lymphatic system but at least partly outside of it and, in particular, in scattered lymphoid tissues. As a matter of anatomical fact, many such processes occur at least partly within intermediate non-lymphoid tissues. For example, a lymphocyte leaving the bone marrow and moving to the thymus.

lymphoid-p x $\equiv_{def}$ (exists yz (and (parts x y) (occurs-in y z) (parts lds z)))

3. *Bodily processes.* Such processes may occur anywhere within the body and are not restricted to either the lymphatic vessels nor to the connections between these and lymphoid organs. For example, a monocyte moving from the aorta towards the left kidney.

Processual communication via routes. The site in which a translocation process occurs is a translocation route for a translocated object. More generally, provided that objects may be translocated in a medium with similar modalities (advection and diffusion), these routes have the potential of being used by any such objects. There is a number of constraints and qualifications that, in finer analysis, could be added to this notional generalisation of routes (there are, for example, physical or chemical barriers for certain agents). Indeed, the regulation of translocation within the body is an important part of the regulation of a number of immune phenomena as well as the functioning of the body. Here we take a simple and generic view: we say that two sites are communicating according to one processual modality when they are connected by a path that affords processes of translocation of one of the kinds surveyed above. We thus recognise the following relations between two sites:

1. advective communication for an advective affordance, *advective-comm*
2. diffusive communication for a diffusive affordance, *diffusive-comm*
3. convective communication for a convective affordance, *convective-comm*.

Although here we take the above relations as formally primitive, they involve some implicit existential quantification on a path between communicating sites which affords the relevant kind of translocation. When such a path exists—or any of the above relations holds—between two sites, we say that these sites communicate translocatively and use the *communcation* relation. We leave to a more extensive treatment of these notions the explicitation of relationships between, and combinations of, affordances created by combinations of paths, heterogenous ones in particular. While in finer analysis, relationships between communication relations may prove to exist only under certain conditions that depend on properties of sites and moving objects (diffusivity, permeability of membranes and so on), the present treatment ignores such qualifications—see [12] for a relevant approach.

Here, we assume a non-qualified communication and that translocative modalities are compatible. For example, if a path between two sites, A and B, affords advection, and a path between B and another site, C, affords convection, then there is a path between A and C that affords communication. For similar reasons, the above relations are transitive.

forall xyz (implies (and (communication x y) (communication y z))
                (communication x z))

Topology in the lymphatic system. We distinguish two main types of component in the lymphatic system: i) lymphatic vessels and ii) lymphatic nodes. Lymphatic vessels are conduits along which lymph flows. They form a network that is marked out by the nodes. Lymphatic nodes are encapsulated lymphoid tissues with sinuses contiguous with the lumen of afferent and efferent lymphatic vessels. At the level of granularity of the present account, we ignore the special internal structure of lymphatic nodes and regard them too as a type of conduit. Conduits have boundaries through which fluid passes by way of entry or exit. Two conduits that share such a boundary are connected so as to form a longer conduit. A lymphatic tree is an elongated conduit and it is a tree because it has branching parts—conduits which share a boundary with two or more. Figure 4 recollects the main kinds of lymphatic tree elements.

The connection between conduits in the lymphatic system may be intuitively oriented. We orientate connection here, not according to flow, because that account relies on features that we have left aside (in particular, valves and peristalsis). We orientate connection from *proximal* (linking to the venous system) to *distal* (immersed in tissue fluids). Thus extremal vessels of type (ii) in Figure 4-a are most proximal and those of type (i) are most distal.

Two lymphatic elements are in the (lymphatic) distal-proximal relation of connection when they share a boundary which is a lymphatically proximal for the first and distal for the second. Here, we adopt a simple treatment without relying explictly on boundaries—see [13] for a relevant approach.

We use *ld-connection* for the relation of direct (or immediate) connection in the distal-proximal direction between lymphatic conduits. Consider (iii) in Figure 4-a as a branching of three lymphatic vessels. Suppose that the right end of the picture is in the proximal direction. Both branching segments on the left

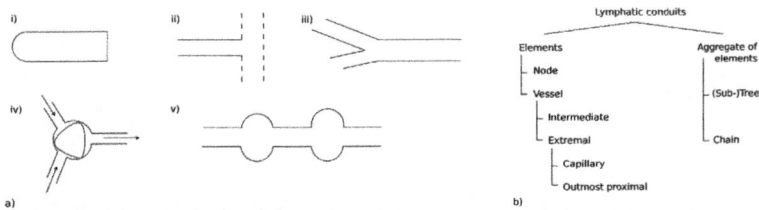

Fig. 4. The basic elements of the lymphatic network. a) In relation to their topological characteristics: i) lymphatic capillaries are one-sided open ended (the broken line is a boundary shared with another lymphatic conduit), ii) terminal vessels of the lymphatic system are connected to cardiovascular vessels (dashed lines), iii) lymphatic vessels are at least two-sided open ended, iv) lymphatic nodes have a number of lymphatic vessels connected to them (afferent or efferent) and, in certain cases, v) certain nodes and vessels form chains. b) A classification of lymphatic conduits: elements and salient kinds of aggregates thereof.

are in the *ld-connection* relation to the segment on the right. It is also useful and easy to define a correlative indirect relation, mediated by successions of direct connections; a relation which is transitive (*lt-connection*). It is now immediate that connections and, by transitivity, chains of connections represent advective routes of lymphatic translocation:

forall xy (implies (ld-connection x y) (advective-comm x y))

Extremal connections of the lymphatic system. The lymphatic system is a network of vessels that starts in regions surrounded by tissue fluid and ends with its connections to the cardiovascular system where lymph advects into the blood stream. This is because i) most distal lymphatic vessels (lymphatic capillaries) collect tissue fluid and ii) most proximal lymphatic vessels, which are connected to blood circulation ('proximal lymphatics' for short), have lymph collected from them by blood vessels. Such extremal elements are at the interfaces between bodily fluid systems—we use the *collects-from* relation for such interfacing elements (Figure 5).

The passage of fluid into lymphatic capillaries (Figure 5-a) occurs through interstices between lymphatic endothelial cells that are partially surrounded by tissue fluid (the regulation of flow in these spaces is too fine grained for the present account and involves barrier operations the treatment of which we have left aside). In the case of proximal lymphatics (Figure 5-b), lymphatic vessels directly connect to the cardiovascular system. In both cases, these interfaces represent convective routes of lymphoid translocation.

Drainage and supply. The lymphatic system's function is to collect fluid from tissues and convey it to the cardiovascular circulation. The whole lymphatic system drains the whole body (but for areas of immune privilege such as the brain and testes) but it is only parts of it that drain tissue fluid from specific

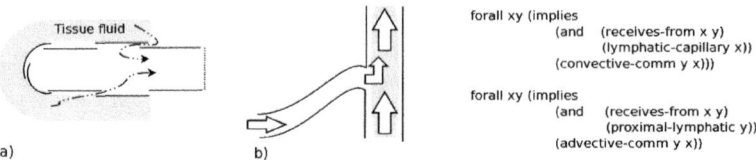

Fig. 5. Extremal lymphatics. a) Extremal connection in capillaries; lymphatic capillaries are (partially) surrounded by tissue fluids trickling through spaces between the cells' walls (a case of convection). b) Extremal connection to the blood system; these proximal lymphatics are connected to, and their content advects, into blood vessels.

regions. However, the branching topology of the lymphatic system does not make it entirely straightforward to account for the drainage of a given body part.

Assuming a complete knowledge of all lymphatic conduits in the body, for each region, it may be possible to identify the lymphatic capillaries collecting tissue fluid from a given region. Following a path of lymphatic connection from these capillaries to proximal lymphatics, the lymphatic drainage of a region can be defined as the part of the lymphatic system that contains the lymphatic vessels belonging to any such path for that region. Defined in this way, the lymphatic drainage of a region contains parts that are not necessarily specific to a region (consider, for example, the throacic duct into which advect numerous lymphatic vessels). Thus, in particular, the lymphatic drainage of a region is distinct from the portion of the lymphatic system in that region. Contrast the thoracic duct (part of the lymphatic system in the thorax and part of the drainage of the right lower limb) and the right external iliac lymphatic chain (part of both the lymphatic tree of the right lower limb and its drainage).

We say that a lymphatic conduit *drains* a region when there is a lymphatic capillary in the *collects-from* relation to that region and in the *ld-connection* to that lymphatic conduit. It follows that drainage in that sense represents a lymphoid translocative route (by transitivity of *communication*).

drains x y $\equiv_{def}$ exists z (and (collects-from z y) (lt-connection z x))

Connectivity routes and communication affordances. Our account of topology in the immune system transforms connectivity routes in the lymphatic systems into routes of advective communication. Through extremal connections of the lymphatic system, we obtain i) advective communication routes to cardiovascular circulation and ii) convective communication routes from tissue fluid. Applying a similar treatment to cardiovascular circulation (advective), tissue fluid (convective), and their interface (convective), we obtain a complete picture of lymphoid and, more generally, bodily communication routes, Figure 6-b. We may thus navigate the immune system and trace relevant bodily processes using, as a basis, the ontology presented here (Figure 6-a).

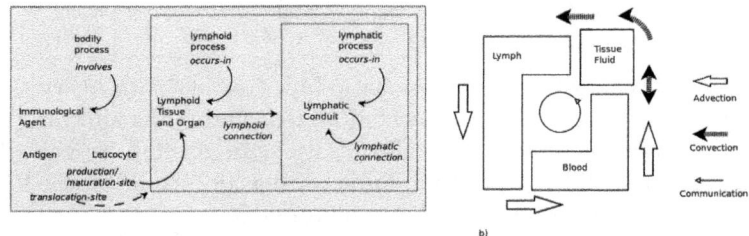

Fig. 6. Overview. a) The immune system, as a system of moving objects, animated by regionalised processes relating to connection routes (a dashed arrows indicates the partial relation of translocation to lymphoid sites). b) Connection routes correspond to compatible communication modalities (advection and convection at the depicted level) underlying body fluid flow and regional and transregional translocations of agents.

3   Knowledge – Integration – Application

The theory presented allows to record a number of locational and connection facts. For example, a specific fact such as that the thoracic duct (td) connects to the left brachiocephalic vein (lbv): (collects-from lbv td). Or a generic fact such as that T-lymphocytes mature in the thymus (thym): forall x (implies (t-lymphocyte y) (maturation-site x thym)). Inferences can be drawn from these (and additional similar facts) such as, for example, that the thoracic duct is a proximal lymphatic or to find a route of translocation for a lymphocyte from the thymus to an organ. On this basis, knowledge representation and reasoning can be expanded via the development of the theory (including definitional extension). The population of a knowledge base involves the sort of facts mentioned in section 1 and also the acquisistion of more background knowledge, in particular regarding anatomy and various cellular mechanisms.

We are developing a prototype implementation of the theory presented in this paper using the PowerLoom system [14]. PowerLoom, 'PLM' hereafter, allows for knowledge representation using the logic-based KIF language [15] which provides suitable expressivity for our theory. We can thus assert ground facts for our theory and query the resulting knowledge base (using classification and rule-based inferencing). The knowledge base can be primed by harvesting the FMA. We take the FMA—that purports to be a canonical model of human anatomy—as representing the anatomy of a particular individual (modulo sex). While a PLM connection to MySQL allows access to the SQL version of the FMA, it proves sometimes more efficient and useful to cache ground facts extracted from the FMA producing smaller KBs. This is not least because integration and curation of FMA extract is required, but we lack room here to discuss the intricacies of such mapping. As an illustration, we extracted the FMA relationships 'afferent to' and 'efferent to' to populate *ld-connection* (and also *collects-from*, in particular in the case of proximal lymphatics). Also extractible and relevant are direct high level drainage and anatomical parthood facts. It is also possible to extract more knowledge but in connection with a theory not discussed here.

The resulting system can be applied in a variety of ways illustrated in increasing order of complexity and cumulative order of development by the following.

- *Reasoning on raw data.* The most basic functionality is to query the connectivity knowledge base, finding connected regions and paths affording communication of different modality and regionalisation. In general, we gain the ability to navigate a knowledge acquisition source such as, for example, the FMA. Also, inference and classification results become resuable.

- *Variabity in annotation of raw data.* This approach supports the annotation of raw data, for example, patient radiological data, that presents variability in the connection of lymph vessels. The acquisistion of knowledge from sources, such as the FMA, as knowledge about an individual allows the alternative grounding of our knowledge base and the combination of canonical knowledge with atypical facts to account for variation.

- *Integration of biomedical terminologies.* There are many sources of annotation of biomedical data. A potential use of the ontology presented and an associated knowledge base is to define terms from biomedical vocabularies (NCI Thesaurus) and nomenclatures (ICD-10), as well as from other ontologies. Such contribution lies in providing formal definitions of terms (which can then be reasoned upon) and the resulting potential for integration of terminological resources.

- *Reasoning with knowledge from additional domains.* As a result of integration with related ontologies, new definitions and queries become possible. More complex scenarios relating to pathologies of the lymphatic (and cardiovascular) circulation can be devised so as to explore the consequences of certain disease conditions. For example, querying the knowledge base will allows us to predict regions that could develop an oedema as a consequence of the blockage of a given vessel or set of vessels. A second scenario would apply to the differential diagnosis of regional oedema, for example swelling of the leg due to pregnancy, radiotherapy, parasitic infiltration, or congestive heart failure.

4   Conclusion

In this paper, we have presented the core elements of a treatment of the immune system as a topological system, focusing primarily on routes of trafficking of immune biological agents within the lymphatic system. We assumed a similar representation of the cardiovascular system in relation to the body at large.

While the work described here is at an early stage, it has achieved a core representation based on the topology of the immune system. This work extends in two main directions. The first corresponds to filling a number of gaps in the account of the core immunological phenomena. Our discussion of biological agents was largely instrumental as these are the objects navigating the network with which we were primarily concerned. The next step is to further the definition of the variety of biological agents and also to link them to the various sites within the lymphoid system. This combines integration with other biomedical ontologies. The second line of developement is to consolidate our topological theory of the immune system and to continue its integration with other similar accounts of topologies in other systems (blood, but also nervous and digestive systems). In that respect the present work contributes a module to a general topology of human physiology.

Acknowledgement. Support by the EC projects RICORDO (www.ricordo.eu) and DDMORE (www.ddmore.eu) is gratefully acknolwedged. We are thankful to the reviewers of ICARIS for their comments on an earlier version of this paper.

References

1. Smith, B.: Ontology. In: The Blackwell Guide to the Philosophy of Computing and Information, pp. 153–166. Blackwell Publishing Ltd, Malden (2008)
2. Grenon, P., de Bono, B.: Cardiovascular System Ontology: Topology (manuscript in preparation)
3. Open Biomedical Ontologies, http://www.obofoundry.org
4. Bioportal, http://bioportal.bioontology.org/
5. Rosse, C., Mejino, J.: A Reference Ontology for Bioinformatics: The Foundational Model of Anatomy. Journal of Biomedical Informatics 36, 478–500 (2003)
6. Bard, J., Rhee, S., Ashburner, M.: An ontology for cell types. Genome Biology 6(2) (2005)
7. Grenon, P., Smith, B.: SNAP and SPAN. Spatial Cognition and Computation 4(1), 69–104 (2004)
8. Casati, R., Varzi, A.: The Structure of Spatial Localization. Philosophical Studies 82(2), 205–239 (1996)
9. Smith, B., Broogart, B.: Sixteen Days. The Journal of Medicine and Philosophy 28(1), 45–78 (2003)
10. Smith, B., et al.: Relations in Biomedical Ontologies. Genome Biology 6 (2005)
11. Smith, B., Grenon, P.: The Cornucopia of Formal-Ontological Relations. Dialectica 58(3), 279–296 (2004)
12. Pool, M.: An Applied Calculus for Spatial Accessibility Reasoning. Journal of Universal Computer Science 9(9), 986–1007 (2003)
13. Smith, B.: Mereotopology: A Theory of Parts and Boundaries. Data and Knowledge Engineerring 20, 287–303 (1996)
14. PowerLoom, http://www.isi.edu/isd/LOOM/PowerLoom/
15. Knowledge Interchange Format (dpANS),
   http://logic.stanford.edu/kif/dpans.html

Refitting Harel Statecharts for Systemic Mathematical Models in Computational Immunology

Chris H. McEwan[1,2], Hugues Bersini[3], David Klatzmann[1],
Veronique Thomas- Vaslin[1], and Adrien Six[1]

[1] UPMC Univ Paris 06, UMR7211, I2D3 Integrative Immunology: Differentiation,
Diversity, Dynamics, 83 Bd de l'Hôpital F-75013 Paris, France
[2] CNRS UMR7606, LIP-6, Agents Cognitifs et Apprentissage Symbolique
Automatique, 4 Place Jussieu 75005 Paris, France
[3] IRIDIA Université Libre de Bruxelles, 50 Av. F. Roosevelt, Brussels, Belgium

Abstract. In this abstract we report progress in applying techniques,
traditionally used by computer scientists in specifying finite state machines, to concisely express complex mathematical models. These techniques complement existing graphical methods in Systems Biology by
allowing a systems approach to be taken at a coarser granularity than
biochemical reactions – where parallel, multi-level interactions within
and between systems must be communicated and simulated.

1 Introduction

Modelling of complex systems is a persistent problem in science. In principle,
modelling is the means by which empirical observations can be explained and
predicted by mechanistic reasoning. In practice, modelling is fraught with many
methodological and pragmatic trade-offs, such as the choice between homogeneous population-based and heterogeneous individual-based methods. Non-
negligible technical details of modelling efforts tend to be largely opaque to
experimentalist collaborators, whose complex systems these models claim to
offer insight into. A complementary problem exists, communicating subtle biological phenomenon to formally trained collaborators. Our proposed attack on
these problems utilises techniques developed by computer scientists for specifying Finite State Machines (FSM). FSM are the *de facto* engineering approach
to developing many real-time safety critical systems, such as those in the avion-
ics industry [4] and these systems tend to be significantly more complex than
typical mathematical models in science. The key observation here is that, although the semantics of these formalisms may be quite different, the techniques
introduced below largely operate on a common underlying graph structure, *not
the semantics of these graphs*. This combinatorial perspective allows us to resolve a difficult issue with developing and communicating complex mathematical
models. In turn, this allows mathematical models to approach the intuitiveness
and heterogeneity of individual-based methods, while retaining the strong formal
methodology and computational efficiency lacking in the latter.

P. Liò, G. Nicosia, and T. Stibor (Eds.): ICARIS 2011, LNCS 6825, pp. 44–50, 2011.

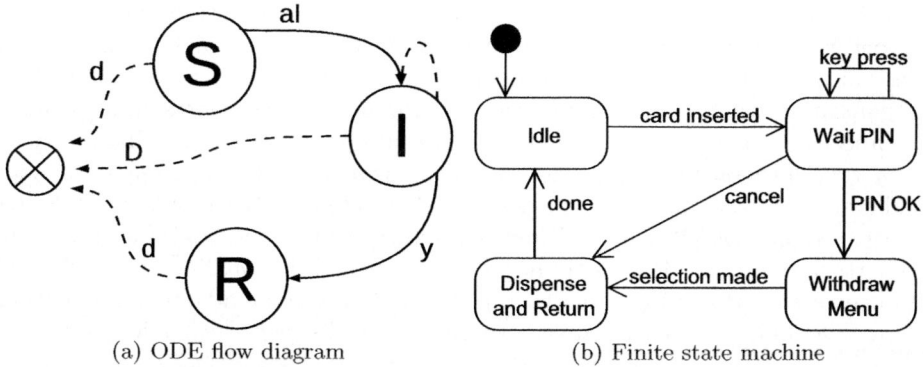

(a) ODE flow diagram   (b) Finite state machine

Fig. 1. ODE and FSM models as directed graphs. (a) The classic "susceptible, infected, recovered" model from epidemiology, parametrised by rates of flow between population compartments. The ODE can be read off from this diagram, e.g. $\frac{dI}{dt} = aIS - DI - yI$. (b) A simple finite-state representation of a cash machine. Transitions occur in response to discrete external events generated as the customer interacts with the machine.

2   Background and Related Work

Classically, an ODE model is presented as an n-dimensional state vector $x(t)$, representing the n quantities of interest at time t, and a system of n coupled differential equations of the general form

$$\frac{dx_i}{dt} = f_i(x,t) = \sum_j^n f_{ij}(x,t) - \sum_j^n f_{ji}(x,t), \tag{1}$$

where each f_{ij} quantifies the flow of "mass" into x_i from x_j. For maximal generality, each f_{ij} is presented as an arbitrary function of the current state x. In practice, f_{ij} may be a function of x_j, $x_j x_k$ for some $k \in [1, n]$, or a constant. Typically, many $f_{ij} = 0$ and none of them depend explicitly on time t. This deliberately over-general presentation makes the graphical form of an ODE readily apparent (see Fig. 1(a)): each variable x_i can be represented as node and each f_{ij} as a directed edge. Such graphical approaches are sometimes used for pedagogical purposes, under the the moniker of *flow charts* [7]. Graphical modelling is also popular in Systems Biology (see e.g. [5]) although the approach we introduce here will be more widely applicable than chemical kinetics.

In contrast, Finite State Machines are a computational formalism that are explicitly based on directed graphs (see Fig. 1(b)). Here, each node represents a possible "state" of the machine; each edge represent the change of state that occurs in response to a discrete "event". There are several flavours of this formalism, though the details are not important here. Although Fig. 1(b) is intuitive, as FSM become more elaborate the complexity of the graph structure rapidly grows beyond that of the behaviour it describes. In the worst case, introducing a state may result in a combinatorial increase in the elements of the graph.

To address this problem, Harel introduced statecharts [3], a graphical formalism for the unambiguous representation of complex finite state machines. The impetus for this increased level of abstraction was concern not unlike that we see voiced today in biological modelling, e.g. a need for hierarchical, multi-level organisation with a controllable level of granularity; and representing systems composed of complex internal sub-systems that operate in parallel. Indeed, Harel is a vocal proponent of applying this formalism to modelling complex biological systems [1,2,9], albeit as an agent-based paradigm. Others have incorporated state machine and ODE formalisms in so-called "hybrid models". Recently, statecharts were proposed as an aid in producing logical (i.e. qualitative) models [8]. In contrast to preceding work, we apply statecharts to quantitative, population-based modelling of continuous-deterministic and discrete-stochastic systems.

3   Cellular Processes: A Motivating Example

To avoid digressions that distract from the technique itself, we develop a toy model that can be easily followed and succinctly explained. We also take some liberties with the biology in order to demonstrate specific points. This illustrative model is based on modelling work currently being developed in immunology.

3.1   The Complexity of Systemic Models Grows Multiplicatively

Consider a hypothetical model of a lymphocyte that, after an initial period of "naivety", has its receptor bind to its ligand. This induces the cell to become an "effector", performing some function not relevant here. After a period, effector functionality wears off and this binding process can repeat indefinitely, but the cell is now upgraded to a "memory", rather than "naive", cell. Perhaps effector cells proliferate more heavily and memory cells have a lower death rate. Such models are typical in theoretical immunology and a likely model might be

$$\frac{dN}{dt} = b + p_1 N - (d_1 + a(N, M, L))N \tag{2}$$

$$\frac{dE}{dt} = p_2 E + a(N, M, L)N + a(M, N, L)M - (d_2 + y)E \tag{3}$$

$$\frac{dM}{dt} = p_1 M + yE - (d_2 + a(M, N, L))M \tag{4}$$

where N, E, and M represent naive, effector and memory cell populations, respectively, and b, d_i, p_i and y are rates of birth, death, proliferation and maturation. The non-linear function a quantifies competition for and binding to ligand L, the details of which have no immediate bearing on our presentation. Now, lymphocytes spend their life between peripheral tissues in the body and the lymph nodes, where antigenic debris is drained and collected. Not only is there a greater concentration of ligand in the lymph node, but also the appropriate chemical environment for sustained proliferation. We need to expand our model to account for these facts, which requires replicating Eqs. (2)-(4) to represent dynamics inside and outside the lymph node, as well as flow into and out of the lymph node itself. Perhaps

$$\frac{dN}{dt} = b + p_1 N - (d_1 + j + a(N, M, L))N + kN' \tag{5}$$

$$\frac{dE}{dt} = p_2 E + a(N, M, L) + a(M, N, L) - (d_2 + j + y)E + kE' \tag{6}$$

$$\frac{dM}{dt} = p_1 M + yE - (d_2 + j + a(M, N, L))M + kM' \tag{7}$$

$$\frac{dN'}{dt} = p_1 N' - (d_1 + k + a(N', M', L'))N' + jN \tag{8}$$

$$\frac{dE'}{dt} = p_3 E' + a(N', M', L') + a(M', N', L') - (d_2 + k + y)E' + jE \tag{9}$$

$$\frac{dM'}{dt} = p_1 M' + yE' - (d_2 + k + a(M', N', L'))M' + jM \tag{10}$$

where primed variables represent lymph-node specific quantities, j and k represent flow into and out of the lymph node, respectively, and p_3 represents the increased proliferation rate due to the favourable environment.

We now introduce an experimental treatment where dividing cells can be induced to initiate apoptosis, or cell death (see e.g. [10]). To emphasise our point, at some cost to biological plausibility, we will assume that this treatment takes effect at any checkpoint during the cell-cycle and that there is sufficient reason and data to warrant modelling at this level of detail. This simply provides a finer-granularity to the modelling task while avoiding contrived realism. We omit the full mathematical derivation, which would require replicating Eq. (5) - (10) for each stage of cell-cycle, with additional terms to account for movement between these stages and the absence or presence of treatment. For a basic 5-stage cell-cycle, the result is a system of 30 equations with over 125 individual terms. Although by no means a complex phenomenological description by biological standards, its mathematical expression has already become incommensurately complex, tedious and fragile.

3.2 Using Statecharts to Factor Model Complexity

Figure 2 provides a statechart description of our motivating example, including cell-cycle. Notice how the diagram complexity is closer to the complexity of the biological description. This is in large part due to the introduction of *hierarchy* and *orthogonal parallelism* as organisational constructs (see [6] for a more formal exposition of statechart constructs in the context of this model). In contrast, the directed graph represented by this statechart is shown below and, like Fig. 1(a), is of proportional complexity to the mathematical description. Recall, even though this complex model may be what is ultimately *executed*, it is the statechart that is *communicated* and *developed* amongst collaborators.

Much like the flow diagram depicted in Fig. 1(a), each node in the directed graph is a component of the state vector x and each transition a term $f_{ij}(x)$.

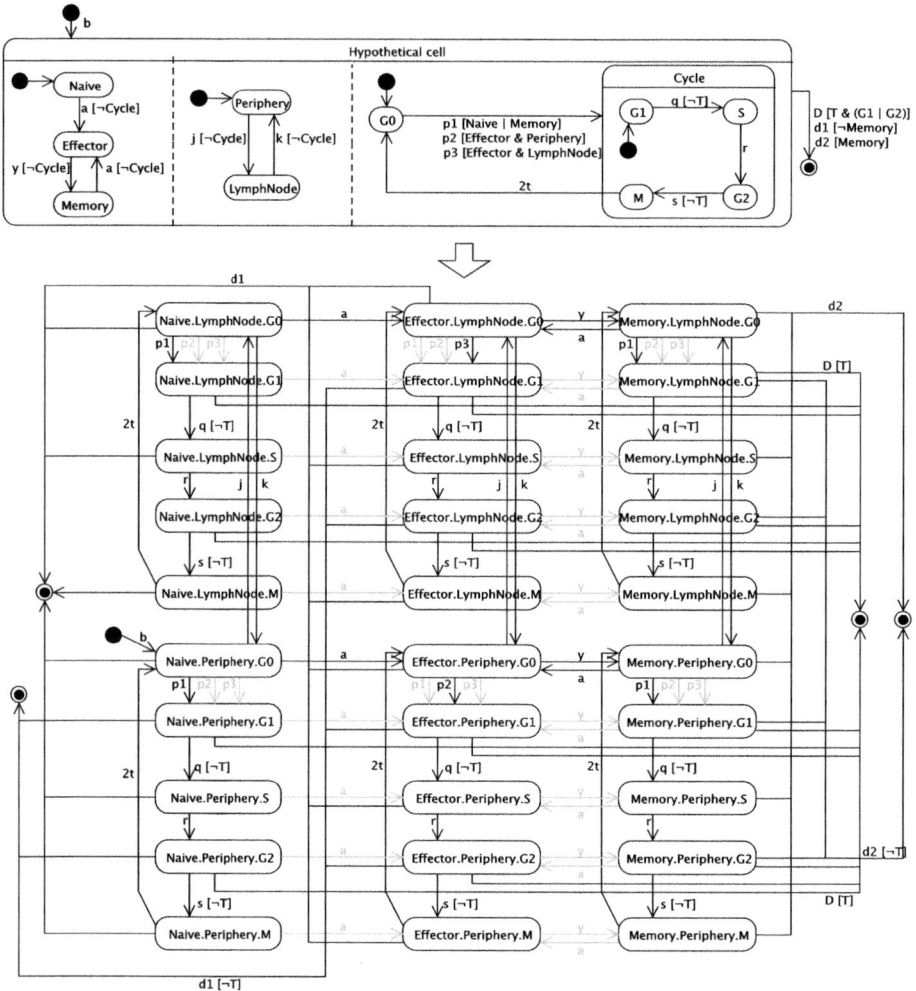

Fig. 2. The statechart (top) and underlying directed graph (bottom) representing the illustrative model. The former remains closer to the conceptual complexity of the model, while retaining the necessary expressive power to specify all possible execution paths in the latter. Hierarchy in the model is demonstrated with the expanded detail in cell-cycle states. Orthogonal parallelism allows us to express the three phenomenon *as if* they were independent, with dependencies annotated on the diagram (e.g. a cell cannot move while in cell cycle). From the concise statechart description, it is possible to automatically derive the directed graph which can then be translated into ODEs or simulated in place. Greyed-out transitions have guards (the logical expressions in square brackets) that can be evaluated as false and removed prior to simulation.

What we gain, over Fig. 1(a), is the ability to finesse the homogeneity assumption by introducing fine-grained structuring of the population without incurring the cognitive costs of maintaining and communicating the accompanying mathematical or graphical structure.

3.3   Beyond Model Representation

The directed graph structure in Fig. 1(a) is readily translated into a form expected by traditional numerical integration libraries or intermediate formats such as SBML. Going further, we have implemented a prototype system that produces simulations automatically from a statechart description expressed in XML. It is a relatively straight-forward exercise to translate traditional vector-based numerical methods for continuous-deterministic and discrete-stochastic scheduling, parameter fitting and sensitivity analysis to the directed graph structure employed here. Further, given their simpler semantics, ODE models have proven to be more readily amenable to the model-driven development and automatic code-generation philosophy behind statecharts proper.

A compelling feature of this graphical formalism, not discussed in the preceding material, is its malleability and extensibility. States, transitions and parameters are all first-class objects that can be easily rewired and reparameterised even, in principle, by experimentalist collaborators. State and transition classes can be extended to represent e.g. arbitrary non-linear functional forms or common modelling patterns such as temporally-constrained states. This allows theorists, experimentalists and even reverse-engineering algorithms to explore structural and functional forms of a model without maintaining the underlying numerical realisation. Although existing graphical modelling languages may claim similar benefits, to our knowledge none are able to generate the substantial bulk of a model automatically from a concise human-friendly description.

4   Conclusion

The ability to model sub-system parallelism and multi-level hierarchy is a powerful feature of Harel statecharts – a feature that is sometimes lost in the literature under computer science and software engineering nomenclature. We have shown how a formalised subset of Harel statecharts can be applied to scaling mathematical descriptions of systemic phenomena. In addition to finessing the associated increase in underlying model complexity for the modeller, this approach provides a graphical communication medium that, in our experience, is readily accepted by non-technical collaborators and can be productively discussed, questioned and reformulated without excessive concern for underlying technical details. We submit that with some minor enrichment of the statechart diagram language, to better align it with scientific investigation and reporting, statecharts could serve as an effective medium of communication and development for experimentalists and theorists that supports both computational and mathematical approaches.

References

1. Efroni, S., Harel, D., Cohen, I.R.: Emergent dynamics of thymocyte development and lineage determination. PLoS Computational Biology 3(1) 13 (2007)
2. Harel, D.: Concurrency in Biological Modeling: Behavior, Execution and Visualization. Electronic Notes in Theoretical Computer Science 194(3), 119–131 (2008)
3. Harel, D.: Statecharts: a visual formalism for complex systems. Science of Computer Programming 8, 231–274 (1987)
4. Harel, D.: Statecharts in the Making: A Personal Account. In: HOPL III Proceedings of the Third ACM SIGPLAN Conference on History of Programming Languages (2007)
5. Kitano, H., Funahashi, A., Matsuoka, Y., Oda, K.: Using process diagrams for the graphical representation of biological networks. Nature Biotechnology 23(8), 961–966 (2005)
6. McEwan, C.H., Bersini, H., Klatzmann, D., Thomas-Vaslin, V., Six, A.: A computational technique to scale mathematical models towards complex heterogeneous systems. Submitted to COSMOS 2011 Workshop on Complex Systems Modelling (2011)
7. Otto, S.P., Day, T.: A biologist's guide to mathematical modeling in ecology and evolution. Princeton University Press, Princeton (2007)
8. Shin, Y.-J., Nourani, M.: Statecharts for gene network modeling. PLoS ONE 5(2) (2010)
9. Swerdlin, B.N., Cohen, I.R., Harel, D.: The Lymph Node B Cell Immune Response: Dynamic Analysis In-Silico. Proceedings of the IEEE (2008)
10. Thomas-Vaslin, V., Altes, H.K., de Boer, R.J., Klatzmann, D.: Comprehensive Assessment and Mathematical Modeling of T Cell Dynamics and Homeostasis. The Journal of Immunology 180, 2240–2250 (2008)

In Silico Investigation into CD8Treg Mediated Recovery in Murine Experimental Autoimmune Encephalomyelitis

Richard A. Williams[1], Mark Read[1], Jon Timmis[1,2],
Paul S. Andrews[1], and Vipin Kumar[3]

[1] Department of Computer Science, University of York, UK
{rawillia,markread,jtimmis,psa}@cs.york.ac.uk
[2] Department of Electronics, University of York, UK
[3] Laboratory of Autoimmunity, Torrey Pines Institute for Molecular Studies,
La Jolla, USA

Extended Abstract

Experimental autoimmune encephalomyelitis (EAE) is an animal model of human autoimmune diseases in general, and multiple sclerosis (MS) in particular [2]. The animal disease is mediated through a network of cells; encephalitogenic CDThelper (CD4Th1) cells are activated in the peripheral lymph nodes following immunization for EAE[1], and migrate to the central nervous system where they induce activation of microglia, macrophages and dendritic cells (DCs). The resultant inflammation causes demyelination of neurons, prompting the presentation of myelin basic protein (MBP) to additional encephalitogenic T cell populations in the cervical lymph nodes by migratory DCs. The spontaneous recovery that occurs following autoimmune episodes is associated with the induction of apoptosis in encephalitogenic CD4Th1 cells by a CD8 regulatory T cell (CD8Treg) population [1,6]. Tang et al [7] demonstrated a mechanism where CD4Treg cells assist DCs in priming CD8Treg cells, which mediate down-regulation of the autoimmune response through selective apoptotic elimination of CD4Th1 cells.

The exact location of this down-regulation of the autoimmune response by CD8Treg cells is unknown. One possibility is that DCs migrating from the central nervous system, potentially carrying both MBP (from neurons) and T cell receptor (TCR) derived peptides (Fr3 and CDR1/2; from encephalitogenic CD4Th1 cells), are simultaneously priming both CD4Th1 and Treg cell populations, and that regulation of autoimmunity is taking place around the DC. In this paper we investigate the effect of regulation of CD4Th1 cells by CD8Treg cells through use of a simulation (ARTIMUS) we have developed to support investigation into EAE [5]. We investigate the hypothesis that a significant portion of CD4Th1 regulation by CD8Treg cells occurs around DCs that prime both T cell populations, and hence that regulation occurring around such DCs is critical for recovery from disease.

---

[1] Immunization is through MBP, a myelin derivative, complete Freund's adjuvant and pertussis toxin, which are both powerful immunopotentiators.

P. Liò, G. Nicosia, and T. Stibor (Eds.): ICARIS 2011, LNCS 6825, pp. 51–54, 2011.
© Springer-Verlag Berlin Heidelberg 2011

In [9] we examined the peptide presentation profiles for DCs *in silico* using ARTIMUS, and showed that the vast majority of DCs (circa 90%) do not present antigenic peptides, and of those that do, the overwhelming majority (circa 90%; or 9% of total DCs) present either MBP or TCR-derived peptides, but not both. In fact, only 1% of DCs present both MBP and TCR-derived peptides. To further investigate peptide presentation dynamics, we have augmented ARTIMUS such that presentation of antigenic peptide by DCs is *mutually exclusive*; DCs are no longer able to present both MBP and TCR-derived peptides.

This manipulation to ARTIMUS allows DCs to phagocytose cells as normal, however only the first processed peptide type (MBP or TCR) can become presented on Major Histocompatibility Complexes (MHCs) of the DC. This negates the ability of a single DC to prime both CD4Th1 and CD4Treg cells, and prevents regulation taking place around priming DCs, therefore allowing us to observe the effects on the system. If killing is not significantly altered by this augmentation, then regulation around DCs cannot be critical for recovery from the autoimmune response.

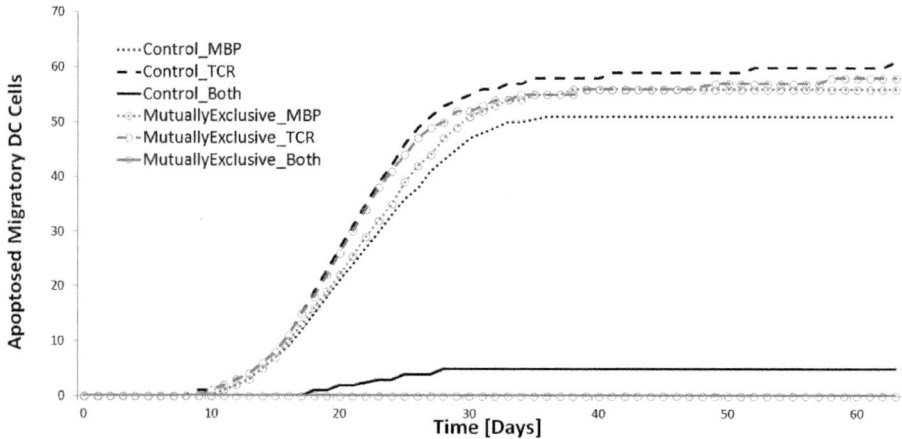

Fig. 1. Median averages from 1,000 runs were taken for each of the control and *mutually exclusive* DC simulation runs. To ensure individual DCs were only counted once, counts were taken of DCs that had entered apoptosis by the end of the simulation. A-Test scores confirmed that the *mutually exclusive* DC simulation experiments resulted in no DCs presenting both MBP and TCR-derived peptides (score = 0.002), a small effect size difference in TCR-derived expression (score = 0.427) and MBP presentation (score = 0.635), although no real scientific significance, and virtually no effect size difference in total DCs (score = 0.503) or cells presenting no antigen (score = 0.478).

Non-parametric A-Tests [8] are used to measure scientific significance (effect size) of the differences between cell populations from the augmented simulator with respect to control (un-augmented simulation) cell populations. The A-Test provides a score between 0 and 1 representing the probability that a randomly selected sample for distribution one is larger than a randomly selected sample for distribution two. Vargha and Delaney [8] provide thresholds to indicate the magnitude of difference between two distributions. They indicate scores >0.71 and <0.29 to represent *large* differences, and we assume these boundaries to indicate scientific significance.

A-Test scores show that the *mutually exclusive* presentation of antigenic peptides by DCs result in a small decrease in the number of DCs presenting TCR-derived peptides (A-Test score = 0.427) and a small increase in the number of DCs presenting MBP-derived peptides (A-Test score = 0.635) with respect to the control (figure 1). This leads to an approximate 10% reduction in the priming of CD8Treg cells within the system, which leads to an approximate 5% reduction overall in the total number of CD4Th1 cells which are apoptosed by CD8Treg population. Our primary focus however, is the effect of *mutually exclusive* presentation on priming DCs within the CLN where DCs prime both populations of T cells (CD4Th1 and CD4Treg). A-Test scores for total CD4Th1 apoptosis and CD4Th1 apoptosis within the CLN (A-Test scores of 0.415 and 0.44) indicate a small difference in the CD4Th1 killing facilitated by CD8Treg cells with respect to control.

In Conclusion

This paper has sought to investigate, through simulation, the extent to which regulation of the autoimmune response in EAE takes place around DCs that prime both autoimmune and Treg cell populations. Observation of DC peptide presentation profiles has established that only 10% of DCs that are able to prime T cells simultaneously prime *both* CD4Th1 and Treg populations. Therefore, with only 1% of total DCs simultaneously presenting both MBP and TCR-derived peptides, it seems unlikely that the hypothesis is true. Furthermore, given our criteria for scientifically significant results, A-Test scores indicate that no significant difference in the ability of CD8Treg cells to regulate the CD4Th1 population arises from this manipulation. We therefore reject the hypothesis that a significant portion of CD4Th1 regulation by CD8Treg cells occurs around DCs that prime both T cell populations, and conclude that the apoptosis of CD4Th1 cells as induced by CD8Treg cells does not critically rely on these T cell populations being primed on the same DCs.

Simulation results can not, as yet, be confirmed using *in vitro* or *in vivo* testing due to limitations in current wet-lab technology. Our approach to simulation based investigation employs close liaison between the modellers and domain expert to get a firm handle on the domain model [4], and rigorous statistical methods to best align simulation work with the real domain, notably through careful calibration and sensitivity analysis [3].

This work forms part of ongoing work to further understand the CD8Treg mediated regulatory pathway in EAE through complementing wet-lab work with *in silico* experimentation.

References

1. Kumar, V., Sercarz, E.: An integrative model of regulation centered on recognition of TCR peptide/MHC complexes. Immunological Reviews 182, 113–121 (2001)
2. Pender, M.P.: Experimental autoimmune encephalomyelitis. In: Pender, M.P., McCombe, P.A. (eds.) Autoimmune Neurological Disease, pp. 26–88. Cambridge University Press, Cambridge (1995)
3. Read, M., Andrews, P., Timmis, J., Kumar, V.: Techniques for grounding agent-based simulations in the real domain: a case study in experimental autoimmune encephalomyelitis. Mathematical and Computer Modelling of Dynamical Systems (accepted)
4. Read, M., Timmis, J., Andrews, P.S., Kumar, V.: A domain model of experimental autoimmune encephalomyelitis. In: Stepney, S., Welch, P.H., Andrews, P.S., Timmis, J. (eds.) CoSMoS, pp. 9–44. Luniver Press (2009)
5. Read, M., Timmis, J., Andrews, P.S., Kumar, V.: An in-silico simulation of experimental autoimmune encephalomyelitis (in Preparation)
6. Smith, T.R.F., Kumar, V.: Revival of CD8+ Treg-mediated suppression. Trends in Immunology 29, 337–342 (2008)
7. Tang, X., Kumar, V.: Specific control of immunity by regulatory CD8 T cells. Cellular and Molecular Immunology 2, 11–19 (2005)
8. Vargha, A., Delaney, H.D.: A critique and improvement of the CL common language effect size statistics of McGraw and Wong. Journal of Educational and Behavioral Statistics 25, 101–132 (2000)
9. Williams, R.A. In Silico Experimentation using Simulation of Experimental Autoimmune Encephalomyelitis. Master's Thesis, University of York, York, UK (2010)

Classification of MHC I Proteins According to Their Ligand-Type Specificity

Eduardo Martínez-Naves[2], Esther M. Lafuente[2], and Pedro A. Reche[1,2,*]

[1] Laboratory of Immunomedicine
[2] Department of Microbiology I–Immunology, Facultad de Medicina,
Universidad Complutense de Madrid, Av. Complutense, s/n, Madrid 28040, Spain
{emnaves,melafuente,parecheg}@med.ucm.es

Abstract. Major histocompatibility complex class I (MHC I) molecules belong to a large and diverse protein superfamily whose families can be divided in three groups according to the type of ligands that they can accommodate (ligand-type specificity): peptides, lipids or none. Here, we assembled a dataset of MHC I proteins of known ligand-type specificity (MHCI^{556} dataset) and trained k-nearest neighbor and support vector machine algorithms. In cross-validation, the resulting classifiers predicted the ligand-type specificity of MHC I molecules with an accuracy $\geq 99\%$, using solely their amino acid composition. By holding out entire MHC I families prior to model building, we proved that ML-based classifiers trained on amino acid composition are capable of predicting the ligand-type specificity of MHC I molecules unrelated to those used for model building. Moreover, they are superior to BLAST at predicting the class of MHC I molecules that do not bind any ligand.

Keywords: classical MHC class I molecules, non-classical MHC class I molecules, machine learning, ligand, prediction.

1 Introduction

The major histocompatibility complex class I (MHC I) protein family encompass a large number of diverse glycoproteins that can be divided into classical MHC I molecules and non-classical and MHC I-like molecules [1]. Because of their crucial role in graft rejection and antigen presentation, classical MHC I molecules (hereafter MHC Ia) were the first to be discovered and studied. In humans, MHC molecules are, for historical reasons, known as human leukocyte antigens (HLAs).

MHC Ia molecules are cell surface expressed glycoproteins consisting of an α chain (encoded inside the MHC gene region) paired with β2-microglobulin (β2m), and their function is to present peptides for immune recognition by CD8 T cells [2]. MHC I-bound peptides are nested in a cleft of the α1α2 domain of the MHC I molecule (MHC I α1α2 domain), which comprises two α-helices lying above a floor of 8 antiparallel β-strands.

---

* Corresponding author.

P. Liò, G. Nicosia, and T. Stibor (Eds.): ICARIS 2011, LNCS 6825, pp. 55–65, 2011.
© Springer-Verlag Berlin Heidelberg 2011

Non-classical and MHC I-like molecules (hereafter MHC Ib molecules) were discovered later and differ in many aspects from MHC Ia molecules [3]. MHC Ib molecules can be encoded inside or outside the MHC locus, display a wide range of functions and, in contrast to MHC Ia molecules, are either non-polymorphic or exhibit little polymorphism [3]. Moreover, while MHC Ia molecules can only bind peptides, there are known examples of MHC Ib molecules that bind peptides, others that bind lipids and some that do not have any ligand –they have an empty groove.

Relevant examples of peptide-binding MHC Ib molecules are HLA-E and HLA-G, and their mouse functional counterparts Qa1 (H2-T23) and Qa2 (H2-Q9), respectively. All these molecules behave much as MHC Ia molecules [4-7]: peptide binding is necessary for stable cell surface expression and T cells can recognize the bound peptides. However, in addition to antigen presentation, they are also involved in immunoregulation, bridging innate immunity and adaptive immunity through their interaction with Natural Killer (NK) cells [8].

MHC Ib molecules that are known to bind lipids include CD1 antigens, which present them to $\alpha\beta$ T cells [9]; AZGP1 (zinc-binding alpha-2-glycoprotein 1; ZAG), a soluble lipid mobilizing factor that binds fatty acid and fatty acid analogues [10]; and PROCR (Endothelial Protein C Receptor; EPCR), which binds phospholipids and plays an important role in the inhibition mechanism of coagulation mediated through protein C activation [11]. The distinct families of MHC Ib molecules that bind lipids differ not only functionally but also structurally. Thus, while the 3D-structure of CD1 antigens resemble closely that of MHC Ia molecules, ZAG does not pair with β2m [12] and EPCR in addition also lacks the α3 domain [13].

The group of MHC Ib molecules without bound ligands includes TLA (H2-T3), a mouse thymus leukemia antigen involved in intestinal intraepithelial immunity and the molecules T9 (H2-T9), T10 (H2-T10) and T22 (H2-T22). Despite de lack of ligand, TLA, T9, T10 and T22 all encompass β2m and are capable of interacting directly with TCRs, yet without presenting any antigen [14, 15]. In contrast, other ligand-free MHC Ib molecules such as MICA and B and ULBP (1, 2 & 3) are distantly related to MHC Ia molecules, do not pair with β2m and interact with activating receptors from NK and T cells [16]. Finally, there are also MHC Ib molecules without bound ligands, like FcRn (FCGRT) and HFE, that do not interact with NK or T cells. FcRn is an immunoglobulin G (IgG) Fc receptor that mediates the transfer of IgG from the mothers' plancenta and milk to fetuses and newborns, respectively [17], whereas HFE is involved in regulation of iron levels [18]. Both, FcRn and HFE, encompass β2m [19, 20].

Functional characterization of MHC I molecules generally requires identifying their cognate ligands. The quest to identify the ligands of MHC I proteins is, however, not an easier task and requires having an *a priori* knowledge of their nature/type so that the experimental efforts can be appropriately directed. Therefore, anticipating the type of bound ligands –if any– of MHC I proteins is worth the effort. In this work we have approached the problem of predicting the ligand-type specificity of MHC I molecules using machine learning. Specifically, we trained k-nearest neighbor and support vector machine classifiers that in cross-validation predict the ligand-type specificity of MHC I molecules with great accuracy and just using the amino acid composition as input features

2   Materials and Methods

2.1   Sequence Collection and Processing

We collected the amino acid sequences of MHC I molecules of known ligand-type specificity (P:Peptides, L:Lipids or N:No ligand) from specialized databases –the IMGT/HLA and IPD-MHC databases at EBML-EBI (http://www.ebi.ac.uk)– and from pre-computed BLAST similarity searches. Pre-computed BLAST similarity searches were obtained for selected query sequences using the BLINK utility at NCBI. Sequences obtained from specialized databases consisted of MHC Ia molecules –belonged to the peptide-binding group– whereas the sequences collected from pre-computed BLAST searches were assigned to have the same type of ligand than that of the sequence queries. Sequences that were collected after each query was decided upon visual inspection of the BLAST hits.

We selected the of α1α2 domain of the collected sequences by aligning them to a profile hidden Markov model (pHMM) of the MHC I α1α2 domain, using the HMMER package [21]. We discarded any domain sequence with less that 170 amino acids or more than 190 amino acids, keeping only unique and non-overlapping sequences. The pHMM employed in this task (PF00129, class I Histocompatibility antigen, domains alpha 1 and 2) was obtained from PFAM [22].

2.2   Sequence Similarity Reduction and Similarity Analyses

To reduce sequence similarity in datasets we used the *purge* utility of the Gibbs Sampler [23], using an exhaustive method and maximum blosum62 relatedness score of 925. We analyzed the sequence identity in datasets from pairwise sequence alignments that were obtained using the Needleman–Wunsch global alignment algorithm implemented with the *needle* application of the EMBOSS package [24]. For any given dataset of N sequences, we analyzed $N!/2*(N-2)$ distinct pairwise sequence alignments and computed the mean sequence identity in the dataset and the respective standard deviation.

2.3   Model Building and Evaluation

We used the Waikato Environment for Knowledge Analysis (WEKA)[25] to built and evaluate machine learning (ML)-based classification models. As input for WEKA, we provided datasets in Attribute-Relation Format (ARFF), using the amino acid composition of the α1α2 domain as attributes and the known ligand-type class (P:Peptides, L:Lipids and N:No ligand) as classification instances. The amino acid composition of any protein sequence consists of a fixed vector of 20 dimensions (f_i), each specific for every distinct amino acid (i) and computed using equation 1.

$$fi = \frac{n_i}{N} \tag{1}$$

where i refers to any of the 20 amino acid types, N is the total number of amino acids (sequence length), and n_i is the number of i amino acids.

WEKA provides a large collection of ML algorithms for data classification. In this study, we selected k-Nearest Neighbor algorithm (kNN) and support vector machines (SVMs) [26, 27]. Briefly, kNN classification first finds a number, k, of examples in the training dataset that are closest to the test example, which is then assigned to the predominant class. SVM classification relies on mapping the input feature vector onto a higher m-dimensional feature space using some non-linear function (kernel), where an optimal separation of the data can be achieved with a linear model. As kernels for SVMs, we used a Radial Basis Function (RBF-kernel) and Polynomial functions (P-kernel). Moreover, we used the sequential minimal optimization (SMO) algorithm [28] to train SVMs. Model optimization was achieved by varying the relevant parameters of the selected ML algorithms on multiple classification experiments: k for kNN classification, C an G for the RBF-Kernel and E and C for the P-kernel.

The performance of models was evaluated estimating the percentage of properly corrected instances (*ACC, accuracy*) in 10-fold cross-validation experiments. In a 10-fold cross-validation, the data is randomly partitioned into 10 sets, and the instances in each set are tested using classifiers trained on all of the remaining data. Thus, the data is never tested with models trained on them. We repeated the 10-fold cross-validation experiments 10 times, obtaining average and standard deviations noted measures of performance from 100 different values.

2.4 Classification of MHC I Sequences Using BLAST

To predict the ligand-type specificity (P, L, N) MHC I molecules using BLAST we utilized BLAST-formatted databases derived from the relevant training datasets. BLAST searches were executed with default settings and BLAST-formatted databases were derived from FASTA files in which each distinct MHC I sequence had a header with a label indicating the nature of its ligand (P: peptides, L:lipids and N: No ligand).

3   Results and Discussion

3.1   Dataset of MHC I Molecules of Known Ligand-Type Specificity

The type of ligands that MHC I molecules can bind can be inferred from that of MHC I molecules of known ligand-type specificity. All MHC I protein family members that have been characterized so far can either bind peptides (P), lipids (L) or have no ligand (N). Therefore, we assembled a dataset consisting of 556 unique, non-overlapping amino acid sequences of members of this family (hereafter MHCI[556] dataset) comprising 395, 84 and 117 sequences that binding peptides (P), lipids (L) or have no ligand (N), respectively. The distinct MHC I families –and their ligand type-specificity– included in the MHCI[556] dataset are listed Table 1. In this dataset, we only incorporated the sequence of the α1α2 domain, for this domain bears the binding groove whose physicochemical properties and shape determine the binding ability of the MHCI molecule. Moreover, to avoid incomplete domains and domains with translated introns, we only included sequences that ranged from 170 to 190 amino acid residues –the average size of the MHC I α1α2 domain is ~ 180 residues.

Table 1. MHC I molecules in MHCI[556] dataset

MHCI	Species	Seqs.	Ligand
HLA-[ABC]	Human	111	P
DLA-88	Dog	22	P
SLA-[123]	Swine	51	P
BoLA-N	Cattle	39	P
OLA-N	Sheep	12	P
ONMY-UBA	Rainbow trout	29	P
SASA-UBA	Atlantic Salmon	27	P
RT1-A	Rat	21	P
H2-X	Mouse	26	P
HLA-E	Human and Primates	6	P
HLA-G	Human and primates	1	P
H2-T23(Qa1)	Mouse and Rat	4	P
H2-Q9	Mouse	2	P
H2-M3	Mouse and Rat	4	P
CD1[A-E]	Vertebrates	71	L
ZAG	Vertebrates	6	L
EPCR	Vertebrates	7	L
MICA&B	Vertebrates	38	N
HFE	Vertebrates	6	N
MILL1&2	Mouse and Rat	4	N
FcRN	Vertebrates	9	N
ULPB	Vertebrates	45	N
H2-T3(TLA)	Mouse and Rat	15	N

Dataset is available from corresponding author upon writing request.

Large sequence similarity in datasets can be detrimental for the generalization power of predictive methods and, in general, can inflate predictions rates [29]. Therefore, in the MHCI[556] dataset we also included those sequences that remained after applying a sequence-similarity reduction schema (See Material and Methods). Sequence similarity between the proteins belonging to the P, L and N group is 63.69 ± 17.62, 41.8 ± 15.37, 36.37 ± 21.07, respectively.

3.2 ML-Based Classifiers Predicting the Ligand-Type Specificity of MHC I Molecules

We built and evaluated our predictive models by training several ML algorithms on the amino acid composition of the sequences included in the MHCI[556] dataset. Specifically, we used k-Nearest Neighbor algorithm (kNN) and support vector machines (SVMs) with polynomial (SVM-Pk) and RBF-kernels (SVM-RBFk). We selected these algorithms because of their reliability, simplicity and speed [26]. Moreover, in preliminary experiments, they outcompeted other popular algorithms such as artificial neural networks (data not shown). For model optimization, we trained the algorithms in combination with multiple variable parameters (details in Materials and Methods).

The performance of the resulting ML-based classifiers was remarkable (Fig. 1A). The best classification results were obtained using SVM-RBFk, which reached an *ACC* of 100.00 ± 0.00%; not a single MHC I molecule was misclassified in any of the 10-fold cross-validation experiments that were carried out (Fig. 1B). Next to these results were those obtained using kNN (*ACC* = 99.93 ± 0.35%), which during repeated 10-fold cross-validation experiments only misclassified one of the MHC I molecules of the L group into the N group (Fig. 1B). The classification performance achieved using SVM-Pk (*ACC* = 99.46 ± 0.87) was slightly lower than that obtained with kNN (one-side two sample *t*-test of average *ACC* values; p ≤ 0.05), and two molecules were consistently misclassified (Fig. 1B).

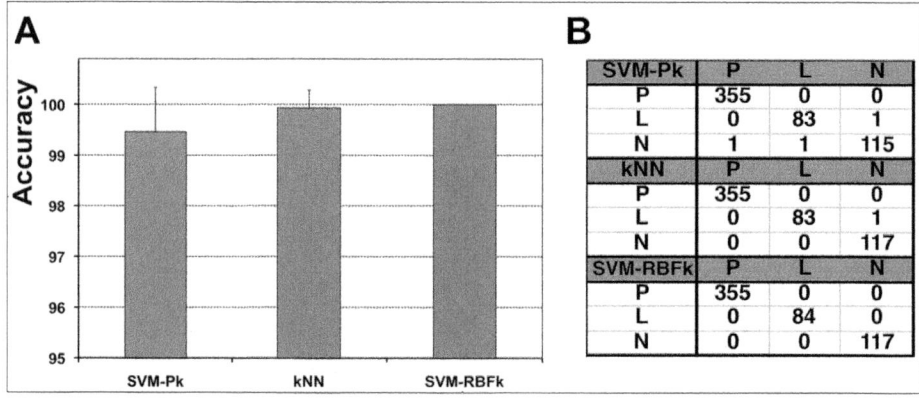

Fig. 1. *Predictive performance of ML-based classifiers.* A) Graph depicting the *ACC* achieved by the ML-based classifiers (abscissas) on the MHCI[556] dataset in cross-validation. ML-based classifiers consisted k-Nearest Neighbor (kNN) and SVM with polynomial (SVM-Pk) and RBF (SVM-RBFk) kernels. The performance was evaluated in 10-fold cross-validations experiments that were repeated 10 times, and in consequence we represent average values of *ACC*. Note that the y-axis is higher than 100% simply to display the standard deviation of the performance measures (error bars). B) Confusion matrix corresponding to the classification results obtained in a representative 10-fold cross-validation experiment. The performance of ML-based classifiers shown in the figure was achieved using the following parameters: kNN: $K = 4$; SVM-Pk: $E = 3, C = 1$; SVM-RBFk: $G = 4, C = 4$.

The fact that the numerous and highly diverse MHC I molecules could be classified into their appropriated ligand-type specificity (P, L, N) on the solely basis of the amino acid composition of the α1α2 domain is certainly noteworthy. In fact, accurate classification of biological sequences using ML has generally been accomplished using many more input features (*e.g.* dipeptide composition of proteins and/or input resulting of combining several sequence encoding schemes), and still, the results were not as good [30-32]. Nonetheless, it is true than those studies involved binary classifications, in which a group of related proteins (*e.g.* Histones) was classified from the remaining universe of proteins (*e.g.* non-Histones). Instead, here we performed a multiclass classification.

That the performance of all the classifiers was that high reflects on the one hand the quality of the dataset that we assembled for training and on the other suggests that the ligand-type specificity of MHC I molecules is readily imprinted on their amino acid composition.

3.3   Comparison of the Generalization Power of ML-Based Classifiers and BLAST

In order to examine the generalization power of our ML-based approach, we carried out several experiments in which we remove entire groups of proteins from the MHCI[556] dataset prior to model building, and latter applied the models to predict the class (P, L, N) of the holdout sequences. These models were built and optimized as described previously, in 10-fold cross-validation experiments that were repeated 10 times. In addition, we also predicted the ligand-type specificity of the holdout sequences using BLAST [33]. In the BLAST approach, the class of the sequences (P, L, N) was assigned to that of the closest match in the MHCI[556] dataset, previously depleted of the holdout sequences (details elsewhere in Materials and Methods). Note that our goal behind these evaluations is not to select the optimal parameters of the algorithms but to explore the ability of ML-based classifiers produced in cross-validation, to predict unseen data differing from that used for training. The results of these analyses are depicted on Table 2 and are reviewed next but first it is worth stressing that in these experiments one should not tally the errors across different holdout evaluations. The number of sequences in each of the distinct holdout groups differs form one to another and so the models used for testing. Therefore, the conclusions from these experiments must be drawn upon analyzing the results obtained in each holdout group independently. Cleary, the goal behind these evaluations is to explore whether ML-based classifiers built and optimized in cross-validation –conditions in which they attaining an extremely good performance– can also predict the ligand-type specificity of MHCI molecules that differ entirely from those used for model building and compare the results with those that one would obtain using BLAST.

The performance of the ML-based classifiers trained on datasets depleted of holdout sequences was extremely good (always $\geq$ 99.4 %) and mirrored the results obtained with classifiers developed on the full MHCI[556] dataset.   The best performance was achieved with SVM-RBFk models, which attained 100% accuracy in most of the tests (see Table 2). kNN were next followed by SVM-Pk.   The difference in accuracy achieved by the different ML algorithms in cross-validation appear minor but they were statistically significant (one-side two sample t-test of average ACC values; $p \leq 0.05$). More importantly, the models that attained the larger accuracy in cross-validation yielded also the better results in the holdout tests. For example, in the predictions involving HFE, the SVM-RBFk model (ACC = 100.00 $\pm$ 0.00 %) predicted the correct class of all the sequences, while SVM-Pk (ACC = 99.44 $\pm$ 0.98) and kNN models (99.96 $\pm$ 0.25) did not.

ML-based models and in particular SVM-RBFk models exhibited an excellent generalization power, as they were able to predict the right class (P, L, N) of the sequences in distinct holdout tests. There were however exceptions. ML-based models were unable to predict the ligand-type specificity of proteins belonging to the ZAG and TLA groups and made some errors predicting both, the lack of ligand of ULPB and FcRN proteins and the peptide-binding of classical MHC I molecules from

Table 2. Evaluation of ML-based models and BLAST on MHC I holdout groups

Holdout group			[3] Performance in holdout group depleted datasets		[4] Classification		
	Lg[1]	Sq.[2]	Algorithm	ACC	P	L	N
HLA-[ABC]	P	111	kNN (K = 1)	99.97± 0.22	111	0	0
			SVM-Pk (E = 5, C = 1)	99.33 ± 1.17	111	0	0
			SVM-RBFk (G = 2, C = 1)	100.00 ± 0.00	111	0	0
			BLAST		111	0	0
RT1-A & H2-X (murine)	P	47	kNN (K = 1)	99.90 ± 0.42	47	0	0
			SVM-Pk (E = 5, C = 1)	99.53 ± 0.96	47	0	0
			SVM-RBFk (G = 3, C = 1)	100.00 ± 0.00	47	0	0
			BLAST		47	0	0
SASA- & ONMY-UBA (fish)	P	56	kNN (K = 1)	100.0 ± 0.00	23	19	14
			SVM-Pk (E = 5, C = 1)	99.42 ± 1.02	18	6	32
			SVM-RBFk (G = 2, C = 1)	100.00 ± 0.00	28	10	18
			BLAST		56	0	0
EPCR	L	7	kNN (K = 4)	99.98 ± 0.18	0	7	0
			SVM-Pk (E = 5, C = 1)	99.41 ± 1.02	0	7	0
			SVM-RBFk (G = 2, C = 2)	100.00 ± 0.00	0	7	0
			BLAST	100.00 ± 0.00	0	7	0
ZAG	L	6	kNN (K = 4)	99.94 ± 0.31	4	0	2
			SVM-Pk (E = 5, C = 1)	99.75 ± 0.63	5	0	1
			SVM-RBFk (G = 2, C = 1)	100.00 ± 0.00	2	0	4
			BLAST		6	0	0
MICA&B	N	38	kNN (K = 3)	99.96 ± 0.26	0	0	38
			SVM-Pk (E = 5, C = 1)	99.54 ± 0.99	0	0	38
			SVM-RBFk (G = 3, C = 2)	99.96 ± 0.27	0	0	38
			BLAST		28	0	10
HFE	N	6	kNN (K = 1)	99.96 ± 0.25	1	0	5
			SVM-Pk (E = 5, C = 1)	99.44 ± 0.98	3	0	3
			SVM-RBFk (G = 2, C = 4)	100.00 ± 0.00	0	0	6
			BLAST		1	5	0
ULPB	N	45	kNN (K = 1)	99.80 ± 0.59	3	21	21
			SVM-Pk (E = 5, C = 1)	99.61 ± 0.87	9	11	25
			SVM-RBFk (G = 1, C = 8)	99.88 ± 0.46	1	7	37
			BLAST		9	1	35
FcRN	N	9	kNN (K = 1)	99.96 ± 0.25	6	0	3
			SVM-Pk (E = 5, C = 1)	99.44 ± 0.92	0	3	6
			SVM-RBFk (G = 2, C = 1)	100.00 ± 0.00	0	3	6
			BLAST		0	8	1
TLA	N	15	kNN (K = 1)	99.94 ± 0.31	15	0	0
			SVM-Pk (E = 4, C = 1)	99.94 ± 0.41	15	0	0
			SVM-RBFk (G = 2, C = 1)	100.00 ± 0.00	15	0	0
			BLAST		15	0	0

[1] Known ligand-type class of the holdout sequences (P:bind peptides; L:bind lipids; N: No ligand) [2] Number of holdout sequences. [3] Models were built and optimized on MHC I datasets depleted of the holdout data in 10-fold cross-validation experiments that were repeated 10 times. *ACC* depicted in table was achieved using the indicated parameters. [4] Class assignment (predicted ligand-type specificity: P, L, N) of holdout sequences using models built and optimized on datasets lacking the holdout sequences. Shadowed cells point to the right outcome of the predictions. BLAST-predictions were obtained upon a BLAST search against a reference dataset lacking the holdout sequences, encompassing the same sequences than the relevant training set used for ML.

fish. In comparison, BLAST correctly predicted the peptide binding of all classical MHC I molecules from fish but it also failed to predict the ligand-type specificity of proteins belonging to the ZAG and TLA groups. Moreover, BLAST made more mistakes than the SVM-RBFk model predicting the lack of ligand of ULPB and FcRN proteins, and unlike the ML-based models failed to predict the lack of ligand of most proteins in the HFE and MICA&B groups.

Overall, these results highlight ML-based models trained on amino composition are capable of predicting the ligand-type specificity of MHC I molecules that are not related to those used for training. Moreover, ML-based models, particularly those based on SVM-RBFk, were clearly superior to BLAST at predicting the class of proteins that do not bind any ligand. However, the ML-based also showed limitations. Therefore, one should regard the BLAST- and ML-based approaches as complementary and furthermore is important to train the ML-based classifiers on the complete MHCI^{556} dataset.

4 Conclusions and Limitations

There is a plethora of methods that can actually predict peptide binding to MHC Ia molecules [34]. Surprisingly, until now, no method was available to predict whether a given member of the MHCI protein family can bind any ligand at all, and if so, the nature of such ligand (Peptides or Lipids). Upon assembling a dataset of MHC I molecules of known ligand-type specificity (P, L, N), we trained ML-based models that achieve that task through a classification approach.

These models along with a BLAST classifier built on the same dataset are readily available for public free use at http://imed.med.ucm.es/MHCLIG/. The identification of potential ligands frequently handicaps MHC I research and we believe this resource ought to be became instrumental on that quest. It is important to stress that the methods developed here can only predict the three known ligand-type specificities of MHC I molecules (P, L and N). If there would be MHC I molecules with other, yet to be characterized, type of ligands (*e.g.* sugars, nucleotides, etc) the breath of our predictions will be clearly limited.

Acknowledgments

We wish to tank Dr. Alfonso Valencia for helpful comments. This work was supported by the Ministerio de Ciencia e Innovación of Spain (SAF2009-08103 to PAR and grant SAF2007-60578 to EML), the Spanish Ministry of Health (grant PI080125 to EMN), the Comunidad Autonoma de Madrid (grant CCG08-UCM/BIO-3769 to PAR) and the Universidad Complutense de Madrid (grant Gr58/08 920631 to EMN, ELN and PAR).

References

1. Maenaka, K., Jones, E.Y.: MHC superfamily structure and the immune system. Curr. Opin. Struct. Biol. 9, 745–753 (1999)
2. Townsend, A., Bodmer, H.: Antigen recognition by class I-restricted T lymphocytes. Annual Review of Immunology 7, 601–624 (1989)

3. Braud, V.M., Allan, D.S., McMichael, A.J.: Functions of nonclassical MHC and non-MHC-encoded class I molecules. Curr. Opin. Immunol. 11, 100–108 (1999)

4. Clements, C.S., Kjer-Nielsen, L., Kostenko, L., Hoare, H.L., Dunstone, M.A., Moses, E., Freed, K., Brooks, A.G., Rossjohn, J., McCluskey, J.: Crystal structure of HLA-G: a nonclassical MHC class I molecule expressed at the fetal-maternal interface. Proc. Natl. Acad. Sci. USA 102, 3360–3365 (2005)

5. He, X., Tabaczewski, P., Ho, J., Stroynowski, I., Garcia, K.C.: Promiscuous antigen presentation by the nonclassical MHC Ib Qa-2 is enabled by a shallow, hydrophobic groove and self-stabilized peptide conformation. Structure 9, 1213–1224 (2001)

6. Lu, L., Werneck, M.B., Cantor, H.: The immunoregulatory effects of Qa-1. Immunological Reviews 212, 51–59 (2006)

7. Hoare, H.L., Sullivan, L.C., Pietra, G., Clements, C.S., Lee, E.J., Ely, L.K., Beddoe, T., Falco, M., Kjer-Nielsen, L., Reid, H.H., McCluskey, J., Moretta, L., Rossjohn, J., Brooks, A.G.: Structural basis for a major histocompatibility complex class Ib-restricted T cell response. Nat. Immunol. 7, 256–264 (2006)

8. Rodgers, J.R., Cook, R.G.: MHC class Ib molecules bridge innate and acquired immunity. Nature Reviews Immunology 5, 459–471 (2005)

9. Barral, D.C., Brenner, M.B.: CD1 antigen presentation: how it works. Nature Reviews Immunology 7, 929–941 (2007)

10. Kennedy, M.W., Heikema, A.P., Cooper, A., Bjorkman, P.J., Sanchez, L.M.: Hydrophobic ligand binding by Zn-alpha 2-glycoprotein, a soluble fat-depleting factor related to major histocompatibility complex proteins. The Journal of Biological Chemistry 276, 35008–35013 (2001)

11. Esmon, C.T.: The endothelial protein C receptor. Current Opinion in Hematology 13, 382–385 (2006)

12. Sanchez, L.M., Chirino, A.J., Bjorkman, P.: Crystal structure of human ZAG, a fat-depleting factor related to MHC molecules. Science 283, 1914–1919 (1999)

13. Oganesyan, V., Oganesyan, N., Terzyan, S., Qu, D., Dauter, Z., Esmon, N.L., Esmon, C.T.: The crystal structure of the endothelial protein C receptor and a bound phospholipid. J. Biol. Chem. 277, 24851–24854 (2002)

14. Liu, Y., Xiong, Y., Naidenko, O.V., Liu, J.H., Zhang, R., Joachimiak, A., Kronenberg, M., Cheroutre, H., Reinherz, E.L., Wang, J.H.: The crystal structure of a TL/CD8alphaalpha complex at 2.1 A resolution: implications for modulation of T cell activation and memory. Immunity 18, 205–215 (2003)

15. Wingren, C., Crowley, M.P., Degano, M., Chien, Y., Wilson, I.A.: Crystal structure of a gammadelta T cell receptor ligand T22: a truncated MHC-like fold. Science 287, 310–314 (2000)

16. Bahram, S., Inoko, H., Shiina, T., Radosavljevic, M.: MIC and other NKG2D ligands: from none to too many. Current Opinion in Immunology 17, 505–509 (2005)

17. Roopenian, D.C., Akilesh, S.: FcRn: the neonatal Fc receptor comes of age. Nature Reviews Immunology 7, 715–725 (2007)

18. Feder, J.N., Gnirke, A., Thomas, W., Tsuchihashi, Z., Ruddy, D.A., Basava, A., Dormishian, F., Domingo, R., Ellis Jr, M.C., Fullan, A., Hinton, L.M., Jones, N.L., Kimmel, B.E., Kronmal, G.S., Lauer, P., Lee, V.K., Loeb, D.B., Mapa, F.A., McClelland, E., Meyer, N.C., Mintier, G.A., Moeller, N., Moore, T., Morikang, E., Prass, C.E., Quintana, L., Starnes, S.M., Schatzman, R.C., Brunke, K.J., Drayna, D.T., Risch, N.J., Bacon, B.R., Wolff, R.K.: A novel MHC class I-like gene is mutated in patients with hereditary haemochromatosis. Nature Genetics 13, 399–408 (1996)

19. Burmeister, W.P., Huber, A.H., Bjorkman, P.J.: Crystal structure of the complex of rat neonatal Fc receptor with Fc. Nature 372, 379–383 (1994)
20. Lebron, J.A., Bennett, M.J., Vaughn, D.E., Chirino, A.J., Snow, P.M., Mintier, G.A., Feder, J.N., Bjorkman, P.J.: Crystal structure of the hemochromatosis protein HFE and characterization of its interaction with transferrin receptor. Cell 93, 111–123 (1998)
21. Wistrand, M., Sonnhammer, E.L.: Improved profile HMM performance by assessment of critical algorithmic features in SAM and HMMER. BMC Bioinformatics 6, 99 (2005)
22. Sonnhammer, E.L., Eddy, S.R., Durbin, R.: Pfam: a comprehensive database of protein domain families based on seed alignments. Proteins 28, 405–420 (1997)
23. Neuwald, A.F., Liu, J.S., Lawrence, C.E.: Gibbs motif sampling detection of bacterial outer membrane protein repeats. Prot. Sci. 4, 1618–1632 (1995)
24. EMBOSS: the European Molecular Biology Open Software Suite. Trends Genet. 16, 276–277 (2000)
25. Frank, E., Hall, M., Trigg, L., Holmes, G., Witten, I.H.: Data mining in bioinformatics using Weka. Bioinformatics 20, 2479–2481 (2004)
26. Wu, X., Kumar, V., Quilan, J.R., Ghosh, J., Yang, Q., Motoda, H., McLachlan, G.J., Ng, A., Liu, B., Yu, P.S., Zhou, Z.-H., Steinbach, M., Hand, D.J., Steinberg, D.: Top 10 algorithms in data mining Knowledge and Information Systems. Springer, Heidelberg (2008)
27. Dasarathy, B.V.: Nearest Neighbor (NN) Norms: NN Pattern Classification Techniques. McGraw-Hill Computer Science Series. IEEE Computer Society Press, Los Alamitos, California (1991)
28. Platt, J.C.: Fast Training of Support Vector Machines using Sequential Minimal Optimization Advances in Kernel Methods - Support Vector Learning. In: Schölkopf, B., Burges, C., Smola, A.J. (eds.), pp. 185–208. MIT Press, Cambridge (1999)
29. Diez-Rivero, C.M., Chenlo, B., Zuluaga, P., Reche, P.A.: Quantitative modeling of peptide binding to TAP using support vector machine. Proteins 14, 14 (2009)
30. Bhasin, M., Reinherz, E.L., Reche, P.A.: Recognition and classification of histones using support vector machine. J. Comput. Biol. 13, 102–112 (2006)
31. Chen, K., Kurgan, L.A., Ruan, J.: Prediction of protein structural class using novel evolutionary collocation-based sequence representation. J. Comput. Chem. 29, 1596–1604 (2008)
32. Saha, S., Zack, J., Singh, B., Raghava, G.P.: VGIchan: prediction and classification of voltage-gated ion channels. Genomics Proteomics Bioinformatics 4, 253–258 (2006)
33. Altschul, S.F., Madden, T.L., Schaffer, A.A., Zhang, J., Zhang, Z., Miller, W., Lipman, D.J.: Gapped BLAST and PSI-BLAST: a new generation of protein database search programs. Nucleic Acids Res. 25, 3389–3402 (1997)
34. Lafuente, E.M., Reche, P.A.: Prediction of MHC-peptide binding: a systematic and comprehensive overview. Curent Pharmaceutical Design 15, 3209–3220 (2009)

Towards Argument-Driven Validation of an *in silico* Model of Immune Tissue Organogenesis

Kieran Alden[1,2], Paul S. Andrews[2], Jon Timmis[2,3],
Henrique Veiga-Fernandes[4], and Mark Coles[1]

[1] Centre for Immunology and Infection, Hull York Medical School and
Department of Biology, University of York, UK
[2] Department of Computer Science, Deramore Lane, University of York, UK
[3] Department of Electronics, Heslington, University of York, UK
[4] Immunology Unit, Institute of Molecular Medicine, University of Lisbon, Portugal

1 Introduction

Specialised tissues of the immune system including lymph nodes, tonsils, spleen and Peyer's Patches have key roles in the initiation of adaptive immune responses to infection. To understand the molecular mechanisms involved in the development of this tissue, mice deficient for key genes in this process have been developed and analysed, leading to a basic model describing tissue formation. Although this approach has provided some key insights into the molecular mechanisms involved, due to the complexity of gene expression patterns it has not been possible to fully understand the process of lymphoid tissue organogenesis.

In an attempt to further explore the mechanisms involved, we intend to utilise an iterative approach which combines imaging, gene expression, and gene-knockout data with stochastic multi-agent modelling. We have developed an agent-based simulation with which we can investigate the effect of the molecular and biophysical mechanisms involved in such complex biological systems. Our simulation captures the development of Peyer's Patches (PP), specialised lymphoid tissue found within the intestine which plays a key role in the induction of antibody responses to pathogenic bacteria and viruses in the gut [1,2]. This tissue forms during embryonic development as a result of a stochastic process which leads to the formation of 8-12 PP in mice, and around 300 PP in humans [3].

We have found that results from our agent-based simulation do not exactly match those seen *in vivo*. However, we believe that this will often be the case for computer simulations of biology that simplify various aspects of the real system. Consequently, we need to explain and justify how the simulation results have been generated so that these results can be interpreted in the context of the real biological system. We describe in this abstract how we plan to apply goal-structuring notation (an argumentation technique) to provide this explanation and justification.

P. Liò, G. Nicosia, and T. Stibor (Eds.): ICARIS 2011, LNCS 6825, pp. 66–70, 2011.

2   Model and Simulation

Using a principled approach to the development of a separate domain model and simulation [4] we have completed an initial modelling iteration. This forms a baseline simulation to use for further analysis of the mechanisms underlying the tissue development process.

2.1   Domain Model

Analysis of gene knock-out mice identifies key roles in PP development for lymphoid tissue inducing (LTi) and initiating (LTin) cells. In the mouse, these cells migrate into the developing intestine tract 14.5 days into embryonic development (E14.5) and cluster around lymphoid tissue organiser cells (LTo) on the tract surface, forming patches of cells 72 hours later that mature into fully functional Peyers Patches. Taking a reductionist approach which examines each of these cell types cannot explain the behaviour which emerges at the end of the process, the formation of Peyer's Patches. Instead, we have taken an holistic approach through the construction of an agent-based model, an approach which we hope will complement experimental studies [7,8,9]. The LTin, LTi and LTo cells comprise the agents in our simulation. Interactions between these cells take place on the surface of the developing tract, thus requiring our model to represent this environment. Agent-based simulation allows for easy representation of our space, essential to this specific problem. Through working closely with experimental biologists, we have attempted to ensure our model constitutes an accurate representation of the biological domain. The behaviour of the agents, and how this is influenced by interactions between cell surface receptors and chemokines expressed in the gut, RET ligand interactions, and lymphotoxin beta receptor signalling [1,5,6] has been fully documented using state and activity diagrams in a way similar to other work undertaken using the CoSMoS approach [10].

2.2   Platform Model

The domain model is then used to generate a further model which translates the biological understanding into a specification for how the agents and interactions will be encoded in a computer simulation. It is important to note that the domain and platform model are not the same. The domain model captures any emergent behaviours that we might expect to see in domain, but these behaviours are not encoded in the platform model directly, otherwise they would not be emergent behaviours. Where possible, we have derived parameters for the simulation from those identified in experimental work. Environment dimensions have been derived from measurements of the mouse gut taken at different stages of development. Cell distribution and input rates, and cell attributes such as size and velocity have been determined through analysis of time-lapse imaging and flow cytometric analysis performed locally and literature mining. When data is not available, our assumptions have been reviewed by biological domain experts and documented for full scientific scrutiny. A two-dimensional abstraction of the environment has been created to represent the surface of the developing gut on which the interactions between the agents take place. The MASON agent-based framework [11] was used for the implementation of the simulation.

3   Analysis of Initial Results

We have batch-run the simulation under a variety of conditions, including varying the percentage of LTo cells on the intestine tract surface which may be active in the process (a percentage which cannot currently be discovered experimentally), and analysed the output generated. Our aim was to replicate experimental results which identify 8-12 such patches along the length of the tract.

We have found that the cellular behaviour captured in the agents of the simulation accurately replicates that seen in ex vivo experiments which track cell behaviour (in terms of velocity, displacement, and length of track) for a period of one hour. Through interactions between these agents, patches of cells (immature Peyer's Patches) are formed along the length of the gut. Though each patch is of a similar size to those which can be identified experimentally, we have found that our model is more efficient at producing a number of such patches along the gut length than is biologically observed. In simulation, activating only a small percentage of LTo cells on the tract surface is enough to result in up to 40 such patches developing, far larger than the 8-12 that was expected.

4   Explaining the Differences Between the *in vivo* and *in silico* Results

Our result could suggest that either the abstraction of the model is incorrect, or that the biological understanding upon which the model has been developed is not complete. The split between the domain and platform models, encouraged in the CoSMoS process [4], provides an early opportunity to agree and document how the understanding of the biology will be taken forward into the computer simulation. It would be tempting to assume that, with the domain model heavily influenced by our biological expert's current understanding of the system, the translation to the platform model would be the first point at which the model should be reassessed to seek the source of the discrepancy.

However, we propose that a structured technique should be adopted to investigate the reasons behind discrepancies between our simulation and biological results. As previously shown by Ghetiu et al [12], argument-driven validation techniques (ADV) provide such a method. These techniques, such as goal-structuring notation (GSN), provide a way of structuring our reassessment of the model in such a way that each step in the model is validated, the reasoning behind the inclusion or exclusion of a feature or assumption is provided, and evidence given as to why this conclusion has been drawn. Thus, features included from the domain and platform models are both reassessed. The overall objective is to go through the model in steps, linked together by the available evidence to support that step, leading to increased confidence that certain parts of the model are correct, while identifying areas which need further examination. This may identify features where assumptions have been made which need further investigation, or identify clarifications needed from the biological experts. The latter may then feed into wet-lab experimentation in order to assess a feature, or lead to an assessment of the reliability of biological results gathered from external sources such as published literature.

Through the use of this structured approach, the current baseline simulation will undergo a validation phase which both supports and identifies alterations needed to resolve the discrepancy.

5   Conclusion

Computer simulation is a powerful experimental tool that has not previously been exploited when seeking to understand the role of mechanisms involved in lymphoid tissue development. Through integrating this technique with traditional biological experimentation we have developed a baseline model which, through consultation with domain experts, we believed to be an accurate representation of the domain to be modelled. As we have discussed, the behaviour which emerges from the simulation does not faithfully replicate that seen experimentally. Adopting a formal argumentation technique such as goal structuring notation is a necessity for structured examination of a model when attempting to explain and justify the results generated. This method may identify whether a discrepancy occurs as an artefact of the way the simulation has been created, or whether the biological foundations upon which the domain model is built are incomplete and require further investigation.

Acknowledgment

The authors would like to acknowledge those associated with the CoSMoS project for their input into the design and creation of our agent-based model. Paul Andrews is part of this project, funded by EPSRC grants EP/E053505/1 and EP/E049419/1.

References

1. Randall, T.D., Carragher, D.M., Rangel-Moreno, J.: Development of secondary lymphoid organs. Annual Review Immunology 26, 627–650 (2008)
2. Mebius, R.E.: Organogenesis of lymphoid tissues. Nature Reviews Immunology 3, 292–303 (2003)
3. Cornes, J.S.: Number, size, and distribution of Peyers Patches in the human small intestine: Part I The development of Peyer's Patches. Gut. 6, 225–229 (1965)
4. Andrews, P., Polack, F.A.C., Sampson, A.T., Stepney, S., Timmis, J.: The CoSMoS Process, Version 0.1: A process for the Modelling and Simulation of Complex Systems (2010)

5. Veiga-Fernandes, H., Coles, M.C., Foster, K.E., Patel, A., Williams, A., Natarajan, D., Barlow, A., Pachnis, V., Kioussis, D.: Tyrosine kinase receptor RET is a key regulator of Peyers Patch organogenesis. Nature 446, 547–551 (2007)
6. van de Pavert, S., Mebius, R.E.: New insights into the development of lymphoid tissues. Nature reviews Immunology 10, 1–11 (2010)
7. Forrest, S., Beauchemin, C.: Computer Immunology. Immunological Reviews 216, 176–197 (2010)
8. Katare, S., Venkatasubramanian, V.: An agent-based learning framework for modeling microbial growth. Engineering Applications of Artificial Intelligence 14, 715–726 (2001)
9. Chakraborty, A., Das, J.: Pairing computation with experimentation: a powerful coupling for understanding T cell signalling. Nature Reviews Immunology 10, 59–71 (2010)
10. Read, M., Timmis, J., Andrews, P.S., Kumar, V.: A Domain Model of Experimental Autoimmune Encephalomyelitis. In: 2nd Workshop on Complex Systems Modelling and Simulation, pp. 9–44 (2009)
11. Luke, S.: MASON: A Multiagent Simulation Environment Simulation, vol. 81, pp. 517–527 (2005)
12. Ghetiu, T., Polack, F.A.C., Bown, J.: Argument-driven Validation of Computer Simulations A Necessity Rather Than an Option. In: VALID 2010: The Second International Conference on Advances in System Testing and Validation Lifecycle (2010)

Simulating the Dynamics of T Cell Subsets throughout the Lifetime

Stephanie J. Foan[1], Andrew M. Jackson[1], Ian Spendlove[1], and Uwe Aickelin[2]

[1] Academic Unit of Clinical Oncology
[2] Intelligent Modelling and Analysis Research Group, University of Nottingham

Abstract. It is widely accepted that the immune system undergoes age-related changes correlating with increased disease in the elderly. T cell subsets have been implicated. The aim of this work is firstly to implement and validate a simulation of T regulatory cell (T_{reg}) dynamics throughout the lifetime, based on a model by Baltcheva. We show that our initial simulation produces an inversion between precursor and mature T_{reg}s at around 20 years of age, though the output differs significantly from the original laboratory dataset. Secondly, this report discusses development of the model to incorporate new data from a cross-sectional study of healthy blood donors addressing balance between T_{reg}s and T_h17 cells with novel markers for T_{reg}. The potential for simulation to add insight into immune aging is discussed.

1 Introduction to System Dynamics Modelling of Immunity

Simulation has been defined as methods and applications mimicking the behaviour of a real system [1]. The benefits of simulation to immunology include time- and cost-effectiveness as well as less labour- and resource-intensiveness resulting from removal from the biological environment. *In vitro* experimentation is useful for investigating individual interactions but is far removed from the whole picture, and *in vivo* experimentation is useful for the whole picture but is unlikely to answer specific questions [2]. Using simulation, flexibility is available for systematically generating hypotheses and conducting experiments impossible to do practically, yet informed by robust data and literature.

System dynamics simulations are useful for looking at complex systems over time. They are characterised by stocks of an entity and flows between stocks [3]. Immune system examples of stocks include precursor and mature T cell pools and flows might represent transition of cells from precursor to mature. This technique is useful for modelling relationships defined by differential equations. An example of a differential equation describing T cell dynamics is the change in number of precursor cells equated to proliferation of precursors minus death and maturation rates. This ongoing work will apply system dynamics simulation technique to complement *in vitro* studies of T_h17s and T_{reg}s throughout the lifetime.

2 The Need for Balance: T_h17s and T_{reg}s throughout the Lifetime

The immune system maintains a balance between mounting an adequate immune response to protect from infection and restricting the size of the immune response to

P. Liò, G. Nicosia, and T. Stibor (Eds.): ICARIS 2011, LNCS 6825, pp. 71–76, 2011.
© Springer-Verlag Berlin Heidelberg 2011

prevent damage to self. There is evidence to suggest an age-related tendency to a pro-inflammatory environment [4] contributing to more collateral damage and autoimmune diseases. This work addresses the hypothesis that important contributors to this state of imbalance are T_h17 cells (amplifying immune responses) and $T_{reg}s$ (dampening down immune responses). Although some studies have shown an age-related increase in the number of $T_{reg}s$ in human peripheral blood [5][6], it has also been shown that homeostasis is maintained [7]. One study concluded upon the oscillatory nature of T_{reg} numbers through life, with peaks in adolescence and in over 60 year olds [8]. A recent study in T_h17 cells with age showed a small decrease in the frequency of T_h17 cells in the $CD4^+$ memory population in elderly donors relative to young [9]. However, for the balance between $T_{reg}s$ and T_h17 cells, there is currently no published literature.

There is evidence that the balance between $T_{reg}s$ and T_h17s is altered in age-related diseases such as acute coronary syndrome [10]. Thus it is intuitive that this balance should be examined with a cross sectional study in healthy donors of different ages. Laboratory experimentation will begin by using flow cytometry to enumerate peripheral blood cells expressing CD4, CD25 and signature transcription factors of these subsets: Foxp3 and Helios for $T_{reg}s$ and ROR_c for T_h17 cells.

3   Method: Simulation of T_{reg} Dynamics

Ultimately we wish to build a model of the dynamics of $T_{reg}s$ and T_h17 cells throughout life from data currently being collected. Preliminary work for this has involved building a system dynamics simulation in AnyLogic 6.5.0 University Edition, based on a mathematical model by Baltcheva [11]. This model was selected as it comprehensively incorporates the functional dynamics of $T_{reg}s$ in terms of homeostasis and during an acute immune response. It characterises the changing precursor and mature T_{reg} populations throughout the human lifetime. Key assumptions include that there is no change in function or responsiveness throughout the lifetime, nor a change to other influential factors on their dynamics such as dendritic cell number and function [11]. Also, the immune response considered includes an expansion and contraction phase, and only one response can occur at a given timepoint [11]. The original model was based on numbers of $CD4^+CD25^+CD45RO^-$ (precursor) and $CD4^+CD25^+CD45RO^+$ (mature) populations in 119 peripheral blood samples of donors aged 19 to 81 [11]. Although total numbers of $CD4^+CD25^+$ cells remained constant, the ratio of precursor to mature was inverted in early adulthood. This represents an important dimension to the observed homeostasis in T_{reg} numbers throughout the lifespan, especially when considering thymic involution from adolescence, reducing the number of new cells entering the system.

Ordinary differential equations describe the dynamics of the above mentioned cells, and stochastic processes control the frequency, duration and antigen-specific nature of primary and secondary immune responses on the different cell compartments [11]. In this work, a simple scenario was chosen in order to test the hypothesis that the model could be implemented in AnyLogic. The scenario assumes a lack of antigen-induced proliferation and death of both precursor and mature $T_{reg}s$, no density-dependent proliferation and death and thymic output as the only external input into the various T_{reg} subsets [11]. The parameter values used correspond to means of the distributions for scenario 2iiia given in Baltcheva's work [11]. The simulation is shown below:

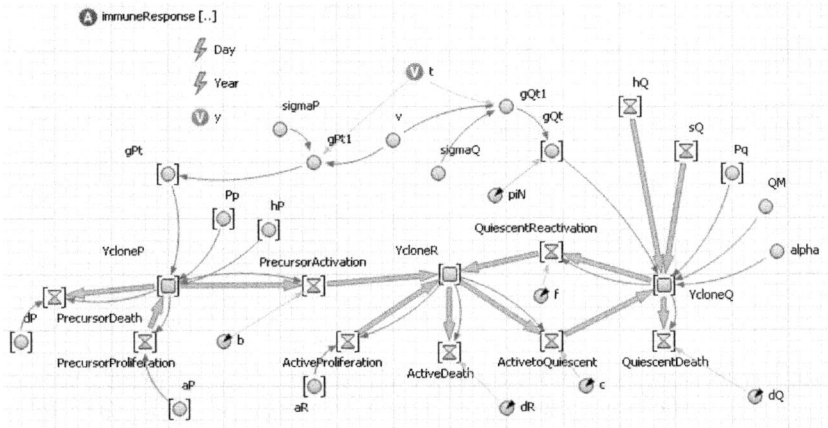

Fig. 1. Main View. Events are shown with ⚡ for time in days (t) and years (y). Flow variables given by ⊠ involve a rate of conversion ◦ multiplied by the number of cells in the stocks named $YcloneP$, $-R$ and $-Q$. P corresponds to precursors, R to active matures and Q to quiescent matures. These stocks are prefixed by $Yclone$ as they represent total and antigen-specific T_{reg}s determined by an array. Homeostatic parameters apply to the total T_{reg} population, whereas immune response parameters are applied to a proportion given by piN. For example, flow of specific precursors into the active mature stock is given by specific precursor stock multiplied by the maturation rate. Each time point, AnyLogic recalculates each stock using the flows defined.

An additional class (immuneResponse) controls the immune system functional status using $IRstatechart$:

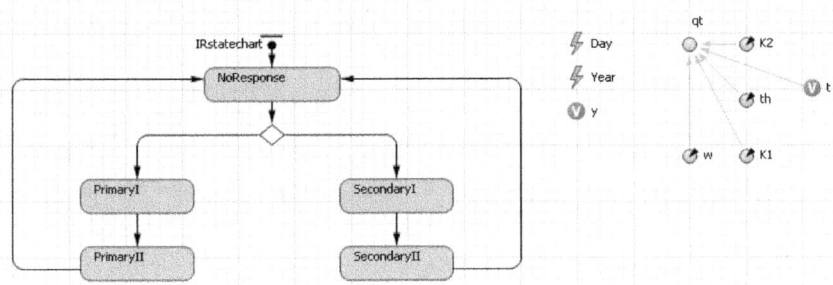

Fig. 2. immuneResponse View. At the beginning of a run the immune system is in the $NoResponse$ state. Every 100.95 time steps, the immune system mounts a primary immune response with probability qt or defaults to a secondary response. $PrimaryI$ and $SecondaryI$, represent the expansion phase. $PrimaryII$ and $SecondaryII$, represent the contraction phase which continues until a new response is instigated. During $PrimaryI$, parameter b is applied. During $PrimaryII$, b is set to zero and parameters c, dR and dQ are applied. In $SecondaryI$ parameters b and f are applied and in $SecondaryII$ these are set to zero and c, dR and dQ are applied.

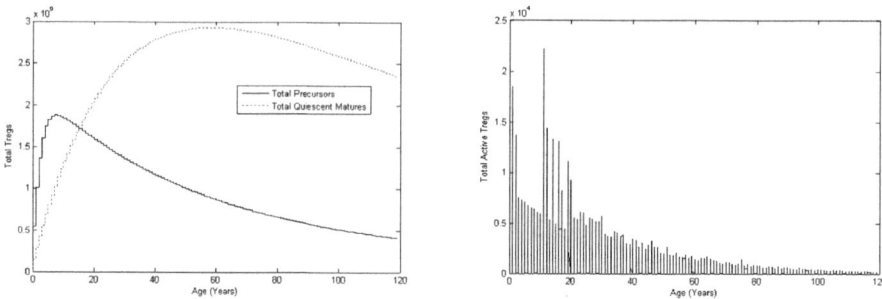

Fig. 3. (generated using MATLAB R2010a): Output data from AnyLogic over a complete run. a) Total precursor and quiescent mature T_{reg} stocks. b) Total active T_{reg}s. Each peak corresponds to antigen-specific clones experiencing either primary or secondary immune responses.

Figure 4 shows simulation output compared to the original dataset. Data has been collected for each stock over 3 complete replications. The maximum standard deviation between three runs for the total precursors was 2.753×10^{-7}. The maximum standard deviation for total quiescent matures was 9411.

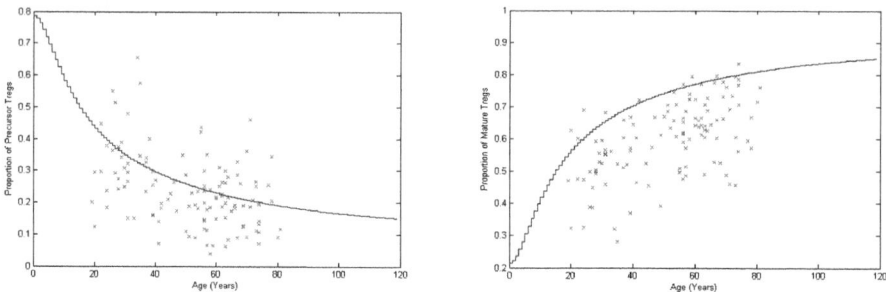

Fig. 4. Output data compared to Baltcheva's dataset. a) The proportion of total T_{reg}s in the precursor stock. b) The proportion of total T_{reg}s in the quiescent stock.

In order to quantify how similar the simulation output was to the laboratory data, both datasets were split into 10-year age groups. The median was calculated for these groups, and the difference between medians for simulation output data and laboratory data have been documented below. A Mann Whitney test was then performed for the null hypothesis of no difference between laboratory and output data and the p values are given below:

Table 1. Comparison of median output and laboratory data for each 10-year age group

Age (Years)	Median Difference		Mann Whitney Test	
	Proportion of Precursors	Proportion of Matures	Proportion of Precursors	Proportion of Matures
10-19	0.3101	0.0207	p=0.083	p=0.658
20-29	0.0525	0.1092	p<0.001	p<0.001
30-39	0.0290	0.1227	p=0.034	p<0.001
40-49	0.0690	0.1182	p=0.001	p<0.001
50-59	0.0587	0.1007	p<0.001	p<0.001
60-69	0.0072	0.1230	p=0.127	p<0.001
70-79	0.0011	0.1204	p=0.808	p<0.001
80-89	0.0805	0.0775	p=0.014	p=0.014

4   Discussion and Concluding Remarks

The implementation of Baltcheva's model as a system dynamics simulation has been documented here and compared to experimental evidence. It has been shown that the simulation mimics the key feature of inversion of precursor and memory cells in early adulthood. The lack of statistical similarity between simulation output and laboratory data indicates that further validation of this model is necessary and will involve a comparison of other scenarios proposed in Baltcheva's work. Ultimately we will develop and validate a simulation of our novel dataset of T_{reg} and T_h17 cells using this sort of approach. $CD4^+CD25^+Foxp3^+$ and $CD4^+Foxp3^+Helios^+$ cell numbers instead of $CD4^+CD25^+$s for T_{reg}s will also be collected as they are arguably more specific markers [12][13]. In terms of improving the simulation, alternatives to continually reactivating a single T_{reg} clone are required, as is simulation of more than one immune stimulus at a time. Baltcheva discloses various assumptions including no difference in T_{reg} function [11]. It may be possible to improve this model by considering functional as well as numerical changes to T_{reg} subsets with age.

A more abstract research question is whether a simplistic model of immunosenescence can lend useful insight into the biological problem. It can be argued that the process of simulation alone might allow researchers to address assumptions and allow for systematic generation of hypotheses. Also, hypotheses which are difficult to test in the laboratory might be testable with a simulation. For example, we might introduce an intervention to mimic ablative chemotherapy by depleting each stock at a single time point. Total values of each stock might then be compared for simulation runs with or without intervention to make hypotheses about T_{reg} recovery. Simulating the dynamics of T_h17 cells in parallel to T_{reg}s may also allow us to make predictions about the maintenance of their balance throughout life, would allow for extreme parameter values to be tested and may indicate a maximum length of time for homeostasis to be maintained.

Our primary hypothesis is that age alters T_{reg} and T_h17 cells with consequences for health in older age and we aim to conduct a cross sectional study to obtain the distribution of particular changes. We anticipate that a strategy of both laboratory investigation and system dynamics simulation as exemplified by Baltcheva's work will be useful to address relationships between T cell subsets over time. The model might also be developed to consider new questions about response to interventions and the length of time the immune system might be able to maintain T_{reg} and T_h17 cell homeostasis.

Acknowledgement. With thanks to Irina Baltcheva for providing her raw data.

References

1. Kelton, W.D., Sadowski, R.P., Swets, N.B.: Simulation with Arena, 5th edn. McGraw-Hill, New York (2010)
2. Kim, P.S., Levy, D., Lee, P.P.: Modeling and Simulation of the Immune System as a Self-Regulating Network. Methods in Enzymology, vol. 467, pp. 79–109. Academic Press, London (2009)
3. Figueredo, G., Aickelin, U.: Investigating immune System aging: System dynamics and agent-based modelling. In: Proceeding of the Summer Computer Simulation Conference (2010)
4. Boren, E., Gershwin, M.E.: Inflamm-aging: Autoimmunity, and the Immune-Risk Phenotype. Autoimmunity Reviews 3, 401–406 (2004)
5. Rosenkranz, D., Weyer, S., Tolosa, E., Gaenslen, A., Berg, D., Leyhe, T., Gasser, T., Stoltze, L.: Higher Frequency of Regulatory T Cells in the Elderly and Increased Suppressive Activity in Neurodegeneration. Journal of Neuroimmunology 188, 117–127 (2007)
6. Gregg, R., Smith, C.M., Clark, F.J., Dunnion, D., Khan, N., Chakraverty, R., Nayak, L., Moss, P.A.: The Number of Human Peripheral Blood $CD4^+$ $CD25^{high}$ Regulatory T Cells Increases with Age. Clinical and Experimental Immunology 140, 540–546 (2005)
7. Hwang, K.A., Kim, H.R., Kang, I.: Aging and Human $CD4^+$ Regulatory T Cells. Clinical Immunology 130, 509–517 (2009)
8. Faria, A.M., de Moraes, S.M., de Freitas, L.H., Speziali, E., Soares, T.F., Figueiredo-Neves, S.P., Vitelli-Avelar, D.M., Martins, M.A., Barbosa, K.V., Soares, E.B., Sathler-Avelar, R., Peruhype-Magalhaes, V., Cardoso, G.M., Comin, F., Teixeira, R., Eloi-Santos, S.M., Queiroz, D.M., Correa-Oliveira, R., Bauer, M.E., Teixeira-Carvalho, A., Martins-Filho, O.A.: Variation Rhythms of Lymphocyte Subsets During Healthy Aging. Neuroimmunomodulation 15, 365–379 (2008)
9. Lee, J.S., Lee, W.W., Kim, S.H., Kang, Y., Lee, N., Shin, M.S., Kang, S.W., Kang, I.: Age-associated alteration in naive and memory th17 cell response in humans. Clinical Immunology (2011) (in Press, Corrected Proof)
10. Li, Q., Wang, Y., Chen, K., Zhou, Q., Wei, W., Wang, Y., Wang, Y.: The Role of Oxidized Low-Density Lipoprotein in Breaking Peripheral T_h17/T_{reg} Balance in Patients with Acute Coronary Syndrome. Biochemical and Biophysical Research Communications 394, 836–842 (2010)
11. Baltcheva, I., Codarri, L., Pantaleo, G., Boudec, J.Y.L.: Lifelong Dynamics of Human $CD4^+CD25^+$ Regulatory T Cells: Insights from in vivo Data and Mathematical Modeling. Journal of Theoretical Biology 266, 307–322 (2010)
12. Thornton, A.M., Korty, P.E., Tran, D.Q., Wohlfert, E.A., Murray, P.E., Belkaid, Y., Shevach, E.M.: Expression of Helios, an Ikaros Transcription Factor Family Member, Differentiates Thymic-Derived from Peripherally Induced Foxp3$^+$ T Regulatory Cells. The Journal of Immunology 184, 3433–3441 (2010)
13. Ziegler, S.F., Buckner, J.H.: Foxp3 and the Regulation of T_{reg}/T_h17 Differentiation. Microbes and Infection 11, 594–598 (2009)

Modelling Containment Mechanisms in the Immune System for Applications in Engineering
(Extended Abstract)

Amelia Ritahani Ismail and Jon Timmis

Department of Computer Science, University of York,
Heslington, YO10 5DD, UK
Department of Electronics, University of York,
Heslington, YO10 5DD, UK
Kulliyyah of ICT, IIUM, P.O. Box 10,
50728 Kuala Lumpur, Malaysia
{ritahani,jtimmis}@cs.york.ac.uk

Granuloma Formation

Granuloma formation is a complex process involving a variety of mechanisms acting in concert to afford an inflammatory lesion that is able to contain and destroy intracellular pathogens. While it is crucial for host defence, inappropriate granulomatous inflammation can also damage the host. Granuloma formation is comprised of four main steps : (1) the triggering of T cells by antigen presenting cells, represented by alveolar macrophages and dendritic cells; (2) the release of cytokines and chemokines by macrophages, activated lymphocytes and dendritic cells. Cytokines and chemokines attract and retain in the lung the immuno-inflammatory cell populations in the lung, inducing their survival and proliferation at the site of ongoing inflammation, favouring (3) the stable and dynamic accumulation of immunocompetent cells and the formation of the organised structure of the granuloma. In granulomatous diseases, the last phase (4) of granuloma formation generally ends in fibrosis. Granuloma formation is initiated when an infectious diseases enters the host. Macrophages will *'eat'* or engulf bacteria to prevent it from spreading. However, bacteria will infect macrophages and duplicate. Despite the fact that macrophages are able to stop the infection, bacteria will use macrophages as a *'taxi'* to spread the disease within the host leading to cell lysis or the breaking down of the structure of the cell. Infected macrophages then will emit a signal which indicates that they have been infected and this signal will lead other macrophages to move to the site of infection, to form a ring around the infected macrophages thus isolating the infected cells from the uninfected cells. This will finally lead to the formation of a granuloma that represents a chronic inflammatory response initiated by various infectious and non-infectious agents.

Conceptual Framework of AIS and CoSMoS Process

Our work is ultimately concerned with the development of an immune-inspired algorithm. Using the principles from conceptual framework of AIS [1] and

P. Liò, G. Nicosia, and T. Stibor (Eds.): ICARIS 2011, LNCS 6825, pp. 77–80, 2011.
© Springer-Verlag Berlin Heidelberg 2011

immuno-engineering [2], we adopt a combined modelling and application oriented approach. Our engineering domain is swarm robotics and in particular the development of swarm robotic systems that are able to contain certain type of errors and initiate repair strategies for certain types of faults that may occur within a swarm robotic system. We observe a natural analogy between the domain and the immunological principles surrounding granuloma formation: containment and repair and focus our attention here.

Following the CoSMoS process [3], we have developed a model and simulation of the general formation and progression of granuloma formation, rather than in the case of a specific disease. This is due to the fact that we do not wish to model the formation to provide insight from a biological perspective, but understand the dynamics of a general model to allow us to distill a series of design principles that we can use to create bio-inspired systems.

We use the Unified Modelling Language (UML) model [4] and agent-based simulation [5] throughout the modelling and simulation process. We first use activity diagrams to indicate the necessary sequence of actions between cells in the system. Secondly, we use state machine diagrams to depict behaviour of individual cells. These are constructed for all entities that either actively change the state of the system and those that play important role in system dynamics. Figure 1 represents the state machine diagram for a macrophage. In this figure we show the different stages of macrophages: uninfected, infected, activated and chronically infected macrophage. Uninfected macrophages take up bacteria and if it is not activated quickly infection will occur. Infected macrophages can still phagocytose and kill, however their ability to function properly decreases with increasing bacterial load. Activated macrophages are extremely efficient at killing their intracellular bacteria load.

These models are then implemented as an agent-based simulation (ABS) [6]. The effectiveness of applying ABS to immunology has been discussed in [7]. The approach we have taken to model the environment is based on the previous work done by [8], who have modelled granuloma formation and the interactions of cells during the formation of granuloma due to chemical gradients. In their work, they have combined continuous representations of chemokines with discrete macrophages and T-cells agent in a cellular automata-like environment. In our model, in representing the environment, we build a two-dimensional (2-D) grid of cells where the infection and formation of granuloma occur. The environment is consist of chemokine space and agent based. The agent space is where the agent can interact and communicate whilst the chemokine space models the chemokines produced by the agents when it is infected by the bacteria to attract T-cells to moves to the site of infections. We observe the phenomena of containment, which is an emergent property of the interactions of the various cells in the simulation.

Towards and Engineering Solution

The model and simulations we have developed have allowed us to gain insight into the process of granuloma formation from an engineering perspective. We

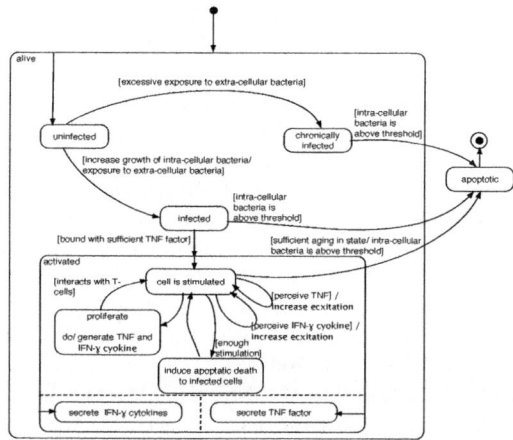

Fig. 1. State diagram showing different stages of macrophages during the formation of granuloma. An uninfected macrophage will become infected when there is an increase growth of bacteria. The uninfected macrophage will also become chronically infected when there is an excessive exposure to extracellular bacteria. With the activation from T-cells, the infected macrophage will become activated.

propose that there is a natural analogy between the potential repair of a swarm of robot and the formation of a granuloma and removal of pathogenic material which has been described in [9]. We can draw four key design principles from the models and simulation:

1. The communication between agents in the system is indirect consisting number of signals to facilitate coordination of agents:
2. Agents in the systems react to defined failure modes by means of faulty from non-faulty using self-organising manner
3. Agents must be able to learn and adapt by changing their role dynamically.
4. Agents can initiate a self-healing process dependant to their ability and location.

These design principles have been taken forward and used as a basis to create a self-healing swarm robotic system where robots are able to recover from certain types of power failure and are collectively able to recharge and continue operation.

References

1. Stepney, S., Smith, R.E., Timmis, J., Tyrrell, A.M., Neal, M.J., Hone, A.N.W.: Conceptual frameworks for artificial immune systems. International Journal of Unconventional Computing 1, 315–338 (2005)
2. Timmis, J., Hart, E., Hone, A., Neal, M., Robins, A., Stepney, S., Tyrrell, A.: Immuno-engineering. In: 2nd International Conference on Biologically Inspired Collaborative Computing. IFIP, vol. 268, pp. 3–17 (2008)

3. Andrews, P.S., Polack, F.A.C., Sampson, A.T., Stepney, S., Timmis, J.: The cosmos process, version 0.1: A process of the modelling and simulation of complex systems (2010)
4. Fowler, M.: UML Distilled. Addisson-Wesley, London (2004)
5. Gilbert, N.: Agent-based models. SAGE Publications, Thousand Oaks (2008)
6. Ismail, A.R., Timmis, J.: Towards self-healing swarm robotic systems inspired by granuloma formation. In: Special Session: Complex Systems Modelling and Simulation, part of ICECCS 2010, pp. 313–314. IEEE, Los Alamitos (2010)
7. Forrest, S., Beauchemin, C.: Computer immunology. Immunological Reviews 216, 176–197 (2007)
8. Segovia-Juarez, J.L., Ganguli, S., Kirschner, D.: Identifying control mechanisms of granuloma formation during m. tuberculosis infection using an agent-based model. Theoretical Biology 231, 357–376 (2004)
9. Timmis, J., Tyrrell, A., Mokhtar, M., Ismail, A.R., Owens, N., Bi, R.: An artificial immune system for robot organisms. In: Levi, P., Kernbach, S. (eds.) Symbiotic Multi-Robot Organisms. Cognitive Systems Monographs, vol. 7, pp. 279–302. Springer, Heidelberg (2010)

Systems Dynamics or Agent-Based Modelling for Immune Simulation?

Grazziela P. Figueredo, Uwe Aickelin, and Peer-Olaf Siebers

Intelligent Modelling and Analysis Research Group, School of Computer Science,
The University of Nottingham, NG8 1BB, UK
{gzf,uxa,pos}@cs.nott.ac.uk

Abstract. In immune system simulation there are two competing simulation approaches: System Dynamics Simulation (SDS) and Agent-Based Simulation (ABS). In the literature there is little guidance on how to choose the best approach for a specific immune problem. Our overall research aim is to develop a framework that helps researchers with this choice. In this paper we investigate if it is possible to easily convert simulation models between approaches. With no explicit guidelines available from the literature we develop and test our own set of guidelines for converting SDS models into ABS models in a non-spacial scenario. We also define guidelines to convert ABS into SDS considering a non-spatial and a spatial scenario. After running some experiments with the developed models we found that in all cases there are significant differences between the results produced by the different simulation methods.

1   Introduction

Simulation presents paradigms that allow us to build models for various problem domains. Some of the important simulation approaches are System Dynamics Simulation (SDS) and Agent-Based Simulation (ABS). SDS is a continuous simulation approach that uses stocks, flows and feedback loops as concepts to study the behaviour of complex systems [1]. The models in SDS consist of a set of differential equations that are solved for a certain time interval [2]. ABS, on the other hand, is a modelling technique that employs autonomous agents that interact with each other. The agents' behaviour is described by rules that determines how they learn, interact with each other and adapt. The overall system behaviour is given by the agents individual dynamics as well as their interactions. Table 1 shows a summary of ABS and SDS features considering their main aspects and differences.

SDS is widely applicable at a high level of abstraction. ABS, on the other hand, is a paradigm that can be used at any level of abstraction, including those levels covered by SDS. As there is an intersection, a range of simulation problems can be solved either by SDS or ABS. In [4], the authors state that ABS is ideal for tissue patterning events because it explicitly represents individual cells in space and time. Moreover, ABS indicates how the tissue behaviour emerges from the interactions of individual cells. On the other hand, ABS requires computational

P. Liò, G. Nicosia, and T. Stibor (Eds.): ICARIS 2011, LNCS 6825, pp. 81–94, 2011.
© Springer-Verlag Berlin Heidelberg 2011

Table 1. Main differences between SDS and ABS (obtained from [3])

Feature	SDS	ABS
Perspective	top-down	bottom-up
Building block	feedback loop	agent
Unit of analysis	system structure	agent's rules
Level of modelling	aggregate	individual
System structure	fixed	not fixed
Time handling	continuous	discrete

power and may produce large sets of data, which could be difficult to analyse [4]. In addition, ABS requires all system's properties to be modelled discretely. SDS, however, deals with continuum approximations. For the simulation of biological systems, therefore, both approaches are useful and should be selected carefully according to the research question to be addressed.

We believe that these two approaches can be very useful for the simulation of parts of the immune system, based on the findings of [4]. However, there is still little knowledge on how to determine the best approach for a given immune problem. Moreover, little is known concerning the comparison of SDS and ABS for simulation in immunology. Hence, our study aims to establish a framework to help with the choice between SDS and ABS approaches for immune system problems.

In previous work [5] we compared the use of ABS and SDS for modelling non-spatial static agents' behaviour in an immune system ageing problem. By static we mean that there is no movement or interactions between the agents. We concluded that for these types of agents, it is preferable to use SDS instead of ABS. When contrasting the results of both simulation approaches, we saw that SDS is less complex and takes up less computational resources, producing the same results as those obtained by the ABS model. In addition, SDS is more robust when the number of cells increase considerably. There were cases where there was not enough computational resources to run the ABS.

More recently, we used case studies which included interactions between tumour cells and immune effector cells, reviewed in [6]. We began with the simplest (single equation) models for tumor growth and proceed to consider two-equation models involving effector and tumour cells. We used mathematical models as basis for both ABS and SDS. The idea was to check if the results are similar and if we can use SDS and ABS for our case studies interchangeably. In our experiments we obtained different outputs from the ABS and the SDS. This is due to the fact that SDS is a deterministic method while ABS is a stochastic method. To proceed with our tests, we considered tumour cells growth together with their interactions with general immune effector cells. In this case, there were also differences in the output because the effector cell numbers change continuously in the SDS, while for the ABS, they change in a discrete pattern. For example, in the SDS it is possible to consider cases where there are 0.5 cells, while for the ABS it is either 0 or 1 cell (agent).

To advance our study, we have two research objectives. Nuno *et al.* [7] mention that most of what has been done in simulation of the immune system is based on differential equations, which can be easily implemented using SDS, as long as feedback loops are expressed in the equations. We believe that the conversion of current well established mathematical or SDS models into ABS would be a first step to investigate individual behaviour and emergence on the existing models. Hence, the first objective is to develop and test our own set of guidelines for converting SDS models into ABS models. For this we will use a non-spatial model involving interactions between the immune system and cancer. Our second objective is to define guidelines to convert ABS into SDS considering a non-spatial and a spatial scenario.

The remainder of the paper is organized as follows. Section 2 presents a literature review of works comparing SDS and ABS for biological problems. In Section 3, we address our first research objective by presenting an example of conversion from SDS to ABS as well as the results comparison. In Section 4, we present two simulation models implemented in ABS and their conversion into SDS models and compare their results. Finally, in Section 5, we draw the conclusions and present ideas to continue our study.

2   Related Work

In this section, we describe the literature concerned with the comparison between ABS and SDS for biological problems. We found that there is hardly any literature comparing the two approaches for immune simulation.

Wayne *et al.* [8] show the application of both SDS and ABS to simulate non-equilibrium cellular ligand-receptor dynamics over a broad range of concentrations. They concluded that both approaches are powerful tools and are also complementary. In their case study, they did not indicate a preferred paradigm, although they state that intuitively SDS is an obvious choice when studying systems at a high level of aggregation and abstraction. On the other hand, SDS is not capable of simulating receptors and molecules and their individual interactions, which can be done with ABS.

Rahmandad and Sterman   [9] compare the dynamics of a stochastic ABS model with those of the analogous deterministic compartment differential equation model for contagious disease spread. The authors convert the ABS into a differential equation model and examine the impact of individual heterogeneity and different network topologies. The deterministic model yields a single trajectory for each parameter set, while stochastic models yield a distribution of outcomes. Moreover, the differential equation model and ABS dynamics differ for several metrics relevant to public health. The response of the models to policies can also differ when the base case behaviour is similar. Under some conditions, however, the differences in means are small, compared to variability caused by stochastic events, parameter uncertainty and model boundary.

As we mentioned before, in our previous work [5], we compared SDS and ABS for a naive T cell output model. We had a scenario where the agents had no interactions and SDS and ABS produced similar outputs, although SDS takes up less computational resources. We concluded, therefore, that SDS is more suitable. More recently, we used case studies which included interactions between tumour cells and immune effector cells. We wanted to know if the results would be similar and if we can use SDS and ABS for our case studies interchangeably. In our experiments, the stochastic behaviour of the agents made the output from ABS different from the SDS output. Moreover, there were differences in the outcomes due to the continuous character of SDS contrasted to the discrete behaviour of ABS.

Macal [2] shows how to translate a SDS into an equivalent time-stepped, stochastic agent-based simulation. Probabilistic elements in the SDS model were identified and translated into probabilities that were used explicitly in the ABS model. The author uses as an example the SIR model proposed by Kermack and McKendrick [10]. This model was built to understand and predict the spread of epidemics. In the model, the population is divided in three groups of individuals, susceptible (S), infected (I) and recovered (R). To convert the model from SDS to ABS, the author considers two agent-based formulations. Model 1 was defined as a *"naive ABS model, because it provides no additional information or implementation advantages over the SDS model"*. There is a set of agents containing a state (S, I or R), which is the only information dynamically updated. The author claims that Model 1 produces exactly the same results for the numbers of S, I and R over time as does the SDS model for a fixed-time step, Δt of length one. Model 2, on the other hand, is fully individual-based agent model and provides additional information over the SDS model. As for example, in some of the ABS simulation runs of Model 2 an epidemic does not occur. In a significant number of cases, the number of contacts and the number of infected individuals (I) is not large enough to spread the infection. These cases occur because of the agent's probabilistic rules. Hence, Model 2 presents similar results from SDS, but not exactly the same because of the runs where there was not epidemic. The author, therefore, concludes that the ABS model is able to provide additional information over what the SDS model provides given its stochastic nature.

In this paper we want to use examples from the immune area to convert from SDS to ABS, similarly to how it was done in [2]. Moreover, we define explicit guidelines for this conversion and bring some other questions concerned with the choice of SDS and ABS. In the next section, we perform the SDS to ABS conversion for a mathematical model of the interactions between tumour cells and effector cells.

3 From SDS to ABS

In this section we address our first research objective by using a mathematical model to build a non-spatial SDS model and then convert it into an ABS model.

3.1 The Mathematical Model

The mathematical model we use to build our SDS was obtained from [11]. The model's equations illustrate the non-spatial dynamics between effector cells (E), tumour cells (T) and the cytokine IL-2 (I_L). The model is described by the following differential equations:

$$\frac{dE}{dt} = cT - \mu_2 E + \frac{p_1 E I_L}{g_1 + I_L} + s1, \tag{1}$$

Equation 1 describes the rate of change for the effector cell population E [11]. Effector cells grow based on recruitment (cT) and proliferation ($\frac{p_1 E I_L}{g_1 + I_L}$). The parameter c represents the antigenicity of the tumour cells (T) [11,12]. μ_2 is the death rate of the effector cells. p_1 and g_1 are parameters used to calibrate the recruitment of effector cells and $s1$ is the treatment that will boost the number of effector cells.

$$\frac{dT}{dt} = a(1 - bT) - \frac{a_a E T}{g_2 + T}, \tag{2}$$

Equation 2 describes the changes that occur in the tumour cell population T over time. The term $a(1 - bT)$ represents the logistic growth of T (a and b are parameters that define how the tumour cells will grow) and $\frac{a_a E T}{g_2 + T}$ is the number of tumour cells killed by effector cells. a_a and g_2 are parameters to adjust the model.

$$\frac{dI_L}{dt} = \frac{p_2 E T}{g_3 + T} - \mu_3 I_L + s2. \tag{3}$$

The IL-2 population dynamics is described by Equation 3. $\frac{p_2 E T}{g_3 + T}$ determines IL-2 production using parameters p_2 and g_3. μ_3 is the IL-2 loss. $s2$ also represents treatment. The treatment is the injection of IL-2 in the system.

3.2 The SDS Model

The SDS model contains three stock variables, tumour cells, effector cells and IL-2. The stock of effector cells, described by Equation 1, is changed by the recruitment of new effector cells, according to the number of tumour cells, death, proliferation and treatment (insertion of new effector cells). The conversion of Equation 1 into a stock and flow diagram can be seen in Figure 1(a). The number of tumour cells is changed by its natural proliferation and death as well as by the number of cells killed by effector cells (Figure 1(b)). IL-2 stock changes with the production of new IL-2 molecules from effector cells (the production also depends on the number of tumour cells), loss and treatment (insertion of IL-2) (Figure 1(c)). The final SDS stock and flow diagram is depicted in Figure 2. We obtain this diagram by associating the flows with the stocks that will influence them. This information is obtained by to the equations of the mathematical model. For example, we know that the number of tumour cells killed is dependent on

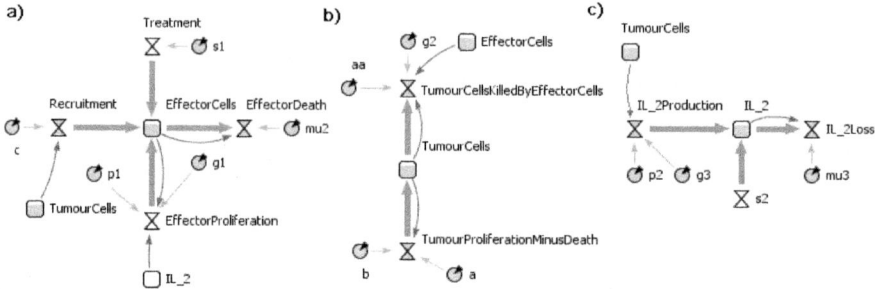

Fig. 1. Equations 1, 2 and 3 converted into stock and flow diagrams (squares = stocks, hourglasses = flows, circles = parameters and arrows = information flows)

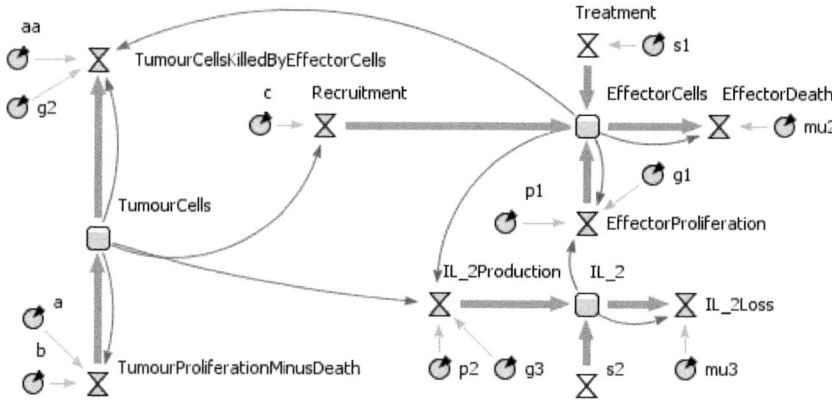

Fig. 2. SDS diagram for the three-equation mathematical model

the number of effector cells. Hence, we have to add the number of effector cells on the mathematical equation of the flow $TumourKilledByEffectorCells$.

3.3   The ABS Model

In order to convert the SDS into an ABS model, we propose the following steps:

1. Identify the possible agents. To do so we use some characteristics defined in [13]. An agent is: (1) self-contained, modular, and uniquely identifiable individual; (2) autonomous and self-directed; (3) a construct with states that varies over time and (4) social, having dynamic interactions with other agents that impact its behaviour. In the SIR model discussed in [2], the author defines two possible ABS. However, in our case we believe that the best way to address the modelling problem is by defining one ABS with three groups of agents, similar to the implementation of Model 2 in [2]. Our agents will be corresponding to the stocks in the SDS model. Hence, the populations of agents are the effector cells, tumour cells and IL-2s. It is important to mention that we converted stocks into agents for this specific problem. However, there are cases where stocks might not be agents. For instance, in our simulation experiments performed for the naive T cell output model in [5], the stocks were states of only one agent representing a T cell.

2. Identify the behaviour of each agent. As we are building the ABS model from an SDS model, the agent's behaviours will be determined by mathematical equations converted into rules. The behaviour of each agent can be seen in Table 2. Each agent has two different types of behaviours: reactive and proactive behaviours. The reactive behavior occurs when the agents perceive the context in which they operate and react to it appropriately. The proactive behaviour describes the situations when the agent has the initiative to identify and solve an issue in the system.

3. Build the agents. Based on the conceptual model derived from step 2 (Table 2) we have developed some state charts, one for each agent type (Figure 3). In the state charts we model states and state transitions.

Table 2. Agents' conceptual model (informed by Equations 1, 2 and 3)

Agent	Parameters	Reactive behaviour	Proactive behaviour
Effector Cell	(1)Death Rate (2)Reproduction Rate	(1)Dies with age (2)Is recruited (3)Is injected as treatment	Reproduces
Tumour Cell	(1)Death Rate 2)Reproduction Rate	(1)Dies killed by effector cells (2)Dies with age	Reproduces
IL-2		(1)Is produced (2)Is lost (3)Is injected	

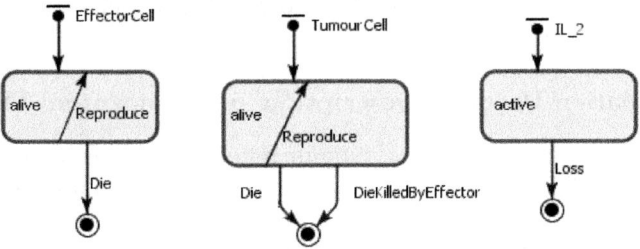

Fig. 3. ABS state charts for the agents of the mathematical model (squares = agent's states, arrows = transitions and filled circles with a ring = final states

3.4 Results Comparison

First we validated our SDS model by comparing its outputs to the outputs produced by the mathematical model derived from [11]. Both produced very similar results. Here we validate our ABS model by comparing its outputs to the outputs produced by the SDS model (i.e. our base model for the comparison).

We ran the simulations on an *Intel Core^{TM}* Duo CPU 2GHz and 2GB RAM. We simulated a period of 400 days. As ABS is a stochastic simulation method we had to conduct several replications. We decided to run 50 replications and calculated the mean values for the outputs. The results for both simulations are shown in Figure 4. From the graphs it is very obvious that the results are very different for the two different simulation approaches.

In the SDS results, tumour cells decrease as effector cells increase, following a predator-prey trend curve. As SDS works with continuous numbers, by 200 days tumour cells and effector cells asymptotically tend to zero. This allows for the populations to increase again, as they never reach zero. On the other hand, for the ABS, the number of effector cells decreases until zero and therefore, proliferation stops. Further investigation needs to be done to see if this is a unique case of if we produce similar results when converting related problems. Moreover, we intend to modify the SDS so that it will consider only discrete numbers of effector cells and investigate the results.

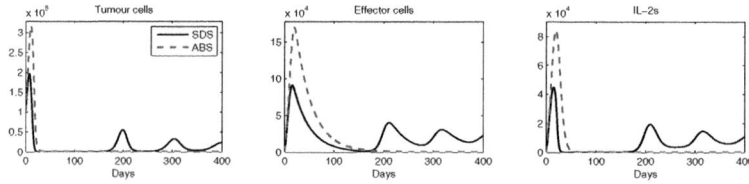

Fig. 4. SDS and ABS results

4   From ABS to SDS

In this Section we address our second objective, which is to define some guidelines to convert a simple ABS model into an SDS model. Next, we present the simulation scenario description.

4.1   Simulation Problem Description and Conceptual Modelling

Effector cells are recruited after a tumour is detected in the organism. Their role is to search and kill tumour cells inside the tumour. Tumour cells reproduce and die with age or are killed by effector cells. For the simulation, we defined the following agents (classes): tumour cell and effector cell. The conceptual model of our agents is given in Table 3. For each agent we present the class specification (parameters and behaviours).

For our experiments, we considered two ABS implementations. The first implementation does not consider cellular movement. The second ABS model allows for effector cell movement. We decided to add space as an additional variable for our simulations because it makes a better match between the simulation and the real world.

Table 3. Agents' conceptual model

Agent	Parameters	Reactive behaviour	Proactive behaviour
Effector Cell	(1)Death Rate (2)Reproduction rate	(1)Dies with age (2)Is recruited	(1)Reproduces (2)Kills tumour cells
Tumour Cell	(1)Death Rate (2)Reproduction rate	(1)Dies with age (2)Is killed by effector cells	(1)Reproduces

4.2 ABS for Model 1

From the conceptual model we have built the ABS model shown in Figure 5. The figure shows the state charts for effector cells and tumour cells agents.

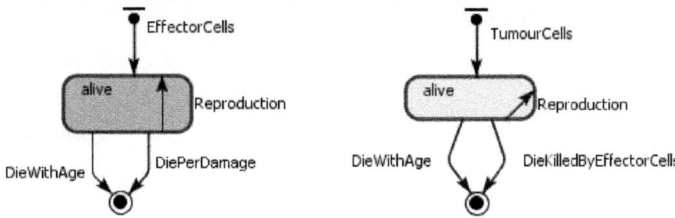

Fig. 5. ABS diagram for Model 1

4.3 SDS for Model 1

For converting the ABS model into an SDS model, we propose the following steps:

1. Identify the system structure. First we have to recognize the system structure and assume a high level of aggregation for the objects being modelled. It is necessary to generalise from the specific events and consider patterns of behaviour that characterise the situation. The cells, therefore, will no longer respond individually. The simulation outcome will be given by the collection of cells and its dynamics as a group. In our case, we have two cell populations (aggregations). Looking at the ABS diagram of Figure 5, the tumour cell population changes with time by reproduction, natural death and death caused by immune cells. The second population are the effector cells. They die with age or apoptosis/damage and reproduce. We know that the effector cell population negatively impacts the amount of tumour cells because effector cells kill tumour cells with time. The reproduction of effector cells increases as the number of tumour cells increase. In addition, as effector cells kill tumour cells they get damaged. Therefore, the tumour cell population impacts the effector cells population in both positive and negative ways.

2. Identify the stocks in the system. Stocks are physical entities which can accumulate over time. In our example, we defined as stocks the effector cells and tumour cells.

3. Define the stocks and their flows. Having the stocks (step 2) and the information about the structure of the model (step 1) we can depict how each stock is changed over time by the flows and the information about how a stock would influence a flow. The effector cells stock will be decreased by death and apoptosis. Moreover, this will be increased by proliferation. The number of effector cells in the system also influences the number of cell's death, proliferation and apoptosis. Therefore, we will have a stock and flow diagram shown in Figure 6(a). The same happens with the tumour cell stock, which is changed by proliferation and death (Figure 6(b)).

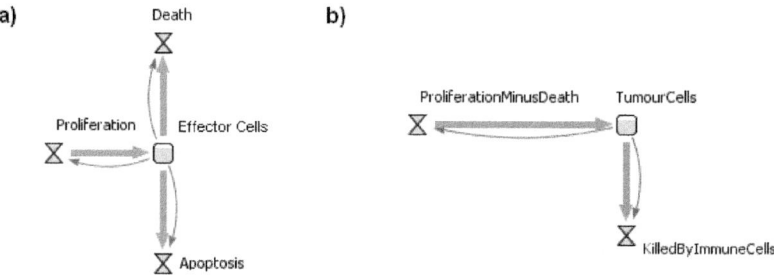

Fig. 6. Stock and flow diagram for effector cells (a) and tumour cells (b)

4. Define the final stock and flow diagram. After defining the diagrams for each stock, it is necessary to go back to the system structure and define how the stocks will interact or influence each other. As we mentioned before, tumour cells impact on the proliferation and death of effector cells, and effector cells influence the growth of tumour cells (Figure 7).

$$\frac{dT}{dt} = p_T(T) - d1_T(T) - d2_T(T, E) \tag{4}$$

5. Define the mathematical model. For SDS, a set of mathematical equations is necessary to describe how the stocks will change over time. By looking at the

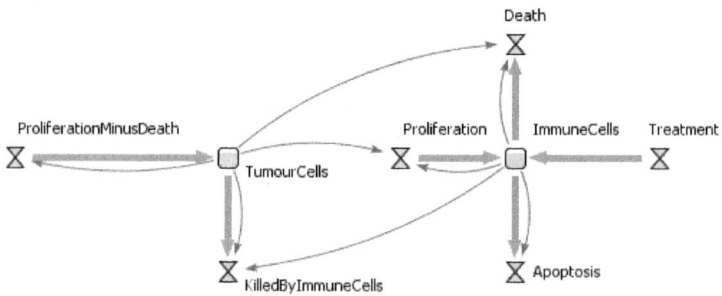

Fig. 7. SDS diagram for Model 1

diagram of Figure 7, the interactions between tumour cells and immune effector cells can be defined by the equations:

$$\frac{dE}{dt} = p_E(T,E) - d_E(T,E) - a_E(E), \tag{5}$$

where: T is the number of tumour cells, E is the number of effector cells, $p_T(T) - d1_T(T)$ is the growth of tumour cells ($proliferation - natural\_death$), $d2_T(T,E)$ is the number of tumour cells killed by effector cells, $p_E(T,E)$ is the proliferation of effector cells and $a_E(E)$ is the death (apoptosis) of effector cells.

For SDS the information provided by the ABS is not enough, because we do not have the equations and rates defining the growth or death of each cell population. Therefore, to continue building the model we need extra information. For example, a data set or a well established model that describes mathematically how the system changes over time would be necessary. For our case study, we used the data and equations defined in [14]:

$$p_T(T) - d1_T(T) = Ta(1 - bT), \tag{6}$$

$$d2_T(T,E) = TE, \tag{7}$$

$$p_E(E,T) = \frac{pTE}{g+T}, \tag{8}$$

$$d_E(E,T) = mTE, \tag{9}$$

$$a_E(E) = dE, \tag{10}$$

Where: $a = 1.636$, $b = 0.002$, $d = 0.3743$, $g = 20.19$, $m = 0.00311$ and $p = 1.131$. We got these values from [6] and used these parameters on the ABS. The models validation was based on the results shown in [6].

4.4   Results for Model 1

We validated our simulation models by comparing its outputs to the outputs produced by the mathematical model derived from [14], as we have done in Section 3.4. We simulated Model 1 for a period of 100 days using both approaches. We ran 50 replications for the ABS and calculated the mean values for the outputs. The results are shown in Figure 8. In the figure, we plotted the results for the first 60 days, where the simulations reach a steady-state.The outputs produced by the SDS model are the same as the mathematical model and different from the results produced by the ABS model. The growth of tumour cells happens faster in the ABS. Another difference is in the decay of effector cells. By 20 days, there is an increase in the number of effector cells for the SDS, while in the ABS it does not increase. We believe this is due to the continuous character of SDS compared to ABS. Therefore, once effector cells population decreases to zero

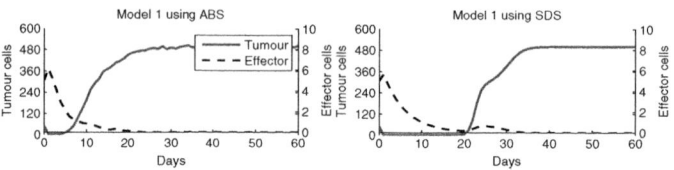

Fig. 8. ABS and SDS results for Model 1

in the ABS, it does not increase again. The SDS the effector cells decrease to zero asymptotically. As they do not reach the value zero, they grow back again, according to the mathematical definitions (Equations 4 and 5).

4.5   ABS for Model 2

As Model 1 is non-spatial, the effector cells do not move to reach a tumour cell. It impacts on the results of the simulations because tumour cells die in a rate that considers the entire population of effector cells. If we want to simulate a scenario closer to reality, a certain effector cell E_{c_i} has to move towards a tumour cell T_{c_i} and kill it. The remaining effector cells in the population will not have any impact on the death of T_{c_i}. Therefore, we decided to introduce space in Model 2. Our goal is to verify the differences in the model's behaviour over time, compared to Model 1. We also want to investigate how the movement of effector cells would impact on the SDS model development. The agents of Model 2 will be the same considered in Model 1 (Figure 5), as well as their behaviours (Table 3). However, we added an additional rule to the effector cell agents: they have to move towards the closest tumour cell and then kill it.

4.6   SDS for Model 2

Although the stock and flow diagram for Model 2 remained the same as for Model 1 (Figure 7), we had to adapt the mathematical model to include effector cell movement. At each time step in the simulation, the maximum number of tumour cells killed will be equal to the number of effector cells. Hence, Equation 4 will be replaced by Equation 11:

$$\frac{dT}{dt} = p_T(T) - d1_T(T) - d2_T(E) \tag{11}$$

where: $d2_T(E) = E$

4.7   Results for Model 2

The simulation results for Model 2 are shown in Figure 9. For the ABS results, we display the mean value of 50 runs. The outcomes for both simulations strategies is similar, although the mean number of effector cells in the ABS is 40% higher. With these results we show that for this example, the cellular movement can be also simulated in the SDS.

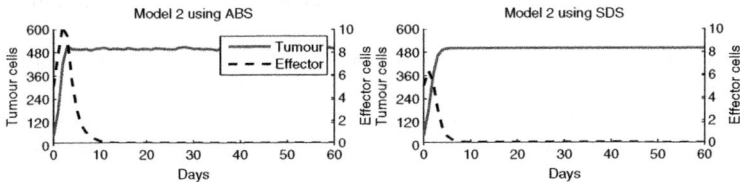

Fig. 9. ABS and SDS results for Model 2

5   Conclusions

In the literature there is little guidance on how to choose between SDS and ABS for a specific immune problem. Our overall research aim is to develop a framework that helps with this choice. In this work we investigated the question if it is possible to easily convert simulation models between these two approaches. As there are no explicit guidelines available from the literature, we developed and tested our own set of guidelines for converting SDS models into ABS models and vice-versa. While in the first case we only considered a non-spatial scenario, in the latter case we looked at a non-spatial and a spatial scenarios. Our results showed that it is possible to obtain an ABS model based on the information inherited in a SDS model. However, the outcomes for the two approaches were different. For the conversion of ABS into an SDS we realized that, for our case study, extra information was necessary to build some of the mathematical equations required for the SDS model. Hence, we had to use a mathematical model established in the literature to continue building the simulation. We obtained different outcomes in our non-spatial scenario. When we added spatial dimension to the agents in the ABS we still managed to adapt the SDS model, with similar results. As future work, we intend to investigate further the reasons why our conversion from SDS into an ABS produced different results. We will implement further models to see if there is a systematic error behind these mismatches.

References

1. Forrester, J.W.: Urban Dynamics. Pegasus Communications (1969)
2. Macal, C.M.: To agent-based simulation from system dynamics. In: Proceedings of the 2010 Winter Simulation Conference (2010)
3. Schieritz, N., Milling, P.M.: Modeling the forrest or modeling the trees: A comparison of system dynamics and agent based simulation. In: Proceedings of the XXI International Conference of the System Dynamics society (2003)
4. Thorne, B.C., Bailey, A.M., Pierce, S.M.: Combining experiments with multi-cell agent-based modeling to study biological tissue patterning. Briefings in Bioinformatics 8, 245–257 (2007)
5. Figueredo, G.P., Aickelin, U.: Investigating immune system aging: System dynamics and agent-based modelling. In: Proceedings of the Summer Computer Simulation Conference (2010)
6. Eftimie, R., Bramson, J.L., Earn, D.J.: Interactions between the immune system and cancer: A brief review of non-spatial mathematical models. Bull. Math. Biol. (2010)

7. Fachada, N., Lopes, V., Rosa, A.: Agent-based modelling and simulation of the immune system: a review. In: Neves, J., Santos, M.F., Machado, J.M. (eds.) EPIA 2007. LNCS (LNAI), vol. 4874, pp. 2007–2013. Springer, Heidelberg (2007)
8. Wakeland, W.W., Gallaher, E.J., Macovsky, L.M., Aktipis, C.A.: A comparison of system dynamics and agent-based simulation applied to the study of cellular receptor dynamics. In: Hawaii International Conference on System Sciences, vol. 3 (2004)
9. Ramandad, H., Sterman, J.: Heterogeneity and network structure in the dynamics of diffusion: Comparing agent-based and differential equation models. Management Science 5 (2008)
10. Kermack, W.O., McKendrick, A.G.: Contributions to the mathematical theory of epidemics. Proc. Roy. Soc. (1927)
11. Kirschner, D., Panneta, J.C.: Modelling immunotherapy of the tumor immune interaction. J. Math. Biol. 1, 235–252 (1998)
12. Arciero, J.C., Jackson, T.L., Kirschner, D.E.: A mathematical model of tumor-immune evasion and siRNA treatment. Discrete and Continumour Dynamical Systems - Series B 4, 39–58 (2004)
13. Macal, C.M., North, M.J.: Tutorial on agent-based modeling and simulation. In: Proceedings of the 2005 Winter Simulation Conference (2005)
14. Kuznetsov, V.A., Makalkin, I.A., Taylor, M.A., Perelson, A.S.: Nonlinear dynamics of immunogenic tumors: parameter estimation and global bifurcation analysis. Bulletin of Mathematical Biology 56, 295–321 (1994)

Implementation of a Computational Model of the Innate Immune System

Alexandre Bittencourt Pigozzo, Gilson Costa Macedo,
Rodrigo Weber dos Santos, and Marcelo Lobosco

Universidade Federal de Juiz de Fora, 36036-330, Juiz de Fora, MG, Brazil
alexbprr@gmail.com, {gilson.macedo,marcelo.lobosco}@ufjf.edu.br,
rwdsantos@yahoo.com

Abstract. In the last few years there has been an increasing interest in mathematical and computational modelling of the human immune system (HIS). Computational models of the HIS dynamics may contribute to a better understanding of the complex phenomena associate to the immune system, and support the development of new drugs and therapies for different diseases. However, the modelling of the HIS is an extremely hard task that demands huge amount of work to be performed by multidisciplinary teams. In this scenario, the objective of this work is to model the dynamics of some cells and molecules of the HIS during an immune response to lipopolysaccharide (LPS) in a section of the tissue. The LPS constitutes the cellular wall of Gram-negative bacteria, and it is a highly immunogenic molecule, which means that it has a remarkable capacity to elicit strong immune responses.

Keywords: Immune Modelling, Innate Immune System, Acute Inflammation, Partial Differential Equations, Finite Difference Method.

1 Introduction

The development of computational systems that simulates an entire living system was proposed by the UK Computing Research Committee as one of the grand challenges in computing research for 2010 and beyond [1]. This class of system is known as iViS (in Vivo-in Silico). The potential benefits of iViS are enormous, so are the challenges along this long way. Currently, the development of such iViS systems is in its early stages. Also, the Brazilian Computing Society has proposed five Grand Research Challenges in Computer Science in Brazil [2], one of them is the computational modeling of complex systems.

In this scenario, our work aims to develop and implement a mathematical and computational model of the Human Immune System (HIS). The complete modeling of the HIS demands large amount of work to be performed by multidisciplinary teams. In this work we focus on one specific task: the simulation of the immune response to lipopolysaccharide (LPS) in a microscopic section of a tissue, reproducing, for this purpose, the initiation, maintenance and resolution of immune response. The LPS endotoxin is a potent immunostimulant that

P. Liò, G. Nicosia, and T. Stibor (Eds.): ICARIS 2011, LNCS 6825, pp. 95–107, 2011.

can induce an acute inflammatory response comparable to that of a bacterial infection.

Our model is based on a previous work [3] that describes a set of Partial Differential Equations (PDEs) used to reproduce important phenomena such as the temporal order of cells arriving at the local of infection, presentation of LPS by dendritic cells, the macrophage and T regulatory participation in the immune response termination, the production of pro-inflammation and anti-inflammation cytokines and the chemotaxis phenomenon.

In this work, we present a reduced model of the immune system that simulates the spatial and temporal behavior of LPS, neutrophil and cytokine during the first phase of the innate response. The main contributions of this work are the following: a) the model proposed in this work introduces a new way to model the permeability of the endothelium, inserting a dynamic permeability term that depends on the cytokine concentration; b) it presents new boundary conditions; and c) it can qualitatively reproduce the behavior of neutrophils during an immune response to an LPS.

The remainder of this work is organized as follows. Section 2 includes the biological background necessary for understanding this work. Section 3 describes the mathematical model implemented in this work. Section 4 describes the implementation of the mathematical model. Section 4.1 presents the simulation results obtained with the model proposed. Our conclusions and plans of future works are presented in Section 5.

2   Biological Background

Body surfaces are protected by epithelia, which constitutes a physical barrier between the internal and external environments. The body's epithelia form an effective block against the external environment, but eventually they can be crossed or settled by pathogens, causing infections. After crossing the epithelium, the pathogens encounter cells and molecules of the innate immune system that immediately develop a response. Reinforcing the innate immune response but taking days instead of hours to develop, the adaptive immune system is capable of eliminating the infection more efficiently than the innate immune system. The adaptive immune system is only present in vertebrates and depends primarily on the recognition executed by lymphocytes, that posses the ability to distinguish a pathogen and direct to it a stronger immune response.

The initial response of the body to an acute biological stress, such as a bacterial infection, is an acute inflammatory response [4]. The strategy of the HIS is to keep some resident macrophages on guard in the tissues to look for any signal of infection. When they find such a signal, the macrophages alert the neutrophils that their help is necessary. The cooperation between macrophages and neutrophils is essential to mount an effective defense, because without the macrophages to recruit the neutrophils to the location of infection, the neutrophils would circulate indefinitely in the blood vessels, impairing the control of huge infections.

The LPS endotoxin is a potent immunostimulant that can induce an acute inflammatory response comparable to that of a bacterial infection. After the lyse of the bacteria by the action of cells of the HIS, the LPS can be released in the host, intensifying the inflammatory response and activating some cells of the innate system, such as neutrophils and macrophages.

The LPS can trigger an inflammatory response through the interaction with receptors on the surface of some cells. For example, the macrophages that resides in the tissue recognizes a bacteria through the binding of TLR4 with LPS. The commitment of this receptor activates the macrophage to phagocytose, degrading the bacteria internally and secreting proteins known as cytokines and chemokines, as well as other molecules.

The inflammation of an infectious tissue has many benefits in the control of the infection. Besides recruiting cells and molecules of innate immunity from blood vessels to the location of the infected tissue, it increases the lymph flux containing microorganisms and cells that carry LPS to the neighbors lymphoid tissues, where these cells will present the LPS to the lymphocytes and will initiate the adaptive response. Once the adaptive response is activated, the inflammation also recruits the effector cells of the adaptive immune system to the location of infection.

3   Mathematical Model

The model proposed in this work is based on a set of Partial Differential Equations (PDEs) originally proposed by [3]. In our model, a set of equations describe the dynamics of the immune response to LPS in a microscopic section of tissue. In particular, the interactions among LPS, neutrophil and cytokine are modeled. In the current model, the variable CH represents the functions and interactions of two distinct types of cytokines, the TNF-α and IL-8.

The main differences between our model and the original one[3] are: a) the current work does not consider the dynamics of the T cytotoxic cells, T regulatory cells, dendritic cells and the cytokines produced by these types of cells, and b) the boundary conditions of neutrophils and LPS was modified. In the case of neutrophils, the model proposed in this work includes a new term for the endothelium permeability. This permeability depends on the pro-inflammatory cytokine concentration, and defines how many neutrophils leaves the blood vessels and enters the infected tissue. This influx of cells occurs not only on the borders of the domain, but also along the entire domain. Finally, in the case of LPS, we used a Neumann boundary condition, instead of the Dirichlet boundary condition originally proposed in [3].

Another difference between our work and the original one are the values used as parameters in simulations: the original work uses values obtained from distinct species[3], while we use values obtained from a single species, the human species, whenever possible.

Figure 1 presents schematically the relationship between neutrophils, pro-inflammatory cytokines and LPS. The LPS diffuse and cause a response in the neutrophils, that recognize these LPS and phagocyte them. The process

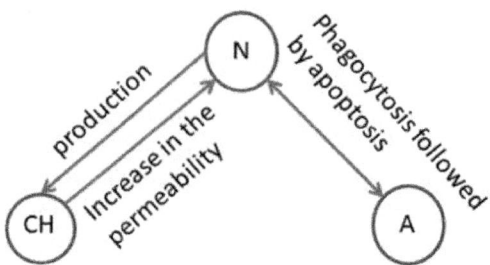

Fig. 1. Relationship between the components

of phagocytosis induces, in a rapid way, the apoptosis of neutrophils. This induction is associated with the generation of reactive oxygen species (ROS) [5].

The pro-inflammatory cytokine is produced by neutrophils after the membrane receptors of these neutrophils recognize the LPS. The pro-inflammatory cytokine induces an increase in the endothelial permeability allowing more neutrophils to leave the blood vessels and enter the infected tissue. Besides, the pro-inflammatory cytokine is chemoattractant of neutrophils, guiding their movement. As a result the neutrophils move in the direction of the gradient of the pro-inflammatory cytokine.

The main characteristics of the mathematical model are:

- Neutrophils interact with pro-inflammatory cytokines and LPS;
- The interaction between neutrophils and LPS increases the production of cytokines;
- Cytokines induce an increase in the endothelial permeability and allows more neutrophils to come to the infected tissue;
- In the tissue, neutrophils move in the direction of the gradient of the pro-inflammatory cytokines (chemotaxis);
- Pro-inflammatory cytokines attracts the neutrophils to the location where the LPS concentration is higher.

Our set of equations is given below, where A, N and CH represent the population of LPS, neutrophils and pro-inflammatory cytokines, respectively.

The LPS equation is shown in Equation 1.

$$\begin{cases} \frac{\partial A}{\partial t} = -\mu_A A - \lambda_{N|A} A.N + D_A \Delta A \\ A(x,0) = A_0 \quad | \quad 0 \leq x < 1, \frac{\partial A(.,t)}{\partial n}|_{\partial\Omega} = 0 \end{cases} \quad (1)$$

The term $\mu_A A$ models the decay of the LPS, where μ_A is its decay rate. The term $\lambda_{N|A} A.N$ models the phagocytosis of LPS by neutrophils, where $\lambda_{N|A}$ is the phagocytosis rate. The term $D_A \Delta A$ models the diffusion of the LPS, where D_A is the diffusion coefficient.

The neutrophil equation is shown in Equation 2.

$$
\begin{cases}
permeability = ((Pmax - Pmin).CH/(CH + Keqch) + Pmin) \\
sourceN = permeability.(NmaxTissue - N) \\
\frac{\partial N}{\partial t} = -\mu_N N - \lambda_{A|N} A.N + D_N \Delta N + sourceN - \nabla.(\chi_N N \nabla CH) \\
N(x,0) = N_0, \frac{\partial N(.,t)}{\partial n}|_{\partial\Omega} = 0
\end{cases}
\tag{2}
$$

The term $((Pmax - Pmin).CH/(CH + Keqch) + Pmin)$ uses a Hill equation [6] to model how permeability of the endothelium of the blood vessels depends on the local concentration of cytokines. Hill equations are also used, for example, to model drug dose-response relationships [7]. The idea is to model the increase in the permeability of the endothelium according to the concentration of the pro-inflammatory cytokines into the endothelium. In the Hill equation, $Pmax$ represents the maximum rate of increase of endothelium permeability induced by pro-inflammatory cytokines, $Pmin$ represents the minimum rate of increase of endothelium permeability induced by pro-inflammatory cytokines and $keqch$ is the concentration of the pro-inflammatory cytokine that exerts 50% of the maximum effect in the increase of the permeability.

The term $\mu_N N$ models the neutrophil apoptosis, where μ_N is the rate of apoptosis. The term $\lambda_{A|N} A.N$ models the neutrophil apoptosis induced by the phagocytosis, where $\lambda_{A|N}$ represent the rate of this induced apoptosis. The term $D_N \Delta N$ models the neutrophil diffusion, where D_N is the coefficient of diffusion. The term $sourceN$ represents the source term of neutrophil, that is, the number of neutrophils that is entering the tissue from the blood vessels. This number depends on the endothelium permeability ($permeability$) and the capacity of the tissue to support the entrance of neutrophils ($NmaxTissue$), that can also represent the blood concentration of Neutrophils. In this model we consider it, $NmaxTissue$, constant over time. The term $\nabla.(\chi_N N \nabla CH)$ models the chemotaxis process of the neutrophils, where χ_N is the chemotaxis rate.

Finally, the cytokine equation is shown in Equation 3.

$$
\begin{cases}
\frac{\partial CH}{\partial t} = -\mu_{CH} CH + \beta_{CH|N}.N.A + D_{CH} \Delta CH \\
CH(x,0) = 0, \frac{\partial CH(.,t)}{\partial n}|_{\partial\Omega} = 0
\end{cases}
\tag{3}
$$

The term $\mu_{CH} CH$ models the pro-inflammatory cytokine decay, where μ_{CH} is the decay rate. The term $\beta_{CH|N}.N.A$ models the production of the pro-inflammatory cytokine by the neutrophils, where $\beta_{CH|N}$ is the rate of this production. The term $D_{CH} \Delta CH$ models the diffusion of the pro-inflammatory cytokines, where D_{CH} is the diffusion coefficient.

This set of equations tries to model the role of chemotaxis in the migration of immune cells to sites of inflammation and infection. Neutrophils and cytokines are of fundamental importance in this process. We believe that our mathematical and computational models can enhance the comprehension of inflammatory and immune processes. A better understanding of these processes is essential since they trigger a cascade of events that activate and coordinate the global response of the immune system [8]. The understanding of the neutrophils role is also important because of its specific regulatory effectors of immunity: they orchestrate immature DC, recruit T cells, and the chemokines released by them display chemotactic activity for macrophages, dendritic cells, NK cells, and T cells [9].

The table 1 presents the initial conditions and the values of the parameters used in the simulations.

Table 1. Initial conditions and parameters

Parameter	Value	Unit	Reference
N_0	$2, 0 < x < 5$	cell	estimated
CH_0	$0, 0 < x < 5$	cell	estimated
A_0	$50, 0 < x < 1$	cell	estimated
$Pmax$	10	1/day	estimated based on [10]
$Pmin$	1	1/day	estimated based on [10]
$NmaxTissue$	5	cell	estimated
$keqch$	1	cell	estimated
μ_A	0.005	1/day	[3]
$\lambda_{N|A}$	0.55	1/cell.day	[3]
D_A	2000	μm^2/day	estimated
μ_N	3.43	1/day	[3]
$\lambda_{A|N}$	0.55	1/cell.day	[3]
X_N	14400	μm^2/day	[11]
D_N	12096	μm^2/day	[12]
μ_{CH}	7	1/day	estimated
$\beta_{CH|N}$	0.4	1/cell.day	[3]
D_{CH}	9216	μm^2/day	[3]

4 Implementation

The numerical method employed was the finite difference method [13] that is used in the discretization of PDEs. This numerical method is based on the approximation of derivatives with finite differences.

A complex part of the resolution of the PDEs is the resolution of the convective term, the chemotaxis term. The development of numerical methods to approximate convectives terms (that in most cases are not linear) have been subject of intense research in the last years [14,15,16,17].

Different numerical approaches have been proposed [18,19] to solve this kind of equations. Our implementation is based on the finite difference method for the spatial discretization and the explicit method for the time evolution with an upwind scheme for the convective term of the equation. The upwind scheme discretize the hyperbolic PDEs using a bias for the flux direction given by the signal of the characteristic speeds. The upwind scheme uses an adaptive or solution-sensitive stencil to precisely simulate the direction of information propagation.

The discretization of the chemotaxis term $(\nabla.(\chi_N N \nabla CH))$ uses a first order upwind scheme called FOU (First-Order Upwind scheme)[20]. In one-dimension, the upwind scheme approximates the chemotaxis flux at the point $x + \frac{deltaX}{2}$ in the following way:

```
if (ch[x+deltaX] − ch[x−deltaX] > 0) {
    flux = ((n[x] − n[x−deltaX])/deltaX)*(ch[x+deltaX] − ch[x−deltaX])/(2*deltaX);
}
else{
    flux = ((n[x+deltaX] − n[x])/deltaX)*(ch[x+deltaX] − ch[x−deltaX])/(2*deltaX);
}
```

In this code, *ch* represents the discretization of the pro-inflammatory cytokine, *n* represents the discretization of neutrophils, *x* is the position in space and *deltaX* is the spatial discretization. The test made is to define what is the signal of the characteristic speed, where the speed of the movement of $N(x)$ is given by the term ∇CH. This value is then used to choose between two schemes of finite differences: forward or backward.

We decided to implement our own numerical method to solve the systems of PDEs because a) we have the possibility to parallelize the code; and b) most of the numerical libraries offer few functions that are suitable to our problem.

The sequential code was implemented in C. Then the code was parallelized using three distinct models. The first one uses the shared memory model, the second one the message passing model, whereas the third one uses an hybrid model [21].

Both OpenMP and MPI versions use the domain decomposition technique to divide the work between threads/processes. More specifically, the calculus of the PDEs are divided between threads/processes in such way that each thread/process is responsible for calculating the system of PDEs for some portions of the spatial domain. In the hybrid approach, the domain is divided into sub-domains and these are sent to MPI processes. The MPI processes are the responsible for dividing the calculus of its sub-domain between the threads they have created. The MPI processes exchange the values of the boundaries of its sub-domains at the end of each time step [21].

4.1   Numerical Results

To show the importance of some cells, molecules and processes in the dynamics of the innate immune response, a set of simulations were performed under different scenarios. The simulations start with a simple scenario were the cells of the HIS are not considered (case 1). More complex scenarios are then considered: in each scenario, a new set of equations and terms are added to the previous one, until the complete scenario is reached in the last case (case 5).

The descriptions for each case are given below:

- case 1: only LPS are considered, that is, cells and molecules of the immune system are not considered. The LPS simply diffuses through the tissue.
- case 2: the neutrophils are added to the dynamics. In this case, the LPS are phagocyted by the neutrophils that suffer apoptosis after the phagocytosis. In this case, we do not consider the production of cytokines when the neutrophil recognizes the LPS.

– case 3: a source term is added to the neutrophil equation. Neutrophils enter the tissue by considering a constant endothelium permeability *permeability*: $sourceN = permeability.(NmaxTissue - N)$.
– case 4: the cytokine equation is added to the model. In this case the neutrophils produce cytokines when it recognizes the LPS. Also, the permeability term depends on the cytokine concentration.
– case 5: the chemotaxis process is added to the neutrophil equation. The neutrophils move in the direction of the cytokine gradient, being attracted to the regions where the LPS concentration is higher.

In all cases we considered an one-dimensional domain with of $5mm$ and the number of time steps used represents an interval of approximately 1 day.

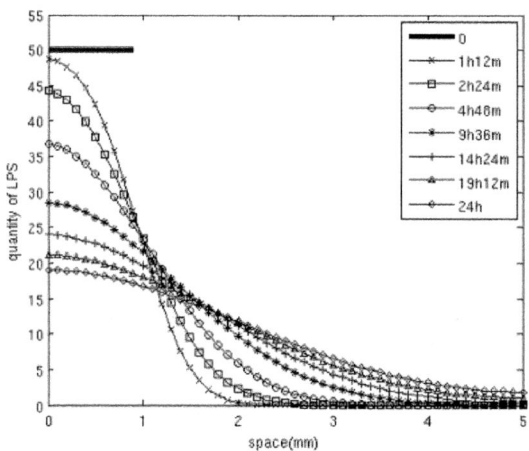

Fig. 2. Temporal evolution of the spatial distribution of LPS. The x-axis represents the space (in mm) and the y-axis represents the number of LPS.

CASE 1. In this scenario, without the immune system acting, the LPS (Fig.2) simply diffuses over the entire domain.

CASE 2. The neutrophils diffuse through the domain looking for any signs of inflammation or infection. When a neutrophil finds an LPS and occurs a successful binding, the neutrophil phagocytes the antigen and after this it undergo apoptosis. The phagocytosis of the antigen (Fig.3, left) is responsible for a significant decrease in the antigen population when compared to the previous case, mainly in the region with more LPS.

The neutrophil population (Fig.3, right) decreases until zero because they suffer apoptosis induced by the phagocytosis and there is not a source of neutrophils to replenish the population. In this case, the production of pro-inflammatory cytokines is not considered.

CASE 3. At first, the neutrophils start to decrease (Fig.4, right) due to the apoptosis induced by the phagocytosis. However, after some time they start to increase because the number of neutrophils that are entering into the tissue becomes greater than the number of neutrophils that dies due to the use of the new term used to express the endothelium permeability. So the neutrophils population does not approximate to zero and maintains a minimal concentration that is capable to handle infections more efficiently than in the previous case because the influx of neutrophils occurs not only on the borders of the domain, but also along the entire domain. Due to all the previously mentioned facts the antigen population (Fig.4, left) decreases more in this case than in the previous one.

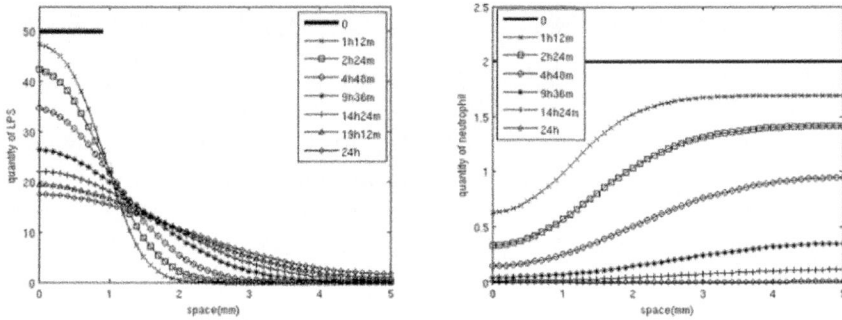

Fig. 3. Temporal evolution of the spatial distribution of LPS and neutrophils. The x-axis represents the space (in mm) and the y-axis represents the number of LPS and neutrophils, respectively.

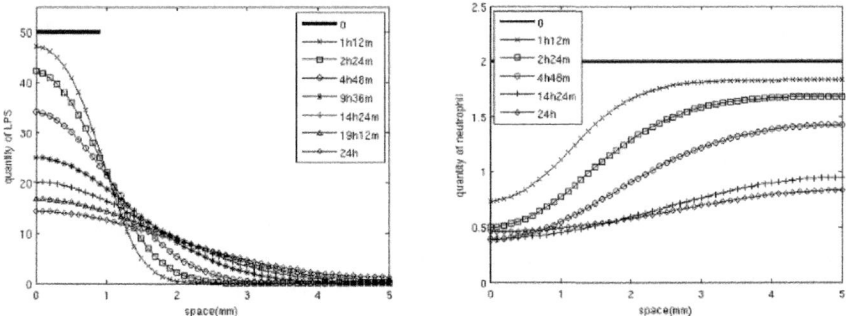

Fig. 4. Temporal evolution of the spatial distribution of LPS and neutrophils. The x-axis represents the space (in mm) and the y-axis represents the number of LPS and neutrophils, respectively.

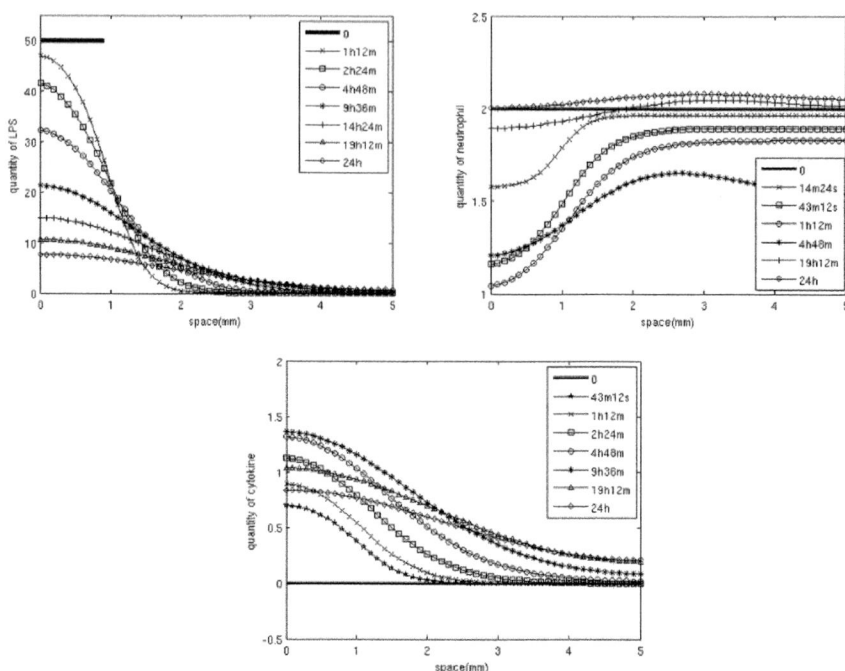

Fig. 5. Temporal evolution of the spatial distribution of LPS, neutrophils and cytokines. The x-axis represents the space (in mm) and the y-axis represents the number of LPS, neutrophils and cytokines, respectively.

CASE 4. As in the previous case, it can be observed that the neutrophil population start to decrease but after some time, it starts to increase rapidly and vigorously (Fig.5, upper right). The insertion of the term that models the production of pro-inflammatory cytokine and the term that models the variable permeability allow a great influx of neutrophils in the regions of locally high concentration of antigen. These are regions where the neutrophils produce more cytokine (Fig.5, lower left). As a result of this great influx of neutrophils, the immune response is more efficient in the control of the infection: neutrophils almost completely eliminate the LPS (Fig.5, upper left).

CASE 5. In this case the inclusion of the chemotaxis process results in a movement of neutrophils in the direction of the gradient of the pro-inflammatory cytokines. As a consequence of this movement, the spatial distribution of the neutrophils changes significantly (Fig.6, upper right). These neutrophils that are attracted also contributes to produce even more cytokines (Fig.6, lower left) in the locations of the tissue where the LPS are more concentrated (Fig.6, upper left), resulting in a more vigorous and rapid immune response.

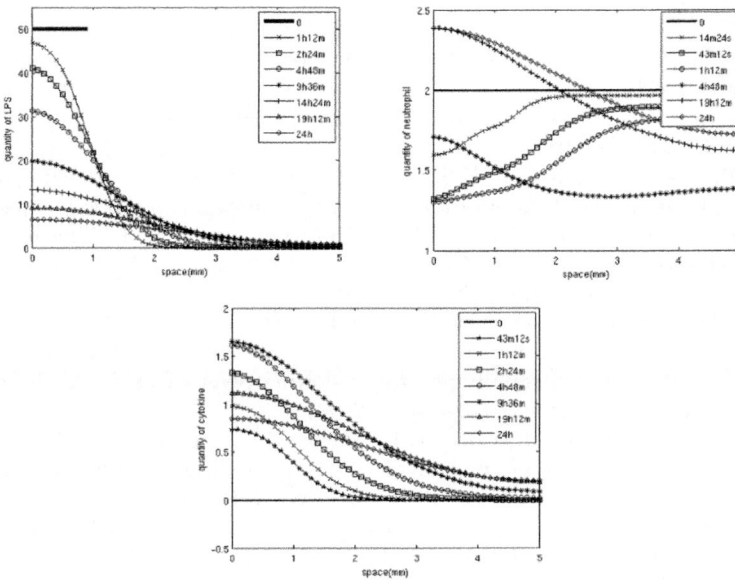

Fig. 6. Temporal evolution of the spatial distribution of LPS, neutrophils and cytokines. The x-axis represents the space (in mm) and the y-axis represents the number of LPS, neutrophils and cytokines, respectively.

5 Conclusions and Future Works

In this work we presented a mathematical and computational model that simulates the immune response to LPS in a microscopic section of a tissue. To achieve this objective, the model reproduces the initiation, maintenance and resolution of immune response. A set of PDEs are used to model the main agents involved in this processes, like the antigen, chemokines and neutrophils.

The main contribution of this work is the new way proposed to model the permeability of the endothelium, inserting a dynamic permeability that is dependent of the cytokine concentration. Also, we believe that our simple model is capable of reproducing qualitatively the dynamics of the modeled process, more specifically, the interaction between neutrophils and cytokines in the establishment of an immune response against the antigens.

As future works, we plan to implement a more complete mathematical model including, for example, new cells (Natural Killer, dendritic cells or the complement system), others pro-inflammatory cytokines, anti-inflammatory cytokine, molecules and others processes envolved in the immune responses.

Acknowledgment

The authors would like to thank FAPEMIG (CEX APQ 01326/08), CNPq (481535/2008-0, 479201/2010-2), CAPES (for the M.Sc. scholarship to the first author) and UFJF for supporting this study.

References

1. Hoare, T., Miller, R.: Grand Challenges in Computing Research. British Computer Society (2004)
2. Medeiros, C.B.: Grand research challenges in computer science in brazil. Computer 41, 59–65 (2008)
3. Su, B., Zhou, W., Dorman, K.S., Jones, D.E.: Mathematical modelling of immune response in tissues. Computational and Mathematical Methods in Medicine: An Interdisciplinary Journal of Mathematical, Theoretical and Clinical Aspects of Medicine 10, 1748–6718 (2009)
4. Janeway, C., Murphy, K.P., Travers, P., Walport, M., Janeway, C.: Immunobiology, 5th edn. Garland Science, New York (2001)
5. Zhang, B., Hirahashi, J., Cullere, X., Mayadas, T.N.: Elucidation of molecular events leading to neutrophil apoptosis following phagocytosis. The Journal of Biological Chemistry 278, 28443–28454 (2003)
6. Goutelle, S., Maurin, M., Rougier, F., Barbaut, X., Bourguignon, L., Ducher, M., Maire, P.: The hill equation: a review of its capabilities in pharmacological modelling. Fundamental & Clinical Pharmacology 22(6), 633–648 (2008)
7. Wagner, J.G.: Kinetics of pharmacologic response i. proposed relationships between response and drug concentration in the intact animal and man. Journal of Theoretical Biology 20(2), 173–201 (1968)
8. Byrne, H.M., Cave, G., McElwain, D.L.S.: The effect of chemotaxis and chemokinesis on leukocyte locomotion: A new interpretation of experimental results. Mathematical Medicine and Biology 15(3), 235–256 (1998)
9. di Carlo, E., Iezzi, M., Pannellini, T., Zaccardi, F., Modesti, A., Forni, G., Musian, P.: Neutrophils in anti-cancer immunological strategies: Old players in new games. Journal of Hematotherapy & Stem Cell Research 10, 739–748 (2001)
10. Price, T., Ochs, H., Gershoni-Baruch, R., Harlan, J., Etzioni, A.: In vivo neutrophil and lymphocyte function studies in a patient with leukocyte adhesion deficiency type ii. Blood 84(5), 1635–1639 (1994)
11. Felder, S., Kam, Z.: Human neutrophil motility: Time-dependent three-dimensional shape and granule diffusion. Cell Motility and the Cytoskeleton 28(4), 285–302 (1994)
12. Chettibi, S., Lawrence, A., Young, J., Lawrence, P., Stevenson, R.: Dispersive locomotion of human neutrophils in response to a steroid-induced factor from monocytes. J. Cell. Sci. 107(11), 3173–3181 (1994)
13. LeVeque, R.J.: Finite Difference Methods for Ordinary and Partial Differential Equations. Society for Industrial and Applied Mathematics (2007)
14. Harten, A.: High resolution schemes for hyperbolic conservation laws. J. Comput. Phys. 135, 260–278 (1997)
15. Leonard, B.P.: Simple high-accuracy resolution program for convective modelling of discontinuities. International Journal for Numerical Methods in Fluids 8(10), 1291–1318 (1988)
16. Shu, C.W., Osher, S.: Efficient implementation of essentially non-oscillatory shock-capturing schemes,ii. J. Comput. Phys. 83, 32–78 (1989)
17. Sod, G.A.: A survey of several finite difference methods for systems of nonlinear hyperbolic conservation laws. Journal of Computational Physics 27(1), 1–31 (1978)

18. Marrocco, A.: Numerical simulation of chemotactic bacteria aggregation via mixed finite elements. Math. Mod. Num. Analysis 37, 617–630 (2003)
19. Filbet, F.: A finite volume scheme for the patlak–keller–segel chemotaxis model. Numerische Mathematik 104, 457–488 (2006)
20. Hafez, M.M., Chattot, J.J.: Innovative Methods for Numerical Solution of Partial Differential Equations. World Scientific Publishing Company, Singapore (2002)
21. Pigozzo, A.B., Lobosco, M., dos Santos, R.W.: Parallel implementation of a computational model of the his using openmp and mpi. In: International Symposium on Computer Architecture and High Performance Computing Workshops, pp. 67–72 (2010)

Relevance of Pattern Recognition in a Non-deterministic Model of Immune Responses

Anastasio Salazar-Bañuelos

Department of Surgery, Division of Transplantation, Foothills Medical Centre,
1403 – 29 street NW, Calgary, AB, Canada T2N 2T9
salazara@ucalgary.ca

Abstract. An artificial immune system model which lacks an explicit pattern recognition mechanism, yet appears to explain immunological memory and immune responses had been proposed[1, 2]. In this study, I asked whether inclusion of a pattern recognition mechanism (antigen-antibody) in the same computer simulation would substantially change the outcomes and thus the explanatory power of the proposed model. Our results suggest that although antigen-antibody interactions can elicit the emergence of an immune response, their relevance is contingent on the previous condition of the system, that is, the starting balance between suppressive and reactive agents (attractor) and its distance from the threshold for an inflammatory response. I conclude that changing the attractor (which maintain the level of reactivity in the background) is more important for the emergence or non-emergence of immune responses than modifying the pattern recognition system.

Keywords: Pattern Recognition, Artificial Immune Systems, Simulation.

1 Introduction

Since the foundation of immunology as a scientific discipline, pattern recognition has been central to the explanation of immune responses. Most research programs in immunology are focused on the search for recognition agents and determination of their properties and mechanisms to explain how antigen recognition takes place - how the recognizer (antibody or lymphocyte receptor) recognizes an antigenic molecular pattern. With a few exceptions, this has been taken as a sine-qua-non condition for the explanation of immune responses, and the only problem to solve becomes the mechanisms responsible for the creation of antibodies and the recognition of their complementary antigenic pattern [3, 4]. This approach is evidenced by the evolution of the theoretical framework in immunology from the "side chain" and "template" theories to the clonal selection theory [5]. From this perspective, pattern recognition is the ultimate and direct cause of immune responses. Indeed, antigen recognition as the core for the explanation of immune responses is supported by several observations: antibody-antigen specificity, responses to specific antigens, responses to Pathogen-Associated Molecular Patterns (PAMPs), specificity of antitoxins, responses to Human Leukocyte Antigens (HLA) in transplanted tissue, and the specificity of antibodies to autoantigens in the case of autoimmune diseases. However, there are

P. Liò, G. Nicosia, and T. Stibor (Eds.): ICARIS 2011, LNCS 6825, pp. 108–116, 2011.
© Springer-Verlag Berlin Heidelberg 2011

also several inconsistencies: responses to third-party antigens [6, 7], adjuvant-dependent responses [8], differential rates of rejection between transplanted organs with same HLA in the same recipient [9], and others. These inconsistencies have been ignored more because of the absence of a better theoretical explanation than a lack of awareness by the immunology community [10].

Artificial Immune System (AIS) [11], have largely been inspired by classical theories in immunology and translate this conceptual framework into the construction of algorithms and simulations centered in pattern recognition, clonal selection, the Self/Non-Self paradigm [12] and Danger Theory [13] with relative success [14, 15]. On the other hand, Complexity Theory, Swarm Intelligence and Artificial Immune Systems have attracted the interest of some biologists as an opportunity for being able to comprehend the immune system in a more holistic way than is possible by the reductionist approach [16]. Within the framework of AIS [11], a model which claims to be non-deterministic and lacks pattern recognition as the core for the explanation of immune responses had been proposed [1].

This theory considers inflammation as the phenomenon that demarcates what I refer to as an immune response, which emerges from a complex, dynamic system composed of all relevant cells and molecules and is located at supra-molecular level - a "Swarm" function defined as the emergence of a new phenomenon from the decentralized collective behavior of agents at lower levels of complexity. In this theory, the relevant agents and interactions are abstracted to only reactive and suppressive events - events that create critical local conditions that either promote or prevent attainment of a threshold for inflammation. This simple abstraction allows the creation of algorithms that resemble the dynamics for the formation of reactive and suppressive lymphocyte clones as a special case of Polya's Urn [2]. The proportions obtained between suppressive and reactive agents constitute the "attractor" for the system, resulting in a stable distance between this attractor and the threshold required for the emergence of inflammation. By manipulating the starting proportion and numbers of reactive and suppressive clones, the attractor set point can be changed and thus the probability that a perturbation of the system will reach threshold and result in an inflammatory response. For example, one attractor set point could be close to threshold and produce a situation in which autoantibodies are relevant for the development of autoimmunity, whereas another attractor set point could be far from threshold and produce a situation in which they are irrelevant, as in a healthy carrier of autoantibodies. Thus, this non-deterministic model gives a different understanding of clonal selection, attempts to explain immunological memory and robustness of immune responses, as well as apparent paradoxes that arise when relying solely on the concept of pattern recognition as a predictor of immune reactions.

Although this theoretical construction may explain the generation of lymphocyte clones, the stability and robustness of immune responses, and immunological memory, it fails to address the fact that an evident molecular pattern recognition occurs in most "immune responses," such as PAMPs and the innate immune response, HLA molecules and transplant rejection, and tissue-specific antigens and autoimmune diseases. Therefore, I asked if adding a pattern recognition process relevant for the reactivity of the system will invalidate the claim that inflammation as an emergent phenomenon which defines an immune response is non-deterministic.

2 Methods

A new region is added to the previously reported simulation [17] by defining specific patches within the space that resemble a tissue with a specific Non-Self marker (graft, autoimmunity, viral infected tissue, cancer cells, etc.). I also created an independent agent (antibody) produced by the central system (bone marrow) with a random and unrestricted movement among the patches. These antibodies increase the patch mediator, (such mediator is produced by the patch at a fixed rate, then diffused to the neighboring patches and dissipates at a constant rate, simulating the generation of lympokines by the cells in a tissue, its secretion and dissipation) but only if a pattern is recognized in the patch where the antibodies are temporarily situated, thus resembling the action of a tissue-specific antibody. The rest of the simulation was unchanged from the original simulation; that is, autoreactive cells can also increase the mediator whereas suppressive cells decrease it.

Table 1. Results: This table shows the overall results after running iteratively the simulations up to a 100 times for each Attractor-Antibody concentration combinations. The time running was until responses emerges, and in the cases where no response was observed the simulation was kept running for at least an hour.

Clone Proportion (Attractor)	Antibody concentration	Response in pattern recognition area (circled area in figures)	Response out-side pattern recognition area	Figure 1
[#]Reactive	*Low N=138	positive +	positive +++	a
[#]Reactive	*Medium N=1104	positive +++	positive +	b
[#]Reactive	Fixed N= 207	positive +++	positive +	c
[#]Suppressive	*High N=3381	positive ++	negative	d
[#]Suppressive	Fixed N= 207	negative	negative	NS
[#]Suppressive	*Low N=106	negative	negative	NS
[#]Suppressive	*Medium N=1035	negative	negative	NS
+ indicates the number of response areas in the simulation field NS=Not shown N = Number of antibodies				

* Low, medium and high are arbitrarily defined and the values are only relative to each other

[#] Suppressive and Reactive refer to the predominance of reactive or suppressive agents in the background (Lymphocytes)

The simulation was run iteratively, exploring different starting conditions: When the proportions of reactive/suppressive agents favor suppressive agents, the attractor is located farther to the threshold for the emergence of the phenomenon (suppressive), when they favor reactive agents the attractor is closer to the threshold (reactive). These two situations of the attractor were tested in different antibody density given by the number of antibodies produced. I tested low, medium and high concentration taken arbitrarily. Because the production of clones is by a stochastic process, round numbers could not be preset.

3 Results

Table 1 shows the results of the simulations. When the simulation was run in a suppressive background, increasing the concentration of antibody 10-fold failed to elicit a response either inside or outside the pattern recognition area. Increasing the antibody concentration to 33-fold elicited a response within the pattern recognition area but not outside it. When the simulation was run in a reactive background, the overall number of responses was similar between conditions of high medium and low antibody concentrations, although there were changes in the number of responses within and outside the pattern recognition area as a function of antibody concentration. When the same number of antibodies ("fixed") was placed within suppressive and reactive backgrounds, different simulation results were obtained. Overall, the results show that the concentration of antibody was not a predictor of the outcome of the simulation, but rather that outcome depended on the background condition.

4 Discussion

Antigen recognition necessarily requires an a priori classification of molecules so as to discriminate which ones will be recognized as either pathogen, Non-Self, or Danger. For the current Self/Non-Self paradigm, such classification is considered to take place according to clonal selection theory [18], by the positive and negative selection of lymphocyte clones, eliminating those that react with host tissue (Self) and keeping those that do not (Non-Self). In doing so, reactivity is kept for all molecular patterns classified as Non-Self, and the causation of an immune response is reduced to antigen recognition. How this recognition takes place has been the principal aim for classical molecular centered immunology [19, 3, 4]. However this construction is problematic since it requires an ill-defined immunological Self [20].

Moreover, this molecular classification needs a qualifier for what is being classified, introducing necessarily teleology, that is always present in classical immune theories and evidenced by the jargon of the discipline: immunology, self, danger, etc. This teleologic aspect has always been inherited throughout immunology theoretical base, from defense against pathogens, to the recognition of self. It is this need for an a priori classification that prevents new theories from escaping finalists approaches as is the case with Danger theory [13]. Although it is recognized that teleologic explanations are only an explicative construct because the "immune system" has no way to know (in the sense of human cognition) what is "good or bad", "own or foreign" "harmless or harmful", it seems to be inescapable to not incorporate teleology and metaphors in immune theoretical constructions.

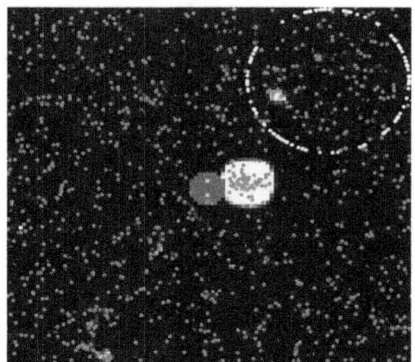

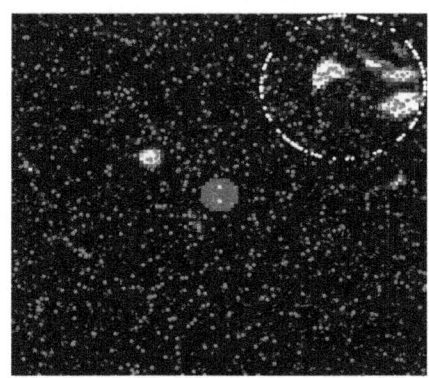

(a) Reactive attractor, with a low concentration of antibodies. The emergence of "inflammation" occurs more frequently outside the antigen area, the antibody fails to "determine" the emergence of "inflammation" in the antigen area. There is not apparent discrimination between areas.

(b) Same attractor as in (a) with increased concentration of antibodies, showing the emergence of "Inflammation" in the "antigen" specific area. An incipient "inflammation" is seen originating outside this area however, the predominance of the activity is clear in the "antigen specific" area over the rest.

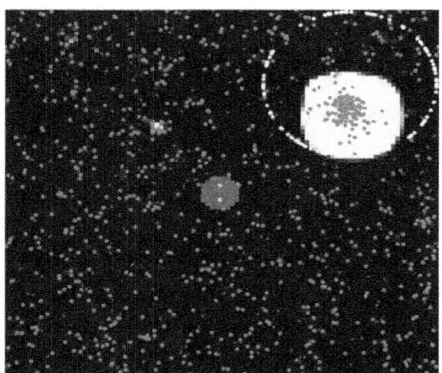

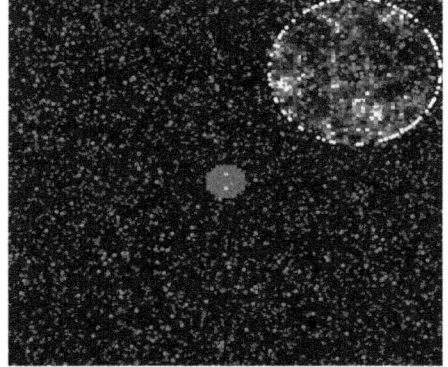

(c) Reactive attractor with increased "antibody" with respect to (a) showing "inflammation" in "antigen" area. The exact same concentration of "antibody" was used in another (NS) simulation with a suppressive instead of reactive attractor, with no emergence of "inflammation", demonstrating the "antibody" relevance dependable upon the attractor.

(d) Suppressive attractor with a "High" concentration of "antibodies" showing that to overcome a suppressive attractor, a very high concentration of "antibody" is required and only then "inflammation" can occur in the "antigen area", indicating that the emergence of the phenomenon is dependable upon the distance between the attractor and the threshold.

Fig. 1. Showing examples of the interface images of simulations run with different initial proportions of pro-inflammatory and suppressive clones (gray dots), and different concentration of "antibodies" (red dots). The central zone represents the "bone marrow", source of both clones and antibodies. The circular area delimited by white dots represents the "antigen" recognized by antibodies, increasing the "chemical mediator" , the area outside the circle is not recognized by the antibodies. All 3 zones have the same relational rules with both reactive or suppressive clones. Inflammation is identified by the escalation in the concentration of "lymphokines" white patches.

Furthermore, the discovery of suppression mechanisms as relevant for the generation or not of immune responses [21], and its derived concept of dominant tolerance [22] show the fallacy of pattern recognition as causal event of immune responses. Since suppression mechanisms are involved in the determination of whether or not an immune response will occur, and since both suppression and reactivity can be specific for the same molecular pattern, it is the predominance between competing reactive and suppressive events and not the molecular pattern of the antigen which is most relevant for the emergence of the response. The importance of this balance between suppression and reactivity for the generation of immune responses has been shown in an increasing numbers of experimental and clinical observations [23, 24, 25]. Therefore, it is not the lack of experimental and clinical observation which prevents our understanding of how suppressive and reactive events interact to produce the phenomena associated with immunity, but rather it is our ignorance of the underlying mechanism "Treg cannot know ahead of time an ideal set-point for immune homeostasis"[26].

The results of our simulations indicate that although an antibody is specifically directed to increase the mediator and thus the probability for a local response, it becomes relevant for the emergence of an inflammatory response only when it overcomes the attractor set by the previous equilibrium between autoreactive and suppressive agents. Therefore, within the limitations that a computer simulation has to reproduce real-life phenomena, we can propose that this equilibrium is more decisive for the emergence or non-emergence of a response than an antibody directed towards a specific area. This is a provocative proposal, since it undermines the importance of pattern recognition for the determination of an immune response and suggests that such patterns are ontologically neutral and contingent on the background wherein such phenomenon occurs. As a consequence, this eliminates the need to define patterns in terms of Self or Non-Self, since such a classification cannot exist before the phenomenon. In other words, the phenomenon (inflammation) is what classifies the antigens a *posteriori*, as those that elicit a response and those that fail to do so. In turn, the phenomenon is the end result of several agents, interactions, and mechanisms acting in a holistic way, which at the same time are contingent on the primordial construction of the system, its history, environmental factors, and any newly formed agents, such as new antibodies. Thus, the response towards an antigen is contingent on the whole system, which explains how antigens can be taken as Self or as Non-Self under different circumstances by the same organism. According to this conceptualization, pattern recognition by an antibody has the same implications as any other factor contributing to reactivity or suppression, being this specific or unspecific. More importantly, in this model, donor-specific interactions lack direct causality, since their relevance for the emergence of inflammation depends upon the level of the background reactivity (attractor).

The results of the present simulations do not only support the non-deterministic character of immune responses, but also add to the theory [1] by explaining the contribution of antigen-specific interactions in the emergence of inflammation. Taken in this context, pattern recognition will not necessarily determine whether a response will occur, but will determine the place or tissue wherein its influence may be relevant. It is interesting that antibody production as it occurs in our model constitutes an amplifier of the response both in the probability in triggering the response and in its intensity, adding an interesting insight since it can explain why in real life, not all interactions with the environment (Non-Self) trigger responses. It can also explain the observations that the presence of autoantibodies does not always result in inflammation, as is the case of autoantibodies in healthy individuals [27, 28, 29, 30, 31], that not all transplant recipients with antibodies against HLA donor molecules reject their grafts, although there is a statistical correlation with their presence [32]; that transplant recipients who do reject at some point have long episodes where the allograft is not rejected; and that such rejection episodes are for the most unpredictable both as an event and in their time of occurrence.

In an antigen-driven explanation of immune responses, the therapeutic strategy has been to try to modify this pattern recognition by eliminating the recognizer or modifying its ability to recognize its target antigen. Our theoretical results indicate that such modifications will have a temporary effect, since they will not affect the attractor of the system, which will tend to return the system to its previous set point after any intervention (robustness). Our results also indicates that changing the attractor, as has been suggested elsewhere [1, 17, 2], is more important for the manipulation of immune responses.

5   Conclusions

Although pattern recognition is a well established molecular phenomenon in immune responses, it is nonetheless problematic as the definitive cause of immune responses on both theoretical and empirical grounds. The results presented here, suggests that the creation of the attractor by the recursive proliferation process of reactive and suppressive clones sets the background reactivity of the system wherein all other influences relevant for the emergence of a response, whether antigen-specific or not, take place. These influences act as disturbances for the level of reactivity, eliciting a response only if they overcome the attractor by reaching a threshold. However, the effectiveness of these influences is dependent on the level of the attractor, not vice versa.

This primordial existence of the system attractor upon which all immune phenomena occur is, for the most part, ignored in classical explanations of immune responses, which consider the individual factors (antibodies, lymphocytes, pathogens, injury) as driven by the recognition of an antigen in the generation of responses. This work shows how immune phenomena can be described at a supramolecular level, how reductionist explanations can be avoided, and how to formalize the system by abstracting at the cellular and molecular level and, in doing so, grasp the holistic character of the response. An explanation for the importance of pattern recognition in the generation of immune responses is proposed which avoids finalist metaphorical concepts. Also this model provides a theoretical explanation for observations which lack understanding within classical theories. How the dynamics of antibody production and elimination as well as the amount of antigen binding antibodies interact with the background attractor is of theoretical interest awaiting further formulation.

References

1. Salazar-Bañuelos, A.: Immune responses: A stochastic model. In: Bentley, P.J., Lee, D., Jung, S. (eds.) ICARIS 2008. LNCS, vol. 5132, pp. 24–35. Springer, Heidelberg (2008)
2. Stibor, T., Salazar-Bañuelos, A.: On immunological memory as a function of a recursive proliferation process. In: 15th IEEE International Conference on Engineering of Complex Computer Systems, IEEE Press, Oxford (2010)
3. Delves, P.J., Roitt, I.M.: The immune system. First of two parts. N. Engl. J. Med. 343, 37–49 (2000)
4. Delves, P.J., Roitt, I.M.: The immune system. Second of two parts. N. Engl. J. Med. 343, 108–117 (2000)
5. Silverstein, A.M.: A History of Immunology. Academic Press, San Diego (1989)
6. Davies, J.D., Leong, L.Y., Mellor, A., Cobbold, S.P., Waldmann, H.: T cell suppression in transplantation tolerance through linked recognition. J. Immunol. 156, 3602–3607 (1996)
7. Charlton, B., Fathman, C.G., Slattery, R.M.: Th1 unresponsiveness can be infectious for unrelated antigens. Immunol. Cell Biol. 76, 173–178 (1998)
8. Zamora, A., Matejuk, A., Silverman, M., Vandenbark, A.A., Offner, H.: Inhibitory effects of incomplete Freund's adjuvant on experimental autoimmune encephalomyelitis. Autoimmunity 35, 21–28 (2002)
9. Calne, R.Y., Sells, R.A., Pena, J.R., Ashby, B.S., Herbertson, B.M., Millard, P.R., Davis, D.R.: Toleragenic effects of porcine liver allografts. Br. J. Surg. 56, 692–693 (1969)
10. Orosz, C.G.: Immune simulation: applying complexity theory to transplant immunology. Canadian Society of Transplantation, Scientific Meeting, Lake Louise, Canada. Personal Communication (2003)
11. Greensmith, J., Whitbrook, A., Aickelin, U.: Artificial Immune Systems. In: Gendreau, M., Potvin, J.-Y. (eds.) Handbook of Metaheuristics, 2nd edn., pp. 421–448. Springer, Heidelberg (2010)
12. Forrest, S., Perelson, A.S., Allen, L., Cherukuri, R.: Self-nonself discrimination in a computer. In: proceedings of the 1994 IEEE Symposium on Research in Security and Privacy, pp. 202–212. IEEE Computer Society Press, Los Alamitos (1994)
13. Matzinger, P.: Tolerance, danger, and the extended family. Annu. Rev. Immunol. 12, 991–1045 (1994)
14. Timmis, J.: Artificial immune systems—today and tomorrow. Natural computing: An International Journal 6(1), 1–18 (2007)
15. Hart, E., Timmis, J.: Application area of AIS: The past, the present and the future. Appl. Soft. Comput. 8(1), 191–201 (2008)
16. Orosz, C.S., Forrest, S., Hoffmeyr, S., Cohen, I.R., Segel, L.A.: How complexity helps to shape alloimmunity. Graft 4, 365–382 (2001)
17. Salazar-Bañuelos, A.: Non-deterministic explanation of immune responses: A computer model. In: Andrews, P.S., Timmis, J., Owens, N.D.L., Aickelin, U., Hart, E., Hone, A., Tyrrell, A.M. (eds.) ICARIS 2009. LNCS, vol. 5666, pp. 7–10. Springer, Heidelberg (2009)
18. Burnet, F.M.: A modification of Jerne's theory of antibody production using the concept of clonal selection. Aust. J. Sci. 20, 67–69 (1957)
19. Von Boehmer, H., Teh, H.S., Kisielow, P.: The thymus selects the useful, neglects the useless and destroys the harmful. Immunol. Today 10, 57–61 (1989)
20. Alfred, I.T.: The Immune Self, Theory or metaphor? Cambridge University Press, Cambridge (1994)

21. Sakaguchi, S.: Regulatory T Cells: key controllers of immunologic self-tolerance. Cell 101, 455–458 (2000)
22. Coutinho, A.: The Le Douarin phenomenon: a shift in the paradigm of developmental self-tolerance. Int. J. Dev. Biol. 49, 131–136 (2005)
23. Salaun, J., Simmenauer, N., Belo, P., Coutinho, A., Le Doarin, N.M.: Grafts of supplementary thymuses injected with allogeneic pancreatic islets protect nonobese diabetic mice against diabetes. Proc. Natl. Acad. Sci. U.S.A. 99, 874–877 (2002)
24. Salaun, J., Corbel, C., Le Douarin, N.M.: Regulatory T cells in the establishment and maintenance of self-tolerance: role of the thymic epithelium. Int. J. Dev. Biol. 49, 137–142 (2005)
25. Carneiro-Sampaio, M., Coutinho, A.: Tolerance and autoimmunity: lessons at the bedside of primary immunodeficiencies. Adv. Immunol. 95, 51–82 (2007)
26. Quintana, F.J., Cohen, I.R.: Regulatory T cells and immune computation. Eur. J. Immunol. 38, 903–907 (2008)
27. Cui, Z., Zhao, M.H., Segelmark, M., Hellmark, T.: Natural autoantibods to myeloperoxidase, proteinase 2, and the glomerular basement membrane are present in normal individuals. Kidney Int. (2010)
28. Levin, E.C., Acharya, N.K., Han, M., Zavareh, S., Sedeyn, J.C., Venkataraman, V., Nagele, R.G.: Brain-reactive autoantibodies are nearly ubiquitous in human sera and may be linked to pathology in the context of blood-brain barrier breakdown. Bran. Res. (2010)
29. Marin, G.G., Cardiel, M.H., Cornejo, H., Viveros, M.E.: Prevalence of antinuclear antibodies in 3 groups of healthy individuals: blood donors, hospital personnel, and relatives of patients with autoimmune diseases. J. Clin. Rheumatol. 15, 325–329 (2009)
30. Trendelenburg, M.: Autoanibodies-physiological phenomenon or manifestation of disease. Praxis (Bern 1994) 96, 379–382 (2007)
31. Nilsson, B.O., Skogh, T., Ernerudh, J., Johansson, B., Lofgren, S., Wikby, A., Dahle, C.: Antinuclear antibodies in the oldest-old women and men. J. Autoimmun. 27, 281–288 (2006)
32. McKenna, R.M., Takemoto, S.K., Terasaki, P.I.: Anti-HLA antibodies after solid organ transplantation. Transplantation 69, 319–326 (2000)

On the Analysis of the Immune-Inspired B-Cell Algorithm for the Vertex Cover Problem

Thomas Jansen[1,*], Pietro S. Oliveto[2,**], and Christine Zarges[3]

[1] University College Cork,
Department of Computer Science, Cork, Ireland
t.jansen@cs.ucc.ie
[2] School of Computer Science,
University of Birmingham, Birmingham B15 2TT, UK
P.S.Oliveto@cs.bham.ac.uk
[3] TU Dortmund, Fakultät für Informatik, LS 2,
44221 Dortmund, Germany
Christine.Zarges@tu-dortmund.de

Abstract. The runtime of the immune inspired B-Cell Algorithm (BCA) for the NP-hard vertex cover problem is analysed. It is the first theoretical analysis of a nature-inspired heuristic as used in practical applications for a realistic problem. Since the performance of BCA in combinatorial optimisation strongly depends on the representation an encoding heuristic is used. The BCA outperforms mutation-based evolutionary algorithms (EAs) on instance classes that are known to be hard for randomised search heuristics (RSHs). With respect to average runtime, it even outperforms a crossover-based EA on an instance class previously used to show good performance of crossover. These results are achieved by the BCA without needing a population. This shows contiguous somatic hypermutation as an alternative to crossover without having to control population size and diversity. However, it is also proved that populations are necessary for the BCA to avoid arbitrarily bad worst case approximation ratios.

1 Introduction

Artificial immune systems (AIS) are nature-inspired algorithms, which are based on the immune system of vertebrates [3]. Besides the natural tasks of anomaly detection and classification, they are often used for optimisation. There are many AIS algorithms for optimisation, e.g., CLONALG [4], the B-Cell Algorithm (BCA) [12] and OPT-IA [2]. All these algorithms are based on the clonal selection principle [3], a theory which describes the basic features of an adaptive immune response to invading pathogens. They work on a population of immune

---

* This material is based in part upon works supported by the Science Foundation Ireland under Grant No. 07/SK/I1205.

** Pietro S. Oliveto was supported by EPSRC under Grant No. EP/H028900/1. The work presented in this paper was started at Dagstuhl seminar N. 10361.

P. Liò, G. Nicosia, and T. Stibor (Eds.): ICARIS 2011, LNCS 6825, pp. 117–131, 2011.

cells (here also called individuals), representing candidate solutions. These individuals proliferate and undergo a hypermutation process called affinity maturation, implying mutations at high rate. The design of the mutation operator can be inspired by various types of immune cells.

In previous theoretical work, the inversely fitness-proportional mutation rate from CLONALG [18,19] as well as somatic contiguous hypermutations (CSM) [10] used in the BCA were considered on simple example problems and within a very simple algorithmic framework. In this paper we further investigate CSM and BCA. In contrast to previous analyses we consider the original framework of the BCA as introduced in [12]. Its convergence is analysed using a Markov chain model in [1]. Examples for applications of the BCA can be found in [17]. We present an analysis of the BCA for the vertex cover problem, taking into consideration instance classes previously studied in the context of EAs [9,14,15].

Given an undirected graph $G = (V, E)$ with $|V| = n$ and $|E| = m$, the vertex cover problem is that of finding a minimum set of vertices $V' \subset V$ such that each edge is covered at least once, i.e., $\forall \{u, v\} \in E\colon \{u, v\} \cap V' \neq \emptyset$. Since the problem is NP-hard it is not expected that any algorithm solves all instances of the problem in polynomial time (unless $P = NP$). But various approximation algorithms exist. The best known returns an approximation of $2 - \Theta(1/\sqrt{n})$ [11]. A lower bound of 1.3606 (if $P \neq NP$) is known [5]. In [15] a lower bound of $2 - o(1)$ was proved for the approximation ratios of random local search (RLS) and the $(1+1)$ EA while they are arbitrarily bad if restarts are not allowed [9]. In [14], it was shown that, for reasonable population sizes, the arbitrarily bad ratios still hold for the $(1+\lambda)$ EA and evidence was given that they also hold for the $(\mu+1)$ EA. These results were achieved for special instances of bipartite graphs.

We follow a similar approach. We show how standard bit mutation and CSM together lead to an efficient optimisation of those instance classes previously used to prove bad EA approximation ratios. We also prove that the BCA can efficiently optimise instances where crossover and a carefully chosen diversity mechanism were previously shown to be effective. Since for these instances we achieve the best upper bounds without a population we conclude that CSM can be an effective and simpler alternative to crossover. On the other hand, we also show limitations of the BCA and that populations can be necessary. We prove that, without a sufficiently large population, the worst case approximation ratio of the BCA can be arbitrarily bad. We add a lower bound of $3/2$ on the approximation ratio of the BCA for all reasonable population sizes. Moreover, we show that a small modification of the BCA leads to improved upper bounds.

In combinatorial optimisation one needs to decide on a representation. The performance of operators such as crossover and CSM depends drastically on the representation [16]. We introduce an ordering heuristic that prefers to place nodes sharing common neighbours close to each other. This is an important practical improvement over previous papers where naively an appropriate representation was assumed.

2   Preliminaries

For a graph $G = (V, E)$ vertex cover is a minimisation problem that maps sub-sets $V' \subseteq V$ to their cost. A subset V' is a feasible solution if each edge is covered. The cost of a cover equals its size $|V'|$. For infeasible solutions V' we define the cost by $(|V| + 1) \cdot |\{e \in E \mid e \cap V' = \emptyset\}|$. The term $|\{e \in E \mid e \cap V' = \emptyset\}|$ counts the number of edges not covered by V'. The factor $|V| + 1$ makes each infeasi-ble solution worse than any feasible one. Note that the choice of $S = \{0, 1\}^{|V|}$ and our definition of cost are not a complete representation. For the node set $V = \{v_1, v_2, \ldots, v_{|V|}\}$ we need to decide about the mapping of the nodes to the bits in a bit string. There are $|V|!$ different mappings $m \colon V \to \{1, \ldots, |V|\}$ since they are permutations. It is not clear how a good one can be found. We suggest a simple heuristic using the following notation.

We abbreviate $\{1, 2, \ldots, k\}$ by $[k]$. The input is the graph $G = (V, E)$ with $V = \{v_1, v_2, \ldots, v_{|V|}\}$. The output is a permutation that we build step-wise in an ar-ray $a[1 \ldots |V|]$ with $a[i] = m^{-1}(i)$. Let $p(a) = \min\{i \in [|V|] \mid a[i+1] = a[i+2] = \cdots = a[|V|] = 0\}$. Let $G_a = (V_a, E_a)$ denote the subgraph of the input graph G with $V_a = \{v_{a[i]} \mid i \in [p(a)]\}$ and $E_a = \{\{u, v\} \mid \{u, v\} \in E, \{u, v\} \subseteq V_a\}$. For G_a and a node $v \in V \setminus V_a$ let $G_{a,v} = (V_{a,v}, E_{a,v})$ denote the subgraph that is created by adding the node v and the corresponding edges to G_a, i.e., $V_{a,v} = V_a \cup \{v\}$, $E_{a,v} = E_a \cup \bigcup_{u \in V_a} (\{u, v\} \cap E)$. For a graph $G' = (V', E')$ and a node $v \in V'$ we denote the degree of v in G' as $\deg_{G'}(v) = |\{\{u, v\} \mid u \in V', \{u, v\} \in E'\}|$. For nodes $u, v \in V'$ let $cn_{G'}(u, v) = |\{w \in V' \mid \{\{u, w\}, \{v, w\}\} \subseteq E'\}|$ denote the number of common neighbours of the nodes u and v in G'.

Algorithm 1. Ordering heuristic for the vertex cover problem

1. $p := 0$; For $i := 1$ to $|V|$ do $a[i] := 0$
2.   While $p < |V|$ do
3.   If $V_a \neq \emptyset$ Then $m_c := \max\limits_{u \in V_a, v \in V \setminus V_a} cn_G(u, v)$ Else $m_c := 0$
4.   If $V_a \neq \emptyset$ Then $m_d := \max\limits_{v \in V \setminus V_a} \deg_{G_{a,v}}(v)$ Else $m_d := 0$
5.   If $m_c = m_d = 0$ Then
6.   Select $v_i \in \left\{ v \in V \setminus V_a \mid \deg_G(v) = \min\limits_{v' \in V} \deg_G(v') \right\}$ uniformly at random.
7.   Else
8.   If $m_c > m_d$ Then
9.   Select $v_i \in \left\{ v \in V \setminus V_a \mid \max\limits_{u \in V_a} cn_G(u, v) = m_c \right\}$ uniformly at random.
10.   Else Select $v_i \in \left\{ v \in V \setminus V_a \mid \deg_{G_{a,v}}(v) = m_d \right\}$ uniformly at random.
11. $p := p + 1$; $a[p] := v_i$

The ordering heuristic tends to group nodes together that share many neigh-bours. It is hoped that reflecting this relation between nodes in the ordering helps the BCA as well as crossover-based EAs. Applying it is tedious but not difficult. We state the resulting orderings on the considered graphs as lemmas but omit the proofs due to space restrictions.

We compare the BCA with mutation- and crossover-based EAs. We consider the (1+1) EA, only using standard bit mutations, and the $(\mu+1)^D_\times$ RLS that in addition incorporates 1-point crossover and a diversity mechanism. These algorithms have already been analysed [9,14,15].

One of the main characteristics of the BCA is the immune-inspired mutation operator. It decides randomly about a contiguous region of the bit string and flips each bit within this region with a given probability $r \in [0,1]$. The parameter r is important. Clark et al. [1] discuss that global convergence requires to avoid the extreme cases $r = 0$ and $r = 1$. But since the BCA also uses standard bit mutation, the algorithm converges also if $r = 1$.

Definition 1 (Somatic Contiguous Hypermutation (CSM) Wrapping Around [10]). *CSM mutates $x \in \{0,1\}^n$ given a parameter $r \in [0,1]$.*
  1.   *Select $p \in \{0, 1, \ldots, n-1\}$ uniformly at random.*
  2.   *Select $l \in \{0, 1, \ldots, n\}$ uniformly at random.*
  3.   *For $i := 0$ to $l - 1$ do*
  4.   *With probability r set $x[(p+i) \bmod n] := 1 - x[(p+i) \bmod n]$.*

As done before [10], we only consider the case $r = 1$ here. The BCA [12] maintains a population of size μ. RSHs are often started with random solutions. In combinatorial optimisation, sometimes a trivial feasible solution is used as starting point. For vertex cover this is the complete set of nodes. We consider a population initialised uniformly at random in most cases in the following and point out where we deviate from this. In each round, first a clonal selection and expansion step is executed. Here, each individual from the population is cloned λ times. Afterwards, for each individual in the population one of these clones (selected uniformly at random) is subject to standard bit mutations, i.e., each bit is flipped with probability $1/n$. Finally, all clones are subject to CSM. For the selection for replacement each individual is compared only with its own offspring. One of the best offspring replaces the individual if it is not worse. The μ individuals in the population evolve independently from each other. In practice small values for λ are used. We consider only the case $\lambda = O(1)$.

The (1+1) EA [7] has a population of size 1 and creates one offspring by standard bit mutations with mutation probability $1/n$ in each round. The new individual replaces the old one if it is not worse.

The $(\mu+1)^D_\times$ RLS [14] maintains μ individuals and performs, in each round, crossover followed by a selection for replacement step with probability p_c as follows. Two offspring y_1 and y_2 are created using 1-point-crossover of two randomly selected individuals x_i and x_j, i.e., one common position in the bit strings is selected uniformly at random and the segments beyond this point are swapped between the two individuals. The two offspring replace the two individuals if they are feasible and if the better offspring is not worse than its worst parent. Afterwards, mutation followed by another selection for replacement is executed. One individual is selected and exactly one bit is flipped. This offspring is inserted into the population if it is not worse than its parent. In both variation procedures offspring are only compared with their parents and replace only them.

As usual in the analysis of RSHs, we investigate the first point of time when a global optimum is reached via the number of function evaluations executed and denote this as the optimisation time of the algorithm. Finally, we define the worst case approximation ratio of an algorithm A on a minimisation problem P as $\max_{I \in P}(A(I)/OPT(I))$, where $A(I)$ is the value of the solution obtained by A on instance I and $OPT(I)$ is the value of the best solution on instance I.

The following lemma will be useful for the proofs of the rest of the paper. Its proof is a straightforward application of the recently introduced multiplicative drift theorem [6].

Lemma 1. *Let $\lambda = O(1)$. The expected time for the BCA to produce a feasible (not necessarily optimal) vertex cover is $O(\mu n^2 \log n)$. The expected time for the whole population to be feasible vertex covers is $O(\mu n^2 \log^2 n)$.*

Proof. Given an individual of the initial population, we want to find the expected time until its number of uncovered edges has been reduced to 0. Let $Z^{(t)}$ denote the number of uncovered edges. We have $1 \leq Z^{(t)} \leq |E| < n^2$.

In the following we only consider 1-bit mutations. Then, we have a probability of $2/n$ that a specific bit covering an uncovered edge flips. The probability that the BCA flips exactly one bit is at least $(1 - 1/n)^n \cdot (1/(n + 1)) \geq 1/(2en)$. This yields $E\left(Z^{(t+1)}\right) \leq (1 - 1/(en^2)) \cdot Z^{(t)}$. Considering the μ independent and parallel runs and setting $\delta = 1/(en^2)$, we get an expected time of at most $\mu \cdot 2en^2 \cdot \ln(1 + |E|) = O(\mu n^2 \log n)$ due to the multiplicative drift theorem [6].

The probability that we need twice the expected number of function evaluations is at most $1/2$ (Markov's inequality). By using the inequality iteratively the probability that the individual fails after $(\log \mu + 1)$ phases of this length is bounded by $1/(2\mu)$. By a union bound the probability that any of the μ individuals fail is less than $1/2$ implying an upper bound on the expected time for all individuals reaching a vertex cover of $O(\mu n^2 \log^2 n)$.   □

The following corollary shows that a simple modification improves the upper bound on the runtime by a factor of n.

Corollary 1. *By modifying the BCA such that CSM is only applied with constant probability $0 < p < 1$, the expected runtime for an individual to produce a vertex cover is $O(\mu n \log n)$ and the whole population is a vertex cover in expected time $O(\mu n \log^2 n)$.*

Proof. The probability of an arbitrary bit flip of exactly one bit is now $(1 - p) \cdot \binom{n}{1} \cdot 1/n \cdot (1 - 1/n)^{n-1} \geq (1 - p) \cdot 1/e = \Theta(1)$. The rest of the proof is unchanged.   □

3   The BCA Outperforms Mutation-Based EAs

We first point out in which situations the BCA outperforms EAs that only use mutation. We consider bipartite graphs. The following instance class $B_{n,\varepsilon}$ was introduced by Friedrich et al. [9] and re-used by Oliveto et al. [15]. For the sake of simplicity we assume that $\varepsilon n \in \mathbb{N}$ holds.

Definition 2. *Let ε be some constant with $0 < \varepsilon < 1$. The graph $B_{n,\varepsilon}$ contains two disjoint sets of vertices $V_1 := \{a_i \mid 1 \le i \le \varepsilon n\}$ and $V_2 := \{b_j \mid 1 \le j \le (1-\varepsilon)n\}$, i. e., $V := V_1 \cup V_2$. It contains the edges $E := \{(x,y) \mid x \in V_1, y \in V_2\}$.*

Lemma 2. *On the $B_{n,\varepsilon}$ graph, the ordering heuristic (Algorithm 1) computes an ordering of the form $b_{i_1}, \ldots, b_{i_{\varepsilon n-1}}, a_{j_1}, \ldots, a_{j_{\varepsilon n}}, b_{i_{\varepsilon n}}, \ldots, b_{i_{(1-\varepsilon)n}}$ with $\{i_1, i_2, \ldots, i_{(1-\varepsilon)n}\} = [(1-\varepsilon)n]$ and $\{j_1, j_2, \ldots, j_{\varepsilon n}\} = [\varepsilon n]$.*

W. l. o. g. $0 < \varepsilon < 1/2$ and thus, $|V_1| \le |V_2|$. There are two covers, V_1 and V_2 that cannot be improved by RLS. We call these local search covers. Of these, V_1 is the unique *global optimum*. In the following, we refer to V_2 as *local optimum*. For the (1+1) EA on $B_{n,\varepsilon}$ the approximation can be made arbitrarily bad [9]. However, using restarts, the (1+1) EA is efficient on $B_{n,\varepsilon}$ [15]. In contrast to the (1+1) EA, the BCA is able to find the optimal solution in expected polynomial time without using restarts. This is due to the fact that it is able to 'jump' from the local optimum to the global one by flipping all bits at once.

Theorem 1. *Let $\varepsilon = i/n$ with $1 < i < n/2$, $\lambda = O(1)$. The expected time for the BCA to find the global optimum of $B_{n,\varepsilon}$ is $O(\mu n^2 \log n)$.*

Proof. Consider one of the μ individuals of the BCA. Starting from a random set of selected vertices in expected time $O(n^2 \log n)$ a feasible vertex cover is found (Lemma 1). In such a solution, either V_1 or V_2 must be selected completely. Assume V_2 is completely in the cover. Then, in order to obtain a local optimum, all vertices in V_1 have to be deselected. Analogously, we can obtain the global optimum if V_1 is completely in the cover. After we have obtained a feasible solution, only mutations preserving this are accepted.

Let i be the number of vertices that have to be deselected. To remove such a vertex, it suffices not to flip any bit during the standard bit mutation and choose this vertex and length 1 for CSM. The probability for such a removal is at least $(1-1/n)^n \cdot (i/n) \cdot (1/(n+1)) \ge i/(2en^2)$. This yields an expected time of at most
$$\sum_{i=1}^{(1-\varepsilon)n} 2en^2/i = O(n^2 \log n)$$
for obtaining either the global or the local optimum.
If we end up in the global optimum, the claim follows immediately. Otherwise, we need to wait for a mutation that directly 'jumps' from the local to the global optimum since no other solution will be accepted. A mutation flipping all bits accomplishes this goal. Such a mutation has probability $1/(n(n+1))$ and thus, in expectation we need to wait $O(n^2)$ generations. Since we have μ independent individuals, this yields an optimisation time of $O(\mu n^2 \log n)$. □

The (1+1) EA using a restart strategy as well as the BCA find the global optimum of $B_{n,\varepsilon}$ in expected polynomial time. As an example for a hard-to-approximate instance class for the (1+1) EA an amplified class $B_{h,\ell,\varepsilon}$ was considered [15]. We consider ℓ concatenated copies of $B_{h,\varepsilon}^{(i)}$, $i \in \{1, \ldots, \ell\}$, where two neighboured copies are connected via an edge between their smaller subsets.

Definition 3. *Let $h, \ell \in \mathbb{N}$ and ε be some constant with $0 < \varepsilon < 1$. Let $n = h \cdot \ell$. The graph $B_{h,\ell,\varepsilon}$ contains the nodes $V := \bigcup_{k=1}^{\ell}(V_1^{(k)} \cup V_2^{(k)})$ with $V_1^{(k)} := \left\{a_i^{(k)} \mid 1 \leq i \leq \varepsilon h\right\}$ and $V_2^{(k)} = \left\{b_j^{(k)} \mid 1 \leq j \leq (1-\varepsilon)h\right\}$. It contains the edges $E := \bigcup_{i=1}^{\ell} E^{(i)}$ with $E := \left\{\left(a_i^{(k)}, b_j^{(k)}\right) \mid a_i^{(k)} \in V_1^{(k)}, b_j^{(k)} \in V_2^{(k)}\right\} \cup \left\{\left(a_{\varepsilon n}^{(k)}, a_1^{(k+1)}\right) \mid 1 \leq k \leq \ell - 1\right\}.$*

There is one unique global optimum that consists of all vertices in the smaller subsets, i.e., $\bigcup_{i=1}^{\ell} V_1^{(i)}$. There are many local optima: each cover, where in at least one component the local optimum is chosen, is a local search cover.

We start with the result of the ordering heuristic. We see that the heuristic clusters vertices from the bipartite components within the bit string. Starting with an arbitrary component, the remaining components are successively added.

Lemma 3. *On $B_{h,\ell,\varepsilon}$ the ordering heuristic (Algorithm 1) computes an ordering of the form $C^{(i_1)}, \ldots, C^{(i_\ell)}$ with $\{i_1, \ldots, i_\ell\} = [\ell]$, where $C^{(i)}$ denotes the ordering of the bipartite components $B_{h,\varepsilon}^{(i)}$. For $C^{(i_1)}$, we have an ordering of the form $b_{j_1}^{(i_1)}, \ldots, b_{j_{\varepsilon n - 1}}^{(i_1)}, a_{k_1}^{(i_1)}, \ldots, a_{k_{\varepsilon n}}^{(i_1)}, b_{j_{\varepsilon n}}^{(i_1)}, \ldots, b_{j_{(1-\varepsilon)n}}^{(i_1)},$ with $\{j_1, j_2, \ldots, j_{(1-\varepsilon)n}\} = [(1-\varepsilon)n]$ and $\{k_1, k_2, \ldots, k_{\varepsilon n}\} = [\varepsilon n]$. For all other orderings, the ordering of the component $B_{h,\varepsilon}^{(i)}$ is $a_1^{(i)}, a_{k_2}^{(i)}, \ldots, a_{k_{\varepsilon n}}^{(i)}, b_{j_1}^{(i)}, \ldots, b_{j_{(1-\varepsilon)n}}^{(i)},$ with $\{j_1, j_2, \ldots, j_{(1-\varepsilon)n}\} = [(1-\varepsilon)n]$ and $\{k_2, \ldots, k_{\varepsilon n}\} = \{2, \ldots, \varepsilon n\}$ if $B_{h,\varepsilon}^{(i)}$ is selected after $B_{h,\varepsilon}^{(i-1)}$ or $a_{\varepsilon n}^{(i)}, a_{k_2}^{(i)}, \ldots, a_{k_{\varepsilon n}}^{(i)}, b_{j_1}^{(i)}, \ldots, b_{j_{(1-\varepsilon)n}}^{(i)},$ with $\{j_1, j_2, \ldots, j_{(1-\varepsilon)n}\} = [(1-\varepsilon)n]$ and $\{k_2, \ldots, k_{\varepsilon n}\} = [\varepsilon n - 1]$ if $B_{h,\varepsilon}^{(i)}$ is selected after $B_{h,\varepsilon}^{(i+1)}$.*

On $B_{h,\ell,\varepsilon}$, the approximation ratio for the (1+1) EA is bounded below by $2 - o(1)$ and restarts do not help [15]. When considering the BCA, the ordering heuristic becomes important. As already seen, the BCA can flip all bits in a single mutation step and 'jump' from the local to the global optimum on $B_{n,\varepsilon}$. This can be repeated in order to optimise the bipartite components of $B_{h,\ell,\varepsilon}$.

Theorem 2. *Let $\varepsilon = i/n$ with $1 < i < n/2$ and $\lambda = O(1)$. The expected optimisation time of the BCA using the ordering from Algorithm 1 to find the global optimum of the $B_{h,\ell,\varepsilon}$ graph is $O\big(\mu(n^2 \log n + \ell n^2)\big)$.*

Proof. Consider one of the μ individuals. We divide the optimisation into three phases. Starting from a random set of selected vertices, we need expected time $O(n^2 \log n)$ to produce a feasible vertex cover (Phase 1, Lemma 1). Afterwards, we obtain a local or global optimum after $O(n^2 \log n)$ steps in exactly the same way as in Theorem 1 (Phase 2). For the third phase, assume that this solution is a local optimum (otherwise nothing is to show) and consider the components separately. For each $B_{h,\varepsilon}^{(i)}$ there are three possible covers: exactly all vertices from $V_1^{(i)}$, exactly all vertices from $V_2^{(i)}$, or all vertices from $V_2^{(i)}$ and one or two vertices from $V_1^{(i)}$, which are connected to the neighbouring components. In the first case, the component is *optimal*. Once a component is optimal, it stays optimal. In the second case, the component can be converted into an optimal component in expected time $O(n^2)$ by flipping the complete region corresponding to $B_{h,\varepsilon}^{(i)}$.

In the third case, such a mutation leads to an infeasible cover. Since we have a local optimum for each connecting edge only one vertex incident to this edge is in the cover. We observe there are only $\ell - 1$ connecting edges and thus, initially there is at least one component of the first or second form. We assume pessimistically that it is not optimal. This component can be converted into an optimal one in expected time $O(n^2)$.

Consider one of the neighbours of the new optimal component, say $B_{h,\varepsilon}^{(j)}$. The vertex incident to the connecting edge must be selected: otherwise the previous cover would not have been feasible. The connecting edge between $B_{h,\varepsilon}^{(i)}$ and $B_{h,\varepsilon}^{(j)}$ is now also covered by the optimal component $B_{h,\varepsilon}^{(i)}$ and thus, the resulting cover is not locally optimal any more. However, we can easily remove this 'free' vertex in $B_{h,\varepsilon}^{(j)}$ via a specific 1-bit mutation. It suffices to perform a 1-bit mutation in the standard bit mutation and have length 0 for the CSM. Thus, the probability for this event is at least $(1/n) \cdot (1 - 1/n)^{n-1} \cdot (1/(n+1)) \geq 1/(en^2)$ and we need expected time $O(n^2)$ to recover a local optimum.

Assume that k components are optimal. They cover $\geq k$ connecting edges. Thus, the remaining $\ell - k$ non-optimal components cover $\leq \ell - k - 1$ connecting edges. Thus, there is always a component of the second form that can easily be converted into an optimal one, possibly followed by a recovering step.

Altogether, we need expected time $O(n^2)$ to convert a single non-optimal component into an optimal component and recover a locally optimal solution. Since there are at most ℓ non-optimal components at the beginning, the expected time for this phase is $O(\ell n^2)$. This yields the claimed expected optimisation time for all three phases and the population. □

We remark that either it is proved (i. e., $(1+\lambda)$ EA) or there is strong theoretical evidence (i. e., $(\mu+1)$ EA, $(\mu+\lambda)$ EA) that EAs with populations are unable to optimise $B_{h,l,\varepsilon}$ in expected polynomial time [14].

4   The BCA Outperforms Crossover-Based EAs

For the following instance class $G_{\ell,h}$ the $(1+1)$ EA requires exponential optimisation time even with restarts if $h = \ell$ [15]. However, the $(\mu+1)_\times^D$ RLS is efficient [14].

Definition 4. *Let $\ell = h = \sqrt{n}$ and $n = \ell \cdot h$. The graph $G_{\ell,h}$ contains the nodes $\{a_{i,j}, \mid 1 \leq i \leq \ell, 1 \leq j \leq h\}$. It contains the edges $\{a_{i,j}, a_{i+1,j}\} \mid 1 \leq i \leq \ell, 1 \leq j \leq h\}$. The graph $G'_{h,\ell}$ additionally contains nodes s_1, s_2 and edges $\{s_1, a_{1,j}\}$, $\{a_{h,j,s_2}\}$ for all $j \in [\ell]$.*

The unique optimal cover of a graph $G_{\ell,h}$ has $(\ell - 1)h/2$ nodes. In [14] it was implicitly assumed that the graph is represented with the nodes inserted in the bit string one column at a time from the leftmost column to the rightmost one. However, no reason for this assumption was given. The heuristic of Algorithm 1 will not give the desired representation as with high probability, the bits representing the nodes of the first column will end up mixed throughout the bit string. As a result neither the BCA nor the $(\mu+1)^D_\times$ RLS would be efficient for the graph. Hence, we modify the instance class slightly by adding a 'single node' connected with all the nodes of one column and another one connected with all the nodes of a different column.

Lemma 4. *On the $G'_{\ell,h}$ graph, the ordering heuristic (Algorithm 1) computes an ordering of the form $s_1, a_{2,j_1}, \ldots, a_{2,j_h}, a_{1,j_1}, \ldots, a_{1,j_h}, a_{3,j_1}, \ldots, a_{3,j_h}, a_{4,j_1}, \ldots, a_{4,j_h}, \ldots, a_{\ell,j_1}, \ldots, a_{\ell,j_h}, s_2$ with $\{j_1, j_2, \ldots, j_h\} = [h]$, or symmetrically the opposite ordering $s_2, a_{\ell-1,j_1}, \ldots, a_{\ell-1,j_h}, a_{\ell,j_1}, \ldots, a_{\ell,j_h}, a_{\ell-2,j_1}, \ldots, a_{\ell-2,j_h}, \ldots, s_1$.*

We consider ℓ to be odd for the sake of having a unique global optimum. The optimum has size $\lfloor(\ell/2)\rfloor h + 2$ and consists of the two nodes s_1 and s_2, plus the nodes of the columns with even j. The largest local search cover has size $(2/3)\ell h + 1$ if ℓ is a multiple of three and size $\lceil(2/3)\ell\rceil h$ otherwise. Such worst local search cover is achieved when s_1 is not in the cover and the first two columns out of every three columns are in the cover (or symmetrically the opposite cover set).

We adopt the notation from [14]. A 0 is used to represent a column where all the nodes are not in the current cover and a 1 to represent a column of nodes that are all in the current cover. Furthermore, the first and the last symbols of a pattern represent s_1 and s_2 respectively (1 for in the cover, 0 for out). Hence the schema 101010101 is the pattern of the global optimum of $G'_{\ell,h}$ for $\ell = h = 7$ and 110010101 is how it is represented by Algorithm 1. On the other hand, the worst local search cover is defined by the schema 011011010. We see that the columns 1 and 2 are exchanged by Algorithm 1. The proof of the following theorem is similar to the one in [13] and omitted here.

Theorem 3. *Let $\mu \geq n^{1+\epsilon}$ and $p_c \leq 1/(\mu\sqrt{n}\log n)$. With probability at least $1 - o(1)$ the $(\mu+1)^D_\times$ RLS algorithm finds the minimum vertex cover of the $G'_{\ell,h}$ graph with the ordering of Algorithm 1 in time $O(\mu^2 n/p_c)$ if $h = \ell = \sqrt{n}$.*

The theorem only gives an upper bound on the runtime. Lower bounds are harder to achieve. The *expected* runtime of the $(\mu+1)^D_\times$ RLS for $G_{\ell,h}$ is infinite and would be exponential if bitwise mutation was used instead of single bit flips (i.e., $(\mu+1)^D_\times$-EA). In the following theorem we show better upper bounds for the runtime of the BCA and prove that it is also efficient in expectation for $G'_{\ell,h}$.

Theorem 4. *Let $\lambda = O(1)$. The expected runtime for the BCA to find the minimum vertex cover of $G'_{\ell,h}$ using the heuristic ordering is $O(\mu \cdot n^3)$.*

Proof. By Lemma 1 a vertex cover is produced in expected time $O(\mu n^2 \log n)$. Once a vertex cover is reached it suffices to flip each bit at least once to reach a local search cover. We follow the upper bound proof of Theorem 1 to show that CSM flips all bits in expected $O(n^2 \log n)$ generations. Since μ fitness function evaluations occur per generation we achieve an expected runtime of $O(\mu n^2 \log n)$ for at least one individual to find a local search cover.

We pessimistically assume that the found local search cover is the worst possible, i.e., 011011011011...01 or 011011011011...110 according to the length of ℓ. In order to improve the fitness it is necessary to flip all the bits of more than one column. In particular, it is sufficient to flip all the bits between two consecutive 11 columns, including the last 1 column of the first 11 couple and the first 1 column of the last 11 couple. Then the current vertex cover decreases in size of h nodes. Once there is only one 11 couple left, it is sufficient to flip all the bits between the first 1 column of the pattern and the single node s_i not in the current cover to find the optimum. The probability for an improvement to happen is $\Theta(1/n^2)$. Once all the 11 columns have been removed, either the global optimum has been found or its complement. In expected time $O(\mu n^2)$ the optimum is reached from its complement by flipping all bits.

We estimate the expected time to remove all the consecutive 11 columns from an individual. Since the number of 11 columns in an individual is at most $(2/3)\ell$, at most this number of CSMs are necessary to remove all the 11 column couples except for the couple starting at columns 1 and 2 (i.e., the s_1 node is a 0). This couple of 11 columns cannot be removed directly by CSM, if it is the last remaining 11 couple, because s_1 and the first column are not contiguous in the bit string. In order to efficiently optimise the first two 11 columns it suffices that bitwise mutation inserts the s_1 node in the cover and then CSM removes all the first column nodes. The probability for this is $(1 - 1/n)^{n-1} \cdot 1/n \cdot 1/(n(n+1))$ implying expected $\Theta(n^3)$ generations for it to occur. Since the other CSMs require $\sum_{i=1}^{\ell/3-1}(\Theta(n^2)/i) = \Theta(n^2)\sum_{i=1}^{\ell/3-1} 1/i = O(n^2 \log n)$ generations, the total expected runtime is $\mu \cdot O(n^3 + n^2 \log n) = O(\mu n^3)$.   □

Corollary 2. *By modifying the BCA such that CSM is only applied with probability p ($0 < p < 1$ constant) the expected runtime for $G'_{\ell,h}$ is $O(\mu n^2 \log n)$.*

Proof. The algorithm can optimise the first 11 column by flipping the s_1 node together with a node of the first column in expected time $O(\mu \cdot n^2/h)$. Then the remaining nodes of the first column may be removed in following steps either by bitwise mutation in expected time $O(\mu n \log n)$ or by separate contiguous mutations in expected time $O(\mu n^2 \log n)$.   □

5   Limitations of the BCA and Bounds on Approximation

Now we show that also the BCA is not always able to find good approximate solutions. We consider a bipartite graph like $B_{n,\varepsilon}$ and equip it with εl additional nodes and εl additional edges. These additional nodes and edges have the consequence that the second best solution for $B_{n,\varepsilon}$ now becomes a large set of second best solutions that form a kind of plateau which is difficult to leave. We start with a formal definition of this graph.

Definition 5. *Let $l \in \mathbb{N}$ and ε be some constant with $0 < \varepsilon < 1$. Let $n := l + \varepsilon l$. The graph $M_{l,\varepsilon}$ contains the nodes $\{a_i, b_i, c_j \mid 1 \le i \le \varepsilon l, 1 \le j \le (1 - \varepsilon)l\}$. It contains the edges $\{\{a_i, b_i\}, \{b_i, c_j\} \mid 1 \le i \le \varepsilon l, 1 \le j \le (1 - \varepsilon)l\}$.*

The main property of $M_{l,\varepsilon}$ is the following. If a vertex cover does not include some node b_i it needs to include the node a_i and all c-nodes. This holds for any $i \in \{1, 2, \ldots, \varepsilon\}$. In order to remove a c-node all b-nodes need to be included. Simply including b-nodes does not work since this increases the size of the vertex cover. This causes difficulties for the BCA. We begin by determining the node ordering due to the ordering heuristic (Algorithm 1).

Lemma 5. *On the graph $M_{l,\varepsilon}$ the ordering heuristic (Algorithm 1) computes an ordering of the form $a_{i_1}, b_{j_1}, b_{j_2}, \ldots, b_{j_{\varepsilon l}}, c_{k_1}, c_{k_2}, \ldots, c_{k_{(1-\varepsilon)l}}, a_{i_2}, \ldots, a_{i_{\varepsilon l}}$ with $\{i_1, i_2, \ldots, i_{\varepsilon l}\} = \{j_1, j_2, \ldots, j_{\varepsilon l}\} = \{1, 2, \ldots, \varepsilon l\}$ and $\{k_1, k_2, \ldots, k_{(1-\varepsilon)l}\} = \{1, 2, \ldots, (1 - \varepsilon)l\}$.*

Since the sub-graph spanned by all b-nodes and all c-nodes is a complete bipartite graph in any vertex cover we have all of the b-nodes or all of the c-nodes. We consider a local search cover. If such a vertex cover contains all b-nodes it contains no other nodes. This is the optimal vertex cover and has size εl. If such a vertex cover contains all c-nodes it additionally contains a selection of in summation εl a-nodes and b-nodes. This is the case since all edges $\{a_i, b_i\}$ need to be covered. This vertex cover has size $(1 - \varepsilon)l + \varepsilon l = l$ and its approximation ratio is $1/\varepsilon$. Before any of the c-nodes can be removed from such a vertex cover we need to include all b-nodes. We have $2^{\varepsilon l}$ of these covers and as long as not all b-nodes are included they are all completely symmetric. This makes it very difficult for any search algorithm to find a vertex cover with b-nodes.

Lemma 6. *Consider the set of all vertex covers $\mathcal{L}$ of $M_{l,\varepsilon}$ such that each cover $x \in \mathcal{L}$ includes exactly l nodes, among them all c-nodes. We have $|\mathcal{L}| = 2^{\varepsilon l}$. All three randomised search heuristics considered here started with some random cover from $\mathcal{L}$ need on average $\Omega(2^{\varepsilon l})$ steps to locate a cover including all b-nodes.*

Proof. Since the vertex cover contains all c-nodes all edges $\{b_i, c_j\}$ with $i \in [\varepsilon l]$ and $j \in [(1 - \varepsilon)l]$ are covered. Any vertex cover also needs to cover also all edges $\{a_i, b_i\}$ with $i \in [\varepsilon l]$. Since $(1 - \varepsilon)l$ c-nodes are in the cover there are only εl nodes left for this. Thus, for each $i \in [\varepsilon l]$ we have either a_i or b_i in the cover. Therefore, there are $2^{\varepsilon l}$ different such covers. The random search heuristics considered here share the property that once a cover in $\mathcal{L}$ is considered this cover will not be discarded for any node selection that is not a vertex cover and neither for any vertex cover with a larger number of nodes. Thus, the search is restricted to vertex covers from $\mathcal{L}$ until a vertex cover including all b-nodes is found. Since all vertex covers in $\mathcal{L}$ have equal size they all have equal function value. Thus, the RSHs perform a random walk on a plateau of size $2^{\varepsilon l}$. Note that all three randomised search heuristics are completely symmetric with respect to all these plateau points. It follows from results in black-box complexity [8] that the expected time to leave $\mathcal{L}$ is $\Omega(2^{\varepsilon l})$. $\square$

Lemma 6 implies that once the BCA only has node selections from $\mathcal{L}$ as current search points it will take $\Omega(2^{\varepsilon l})$ steps to locate an optimal vertex cover. This implies that in this situation the BCA is not able to improve over a $1/\varepsilon$ approximation in expected polynomial time for any constant $\varepsilon > 0$. We prove that this is actually going to happen with a probability that is not completely negligible when the BCA is started with the trivial vertex cover.

Lemma 7. *Consider the BCA with arbitrary μ and λ on $M_{l,\varepsilon}$ with $0 < \varepsilon < 1$ constant, started with only complete covers. There are constants $c, d > 0$, such that the probability that it does not improve over a $(1/\varepsilon)$-approximation in $d \cdot 2^{\varepsilon l}$ steps is bounded below by c^μ. The expected optimisation time is $2^{\Omega(l) - O(\mu)}$.*

Proof. We observe that the statement on the expected optimisation time is a direct consequence of the first statement. Lemma 6 implies that it suffices to prove that the probability for one member of the population to enter $\mathcal{L}$ is bounded below by $c' > 0$. Then (for $0 < c < c'$ sufficiently small) the probability to leave $\mathcal{L}$ in $d \cdot 2^{\varepsilon l}$ steps ($d > 0$ sufficiently small) is bounded below by c. Consequently, the probability for all of them to do so is bounded below by c^μ.

Consider the complete vertex cover. We know (Lemma 5) that all b-nodes are ordered consecutively. There are εl b-nodes. The probability that a hypermutation selects as beginning of the mutated area a position within the b-nodes is bounded below by $\varepsilon l / (l + \varepsilon l) = \varepsilon / (1 + \varepsilon)$. The probability of having a positive length of this interval is $1 - 1/(n + 1)$. If the length extends beyond the b-nodes the mutation will not be accepted since the resulting set is not a vertex cover. Thus, the probability that the first accepted mutation removes only b-notes is bounded below by $\varepsilon / 2$. Note that such a step cannot be undone without removing at least the same number of nodes since otherwise the size of the cover increases. With $c' := \varepsilon / 2$ we obtain the claimed lower bound.   □

We observe that the bounds in Lemma 7 strongly depend on the population size μ. With μ sufficiently large we only obtain trivial bounds. We remark that this matches the truth in the sense that the BCA with sufficiently large population is in fact efficient on $M_{l,\varepsilon}$. With probability $\Omega(1/n^2)$ in the very first step all c-nodes are removed. After that we just need to wait for all a-nodes to be removed, something that will take $O(\mu n^2 \log n)$ steps. It is not difficult to prove that this implies an upper bound of $O(n^{4+\delta})$ (for any constant $\delta > 0$) on the expected optimisation time of BCA with sufficiently large population. We improve on the results on $M_{l,\varepsilon}$ by considering a version that amplifies the effects. We consider concatenated copies of $M_{l,\varepsilon}$.

Definition 6. *Let $k, l \in \mathbb{N}$ and $0 < \varepsilon < 1$ be constant, $n := k(l + \varepsilon l)$. Consider k copies of $M_{l,\varepsilon}$ where the nodes of the m-th copy are $\{a_i^{(m-1)}, b_i^{(m-1)}, c_j^{(m-1)} \mid i \in [\varepsilon l], j \in [(1 - \varepsilon)l]\}$. Rename the edges accordingly. The graph $M_{k,l,\varepsilon}$ contains these k copies and additionally edges $\{b_1^{(m)}, b_{\varepsilon l}^{(m-1)}\}$ for $m \in [k - 1]$.*

Lemma 8. *On the graph $M_{k,l,\varepsilon}$ the ordering heuristic (Algorithm 1) computes an ordering that starts with an arbitrary a-node. For each $m \in \{0, 1, \ldots, k - 1\}$ the nodes b- and c-nodes are arranged consecutively, i. e., in the form $b_{i_1}^{(m)}$, $b_{i_2}^{(m)}$, $\ldots$, $b_{i_{\varepsilon l}}^{(m)}$, $c_{j_1}^{(m)}$, $c_{j_2}^{(m)}$, $\ldots$, $c_{j_{(1-\varepsilon)l}}^{(m)}$ with arbitrary indices $i_1, i_2, \ldots, i_{\varepsilon 1}$ and $j_1, j_2, \ldots, j_{(1-\varepsilon)l}$.*

Theorem 5. *Consider the BCA with arbitrary $\mu = n^{O(1)}$ and λ on $M_{k,l,\varepsilon}$ with $0 < \varepsilon < 1$ constant, started with only complete covers. With probability $1 - e^{-\Omega(k)}$ it does not improve over a $3/2$-approximation in time $2^{o(l)}$.*

Proof. We use the results from the proof of Lemma 7. The situation is slightly different due to connecting edges $\{b_1^{(m)}, b_{\varepsilon l}^{(m-1)}\}$. Since these need to be covered at least one of the nodes $b_1^{(m)}$, $b_{\varepsilon l}^{(m-1)}$ needs to be included. Since this concerns only at most two of the εl b-nodes in each component this does not change the involved probabilities significantly. We know that there is a constant c such that in a single component (any single component, not a fixed one) a vertex cover with all c-nodes selected and $\Omega(l)$ b-nodes not selected is found. This holds in each component. Thus, the expected number of such components is $\geq kc$. We conclude that we expect to see $\leq k(1 - c)$ components with the optimal partial vertex cover. Application of Chernoff bounds yields that only with probability $e^{-\Omega(k)}$ the number of such components exceeds $(1 + \delta)k(1 - c)$ for an arbitrary constant $\delta > 0$. We choose δ later and will make sure that $(1 + \delta)(1 - c) < 1$ holds. Note that this is possible for any constant c with $0 < c < 1$.

Consider such a vertex cover. The size of the optimal vertex cover equals $k\varepsilon l$. Thus, the approximation ratio is given by $1 + (c + \delta(\epsilon + c - \varepsilon c) - \varepsilon c)/\varepsilon$. We set δ in a way that $\varepsilon \leq \delta < c/(1 - c)$ holds. Note that this is always possible if ε is sufficiently small. This implies that $(1 + \delta)(1 - c) < 1$ holds and that the approximation ratio is bounded below by $1 + (c/\varepsilon)$. We remember from the proof of Lemma 7 that we can use any constant $c < \varepsilon/2$. Since $(\epsilon\delta + \delta c - \varepsilon c - \varepsilon\delta c)/\varepsilon > 0$ due to our choice we obtain a ratio of $1 + 1/2 = 3/2$. We have the lower bound of $2^{\Omega(l)}$ from Lemma 7 and the claimed bound follows. $\square$

6   Conclusions

An analysis of the BCA for vertex cover has been presented. This is the first theoretical analysis on a realistic problem class for exactly the same algorithm used in practical applications and not simplified versions. The BCA outperforms mutation-based EAs on vertex cover instance classes that are known to be hard for RSHs. With respect to the expected optimisation time, it also outperforms a crossover-based EA on an instance class with characteristics that were previously used to show the effectiveness of crossover. However, including restarts both algorithms are efficient there. All the presented positive results do not require a population of immune cells, indicating that CSM is a valid alternative to crossover without having to deal with diversity and population size issues. Thus, our results seem to confirm that small population sizes suffice as used in practice. But populations can be essential to avoid arbitrarily bad worst case approximations. For crossover and CSM to be effective it is necessary that related nodes are close to each other. We have proposed an ordering heuristic to achieve this and have proved that it works for the optimisation of several instance classes. Finally, the analysis suggests a modification of the BCA applying CSM not always but only with some constant probability < 1.

Many open problems remain. Concerning parameter settings, the role of the number of clones λ is not investigated. Concerning runtime, although we have proved that the BCA outperforms the $(\mu+1)_{\times}^{D}$ RLS in expectation we have no such results with high probability. Concerning negative results, we have only proved a lower bound of $3/2$ on the worst case approximation ratio. Finally, further study of the ordering heuristic is needed.

References

1. Clark, E., Hone, A., Timmis, J.: A markov chain model of the B-cell algorithm. In: Jacob, C., Pilat, M.L., Bentley, P.J., Timmis, J.I. (eds.) ICARIS 2005. LNCS, vol. 3627, pp. 318–330. Springer, Heidelberg (2005)
2. Cutello, V., Nicosia, G., Pavone, M.: Exploring the capability of immune algorithms: A characterization of hypermutation operators. In: Nicosia, G., Cutello, V., Bentley, P.J., Timmis, J. (eds.) ICARIS 2004. LNCS, vol. 3239, pp. 263–276. Springer, Heidelberg (2004)
3. Dasgupta, D., Niño, L.F.: Immunological Computation: Theory and Applications. Auerbach (2008)
4. de Castro, L., Zuben, F.: Learning and optimization using the clonal selection principle. IEEE T. on Evol. Comp. 6(3), 239–251 (2002)
5. Dinur, I., Safra, S.: On the hardness of approximating vertex cover. A. of Mathematics 162(1), 439–485 (2005)
6. Doerr, B., Johannsen, D., Winzen, C.: Multiplicative drift analysis. In: Proc. of GECCO 2010, pp. 1449–1456 (2010)
7. Droste, S., Jansen, T., Wegener, I.: On the analysis of the (1+1) evolutionary algorithm. Theoretical Computer Science 276(51), 51–81 (2002)
8. Droste, S., Jansen, T., Wegener, I.: Upper and lower bounds for randomized search heuristics in black-box optimization. Theory of Comp. Sys. 39(4), 525–544 (2006)
9. Friedrich, T., Hebbinghaus, N., Neumann, F., He, J., Witt, C.: Approximating covering problems by randomized search heuristics using multi-objective models. Evol. Comp. 18(4), 617–633 (2010)
10. Jansen, T., Zarges, C.: Analyzing different variants of immune inspired somatic contiguous hypermutations. Theoretical Computer Science 412(6), 517–533 (2011)
11. Karakostas, G.: A better approximation ratio for the vertex cover problem. ACM Trans. on Algorithms 5(4), 41:1–41:8 (2009)
12. Kelsey, J., Timmis, J.: Immune inspired somatic contiguous hypermutation for function optimisation. In: Cantú-Paz, E., Foster, J.A., Deb, K., Davis, L., Roy, R., O'Reilly, U.-M., Beyer, H.-G., Kendall, G., Wilson, S.W., Harman, M., Wegener, J., Dasgupta, D., Potter, M.A., Schultz, A., Dowsland, K.A., Jonoska, N., Miller, J., Standish, R.K. (eds.) GECCO 2003. LNCS, vol. 2724, pp. 207–218. Springer, Heidelberg (2003)

13. Oliveto, P.S.: A proof that crossover helps to optimise vertex cover problems. Technical report, University of Birmingham (2011),
http://www.cs.bham.ac.uk/~olivetps
14. Oliveto, P.S., He, J., Yao, X.: Analysis of population-based evolutionary algorithms for the vertex cover problem. In: Proc. of CEC 2008 (WCCI 2008), pp. 1563–1570 (2008)
15. Oliveto, P.S., He, J., Yao, X.: Analysis of the (1+1)-EA for finding approximate solutions to vertex cover problems. IEEE T. Evol. Comp. 13(5), 1006–1029 (2009)
16. Rothlauf, F.: Representations for Genetic and Evol. Algorithms. Springer, Heidelberg (2006)
17. Trojanowski, K., Wierzchoń, S.: On some properties of the B-cell algorithm in nonstationary environments. In: Advances in Information Processing and Protection, pp. 35–44. Springer, Heidelberg (2008)
18. Zarges, C.: Rigorous runtime analysis of inversely fitness proportional mutation rates. In: Rudolph, G., Jansen, T., Lucas, S., Poloni, C., Beume, N. (eds.) PPSN 2008. LNCS, vol. 5199, pp. 112–122. Springer, Heidelberg (2008)
19. Zarges, C.: On the utility of the population size for inversely fitness proportional mutation rates. In: Proc. of FOGA 2009, pp. 39–46 (2009)

Variation in Artificial Immune Systems: Hypermutations with Mutation Potential

Thomas Jansen[1,*] and Christine Zarges[2]

[1] University College Cork, Department of Computer Science, Cork, Ireland
t.jansen@cs.ucc.ie
[2] TU Dortmund, Fakultät für Informatik, LS 2, 44221 Dortmund, Germany
Christine.Zarges@tu-dortmund.de

Abstract. Specific hypermutation operators are one of the distinguishing features of artificial immune systems. They can be considered in isolation and compared with other variation operators. For a specific immune-inspired hypermutation operator, hypermutations with inversely proportional mutation potential, an analysis of its ability to locate optima precisely and in large distance from other promising regions of the search space is presented. Four different specific variants of this mutation operator are considered. Two of these turn out to be very inefficient in locating optima precisely while the other two are able to do this efficiently. Based on these findings an improved version of this kind of mutation is introduced that removes some of the deficiencies and allows to parameterize the trade-off between efficiency in local search and the ability to perform huge changes in single mutations.

1 Introduction

Artificial immune systems (AIS) are a special class of biologically inspired algorithms, which are based on the immune system of vertebrates and derived from various immunological theories, namely the clonal selection principle, negative selection, immune networks or the danger theory [9,10]. Besides the natural tasks of anomaly detection and classification, they are often applied to function optimization. In this context, mostly algorithms based on the clonal selection principle [2], a theory which describes the basic features of an adaptive immune response to invading pathogens (antigens), are used. During the last years, many clonal selection algorithms to tackle optimization problems have been developed, for example: CLONALG [11], OPT-IA [6], the B-Cell algorithm [18], and MISA [3]. These algorithms share a common approach in a broad sense. They work on a population of immune cells or antibodies that represent candidate solutions of the considered problem, i. e., the function to be optimized. The antibodies proliferate and undergo a hypermutation process called affinity maturation, implying mutations at high rate. The design of the mutation operator can be inspired by various types of immune cells found in the immune system.

---

* This material is based in part upon works supported by the Science Foundation Ireland under Grant No. 07/SK/I1205.

P. Liò, G. Nicosia, and T. Stibor (Eds.): ICARIS 2011, LNCS 6825, pp. 132–145, 2011.

In previous work, the inversely fitness proportional mutation rate from CLON-ALG as well as somatic contiguous hypermutations used in the B-Cell algorithm were considered. In both cases, the performance was analyzed within a very simple algorithmic framework. In algorithms using inversely fitness proportional mutation rates, the mutation rate of a search point depends on the function value of the search point to be mutated, i. e., the larger the function value the smaller the mutation rate. It was shown that the operator used in CLONALG is inefficient for a very simple optimization problem tackled with a kind of hill-climber [22]. However, when used together with a population, its performance increases drastically [23]. Somatic contiguous hypermutations only flip bits within a randomly chosen, contiguous interval of a search point. It was shown that somatic contiguous hypermutations may lose in comparison with standard bit mutations on functions where mutations of single bits suffice but win when specific b-bit mutations are needed [17].

Here, we consider the mutation operator used in OPT-IA. The number of mutations is determined by a function called mutation potential. Different variants of mutation potentials are known, i. e., inversely proportional, proportional, or static. Since inversely proportional hypermutations are quite common in AIS, we restrict our analyses to these kind of mutation potentials. A convergence analysis of an algorithm using hypermutation with mutation potential is presented in [8]. The motivation for our study is to contribute to a solid understanding of artificial immune systems. Thus, we analyze an operator used in practice, point out strengths and weaknesses, and suggest ways of improving it.

We prove that the simple version of this operator is unable to locate a target point efficiently (Section 3). If the operator is modified so that it stops at the first improvement this changes drastically (Section 4). Motivated from the results of our analysis we suggest a new variant of the mutation potential that removes some of the difficulties (Section 5).

2   Definitions, Algorithms and Notations

We consider a specific class of immune-based hypermutation operators where a hypermutation comprises of a sequence of local mutation steps. The number of local mutation steps that may be carried out in a single hypermutation is determined by a function called *mutation potential* [4,6]. There exist different classes of mutation potentials, namely *static, inversely proportional,* or *proportional.* Moreover, the concrete definition of such mutation potentials may differ. Here, we restrict ourselves to the definition of an inversely proportional mutation potential for minimization problems due to Cutello et al. [7]. Additionally we restrict ourselves to functions f with strictly positive function values, i. e., $f \colon S \to \mathbb{R}^+$. This simplifies the definition of the mutation potential slightly.

Definition 1. *For some objective function $f \colon S \to \mathbb{R}^+$ and a constant $c \in {]}0,1[$ we define an inversely proportional mutation potential M_c for minimization of f as $M_c(v) = \lceil (1 - f_{\mathrm{OPT}}/v) \cdot c \cdot n \rceil$, where f_{OPT} is the minimum function value for the considered objective function and $n = \lceil \log_2 |S| \rceil$.*

In practice, the optimal function value is not known. In this case, an upper bound on the optimal value can be used. If hypermutation with mutation potential are used with a collection of search points, the currently best known function value from the collection of search points may be used alternatively for the other search points. For the analysis we assume that f_{OPT} is known.

Each time the mutation operator is applied to a search point $x \in S$ with $f(x) = v$, it tries to mutate x at most $M_c(v)$ times. We call such an event *mutation step*. The series of at most $M_c(v)$ mutation steps is called *mutation*. Note, that we round up in order to guarantee $M_c(v) \geq 1$ if x is not optimal. Moreover, the number of mutation steps should be an integral number. We remark that $v = f_{\mathrm{OPT}}$ yields $M_c(v) = 0$, i. e., no mutation step is performed. When using the currently best known function value as estimate for f_{OPT}, this is unfavorable if the best function value from the collection of search points is not optimal as it can never be improved in this situation. If the whole collection of search points consists of copies of the current best, the algorithm is stuck.

Within this paper we consider the search space $S = \{0,1\}^n$, the most commonly used and in some sense universal finite search space. Unfortunately, there are no details on how mutation steps are actually executed given in the aforementioned papers. We interpret the concrete procedure as simple as possible. The considered operator sequentially draws $M_c(v)$, not necessarily distinct, positions in the bit string and flips them independently. Note, that if, e. g., a position is chosen twice, it will be left unchanged in the resulting bit string.

Another possible realization of mutation potentials is to hinder the operator to chose a specific position several times. This is somehow similar to tabu search [15]. We define this variant in the following.

A mechanism often used in conjunction with mutation potentials [6,7] and also in other contexts [5] is the so-called *stop at first constructive mutation* (FCM). During the mutation of x an evaluation of the objective function is performed after every single mutation step. If the mutation operator yields a search point y with $f(y) < f(x)$, we call such a mutation *constructive*. The mutation procedure stops at the first occurring constructive mutation. This mechanism is meant to slow down (premature) convergence. We will see that FCM is crucial for the performance of mutation potentials already on very simple optimization problems. We combine FCM with the two operators defined above and summarize all four variants in the following definition

Definition 2. *For the tabu variant let* $tabu = 1$, *else* $tabu = 0$. *For the variant with stop at first constructive mutation let* $fcm = 1$, *else* $fcm = 0$. *The inversely proportional hypermutation operators mutate* $x \in \{0,1\}^n$ *in the following way:*

1. *Set* $y := x$. *Set* $v := f(x)$.
2. *Repeat the following* $M_c(v)$ *times:*
   (a) *If* $tabu = 0$ *select* $i \in \{1, \ldots, n\}$ *uniformly at random*
       else select $i \in \{1, \ldots, n\}$ *uniformly at random, i not previously chosen.*
   (b) $y[i] := 1 - y[i]$
   (c) *If* $fcm = 1$ *and* $f(y) < f(x)$ *Then break*

To analyze the performance of the proposed mutation operators, we embed them into an algorithmic framework. We focus on the analysis of mutation potentials and omit other features of AIS. Thus, we use a minimal substrate as our experimentation platform. The following very simple algorithm (Algorithm 1) minimizes some pseudo-Boolean function $f \colon \{0,1\}^n \to \mathbb{R}^+$. It uses a collection of search points of size one and produces one new search point via mutation. This point is accepted if and only if its function value is at least as small.

Algorithm 1 (Algorithmic Framework)

1. *Choose $x \in \{0,1\}^n$ uniformly at random.*
2. *Create $y := mutate(x)$.*
3. *If $f(y) \leq f(x)$ then set $x := y$.*
4. *Continue at 2.*

We use the mutation operators based on mutation potentials defined above in step 2 of the algorithm resulting in a very simple AIS. We call the respective variants SiMPA (tabu = fcm = 0), SiMPA-tabu (tabu = 1, fcm = 0), SiMPA-fcm (tabu = 0, fcm = 1), and SiMPA-tabu-fcm (tabu = fcm = 1), where SiMPA stands for Simple Mutation Potential Algorithm. We sometimes denote the search point x in the beginning of the t-th iteration of the algorithm by x_t.

In evolutionary computation standard bit mutations are most common [12]. There, each bit is flipped independently with mutation probability $1/n$. Plugging standard bit mutations into our framework yields a very simple evolutionary algorithm, known as (1+1) EA [13]. Note that using other mutation operators algorithms like local search or tabu search may be obtained. Since the (1+1) EA is well investigated and well understood a multitude of results is available and may be used for comparisons, see for example [1,21].

Probably the best-known example function in the context of randomized search heuristics (RSHs) is ONEMAX [13]. The function value simply equals the number of 1-bits, $\text{ONEMAX}(x) = \sum_{i=0}^{n-1} x[i]$. ONEMAX is a function that is very easy to optimize since it gives clear hints for the appropriate search direction. Thus, it is a good benchmark for investigating whether a given algorithm is generally capable of finding a local or global optimum of a reasonable and well-structured function. It has also been studied in the context of AIS [22,23] for inversely fitness proportional mutation rates and somatic contiguous hypermutations [17]. Since we consider minimization problems, we consider $\text{ZEROMIN}(x) := n + 1 - \text{ONEMAX}(x)$ instead which is obviously almost equivalent to ONEMAX. For search heuristics that treat 0-bits and 1-bits symmetrically the only difference is the addition of +1 that causes ZEROMIN to be strictly positive. Note, that these modifications have no significant effect on the performance of the algorithms we consider and thus, we essentially execute an analysis for ONEMAX.

As usual in the analysis of general RSHs, there is no stopping criterion in the algorithm and we investigate the first point of time when a global optimum of f is reached. Note, that in our case this does not necessarily correspond to the number of iterations until a global optimum is found since for mutation operators using FCM there may be more than one function evaluation per iteration. We denote the number of function evaluations as the optimization time of the algorithm which is a common measure for the run time of RSHs. It is important to notice that the algorithm itself does not know that it has found an optimum. In the following, let $T_{A,f}$ denote the optimization time of an algorithm A and $E(T_{A,f})$ be its expected value. We use standard notation from the analysis of randomized algorithms [19].

3 Hypermutations with Mutation Potential

In this section we highlight a weakness of hypermutations with mutation potential if those are carried out blindly, i.e., without checking for an improvement after each local mutation step. The main problem is the large number of local mutation steps carried out. A random walk of this length in a search space of size 2^n has hardly any chance of locating a specific search point. We begin with a lower bound on the number of local mutation steps and establish bounds on the mutation potential on ZeroMin for this purpose.

Lemma 1. *For* ZeroMin *the mutation potential* M_c *is always bounded by* $(c/2)n \leq M_c(v) < cn$ *as long as the global optimum is not found.*

Proof. The mutation potential is defined by $M_c(v) = (1 - f_{OPT}/v) \cdot cn$ for an objective function with local optimum f_{OPT} and a search point with function value $v \geq f_{OPT} > 0$. It becomes minimal for minimal v and maximal for maximal v. For ZeroMin, we have $f_{OPT} = 1$, ZeroMin$(x) \in \{1, 2, \ldots, n+1\}$ and thus $(1 - 1/2)cn \leq M_c(v) \leq (1 - 1/(n+1))cn$ holds. This is equivalent to $(c/2)n \leq M_c(v) < cn$.   □

We now show that SiMPA is very inefficient on ZeroMin: It fails to locate the global optimum efficiently on average and with overwhelming probability.

Theorem 1. $E(T_{SiMPA,\text{ZeroMin}}) = 2^{\Omega(n)}$, $Prob\left(T_{SiMPA,\text{ZeroMin}} < 2^{(c/6)n}\right) = 2^{-\Omega(n)}$.

Proof. Let $d := c/3$. Note that d is a constant with $d \in]0, 1/3]$ since c is a constant with $c \in]0, 1]$. With probability $1 - 2^{-n}$ the initial search point x_1 is different from the unique global optimum 1^n. We consider the very last mutation leading from $x_{T_{SiMPA,\text{ZeroMin}}-1}$ to 1^n. In this very last mutation we consider the final dn local mutation steps. Since $dn < (c/2)n$ we know that these last dn local mutation steps actually exist (Lemma 1). If in these dn last local mutation steps the Hamming distance to the unique global optimum becomes larger than dn the optimum cannot be reached since each local mutation step decreases this Hamming distance by at most 1. This also holds in the beginning. Thus, we only increase the probability of seeing the global optimum reached if we assume that the Hamming distance is always at most dn. Under this assumption the probability for decreasing the Hamming distance is always bounded above by d

and the probability of increasing it is at least $1 - d$. We obtain an upper bound for the probability of reaching the global optimum by applying results from the gambler's ruin problem [14, Sect. XIV.2] with player A starting with $s_A = dn$, player B starting with $s_B = 1$, player A winning a round with probability $1 - d$ and player B winning a round with probability d. This yields the upper bound $\left((d/(1-d))^{dn} - (d/(1-d))^{dn+1}\right) / \left(1 - (d/(1-d))^{dn+1}\right) < (d/(1-d))^{dn}$ and proves $\mathrm{E}\left(T_{\mathrm{SiMPA,ZeroMin}}\right) > (1 - 2^{-n}) \cdot ((1-d)/d)^{dn} = 2^{\Omega(n)}$ and thus the first part of the theorem. For the second part we apply the union bound and obtain $\mathrm{Prob}\left(T_{\mathrm{SiMPA,ZeroMin}} < ((1-d)/d)^{(d/2)n}\right) < 2^{-n} + ((1-d)/d)^{(d/2)n} \cdot (d/(1-d))^{dn} = 2^{-\Omega(n)}$ as upper bound. $\qquad\square$

The hypermutation in SiMPA may flip a bit several times. In SiMPA-tabu this is avoided by restricting local mutation steps to bits that have not been touched before by another local mutation step in the same hypermutation. We show that this does not help in locating the global optimum.

Theorem 2. *Let* $d := \min\{c/2, 1 - c\}$. $E(T_{\mathit{SiMPA\text{-}tabu},\mathrm{ZeroMin}}) = 2^{\Omega(n)}$, $Prob\left(T_{\mathit{SiMPA\text{-}tabu},\mathrm{ZeroMin}} < 2^{(d/2)n}\right) = 2^{-\Omega(n)}$.

Proof. Like in the proof of Theorem 1 we consider the very last mutation leading from $x_{T_{\mathrm{SiMPA,ZeroMin}}-1}$ to 1^n. Since we are considering SiMPA-tabu we know that the number of bits changed in a single hypermutation of x equals $M_c(v)$. Thus, $h := \mathrm{H}\left(x_{T_{\mathrm{SiMPA,ZeroMin}}-1}, 1^n\right) = M_c(v)$ holds. We have $(c/2)n \le h < cn$ (Lemma 1). There are $\binom{n}{h}$ ways of selecting the h bits that are changed by the hypermutation. Out of these only one selection leads to the unique global optimum. Thus, the probability of hitting the global optimum in this mutation equals $1/\binom{n}{h}$. Note that $\binom{n}{h} = \binom{n}{n-h}$. Remember $d = \min\{c/2, 1 - c\}$. We see that $\binom{n}{h} \ge \binom{n}{dn}$ holds and use $\binom{n}{dn} \ge (n/(dn))^{dn} = d^{-dn}$ [19, Appendix B] to prove the first statement. For the second statement we use the union bound in the same way as in the proof of Theorem 1. $\qquad\square$

4   Adding 'Stop at the First Constructive Mutation Step'

We have seen that SiMPA and SiMPA-tabu, i.e., the algorithms without FCM, are inefficient on the considered example function ZeroMin. It is known, that the expected optimization time of Algorithm 1 using standard bit mutations (known as (1+1) EA) equals $\mathrm{E}\left(T_{(1+1)\,\mathrm{EA,ZeroMin}}\right) = \Theta(n \log n)$ [13] This can be achieved with single bit mutations, only. We now show that using hypermutations with mutation potential and FCM leads to considerably longer but still polynomial optimization times. We start with the tabu variant of the algorithm.

Theorem 3. $E(T_{\mathit{SiMPA\text{-}tabu\text{-}fcm},\mathrm{ZeroMin}}) = \Theta\left(n^2 \log n\right)$.

Proof. The upper bound follows easily from fitness layer arguments. Assume that the current bit string has i 0-bits. Due to the FCM mechanism it suffices that the first bit chosen by the mutation operator is one of those 0-bits in order to have an improvement. This event has probability i/n and the expected waiting time is n/i. If the mutation operator fails in flipping a 0-bit first, it chooses less than cn additional bits (Lemma 1). Note, that after each of these steps a function evaluation is performed. As for each number of 0-bits $i \in \{1, 2, \ldots, n\}$ at most one such improvement is needed, this yields the claimed upper bound

$$\mathrm{E}\left(T_{\text{SiMPA-tabu-fcm},\text{ZeroMin}}\right) < \sum_{i=1}^{n} cn \cdot n/i = O\left(n^2 \log n\right).$$

For the lower bound, we first observe that the mutation operator can only achieve improvements of 1 since it stops after the first improvement. Let again i be the number of 0-bits in a search point x_t. Note, that $i \geq n/3$ holds for the initial search point x_1 with probability $1 - 2^{-\Omega(n)}$ due to Chernoff bounds [19, Sect. 4.1]. Thus, we require at least $n/3$ improving iterations with high probability, one for each $i \in \{1, 2, \ldots, n/3\}$. Note, that the case that the initial search point contains less than $n/3$ ones only has an exponentially small contribution to the expected value.

For the rest of the proof, we only consider the last $n/3$ improving iterations and thus can assume $i \leq n/3$. In order to prove our lower bound on the optimization time, we need to derive an upper bound on the probability for a constructive mutation step in a mutation, i. e., $\mathrm{Prob}\left(f(x_{t+1}) < f(x_t)\right)$.

We see that the underlying random process is similar to the process considered in the classical ballot theorem [14, Sect. 3.1] which can be stated as follows: *Consider a ballot with two candidates A and B where A receives p votes and B receives $q < p$ votes. Assuming that all possible counting orderings have the same probability, the probability that throughout the counting of the ballot A is strictly ahead of B is exactly $(p-q)/(p+q)$.* Note, that the counter event in this setting is the event that there is a point in time throughout the counting where the number of votes for B is at least as large as the number of votes for A.

Since we assume $i \leq n/3$, in our case p corresponds to the number of 1-bits while q corresponds to the number of 0-bits, i. e., $p = n - i$, $q = i$ and $p + q = n$. There are two differences between the considered process and the process from the ballot theorem. First, we are interested in the probability that there is a point in time where B is strictly ahead of A, since this corresponds to the event of a constructive mutation step. Clearly, this can be bounded above by the probability for the above mentioned counter event. Second, we are only considering $M_c(v) < cn < n$ steps of the counting. Since considering a smaller number of steps can only decrease the probability to see B strictly ahead of A, the ballot theorem yields an upper bound on the probability sought. $\mathrm{Prob}\left(f(x_{t+1}) < f(x_t)\right) \leq 1 - ((n-i) - i)/n = 2i/n$. This implies that the waiting time for an improvement is at least $n/(2i)$. If the mutation operator fails in improving the current search point, it chooses at least $cn/2$ bits (Lemma 1). As we are only able to achieve improvements of 1, this leads to the claimed lower bound on the optimization time in very much the same way as we derived the upper bound. $\mathrm{E}\left(T_{\text{SiMPA-tabu-fcm},\text{ZeroMin}}\right) \geq \sum_{i=1}^{n/3} \frac{cn}{2} \cdot \frac{n}{2i} = \Omega\left(n^2 \log n\right)$ □

In contrast to SiMPA-tabu-fcm, in SiMPA-fcm certain bits can flip several times. This provides the possibility to reverse a 'bad' earlier choice. Since this might increase the probability for a constructive mutation step, we need to be more careful when analyzing this algorithmic variant. In particular, we cannot apply the ballot theorem due to the potential multiple flipping of a single bit.

Theorem 4. $E(T_{SiMPA\text{-}fcm,\text{ZeroMin}}) = \Theta(n^2 \log n)$.

Proof. The proof for the upper bound is exactly the same as in Theorem 3.

For the lower bound, remember, that the parameter c used in the definition of the mutation potential (Definition 1) is a constant with $c \in]0, 1[$. Thus, there exists a constant $\varepsilon > 0$ such that $c \leq 1 - \varepsilon$ holds.

Let again be i the number of 0-bits in the current search point. We see that a mutation in this situation is a random walk. When starting in i, the probability to reach state $i - 1$ is i/n in the first mutation step. We observe that for each step into the wrong direction, we need to use the corresponding edge into the correct direction in order to be able to reach state $i - 1$ during the mutation. To be more precise, for an edge with probability $(i + k)/n$ the corresponding edge with probability $(n - i - (k - 1))/n$ has to be used, $k \in [1, \dots, n - i]$. Then, the event to use this pair of edges has probability $p(i) = (i + k)(n - i - (k - 1))/n^2$. We substitute $j = i + k$ for the sake of readability and get $p(j) = j(n - j + 1)/n^2$.

Additionally, the edge from i to $i - 1$ has to be the last edge used and all paths that reach state $i - 1$ have odd length. Moreover, once the random walk has distance at least $\lfloor (M_c(v) - 1)/2 \rfloor + 1$ from i, it is not possible to reach state $i - 1$. This implies that this holds for any random walk with length $\geq M_c(v)/2$.

Remember that the function value can only decrease by 1. The initial search point x_1 contains at least $(\varepsilon/4)n$ 0-bits with probability $1 - 2^{-\Omega(n)}$ due to Chernoff bounds. Thus, we may only consider the last $(\varepsilon/4)n$ improving iterations and assume $i \leq (\varepsilon/4)n$. We conclude that a 'successful' random walk reaches only nodes with at most $(\varepsilon n/4) + (M_c(v)/2) = (\varepsilon n/4) + (1 - \varepsilon)n/2 = ((1/2) - (\varepsilon/4))n$ 0-bits. The probability to use a specific pair of edges as discussed above, is maximal for $j = (1/2 - \varepsilon/4)n$ in the interval $[0, (1/2 - \varepsilon/4)n]$. Plugging this into our equation for $p(j)$ yields: $(((1/2) - \varepsilon/4)n(n - ((1/2) - \varepsilon/4)n + 1))/n^2 = (1/4) - (\varepsilon^2/16) + ((1/2) - \varepsilon/4)/n$. We see that each of these pairs is used with a constant probability smaller than $1/4$, say $1/4 - \delta$ for some constant $0 < \delta < 1/4$, during the random walk if n is sufficiently large.

Let p_t be the probability that after exactly $2t + 1$ steps in a mutation the first constructive mutation step occurs. Since there are at most $\binom{2t}{t}$ different paths of length $2t$ ending in state $i - 1$, we can bound the probability for a constructive mutation step as follows.

$$\text{Prob}\left(f(x_{t+1}) < f(x_t)\right) = \frac{i}{n} + \sum_{t=1}^{\lfloor \frac{M_c(v)-1}{2} \rfloor} p_t < \frac{i}{n} + \sum_{t=1}^{\lfloor \frac{M_c(v)-1}{2} \rfloor} \frac{i}{n} \cdot \binom{2t}{t} \cdot \left(\frac{1}{4} - \delta\right)^t$$

$$< \frac{i}{n} + \frac{i}{n} \cdot \sum_{t=1}^{\lfloor \frac{M_c(v)-1}{2} \rfloor} \frac{4^t}{\sqrt{t}} \cdot \left(\frac{1}{4} - \delta\right)^t = \frac{i}{n} + \frac{i}{n} \cdot \sum_{t=1}^{\lfloor \frac{M_c(v)-1}{2} \rfloor} \frac{(1 - 4\delta)^t}{\sqrt{t}} = O\left(\frac{i}{n}\right)$$

As in Theorem 3, this yields the claimed lower bound $\mathrm{E}\left(T_{\text{SiMPA-fcm,ZeroMin}}\right)$
$$\geq \sum_{i=1}^{n/3} (cn/2) \cdot \Omega(n/i) = \Omega\left(n^2 \log n\right). \qquad \Box$$

We have seen that in both algorithms using FCM we lose a factor of n in comparison to the $(1+1)$ EA on ZeroMin. This is due to the fact that in an unsuccessful mutation, we perform $M_c(v)$ function evaluations. Clearly, using other mutation potentials leads to different optimization times. Note, that in general, we have $\mathrm{E}\left(T_{A,\text{ZeroMin}}\right) = \Theta(\sum_{i=1}^{n}(n/i) \cdot M_c(i+1))$ for a given mutation potential M_c and the FCM-variants. We come back to this point in Section 5.

In the remainder of this section, we examine where hypermutations with mutation potential provably excel over other randomized search heuristics like for example the $(1+1)$ EA. For this purpose, we consider an example function that was introduced by Neumann et. al [20] in order to show benefits of combining ant colony optimization and local search. The function is called SP-Target (short path with target) and can be described as follows.

Let $|x|_1$ denote the number of 1-bits and $|x|_0$ the number of 0-bits in a search point x. In the vast majority of the search space the function value guides the search heuristic towards 0^n. There, a path with increasing function values starts, leading the algorithm towards the local optimum 1^n. The set of points on the path is denoted as $\text{SP} = \{1^i 0^{n-i} \mid 0 \leq i \leq n\}$. The global optimum (target) is a large area containing points with at least $3n/4$ 1-bits and a minimal Hamming distance to the SP-path and can be defined as follows where $0 < \gamma \leq (3/20) - \alpha$ ($\alpha > 0$ a small constant) is chosen arbitrarily with $\gamma = \omega(1/n)$.

$$\text{OPT} = \{x \mid |x|_1 \geq 3n/4 \text{ and } \mathrm{H}(x,\text{SP}) \geq \gamma n\}$$

A visualization of SP-Target can be found in Figure 1.

Definition 3. *Let* SP *and* OPT *be defined as described above. Then, for $n \in \mathbb{N}$ the function* SP-Target$(x)\colon \{0,1\}^n \to \mathbb{N}$ *is defined for all $x \in \{0,1\}^n$ by*

$$\text{SP-Target}(x) := \begin{cases} |x|_0 & x \notin (\text{SP} \cup \text{OPT}) \\ n+i & x = 1^i 0^{n-i} \in \text{SP} \\ 3n & x \in \text{OPT} \end{cases}.$$

Note, that in contrast to the original definition of SP-Target, we allow larger Hamming distances. Moreover, we switch to a minimization problem by considering $3n + 1 - \text{SP-Target}(x)$ instead. We remark that the $(1+1)$ EA is not efficient on SP-Target as long as $\mathrm{H}(\text{OPT},\text{SP}) = \gamma n = \omega(\log n/\log\log n)$ [16]. We consider SiMPA-tabu-fcm and show that as long as the parameter c from the mutation potential is chosen large enough, the algorithm is efficient on SP-Target.

Theorem 5. *Let $8\gamma/(3-4\gamma) < c < 1$, constant (with $0 < \gamma \leq (3/20)-\alpha$, $\alpha > 0$ some small constant, $\gamma = \omega(1/n)$).*
Then, $\mathrm{E}(T_{\text{SiMPA-tabu-fcm},\text{SP-Target}}) = O(n^3)$.

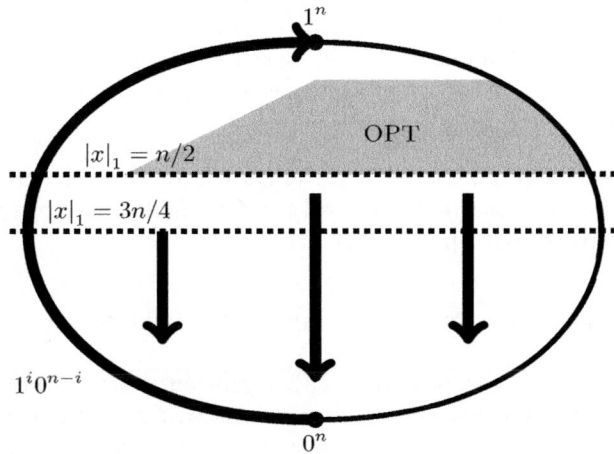

Fig. 1. Visualization of the objective function SP-Target

Proof. We partition the search space $\{0,1\}^n$ in three disjoint sets that match the structure of SP-Target. Let $C := \text{OPT}$, $B := \text{SP}$ and $A = \{0,1\}^n \setminus (B \cup C)$. It is easy to see that these sets form a fitness-based partition with $A >_{\text{SP-Target}} B >_{\text{SP-Target}} C$ [13]. Let T_X for $X \in \{A,B,C\}$ denote the number of function evaluations where we have $x_t \in X$. Clearly, $T_{\text{SiMPA-tabu-fcm,SP-Target}} = T_A + T_B + T_C$ holds. Due to Theorem 3 we know that $T_A = O(n^2 \log n)$. In very much the same way we can show $T_B = O(n^3)$.

Let y denote the search point during mutation. We pessimistically assume that we have not found a globally optimal search point until $x_t = 1^n$ holds, i.e., the algorithm has reached the local optimum. We now show that in this situation $y \in \text{OPT}$ holds after one of the mutation steps in the mutation with high probability. For this event two conditions have to be fulfilled: $|y|_1 \geq 3n/4$ and $H(y, \text{SP}) \geq \gamma n$.

The first condition is satisfied as long as less than $n/4$ mutation steps are performed. Thus, we only consider the first at most $n/4$ mutation steps of a mutation when showing the second condition. After these $\leq n/4$ steps we have $|y|_1 \geq 3n/4$ and thus, the second condition is trivially fulfilled for all $z \in \text{SP}_{\text{low}} = \{1^i 0^{n-i} \mid 0 < i < 3n/4 - \gamma n\}$.

For $z \in \text{SP}_{\text{high}} = \{1^i 0^{n-i} \mid i \geq 3n/4 - \gamma n\}$ we consider the first $3n/4 - \gamma n$ bits of y. Note, that the number of 1-bits in y decreases by exactly 1 in each mutation step since we consider the tabu-variant of the hypermutation variant. Thus, we need at least γn mutation steps in order to be able to reach OPT. Moreover, we know that in the considered situation $M_c(v) = cn/2$ holds.

After k mutation steps the expected number of 0-bits in the prefix of length $(3/4 - \gamma)n$ equals $k(3/4 - \gamma)$. Consider $k = ((4\gamma/(3-4\gamma)) + (1/4) - (3-19\alpha)/(12 + 20\alpha))n$ mutation steps. Since we have $\gamma \leq (3/20) - \alpha$, $k \leq n/4$ holds for our choice of k. Since we have $c > (8\gamma/(3-4\gamma))$, we also have $k \leq cn/2$. Altogether, we can conclude that the expected number of 0-bits in the prefix is by a constant factor bigger than $4\gamma/(3 - 4\gamma) \cdot ((3/4) - \gamma) \cdot n = \gamma n$. Using Chernoff bounds, we have that the probability to have less than γn bits in the prefix is $2^{-\Omega(\gamma n)}$. Since this yields, $\mathrm{H}(y, \mathrm{SP_{high}}) \geq \gamma n$, we have that with probability $1 - 2^{-\Omega(\gamma n)}$ we sample $y \in \mathrm{OPT}$ during a mutation.   □

We remark that a similar result can be shown for SiMPA-fcm. However, the proof is, for the same reasons discussed for ZeroMin, more complicated and is therefore omitted due to space restrictions.

5   Improving Hypermutations with Mutation Potential

We have seen that hypermutations with mutation potential are not helpful in locating local or global optima when used blindly, i. e., without checking for an improvement after each local step. If such checks are carried out the search is still less efficient than when other much simpler mutation operators are used. More-over, hypermutations with mutation potential also suffer from further weaknesses that are similar to problems observed in evolutionary algorithms when fitness-proportional selection is employed. The operator is only defined for strictly pos-itive objective functions. Moreover, it is highly sensitive with respect to scaling of the objective functions. It is known that going from the consideration of the actual function values to their ranks removes these difficulties. We take exactly the same route here in the following. Note that the following definition cannot be used for continuous search spaces S since it assumes that S is countable.

Definition 4. *In rank-based hypermutations with mutation potential the mu-tation potential* $\widehat{M}_{c,\rho}(v)$ *for a search point x is defined in the following way. Let $\{f(x) \mid x \in S\} = \{v_1, v_2, \ldots, v_{|S|}\}$ with $v_1 < v_2 < \cdots v_{|S|}$. $\widehat{M}_{c,\rho}(v_i) = \lceil (1 - n^\rho/(n^\rho + i - 1)) \cdot cn \rceil$ for some constant $0 < c < 1$ and $\rho \in \mathbb{R}_0^+$.*

The rounding in the definition of the rank-based mutation potential $\widehat{M}_{c,\rho}$ is necessary since the mutation potential needs to be an integer. We round up to have $\widehat{M}_{c,\rho}(v_i) > 0$ for any non-optimal v_i.

The critical remarks about the limited practicality of the mutation poten-tial M_c also apply to the rank-based mutation potential $\widehat{M}_{c,\rho}$. In general, neither the optimal value $f_{\mathrm{OPT}} = v_1$ nor the rank of a specific function value are known. In practice, one will use estimates that will be based on a priori knowledge of the objective function (where available) and observations made during the run. Investigating the effects these estimates have on the performance in practice is beyond the scope of this paper.

The rank-based mutation potential $\widehat{M}_{c,\rho}$ coincides with the mutation poten-tial M_c when the function value v_i is transformed to $1 + (i - 1)/n^\rho$. Remember that i is the rank of the function value v_i. The parameter $\rho \in \mathbb{R}_0^+$ controls the degree of mutation aversion the hypermutation operator has. With its minimal value, $\rho = 0$, the rank-based mutation potential equals $\widehat{M}_{c,0}(v_i) = \lceil (1 - 1/i)cn \rceil$ and is similar to the original mutation potential. In fact, it is equal for ZeroMin.

With increasing ρ it decreases and $\lim_{\rho\to\infty} \widehat{M}_{c,\rho}(v_i) = 1$ holds for any fixed function value v_i. Thus, the search converges to a pure local search with increasing ρ.

We assess the effects of the rank-based mutation potential $\widehat{M}_{c,\rho}$ by considering the example function ZeroMin. Since we already noted that for ZeroMin the rank-based mutation potential $\widehat{M}_{c,0}$ and the mutation potential M_c coincide the following are direct corollaries from Theorem 3 and Theorem 4.

Corollary 1. $E(T_{SiMPA\text{-}fcm,\text{ZeroMin}}) = \Theta(n^2 \log n)$, $E(T_{SiMPA\text{-}tabu\text{-}fcm,\text{ZeroMin}}) = \Theta(n^2 \log n)$ *hold for* $\widehat{M}_{c,0}$.

With $\rho > 0$ we can observe improved performance. The improvement depends on ρ and is caused by the reduced cost of one hypermutation.

Theorem 6. *Let SiMPA-fcm and SiMPA-tabu-fcm denote the two algorithms employing the rank-based mutation potential $\widehat{M}_{c,\rho}$ with $\rho \in \mathbb{R}^+$, ρ constant. For $\rho \in [0,1]$, $E(T_{SiMPA\text{-}fcm,\text{ZeroMin}}) = \Theta(n^2 \log n)$, $E(T_{SiMPA\text{-}tabu\text{-}fcm,\text{ZeroMin}}) = \Theta(n^2 \log n)$ hold. For $\rho > 1$, $E(T_{SiMPA\text{-}fcm,\text{ZeroMin}}) = \Theta(n \log n + n^{3-\rho})$, $E(T_{SiMPA\text{-}tabu\text{-}fcm,\text{ZeroMin}}) = \Theta(n \log n + n^{3-\rho})$ hold.*

Proof. In the proofs for the hypermutation variants that use stop at the first constructive mutation (Theorem 3 and Theorem 4) we noticed that for algorithms $A \in \{\text{SiMPA-fcm, SiMPA-tabu-fcm}\}$ $E(T_{A,\text{ZeroMin}}) = \Theta\left(\sum_{i=1}^{n} \frac{n}{i} \cdot M_c(i+1)\right)$ holds. Here we use the rank-based mutation potential $\widehat{M}_{c,\rho}$ and have $\widehat{M}_{c,\rho}(v_i) = \lceil (1 - n^\rho/(n^\rho + i - 1)) \cdot cn \rceil = \Theta(in/n^\rho + i)$. This yields $E(T_{A,\text{ZeroMin}})$

$$= \Theta\left(\sum_{i=1}^{n}(n/i) \cdot \min\{1, in/(n^\rho+i)\}\right) = \Theta\left(\sum_{i=1}^{\min\{n,\lceil n^{\rho-1}\rceil\}}(n/i) + n^2\sum_{i=\lceil n^{\rho-1}\rceil}^{n} 1/(n^\rho + i)\right)$$

$$= \Theta(n \log n) + \Theta\left(n^2 \cdot \left(\sum_{i=n^{\rho-1}}^{\min\{n,n^\rho\}} 1/n^\rho + \sum_{i=n^\rho}^{n} 1/i\right)\right). \text{ For } \rho > 2 \text{ we have } n^\rho > n$$

so that the second sum is empty. Moreover, $n^{\rho-1} > n$ holds so that the first sum is also empty. This yields $\Theta(n \log n)$ as bound. For $\rho = 2$ we obtain the same bound. For $1 < \rho < 2$ we have $n^\rho > n$, so the second sum is empty. This yields

$$E(T_{A,\text{ZeroMin}}) = \Theta(n \log n) + \Theta\left(n^2 \cdot \sum_{i=n^{\rho-1}}^{n} 1/n^\rho\right) = \Theta(n \log n) + \Theta(n^{3-\rho}) \text{ as}$$

bound and together the statement for $\rho > 1$ follows. Finally, for $0 \le \rho \le 1$ we have $E(T_{A,\text{ZeroMin}}) = \Theta(n \log n) + \Theta\left(n^2 \cdot \left(\sum_{i=1}^{n^\rho} \frac{1}{n^\rho} + \sum_{i=n^\rho}^{n} \frac{1}{i}\right)\right) = \Theta(n \log n)$ $+\Theta(n^2 \cdot (1 + \log n))$ and the statement for $\rho \le 1$ follows. $\square$

6   Conclusions

We have considered a class of hypermutation operators known from artificial immune systems, namely hypermutations with inversely proportional mutation potential. These operators perform potentially large mutations by a sequence of local mutation steps where the length of the sequence is defined by the mutation potential and increases with decreasing quality of the search points. We considered four different variants of this operator by either allowing or forbidding local mutation steps to undo each other and by either allowing or forbidding to check for a successful mutation after each local mutation step. We embedded these operators in a minimal framework and performed an analysis to find out about their properties with respect to locating a global or local optimum of a simple objective function.

When the hypermutation is performed blindly, i. e., checking for a success only after carrying out all local mutation steps, the hypermutation operator is completely unable to locate optimal points. Only when such checks for constructive mutations are included the algorithm becomes efficient. The question if local mutation steps may undo each other turns out to be far less important. In this informed way the resulting algorithm is able to locate optimal points but is slower in doing this than similar evolutionary algorithms with standard bit mutations. This disadvantage is counter-balanced by the advantage of being able to locate optima that are very far from any path of increasing function values, something that standard bit mutations cannot do.

Inversely proportional mutation potential comes with the same disadvantages as fitness proportional selection: It is highly sensitive with respect to scaling of the objective function and not defined for objective functions that may yield non-positive values. We cope with both problems by introducing a novel variant that is rank-based. By introducing a new parameter that allows to adjust the mutation aversion we are able to tune the performance and achieve a performance on simple problems that is asymptotically equal to what standard bit mutations can achieve.

Many questions are still open. Beyond the observations with respect to localization of specific optima and being able to locate optima far from paths of increasing function value one needs to find out about the performance of hypermutations with inversely proportional mutation potential in more practical settings. We have not at all touched the question how the algorithm reacts when instead of the actual optimal value the mutation potential is computed using an estimate based on the current search. Finally, embedding the operator in a more complete artificial immune system and analyzing its interplay with the other components is an important topic of future research.

References

1. Auger, A., Doerr, B. (eds.): Theory of Randomized Search Heuristics. World Scientific Review (2011)
2. Burnet, F.M.: The Clonal Selection Theory of Acquired Immunity. Cambridge University Press, Cambridge (1959)
3. Cortés, N.C., Coello Coello, C.A.: Multiobjective optimization using ideas from the clonal selection principle. In: GECCO 2004, pp. 158–170 (2003)
4. Cutello, V., Narzisi, G., Nicosia, G., Pavone, M.: Clonal selection algorithms: A comparative case study using effective mutation potentials. In: Jacob, C., Pilat, M.L., Bentley, P.J., Timmis, J.I. (eds.) ICARIS 2005. LNCS, vol. 3627, pp. 13–28. Springer, Heidelberg (2005)

5. Cutello, V., Nicosia, G., Oliveto, P.: Analysis of an evolutionary algorithm with hypermacromutation and stop at first constructive mutation heuristic for solving trap functions. In: Proc. of the 2006 ACM Symp. on Applied Computing (SAC 2006), pp. 945–949 (2006)

6. Cutello, V., Nicosia, G., Pavone, M.: Exploring the capability of immune algorithms: A characterization of hypermutation operators. In: Nicosia, G., Cutello, V., Bentley, P.J., Timmis, J. (eds.) ICARIS 2004. LNCS, vol. 3239, pp. 263–276. Springer, Heidelberg (2004)

7. Cutello, V., Nicosia, G., Pavone, M., Timmis, J.: An immune algorithm for protein structure prediction on lattice models. IEEE Trans. on Evolutionary Comp. 11(1), 101–117 (2007)

8. Cutello, V., Nicosia, G., Romeo, M., Oliveto, P.S.: On the Convergence of Immune Algorithms. In: Proc. of the IEEE Symp. on Foundations of Computational Intelligence (FOCI 2007), pp. 409–415 (2007)

9. Dasgupta, D., Niño, L.F.: Immunological Computation: Theory and Applications. Auerbach (2008)

10. de Castro, L.N., Timmis, J.: Artificial Immune Systems: A New Computational Intelligence Approach. Springer, Heidelberg (2002)

11. de Castro, L.N., Von Zuben, F.J.: Learning and optimization using the clonal selection principle. IEEE Trans. on Evolutionary Computation 6(3), 239–251 (2002)

12. De Jong, K.A.: Evolutionary Computation. MIT Press, Cambridge (2006)

13. Droste, S., Jansen, T., Wegener, I.: On the analysis of the (1+1) evolutionary algorithm. Theoretical Computer Science 276(1-2), 51–81 (2002)

14. Feller, W.: An Introduction to Probability Theory and Its Applications, 3rd edn. John Wiley & Sons, West Sussex (1968)

15. Glover, F., Laguna, M.: Tabu Search. Kluwer, Dordrecht (1997)

16. Jansen, T., Wegener, I.: On the choice of the mutation probability for the (1+1) EA. In: Deb, K., Rudolph, G., Lutton, E., Merelo, J.J., Schoenauer, M., Schwefel, H.-P., Yao, X. (eds.) PPSN 2000. LNCS, vol. 1917, Springer, Heidelberg (2000)

17. Jansen, T., Zarges, C.: Analyzing different variants of immune inspired somatic contiguous hypermutations. Theoretical Computer Science 412(6), 517–533 (2011)

18. Kelsey, J., Timmis, J.: Immune inspired somatic contiguous hypermutation for function optimisation. In: Proc. of the 5th Annual Conf. on Genetic and Evolutionary Computation (GECCO 2003), pp. 207–218 (2003)

19. Motwani, R., Raghavan, P.: Randomized Algorithms. Cambridge University Press, Cambridge (1995)

20. Neumann, F., Sudholt, D., Witt, C.: Rigorous analyses for the combination of ant colony optimization and local search. In: Dorigo, M., Birattari, M., Blum, C., Clerc, M., Stützle, T., Winfield, A.F.T. (eds.) ANTS 2008. LNCS, vol. 5217, pp. 132–143. Springer, Heidelberg (2008)

21. Neumann, F., Witt, C.: Bioinspired Computation in Combinatorial Optimization – Algorithms and Their Computational Complexity. Springer, Heidelberg (2010)

22. Zarges, C.: Rigorous runtime analysis of inversely fitness proportional mutation rates. In: Rudolph, G., Jansen, T., Lucas, S., Poloni, C., Beume, N. (eds.) PPSN 2008. LNCS, vol. 5199, pp. 112–122. Springer, Heidelberg (2008)

23. Zarges, C.: On the utility of the population size for inversely fitness proportional mutation rates. In: Proc. of the 10th ACM SIGEVO Conf. on Foundations of Genetic Algorithms (FOGA 2009), pp. 39–46 (2009)

Stochastic Search with Locally Clustered Targets: Learning from T Cells

Rüdiger Reischuk and Johannes Textor

Institut für Theoretische Informatik
Universität zu Lübeck, 23538 Lübeck, Germany
{reischuk,textor}@tcs.uni-luebeck.de

Abstract. Searching a space with locally clustered targets (think picking apples from trees) leads to an optimization problem: When should the searcher leave the current region, and invest the time to travel to another one? We consider here a model of such a search process: infection screening by T cells in the immune system. Taking an AIS perspective, we ask whether this model could provide insight for similar problems in computing, for example Las Vegas algorithms with expensive restarts or agent-based intrusion detection systems. The model is simple, but presents a rich phenomenology; we analytically derive the optimal behavior of a single searcher, revealing the existence of two characteristic regimes in the search parameter space. Moreover, we determine the impact of perturbations and imprecise knowledge of the search space parameters, as well as the speedup gained by searching in parallel. The results provide potential new directions for developing tools to tune stochastic search algorithms.

1 Introduction

Natural resources such as fruit, drinking water, minerals, or prey are most often unevenly distributed in the environment. Moreover, these resources are not infinite, and may be depleted by consumption. Animals thus need to adjust their foraging behaviour accordingly. For example, many predators migrate to different hunting grounds from time to time to ensure a continuous supply with prey. *Foraging theory* [1] is a mathematical treatment of animal foraging behaviour based on the hypothesis that animals evolve to maximize their energy intake, and thus find ways to use their environment optimally. This gives rise to optimization problems such as the *giving up time:* when should a forager give up its current hunting ground, and invest the energy necessary to find a new one?

In this paper, we introduce a "foraging-type" model that we developed to understand the stochastic search of T cells for antigen. Taking an AIS perspective, we ask: what could we learn from this model that could be useful for similar optimization processes in computing and operations research? Scenarios that lead to optimization problems of this type include the following:

- *Security:* Immune-inspired distributed intrusion detection systems (e.g. [2], [3]) mimicking the function of T cells: They consist of large numbers of

P. Liò, G. Nicosia, and T. Stibor (Eds.): ICARIS 2011, LNCS 6825, pp. 146–159, 2011.

agents, each specialized to detecting a certain type of intrusion, which continuously migrate between different hosts or switches in the network.
- *Economy:* Quality control procedures in companies that are organized into branches. The employees in charge of quality control divide their time between inspecting branches and travelling between branches.
- *Algorithms:* Optimal restart of Las Vegas algorithms with expensive restarts. A Las Vegas algorithm is an algorithm with deterministic output whose runtime is a random variable. Such algorithms can be accelerated by restarting them when an unfavorable region of the run time distribution is reached; a well-known example is Schöning's probabilistic SAT solver [4]. An optimal strategy for restarting such algorithms was given by Luby et al. [5]. However, this strategy does not take into account the time needed for restarting the algorithm, which may be substantially larger than the cost of a single search step [4]. Taking this into account leads to a "foraging-type" optimization problem.

1.1 Model Definition and Contributions

The general case of our model can be stated as follows. Consider an indexed set of compartments, which we call *bags*. For each bag i, we have a discrete probability density function $P_i(t)$, giving the probability of hitting the target at time t in bag i, where $t = 0$ is the time that the bag is entered. Furthermore, we have a function $T(i, j)$ denoting the time needed to travel from bag i to bag j. We will assume that the searcher has no knowledge about the *local* target densities (it does not know the $P_i(t)$ for the bags i it visits), and thus simply chooses the next bag uniformly at random. However, the searcher may have some knowledge about the *global* target density (e.g., a suitable average of all the $P_i(t)$).

A searcher like this learns nothing as it progresses, because the search is already finished upon encountering the target. As proved by Luby et al. [5], the optimal strategy in such a case is to restart the search in fixed time intervals. A *strategy* can thus be defined simply as a constant *residence time R* to be spent in each bag before travelling to a different one. Denote by H the *first hitting time*, i.e., the random variable giving the time that the searcher finds the first target. Our goal is to set R such as to minimize the expected hitting time $E[H]$. In more complex cases, one might consider R as a function whose input reflects the searcher's knowledge about its environment.

In the present paper we focus on a special case of our model where the transit time $T(i, j)$ is constant, and sampling in the bags is by drawing with replacement. This special case is a reasonable model of T cell infection screening in the immune system, which is justified in detail in Section 1.2. Readers who are not interested in the immunological background can skip the rest of this introduction and move directly to the technical part, which starts in Section 2. Our technical contributions are the following:

- We obtain both exact and asymptotic results for a single searcher's optimal behaviour (Section 3). This analysis clearly identifies two distinct parameter regimes with quite different asymptotics.

- We then apply these results to characterize the impact of parameter perturbations on the search performance (Section 3.5). This gives insight into the robustness of an optimal searcher against such perturbations, as well as bounds for the search performance when only imprecise estimates of the search space parameters are available.
- Finally, we analyze the performance of a parallel search by multiple independent searchers (Section 4).

1.2   Background: Modelling T Cell Immune Surveillance

The T cells of the immune system [6] screen for antigen (e.g. viruses, bacteria) presented on specialized cells in lymph nodes. A mouse, for instance, has 30-35 lymph nodes distributed strategically across its body. Detection of antigen by T cells is an important step for the initiation of an immune response. T cells are highly specialized: It was estimated that for a given antigen, a mouse has only around 100-200 T cells capable of detecting that antigen [7]. Because many infections are localized (e.g. in the respiratory tract or the intestine), T cells continuously circulate around the body in search for antigen, and migrate to a different lymph node approximately once per day [8]. The cells are carried to the lymph nodes via the blood stream, and hence essentially circulate at random. Mapping this to the previously defined notation, the bags are the lymph nodes, R corresponds to the time spent in the lymph node, and $T(i,j)$ becomes a constant T equal to the time spent travelling between lymph nodes. Since T cells spend around 2/3 of their lifetime in lymph nodes [9], $R \approx 18h$ and $T \approx 6h$.

The most interesting question is whether drawing with replacement is an accurate model for antigen sampling within lymph nodes. By means of two-photon microscopy, it has become possible to observe T cells in lymph nodes in the living, intact animal. These experiments revealed that the search of T cells for antigen is essentially a 3D random walk through the lymph node tissue [10]. Thus, we can indeed justify the drawing with replacement model as it is a quite reasonable approximation of a 3D random walk. In the rest of this section we give some more detail about this correspondence (note however, that this is a mere exposition of well-known facts from random walk theory).

Consider a random walk in the lattice $\mathbb{Z}^3$, and let p_n denote the probability that the vertex reached by the random walk in its n-th step has been visited before. S_n denotes the expected number of different vertices covered within the first n steps, and r_n the probability that the random walk returns to its point of origin at least once within the first n steps. By reversing the random walk in time, it is clear that $p_n = r_n$, and it is known that

$$r_\infty := \lim_{n \to \infty} r_n = \sup_{n \in \mathbb{N}} r_n = 1 - \frac{1}{u(3)} = 0.3405373\ldots, \qquad (1)$$

which is Polya's random walk constant [11]. Thus, we obtain the following asymptotic bound on S_n:

$$\mathrm{E}[S_n] \approx (1 - r_\infty)\, n \qquad (2)$$

Hence, every time a node is visited, we have a chance of at least 66% that it is a node we have not visited before. Now assume that targets are distributed in this lattice such that every vertex is a target with probability c. We are interested again in the first hitting time, i.e. the number of steps it takes a random walk to hit a target for the first time, denoted by $H = H(c)$. Its expectation can be evaluated as follows:

$$E[H] = \sum_{j=1}^{\infty} j \cdot \Pr[H = j] = \sum_{j=1}^{\infty} j \cdot (\Pr[H > j-1] - \Pr[H > j]) \tag{3}$$

$$= \sum_{j=0}^{\infty} \Pr[H > j] = \sum_{j=0}^{\infty} E[(1-c)^{S_j}] \tag{4}$$

For $c \ll 1$, i.e. when $(1-c)^n$ decreases very slowly, the last expression can be approximated by

$$E[H] \approx \sum_{j=0}^{\infty} (1-c)^{E[S_j]} \approx \sum_{j=0}^{\infty} (1-c)^{(1-r_\infty)\,j} \tag{5}$$

$$= \frac{1}{1 - (1-c)^{(1-r_\infty)}} = \frac{1}{1 - (1-c)^{0.659462670\ldots}} \,. \tag{6}$$

This approximation, called the *Rosenstock approximation* [12], is known to give quite good estimates for $c < 0.05$. Using the binomial series expansion, and setting $t_\infty = 1 - r_\infty$, we obtain for the (per step) success probability of the random walk:

$$\frac{1}{E[H]} \approx 1 - (1-c)^{t_\infty} = 1 - \sum_{k=0}^{t_\infty} \binom{t_\infty}{k}(-c)^k = c\,t_\infty - O(c^2) \,. \tag{7}$$

Comparing this random walk search to a systematic search of the lattice vertex by vertex (which is equivalent to drawing with replacement), we see that both methods give rise to a geometric hitting time distribution. For small c, the systematic search outperforms the random walk in terms of expected hitting time by a factor of at most 1.5. Note that at least three spatial dimensions are needed to make the random walk search competitive with the systematic search – the random walk search strategy would be far less effective in a one- or two-dimensional environment.

2   Formal Statement of the Special Case

Recall the definitions of *bags* with according hitting time distributions $P_i(t)$ and transit times $T(i, j)$ from Section 1.1 We assume that the local search in a bag is by sampling with replacement, i.e., for all bags i we have $P_i(t) = c_i$. Hence, the hitting time within bag i is geometrically distributed with parameter c_i. We distinguish between two types of bags, called *good* bags and *bad* bags[1]. We fix some constant c such that $c_i = c$ for all good bags c_i. For the bad bags c_j, we set $c_j = 0$. Furthermore, we assume the travel time $T(i, j) = T$ to be constant. Let n_{good} denote the number of good bags, and n be the number of all bags. Then $\nu := n_{good}/n$ gives the fraction of good bags[2] Hence, when sampling the bag i, the success probability in the current bag (which was drawn uniformly at random from $\{1, \ldots, n\}$) is c with probability ν and 0 with probability $1 - \nu$. Because the next bag to travel to is chosen at random, our special case is now fully characterized by the parameters c, T, and ν, and we will only consider the nontrivial cases with $0 < \nu < 1$.

As mentioned in Section 1.1, it follows from Luby et al. [5] that the optimal strategy is to transit to a new bag after a fixed residence time time R_{opt}. Even though we have yet to determine R_{opt}, this means that we can restrict our attention to searchers of the following type: The searcher picks a bag i uniformly at random, spends time R in the bag drawing one sample per time step, and then spends time T in transit to the next bag. This is iterated until a target is found. Despite its simplicity, our special case gives rise to surprisingly rich asymptotic behaviour, as we will see in the upcoming analysis.

3   Optimizing a Single Searcher

Since the parameters T, ν and c characterize the search problem and are thus beyond our control, our goal is to tune the parameter R in order to maximize search performance. This leads to an optimization problem: If a searcher spends too much time in a bag i, it risks that i is a bad bag, in which case the time would better be spent searching somewhere else. On the other hand, leaving the bag i carries the risk that i could have been a good bag and the target might soon have been found. If the searcher could detect which type of bag it is currently in, then the optimal strategy would obviously be to transit immediately to new bags until a good one is reached. However, because this is not possible, R must be set to a value that balances between the two risks. We derive the following results analytically:

- Expectation $E[H]$ of the hitting time H (Proposition 1);
- Asymptotics of $E[H]$ for large and small R (Propositions 2,3);
- The optimal residence time R_{opt} (Proposition 4); and
- Asymptotic expressions for R_{opt} for *locally dominated* and *globally dominated* parameters (Propositions 5 and 6).

---

[1] Note that there must at least be two different types of bags, otherwise there would of course be no benefit in travelling between bags.

[2] In the immune surveillance model, ν corresponds to the fraction of lymph nodes that are near the area of infection (draining lymph nodes). For instance, in a literature experiment with herpes simplex virus [13], there were 5 draining lymph nodes on average, thus $\nu = 5/35$.

3.1   The Expected Hitting Time

Proposition 1. *Let H denote the first hitting time of a search process according to Section 2 with parameters $R, T, c,$ and ν. Then H has expectation*

$$\mathrm{E}[H] \;=\; \frac{1-c}{c} - \frac{1-\rho}{\rho}\,R + \left(\frac{1-q}{q}\right)\,(R+T) + 1 \tag{8}$$

where $\rho = 1 - (1-c)^R$ and $q = \nu\rho$.

Proof. Let us call a sequence of searching a bag (which takes time R) and transiting to the next bag (which takes time T) a *phase*. Let U be a random variable denoting the number of unsuccessful phases before the searcher finds a target in a good bag in phase $U + 1$, and let S be the number of samples drawn in phase $U + 1$ before the target is found. Then the hitting time is given by

$$H \;=\; (T + R)\,U + S + 1 \;. \tag{9}$$

Since U and S are stochastically independent, it holds that

$$\mathrm{E}[H] = (R + T)\;\mathrm{E}[U] + \mathrm{E}[S] + 1 \;. \tag{10}$$

U is geometrically distributed with parameter q, hence $\mathrm{E}[U] = (1 - q)/q$. S on the other hand has a geometric distribution that is "truncated" to the finite support $\{0, \ldots, R - 1\}$. With some algebra, it can be verified that

$$\mathrm{E}[S] = \frac{1}{\rho}\sum_{k=0}^{R-1} k\,(1-c)^k\,c \;=\; \frac{1-c}{c} - \frac{1-\rho}{\rho}\,R \;. \tag{11}$$

Putting S and U together, we obtain the result. $\qquad\square$

The above formula is indicative of the fact that the search is a combination of two sampling processes with replacement: The global search for a good bag, and the local search for a target in a good bag.

3.2   Asymptotics of the Expected Hitting Time

To understand the dependencies of the expected hitting time, we first analyze its asymptotics for large and small R. For $R \geq M\,c^{-1}$ with $M \gg 1$ the term $(1 - c)^R \leq e^{-M}$ becomes very small, and thus ρ close to 1. This results in the following asymptotics:

Proposition 2. *Let H, R, T, ν, c be defined as above, and fix a large constant $M \gg 1$ such that $R \geq M/c$. Then*

$$\mathrm{E}[H] \;\approx\; \frac{1-c}{c} + \frac{1-\nu}{\nu}(R+T) \;\in\; \Theta(R) \;. \tag{12}$$

Hence, spending significantly more time searching a bag than the expected hitting time c^{-1} for a good bag increases the overall hitting time linearly. On the other hand, if R becomes too small, we get the following:

Proposition 3. *Let H, R, T, ν, c be defined as above, and fix some small nonzero $\epsilon \ll 1$ such that $R \leq \epsilon\, c^{-1}$. Then*

$$\mathrm{E}[H] \approx \frac{1}{\nu c} + \frac{T}{\nu c}\, R^{-1} - T \in \Theta\left(1/R\right) . \tag{13}$$

Proof. If $R \leq \epsilon\, c^{-1}$, we can use the approximation $(1 - c)^R = 1 - R\,c + O((R\,c)^2)$. This implies $\rho \approx c\,R$ and $q = \nu\,c\,R$, which upon insertion into Equation 8 gives the result. □

The $\Theta(1/R)$ asymptotics for small R (i.e., halving an already small R almost doubles the number of phases until a global hit occurs) can be intuitively explained by noting that most of the time is spent in transit between bags since the success probability within a bag $\approx R/(\nu c)$ is very low (Figure 1).

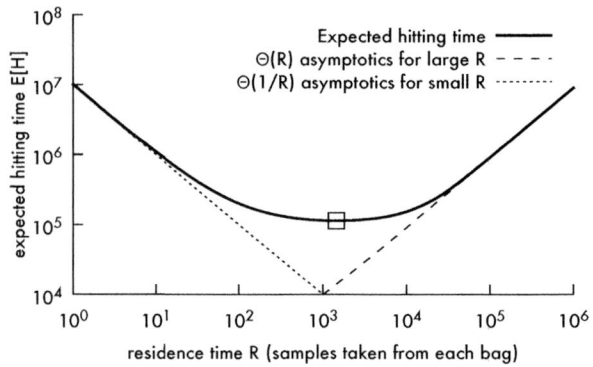

Fig. 1. The expected hitting time $\mathrm{E}[H]$ as per Proposition 8 and its asymptotics as per Propositions 2 and 3 as a function of the residence time R for the parameters $\nu = 0.1, T = 100, c = 0.001$

3.3   The Optimal Residence Time

For given ν, T and c, what is the optimal choice for R, i.e., the one that minimizes $\mathrm{E}[H]$? Let us denote this value by R_{opt}. It is given by the following proposition:

Proposition 4. *Let H, R, T, ν, c be defined as above, and consider $\mathrm{E}[H]$ as a function of R where T, ν, c are constant. Then the $\mathrm{E}[H]$ is minimized by*

$$R_{opt} = W_{-1}\left(-\frac{(1-c)^{\frac{T}{1-\nu}}}{e}\right)\frac{1}{\ln(1-c)} - \frac{T}{1-\nu} + \frac{1}{\ln(1-c)} \tag{14}$$

where W_{-1} is the non-principal branch of the Lambert W function [14].

Proof. We have to solve $\frac{d}{dR}\,\mathrm{E}[H] = 0$, which is equivalent to

$$0 = \frac{d}{dR}\left[\frac{1-\rho}{\rho}R + \frac{1-q}{q}R + \frac{1}{q}T\right] = \frac{d}{dR}\left[\left(\frac{1}{\nu}-1\right)\frac{R+T/(1-\nu)}{1-(1-c)^R}\right]. \quad (15)$$

Now, differentiating we get

$$0 = 1 - (1-c)^R + (R+T/(1-\nu))\,(1-c)^R\,\ln(1-c) \quad (16)$$

$$\Leftrightarrow \quad \left(R + \frac{T}{1-\nu} - \frac{1}{\ln(1-c)}\right)(1-c)^R = -\frac{1}{\ln(1-c)}. \quad (17)$$

This is a transcendental equation and thus cannot be solved for R using only standard algebra. A tool for solving equations of this type, which arise in many applications [14], is the *Lambert W function* defined by

$$x\,e^x = y \iff x = W(y). \quad (18)$$

Using this function, we can express the solutions $\hat{x}$ of the equation $(\hat{x}+\beta)\,\alpha^{\hat{x}} = \gamma$ in closed form with $\hat{y} = \alpha^\beta\gamma\ln\alpha$, because $\hat{x} = \frac{W(\hat{y})}{\ln\alpha} - \beta$. Inserting $\alpha = (1-c)$, $\beta = \frac{T}{1-\nu} - \frac{1}{\ln(1-c)}$ and $\gamma = -\frac{1}{\ln(1-c)}$ in our case gives $\hat{y} = -(1-c)^{\frac{T}{1-\nu}}/e$. Because $-1/e < \hat{y} < 0$, the two branches W_0 and W_{-1} of the Lambert W function both solve the equation. The non-principal branch W_{-1} is the meaningful one in our case because it maps to the interval $(-\infty, -1)$, while W_0 maps to $[-1, 0]$. Inserting α, β, γ and $\hat{y}$ yields the claimed expression.   □

3.4   Asymptotics of the Optimal Residence Time

The exact solution given by Proposition 4 for the optimal residence time is rather complex and yields little insight into the dependencies between R_{opt} and the parameters T, ν, and c. Thus, we now turn our attention to two important regions in the parameter space for which more illustrative asymptotic forms of R_{opt} can be derived. For simplicity, we assume that c is moderately small (e.g. $c < 0.1$); a similar analysis is possible without this assumption, but the asymptotic formulae become more complicated.

We will show the existence of two quite different parameter regimes. The switching point between them is given by a rather unexpected trade-off:

Definition 1. *Let H, T, ν, c be defined as above, and let c be moderately small such that $\ln(1-c) \approx -c$. For*

$$\frac{1}{c} \ll \frac{T}{1-\nu}, \quad (19)$$

we call H transit dominated. Otherwise, if

$$\frac{1}{c} \gg \frac{T}{1-\nu}, \quad (20)$$

then we call H locally dominated.

Note that the parameter ν plays hardly any role in defining these two parameter regimes as in the interesting cases, ν is typically rather small (otherwise the search problem would not be very different from a simple local search in one bag). Thus, surprisingly, *the transit time T is more important than the difficulty of the global search problem*, which can be measured by $1/\nu$ rather than $1/(1-\nu)$.

The upcoming two propositions yield quite interesting differences between transit dominated and locally dominated settings.

Proposition 5. *Let H be transit dominated by T, ν, c. Then*

$$R_{opt} \approx \frac{\ln T - \ln(1 - \nu) + \ln c}{c} . \tag{21}$$

Proof. We use the following power series expansion for $W_{-1}(y)$, which converges quickly for $1/e \ll y < 0$ [14]:

$$W_{-1}(y) = \lambda_1 - \lambda_2 + \sum_{k=0}^{\infty} \sum_{m=1}^{\infty} c_{km} \frac{\lambda_2^m}{\lambda_1^{m+k}} \tag{22}$$

$$= \lambda_1 - \lambda_2 + \sum_{k=0}^{t-1} \sum_{m=1}^{t-k} c_{km} \frac{\lambda_2^m}{\lambda_1^{m+k}} + O\left(\left(\frac{\lambda_2}{\lambda_1}\right)^{t+1}\right) , \tag{23}$$

where $\lambda_1 := \ln(-y)$, and $\lambda_2 := \ln(-\lambda_1) = \ln(-\ln(-y))$. The c_{km} are constants that are not important for our analysis, since we asymptotically approximate W_{-1} for $y \to 0$ by truncating the sum terms of the power series ($t = 0$). For our $\hat{y}$ defined in the proof of Proposition 4 this results in $\lambda_1 = \frac{T}{1-\nu} \ln(1-c) - 1$ and

$$W_{-1}\left(-\frac{(1-c)^{\frac{T}{1-\nu}}}{e}\right) = \lambda_1 - \lambda_2 + O\left(\frac{\lambda_2}{\lambda_1}\right) \tag{24}$$

$$= \frac{T \ln(1-c)}{1-\nu} - 1 - \ln\left(1 - \frac{T \ln(1-c)}{1-\nu}\right) + O\left(\frac{\lambda_2}{\lambda_1}\right) . \tag{25}$$

Inserting this asymptotic expansion into the closed form for R_{opt} given by Proposition 4, some terms cancel out and we arrive at

$$R_{opt} = -\ln\left(1 - \frac{T \ln(1-c)}{1-\nu}\right) \frac{1}{\ln(1-c)} \tag{26}$$

$$+ O\left(\frac{\lambda_2}{\lambda_1 \ln(1-c)}\right) . \tag{27}$$

In the region where $\frac{T}{1-\nu} \gg -\ln(1-c) \approx c$, the argument $1 - \frac{T \ln(1-c)}{1-\nu}$ of the first logarithm is much larger than 1 and can be replaced by $\frac{T}{1-\nu}(-\ln(1-c))$. This gives the approximation

$$R_{opt} \approx \frac{\ln T - \ln(1-\nu) + \ln(-\ln(1-c))}{-\ln(1-c)} . \tag{28}$$

which is valid for any c in a transit dominated setting. Substituting $-\ln(1-c)$ for c yields the claimed expression. $\square$

To understand why this approximation eventually breaks down for $c \to 0$, we look more closely at the O-term of Equation (27) for R_{opt}:

$$R_{\mathrm{opt}} = -\ln\left(1 - \frac{T \ln(1-c)}{1-\nu}\right) \frac{1}{\ln(1-c)} + O\left(\frac{\ln\left(1 - \frac{T \ln(1-c)}{1-\nu}\right)}{\frac{T \ln(1-c)^2}{1-\nu} - \ln(1-c)}\right) \quad (29)$$

Applying De l'Hôpital's Rule it can be shown that R_{opt} *without* the O-term approaches a constant value for $c \to 0$, whereas the O-term starts to dominate. This limit takes us to the locally dominated regime, which we examine next.

Proposition 6. *Let H be locally dominated by T, ν, c. Then we have*

$$R_{opt} \approx \sqrt{\frac{2T}{(1-\nu)c}} . \quad (30)$$

Proof. In the transit dominated regime, the argument of W_{-1} in the closed form of R_{opt} (Proposition 4) is close to $-1/e$, the branch point of the W function. Near this branch point, the power series used in the proof of the previous result is no longer useful (Figure 2, left). From the results of Corless et al. [14] one can derive an alternative power series expansion for W_{-1} near the branch point:

$$W_{-1}(y) = \sum_{t=0}^{\infty}(c_t)^t = -1 + \sigma - \frac{1}{3}\sigma^2 + \frac{11}{72}\sigma^3 + \dots \quad (31)$$

In this expression, $\sigma = -\sqrt{2\,e\,y + 2}$, and thus $|\sigma| \leq 1$. Again the c_t are constants that are irrelevant for our purpose, since we truncate the series after $t = 1$ to obtain an asymptotic approximation. Inserting again the argument for y yields

$$W_{-1}\left(-\frac{(1-c)^{\frac{T}{1-\nu}}}{e}\right) = -1 - \sqrt{2 - 2(1-c)^{\frac{T}{1-\nu}}} + O\left(1 - (1-c)^{\frac{T}{1-\nu}}\right) \quad (32)$$

from which we get the following expression for R_{opt}:

$$R_{\mathrm{opt}} = \frac{-\sqrt{2}}{\ln(1-c)}\sqrt{1 - (1-c)^{\frac{T}{1-\nu}} + O\left(\left(1 - (1-c)^{\frac{T}{1-\nu}}\right)^2\right)} . \quad (33)$$

By the definition of locally dominated parameters, we have $Tc/(1-\nu) \ll 1$. Thus we can substitute $(1-c)^{T/(1-\nu)}$ by $1 - Tc/(1-\nu)$. This yields the claimed expression. $\square$

3.5   Implications for Robustness and Parameter Estimation

The asymptotic results derived in the previous section yield important insight for situations where we have no exact knowledge about the parameters of the search problem. For example, consider the following two questions: (1) A searcher's residence time has been optimally calibrated, and now one of the search parameters

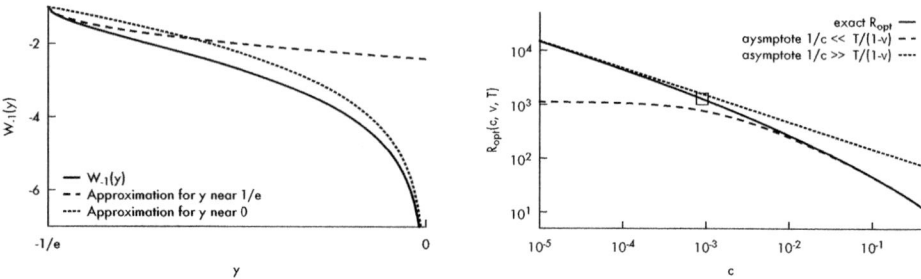

Fig. 2. Left: Illustration of the two different approximations (Equations 22 and 31) used for the Lambert W function in the proofs of Propositions 5 and 6. Right: Transition of the optimal residence time between the two regions described by Proposition 6 (densely dashed) and Proposition 5 (dashed) for $T = 1000, \nu = 0.1$ and varying c. The square marks the point where $\frac{T}{1-\nu} = \frac{1}{c}$.

is perturbed. How much would the perturbation affect the searcher's performance? (2) We determine the search space parameters by statistical estimation. How precise would our estimate need to be to get reasonable performance?

Assume that we set our R to within a factor κ of R_{opt}, i.e., $R_{\text{opt}}/\kappa < R < \kappa R_{\text{opt}}$. Then it follows from the results in Sections 3.1 and 3.2 that $E[H]$ is also within a factor κ of its optimal value. Combining this with the results from the previous section, we see that the situation is very different for the two parameter regimes:

In the *locally dominated* regime (Proposition 6), we have *square root* asymptotics for $1/c, 1 - \nu$, and R, implying that $E[H]$ would be within factor $\sqrt{\kappa}$ of its optimal value if one of these parameters is perturbed by factor κ. Hence, the perturbation has sublinear impact. In the *transit dominated* regime (Proposition 5), the effect of perturbing T and $1 - \nu$ would even be merely *logarithmic*; however, the effect of perturbing c in this regime would be *linear*. Note that in either case, perturbing ν instead of $1 - \nu$ by a small factor κ has virtually no effect if ν is already small.

4   Parallel Search

In this section, we ask how the expected hitting time is reduced by employing several searchers in parallel. We will limit our discussion to the case that the searchers are not synchronized. Note however that being synchronized or not only makes a substantial difference if both ν and c are close to 1, in which case the search problem is anyway not very difficult. We assume that the searchers cannot communicate with each other, and that there is no global control.

Let m denote the number of searchers and H_m the hitting time of such a parallel search. For values of m that are significantly smaller than the expected hitting time $E[H]$ of a single agent, the expectation of the m-parallel search can be approximated by

$$E[H_m] \approx \frac{E[H]}{m} , \tag{34}$$

since in this case the hitting probability of a single step grows approximately by a factor m. This approximation will become invalid for large m, because the bags become saturated with searchers and thus additional searchers will no longer yield substantial speedup. However, in this situation it is still possible to use the following approximation instead:

$$\mathrm{E}\left[H_m\right] = \frac{1}{1 - (1 - R\nu c/(R + T))^m} \tag{35}$$

This approximation is obtained by noting that for a randomly chosen time step, every searcher has an overall chance of $R\nu/(R + T)$ to be in a good bag, and within a good bag the chance of finding a target is c. Assuming that the fraction of searchers in good bags at every timestep is indeed equal to $\gamma = R\nu/(R + T)$ (rather than a random variable with expectation γ), we can approximate the parallel search by random sampling with replacement with a success probability of $1 - (1 - \gamma c)^m$. Note that for $m = 1$, the above equation is equal (up to the constant T) to the equation in Proposition 3 describing the asymptotics of $E[H]$ for small R. Some experimental results are displayed in Figure 3. Notably, while for optimally tuned searchers the speedup is indeed well described by the above equations that predict a linear speedup with saturation, for *non-optimal* residence times it is possible to obtain a *superlinear* speedup by increasing the number of searchers (e.g. in Figure 3, around $m = 100$ for $R = 1$ and around $m = 20$ for $R = 100$).

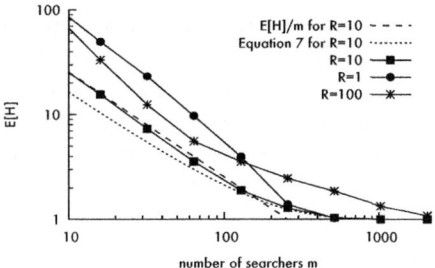

Fig. 3. Speedup of the expected hitting time by m independent parallel searchers. $E[H]$ is plotted as a function of m for $T = 10, \nu = 0.1$, and $c = 0.12591$, which gives $R_{\mathrm{opt}} = 10$. For the optimally tuned population, the approximate expected hitting times as predicted by Equations 34 and 35 are displayed, where Equation 34 describes a power law with slope -1. Per data point we performed 1000 simulations, so that all standard errors of the mean were less than 2%.

5   Conclusions and Future Work

We have stated a "foraging-type" model of stochastic search with locally clustered targets. We performed an in-depth theoretical analysis of the optimal behaviour of a single searcher in this model. The special case corresponds to the behaviour of T cells in the immune system, and is more generally valid for all search processes of this type where the local search is reasonably approximable by drawing with replacement (e.g., the local search is a $\geq 3D$ random walk). As mentioned in the beginning, optimization questions of this type arise in many fields, and we are confident that the model can be applied or extended to many such problems as it is not very immune system-specific. Our work raised many questions to be pursued in the future:

Generalization to other hitting time distributions. The most obvious question is how we can generalize the analytical results obtained for our special case to other scenarios. For instance, concerning our application of modelling infection screening by T cells, there is a hypothesis [15] that the cells need to hit several targets in order to be activated rather than just one. This would give rise to the following generalization of our special case: If c is the probability for a single hit in a good bag per time unit, and k is the number of hits, then the expected hitting time within a good bag would follow a *negative binomial distribution* with parameters c and k instead of a geometric one (which is equal to a negative binomial distribution with $k = 1$). Other distributions of interest include the Weibull distribution which can be used to model the time to failure of systems with constant failure rate; this could be interesting for the quality control scenario.

Parameter estimation and adaptive search. Often we will not know the search space parameters precisely. Thus, the search cannot guarantee to start with an optimal behaviour for the given system. How does a good or optimal strategy look like to estimate the parameters and to adjust the search to the optimal values? Similarly, the parameters may change over time. For instance, an intrusion detection system might face a sequence of intrusions where each intrusion is governed by a certain parameter setting. This setting may change slowly over the time. Knowing the parameters at the beginning or after some period of estimation the searchers could use a strategy optimized for this setting. But later after the change of some parameters this might not longer be the case. How could one adjust in this case?

Application to combinatorial optimization problems. In the introduction, we mentioned the connection of our model to Las Vegas algorithms with expensive restarts. Our model is potentially applicable to combinatorial optimization problems having the property that solutions form clusters in the search space, which e.g. is the case for suitably encoded versions of the traveling salesman problem (TSP). Large instances of the TSP would also have the property that generating a starting point (a tour with a reasonably low weight) takes substantially longer than a local search step in the problem space (e.g. by locally modifying some edges). It remains to be seen whether taking the restart time into account explicitly could lead to substantially faster stochastic algorithms for such problems. In our notation, the bags i for such a problem would be different starting locations in the problem search space[3], and (the cumulants of) the

---

[3] Note that our definition does not require that the bags be disjoint regions in the problem space.

$P_i(t)$ would be the runtime distributions of the algorithm when started at location i. $T(i,j)$ would most likely be a constant function describing the time cost of restarting the algorithm, To extend our theoretical results to such settings, it would hence be crucial to study *arbitrary* distributions $P_i(t)$ with constant $T(i,j) = T$, which would generalize Luby et al. [5] where $T(i,j) = 0$.

References

1. Stephens, D.W., Krebs, J.R.: Foraging Theory. Princeton University Press, Princeton (1987)
2. Hofmeyr, S., Forrest, S.: Architecture for an artificial immune system. Evolutionary Computation 7(1), 1289–1296 (2000)
3. Hilker, M., Luther, K.: Artificial cell communication in distributed systems. In: AINA 2008, pp. 1034–1041. IEEE Computer Society Press, Washington, DC, USA (2008)
4. Hoos, H., Stützle, T.: Stochastic Local Search: Foundations and Applications. Morgan Kaufmann (2005)
5. Luby, M., Sinclair, A., Zuckerman, D.: Optimal speedup of las vegas algorithms. Inf. Process. Lett. 47, 173–180 (1993)
6. Janeway, C., Travers, P., Walport, M., Shlomchick, M.: Immunobiology. Garland Science (2005)
7. Blattman, J.N., Antia, R., Sourdive, D.J., Wang, X., Kaech, S.M., Murali-Krishna, K., Altman, J.D., Ahmed, R.: Estimating the precursor frequency of naive antigen-specific CD8 T cells. Journal of Experimental Medicine 195(5), 657–664 (2002)
8. Westermann, J., Pabst, R.: Distribution of lymphocyte subsets and natural killer cells in the human body. Clin. Investig. 70, 539–544 (1992)
9. von Andrian, U.H.: Intravital microscopy of the peripheral lymph node mirocirculation in mice. Microcirculation 3, 287–300 (1996)
10. Wei, S.H., Parker, I., Miller, M.J., Cahalan, M.D.: A stochastic view of lymphocyte motility and trafficking within the lymph node. Immunological Reviews 195, 136–159 (2003)
11. Glasser, M.L., Zucker, I.J.: Extended watson integrals for the cubic lattices. PNAS 74, 1800–1801 (1977)
12. Weiss, G.H.: Asymptotic form for random walk survival probabilities on three-dimensional lattices with traps. PNAS 77(8), 4391–4392 (1980)
13. Soderberg, K.A., Payne, G.W., Sato, A., Medzhitov, R., Segal, S.S.: Innate control of adaptive immunity via remodeling of lymph node feed arteriole. PNAS 102(45), 16315–16320 (2005)
14. Corless, R.M., Gonnet, G.H., Hare, D.E.G., Jeffrey, D.J., Knuth, D.E.: On the Lambert W function. Advances in Computational Mathematics 5, 329–359 (1996)
15. Mempel, T.R., Henrickson, S.E., von Andrian, U.H.: T-cell priming by dendritic cells in lymph nodes occurs in three distinct phases. Nature 427, 154–159 (2004)

An AIS-Based Mathematical Programming Method

Steven Y.P. Lu[1] and Henry Y.K. Lau[2]

[1] Haitong International Securities Group Limited
22/F, Li Po Chun Chambers, 189 Des Voeux Road Central, Hong Kong
steven.yp.lu@htisec.com
[2] The University of Hong Kong, Pokfulam Road, Hong Kong
hyklau@hku.hk

Abstract. This paper developed an integrated algorithm for the general multi-agent coordination problem in a networked system that is featured by (1) no top-level coordinator; (2) subsystems operate as cooperative units. Through the mapping of such a networked system with human immune system which maintains a set of immune effectors with optimal concentration in the human body through a network of stimulatory and suppressive interactions, we designed a cooperative interaction scheme for a set of intelligent solvers, solving those sub-problems resulted from relaxing complicated constraints in a general multi-agent coordination problem. Performance was investigated by solving a resource allocation problem in distributed sensor networks.

Keywords: Networked system, Lagrangian Relaxation, Artificial Immune Systems, Stimulatory and Suppressive Interactions.

1 Introduction

Motivated by the emergence of large-scale and dynamic networked systems, there has been increasing interest in models and algorithmic developments for the analysis and optimization of networked systems without a centralized coordinator. From an information-processing perspective, the biological immune system (BIS) is a remarkable parallel and distributed adaptive system with decentralized control mechanism [1], which makes it an idea source of inspiration for designing distributed control and optimization algorithms.

There are a number of publications related to distributed continuous or combinatorial optimization algorithms in the Artificial Immune Systems (AIS) community. Continuous optimization deals with the case when the variables assume real values and the domain is infinite (constrained or unconstrained). One of the representative works is the parallel immunological algorithm for continuous global optimization problems, called PAR-IA, developed by Cutello et al. [2]. PAR-IA uses a Master-Slave approach to perform parallel computation. In the Master procedure, the population is partitioned into sub-populations. Then the Master procedure sends each sub-population the Slave procedures and executes Cloning, Hypermutation and Evaluation functions on the original population. Another more recent algorithm is the parallel suppression control algorithm (PSCA) proposed by Lau and Tsang [3]. PSCA

P. Liò, G. Nicosia, and T. Stibor (Eds.): ICARIS 2011, LNCS 6825, pp. 160–172, 2011.

first partitions the population into sub-populations and then adopts the immune-based algorithm to optimize its sub-populations in parallel. The PSCA is essentially an island model where evolution of each sub-population is conducted on an island, and the islands communicate subsets of antibodies with high affinity to one another. The algorithms are tested on eleven numerical benchmark functions, and it produces better results than the other immune algorithms in most cases, but is outperformed by the differential evolution algorithm.

To the best of our knowledge, there has not been any fully developed distributed algorithm for solving combinatorial optimization problems. However, a few centralized algorithms inspired by immunology to solve combinatorial optimization problems are found in the literature. An adaptive optimization algorithm based on the immune network model and MHC peptide presentation is developed by Endo et al. [4] and Toma et al. [5] to solve the n-TSP problem. An AIS-based algorithm utilizing gene libraries and a clonal selection mechanism is developed by Ceollo et al. [6] to solve a series of 31 benchmark job-shop scheduling problems. Ong et al. [7] presents another clonal selection algorithm known as ClonaFlex to solve 12 flexible benchmark job-shop problems.

In this paper, the coordination problem of networked multi-agent systems was modeled as an optimization problem with a decomposable structure. We adopt a modified Lagrangian relaxation method to decompose the original optimization problem into a set of sub-problems, and a novel self-coordination scheme is developed. The novel self-coordination scheme is developed with inspiration from the human immune system. Specifically, the inspiration is obtained from the immune network theory, which assumes that a network of stimulatory and suppressive interactions exists between antibodies in our human body. In the immunity-inspired self-coordination scheme, when a solution to the sub-problem is founded, the subsystem exchanges this solution with its neighbouring subsystems in the network. The individual subsystem then locally evaluates the stimulatory or suppressive effect from each of its neighbours, and updates its associated Lagrange multipliers locally according to the consolidated effect from all of its neighbours. These coordination processes continue iteratively until predefined termination conditions are satisfied.

2 Multi-agent Coordination Problems

Networked systems exist everywhere in our world. Electricity, water, transportation, internet, banking are all brought to us by various physical or social networks. The distributed nature of information and decision-making authority, and the cooperative manner of subsystems make their operations/behavior significantly different from the traditional centralized or hierarchical planning and control paradigms. Coping with these new challenges, there has been increasing interest in recent years in distributed decision-making and control systems. In this paper, we concentrate on the study of the decision-making coordination activities in a networked system, and develop a distributed optimization methodology for the distributed and cooperative structure of information processing and decision-making in a networked system.

2.1   A Mathematical Network Model

In this section, the mathematical model of the multi-agent coordination problem for a general networked system is presented.

We consider a network with a set of agent $V = \{1, 2, \ldots, m\}$. Each agent i has a vector of decision variables X_i and a utility function $f_i(X_i)$ that measures its local operational performance (e.g. the rewards of local resource consumption). There is a set of local constraints $A_i(X_i) \leq b_i$ that restricts the decision-making of agent i. Also, there are sets of coupling constraints $g_{ij}(X_i, X_j) \leq c_{ij}$ between agent i and its neighbouring agents. From each decision-maker's perspective, its local optimization problem is to maximize the value of $f_i(X_i)$ while satisfying both the local constraints and the associated global constraints, as described mathematically in the following Equation (2.1).

$$\text{maxmize} \quad f_i(X_i)$$
$$\text{subject to} \quad A_i(X_i) \leq b_i \tag{2.1}$$
$$g_{ij}(X_i, X_j) \leq c_{ij}, j \in N_i$$

An illustration of this multi-agent coordination problem of a networked system is depicted in Figure 1.

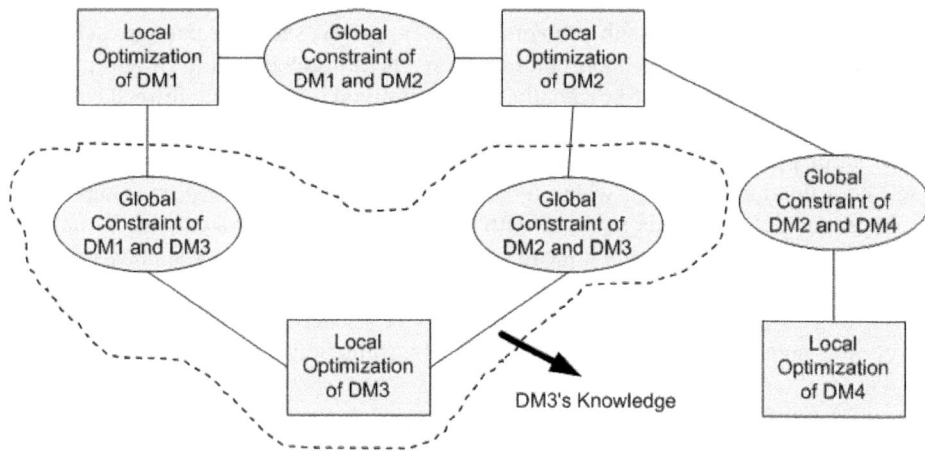

Fig. 1. Multi-agent coordination problem of a networked system

From a centralized perspective, the multi-agent coordination problem of networked systems can be modeled as a multi-objective optimization problem as:

$$\text{maximize} \quad [f_1(X_1), \ldots, f_i(X_i), \ldots, f_m(X_m)]$$
$$\text{subject to}$$

$$\text{All local constraints: } A_i(X_i) \leq b_i, i \in V \tag{2.2}$$
$$\text{All coupling constraints: } g_{ij}(X_i, X_j) \leq c_{ij}, (i, j) \in E$$

In the setting of a networked system, all decision-makers cooperatively pursue a global system objective rather than individually pursuing their local objectives. In this research, we introduce a global system objective to serve as the 'index of evaluation' for measuring the system-wide performance of agents' local interaction. The global system objective is described by Equation (2.3), which is to minimize the sum of deviations from each decision-maker's local optimal.

$$\min \sum_{i=1}^{m} (f_i(X_i^*) - f_i(X_i)) = \max \sum_{i=1}^{m} f_i(X_i) \tag{2.3}$$

So far, the multi-agent coordination problem of a networked system described by Figure 1 can be written mathematically as:

$$\text{maximize} \quad \sum_{i=1}^{m} f_i(X_i)$$

subject to

$$\begin{aligned} &\text{All local constraints: } A_i(X_i) \le b_i, i \in V \\ &\text{All coupling constraints: } g_{ij}(X_i, X_j) \le c_{ij}, (i,j) \in E \end{aligned} \tag{2.4}$$

2.2 Lagrangian Relaxation for Decomposition

In a centralized model given by Equation (2.4) of a multi-agent coordination problem, there are two types of constraints: (1) "easy" constraints where only local variables of one decision-maker appear; (2) "complicating" constraints where local variables of two (or more) coupled decision-makers appear together. By removing the complicating constraints, the problem is split into a set of independent sub-problems, one for each decision-maker. After decomposition, each sub-problem can be optimized locally by a decision-maker in an independent and simultaneous manner. At the same time, information of the sub-problem is gathered, analyzed and stored by each decision-maker separately. In this way, the proposed solution approach then fits in with the actual decision-making and information processing structure of a networked system.

The multi-agent coordination problem defined by Equation (2.4) can be rewritten as a combination of multiple sub-problems. For each decision-maker i, the sub-problem is equivalent to problem defined by Equation (2.1).

$$\text{P: } (\max \sum_{i=1}^{m} f_i(X_i), \text{ s.t. } A_i(X_i) \le b_i, i \in V \text{ and } g_{ij}(X_i, X_j) \le c_{ij}, (i,j) \in E)$$

$$=$$

$$\{ \text{SP}_1 : (\max f_1(X_1), \text{ s.t. } A_1(X_1) \le b_1 \text{ and } g_{1j}(X_1, X_j) \le c_{1j}, j \in N_1),$$

$$\cdots$$

$$\text{SP}_i : (\max f_i(X_i), \text{ s.t. } A_i(X_i) \le b_i \text{ and } g_{ij}(X_i, X_j) \le c_{ij}, j \in N_i),$$

$$\cdots$$

$$\text{SP}_m : (\max f_m(X_m), \text{ s.t. } A_m(X_m) \le b_m \text{ and } g_{mj}(X_m, X_j) \le c_{mj}, j \in N_m) \}$$

We apply Lagrange duality to the coupling constraints of each decision-maker i, such that $g_{ij}(X_i, X_j) \leq c_{ij}, j \in N_i$. These coupling constraints are relaxed with respect to the objective function $f_i(X_i)$ by adding another function $h_i(X_i, X_j, \forall j \in N_i)$, that must reflects the preference of decision-maker i's neighbours. Then, the sub-problem for decision-maker i with augmented objective function can be expressed as:

$$\text{LR-SP}_i(\lambda_{ij}): \{\max(f_i(X_i) + h_i(X_i, X_j, \forall j \in N_i)), \text{ s.t. } A_i(X_i) \leq b_i\}$$

and,   (2.5)

$$h_i(X_i, X_j, \forall j \in N_i) = \sum_{j \in N_i} h_i(X_i, X_j) = \sum_{j \in N_i} \lambda_{ij}(c_{ij} - g_{ij}(X_i, X_j))$$

where, λ_{ij} is the nonnegative Lagrangian multiplier associated with coupling constraint $g_{ij}(X_i, X_j) \leq c_{ij}$ and $h_i(X_i, X_j)$ is the corresponding penalty function.

Therefore, local optimization of sub-problem $\text{LR-SP}_i(\lambda_{ij})$ by decision-maker i is equivalent to the following iterative (optimization) process:

1. Compute an optimal solution X_i^* to $\text{LR-SP}_i(\lambda_{ij})$.
2. Exchange non-private information with neighbouring decision-makers.
3. Update $\lambda_{ij}, \forall j \in N_i$ based on local information and received information from neighbours

2.3 Immunity-Inspired Cooperative Interaction Scheme

In the human immune system, it can be readily observed that part of an antibody (known as paratope) will bind to part of an antigen (known as epitope) in the immunity process. Immune network theory assumes that antibodies also have epitope, which can be bounded by other antibodies' paratopes. These antibodies both stimulate and suppress each other in certain ways that lead to the stabilization of the network of interconnected antibodies. With this assumption, a network of stimulatory and suppressive interactions exists between antibodies that affect the concentrations of each type of antibody. The idiotypic network can be illustrated pictorially by Figure 2, where immunization of an antigen (Ag) may lead to the generation of a chain of antibodies (Ab).

By assuming that there is a single epitope-binding region on each antibody and antigen, and a single paratope-binding region on each antibody, Farmer et al. [8] suggested an abstracted mathematical model of the immune network theory as follows:

$$\frac{dx_i}{dt} = c\left[\sum_{j=1}^{N} m_{ji} x_i x_j - k_1 \sum_{j=1}^{N} m_{ij} x_i x_j + \sum_{j=1}^{n} m_{ji} x_i y_j\right] - k_2 x_i \qquad (2.6)$$

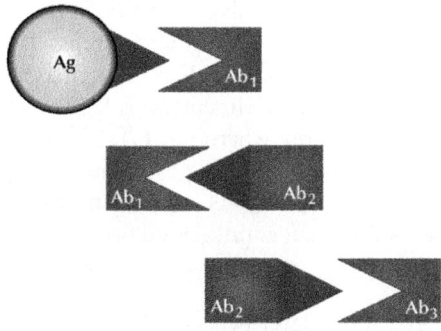

Fig. 2. Idiotypic network

According to Equation (2.6), the change in concentration of an antibody of type i depends on both the stimulation of antigens bounded by antibody i and the aggregated stimulation (or suppression) from antibodies recognized by antibody i.

With inspiration from the immune network theory that a network of stimulatory and suppressive interactions exists between antibodies that affect the concentrations of each type of antibody, in the proposed immunity-inspired cooperation scheme, the selection of the values of λ_{ij}, for $j \in N_i$ by decision-maker i reflects the stimulatory or suppressive effect of both the local objective value $f_i(X_i)$ and the slackness of the relaxed coupling constraint associated with λ_{ij}, $|c_{ij} - g_{ij}(X_i, X_j)|$. Before describing the complete immunity-inspired cooperative interactions scheme, a comparison between the multi-agent coordination problem and the interactions between antibodies in biological immune system is presented, which is given in Table 1.

Table 1. A mapping between networked systems and the biological immune system

Interactions between decision-makers in a networked system	Interactions between antibodies in a biological immune system
Values of decision-maker i's local variables X_i	Concentration of an antibody of type i
Stimulation from local objective value $f_i(X_i)$	Stimulation by binding with antigens
Stimulation from positive values of $c_{ij} - g_{ij}(X_i, X_j)$, for $j \in N_i$	Stimulation by binding with other antibodies
Suppression from negative values of $c_{ij} - g_{ij}(X_i, X_j)$, for $j \in N_i$	Suppression by be recognized by other antibodies

As stated above, each decision-maker i use the updated values of λ_{ij}, for $j \in N_i$ as a tool to determine the stimulatory interactions (when $g_{ij}(X_i, X_j) < c_{ij}$, for $j \in N_i$) and the suppressive interactions with its neighbours (when $g_{ij}(X_i, X_j) > c_{ij}$, for $j \in N_i$) in performing local optimization of sub-problem $\text{LR-SP}_i(\lambda_{ij})$. The updated values of λ_{ij}, for $j \in N_i$ which enables a network of stimulatory or suppressive interactions between decision-makers continues until reaching a stable condition where $g_{ij}(X_i, X_j) = c_{ij}$ is satisfied (or nearly satisfied). According to Lemma 3.2 and the associated analysis given, the satisfaction of the condition $g_{ij}(X_i, X_j) = c_{ij}$ is equivalent to attaining a global optimal solution to the original multi-agent coordination problem.

Prior to the design of the updating policy of λ_{ij}, for $j \in N_i$, an additional property of the parameter λ_{ij} is described as follows:

Lemma 1. If λ_{ij}, for $j \in N_i$ is very big so that $\dfrac{\partial f_i(X_i)}{\partial X_i} - \lambda_{ij} \times \dfrac{\partial g_{ij}(X_i, X_j)}{\partial X_i} < 0$, the interaction between decision-maker i and decision-maker j becomes dominated by decision-maker j. That is to say, the interaction between them will enforce a suppressive effect on the values of X_i in the next iteration of the optimization process performed by decision-maker i. In the contrary, if λ_{ij}, for $j \in N_i$ is very small so that $\dfrac{\partial f_i(X_i)}{\partial X_i} - \lambda_{ij} \times \dfrac{\partial g_{ij}(X_i, X_j)}{\partial X_i} > 0$, the interaction between decision-maker I and decision-maker j becomes dominated by decision-maker i. In addition, the larger the value of $\left| \dfrac{\partial f_i(X_i)}{\partial X_i} - \lambda_{ij} \times \dfrac{\partial g_{ij}(X_i, X_j)}{\partial X_i} \right|$, the bigger the suppressive effect on the value of X_i will be.

Proof: The objective function of decision-maker i for optimizing its sub-problem, $\text{LR-SP}_i(\lambda_{ij})$, can be rewritten as:

$$\max: X_i \times \left[\frac{\partial f_i(X_i)}{\partial X_i} - \lambda_{ij} \times \frac{\partial g_{ij}(X_i, X_j)}{\partial X_i} \right] + \lambda_{ij} \times c_{ij} + \sum_{r \in N_i, r \neq j} \lambda_{ir}(c_{ir} - g_{ir}(X_i, X_r)) \}$$

Considering the first term of the objective function that represents the local interaction between decision-maker i and decision-maker j, if $\dfrac{\partial f_i(X_i)}{\partial X_i} - \lambda_{ij} \times \dfrac{\partial g_{ij}(X_i, X_j)}{\partial X_i} < 0$, the values of X_i will be suppressed to decrease in order to maximize the objective value of its sub-problem $\text{LR-SP}_i(\lambda_{ij})$. Thus, $f_i(X_i) = X_i \times \dfrac{\partial f_i(X_i)}{\partial X_i}$ will decrease, while $h_i(X_i, X_j) = \lambda_{ij} \times c_{ij} - X_i \times \lambda_{ij} \times \dfrac{\partial g_{ij}(X_i, X_j)}{\partial X_i}$ will increase. In order words, the interaction between decision-maker i and decision-maker j becomes dominated by decision-maker j.

According to Lemma 1, in order to ensure that the selection of the values of λ_{ij}, for $j \in N_i$ by decision-maker i reflects the appropriate stimulatory or suppressive effect from neighbouring decision-makers in local interactions, the updating policy for the values of λ_{ij} needs to satisfy the following conditions:

(1) $\dfrac{\partial f_i(X_i)}{\partial X_i} - \lambda_{ij} \times \dfrac{\partial g_{ij}(X_i, X_j)}{\partial X_i}$ $\begin{cases} < 0, & \text{if } g_{ij}(X_i, X_j) > c_{ij} \\ \\ > 0, & \text{if } g_{ij}(X_i, X_j) < c_{ij} \end{cases}$

(2) $\left| \dfrac{\partial f_i(X_i)}{\partial X_i} - \lambda_{ij} \times \dfrac{\partial g_{ij}(X_i, X_j)}{\partial X_i} \right|$ is proportional to $| c_{ij} - g_{ij}(X_i, X_j) |$

Therefore, the following formula is introduced to locally compute the values of λ_{ij}, for $j \in N_i$ by decision-maker i:

$$\frac{\partial f_i(X_i)}{\partial X_i} - \lambda_{ij} \times \frac{\partial g_{ij}(X_i, X_j)}{\partial X_i} = \theta \times (c_{ij} - g_{ij}(X_i, X_j)) \quad (2.7)$$

where θ is a positive constant that is given at the beginning of the optimization process and is known to all decision-makers as their a prior knowledge.

After transforming Equation (2.7), the following expression for λ_{ij} is obtained:

$$\lambda_{ij} = \frac{\dfrac{\partial f_i(X_i)}{\partial X_i} - \theta \times (c_{ij} - g_{ij}(X_i, X_j))}{\dfrac{\partial g_{ij}(X_i, X_j)}{\partial X_i}} \quad (2.8)$$

Once decision-maker i finds an optimal solution X_j to its sub-problem and receives the current optimal solutions X_j of its neighbouring decision-maker j, for $j \in N_i$, it may update λ_{ij} using Equation (2.8).

2.4 The Integrated Algorithm

The proposed algorithm for distributed optimization of multi-agent coordination problem in a networked system is actually a hybrid of Lagrangian relaxation and immunity-inspired cooperative interaction scheme. It is abbreviated as LR-ICI, with procedures described as follows:

Algorithm (LR-ICI for Distributed Optimization)
Initialization (performed **locally at each decision-maker i**):

set $k = 0$, and θ = a positive constant, $0 < \theta < \dfrac{1}{2}$

set $j \in N_i$, K_m = the maximum number of interaction (iteration) k

set data received=1, ε =a small positive constant (acceptable complementary slackness)

For each $(i, j) \in E$, set $\lambda_{ij}(0) = 0$

Main Loop (perform **locally at each decision-maker i**):

while $k < K_m$ **do**

computes an optimal solution

$$X_i^*(k) =$$

$$\underset{A_i(X_i) \leq b_i}{\arg \max} \; \{ f_i(X_i) + \sum_{j \in N_i} \lambda_{ij}(k)(c_{ij} - g_{ij}(X_i, X_j(k-1)))\} \cdot$$

sends $X_i^*(k)$ to decision-maker j, and simultaneously receives $X_j^*(k)$

from decision-maker j, for $j \in N_i$.

if data received = 0, wait; **else**

for each $(i, j) \in E$, calculate $| c_{ij} - g_{ij}(X_i, X_j) |$

if $| c_{ij} - g_{ij}(X_i, X_j) | \leq \varepsilon$, stop; **else**

sets k=k+1;

updates the values of $\lambda_{ij}(k)$, for $j \in N_i$ by

$$\lambda_{ij}(k) = \frac{\dfrac{\partial f_i(X_i)}{\partial X_i} - \theta \times (c_{ij} - g_{ij}(X_i(k-1), X_j(k-1)))}{\dfrac{\partial g_{ij}(X_i, X_j(k-1))}{\partial X_i}}$$

sets data received = 0;

end

end

Repeat the main loop

3   Migration and Maturation of Dendritic Cells

In this Section, the sensor resource allocation problem in a cooperative sensor network [9] was studied to investigate the performance of the proposed distributed solution technique – LR-ICI.

Specifically, we consider the sensor resource allocation problem for the cooperative task of target tracking in a distributed sensor network. It is a distributed observation system with multiple sensors and multiple mobile targets are to be tracked by the sensors. Figure 3 shows an example of a sensor network represented using the grid model with six sensors and two targets. The problem of interest is to find an allocation of sensors to track all the targets, under the constraints that: a) sensors do not have prior information about the targets and their movement; b) sensors have limited sensing range, and only the targets that are inside the neighboring grids of a sensor can be detected by that sensor, as shown in Figure 3(a);

c) sensors have limited sensing resources, and each sensor cannot simultaneously track more than one target. A feasible allocation of the sensors for all targets is shown in Figure 3(b).

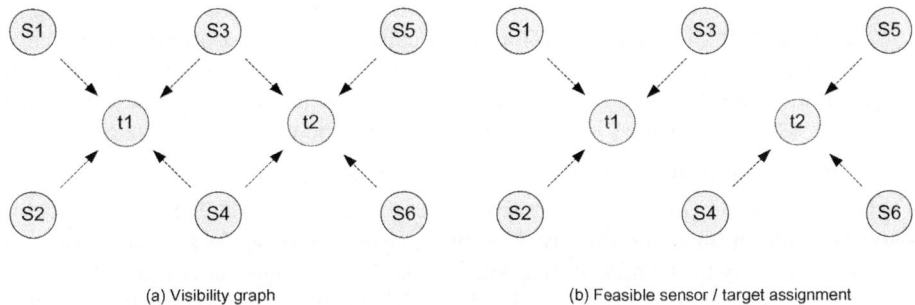

(a) Visibility graph   (b) Feasible sensor / target assignment

Fig. 3. A grid model of sensors network with 6 sensors and 2 targets

In this experiment, there are in total 6 problem types with 5, 7, 9, 11, 13 and 15 mobile targets to be tracked in the sensor grid with a grid size = 100. For each problem type, 10 problem instances were generated by varying the initial position of each target in the target set to be tracked. In the experiments, the parameters of the algorithm were fixed as follows: the maximum number of iteration = 100m (m is the number of targets to be tracked), θ = 0.5, ε =0.1.

We employ two performance metrics for performance measurement and comparison: 1) Percentage of the optimal objective value (to evaluate the "quality of solutions"), and 2) The number of cycles taken to arrive at a global solution (to evaluate the "time to solution" or the "communication overhead"). The experimental results of the proposed algorithm was compared with a distributed constraint optimization technique (ADOPT developed by Modi et al. [10]) and an Auction and Bidding technique, which is modified from the combinatorial auction approach developed by Ostwald et al. [11]. The difference between these distributed algorithms is summarized below:

(1) **ADOPT** is a distributed constraint optimization technique, which conducts constraint-directed search in distributed domains by inference and propagation such that the cost of a set of constraints over the variable is either minimized or maximized. ADOPT is a fully distributed algorithm without centralized coordinator, however, it is difficult to be incorporated with an optimization problem, and the resulted solutions are usually global consistent, instead of global optimal.

(2) **The modified combinatorial auction** is a silent auction in which bidders can bid on sets of items instead of a single item. Each bidder provides sets of items and corresponding prices for each set, and the auctioneer chooses the set of bids that maximizes the payment. Although combinatorial auctions have been shown to be well suited for parallel computation and suggest a significant speedup potential, the existence of an auctioneer (a top-level coordinator) makes it not applicable in networked systems that are considered in this paper.

(3) **LR-ICI** proposed in this research is a distributed algorithm that combines mathematical decomposition and immunity-inspired coordination. In LR-ICI, subsystems solve their sub-problems in local optimization, exchange partial information that depends on specific problem domains with only neighboring subsystems, and then self-coordinate their sub-problems by computing the corresponding Lagrangian multipliers locally with renewed information received through communication. The special features of LR-ICI include: (1) no entity serves as the top-level or centralized coordinator in LR-ICI, and (2) each agent only exchanges just enough information with those in its neighborhood.

The experimental results can be interpreted as below:

(1) As shown in Figure 4, the objective values evaluated by ADOPT is seen to deviate from the optimal solution by 75% in the worst case, while the objective values evaluated by the Combinatorial Auction and LR-ICI algorithms were very close to the optimal values with the worst one at 30% from the optimal value. Particularly, the scalability of LR-ICI outperformed Combinatorial Auction as the number of targets in the sensor grid field increased. The primary reason is that the existence of a top-level coordinator impedes the performance in solving of the problem instances with an increasing number of sub-problems to be coordinated.

(2) As shown in Figure 5, ADOPT outperformed Combinatorial Auction and LR-ICI when the size of the problem instances is small (with targets less than 11 in the experiments). As the number of targets increased up to 11, the number of cycles required by ADOPT to find a global solution increased dramatically, and an exponential growth is observed. For Combinatorial Auction, a linear growth of the number of cycles required to find a global solution with the increase in the problem instance is seen from its scalability curve, while the number of cycles required by LR-ICI seems independent to the number of targets in the sensor grid field.

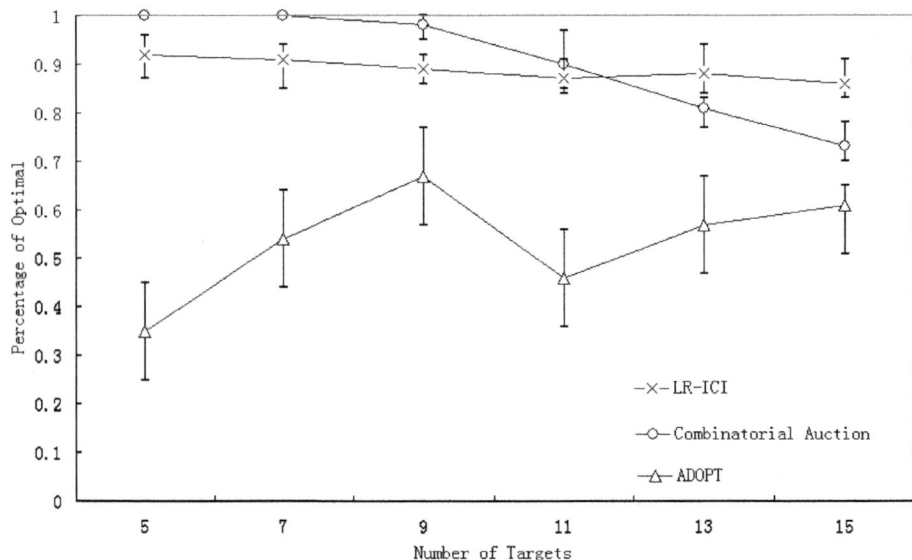

Fig. 4. Comparison of percentage of the optimal objective value

5 Conclusion

In this paper, we first present an optimization model of the coordination problem of networked systems, which can be formulated as a set of local optimization problems of individual decision-makers. A distributed algorithm integrating a modified Lagrangian relaxation technique and an immunity-inspired coordination scheme is then proposed to solve the coordination problem of networked systems. The performance of the proposed algorithm is investigated by solving a cooperative resource allocation problem in wireless sensor networks, where it was shown to have a better scalability in terms of solution quality and speed of convergence.

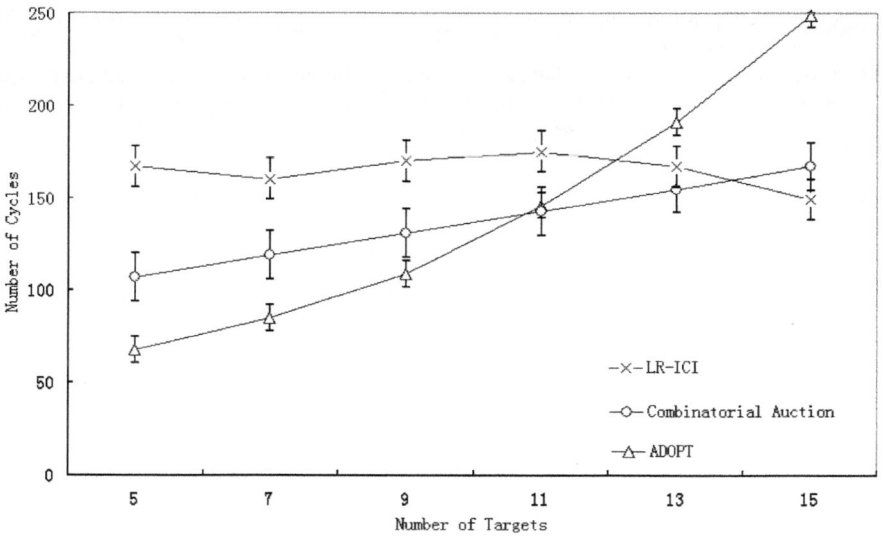

Fig. 5. Comparison of the number of cycles used

References

1. Dasgupta, D.: Advances in artificial immune systems. IEEE Computational Intelligence Magazine 1, 40–49 (2006)
2. Cutello, V., Nicosia, G., Pavia, E.: A Parallel Immune Algorithm for Global Optimization. Computing 5, 467–475 (2006)
3. Lau, Y.K.H., Tsang, W.: A parallel immune optimization algorithm for numeric function optimization. Evolutionary Intelligence 1, 171–185 (2008)
4. Endoh, S., Toma, N., Yamada, K.: Immune algorithm for n-TSP. In: Proceedings of 1998 IEEE International Conference on Systems, Man, and Cybernetics (1998)
5. Toma, N., Endo, S., Yamanda, K.: Immune algorithm with immune network and MHC for adaptive problem solving. In: Proceedings of 1999 IEEE International Conference on Systems, Man, and Cybernetics (1999)

6. Coello Coello, C.A., Rivera, D.C., Cortés, N.C.: Use of an artificial immune system for job shop scheduling. In: Timmis, J., Bentley, P.J., Hart, E. (eds.) ICARIS 2003. LNCS, vol. 2787, pp. 1–10. Springer, Heidelberg (2003)
7. Ong, Z., Tay, J., Kwoh, C.: Applying the Clonal Selection Principle to Find Flexible Job-Shop Schedules. In: Jacob, C., Pilat, M.L., Bentley, P.J., Timmis, J.I. (eds.) ICARIS 2005. LNCS, vol. 3627, pp. 442–455. Springer, Heidelberg (2005)
8. Farmer, J., Packard, N., Perelson, A.: The immune system, adaptation, and machine learning. Physica 22, 187–204 (1986)
9. Mailler, R., Lesser, V., Horling, B.: Cooperative negotiation for soft real-time distributed resource allocation. In: Proceedings of the Second International Joint Conference on Autonomous Agents and Multiagent Systems, pp. 576–583 (2003)
10. Modi, P., Shen, W., Tambe, M., Yokoo, M.: An asynchronous complete method for distributed constraint optimization. In: Proceedings of Autonomous Agents and Multi-Agent Systems (2003)
11. Ostwald, J., Lesser, V., Abdallah, S.: Combinatorial auctions for resource allocation in a distributed sensor network. In: Proceedings of the 26th IEEE International Real-Time Systems Symposium, pp. 266–274 (2005)

Quiet in Class: Classification, Noise and the Dendritic Cell Algorithm

Feng Gu, Jan Feyereisl, Robert Oates, Jenna Reps,
Julie Greensmith, and Uwe Aickelin

School of Computer Science, University of Nottingham,
Nottingham, NG8 1BB, UK
fxg@cs.nott.ac.uk

Abstract. Theoretical analyses of the Dendritic Cell Algorithm (DCA) have yielded several criticisms about its underlying structure and operation. As a result, several alterations and fixes have been suggested in the literature to correct for these findings. A contribution of this work is to investigate the effects of replacing the classification stage of the DCA (which is known to be flawed) with a traditional machine learning technique. This work goes on to question the merits of those unique properties of the DCA that are yet to be thoroughly analysed. If none of these properties can be found to have a benefit over traditional approaches, then "fixing" the DCA is arguably less efficient than simply creating a new algorithm. This work examines the dynamic filtering property of the DCA and questions the utility of this unique feature for the anomaly detection problem. It is found that this feature, while advantageous for noisy, time-ordered classification, is not as useful as a traditional static filter for processing a synthetic dataset. It is concluded that there are still unique features of the DCA left to investigate. Areas that may be of benefit to the Artificial Immune Systems community are suggested.

1   Introduction

The Dendritic Cell Algorithm (DCA) is an immune-inspired algorithm developed as part of the *Danger Project* [1]. Despite being applied to a number of applications, it was originally designed and used as an anomaly detection and attribution algorithm [9]. For the duration of this work, the anomaly detection problem is defined as a binary classification problem, performed on (potentially noisy) discrete time series data. The authors make no assumptions about the relative persistence of anomalous states and normal states, though the persistence of both states is assumed to be sufficiently long to differentiate them from noise. It is also assumed that examples of a system's anomalous behaviour are available for use as training data. This is in contrast to the many alternate definitions of the anomaly detection problem, where there can be the implicit assumption that anomalies are transient or the assumption that only normal behaviour can be studied a priori, reducing the problem to a single class classification. For this investigation a separate, related problem is also defined, termed

P. Liò, G. Nicosia, and T. Stibor (Eds.): ICARIS 2011, LNCS 6825, pp. 173–186, 2011.

"the anomaly attribution problem". This is the problem of attributing causal relationships between the presence of elements in the environment and the occurrence of identified anomalies.

Since its first version [9] the DCA has been subject to many modifications [4,17], empirical tests [2,9,17] and theoretical analyses [12,16,18,22]. This body of work has identified several interesting properties of the DCA. For example, it has been shown that the structure of a single dendritic cell within the DCA is similar in function to the operation of a filter with a dynamically changing transfer function [18,19]. This property could be potentially useful as it allows the algorithm to both exploit the temporal ordering of the input data and remove noisy artefacts from the environmental measurements. However, the effects of the dynamic filter within the DCA to the anomaly detection problem, beneficial or otherwise, have never been demonstrated.

Other theoretical work identifies properties of the DCA that are clearly detrimental to its application to certain problems. One such property is that its classification stage is functionally equivalent to a statically weighted, linear classifier [22]. Such a classifier is neither able to adapt to training data nor meaningfully act on problems which are not linearly separable. Such a criticism is a severe blow to the utility of the DCA in its current form but only strikes at one aspect of a multifaceted algorithm. Within the literature, it has been suggested that replacing the classification stage of the DCA with a trainable, nonlinear, machine learning algorithm would negate much of the criticism made of the DCA while preserving its novel properties [13,20,22].

Modifying the DCA to compensate for the weaknesses identified within the literature, while retaining its original properties, is only a valid course of action if those properties are clearly beneficial. In summary, it is important to identify if the overhead of "fixing" the DCA carries sufficient benefit over creating a new technique for solving the anomaly detection problem. This work is a step towards validating the usefulness of the DCA's novel properties by separating the algorithm into its component parts and assessing their individual contributions. The structure of the paper is as follows, Section 2 provides an outline of the related work; Section 3 gives the research aims in the form of hypotheses; Section 4 presents algorithmic details as mathematical functions; Section 5 details the experimental design; Section 6 shows the results of conducted experiments and the corresponding analysis; finally Section 7 is a discussion of the findings and highlights the future steps for this work.

2   Related Work

2.1   The Dendritic Cell Algorithm

Several different versions of the DCA exist within the literature. The deterministic DCA (dDCA) that was developed for ease of analysis, will be the version considered in this work. The algorithmic details can be found in [10].

The first stage of the DCA is an anomaly detection phase, where the population's classification decisions are monitored in order to identify anomalies within a given dataset. The second phase attempts to correlate the antigen sampled by the cells with the occurrence of detected anomalies.

The DCA receives two types of input, namely signal and antigen. Signals are represented as vectors of real-valued numbers and are periodic measurements of features within the problem environment. An assumption made by the algorithm is that the presence or absence of an anomaly can be detected by observing these features. Antigen are symbols (typically represented as an enumerated type), which represent items of interest within the environment. It is assumed that some of the antigen have a causal relationship with observed anomalies.

The DCA is a population-based algorithm, where several heterogenous agents (cells) monitor the same inputs in parallel. Each cell stores a history of the received input signals, while maintaining a sum of their magnitudes. Upon the sum of the input signal magnitudes reaching a predefined decision threshold, the cell performs a classification based on the signal history. When the decision has been recorded, the cell is reset and instantaneously returned to the population. Each cell is assigned a different decision threshold generated from a uniform distribution, ensuring that cells observe the data over different time scales.

It is demonstrated in [22] that both the classification boundary and the position of the decision boundary can be expressed as hyperplanes, akin to those found in linear classifiers. This premise is used as a foundation for this investigation, so the pertinent machine learning concepts are presented in Section 2.2. As the classification performed by a cell is performed using the history of the sampled signals rather than an instantaneous sample of the environmental features, it can be shown that the DCA exhibits a filtering property which allows it to remove high frequency noise from the input signals [18]. This process relies on the underlying state of the system (normal or anomalous) being persistent for a long enough period of time to distinguish it from the noise. This filtering property is also a key premise of this work and shall be discussed in greater depth in Section 2.3.

2.2   Machine Learning Concepts

In our investigation, the classification stage of the DCA is replaced by a trainable classifier, which is based on the operation of Support Vector Machines (SVM) [3]. Here we present an introduction to this algorithm and the relevant machine learning concepts. SVM models can be described using linear discriminant functions [6], quadratic optimisation [7], and kernel methods [21].

Let $(\mathbf{x}_1, y_1), ..., (\mathbf{x}_n, y_n) \in \mathbf{X} \times Y$ be a given training set with n data instances, where $\mathbf{X} \subseteq \mathbb{R}^d$ is a d-dimensional input feature space and $Y = \{\pm 1\}$ is a set of truths or class labels. For each data instance $\mathbf{x}_i \in \mathbf{X}$ where $i \in [1, n] \cap \mathbb{N}$, a linear discriminant function is defined as $f : \mathbb{R}^d \to \mathbb{R}$,

$$f(\mathbf{x}_i) = \langle \mathbf{w}, \mathbf{x}_i \rangle + b \qquad (1)$$

where $\langle \cdot \rangle$ denotes the inner product of two vectors, $\mathbf{w}$ is the weight vector and b is the bias. The decision boundary of classification is given by $\langle \mathbf{w}, \mathbf{x} \rangle + b = 0$, which corresponds to a $(d - 1)$-dimensional hyperplane within a d-dimensional feature space. A signed measure of the perpendicular distance r from the decision surface to a data point $\mathbf{x}$ can be calculated as,

$$r = \frac{f(\mathbf{x})}{\|\mathbf{w}\|} \tag{2}$$

where $\| \cdot \|$ is the norm operator of a vector.

The linear discriminant functions of SVM models are based on the maximal margin classifier, defined as follows:

$$\langle \mathbf{w}, \mathbf{x}_i \rangle + b \geq +1 \quad \text{if } y_i = +1 \tag{3}$$

$$\langle \mathbf{w}, \mathbf{x}_i \rangle + b \leq -1 \quad \text{if } y_i = -1 \tag{4}$$

Data points lying on the hyperplane $H_1 : \langle \mathbf{w}, \mathbf{x} \rangle + b = 1$ have a perpendicular distance from the origin $|1 - b|/\|\mathbf{w}\|$. Similarly, data points lying on the hyperplane $H_2 : \langle \mathbf{w}, \mathbf{x} \rangle + b = -1$ have a perpendicular distance from the origin $|-1 - b|/\|\mathbf{w}\|$. The margin between the two hyperplanes H_1 and H_2 is equal to $2/\|\mathbf{w}\|$. An optimal decision boundary, defined by $\langle \mathbf{w}, \mathbf{x} \rangle + b = 0$, is found by maximising this margin. It is equidistant and parallel to H_1 and H_2.

The learning task of SVM can be defined as an optimisation problem,

$$\begin{cases} \text{minimise}_{\mathbf{w},b} & \|\mathbf{w}\|^2 \\ \text{subject to} & y_i(\langle \mathbf{w}, \mathbf{x}_i \rangle + b) - 1 \geq 0 \quad \forall i \end{cases} \tag{5}$$

where the constraints are derived from combining Equation 3 and Equation 4. Such an optimisation problem becomes much easier to solve if we introduce Lagrangian multipliers. Let $\alpha_i \geq 0$ be the Lagrangian multipliers, which correspond to the constraints in Equation 5. A primal Lagrangian of the above optimisation problem is defined as

$$L_P = \frac{1}{2}\|\mathbf{w}\|^2 - \sum_{i=1}^{n} \alpha_i[y_i(\langle \mathbf{w}, \mathbf{x}_i \rangle + b) - 1] \tag{6}$$

The primal form L_P is differentiable with respect to $\mathbf{w}$ and b, and an equivalent dual form, known as the Wolfe dual [7], can be derived. The optimisation becomes a convex quadratic programming problem, and all data points that satisfy the constraints also form a convex set [3]. This dual form is defined as

$$L_D = \sum_{i=1}^{n} \alpha_i - \frac{1}{2} \sum_{i,j=1}^{n} \alpha_i \alpha_j y_i y_j \langle \mathbf{x}_i, \mathbf{x}_j \rangle \tag{7}$$

During the training phase of SVM, L_D is maximised with respect to all α_i. The solution of 7 contains feature vectors $\mathbf{x}_i$ such that their corresponding $\alpha_i \neq 0$. These vectors are called support vectors, and they lie on either H_1 or H_2. For non-separable cases, additional constraints are required to allow for outliers.

These constraints are $\sum y_i \alpha_i = 0$ and $0 \leq \alpha_i \leq C$, where C is a parameter that controls the regularisation term. In addition, $\langle \mathbf{x}_i, \mathbf{x}_j \rangle$ can be replaced by $\langle \Phi(\mathbf{x}_i), \Phi(\mathbf{x}_j) \rangle$ through kernel methods. A kernel function is defined as,

$$k(\mathbf{x}_i, \mathbf{x}_j) = \langle \Phi(\mathbf{x}_i), \Phi(\mathbf{x}_j) \rangle \tag{8}$$

where Φ is a mapping from the original input feature space $\mathbf{X}$ to a higher dimensional (inner product) feature space F, where nonlinearly separable problems become more separable [21].

Depending on the applications, a number of kernel functions are available, including linear kernels, polynomial kernels, and Gaussian kernels [21]. A linear kernel only involves performing inner product operations with the input data. Therefore a linear SVM that uses such a kernel is usually simple to train and use. It is more computationally efficient than other SVM models that use more complicated kernel functions [8]. The linear SVM is chosen in this work due to its algorithmic and computational simplicity.

2.3 Signal Processing Concepts

Filters can be viewed as algorithms or structures which apply a gain (ratio of output to input), to their input signal to produce a new output signal. Where filters differ from a simple amplifier, is that the gain applied is a function of the frequency of the input. The mathematical function relating gain to frequency is referred to as the "transfer function" of the filter. In the field of signal processing it is common practice to express filters by providing their transfer functions. For completeness the filters being used for this work will be given here.

The filter with the most analogous behaviour to the DCA is the sliding window filter [18]. A sliding window filter is so called as it can be viewed as a bounding box being translated along the input data. At each step t, the output of the sliding window filter is the average sample size contained within the window. This is expressed in Equation 9,

$$o_t = \frac{1}{W} \sum_{a=(t-W)}^{t} i_a \tag{9}$$

where o_t is the output of the filter at step t, i_a is the input sample at time index a and W is the width of the window in steps.

The transfer function of the sliding window filter is given in Equation 10 [14],

$$G_S(\omega) = \frac{1}{W} \sum_{g=0}^{W-1} e^{-jg\omega} \tag{10}$$

where $G_S(\omega)$ is the transfer function of the sliding window filter, j is the complex number constant and ω is the frequency of the input signal.

A dendritic cell acts like a sliding window filter which only reports its output every W steps [18]. The transfer function for such a filter is given in Equation 11,

$$G_D(\omega) = \frac{1}{W^2} \sum_{g=0}^{W-1} \sum_{b=0}^{W-1} e^{-jb((\omega+(2g\pi)))} \tag{11}$$

where $G_D(\omega)$ is the transfer function of the dendritic cell. However, this transfer function assumes a constant window size W. For a dendritic cell the window size is a function of the magnitude of the input signal being filtered and the decision boundary assigned to the cell. This makes expressing a cell's transfer function extremely difficult as the magnitude of the signal cannot be known a priori. With a given training set, a suitable value to use for the decision boundary could be found by minimising the classification error. However, it is not known if this dynamically changing window size is of any benefit to the algorithm.

3   Research Aims

To justify future work on the DCA it is necessary to assess the importance of its novel features. In the literature, three novel properties of the DCA remain unvalidated: the effect of antigen; the effect of the dynamic filtering; and the effect of having a population of classifiers. Of these, it is arguable that the effect of the dynamic filtering is the most important. This is because the antigen effect is unlikely to yield positive results if the anomaly detection phase is insufficient and the classifier population is unlikely to yield positive results if the dynamic filters used by that population prove to be insufficient.

In order to verify the need for a filter of any kind, it is important to determine if filtering the output from a classifier improves the results of classification when using a time-ordered, noisy dataset. The following null hypothesis will be the first step in this investigation.

H 1 *Filtering the results of a linear classifier presented with time ordered, noisy input data will not result in significant difference of the classification performance.*

This is obviously dependent on designing an appropriate filter as part of the experimental setup.

In order to justify the additional implementation complexity, the dynamic filters should outperform a suitably tuned static counterpart. This yields the following testable null hypothesis.

H 2 *The results from a linear classifier filtered by a dynamic moving window function will have no significant difference to the results from the same classifier using a static moving window function.*

While this investigation is not primarily focussed on the other novel features of the DCA it is of interest to compare the output from the original DCA to that of a filtered and an unfiltered classifier. A trained classifier may have the advantage of being able to adapt to the input data, but the DCA has the additional antigen and multiple perspectives properties, so it will be difficult to definitively identify the reasons for relative performance. However, should the DCA outperform a filtered classifier, it shows that the other properties of the DCA add some information to the decision making process. If on the other hand the DCA is outperformed by a filtered classifier, it would suggest that the benefits of adding a training phase, at the very least, outweigh the possible benefits of the other novel aspects of the algorithm. In either case more experiments would need to be done to assess the merits of the other algorithmic properties. The testable hypothesis from this investigation's perspective is as follows.

H 3 *The classification performance of the DCA will not be signifi-*
cantly different to that of a linear classifier, filtered or otherwise
on a time-ordered, noisy dataset.

If it is possible to reject all of these null hypotheses, then a second set of statistical tests can be performed, assessing the relative benefit of using one technique over the other for the dataset used.

4   Algorithmic Details

To investigate the merits of the sliding window effect of the DCA, it is necessary to separate it from the rest of the algorithm, and use it in conjunction with a better understood classifier. For this investigation, two moving window functions are used as filters for processing the decisions made by a linear SVM. For a given training set, the linear SVM finds an optimal decision boundary and returns the signed orthogonal distance from the decision boundary to each data point, as defined in Equation 2. The moving window functions initialise either a set of window sizes or a set of decision thresholds, and label the data instances within every moving window created. An error function is used to find the optimal window size or decision threshold. The knowledge obtained through training is then applied to classify data instances within the testing set.

For clarity, the algorithmic combinations of a linear SVM with a static and dynamic moving window function that are used in the experiments are defined in the subsequent sections. As the dynamic moving window function cannot be easily defined in a continuous frequency domain, we define both moving window functions in a discrete time domain. For this section time is indexed by $i \in [1, n] \cap \mathbb{N}$ i.e. the index of a data instance in the feature space.

4.1   Static Moving Window Function

Let $A = \{\alpha_l \mid \alpha_l \in \mathbb{N}\}$ be a set of m initial window sizes where $l \in [1, m] \cap \mathbb{N}$, and $k \in [1, \lceil \frac{n}{\alpha_l} \rceil] \cap \mathbb{N}$ be the index of a moving window depending on α_l, where $\lceil \cdot \rceil$ denotes the ceiling function. Let $S_k = [1 + (k-1)\alpha_l, k\alpha_l] \cap \mathbb{N}$ be a set of indexes of the data instances contained within a static moving window. This divides the entire interval $[1, n] \cap \mathbb{N}$ into $\lceil \frac{n}{\alpha_l} \rceil$ partitions. The function for determining the class label of each data instance with respect to a window size α_l is defined as $c : \mathbb{R}^n \times \mathbb{N} \times \mathbb{N} \to \{\pm 1\}$,

$$c(f(\mathbf{x}), \alpha_l, i) = \sum_{k=1}^{\lceil \frac{n}{\alpha_l} \rceil} \mathbb{1}_{S_k}(i) \, \text{sgn} \left(\sum_{s=1}^{n} \frac{f(\mathbf{x}_s)}{\|\mathbf{w}\|} \mathbb{1}_{S_k}(s) \right) \tag{12}$$

where $\mathbb{1}_X(x)$ defines an indicator function that returns one if $x \in X$ holds and zero otherwise, and $\mathrm{sgn}(\cdot)$ denotes a sign function of real numbers defined as,

$$\mathrm{sgn}(x) = \begin{cases} +1 & \text{if } x \geq 0 \\ -1 & \text{otherwise} \end{cases} \tag{13}$$

where $x \in \mathbb{R}$. For each window size α_l, the function c firstly calculates the cumulative distance of all data points, within a generated window, with respect to the decision boundary. It then labels each data instance within such window according to the sign of the calculated cumulative distance. This process is iterative for all the windows generated with respect to a window size.

A mean square error based function is used for evaluating the effectiveness of each window size with respect to the class label, defined as $e : \mathbb{N} \to \mathbb{R}$.

$$e(\alpha_l) = \frac{1}{n} \sum_{i=1}^{n} \|c(f(\mathbf{x}), \alpha_l, i) - y_i\|^2 \tag{14}$$

The static moving window function returns an optimal window size $\alpha_{opt} \in A$ that minimises the resulting classification error, defined as

$$\alpha_{opt} = \arg \min_{\alpha_l \in A} \{e(\alpha_l)\} \tag{15}$$

4.2   Dynamic Moving Window Function

Let $B = \{\beta_l \mid \beta_l \in \mathbb{R}\}$ where $l \in [1, m] \cap \mathbb{N}$ be a set of m initial decision thresholds (lifespans), and $k \in [1, \lfloor \frac{\sum f(\mathbf{x}_i)}{\beta_l} \rfloor] \cap \mathbb{N}$ be the index of a moving window depending on the decision threshold β_l, where $\lfloor \cdot \rfloor$ denotes the floor function. For each decision threshold β_l, the moving windows are found by the following inequality,

$$b_l^{k+1} = \arg \max_{a \in \mathbb{N}} \left\{ a \in (b_l^k, n] \mid \sum_{i=b_l^k}^{a} \left| \frac{f(\mathbf{x}_i)}{\|\mathbf{w}\|} \right| \leq \beta_l \right\} \quad \forall k \tag{16}$$

where $|\cdot|$ is the absolute operator, and each dynamic moving window is bounded by $[b_l^k, b_l^{k+1}] \cap \mathbb{N} \subseteq [1, n] \cap \mathbb{N}$, where b_l^k and b_l^{k+1} are the beginning and end points of the kth moving window and $b_l^1 = 1$. The dynamic window size of a decision threshold β_l is bounded by the cumulative absolute distances $|r_i| = |f(\mathbf{x}_i)/\|\mathbf{w}\||$ from the optimal decision boundary to all the points within it. This is due to the magnitude of $|r_i|$ being closely related to the degree of confidence (sufficient information) for making a decision regarding classification. Let $\tilde{S}_k = [b_l^k, b_l^{k+1}] \cap \mathbb{N}$ be a set of indexes of the data instances contained within a dynamic moving window. This divides the entire interval $[1, n] \cap \mathbb{N}$ into $\lceil \frac{\sum f(\mathbf{x}_i)}{\beta_l} \rceil$ partitions. A similar function to Equation 12 for labelling each data instance with respect to a decision threshold β_l is defined as $\tilde{c} : \mathbb{R}^n \times \mathbb{R} \times \mathbb{N} \to \{\pm 1\}$.

$$\tilde{c}(f(\mathbf{x}), \beta_l, i) = \sum_{k=1}^{\lfloor \frac{\sum f(\mathbf{x}_i)}{\beta_l} \rfloor} \mathbb{1}_{\tilde{S}_k}(i) \, \mathrm{sgn}\left(\sum_{s=1}^{n} \frac{f(\mathbf{x}_s)}{\|\mathbf{w}\|} \mathbb{1}_{\tilde{S}_k}(s) \right) \tag{17}$$

Similar to Equation 14, a mean square error based function with respect to the class label is used for assessing the effectiveness of each decision threshold, defined as $\tilde{e} : \mathbb{R} \to \mathbb{R}$.

$$\tilde{e}(\beta_l) = \frac{1}{n} \sum_{i=1}^{n} \|\tilde{c}(f(\mathbf{x}), \beta_l, i) - y_i\|^2 \tag{18}$$

The dynamic moving window function returns an optimal decision threshold $\beta_{opt} \in B$ that minimises the resulting classification error, defined as

$$\beta_{opt} = \arg \min_{\beta_l \in B} \{\tilde{e}(\beta_l)\} \tag{19}$$

5   Experimental Design

This section details the techniques used to implement the algorithms of interest and the synthetic data required to test the null hypotheses outlined in Section 3. Details of the raw datasets, experimental results and statistical analyses involved in this paper can be found in [11].

5.1   Synthetic Datasets

Synthetic datasets based on two Gaussian distributions are common practice in machine learning, as shown in [22]. This is due to the fact that varying the distance between the distributions allows for control over the separability of the data. For the experiments in Musselle's work [16], where the temporal nature of the data is important, the author uses a Markov chain to generate synthetic datasets, where the probability of state change dictates the relative concentrations of the normal and anomalous behaviour.

For this investigation, both separability and temporal ordering are important. Therefore it was decided to use a dataset based on two Gaussian distributions, then introduce to it an artificial temporal ordering. This is achieved by creating time varying signals representing the class features. Each dataset is divided into quarters, where the first and third quarters are of class I and the second and fourth quarters are of class II. This ordering provides a low frequency underlying change of class, and provides examples of class transitions in both directions. As a consequence, by varying the separability of the classes, one also changes the signal to noise ratio of the time-ordered data, effectively maintaining the same level of noise, but increasing the magnitude of the underlying signal as the separability increases, as illustrated by Fig. 1.

For the generated datasets, class I's mean is fixed at 0.2, and 100 datasets are generated by varying class II's mean from 0.2 (total overlap), to 0.8 (linearly separable) at a regular interval. Both distributions use a standard deviation of 0.1. As the mean of class II increases, the Euclidean distance between the centroids of the two classes increases accordingly. This corresponds to the increment in separability of the two classes. Each dataset contains 2,000 instances, 1,000 for training and 1,000 for testing. By using large numbers of samples, it is intended to reduce artefacts caused by bias in the random number generator.

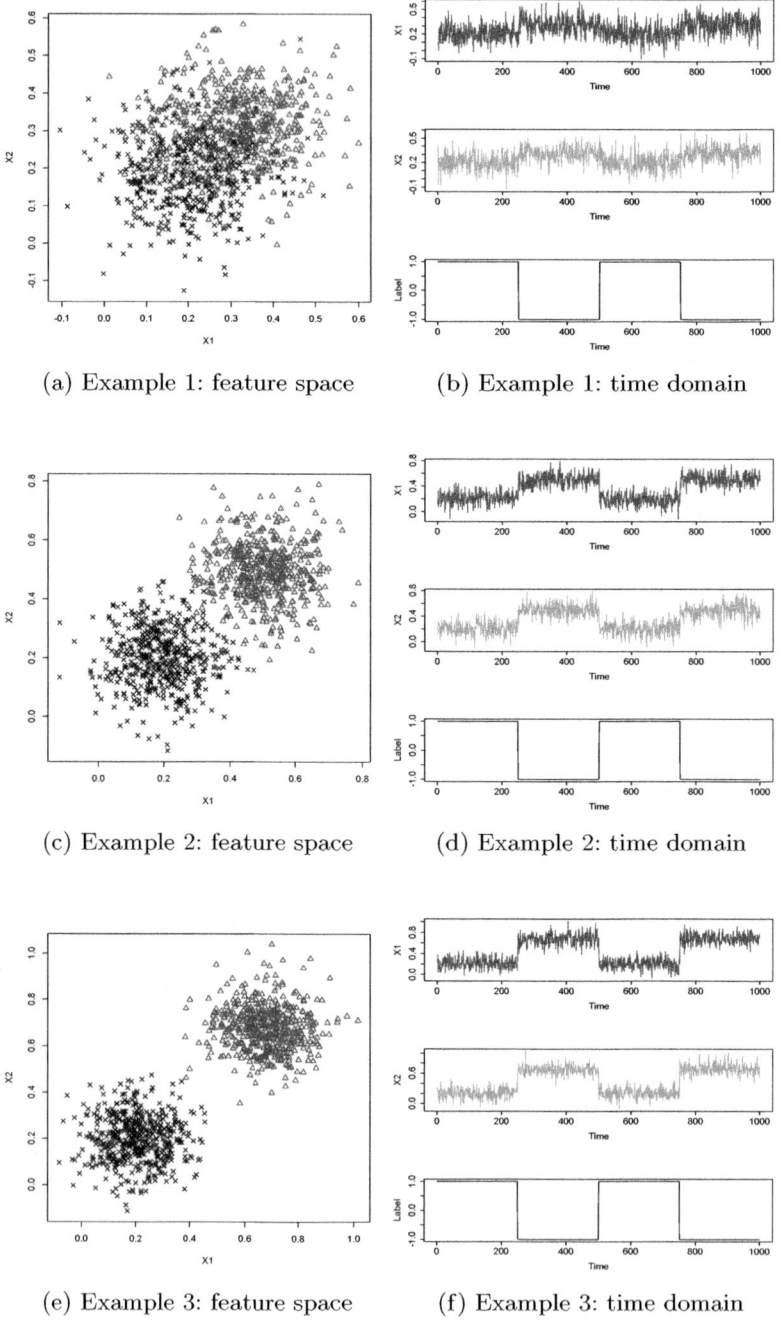

(a) Example 1: feature space   (b) Example 1: time domain

(c) Example 2: feature space   (d) Example 2: time domain

(e) Example 3: feature space   (f) Example 3: time domain

Fig. 1. Feature space and time domain plots of three examples where two classes have different degrees of overlap, and the Euclidean distances between the centroids are 0.17 (a, b), 0.42 (c, d), and 0.68 (e, f)

5.2   Algorithm Setup

Parameters used in the linear SVM are the default values of the R package kernlab [15], and kept the same for both moving window functions. For the static moving window function, the cardinality of the set of initial window sizes $|A|$ is 100, and a window size $\alpha_l \in [1, 100] \cap \mathbb{N}$. For the dynamic moving window function, the cardinality of the set of initial decision thresholds $|B|$ is also 100, and a decision threshold β_l is calculated as,

$$\beta_l = \arg\max_{\mathbf{x}_i \in \mathbf{X}} \left\{ \frac{|f(\mathbf{x}_i)|}{\|\mathbf{w}\|} \right\} \frac{l}{|B|} \lambda \tag{20}$$

where λ is a scaling factor that controls the window sizes considered by the parameter tuning. If $\lambda = 1$, windows are constrained to values typically used within the DCA literature. With $\lambda = 100$, parameters which are equivalent to those used by the static and dynamic moving window functions can also be considered by the tuning process.

The DCA often requires a preprocessing phase that is analogous to the training phase of the linear classifier algorithm, thus only testing sets are used by the DCA. Firstly the two input features are normalised into a range $[0, 1]$ through min-max normalisation. The correlation coefficient between each feature and the class label is then calculated and used to map either of the features to the appropriate signal category. The remaining parameters are chosen according to the values suggested in [10]. The initialisation of lifespans in the DCA uses a similar principle as Equation 20, however the maximisation term is replaced by the signal transformation function of the algorithm and the entire set of lifespans are used for the DC population.

5.3   Statistical Tests

All results will be tested using the Shapiro-Wilk normality test to verify if parametric or nonparametric statistical tests are suitable [5]. All of the null hypotheses in Section 3 are phrased as the absence of a detectable significant difference between pairs of results. The two-sided student t-test will be used for normally distributed samples, and the two-sided Wilcoxon signed rank test will be used for non-normally distributed ones [5].

If differences are detected, the one-sided versions of the relevant difference test will be used to ascertain the relative performance of the results. For all statistical tests a significance level of $\alpha = 0.05$ will be considered sufficient.

6   Results and Analysis

Results from the experiments are presented in terms of the error rates, which are equal to the number of misclassified data instances divided by the total number of instances in the tested dataset. The error rates of the six tested methods across all of the datasets are plotted against the Euclidean distance between the two class

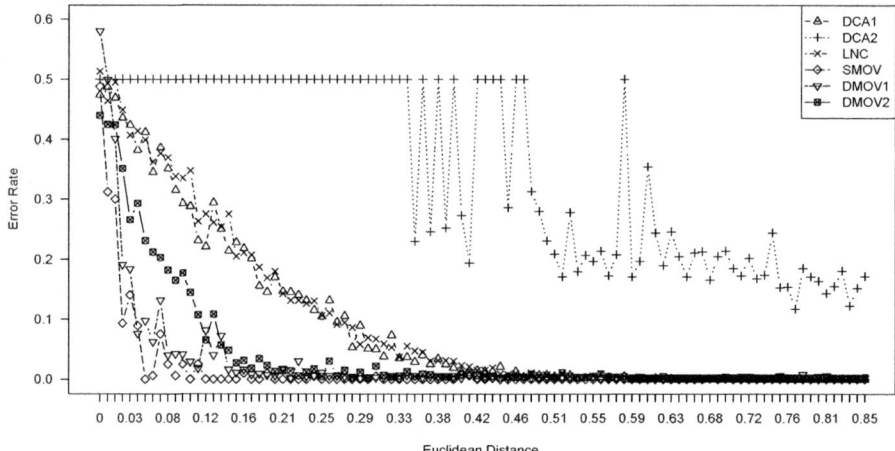

Fig. 2. Error rates of tested methods against the Euclidean distance between centroids of the two classes across all the datasets. DCA1 ($\lambda = 1$) and DCA2 ($\lambda = 100$) denote the Dendritic Cell Algorithm, LNC is the linear SVM, SMOV is the static moving window function, and DMOV1 ($\lambda = 1$) and DMOV2 ($\lambda = 100$) is the dynamic moving window function.

centroids in Fig. 2. For non-separable cases, the classification performance differs from one method to another. In order to determine whether these differences are statistically significant, statistical tests are performed as follows.

The Shapiro-Wilk tests confirm that the data are not normally distributed (p-values are less than 0.05) and therefore the Wilcoxon tests are used to assess the statistical significance for both the two-sided and one-sided comparisons described previously. As all the p-values are less than 0.05, we reject the null hypotheses of all the two-sided Wilcoxon tests with a 95% confidence and conclude that significant differences exist between the results of the different methods. As a result, all of the three null hypotheses presented in Section 3 are rejected.

For completeness Fig. 2 shows results for $\lambda = 1$ (the original DCA parameter range) and the extended search space of $\lambda = 100$. However for analysis, we will only consider the best performing parameterisations of each unique method. From inspection of Fig. 2, it is argued that the order of the methods, in terms of ascending classification performance, is as follows: the linear SVM; the DCA (DCA1); the dynamic moving window function (DMOV2); and the static moving window function. As all the p-values of the one-sided Wilcoxon tests are less than 0.05, this inspection is statistically verified.

7   Discussion and Future Work

The experimental results demonstrate that filtering the decisions of a linear classifier presented with time-ordered and noisy input data significantly changes and improves its classification performance. This was expected to be the case, as even when the datasets are non-separable in the feature space, the temporal ordering means that so long as the hyperplane has a greater than 50% accuracy, it is likely that the average of several instances from the same class, will tend towards the correct class label. This can also be viewed from the frequency domain as non-separability introducing a high frequency noise component into the signal, which can be removed by filtering.

The classification performance of the DCA is significantly different from a linear classifier, filtered or otherwise, on a time-ordered and noisy dataset. In fact, the DCA produces significantly better classification performance than a standard linear classifier, but significantly worse classification performance than the filtered linear classifiers. This implies that the filtering property of the DCA is an important factor of its performance, but that the addition of a training phase to the DCA can add further, substantial improvements.

It is also shown that the classification performance of a linear classifier with a static moving window function is significantly different and better, in comparison to that of a linear classifier with a dynamic moving window function. This is only a valid statement for the datasets used, but infers that the heuristic used by the DCA to alter the transfer function of its filtering component, (i.e. the magnitude of the input signal) is not as good as a simple, static filter.

These results suggest that the problems with the DCA are more deep-rooted than having linear decision boundaries. The DCA's main advantage over the SVM seems to have been its novel filtering technique. However, by substituting the individual components of the DCA with traditional techniques from the domains of signal processing and machine learning, it is clear that it is outperformed. Finding equivalence between the DCA's properties and standard techniques does not necessarily signal an end for the algorithm. However, if those standard techniques can be combined in such a way that their overall structure is the same as the DCA, but their overall performance is better, then there is a danger that "fixing" the DCA will eradicate it entirely. Before clear guidance can be formulated on when, if ever, the DCA is an appropriate choice for a given application, it is important to explore all of its algorithmically unique components. With the classification and filtering properties investigated the next properties that should come under scrutiny are the use of multiple timescales across the cell population and the sampling of antigen.

References

1. Aickelin, U., Cayzer, S., Bentley, P., Greensmith, J., Kim, J., Tedesco, G., Twycross, J.: The Danger Project (2010), http://ima.ac.uk/danger
2. Al-Hammadi, Y.: Behavioural Correlation for Malicious Bot Detection. PhD thesis, School of Computer Science, University of Nottingham (2010)
3. Buerges, C.J.C.: A Tutorial on Support Vector Mahinces for Pattern Recognition. Data Mining and Knowledge Discovery 2, 121–167 (1998)
4. Chelly, Z., Elouedi, Z.: FDCM: A fuzzy dendritic cell method. In: Hart, E., McEwan, C., Timmis, J., Hone, A. (eds.) ICARIS 2010. LNCS, vol. 6209, pp. 102–115. Springer, Heidelberg (2010)

5. Crawley, M.J.: Statistics: An Introduction Using R. Wiley Blackwell (2005)
6. Duda, R.O., Hart, P.E., Stork, D.G.: Pattern Classification, 2nd edn. Wiley-Blackwell (2000)
7. Fletcher, R.: Practical Methods of Optimization. John Wiley and Sons, West Sussex (1987)
8. Fu, Z.Y., Robles-Kelly, A., Zhou, J.: Mixing Linear SVMs for Nonlinear Classification. IEEE Transactions on Neural Networks 21(12), 1963–1975 (2010)
9. Greensmith, J.: The Dendritic Cell Algorithm. PhD thesis, School of Computer Science, University of Nottingham (2007)
10. Greensmith, J., Aickelin, U.: The deterministic dendritic cell algorithm. In: Bentley, P.J., Lee, D., Jung, S. (eds.) ICARIS 2008. LNCS, vol. 5132, pp. 291–303. Springer, Heidelberg (2008)
11. Gu, F., Feyereisl, J., Oates, R., Reps, J., Greensmith, J., Aickelin, U.: Documentation of ICARIS 2011 paper (raw data, experimental results and statistical analysis) (2011), http://www.cs.nott.ac.uk/~fxg/icaris_paper2011.html
12. Gu, F., Greensmith, J., Aickelin, U.: Exploration of the dendritic cell algorithm using the duration calculus. In: Andrews, P.S., Timmis, J., Owens, N.D.L., Aickelin, U., Hart, E., Hone, A., Tyrrell, A.M. (eds.) ICARIS 2009. LNCS, vol. 5666, pp. 54–66. Springer, Heidelberg (2009)
13. Guzella, T.S., Mota-Santos, T.A., Caminhas, W.M.: Artificial immune systems and kernel methods. In: Bentley, P.J., Lee, D., Jung, S. (eds.) ICARIS 2008. LNCS, vol. 5132, pp. 303–315. Springer, Heidelberg (2008)
14. Ifeachor, E., Jervis, P.B.: Digital Signal Processing: A Practical Approach, 2nd edn. Prentice Hall, Englewood Cliffs (2001)
15. Karatzoglou, A., Smola, A., Hornik, K.: Kernel-based machine learning lab. Technical report, Department of Statistics and Probability Theory, Vienna University of Technology (2011)
16. Musselle, C.J.: Insights into the antigen sampling component of the dendritic cell algorithm. In: Hart, E., McEwan, C., Timmis, J., Hone, A. (eds.) ICARIS 2010. LNCS, vol. 6209, pp. 88–101. Springer, Heidelberg (2010)
17. Oates, R.: The Suitability of the Dendritic Cell Algorithm for Robotic Security Applications. PhD thesis, School of Computer Science, University of Nottingham (2010)
18. Oates, R., Kendall, G., Garibaldi, J.: Frequency Analysis for Dendritic Cell Population Tuning: Decimating the Dendritic Cell. Evolutionary Intelligence 1(2), 145–157 (2008)
19. Oates, R., Kendall, G., Garibaldi, J.M.: The limitations of frequency analysis for dendritic cell population modelling. In: Bentley, P.J., Lee, D., Jung, S. (eds.) ICARIS 2008. LNCS, vol. 5132, pp. 328–339. Springer, Heidelberg (2008)
20. Oates, R., Kendall, G., Garibaldi, J.M.: Classifying in the presence of uncertainty: A DCA perspective. In: Hart, E., McEwan, C., Timmis, J., Hone, A. (eds.) ICARIS 2010. LNCS, vol. 6209, pp. 75–87. Springer, Heidelberg (2010)
21. Scholkopf, B., Smola, A.J.: Learning with Kernels: Support Vector Machines, Regularization, Optimization, and Beyond. MIT Press, Cambridge (2002)
22. Stibor, T., Oates, R., Kendall, G., Garibaldi, J.: Geometrical insights into the dendritic cell algorithm. In: Proceedings of the Genetic and Evolutionary Computation Conference (GECCO), pp. 1275–1282 (2009)

A Lymphocyte-Cytokine Network Inspired Algorithm for Data Analysis

Yang Liu[1], Jon Timmis[1,2], and Tim Clarke[1]

[1] Department of Electronics, University of York, UK
{yl520,jt517,tim}@ohm.york.ac.uk
[2] Department of Computer Science, University of York, UK

Abstract. In this paper, we propose an algorithm for cluster analysis inspired by the lymphocyte-cytokine network in the immune system. Our algorithm attempts to optimally represent a large data set by its principle subset whilst maximising the data kernel density distribution. Experiments show that the output data set created by our algorithm effectively represents the original input data set, according to the *Kullback-Leibler* divergence metric. We compare the performance of our approach with the well-known aiNet algorithm and find our approach provides a significant improvement on the representation of the final data set.

1 Introduction

In the context of data analysis, a common task is to attempt to reduce the amount of data that is to be analysed through a pre-processing stage. However, what is important is to maintain the information content in the processed data set with respect to the initial data set.

In statistics, a *kernel* is a weighting function used in non-parametric estimation techniques [1]. Using kernel functions, we can estimate the probability density function of a random variable, usually a finite data set from engineering perspective. This approach is often used for the generation of a smooth distribution to represent the original discrete data set, namely the kernel density distribution (KDD). Therefore, the KDD can be applied to compare two different-sized data sets and thus evaluate the information maintenance of a data analysis algorithm.

In this paper, we make use of kernel density estimations embedded in our approach and proposed the IMSDA (Immune Meta-Stable Data Analysis) algorithm. The aim of the IMSDA algorithm is to represent a large input data set with a smaller subset whilst preserving information content in the smaller, final data set. We take inspiration from the lymphocyte-cytokine network that is present in the immune system to develop our system and test the algorithm on four data sets of different distributions to show the effectiveness of our approach. We then compare our approach with the well established aiNet system. The rest of the paper is structured as follows: Section 2 briefs a well accepted metric for data analysis which allows us to quantify the performance of the algorithm.

P. Liò, G. Nicosia, and T. Stibor (Eds.): ICARIS 2011, LNCS 6825, pp. 187–197, 2011.
© Springer-Verlag Berlin Heidelberg 2011

Section 3 introduces the biological inspiration from the lymphocyte-cytokine connections. Section 4 details the IMSDA algorithm, in which we employ a density estimation method to measure the similarity/differences between the original data set and the compressed data set. Experimental results are provided in Section 5, in comparison with the aiNet algorithm [2].

2   Related Work

In the context of data reduction, the *Kullback-Leibler* (*K-L*) divergence [3] can be used to evaluate the similarity of two data sets where:

$X = \{x \in \Re^N\}$ represents the input data set,
$Y = \{y \in \Re^M\}$ represents the output data set,
$E = \{e \in \Re^N\}$ represents the set of probability densities for X,
$F = \{f \in \Re^N\}$ represents the set of probability densities for Y.

The *Kullback-Leibler* divergence is thus expressed as

$$D_{K-L}(E, F) = \frac{1}{N} \sum_{i=1}^{N} \{ \ln[\frac{1}{M} \sum_{m=1}^{M} K(|x(i) - y(m)|)] - \ln[\frac{1}{N} \sum_{n=1}^{N} K(|x(i) - x(n)|)] \},$$

(1)

where $K(\cdot)$ is a kernel function, usually, a Gaussian kernel. The similarity of two data sets can be assessed by the value of the *K-L* divergence: the smaller *K-L* divergence, the more similarity between them.

Graphically, generating the output data set can be illustrated by Fig. 1, where the grey points represent the original data and the black points represent the output. On the left (Fig. 1(a)) output data points sparsely distributed, which almost entirely covers the original distribution; and on the right (Fig. 1(b)) outputs are densely distributed, which maintains a resembling KDD to the original.

The aiNet algorithm was one of the first generation immune inspired data analysis algorithms and has been widely applied [6], [7]. In general, the aim of the aiNet algorithm is to find a reduced set of points that closely represent the set of

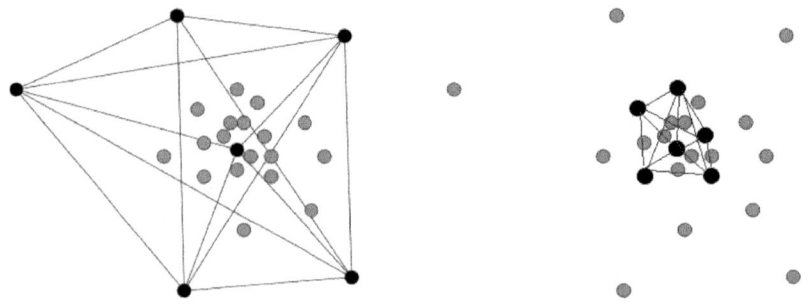

(a) Output loses the input KDD   (b) Output maintains the input KDD

Fig. 1. Data analysis illustration. Figure (a) from [5].

input points. However, as observed by Stibor and Timmis [5], in data compression applications, *'aiNet produced reasonable results on the uniformly distributed data set, but poor results on the non-uniformly distributed data sets, i.e. data sets which contain dense point regions.'* In other words, the original distribution information has mostly gone after compression. Focusing on this problem, work by Von Zuben *et al* [8], [9] introduced an adaptive radius mechanism to the original aiNet. This mechanism automatically adjusts the output distribution according to the original density. Instead of using a kernel estimator, it applies the K-nearest neighbour method (KNN) [1] to evaluate the final information maintenance.

However, in this paper, we propose a lightweight algorithm which seamlessly embeds the K-L divergence to the compression process. The K-L divergence is an inseparable part of the IMSDA algorithm, rather than merely a post-compression evaluation metric [4]. The compression rate is parametrically steerable to the users. When compared with the aiNet algorithm we can note two major differences: 1) the aiNet creates a new data set to present the original instead of a subset and is therefore an *instance creation* algorithm, and 2) it cannot compress the data set under a user-defined compression rate, as an input parameter.

3   Immune Inspiration

Cytokines are signalling chemicals which are secreted by immune cells and mediate many immune functions. As discussed by [10], cytokines have some general properties and are produced in response to antigenic agents. Cytokine secretion is targeted and transient and they often influence the synthesis and actions of other cytokines with their actions often having multiple effects. The cellular response to most cytokines may result in proliferation of the target cells. Different cytokines consequently stimulate a diverse range of immune functions through such cellular communications.

In the lymphocyte-cytokine network, the basic entity is not a lymphocyte but a *type* of lymphocyte, as described in [11] and [12]. Lymphocytes are classified by their chemical properties, i.e. the types of cytokines they produce and by which they are affected. Lymphocytes with identical biological characteristics and behaviours are considered to be of one type. One type of lymphocyte could be affected by a number of types of cytokine which are secreted by other types of lymphocyte (paracrine), or even by itself (autocrine).

In data analysis context, if we consider that the external stimuli is the KDD of the input data, the cytokine secretion of one lymphocyte follows a kernel function [1], and the lymphocytes survive only when the external stimuli meet a certain cytokine concentration. We can then use the surviving lymphocyte to represent the desired output data set. In our work, we take inspiration from the cooperation and competition of the lymphocyte-cytokine network to the development of the IMSDA algorithm.

4   Algorithm

For the purposes of this algorithm, we define $R = \{r \in \Re^N\}$ represents the life index of X. Metaphorically, a type of lymphocyte is a single data element in Y. At each data point n, $e(n)$ and $f(n)$ are defined as

$$e(n) = \frac{1}{N} \sum_{i=1}^{N} K(|x(i) - x(n)|), \tag{2}$$

$$f(n) = \frac{C}{N} \sum_{i=1}^{M} K(|y(i) - x(n)|), \tag{3}$$

where $C \gg 1$ is the input-to-output compression rate.

Taking $e(n)$ as the input stimulus, $f(n)$ is the cytokine concentration produced by the surviving lymphocytes which represent the output data set. The E distribution is fixed when the input data set X is given, but the F distribution fluctuates according to the current output data set Y, which is decided by the cooperation of E, the previous F and the previous life indices, R. For instance, at a certain place n, let

$$s(n) = e(n) - f(n). \tag{4}$$

Define a stochastic proliferation function $P(s)$ as

$$P(s(n)) := \frac{1}{2} \times (|s(n) + 1| - |s(n) - 1|). \tag{5}$$

According to this probability function, we can calculate the proliferation index, and thus the life index at place n is updated by

$$r(n)_{t+1} = r(n)_t + P(s(n)) - \frac{1}{N}, \tag{6}$$

where t is the time stamp and $\frac{1}{N}$ is defined as the natural death rate. If $r(n)$ is higher than a threshold, this data item is considered to be an element of the output data set, otherwise not.

As defined above, the size of the input data set is N, and is fixed. We sequentially stimulate the lymphocyte-cytokine network using the elements in the input data set and then after a number of iterations ($\gg N$) the output data set will be created in a similar manner to the "meta-stable memory" algorithm by [13]. The elements in the output data set are not fixed, i.e., some elements are always in the set, but some others are removed and some new ones are added as the algorithm progresses. However, the size of the output set M also maintains relatively stable: if one element is removed from the set, the absence will immediately affect the equilibrium of the system, according to Equations (2) to (4). At a certain place, when a high value of s is generated from Equation (4), it will probably result in a high increase of life index r by Equation (5). Consequently, there would be a new element placed in the population. Therefore, to relate this approach to data compression, we need to specify a compression rate C *a priori* rather than M. As an integer, M will be very close to (mostly a little larger than) $\frac{N}{C}$. The algorithm terminates when either a predefined small K-L divergence J is achieved or the maximum iteration criterion is reached. The pseudocode of the IMSDA algorithm is detailed in Algorithms 1 and 2 in Appendix A. Source code is available on request.

5   Experiments

5.1   Test Bench

We selected to test our approach with four different data sets, using the same data sets as those presented in [5], which were used to illustrate the data representation capability of the aiNet algorithm. In addition to performing experiments on our proposed system we used aiNet as a comparison system.

Data set 1 was simply generated from a 2D Gaussian distribution (Fig. 2(a)). Set 2 was from a mixture of six Gaussian distributions with different means and covariances (Fig. 3(a)). Set 3 was from a mixture of two Gaussian distributions, with the same mean but different covariances; thus it looks like a denser Gaussian inside another Gaussian (Fig. 4(a)). Set 4 was from a mixture of Gaussian and trigonometric functions; it looks like two Gaussian distributions along two curves separately (Fig. 5(a)).

The size of all testing input data sets was 400. Due to the stochastic nature of our algorithm, each experiment was performed 50 times, and the results were the mean and standard deviation of both the K-L divergence and the size of the output data set, noted by J_μ, J_σ, $|M|_\mu$ and $|M|_\sigma$ respectively. The optimised kernel bandwidth was h=0.96, as suggested by [1].

5.2   Results

As detailed above, the K-L divergence reflects the similarity between two KDDs. The smaller K-L divergence, the higher similarity. If a smaller-sized data set has the same KDD as the larger one, this means that the smaller one can be considered as a reliable compact presentation of the larger. In this section, we compare our results with results obtained from aiNet. The results for each test data set are shown in Tables 1 to 4.

In general, if we compare the results in the columns, we can see that the lower compression rate, the smaller K-L divergence (reflected by the values of J_μ and J_σ), and hence the better performance. Values $|M|_\mu$ and $|M|_\sigma$ illustrate the statistics of the sizes of the output data sets. All the results are close to their desired values ($\frac{400}{C}$), with fluctuations in a small range ($\approx \pm 1$). These figures suggest that the IMSDA algorithm is capable of compressing a non-uniformly distributed data set under the control of a predefined compression rate.

Finally, Table 5 compares the best performance of the aiNet (with the effective compression rate < 1) and the worst of the IMSDA (with the compression

Table 1. IMSDA testing results on data set 1

Data set 1				
C	5	10	20	40
J_μ	-1.969428e-008f	1.988437e-007f	-1.221183e-006f	3.185051e-006f
J_σ	7.811606e-007f	1.798795e-006f	5.528782e-006f	1.903579e-005f
$|M|_\mu$	8.026000e+001f	4.058000e+001f	2.078000e+001f	1.098000e+001f
$|M|_\sigma$	9.216223e-001f	8.351952e-001f	7.899884e-001f	6.223720e-001f

Table 2. IMSDA testing results on data set 2

Data set 2				
C	5	10	20	40
J_μ	6.812991e-009f	1.432075e-007f	4.315232e-007f	-1.285456e-006f
J_σ	5.411515e-007f	1.352140e-006f	4.824157e-006f	1.657471e-005f
$|M|_\mu$	8.026000e+001f	4.108000e+001f	2.120000e+001f	1.146000e+001f
$|M|_\sigma$	1.321873e+000f	8.533248e-001f	8.571429e-001f	6.764252e-001f

Table 3. IMSDA testing results on data set 3

Data set 3				
C	5	10	20	40
J_μ	2.187724e-007f	3.284886e-007f	2.575537e-007f	3.515269e-006f
J_σ	1.092907e-006f	1.955222e-006f	5.166573e-006f	2.552882e-005f
$|M|_\mu$	7.996000e+001f	4.050000e+001f	2.072000e+001f	1.080000e+001f
$|M|_\sigma$	9.889182e-001f	7.889544e-001f	6.401530e-001f	6.700594e-001f

Table 4. IMSDA testing results on data set 4

Data set 4				
C	5	10	20	40
J_μ	3.862265e-008f	-5.032050e-008f	1.623946e-007f	1.492754e-006f
J_σ	5.628660e-007f	1.780854e-006f	3.291327e-006f	1.060585e-005f
$|M|_\mu$	8.002000e+001f	4.086000e+001f	2.064000e+001f	1.108000e+001f
$|M|_\sigma$	1.203566e+000f	7.561989e-001f	57.627919e-001f	6.337449e-001f

rate = 40) for each data set, in terms of the K-L divergence. Results for comparison from aiNet are taken from [5]. In the best cases of aiNet, the mean sizes of the output data set $|M|_\mu$ (484.74, 500.36, 445.72 and 454.04) have exceeded the original size 400. It means that in order to maintain a KDD, aiNet practically generates an inflation of the original data set, rather than compression. Whilst, in the worst cases of the IMSDA, the sizes of the output data set are all around 10. Even though, the K-L distances J_μ by aiNet are still significantly (at least

Table 5. Results comparison between the aiNet and the IMSDA

		J_μ	J_σ	$|M|_\mu$	$|M|_\sigma$
Data set 1	aiNet	-0.009244	0.003484	484.74	9.44
	IMSDA	0.000003185	0.000019036	10.98	0.62
Data set 2	aiNet	-0.002143	0.002816	500.36	11.84
	IMSDA	0.000001285	0.000016575	11.46	0.68
Data set 3	aiNet	-0.024088	0.003718	445.72	7.78
	IMSDA	0.000003515	0.000025529	10.80	0.67
Data set 4	aiNet	0.003771	0.002043	454.04	8.73
	IMSDA	0.000001493	0.000010606	11.08	0.63

hundreds of times) larger than those by the IMSDA. This suggests that the aiNet is less statistically reliable.

In order to illustrate the compression effect, we also randomly choose 5 graphs at compression rates 5, 10, and 20. They are shown in Fig. 2 to 5. We can see that in all cases and at all compression rates, the IMSDA covers the densest areas of the input data sets.

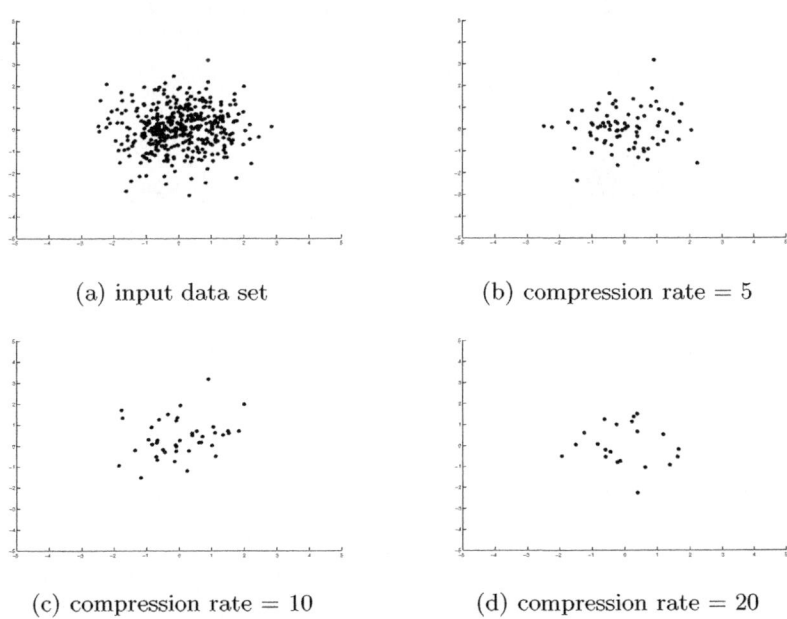

(a) input data set

(b) compression rate = 5

(c) compression rate = 10

(d) compression rate = 20

Fig. 2. IMSDA graphic results on data set 1

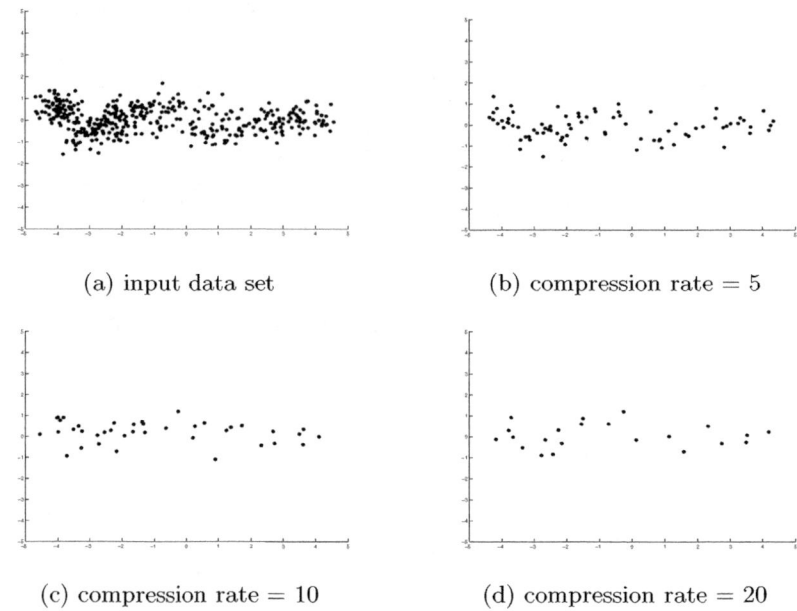

(a) input data set   (b) compression rate = 5

(c) compression rate = 10   (d) compression rate = 20

Fig. 3. IMSDA graphic results on data set 2

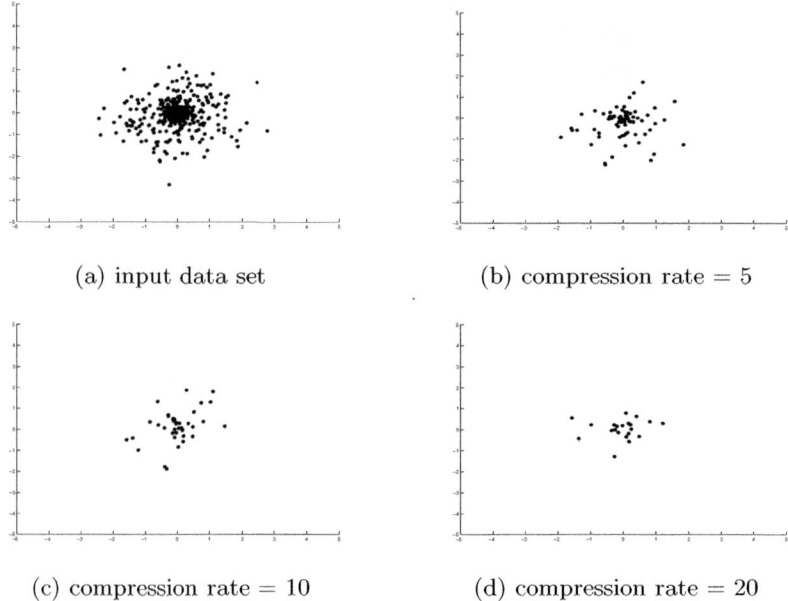

(a) input data set   (b) compression rate = 5

(c) compression rate = 10   (d) compression rate = 20

Fig. 4. IMSDA graphic results on data set 3

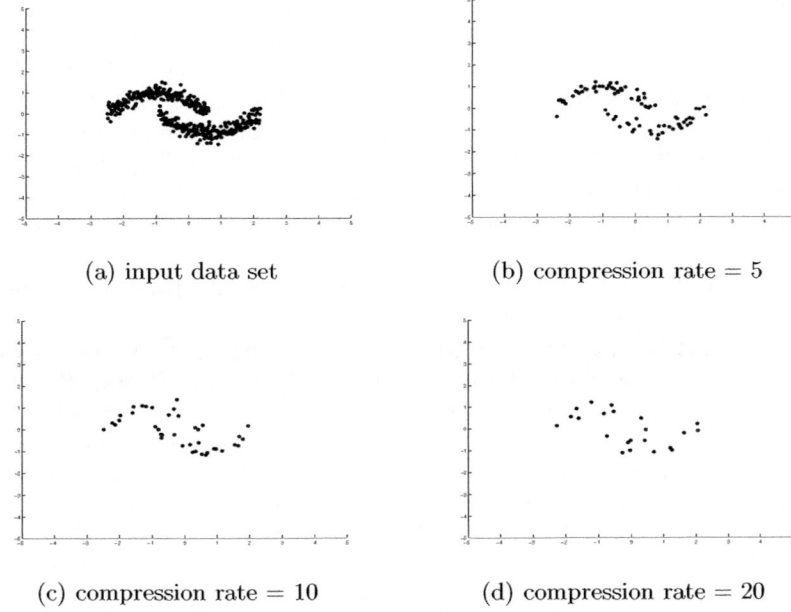

(a) input data set   (b) compression rate = 5

(c) compression rate = 10   (d) compression rate = 20

Fig. 5. IMSDA graphic results on data set 4

6   Conclusion and Future Work

The aim of the IMSDA algorithm is to optimally represent a large data set by its principle subset whilst the data KDD is maximally maintained and has been inspired by the lymphocyte-cytokine interaction in the immune system. The surviving lymphocytes are considered as the output data set, and the cytokine distribution generated by the lymphocytes is taken to represent the output data distribution. The cooperation and competition of the lymphocytes are the key to the IMSDA algorithm. According to the difference between the external stimuli and the internal relationship, the system self-organises its lymphocyte composition, namely the representation of the input data set.

The performance of the algorithm is evaluated by the K-L divergence method which compares the input and output data KDDs. Compared with the aiNet algorithm, the output data set created by the IMSDA algorithm represents the original input data set much more effectively. However, the comparison with the original aiNet was not an end but a start. There are derivatives of the aiNet, such as [9], which will be involved in our future evaluation.

References

1. Silverman, B.W.: Density Estimation for Statistics and Data Analysis. Chapman and Hall, Sydney (1986)
2. de Castro, L.N., von Zuben, F.: Data Mining: A Heuristic Approach. Idea Group Publishing, USA (2001)

3. Kullback, S.: Information Therory and Statistics. John wiley & Sons, West Sussex (1959)
4. Cutello, V., Nicosia, G., Pavone, M., Stracquadanio, G.: An information-theoretic approach for clonal selection algorithms. In: Hart, E., McEwan, C., Timmis, J., Hone, A. (eds.) ICARIS 2010. LNCS, vol. 6209, pp. 144–157. Springer, Heidelberg (2010)
5. Stibor, T., Timmis, J.: An investigation on the compression quality of aiNet. In: Proceedings of the IEEE Symposium on Foundations of Computational Intelligence, pp. 495–502 (2007)
6. Timmis, J.: Artificial immune systems: today and tomorrow. Natural Computing 6, 1–18 (2007)
7. Timmis, J., Hone, A., Stibor, T., Clark, E.: Theoretical advances in artificial immune systems. Theor. Comput. Sci. 403, 11–32 (2008)
8. Bezerra, G.B., Barra, T.V., de Castro, L.N., Von Zuben, F.J.: Adaptive radius immune algorithm for data clustering. In: Jacob, C., Pilat, M.L., Bentley, P.J., Timmis, J.I. (eds.) ICARIS 2005. LNCS, vol. 3627, pp. 290–303. Springer, Heidelberg (2005)
9. Violato, R.P.V., Azzolini, A.G., Von Zuben, F.J.: Antibodies with adaptive radius as prototypes of high-dimensional datasets. In: Hart, E., McEwan, C., Timmis, J., Hone, A. (eds.) ICARIS 2010. LNCS, vol. 6209, pp. 158–170. Springer, Heidelberg (2010)
10. Abbas, A., Lichtman, A., Pillai, S.: Cellular and Molecular Immunology, 6th edn. Saunders Elsevier (2007)
11. Hone, A., van den Berg, H.: Modelling a cytokine network. In: Proceedings of the IEEE Symposium on Foundations of Computational Intelligence, Special session: Foundations of Artificial Immune Systems, pp. 389–393 (2007)
12. Liu, Y., Timmis, J., Clarke, T.: A neuro-immune inspired robust real time visual tracking system. In: Bentley, P.J., Lee, D., Jung, S. (eds.) ICARIS 2008. LNCS, vol. 5132, pp. 188–199. Springer, Heidelberg (2008)
13. Neal, M.: Meta-stable memory in an artificial immune network. In: Timmis, J., Bentley, P.J., Hart, E. (eds.) ICARIS 2003. LNCS, vol. 2787, pp. 168–180. Springer, Heidelberg (2003)

Appendix A: IMSDA Psudocode

```
for n = 1 : N do                          /* Initialisation */
    for i = 1 : N do
    |   e(n) ← 1/N Σ_{i=1}^N K(|x(n) − x(i)|)
    end
    f(n) ← 0,   r(n) ← 0
    M_temp ← 0                /* number of non-zero values in R */
    D ← D_max                 /* D_max can be any large value */
end
```

Algorithm 1. IMSDA initialisation

```
for i = 1 : I do                          /* I is the max iteration criterion */
    for n = 1 : N do
        s(n) ← e(n) − f(n),   r_temp ← r(n)
        r(n) ← r(n) + P(s(n))
        if r(n) > 0 & r_temp = 0 then               /* generate an output point */
            M_temp ← M_temp + 1
            for t=1:N do
                f(t) ← f(t) + (C/N)K(|x(n) − x(t)|)        /* add influence onto F */
            end
        else
            if r(n) ≤ 0 & r_temp > 0 then            /* delete an output point */
                r(n) ← 0,   M_temp ← M_temp − 1
                for t=1:N do
                    f(t) ← f(t) − (C/N)K(|x(n) − x(t)|)   /* remove influence from F
                    */
                end
            end
        end
    end
    Y_temp ← ∅
    for k=1:N do
        if r(k) > 0 then                            /* population control */
            r(k) ← r(k) − 1/N
            if r(k) < 0 then
                r(k) ← 0,   M_temp ← M_temp − 1
                for t=1:N do
                    f(t) ← f(t) − (C/N)K(|x(k) − x(t)|)  /* remove influence from
                    F */
                end
            else
                Y_temp ← Y_temp ∩ x(k)
            end
        end
    end
    D_temp ← D_{K−L}(E, F)                          /* test K-L divergence */
    if D_temp < D then                       /* save if better than previous */
        D ← D_temp,   Y ← Y_temp,   M ← M_temp
        if D_temp < J then                          /* finished */
            return
        end
    end
end
```

Algorithm 2. IMSDA main loop

Inferring Systems of Ordinary Differential Equations via Grammar-Based Immune Programming

Heder S. Bernardino and Helio J.C. Barbosa

Laboratório Nacional de Computação Científica – LNCC,
Av. Getulio Vargas, 333, 25.651-075, Petrópolis-RJ, Brazil
{hedersb,hcbm}@lncc.br
http://www.lncc.br/~hedersb
http://www.lncc.br/~hcbm

Abstract. Grammar-based Immune Programming (GIP) is a method for evolving programs in an arbitrary language using an immunological inspiration. GIP is applied here to solve the relevant modeling problem of finding a system of differential equations –in analytical form– which better explains a given set of data obtained from a certain phenomenon. Computational experiments are performed to evaluate the approach, showing that GIP is an efficient technique for symbolic modeling.

1 Introduction

Metaheuristics in general and Genetic Programming (GP) [13] in particular have been applied with success to several complex real-world search problems. The GP paradigm has become very popular for the automatic generation of programs, such as a mathematical expression. Symbolic regression is a class of problems where one aims at deriving an analytical expression of a function that better fits a given data set. Although there is a large amount of works in the literature using GP, studies using immuno-inspired techniques for such problems are not very common.

An artificial immune system (AIS) proposal for symbolic regression can be found in [12], where a tree-based representation is used. The Immune Programming (IP) [17,15] technique was shown to outperform GP for some symbolic regression problems, including a model of disinfection of *Cryptosporidium parvum*. Another variant is the elitist Immune Programming (eIP) [6], in which the best candidate solution of the population and its hypermutated clone are always kept in the population. This technique was applied to circuit design optimization where it outperformed both the standard IP and Koza's GP [14]. Fault detection systems and symbolic regression problems were used to evaluate and compare the Clonal Selection Programming (CSP) algorithm [9,8], which uses a symbolic string of fixed length. It is important to notice that the majority of such works were published more recently.

Grammatical Evolution (GE) [21,20] is a GP variant which adopts a binary string to represent the candidate solutions, and a formal grammar to define

P. Liò, G. Nicosia, and T. Stibor (Eds.): ICARIS 2011, LNCS 6825, pp. 198–211, 2011.

the syntax of the language. GE's decoding process allows for the use of different search engines, such as genetic algorithms (GA) [20], particle swarm optimization (PSO) [19], differential evolution (DE) [18], and, more recently, AISs [4].

An immune approach using GE ideas can be found in [16] where an evolutionary operator mutates non-terminals according to a specified grammar. This technique was used to infer a kinetic model for the oxidative metabolism of 17β-estradiol (E_2). Grammar-based Immune Programming (GIP) [1,4,3] uses the clonal selection principle to evolve programs. Besides the search mechanism, GIP differs from standard GE with respect to the decoding process. GIP's decoding procedure creates a program (based on the grammar definition) and repairs it (via repair derivation rules) when necessary. GIP was applied to symbolic regression and integration, inference of an ordinary differential equation (ODE), and inference of iterated and discontinuous functions showing to be efficient when applied to these problems. In addition, the repair method was shown to improve the performance also when other search mechanisms were used, such as a GA [4].

The inference of a *system* of ODE's using GIP is studied in this paper. Also, instead of the traditional approach for generating numerical constants in GE used in references [1,4,3], a least-squares approach is incorporated to GIP, thus increasing GIP's efficiency.

The inference of a system of ODEs is presented in Section 2. The GIP approach is discussed in Section 3. Computational experiments, results, and analyses are presented in Section 4. Finally, Section 5 concludes the paper.

2 Inference of System of Ordinary Differential Equations

A set of ODEs is a common description of a physical, chemical, or biological system, involving the time-derivatives of state variables as a function of the current state [23]. The problem considered here consists in finding a symbolic form for $\mathbf{f}(x, \mathbf{y})$ such that the solution of the system composed by ne ODEs

$$\mathbf{y}' = \mathbf{f}(x, \mathbf{y}) = \begin{cases} y_1' = f_1(x, \mathbf{y}) \\ y_2' = f_2(x, \mathbf{y}) \\ \vdots \\ y_{ne}' = f_{ne}(x, \mathbf{y}) \end{cases}$$

matches the given data. In other words, it is to find the differential equation model which better explains the observed data $(x_k, \mathbf{y}_k)$, where $\mathbf{y}_k = \mathbf{y}(x_k)$, $k = 1, \ldots, m$, and m is the size of the available data set.

At least two ways to solve this problem by using symbolic regression techniques can be thought of. The first one consists in taking numerical derivatives from the given data obtaining a set of approximations $\bar{\mathbf{y}}_k' \approx \mathbf{y}'_k$ to which a symbolic regression technique can be applied. Another way is to numerically integrate the system (candidate solution) and compare its output with the observed data pairs $(x_k, \mathbf{y}_k)$.

Both alternative approaches were evaluated in [3] for the case of searching for a single ODE where the second approach was shown to be more accurate while the first one was able to evaluate a candidate solution with much less computational cost.

Here, at different stages, both numerical techniques will be used. Initially, derivatives (via three-point formulae) of the given data are taken. Then, each candidate solution is decoded in the form of a system of ODE's

$$y'_i = f_i(x, \mathbf{y}) \equiv \sum_{j=1}^{nb_i} a_{ij} F_{ij}(x, \mathbf{y}), \quad i \in \{1, \ldots, ne\},$$

where F_{ij} is the j-th basis function in the i-th equation, nb_i is the number of basis functions of the i-th equation, and a_{ij} is the coefficient of the j-th basis function in the i-th equation. To conclude the definition of the system, its numerical coefficients a_{ij} are computed by minimizing the sum of the (squared) discrepancy between the predicted and the numerically obtained derivative value at each data point.

Defining

$$A_i = \begin{pmatrix} F_{i1}(x_1, \mathbf{y}_1) & \ldots & F_{i\,nb_i}(x_1, \mathbf{y}_1) \\ F_{i1}(x_2, \mathbf{y}_2) & \ldots & F_{i\,nb_i}(x_2, \mathbf{y}_2) \\ \vdots & \ddots & \vdots \\ F_{i1}(x_m, \mathbf{y}_m) & \ldots & F_{i\,nb_i}(x_m, \mathbf{y}_m) \end{pmatrix}$$

and denoting transposition by T, one can calculate the vector $\mathbf{a}_i$ of coefficients a_{ij} of the i-th equation by solving, for each i,

$$\left(A_i^T A_i\right) \mathbf{a}_i = A_i^T \, \bar{\mathbf{y}}'_i.$$

This technique was previously used in a GP approach where it was applied either to all candidates [11], or only partially [22].

While derivatives are used to generate the coefficients of each candidate solution (with a reduced computational cost), integration (via 4-th order Runge-Kutta) is then performed in order to calculate its affinity (to be minimized) as the mean of the squared difference between the value obtained by numerical integration and that of the signal (observed data):

$$affinity = \frac{1}{m \times ne} \sum_{i=1}^{ne} \sum_{k=1}^{m} (y_{ki,exact} - y_{ki,approx})^2.$$

as this measure of candidate quality has shown better performance in [3].

3   Grammar-Based Immune Programming

The clonal selection algorithm CLONALG [7] evolves the antibodies inspired by the concept of clonal expansion and selection in which each cell is cloned, hyper-mutated, and those with higher antigenic affinity are selected. In CLONALG, the mutation rate is usually taken inversely proportional to the affinity of the antibody with respect to the antigen. Moreover, inspired by the bone marrow behavior, new candidate solutions could be randomly generated to improve the exploration capability of the algorithm.

The GIP technique uses a binary string to encode each candidate solution and CLONALG as the search engine. Algorithm 1 shows CLONALG's pseudocode (see [2] for more details). To keep the diversity of the population: (i) every

---

Algorithm 1. A CLONALG's pseudocode for optimization problems.

Data: β, ρ, $pRandom$, $populationSize$
Result: $bestSolution$
1 **begin**
2     $antibodies \longleftarrow$ initializePopulation($populationSize$);
3     $affinities \longleftarrow$ evaluate($antibodies$);
4   **while** *stopping criteria is not met* **do**
5        $nAffinities \longleftarrow$ normalize($affinities$);
6        $clones \longleftarrow$ clone($antibodies$, $affinities$, β);
7   hypermutate($clones$, $nFitness$, ρ);
8        $cA \longleftarrow$ evaluate($clones$);
9   select($antibodies$, $affinities$, $clones$, cA);
10   genNew($antibodies$, $affinities$, $pRandom$);
11     $bestSolution \longleftarrow$ getBest($antibodies$);
12 **end**

---

antibody in the population is selected to be cloned, (ii) the number of clones is the same for all candidate solutions, and (iii) each antibody is replaced if a better hypermutated clone has been generated.

In Algorithm 1, the procedure "evaluate" is responsible for transforming a binary string (candidate solution) into a system of ODEs and evaluating it with respect to the objective function in order to define its affinity value. The process to decode an antibody into a program (system of ODEs) is defined in Sections 3.1 and 3.2.

3.1 Grammatical Evolution

In Grammatical Evolution (GE) [21,20], which originally used a GA as the search engine, the genotype is mapped onto terminals by means of a pre-defined grammar. A formal grammar is defined as $G = \{N, \Sigma, R, S\}$, where N is a finite set of non-terminals, Σ is a finite set of terminals or symbols which can appear in the language (such as x, $+$, and cos), R is a finite set of rules, and $S \in N$ is the start symbol. Each rule (or production) from R is described in Backus-Naur Form (BNF) as

$$(\Sigma \cup N)^* N (\Sigma \cup N)^* ::= (\Sigma \cup N)^*, \tag{1}$$

where $\cup$ denotes set union and $*$ is a unary operation widely used for regular expressions in which if N is a set of symbols or characters, then N^* is the set of all strings composed by symbols in N. If the right-hand side of this expression is composed by more than one sequence, the choices are delimited by the symbol "$|$". A non-terminal can be expanded into one or more terminals and non-terminals likewise may self-reference to specify recursion. The context-free grammar used by standard GE has its rules in the form of $N ::= (\Sigma \cup N)^*$.

In GE, the genotype is a binary string representation of an integer array in which each value is encoded by 8 bits [20]. The integer value is used to select a rule from the set of the grammar's productions via the expression

$$rule = (int)mod(nr)$$

where int is the current integer from the integer array and nr is the number of rules for the current non-terminal.

Degeneracy of the genetic code can be observed, as it is not necessary to use all integer values from the array to create the phenotype. Moreover, it is important to notice that during the genotype-to-phenotype mapping process it may happen that after using all integers in the array a complete expression is still not available. In this case, the original strategy presented in [20] is to wrap the integer array and reuse its values (two or more times). However, it is possible that the genotype-to-phenotype mapping process generates an infinite loop. When this happens, it is suggested that the fitness of this candidate solution be set to the worst possible value. Instead we use the repair method [1,4] which generates only valid solutions from the genotype-to-phenotype mapping process. This process is detailed in Section 3.2.

3.2   The Repair Method

According to the CLONALG algorithm presented in Section 3, all antibodies generate hypermutated clones. As a result, a candidate solution which does not belong to the language will probably produce new invalid solutions (see [4]). Here we use a procedure in which an invalid solution phenotype can be repaired during the mapping procedure so as to always be recognized by the grammar. The information about how the repair should operate on an invalid candidate solution is incorporated to the user defined grammar which now is defined by a 5-tuple $G = \{N, \Sigma, R, R_r, S\}$, where N, Σ, R, and S are as previously defined, and R_r is a set of production rules to repair the generated program. Each R_f rule is defined as

$$(\Sigma \cup N)^* N (\Sigma \cup N)^* N (\Sigma \cup N)^* ::= (\Sigma \cup N)^* \Sigma (\Sigma \cup N)^*, \qquad (2)$$

This new set of rules must contain a backward step to create the program when there are no more integers available. Two constraints must be highlighted: (i) the new rule must have less non-terminals than the original one and (ii) given $w \in R_f$ then the inverse transformation of w is in R, or at least can be reached by this one. That is important since a repaired program also must be recognized by the original grammar.

The repair method is performed unstacking the integer values used in the mapping process. Thus, the first integer in the sequence defines which rule from R_r (R_{ij}) will be the repair rule. However, not all possibilities from R_r (R_{ij}) can be considered. The options will be those with a number of non-terminals not larger than the number of non-null children of the invalid sub-program. See [4] for more details.

4   Computational Experiments

Five problems from the literature were used to assess the performance of GIP when solving the problem of finding, in symbolic form, a system of ODEs that better explains a given set of observed data. In each case, the "observed" data $(x_k, \mathbf{y_k})$, $k \in \{1, \ldots, m\}$, were synthetically generated by the numerical integration of the (target) exact model. As mentioned, a 4-th order Runge-Kutta method is used in the evaluation of the candidate solutions, with step-size given by $h = \frac{b-a}{m-1}$.

The grammar used in the experiments is that presented in Section 3 where the production rules for each equation of the system are given by

$$
\begin{aligned}
< base > & ::= & (+ \; < base > < base >) & \quad (0) \\
& & | \; < expr > & \quad (1) \\
< expr > & ::= & (< op > < expr > < expr >) & \; (0) \\
& & | \; < var > & \quad (1) \\
< op > & ::= & + & \quad (0) \\
& & | \; - & \quad (1) \\
& & | \; * & \quad (2) \\
< var > & ::= & 1 & \quad (0) \\
& & | \; y_1 & \quad (1) \\
& & | \; y_2 & \quad (2) \\
& & | \; y_3 & \quad (3)
\end{aligned}
$$

These rules, which are able to generate the expression for a single ODE, are used to build a system of ne ODEs. Thus, each candidate solution is composed by a set of ne binary arrays. Also, R_f is defined as

$$
\begin{aligned}
(+ \; < base > < base >) & ::= \; < base > \; | \; 1 \; | \; y_1 \; | y_2 \; | \; y_3 \\
(< op > < expr > < expr >) & ::= \; < expr > \; | \; 1 \; | \; y_1 \; | y_2 \; | \; y_3 \\
< base > & ::= \quad 1 \; | \; y_1 \; | y_2 \; | \; y_3 \\
< expr > & ::= \quad 1 \; | \; y_1 \; | y_2 \; | \; y_3
\end{aligned}
$$

We have defined this grammar so that it contains exactly the same terminals available in the techniques in the references [5,11,22] which were used for comparison.

GIP's search mechanism is a clonal selection algorithm (CLONALG) with Gray encoding using 8 bits per integer (as suggested by the literature), population size=50, length of each integer array=100, number of clones=1, $\rho = 10$, and percentage of new randomly generated antibodies=5%.

For all problems the stop condition is 100,000 affinity evaluations which is equal to the minimum number of fitness function evaluations considered by all references in all problems. For each experiment 20 independent runs were performed.

We not only present the fitting error (computed in the range $[x_1, x_m]$) but also the prediction error, which is calculated along the extended range $E = [x_m, x_m + 0.1\,(x_m - x_1)]$ at 11 points equally spaced in E. The ratio of prediction to fitting error is an indication of overfitting, and a model with better generalization is usually preferred.

For all experiments we provide: (a) the response of the exact system of ODEs and that of the best approximation found (smallest prediction error); and (b) tables presenting the best, median, average, standard deviation (sd), and worst values (for both fitting and prediction errors) of the solutions found by this approach and the references, as well as the number of affinity/fitness evaluations (ofe) used. In the case of multiple initial conditions, only one curve is shown.

JScheme (http://jscheme.sourceforge.net/jscheme/main.html) and Michael Thomas Flanagan's Java Scientific Library (http://www.ee.ucl.ac.uk/~mflanaga/java) have been used in our implementation. JScheme is an implementation with a very simple interface of the Scheme language while the second library has a large collection of numerical methods, including the Runge-Kutta method and the matrix operations performed here.

4.1   Experiment 1: Artificial Model

The objective of the first numerical experiment, from [22], is to recover the system of ODEs

$$\begin{cases} y_1' = -0.9y_2 + y_3 \\ y_2' = 0.2y_1y_2 \\ y_3' = y_3 - 0.5y_1 \end{cases}$$

from three responses with 101 values for $x \in [0,5]$ each corresponding to initial conditions given by $\mathbf{y}(0) = (0.2, 0.1, 0.3)$, $(0.1, 0.1, 0.1)$, and $(0.2, 0.2, 0.2)$, respectively. Results are given in Figure 1 where it is hard to detect differences between the response curves from the exact and approximated models. In (b), where we compare the best solutions found by the proposed approach and that obtained in [22], it can be seen that GIP performs much better than the reference and uses less affinity evaluations.

4.2   Experiment 2: Chemical Reaction Model

The objective here is to infer a model for the reaction between formaldehyde (y_1) and carbamide in aqueous solution which produces methylol urea (y_2) which

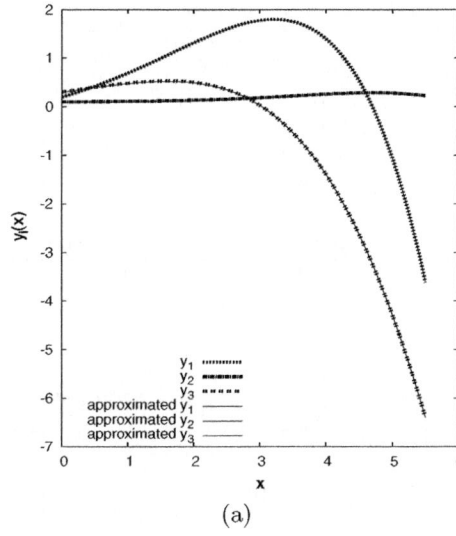

(a)

	Fitting errors	
	GIP	GP [22]
Best	1.33×10^{-34}	6.09×10^{-5}
Median	6.79×10^{-34}	–
Average	9.50×10^{-34}	–
sd	9.04×10^{-34}	–
Worst	4.19×10^{-33}	–
ofe	100,000	300,000
	Prediction errors	
Best	0.00	–
Median	9.61×10^{-33}	–
Average	1.32×10^{-32}	–
sd	1.47×10^{-32}	–
Worst	5.92×10^{-32}	–

(b)

Fig. 1. Experiment 1: The curves of the observed data and the numerical integration of the best approximation (with respect to the prediction error) are presented in (a) while (b) shows the errors of the results found. The first initial condition was used.

in turn continues to react with carbamide and form methylene urea (y_3). The reaction equations are [5]

$$HCHO + (NH_2)_2\, CO \rightarrow H_2N \cdot CO \cdot NH \cdot CH_2OH$$
$$H_2N \cdot CO \cdot NH \cdot CH_2OH + (NH_2)_2\, CO \rightarrow (NH_2CONH)_2\, CH_2$$

By consecutive reactions, the concentrations of the three components in the system satisfy a system of ODEs which can be written as

$$\begin{cases} y_1' = -1.4y_1 \\ y_2' = 1.4y_1 - 4.2y_2 \\ y_3' = 4.2y_2 \end{cases}$$

The initial condition used to generate the "observed" data is $\mathbf{y}(0) = (0.1, 0, 0)$, and 101 pairs of data in $x \in [0,1]$ were generated. Figure 2 shows in (a) the curves of the observed data and the approximate solution. Comparing both sets of curves, as in experiment 1, we can notice that the model inferred by GIP is a good approximation of the exact one. In fact, in (b) it can be seen that GIP's solutions prediction error was zero in all runs. When one considers the results from references [5] and [11], one can verify that GIP produces much more accurate solutions. It is important to notice that this superiority happens for both fitting and prediction errors.

4.3   Experiment 3: Fertility Equation

We consider now the fertility equation from the field of biology [10]. For two alleles B_1 and B_2, there are three possible genotypes, that is, B_1B_1, B_1B_2,

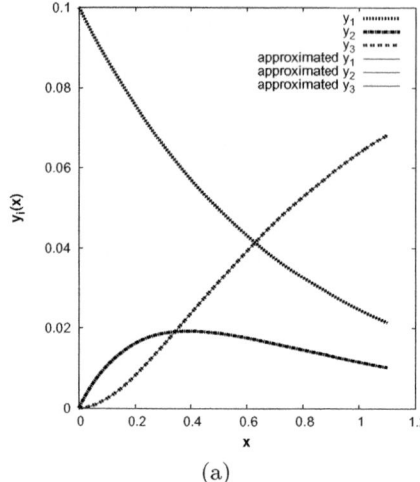

	Fitting errors		
	GIP	GP [5]	GP [11]
Best	$2.07{\times}10^{-38}$	$1.18{\times}10^{-10}$	$1.32{\times}10^{-13}$
Median	$1.12{\times}10^{-37}$	–	–
Average	$1.18{\times}10^{-37}$	–	–
sd	$5.91{\times}10^{-37}$	–	–
Worst	$2.60{\times}10^{-38}$	–	–
ofe	100,000	–	100,000
	Prediction errors		
Best	0.00	$8.03{\times}10^{-10}$	–
Median	0.00	–	–
Average	0.00	–	–
sd	0.00	–	–
Worst	0.00	–	–

(a)   (b)

Fig. 2. Experiment 2: The curves of the observed data and the numerical integration of the best approximation (with respect to the prediction error) are presented in (a) while (b) shows the errors of the results found

and B_2B_2. Let y_1, y_2, and y_3 be the frequencies of B_1B_1, B_1B_2, and B_2B_2, respectively. Then a typical model can be described as

$$\begin{cases} y_1' = 2y_1^2 + 2.5y_1y_2 + 0.375y_2^2 - y_1 P\left(y_1, y_2, y_3\right) \\ y_2' = 0.75y_2^2 + 2.5y_1y_2 + 2.5y_2y_3 + 3y_1y_3 - y_2 P\left(y_1, y_2, y_3\right) \\ y_3' = 1.5y_3^2 + 2.5y_2y_3 + 0.375y_2^2 - y_3 P\left(y_1, y_2, y_3\right) \end{cases}$$
$$P\left(y_1, y_2, y_3\right) = 2y_1^2 + 5y_1y_2 + 1.5y_2^2 + 3y_1y_3 + 5y_2y_3 + 1.5y_3^2$$

Three sequences with 41 values of $x \in [0, 10]$ were generated, and the initial conditions were $\mathbf{y}(0) = (0.5, 0.5, 0)$, $(0.5, 0, 0.5)$, and $(0, 0.5, 0.5)$, respectively. The errors observed in the solutions of this experiment can be found in Figure 3(b) where one can see that, as with the first two experiments, GIP performs better than the techniques from reference [22]. It is important to notice that GIP used one order of magnitude less affinity evaluations (100,000 against 2,700,000) than that reference. Figure 3(a) presents the curves of the observed data and the response of the best solution found by GIP with respect to prediction error. A very small difference between predicted and observed values can be detected.

4.4   Experiment 4: Three-Species Lotka-Volterra Model

The objective here is to infer the Lotka-Volterra model which describes interactions between two or more species of predators and preys. An ecosystem with one predator and two preys can be described by the system of ODEs

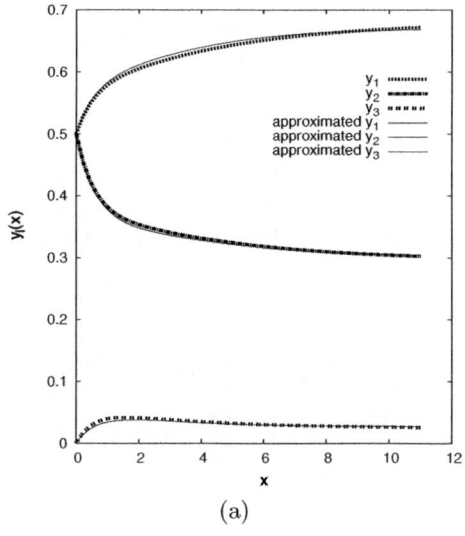

	Fitting errors	
	GIP	GP [22]
Best	1.30×10^{-7}	2.94×10^{-5}
Median	7.43×10^{-7}	–
Average	8.44×10^{-7}	6.22×10^{-5}
sd	3.97×10^{-7}	
Worst	1.51×10^{-6}	–
ofe	100,000	2,700,000
	Prediction errors	
Best	2.25×10^{-8}	–
Median	4.83×10^{-8}	–
Average	5.64×10^{-8}	–
sd	2.97×10^{-8}	–
Worst	1.23×10^{-7}	–

(a)   (b)

Fig. 3. Experiment 3: The curves of the observed data and the numerical integration of the best approximation (with respect to the prediction error) are presented in (a) while (b) shows the errors of the results found. The first initial condition was used.

$$\begin{cases} y_1' = (1 - y_1 - y_2 - 10y_3)\, y_1 \\ y_2' = (0.992 - 1.5y_1 - y_2 - y_3)\, y_2 \\ y_3' = (-1.2 - 5y_1 + 0.5y_2)\, y_3 \end{cases}$$

The initial condition used to generate 101 pairs of data in $x \in [0, 1]$ is $\mathbf{y}(0) = (0.7, 0.2, 0.1)$. Figure 4 presents comparisons for this experiment, where one can notice in (a) that the curves of exact model and the curves of the approximated solution are similar. In (b), comparing the best solutions found, it can be seen that GIP performs much better than reference [11].

4.5   Experiment 5: Identifying a Gene Regulatory Network

In bio-informatics gene regulatory networks have been modeled as S-systems and, using observed time-series data, their numerical coefficients can be identified. The causality model considered here can be approximated by [24]

$$\begin{cases} y_1' = 15y_3y_5^{-0.1} - 10y_1^2 \\ y_2' = 10y_1^2 - 10y_2^2 \\ y_3' = 10y_2^{-0.1} - 10y_2^{-0.1}y_3^2 \\ y_4' = 8y_1^2y_5^{-1} - 10y_4^2 \\ y_5' = 10y_4^2 - 10y_5^2 \end{cases}$$

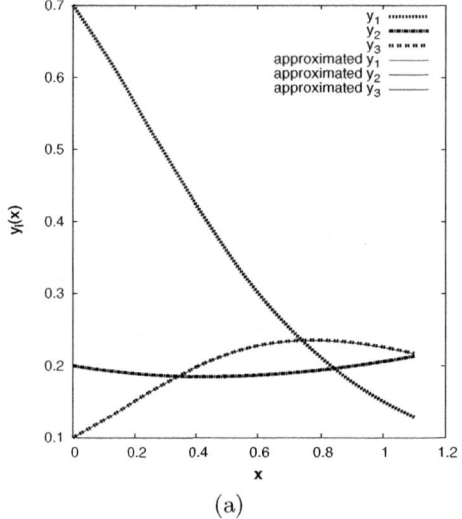

	Fitting errors	
	GIP	**GP [11]**
Best	5.58×10^{-15}	4.78×10^{-11}
Median	3.59×10^{-13}	–
Average	9.02×10^{-13}	–
sd	1.38×10^{-12}	–
Worst	5.45×10^{-12}	–
ofe	100,000	100,000
	Prediction errors	
Best	5.05×10^{-13}	–
Median	1.11×10^{-11}	–
Average	1.53×10^{-11}	–
sd	1.82×10^{-11}	–
Worst	7.34×10^{-11}	–

(a)   (b)

Fig. 4. Experiment 4: The curves of the observed data and the numerical integration of the best approximation (with respect to the prediction error) are presented in (a) while (b) shows the errors of the results found.

It was necessary to modify the grammar for this problem to make this experiment similar to that from reference [11]. The new production rules (R) are

$$< base > \; ::= \qquad\qquad (+ \; < base > \; < base >) \; | \; < expr >$$
$$< expr > \; ::= \qquad\qquad (< op > \; < expr > \; < expr >) \; | \; < var >$$
$$< op > \; ::= \qquad\qquad\qquad + \; | \; - \; | \; *$$
$$< var > \; ::= \qquad y_1 \; | \; y_2 \; | \; y_3 \; | \; y_4 \; | \; y_5 \; | \; y_1^{-1} \; | \; y_2^{-1} \; | \; y_3^{-1} \; | \; y_4^{-1} \; | \; y_5^{-1}$$
$$| \; y_1^{0.1} \; | \; y_2^{0.1} \; | \; y_3^{0.1} \; | \; y_4^{0.1} \; | \; y_5^{0.1} \; | \; y_1^{-0.1} \; | \; y_2^{-0.1} \; | \; y_3^{-0.1} \; | \; y_4^{-0.1} \; | \; y_5^{-0.1}$$

and the rules for repair (R_f) are

$$(+ \; < base > \; < base >) ::= \qquad < base > \; y_1 \; | \; y_2 \; | \; y_3 \; | \; y_4 \; | \; y_5$$
$$| \; y_1^{-1} \; | \; y_2^{-1} \; | \; y_3^{-1} \; | \; y_4^{-1} \; | \; y_5^{-1}$$
$$| \; y_1^{0.1} \; | \; y_2^{0.1} \; | \; y_3^{0.1} \; | \; y_4^{0.1} \; | \; y_5^{0.1}$$
$$| \; y_1^{-0.1} \; | \; y_2^{-0.1} \; | \; y_3^{-0.1} \; | \; y_4^{-0.1} \; | \; y_5^{-0.1}$$
$$(< op > \; < expr > \; < expr >) ::= \qquad < expr > \; y_1 \; | \; y_2 \; | \; y_3 \; | \; y_4 \; | \; y_5$$
$$| \; y_1^{-1} \; | \; y_2^{-1} \; | \; y_3^{-1} \; | \; y_4^{-1} \; | \; y_5^{-1}$$
$$| \; y_1^{0.1} \; | \; y_2^{0.1} \; | \; y_3^{0.1} \; | \; y_4^{0.1} \; | \; y_5^{0.1}$$
$$| \; y_1^{-0.1} \; | \; y_2^{-0.1} \; | \; y_3^{-0.1} \; | \; y_4^{-0.1} \; | \; y_5^{-0.1}$$

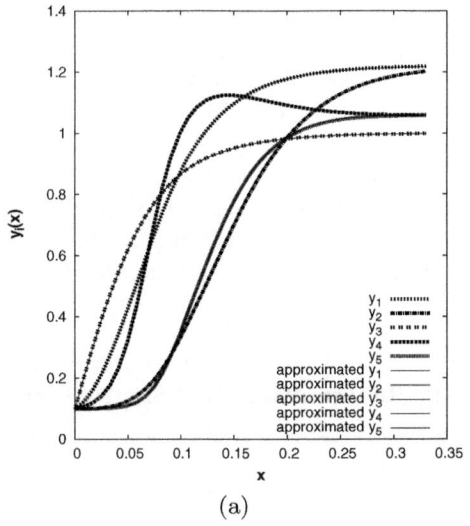

	Fitting errors	
	GIP	GP [11]
Best	1.25×10^{-7}	–
Median	4.80×10^{-7}	–
Average	5.63×10^{-7}	4.53×10^{-6}
sd	3.37×10^{-7}	–
Worst	1.54×10^{-6}	–
ofe	100,000	300,000
	Prediction errors	
Best	9.61×10^{-10}	–
Median	5.42×10^{-9}	–
Average	6.50×10^{-9}	–
sd	3.30×10^{-9}	–
Worst	1.22×10^{-8}	–

(a)   (b)

Fig. 5. Experiment 5: the curves of the observed data and the numerical integration of the best approximation with respect to the prediction error are presented in (a) while (b) shows the errors of the results found.

$$< base >::= \quad y_1 \mid y_2 \mid y_3 \mid y_4 \mid y_5$$
$$\mid y_1^{-1} \mid y_2^{-1} \mid y_3^{-1} \mid y_4^{-1} \mid y_5^{-1}$$
$$\mid y_1^{0.1} \mid y_2^{0.1} \mid y_3^{0.1} \mid y_4^{0.1} \mid y_5^{0.1}$$
$$\mid y_1^{-0.1} \mid y_2^{-0.1} \mid y_3^{-0.1} \mid y_4^{-0.1} \mid y_5^{-0.1}$$
$$< expr >::= \quad y_1 \mid y_2 \mid y_3 \mid y_4 \mid y_5$$
$$\mid y_1^{-1} \mid y_2^{-1} \mid y_3^{-1} \mid y_4^{-1} \mid y_5^{-1}$$
$$\mid y_1^{0.1} \mid y_2^{0.1} \mid y_3^{0.1} \mid y_4^{0.1} \mid y_5^{0.1}$$
$$\mid y_1^{-0.1} \mid y_2^{-0.1} \mid y_3^{-0.1} \mid y_4^{-0.1} \mid y_5^{-0.1}$$

One can verify that the modifications in the production rules lead to the inclusion of the terminals used in [11]. As a result, the definition of the grammar must also be modified, including all terminals considered by the production rules presented above.

Three sequences with 31 values of $x \in [0, 0.3]$ were used, and the initial conditions were $\mathbf{y}(0) = (0.1, 0.1, 0.1, 0.1, 0.1)$, $(0.5, 0.5, 0.5, 0.5, 0.5)$, and $(1.5, 1.5, 1.5, 1.5, 1.5)$, respectively. The results of this experiment are given in Figure 5. Comparing both sets of curves in (a), as in the other experiments, one can notice that the model inferred by GIP is an accurate approximation of the exact one. Also, from (b), GIP produces much better solutions than the GP in reference [11].

5   Concluding Remarks and Future Works

We have presented the application of GIP to the problem of inferring models in the form of a system of ordinary differential equations. Computational experiments demonstrated that GIP was able to produce much better solutions than those from other techniques in the literature. Fitting as well as prediction error were used to verify the quality of the generated solutions. In fact, GIP outperforms the other techniques even using a smaller or equal number of affinity evaluations.

We believe that (i) investigating other ways to determine the numerical constants, (ii) considering noisy data, (iii) guiding the search by minimizing not only the fitting error but also the complexity of the solutions, and (iv) to apply the technique to more complex models are important research avenues for future work.

Acknowledgments. The authors thank the reviewers for their comments and LNCC, CNPq (308317/2009-2) and FAPERJ (grants 26/102.825/2008 and E-26/100.308/2010) for their support.

References

1. Bernardino, H.S., Barbosa, H.J.C.: Grammar-based immune programming for symbolic regression. In: Andrews, P.S., Timmis, J., Owens, N.D.L., Aickelin, U., Hart, E., Hone, A., Tyrrell, A.M. (eds.) ICARIS 2009. LNCS, vol. 5666, pp. 274–287. Springer, Heidelberg (2009)
2. Bernardino, H.S., Barbosa, H.J.C.: Artificial Immune Systems for Optimization. In: Chiong, R. (ed.) Nature-Inspired Algorithms for Optimisation. vol. 193, pp. 389–411. Springer, Heidelberg (2009)
3. Bernardino, H.S., Barbosa, H.J.C.: Comparing two ways of inferring a differential equation model via grammar-based immune programming. In: Proc. of the Iberian-Latin-American Congress on Computational Methods in Engineering (2010)
4. Bernardino, H.S., Barbosa, H.J.C.: Grammar-based immune programming. Natural Computing 10, 209–241 (2011)
5. Cao, H., Kang, L., Chen, Y.: Evolutionary modelling of systems of ordinary differential equations with genetic programming. Genetic Programming and Evolvable Machines (1), 309–337 (2000)
6. Ciccazzo, A., Conca, P., Nicosia, G., Stracquadanio, G.: An advanced clonal selection algorithm with ad-hoc network-based hypermutation operators for synthesis of topology and sizing of analog electrical circuits. In: Bentley, P.J., Lee, D., Jung, S. (eds.) ICARIS 2008. LNCS, vol. 5132, pp. 60–70. Springer, Heidelberg (2008)
7. de Castro, L.N., von Zuben, F.J.: Learning and optimization using the clonal selection principle. IEEE Trans. Evo. Comp. 6(3), 239–251 (2002)
8. Gan, Z., Chow, T.W., Chau, W.: Clone selection programming and its application to symbolic regression. Expert Systems with Appl. 36(2), 3996–4005 (2009)
9. Gan, Z., Zhao, M.-B., Chow, T.W.: Induction machine fault detection using clone selection programming. Expert Systems with Appl. 36(4), 8000–8012 (2009)
10. Hofbauer, J., Sigmund, K.: The Theory of Evolution and Dynamical Systems. Cambridge University Press, Cambridge (1988)
11. Iba, H.: Inference of differential equation models by genetic programming. Information Sciences 178(23), 4453–4468 (2008)
12. Johnson, C.G.: Artificial immune system programming for symbolic regression. In: Ryan, C., Soule, T., Keijzer, M., Tsang, E.P.K., Poli, R., Costa, E. (eds.) EuroGP 2003. LNCS, vol. 2610, pp. 345–353. Springer, Heidelberg (2003)

13. Koza, J.R.: Genetic Programming: On the Programming of Computers by Means of Natural Selection (Complex Adaptive Systems). MIT Press, Cambridge (1992)
14. Koza, J.R., Bennett III, F.H., Andre, D., Keane, M.A.: Synthesis of topology and sizing of analog electrical circuits by means of genetic programming. Computer Methods in Applied Mechanics and Engineering 186(2-4), 459–482 (2000)
15. Lau, A., Musilek, P.: Immune programming models of cryptosporidium parvum inactivation by ozone and chlorine dioxide. Information Sciences 179(10), 1469–1482 (2009)
16. McKinney, B., Tian, D.: Grammatical immune system evolution for reverse engineering nonlinear dynamic bayesian models. Cancer Informatics 6, 433–447 (2008)
17. Musilek, P., Lau, A., Reformat, M., Wyard-Scott, L.: Immune programming. Information Sciences 176(8), 972–1002 (2006)
18. O'Neill, M., Brabazon, A.: Grammatical differential evolution. In: Proceedings of the 2006 International Conference on Artificial Intelligence - ICAI 2006, pp. 231–236. CSREA Press, Las Vegas (2006)
19. O'Neill, M., Brabazon, A., Adley, C.: The automatic generation of programs for classification problems with grammatical swarm. In: Rauterberg, M. (ed.) ICEC 2004. LNCS, vol. 3166, pp. 57–67. Springer, Heidelberg (2004)
20. O'Neill, M., Ryan, C.: Grammatical evolution. IEEE Transactions on Evolutionary Computation 5(4), 349–358 (2001)
21. Ryan, C., Collins, J., Neill, M.O.: Grammatical evolution: Evolving programs for an arbitrary language. In: Banzhaf, W., Poli, R., Schoenauer, M., Fogarty, T.C. (eds.) EuroGP 1998. LNCS, vol. 1391, pp. 83–95. Springer, Heidelberg (1998)
22. Sakamoto, E., Iba, H.: Inferring a system of differential equations for a gene regulatory network by using genetic programming. In: Proceedings of the Congress on Evolutionary Computation, pp. 720–726 (2001)
23. Schmidt, M.D., Lipson, H.: Data-mining dynamical systems: Automated symbolic system identification for exploratory analysis. In: Proc. of the Biennial ASME Conf. on Engineering Systems Design and Analysis, Haifa, Israel (2008)
24. Tominaga, D., Koga, N., Okamoto, M.: Efficient numerical optimization algorithm based on genetic algorithm for inverse problem. In: Proceedings of the Genetic and Evolutionary Computation Conference, pp. 251–258 (2000)

Applying Antigen-Receptor Degeneracy Behavior for Misbehavior Response Selection in Wireless Sensor Networks

Sven Schaust and Helena Szczerbicka

Simulation and Modeling Group, Faculty of Electrical Engineering and Computer
Science, Leibniz University of Hannover, Welfengarten 1, 30167 Hannover, Germany
{svs,hsz}@sim.uni-hannover.de

Abstract. We present a first version of an algorithm producing autonomously responses in wireless sensor networks in order to mitigate
detected malfunction and misbehavior. We were inspired by the low level
mechanisms for response conformation, the degenerate behavior of receptors, of T-cells in the human immune system. The proposed algorithm
uses a co-stimulatory feedback in order to adapt to changing conditions,
thus enabling the system to choose a different response when appropriate. We evaluate the algorithm on a simulation model in OMNet++ and
demonstrate its applicability for wireless sensor networks.

1 Introduction

Wireless Sensor Networks can be subject to many different attacks and intrusions, whereas the motivation for such an attack can range from the desire to
access the network's services to the intention to limit its functionality. Faults,
as the result of a software or hardware failure can be equally severe. The intention of any intrusion detection approach is to detect any of these problems.
Unfortunately, none of the approaches for wireless sensor networks considers an
automatic response mechanism. Typically the approaches assume a human operator intervention, if possible at all. Upon the detection an alert is raised, which
enables a human operator to check the circumstances which caused the alarm.
If indeed an attack is the cause for the misbehavior of a device, the operator can
try to mitigate the effects by selecting an appropriate response from an available
response selection. The selection is typically very specific and highly dependent
on the communication capabilities of the network.

In this article we consider the problem of enabling a decentralized system to
enact autonomously a response against malfunction and misbehavior. The advantage of such an automatic response, enacted without a centralized controller,
is the faster reaction time and thus a smaller impact of the attack on the network.
An approach to provide automatic responses should not only be straightforward
to mitigate the problem, but also be adaptive in order to provide a sufficient
success against unknown malfunctions. Thus a feasible approach should produce
a response decision considering the particular network state. The algorithm we

P. Liò, G. Nicosia, and T. Stibor (Eds.): ICARIS 2011, LNCS 6825, pp. 212–225, 2011.
© Springer-Verlag Berlin Heidelberg 2011

present here enables a single device to react against malfunctions or misbehavior encountered at a neighbor node. We developed this algorithm in accordance with the general framework for artificial immune system algorithms, as introduced by de Castro and Timmis [1], and based its main ideas on the biological processes and their functionality of parts of the cognitive immune system as described by Cohen [2]. As stated before one concern of every response approach is to allow adaptivity towards unknown misbehavior and at the same time allow adaptivity in the reaction considering the network state. To achieve these goals we were inspired by the behavior and the properties of immune agents being involved in the recognition process of a pathogen. The low level mechanism *degeneracy* enables an immune cell not only to recognize a single antigen but many different ones, and at the same time allows to enforce different reactions towards a single antigen.

2   Wireless Ad Hoc and Sensor Networks

Wireless ad hoc and sensor networks are a network class which uses wireless radio for communication. Such networks do not rely on a centralized or fixed infrastructure, instead, the participating devices (*nodes*) use decentralized communication techniques to form a communication topology. All nodes can act as relay stations, enabling data transport from a far away source node to a destination node via intermediate nodes.

Due to the decentralized organization, the unsupervised deployment, as well as the size and material of the device cases, nodes can be subject to different kinds of malfunction or misbehavior. It is therefore necessary to provide such a network with a detection and response mechanism which supports and upholds the radio communication on a sufficient level.

Considering the severe hardware limitations and the intended deployment areas of wireless sensor networks, a suitable detection and response system has not only to be energy aware and computationally friendly but also to act autonomously. Drozda et al. formulated in [5] the basic requirements for such an approach as follows:

1. providing a distributed self-learning and self-tuning mechanism, which minimize the need of human intervention,
2. providing automatic reactions, allowing to eliminate negative effects of an observed malfunction within the network.

3   Problem Formulation

We study the problem of selecting a suitable response for a detected misbehavior, based on the current information available at a network device. Each node is capable of gathering information about its direct neighbors, based on either promiscuous surveillance of the radio communication or due to co-stimulatory data exchange within a two-hop neighborhood. We assume that a functional detection system is present and that the system has a low false positive rate. The algorithm to decide upon which response might be suitable has to be adaptive to changing network conditions, such as changes in data traffic and connectivity. As many different responses might be suitable for the detected misbehavior, the approach needs to determine what a feasible choice might be. Additionally, a single response might be applicable to many different misbehaviors allowing a node to enact the same response for different forms of misbehavior. Therefore a simple one-to-one mapping between a response and a cause seems to be not suitable. On the contrary, we believe that the system needs to allow an adaptive many-to-many mapping in order to allow the system to emerge a suitable selection depending on the current network conditions.

3.1   Cognitive Immune System

The described problem of getting a specific response, based on non-specific information and actions, is also present in parts of the human immune system. The functionality of the immune system can be described as a cognitive system which allows for maintenance and repair of the body [2]. As a cognitive system, the immune system is able to distinguish and bind to different pathogens. Each pathogen is represented by an antigen which is identified and represented by so called antigen-presenting-cells (APC), for example dendritic cells and macrophages. APCs are members of the innate immune system and provide special binding sites (major histocompatibility complex, MHC-II) which can be recognized by the receptors of lymphocytes, in our case T-cells. T-cells are members of the adaptive immune system, and able to learn and memorize previously unknown pathogens. The recognition and binding of receptors is performed in a two step approach. Each lymphocyte receptor consists of two areas: a combining site to recognize a specific APC and a reaction site, which is in charge of triggering a response. Within the immune system, the binding of receptors to APCs is based on several physical and chemical binding forces, which depend on the protein structures of the involved receptors and MHC-II complexes. The main advantage of these bindings is their reversibility. A binding is not longlasting, as otherwise a cell would become useless (and therefore die).

One important part of the interaction between T-cells and APCs is the degenerate behavior of its binding structures. Each receptor is able to bind not only to one specific protein structure, but to many different ones. As Cohen reports in [6], the degenerate nature of antigen-receptors was tested experimentally, and that two different concepts for immune receptor recognition were found:

- Poly-clonality: A single antigen epitope is able to activate different lymphocyte clones.
- Poly-recognition: A single lymphocyte clone is able to recognize different antigen epitopes.

While the first concept allows the recognition of an antigen by many different lymphocyte clones, and hence many different T-cells, the second one enables each single lymphocyte to trigger a conformation to more than one antigen epitope.

We took the described interactions between the innate and the adaptive system as a good starting point for developing an algorithm that exploits the poly-recognition property.

Degeneracy and its applicability to AIS algorithms has been investigated by Andrews et al. [7] in 2006. They originally formulated the advantage of using degeneracy in biologically inspired computational systems in accordance to the conceptual framework by de Castro et al [1]. In 2007 Mendao et al. [8] proposed an extended clonal selection algorithm for classification problems based on the degenerate behavior of B-cells, with the emphasis to classify G-Protein coupled receptors.

3.2 Pathogen Recognition Model

Our simplified model of the immune system interaction [9] between antigens, APCs and T-cells is as follows: Consider a pathogen entering the human body. Cells of the innate immune system recognize the pathogen by its antigens and which become represented by an APC. As we talk about a biological system, we do not have just one instance but many thousands of each. Depending on the chemokine concentration due to the presence of antigens and APCs, T-cell receptors are able to bind to the MHC-II complex of an APC. Thus an activation, and based upon this a conformation can take place. The conformation is achieved by the binding strength (affinity) between the APC and the T-cell. Each T-cell has several possible responses which can be triggered depending on this conformation.

4 Towards an Active Response Selection Mechanism

De Castro and Timmis introduced in 2002 [1] a general framework for developing AIS algorithms. Based on this framework, we formulated our computational concept of a response selection mechanism, which we call *Active Response Selection Mechanism*. The first step within this framework targets the domain of the problem. A suitable mapping between the immunological components and the components of the engineering solution has to be found. The engineering domain of our problem consists of network characteristics (called features from here on), which are used to identify malfunction and misbehavior due to its effects on the network traffic and data delivery. Each feature is a calculated real-value based on measurements within a time window of size t. Based on prior research by Drozda et al. [10], the following features will be used in our system:

1. *Forwarding Index*: Number of data packets received by a node and then forwarded to the next hop of a route.
2. *Process Delay*: Delay of a received data packet, before being forwarded at a node.
3. *Data Rate Index*: Number of data packets being forwarded by a node.
4. *Routing Activity Index RREQ*: Number of RREQ packets, received by a node and normalized for the time window size.

5. *Routing activity Index RREP*: Number of RREP packets, received by a node and normalized for the time window size.
6. *Forwarding Manipulation Index*: Number of data packets received and furthermore manipulated by the receiver before being forwarded.
7. *Injection Delay Index*: avg. Delay between data packets sent by a neighbor node.

For each time window, a feature vector is composed including all available feature measures. On the immunological side, we have antigens and receptors which specify the systems components to identify and detect a pathogen. The mapping of antigen and receptors on feature vectors is straightforward. The response confirmations of the immune system and their binding behavior have to be represented by metrics which can be applied to the feature vectors. We considered two distance metrics and one similarity metric for this task in order to evaluate the appropriateness of each metric.

Consider two real-valued vectors A and B of length n, where A_i and B_i denote the value at position i. We considered the commonly known Euclidean distance for n dimensional vectors as well as the Manhattan distance which are defined as follows:

Euclidean distance:
$$\sqrt{\sum (A_i - B_i)^2} \tag{1}$$

Manhattan distance:
$$\sum |A_i - B_i| \tag{2}$$

We also considered a similarity metric based on the cosine angle between two real valued vectors of length n: If the result of the calculation is equal to 1, the angle between the two vectors is 0 and therefore they point in the same direction (and are actually identical). If the value is less than 1 the vectors differ. The cosine similarity is calculated as follows:

$$\frac{\sum_{i=0}^{n} A_i \times B_i}{\sqrt{\sum A_i^2} \times \sqrt{\sum B_i^2}} \tag{3}$$

When using a metric on real-valued vectors, a n dimensional shape space is generated in which receptors and antigen vectors are mapped and matched. Depending on the distance (or similarity), receptor vectors will cluster around antigen vectors. In order to find a suitable response, a selection algorithm is necessary. We decided to use the k-nearest neighbor classification algorithm to categorize the receptor vectors in order to find a suitable response. Each receptor in our system is assigned to all available responses in the beginning which equal opportunities for each response.

Thus, the presented vectors are able to bind without a response specificity. We decided to use masking vectors on-top of the receptor vectors to limit the binding affinity towards antigens and responses, and thus to enable more specific response confirmations. A masking vector m is a real-valued vector of the same length n as an antigen or receptor vector storing weights m_i for each entry.

A masking vector represents an additional limitation of the responses towards specific misbehavior. Each formula was updated accordingly. The final metric formulas are therefore as follows:

For the Euclidean distance:

$$\sqrt{\sum (m_i A_i - m_i B_i)^2} \tag{4}$$

For the Manhattan distance:

$$\sum |m_i A_i - m_i B_i| \tag{5}$$

For the cosine affinity:

$$\frac{\sum_{i=0}^{n} m_i A_i \times m_i B_i}{\sqrt{\sum (m_i A_i)^2} \times \sqrt{\sum (m_i B_i)^2}} \tag{6}$$

In our simplified model, the complexity of the conformation mechanism in the immune model is embodied by the ability of masking vectors to get assigned to responses and to be alterable. How this is achieved will be explained in the following sections. The benefit of using such masks lies in the ability to have a simple model without the need of modeling chemokines and other agents of the biological system.

4.1   Antigen Receptor Response Selection Mechanism

The final step of the general AIS framework is the development of an algorithm based on the considered immune model. The algorithm is intended to target the problem of choosing a suitable response for a detected malfunction or misbehavior. Our algorithm is based upon the following basic ideas: Similar to the representation of pathogens in the immune system, a technical system needs to represent misbehavior and malfunction. A detection system is therefore necessary to decide whether suspicious feature vectors are representing misbehavior. Once a vector is marked as misbehaving, it is used in our response selection approach as antigen represented by an APC. Depending on the interaction of the antigen vector with the available response receptors, a specific response is chosen and enacted. The quality of the response and its impact towards the misbehavior need to be measured during a specific feedback time period. The feedback evaluation is triggered after a response specific settling time. We allow both negative and positive feedback. In case of a negative feedback, the response is undone (if possible) and the affinity towards the misbehavior is reduced. In case of a positive feedback the responses affinity towards the misbehavior is increased. Thus the system is able to learn which responses are suitable for a specific misbehavior, with regard to the current network status. The re-usage of a response is therefore proportional to its success. In case of a negative feedback, the re-usage of a response is less likely for the specific misbehavior. By applying such a feedback loop to the selection mechanism, the system eventually develops a form of cognitive memory.

Requires: Initial receptor set Θ with response matching, k value for kNN
Input: Time window based antigen vector A with an anomaly indication from the detection unit

for *each A* **do**
   $m \longleftarrow$ misbehavior specific mask
   for *each $\theta \in \Theta$* **do**
      $d_{cosine}(\theta, A) = \frac{\sum_{i=0}^{n} m_i A_i \times m_i \theta_i}{\sqrt{\sum (m_i A_i)^2} \times \sqrt{\sum (m_i \theta_i)^2}}$
   end
   $\sigma = k$-nearest vectors for $d_{cosine}(\theta, A)$
   if *($\forall \sigma$ the response res_i is available)* **then**
      Select correlated response res_i
   end
   else
      $res_i =$ response of $minDistance(\forall \sigma_k \in \sigma_k , A)$
   end
   Initiate res_i and set *OngoingResponse* = true
   Inform Detection Unit about response activation
   Wait t_w to trigger 2-hop feedback analysis for res_i
   Wait t_{feed} for feedback ACK
   if *FeedbackAnalysisIsPositiv* **then**
      Increase weights by w_{pos} in m for A
      Add A to receptor set
      Connect res_i with A under m
   end
   else
      Decrease weights by w_{neg} for A under m
      Add A to receptor set and link all responses equally to it
   end
   Inform Detection Unit about response finish
   Set *OngoingResponse* = false
end

Algorithm 1. Antigen Receptor Degeneracy Algorithm: ARDA using cosine similarity as comparison metric

Our approach considers responses in case of network malfunction, which can range from simple mechanisms as rebooting, re-routing, black listing of a node or multi-path data routing, up to the replacement of software or hardware of a node. The responses are defined using the knowledge about the available OSI layer protocols of the investigated network, the limitations of the hardware/software and the possibilities of an interaction with a human operator.

4.2   The Algorithm

Based on the previous basic description, the algorithm (the pseudo code is given in algorithm 1) proceeds in three stages:

First, an initial receptor set Θ is provided by a combination of expert knowledge and a decision tree classification approach. Once the receptor set has been created from the available misbehavior vectors, which were collected from several independent simulation runs, a mask set M is created and assigned to the receptor set, by assigning at least one mask to each receptor in the set according to the represented misbehavior. If a receptor represents different forms of misbehavior each suitable mask gets assigned. The masking allows a receptor to have different affinities towards an antigen, depending on the assumed misbehavior. After this initialization process, the available responses res_i are mapped to the available receptors θ_i and masks m_i. This was done manually by considering carefully the simulation results. Note that each receptor is able to bind to more than one response, but at least one response must be assigned to a receptor. Currently the assignment is based on expert knowledge only. However we plan to replace this approach by a learning classifier approach in later versions of our algorithm as any human intervention needs to be minimized. Once the initialization is finished the algorithm is able to react upon detected misbehavior (antigens), which it gets from an accompanied detection system. Antigens (A) are collected continuously by a logging mechanism which analyses the communication channels and extracts the relevant feature values for a specific time period Δt. A classification of the misbehavior is performed which enables the system to choose the most appropriate mask m for the following selection process. The antigen vector A is mapped into the receptor shape space and the distances and similarity to the available receptor vectors Θ are computed (under consideration of m). Based on the calculated distance (or similarity) the k-nearest receptor set σ is computed using the k-nearest neighbor algorithm (kNN) [11]. Each receptor in σ is a real-valued vector with entries representing network conditions correlated with misbehavior. The next step is to evaluate the receptors and the possible responses. In order to select a response, the receptors in σ get evaluated for each response. If one response is present in all receptors of σ, it is chosen. If no explicit response is found, a decision based on the most frequent occurrences of responses in the past, during the working of the system, is made. For each of the correlated responses the minimum distance (maximum similarity) of the assigned receptor to the antigen is considered, and the best fitting (min distance, max similarity) is chosen. Afterwards, the response is enacted and a *response timer* is activated. The timer is necessary to cancel responses which cannot be enacted due to communication errors or which simply lack to react to the misbehavior in a reasonable time span. In such cases the response will get a negative feedback. If the response is completed within the time interval, a feedback analysis is started. This marks the final phase of our approach. The feedback analysis starts with a wait period $t_w \geq 1.5 \times \Delta t$, in order to allow the network to settle after the application of a response. After this initial waiting time, the recent network conditions (features) are measured and compared to the network conditions (antigen) which started the response. This is done by a two-hop acknowledgment on the involved route. Again a timer t_{feed} was used to limit the waiting time for the expected acknowledgment. Only if the network quality of service parameters have improved, the feedback is positive. In this case the weights of the masking vector m are increased and the response

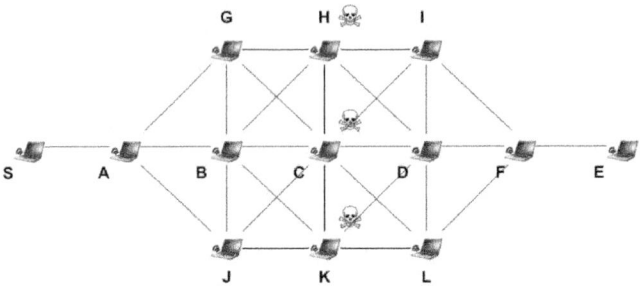

Fig. 1. WSN Topology for the experiments. Possible misbehaving nodes are H, C, K. S is the sender, E the receiver of global traffic. G, B, J are capable to detect misbehavior and to respond to it. I, D, L are used for the feedback analysis.

receptor binding tightened. The values for increasing the masking vector entries are in this first version fixed. Additionally the antigen vector is inserted into the receptor set Θ and linked to the available responses. Once the feedback is finished, the response selection algorithm goes back to "normal", waiting for incoming antigen vectors. Note that during a local response selection and action, incoming antigens are ignored for the involved nodes, as a response node cannot enact several responses at once for the same misbehaving node.

5   Experimental Setup

Our experimental analysis was performed on a simulation model, that consists of a wireless sensor network scenario with a total number of 13 nodes, including one sender and one receiver. The scenario was implemented in OMNet++ 4.0 [12], a common discrete event simulator. Between the sender and the sink several paths exist (see figure 1). Three strategically placed intermediate nodes were modified to enact misbehavior upon request. Depending on the data path established by the routing protocol, between source and destination, the misbehavior was enacted on the one modified node which was part of the route. As it was necessary to learn and train the system within an initial setup phase, misbehavior was started 5 minutes (of simulated time) after the network initialization was finished. The total simulated run time for each scenario was 60 minutes. A constant bit data traffic between source and sink was established with a data rate of 1 packet per second. The logging time window Δt for antigen vectors was 10 seconds. The response fail timer t_w was set to 15 seconds. The feedback timer t_{feed} was set to 5 seconds.

5.1   Misbehavior

For our analysis of ARDA we implemented a basic misbehavior module which allows to enact the following misbehaviors:

- *Selective packet forwarding*: a node drops packets from specific routes thus limiting the available data.
- *Artificial packet injection*: a node injects artificially generated information into the network with the intention to falsify the collected information or to limit the available bandwidth.
- *Manipulation of packet content*: a node changes the payload of a packet thus falsifying the collected information. This is in conjunction with a time delay at the misbehaving node. Thus we measured the time delay between two consecutive sends of a packet.

5.2   Responses

To test our response selection approach we implemented four different responses, all being applicable for the intended misbehaviors in our scenario:

1. *No Response*: The default action if the misbehavior is hardly detectable and very similar to normal behavior.
2. *Shut down*: A node gets shut down by an over the air command, thus being no longer part of the network.
3. *Flashing*: A node's operating system gets replaced by an over the air reprogramming approach. This is emulated by a packet transmission of the size of a typical OS image for a sensor node.
4. *Blacklisting*: A node is temporally black-listed in the routing table and hence during this time period no longer available for routing.

Each response was evaluated for its applicability in the test scenario. Table 1 gives a summary of the responses impact on the network in terms of data overhead and measured duration and whether the responses can be revoked. This is an important feature for responses, when getting a negative feedback. In such a case the QoS parameters of the network are even worse than the QoS parameters measured during the misbehavior. In such circumstances it should be possible to revoke a response.

Table 1. Response actions considered for the scenario, their overhead, duration and revocation. The latter is either manually by a human operator or automatically by a command signal.

Action	Overhead	Duration	Revocation
"no response"	0 byte	0 sec.	-
"shut down"	236 bytes	0.4 sec.	manually
"flashing"	119000 bytes	12 sec.	manually
"blacklisting"	1110 bytes	1.04 sec.	automatically

5.3   Results

Our analysis consists of the following parts: First, we examined the suitability of the response selection towards the considered misbehaviors by evaluating
the feedback for each enacted response. Second, we measured the impact of the
misbehavior and the responses on the network, by collecting quality of service
parameters (received packets, good-put and delivery time). Third, we examined
the different metrics and their impact on the response selection. For these tasks
we conducted 20 independent simulation runs per scenario. The obtained results
are given in tables 2 and 3 as well as in figure 2. We observed a 75% ratio of
positive feedbacks for each response. As we expected a better ratio, we additionally examined the negative feedback and found out that most of it was caused
by time outs during the feedback evaluation period. We tracked the problem
down to a difficult bug in the routing protocol which we used in our simulation.
Without this problem the positive feedback ratio would have been around 90%.
In table 3 the QoS values for the different scenarios and enacted responses are
shown. We observed a significant mitigation of misbehavior for packet dropping
and measurable mitigations for the other two. In figure 2 the obtained results for
the metric survey are given. We observed no significant differences for the three
metrics and thus can for the given scenario conclude, that all metrics are equally
suitable for the selection. Based on this observation, we decided to use the cosine
similarity metric as our default metric for the algorithm. The response selection
algorithm was tested for the different occurrences of misbehavior. Sometimes in
the packet dropping misbehavior scenario our detection module was not able to
correctly identify which of the three modified nodes was part of the current route
and thus a false positive was produced. For these cases the algorithm selected
the "no response" action, as the proposed antigen was obviously very similar to
normal behavior.

In each scenario we allowed up to 60 subsequent occurrences of misbehavior
and thus up to 60 response actions during a single simulation run. The results
are shown in table 2. For the packet dropping misbehavior 59 responses were
enacted during an avg. simulation run. Of these, 45 had a positive feedback and
14 a negative feedback. The high value of negative feedback is due to problems

Table 2. Response feedback results for each of the three misbehavior scenarios. Values
are averages in total over 20 simulation runs. Standard deviation given only for total
no. of positive and negative feedback. Confidence levels are listed in brackets and were
calculated for $\alpha = 0.05$. For the negative feedback, the results for the analysis based
and time out based decision are given too.

Misbehavior	Feedback Result					
	positive		negative			
	total no.	std. dev.	total no.	std. dev.	analysis	time out
Packet dropping	45.05	3.71 (1.62)	14	3.68 (1.61)	5.15	8.85
Packet delay	45.39	2.2 (0.96)	12.94	2.21 (0.97)	1.44	11.5
Packet injection	42.37	3.34 (1.46)	16.63	3.15 (1.38)	5.05	11.58

Table 3. QoS parameter comparison of the network condition when exposed to the three types of misbehavior and the improvements achieved by each response type 21 seconds after the response was performed. For comparison, the QoS parameters for normal traffic are shown in the last row.

Misbehavior (Mis) & Response	Received Packets	Goodput	Delivery time
Mis: 70 % packet dropping	71.83%	57.56 Bit/sec	0.230465 sec.
shutdown	92.22%	73.7 Bit/sec.	0.21294 sec.
flashing	91.83%	73.5 Bit/sec.	0.21351 sec.
blacklisting	91.3%	73.05 Bit/sec.	0.2156 sec.
Mis: 0.5 sec. packet delay	92%	73.6 Bit/sec	0.37298 sec.
shutdown	97.1%	77.7 Bit/sec.	0.0878 sec.
flashing	98.3%	78.7 Bit/sec.	0.0871 sec.
blacklisting	98.1%	78.5 Bit/sec.	0.0872 sec.
Mis: 5 packets/sec. packet injection	92.5%	74.2 Bit/sec	0.213195 sec.
shutdown	98%	78.13 Bit/sec.	0.0751 sec.
flashing	97%	77.6 Bit/sec.	0.0752 sec.
blacklisting	96%	76.7 Bit/sec.	0.0903 sec.
normal traffic	94.3%	75.5 Bit/sec.	0.20907 sec.

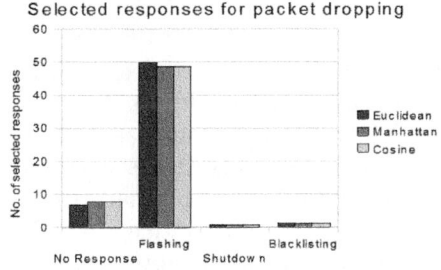

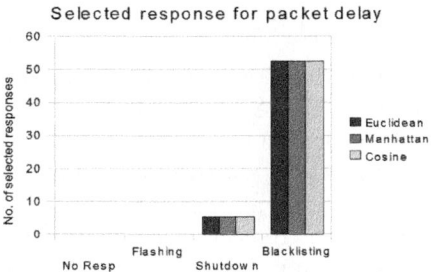

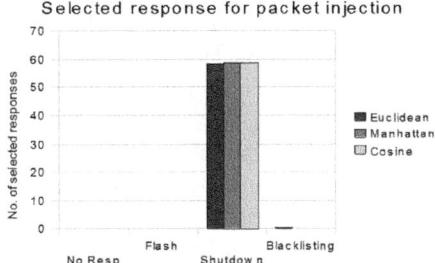

Fig. 2. Impact of metric on the response selection based on 20 simulation runs. Each figure shows the total number of selected responses over all simulation runs for the three types of misbehavior.

in receiving the feedback acknowledgment in time. Only 5 negative feedbacks were based upon a negative evaluation of the response. This in conjunction with the decision of using the "no response" at some occurrences of the misbehavior.

For the packet delay misbehavior 58 responses were enacted during an avg. simulation run. Of these, again 45 had a positive feedback and 13 a negative feedback. Almost all negative feedbacks were based on a missing acknowledgment after the feedback timer had run out. For the packet injection misbehavior 59 responses were enacted during an avg. simulation run. Of these, 42 had a positive feedback and 16 a negative feedback. Again a high number of negative feedback (> 11) was caused by the feedback timer. Only 5 were caused by the response itself.

Unfortunately we found out that our experiment was not significant enough to fully analyze the feedback algorithm. The observed negative feedback values were rather caused by the non-perfect routing algorithm and not by the properties of our algorithm. The problem was to establish a two hop acknowledgment in a given time period, which unfortunately took quite often longer than expected. We used the DYMO [13] routing protocol provided for OMNet++. DYMO is a common example of an appropriate sensor network routing protocol. Our next simulation experiments will consider a different routing protocol to minimize the effect of the protocol on the performance of the algorithm. This should allow a more significant analysis of our approach.

6   Conclusion

In this article we proposed a first version of an antigen receptor degeneracy algorithm (ARDA) which allows for an autonomous response selection for certain misbehavior from a predefined response set. The basic algorithm was developed in conjunction with the conceptual framework for AIS algorithms introduced by Timmis et al. The main idea behind this algorithm is to ensure that no fixed single connection between a response receptor and an antigen is defined in the beginning. Instead a more general and thus non-specific approach is considered which allows specificity to emerge during the runtime of the algorithm. The algorithm was only able to select a stable response for each misbehavior, it additionally turned out to be robust against misclassification of antigens and false positives. Misclassification was caused by wrongly chosen masks m for the matching part, false positives were caused by the too simplistic detection module. Although the algorithm is able to function in this simplistic scenario, we believe that further exploration and improvements are necessary in order to provide a stable and robust version which finally can deal with many different malfunctions and misbehaviors. The first improvement will be the introduction of a cloning and mutation strategy for newly added receptors to improve the response matching and learning. This will be accompanied by a removal strategy to limit the number of available receptors and thus to limit the computational demands. Although the feedback analysis provided the system with reasonable results, further improvements are possible. First, the timer for the analysis needs to be calibrated better, and second, an adaptive timer which considers the response duration might even further improve the results of the feedback analysis. The problems with the considered DYMO routing protocol, call for the consideration of different routing protocols and a further analysis of their impact on the algorithm. Finally, the automatic building of an initial receptor set is still an open problem. For this experimental study we built the receptor set based on observation of the misbehaviors during test runs, using a classifier and expert knowledge. This however is not suitable for an autonomous system. Instead, we want an initial receptor set to be created by an unsupervised learning strategy. During the runtime of the algorithm this initial set should be updated and changed according to the results of the algorithm.

References

1. De Castro, L., Timmis, J.: Artificial immune systems: a new computational intelligence approach. Springer, Heidelberg (2002)
2. Cohen, I.: Tending Adam's Garden: evolving the cognitive immune self. Academic Press, San Diego (2000)
3. Loo, C., Ng, M., Leckie, C., Palaniswami, M.: Intrusion Detection for Routing Attacks in Sensor Networks. International Journal of Distributed Sensor Networks 2(4), 313–332 (2006)
4. Drozda, M., Schaust, S., Szczerbicka, H.: Immuno-inspired knowledge management for ad hoc wireless networks. In: Szczerbicki, E., Nguyen, N.T. (eds.) Smart Information and Knowledge Management. Studies in Computational Intelligence, vol. 260, pp. 1–26. Springer, Heidelberg (2010)
5. Drozda, M., Schildt, S., Schaust, S., Einhellinger, S., Szczerbicka, H.: A tool for prototyping AIS based protection systems for ad hoc and sensor networks. Cybernetics and Systems 39(7), 719–742 (2008)
6. Cohen, I., Hershberg, U., Solomon, S.: Antigen-receptor degeneracy and immunological paradigms. Molecular Immunology 40(14-15), 993–996 (2004)
7. Andrews, P., Timmis, J.: A computational model of degeneracy in a lymph node. Artificial Immune Systems, 164–177 (2006)
8. Mendao, M., Timmis, J., Andrews, P., Davies, M.: The immune system in pieces: Computational lessons from degeneracy in the immune system. In: IEEE Symposium on Foundations of Computational Intelligence FOCI 2007, pp. 394–400. IEEE Computer Society Press, Los Alamitos (2007)
9. Murphy, K., Travers, P., Walport, M.: Janeway's immunobiology. Garland Pub. (2008)
10. Drozda, M., Schildt, S., Schaust, S., Szczerbicka, H.: An Immuno-Inspired Approach to Misbehavior Detection in Ad Hoc Wireless Networks. Computing Research Repository (CoRR) arXiv.org/abs/1001.3113 (2010)
11. Dudani, S.: The distance-weighted k-nearest-neighbor rule. IEEE Transactions on Systems, Man and Cybernetics 4, 325–327 (1976)
12. OMNeT++ Community Web Site, http://www.omnetpp.org
13. Chakeres, I., Perkins, C.: Dynamic MANET on-demand (DYMO) routing. draft-ietf-manet-dymo-19. txt (2010) (work in progress)

Parameter Optimisation in the Receptor Density Algorithm

James A. Hilder, Nick D.L. Owens, Peter J. Hickey, Stuart N. Cairns,
David P.A. Kilgour, Jon Timmis, and Andy Tyrrell*

Department of Electronics, University of York, Heslington, UK, YO10 5DD
jah128@ohm.york.ac.uk

Abstract. In this paper a system which optimises parameter values for
the Receptor Density Algorithm (RDA), an algorithm inspired by T-
cell signalling, is described. The parameter values are optimised using
a genetic algorithm. This system is used to optimise the RDA parameters to obtain the best results when finding anomalies within a large
prerecorded dataset, in terms of maximising detection of anomalies and
minimising false-positive detections. A trade-off front between the objectives is extracted using NSGA-II as a base for the algorithm. To improve
the run-time of the optimisation algorithm with the goal of achieving
real-time performance, the system exploits the inherent parallelism of
GPGPU programming techniques, making use of the CUDA language
and tools developed by NVidia to allow multiple evaluations of a given
data set in parallel.

Keywords: Receptor Density Algorithm, Genetic Algorithms, NSGA-
II, GPGPU, CUDA, Artificial Immune Systems.

1 Introduction

The RDA, is an Artificial Immune System which is inspired by the cell signalling mechanisms found in T-cells [12]. We have adapted the RDA for use in
chemical detection systems, and when combined with a signature matching algorithm, the pair can be used to detect and identify known or unknown chemicals
substances [14]. The ability to perform fast and accurate detection of chemical
substances has many applications, including the detection and identification of
chemical/biological agents, explosives and drugs, and background environmental monitoring [6]. Currently, there are two main alternatives to address this
detection problem: highly trained canines (better known as sniffer dogs) and
analytical chemical detectors. Whilst sniffer dogs are an effective widely utilised
solution, they have drawbacks such as the resources required to train and keep
a dog and the effectiveness of the animal decreasing as it tires [7]. The alternative method of detecting chemical substances is the use of analytical chemical

---

* James Hilder, Nick Owens, Jon Timmis and Andy Tyrrell are with the Department
of Electronics, University of York. Peter Hickey, Stuart Cairns and David Kilgour
are with DSTL Fort Halstead, Sevenoaks, Kent, UK, TN14 7BP.

P. Liò, G. Nicosia, and T. Stibor (Eds.): ICARIS 2011, LNCS 6825, pp. 226–239, 2011.

detectors, which take measurements of chemical or physical properties of an environment and produce spectra describing the local conditions. In this paper we will refer to such a device as a *spectrometer*.

Previous work has seen the RDA being utilised for the purpose of chemical detection through the use of a such a spectrometer mounted to a robotic platform [14]. Through the careful hand-tuning of algorithm parameters to match the given sensor and environment, the system could effectively identify anomalous chemicals and descriminate between those considered hazardous and those considered safe. In an ideal world, this process of parameter tuning should be fully automated in rapid timeframes, allowing the system to adapt to both new environments and sensors without the need of skilled human intervention. In this paper, a process to achieve this parameter automation is described, which exploits the multi-objective selection offered by the Non-Dominated Sorting Genetic Algorithm II (NSGA-II) [5] to find parameter sets which aim to maximum anomaly detection whilst minimising false-positive detection rates.

The paper then describes a method by which the optimisation algorithm can be accelerated to offer near real-time optimisation of parameters, as required in a robot-mounted field deployment. This is achieved through the parallel computing resources offered by General-Purpose computing on Graphics Processing Units (GPGPU). The RDA is re-implemented in the CUDA programming language, allowing parallel execution of multiple instances of the algorithm which use different parameter choices to accelerate the NSGA-II algorithm [9].

The structure of this paper is as follows: the following section describes the background and basic operation of the RDA and the signature-matching algorithm. Section 3 describes the GA used to automate the process of parameter selection, with results obtained from a conventional (CPU-based) implementation of the algorithm discussed in Section 4. The implementation of the algorithm in CUDA and the methods used to optimise performance with are given in Section 5, including a discussion the relative performance merits in terms of time, cost and energy over the conventional CPU-based implementation. Concluding remarks are given in Section 6.

2   The Receptor Density and Signature Matching Algorithms

In this section the operation of a two stage approach to substance detection is described, in terms of a pair of general algorithms which may be applied to any spectrum to learn and identify signatures of substances. We refer to the appearance of the signature of a chemical substance in a spectrum as an *anomaly*, in the sense that it is by assumption different from the preceding background spectra, and so we discuss *anomaly detection* in spectra. It is noted that the substances discussed in this paper are not pure compounds, but rather complex mixtures of chemicals, which we attempt to identify and distinguish in their entirety rather than adopting a reductionist approach of componentisation followed by analysis.

The primary stage of this approach uses a novel algorithm to generate signatures of anomalies, the RDA. The RDA is able to detect the existence of an anomaly, and then produce a signature in which the background and noise are removed. Second, we correlate the signatures against a library of known substances, with the option of adding a new library entry for below-threshold signatures. The complexity here lies in the first stage, and so we assume that if the first stage can produce high quality signatures, then a simple matching algorithm will prove effective for the second stage. Many different algorithms for matching signatures exist of varying complexity and effectiveness, in particular neural-networks have been used to high success with mass-spectrometers [2,15]; in this paper, the accurate recognition of anomaly-instances is considered the primary objective, with the classification of the anomaly based on its signature considered a secondary goal, hence a simple signature-matching algorithm is used. Previous studies on the data sets used have indicated that provided effective parameter choices are made for the RDA, the resulting chemical signatures created are suitably unique and well-defined to allow a simple matching algorithm to be used without inducing errors. Formal definitions of the mathematical models the sensors, spectra and signatures can be found in [14].

2.1   The Receptor Density Algorithm

To generate clean (noise-removed, background subtracted) signatures we employ an anomaly detection system: the RDA [10,12]. The RDA is an Artificial Immune System (AIS), which is an algorithm developed by inspiration of the vertebrate immune system. Specifically, the RDA is developed from models of the immunological T-cell and the T-cell receptor's ability to contribute to T-cell discrimination [11]. The details of the conception behind the algorithm and a detailed breakdown of its relation to biology are not important to its functioning within this paper; we direct the interested reader to [11] for models of the biology and to [10,12] for further details on the algorithm's construction from the models, and theoretical analysis of algorithm behaviour.

The RDA places a *receptor* at each discretised location within the spectrum. At each time step each receptor takes input $s_{i,t}$ and produces a binary classification $c_t \in 0, 1$ which describes whether that location is considered anomalous. The classification decision is performed via the dynamics of two variables associated with each receptor: the receptor position p and negative feedback n. The behaviour of a receptor is depicted in figure 1, and is as follows: A receptor has a length ℓ and a position p. The receptor has a negative feedback barrier $\beta \in (0, \ell)$, if $p > \beta$ then negative feedback is linearly generated which acts to reverse the progression of p. If $p \geq \ell$, then the receptor generates an anomaly classification $c_t = 1$, this classification signal is $c_t = 0$ at all other times.

More concretely, the dynamics of p and n at spectrum location i can be described by the following recurrence equations:

$$p_{i,t} = bp_{i,t-1} + S_t - n_{i,t-1}$$
$$n_{i,t} = dn_{i,t-1} + gH(p_{i,t-1} - \beta) \tag{1}$$

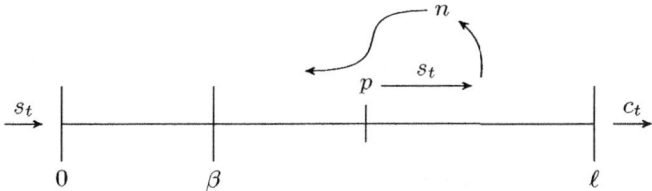

Fig. 1. The receptor receives in input s_t and advances the receptor position p. If $p \geq \beta$ the receptor linearly generates negative feedback which arrests and reverses the progression of p. Should $p = \ell$ then the receptor generates a classification signal $c_t = 1$, if the receptor position is $p < \ell$ then the classification signal is $c_t = 0$ [13].

with $0 < b, d < 1$ the position and negative feedback decay rates respectively; S_t the spectrum at time t; $g > 0$ the negative feedback growth rate; $0 < \beta < \ell$ the negative feedback barrier; $H(\cdot)$ the Heaviside step function. The parameters b, d, g, β, ℓ define a scale with which to interpret the input from the spectrum S_t. The range of input s_i results in four regions of equilibrium of the receptor position p_e and negative feedback n_e. The four regions, depicted in figure 2, are defined as follows:

1. For $s_i < (1 - b)\beta$ the negative feedback barrier β will not be broken, no negative feedback will be generated. As such, $p_e = u/(1 - b)$, $n_e = 0$.
2. For $(1 - b)\beta < s_i < (1 - b)\beta + g/(1 - d)$, negative feedback will be generated and it will grow and arrive approximately at position $p_e \approx \beta$, with $n_e \approx s_i - \beta(1 - b)$.
3. For $(1 - b)\beta + g/(1 - d) < s_i < (1 - b)\ell + g/(1 - d)$, the negative feedback will not be able to hold $p_e = \beta$ and will rise to a maximum $n_e = g/(1 - d)$.
4. For $s_i > (1-b)\ell+g/(1-d)$ the equilibrium positions are calculated identically as in region 3, but now $p > \ell$ and so this situation is not of interest.

In regions 1, 3 & 4, p and n will asymptotically approach the equilibrium positions p_e and n_e from any initial p_0, n_0 with a suitable choice of parameters. However, the equilibrium positions in region 2 are approximate: if the recurrences from Equation 1 are placed at the equilibrium position they will not remain at this point, but will cycle anticlockwise in the (p, n)-plane. This cycle is a stable limit cycle, and its size and shape are dependent on the parameters b, d, g, as discussed in [12]. Figure 3(a) illustrates the point, the RDA takes input from a model $\mathcal{M}$ with 200 locations and constant in time rate function $\rho_i = \alpha(N(60, 8.9) + N(120, 20))$ for a positive constant α and $N(\mu, \sigma)$ a normal distribution with mean μ and standard deviation σ. In the regions where $\mathcal{M} > \beta$ the negative feedback is a weighted density estimate of $\mathcal{M}$ (see [12] for details on the weighted density estimate). The anomaly detection occurs when there is a change in input in time. This is demonstrated in figure 3(b), the rate function of the model sensor is changed causing an increase in p resulting in the anomaly condition $p > \ell$ being satisfied.

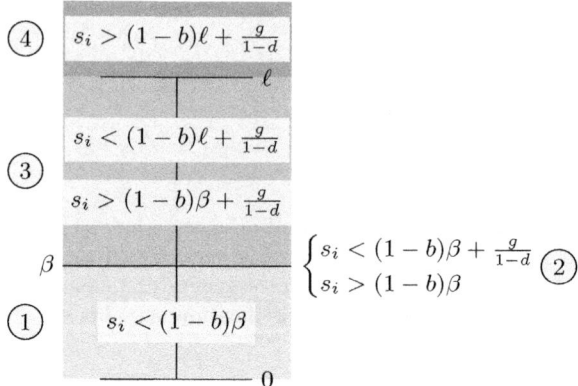

Fig. 2. The equilibrium values of p_e and n_e for ranges of s_i defined by regions 1, 2, 3, 4, see text for details

2.2 The RDA for Anomaly Detection in Spectra

From the previous section it should be clear that the negative feedback will track with the input (if the input is within a suitable range defined by RDA parameters). Anomalies are detected when new peaks appear in the spectra with sufficient size to push $p > \ell$. The RDA can be used to generate a signature of the new features in the spectra, we describe this via two concepts: the *anomaly time* and the *anomaly signature*:

Definition 1. *The time of an anomaly is $t_a = t_e - t_s$, with t_s the time step where the first receptor $p_{i,t_s} \geq \ell$ and t_e is the first time point after t_s where no receptor is above ℓ, that is $p_{i,t_e} < \ell, \forall i$.*

Definition 2. *The signature of an anomaly is average of the distance of each receptor above β taken over the time of the anomaly. For an anomaly A its signature is $\sigma(A)$:*

$$\sigma(A) = (\sigma_{A_0}, \sigma_{A_1}, \ldots, \sigma_{A_{w-1}}) \tag{2}$$

$$\sigma_{A_i} = \frac{1}{t_e - t_s} \sum_{t=t_e}^{t_s-1} (p_t - \beta) H(p_t - \beta) \tag{3}$$

2.3 Signature Matching and Libraries

We now discuss stage two of our anomaly detection process, the correlation of signatures. The intent here is keep general signature mapping relatively simple for two reasons. First, established signature matching/generation techniques spend time compensating for issues that we have addressed with the RDA [1]. Second, it is likely that signature matching will need to be tailored to the specifics of the mass spectrometery device. In general the we match two different anomalies by correlating their signatures:

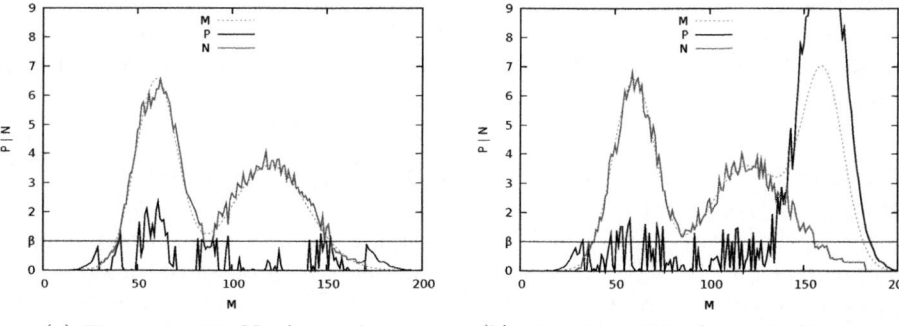

(a) Timestep=50, No Anomaly.   (b) Timestep=101, Anomaly Detected.

Fig. 3. Demonstration of the RDA. A model sensor $\mathcal{M}$ is applied to the RDA with parameters: $b = 0.84$; $d = 0.98$; $g = 0.35$; $\beta = 1$, with initial $p_0, n_0 = 0$. Plot a) shows timestep $t = 50$. In the regions where $\mathcal{M} > \beta$ the negative feedback is a density estimate of $\mathcal{M}$ and p is held close to β. Plot b) shows timestep $t = 101$, with a large increase in p: receptors 151–169 would register $c = 1$ an anomaly state. If the RDA recurrences are further applied the negative feedback will grow to match the new input and the p will drop back toward β [14].

Definition 3. *The match between two anomalies A and B is written $\mu(A, B)$ and is the correlation between their signatures:*

$$\mu(A, B) = \frac{1}{\|\sigma(A)\|\|\sigma(B)\|} \sum_{i=0}^{w-1} \sigma_{A_i}\sigma_{B_i} \qquad (4)$$

We expect spectrometers to have associated spectral defects, for example, drift of peaks to nearby locations, variable relative peak heights, identical substances generating different sets of peaks. The above definition of matches between signatures should be more robust to some of these variations than distance metrics such as Euclidean distance. We combine many anomalies generated from the same substance to create a signature library entry for that anomaly by taking the average of the anomaly signatures. We denote the sum S_A of n anomalies $A_0, A_1, \ldots A_{n-1}$ of substance A as follows:

$$S_A = \sum_{k=0}^{n-1} \sigma(A_k) = \left(\sum_{k=0}^{n-1} \sigma_{A_{k_0}}, \sum_{k=0}^{n-1} \sigma_{A_{k_1}}, \ldots, \sum_{k=0}^{n-1} \sigma_{A_{k_{w-1}}} \right) \qquad (5)$$

Then a library entry for a particular substance is a pair $(\mathcal{L}, L_A)$, with $\mathcal{L}$ a substance label and L_A the normalised sum of signatures:

$$L_A = S_A/\|S_A\| \qquad (6)$$

For operation an implementation of the RDA system can be supplied with a library of pre-built signature label instances. Upon detecting a new anomaly its signature can be correlated against all library instances, it is then assigned to the class with which it has the highest correlation. If the maximum correlation with all library entries falls below a threshold τ_L then the substance can be considered unknown, and added to the library as a new label-less entry for that substance.

3   Genetic Algorithm for Optimising Parameters

Prior to the research described in this paper, the process of determining the parameters for the RDA was based on a iterative process of analysis of the spectral data and RDA output in MATLAB [12]. The parameters are determined by the typical range of values presented in the spectra of the sensor being used. The gb scaling factor is adjusted to a level which provides background noise levels in the range 0 - 10 at each receptor, with spikes at anomalies ranging from roughly 10 up to over 1000 for very strong signals. Once sensible values have been chosen based on the ranges, the decay and efficacy parameters a, b, d and g are adjusted to find optimal balances in the trade-offs between response-time against quality, interleave-time against quality and false-positive anomalies against missed anomalies.

Generally, given the target function of the algorithm, it is likely that it will be safer and more useful to choose parameters biased towards fewer missed anomalies at the expense of a higher rate of noise-induced false positives. To assist this process it is necessary to compare the statistics from the largest noise signals to those of the smallest anomalies which need to be detected; from experimentation with the IMS data there is statistically very little difference between strong noise signals and weak anomalies, so a certain degree of compromise must be made if the weakest anomalies are to be detected; generally, a false-positive detection caused by noise will have a very weak correlation to any known signatures and can be dismissed by the identification algorithm. Whilst this process of parameter selection provides acceptable results, it is both time consuming and requires knowledge of the sensor, the environment and the inner operation of the RDA. As the target goal for this application is a semi-autonomous field robot, which may potentially carry a number of diverse sensors and be used in widely varying background conditions, the described approach for parameter selection is unsuitable.

To automate the process of parameter selection, a genetic algorithm has been implemented that automatically optimises the main set of parameters to provide a balance of minimised missed anomalies and false-positive detections. In its initial implementation, this algorithm was devised to run on a cluster of standard (X86) processors. The genetic algorithm is based the NSGA-II multi-objective selection algorithm, which ranks the population of parameter sets in pareto-fronts based on the two objective scores at the end of each generation, with priority given to the diversely spread solutions in a given front through the use of a crowding-distance measure. Further details of the NSGA-II algorithm and its operation can be found in [5].

3.1   Algorithm Description

The algorithm uses a floating-point genotype[1] with a length determined by the number of parameters to be optimised; in the tests conducted this ranges between five and eight values, as discussed in the Section 4. Each gene is linearly scaled to the relevant parameter value between a preset low and high range value in the genotype-phenotype mapping process.

The algorithm uses only mutation as a genetic operator, with the number of genes mutated determined by a shifted $\alpha = 1$ Poisson distribution, resulting in a 73.6% probability on 1 gene being mutated, an 18.4% of 2 gene mutations and an 8.0% of 3 or more genes mutated in each operation. When a gene is mutated, a randomly selected Cauchy-Lorentz distributed value is selected and added to its previous value, with bounds-checking to ensure it remains between zero and one. The γ value for the Cauchy distribution decays with generation, determined by the function below, which promotes wide-ranging mutations in lower generations and fine-grained optimisation in later generations.

$$\gamma = \frac{1}{\sqrt[3]{\text{generation}}} \tag{7}$$

3.2   Mass Spectrometry Benchmark

The test data used for the experiments described in this paper are based on the Mass Spectrometry data associated with the DSTL ICARIS 2009 & 2010 competitions [8]. This data was collected in laboratory conditions using a highly sensitive time-of-flight proton-transfer mass spectrometer (PTRMS). The data is presented as a spectrum of width 270 with a data-rate of 3Hz; in total approximately 200,000 timesteps (around 18 hours of data) are available. At various intervals a number of different substances are introduced to the sensor at different distances and strengths, which are loosely categorised as 'weak','medium' and 'strong'. Across the complete test set, seven different substances are introduced a total of 245 times, shown in Table 1.

4   Results

Testing was initially carried out using manually selected parameter settings, to observe correct functionality of the algorithm and to provide a benchmark for evaluating the optimisation process. These parameters were selected through extensive study of the data in MATLAB and following the parameter selection guidelines given in [12]. It is important to note that the process of selecting these parameters amounted to several hours work by the author of the algorithm; a process which is not realistic for a dynamic real-world deployment where neither the expertise nor time would be available. It should also be noted that the RDA is a deterministic algorithm, thus a given parameter set will yield identical output every time it is evaluated. Table 1 contains further information about

---

[1] Floating-point values range from 0.0 to 1.0.

Table 1. Substances in PTRMS Data and Detection Rates using Manual Parameters

Substance	Total	Matched[1]	Missed[2]	Detection Rate	Strength[3]
Shower Gel	31	28	3	90.3%	3,505
Shampoo	37	36	1	97.3%	5,820
Shaving Gel	25	25	0	100.0%	6,126
Brewed Coffee	39	39	0	100.0%	2,415
Coffee Beans	40	34	6	85.0%	3,413
Olive Oil	40	33	7	82.5%	393
Smoked Ham	33	17	16	51.5%	187
Overall	245	212	33	86.5%	21,859

[1] Number of instances of anomaly which were correctly identified.
[2] Number of instances of anomaly which were not identified.
[3] Cumulative strength of anomalous-receptor values.

the anomalies detected using this manual parameter set. The matched instances column contains the sum of the anomalies for each substance that was correctly detected from the test-set. The missed instances column contains the number of times the given substance was present in the test-set but not detected by the algorithm. The overall strength is the cumulative count of all receptors that are above the l threshold; the higher this value, the more detailed and accurate the corresponding signature will be. From the results it is clear that the RDA with the chosen parameter set effectively detects most instances of shower gel, shampoo, shaving gel and brewed coffee. It is less effective at detecting instances of coffee beans and olive oil, and detects less than half the instances of smoked ham. In total, 33 of the 245 anomalies are missed, with a successful detection rate of 86.5%, and a total of 7 false-positive detections are incurred (a false-positive rate of 3.2%).

It is important to note here that in the process of selecting this parameter set, others were found which either increase the detection rate and the expense of more false-positives, and also sets which decreased the false-positive rate whilst make fewer successful detections. However, the results above were considered the best found to suit the data and target problem; the false-positive rate expanded rapidly if the algorithm was made more sensitive to anomaly detection (achievable through lowering the positive feedback threshold, lowering the decay rate of feedback or increasing the scaling factors), and methods to lower the false-positive rate caused many more anomalies to not be correctly detected. As the data set contains real experimental data taken from a noisy environment, there are a number of instances where background events such as a door opening cause spikes in the PTRMS spectral data which a far larger than some of the known anomaly instances. As a result of this, the authors would consider that it is highly unlikely that any anomaly detection system could achieve a false-positive rate of less than 4 given the same detection rate, and it is further unlikely that all anomaly instances could be detected without a far greater false-positive rate due to the very minor SNR of the weakest anomalies.

The first set of tests using the GA to optimise parameter values evolved parameter sets for eight of the main algorithm parameters: ℓ, β. gb, h, a, b, d and g. Each parameter was allowed a range covering one decade, with the central value falling close to the value extracted from the previously described manual optimisation. A population size of 40 was chosen, with the 10 fittest parents as ranked by the NSGA-II selection process advanced to the following generation, each producing three mutated offspring. The population size was chosen as it proved the most efficient when run on the available 40-node cluster computer in early tests. In this batch of tests, the each algorithm was run for 250 generations, with the Pareto-optimal results extracted at the end of the final generation. A total of 100 runs of the test were conducted, with the results illustrated in Figure 4.

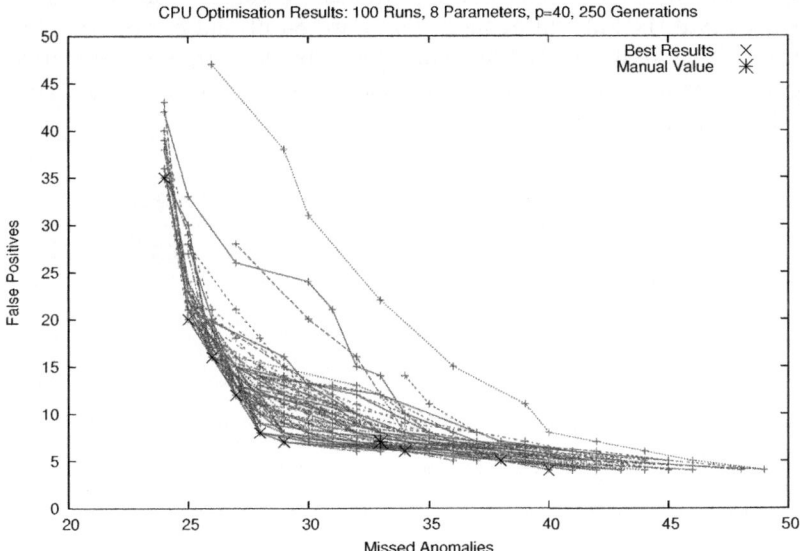

Fig. 4. The Pareto-optimal fronts extracted after 250 generations of each run in the GA evolving 8 RDA parameters. The results for the manually selected parameter set are included for comparison purposes.

After 250 generations, 58% of the runs had found a solution which equalled or better the manual chosen parameters when compared in terms of false positives. Of these, 6 runs had equalled the manual parameters rate of 33 missed anomalies for 7 false positive detections, whilst 52 runs had solutions with 32 or fewer missed anomalies for 7 false positives. When compared in terms of missed anomalies, no run found a solution with under 7 false positives for 33 missed anomalies, although 14% of runs did find solutions with 34 missed anomalies and 6 false positives. It is clear that in the majority of runs, a spread of parameter sets could be obtained from the final populations which offered a range of missed-anomaly:false-positive trade-offs that were comparable with the manually discovered bests. However, these results come at considerable computational expense; the size of the data-set results in a processing time of roughly 10 seconds for each individual; as a consequence a single run can take around 24 hours to finish if parallel techniques are not employed[2].

A second set of tests was then evaluated to attempt to speed up the optimisation time through the reduction of the number of parameters optimised. To achieve this goal, three of the previously evolved parameters, ℓ, β and gb were preset to the values used in the manually obtained parameters. The feedback threshold values of $\ell = 5$ and $\beta = 1$ have been found to be effective for a wide range of problems when the scaling factor gb is set such that the weakest anomalies are scaling such that the received receptor value is equal to 10; analysis of these parameter settings can be found in [12]. The optimisation process was run for 125 generations with all other settings the same as in the previous experiment to determine if the reduction in parameter quantity could produce similar results after half the amount of time. The Pareto-optimal fronts from 30 runs of this experiment are illustrated in Figure 5. From these results, 50% of the runs had equalled or bettered the manually determined rate of 33 missed anomalies for 7 false positive detections.

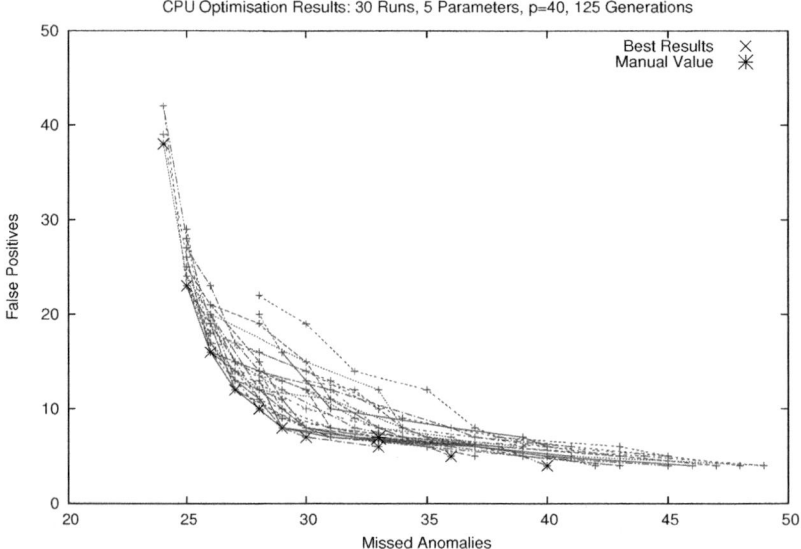

Fig. 5. The Pareto-optimal fronts extracted after 125 generations of each run in the GA evolving 5 RDA parameters

Further efforts were also made to reduce the computational time whilst retaining similar results. Through the caching of the entire dataset in memory and removal of all disk access, a 70% reduction in run-time was achieved. Reducing

---

[2] Runtime based on a single thread on a Core 2 2.6GHz machine, running 64-bit Ubuntu 10.04.

the test-set size to one-tenth its original size through careful selection of a most relevant areas offered similar ten-fold reduction in run-time whilst still producing comparable results to the manual selected parameters when evaluated over the whole test-set. However, even with such techniques to improve optimisation time, the results are still not suited to a real-world deployment in which calibration to new environments and sensors would be required in rapid timeframes. As a consequence, methods to migrate the RDA to allow parallel analysis of data using multiple parameter sets on a GPGPU architecture were investigated.

5   Acceleration of Genetic Algorithm Using CUDA

The functional block of the RDA, originally implemented in C, was converted to CUDA code, using CUDA Toolkit 3.1. The operation of the implementation had the NSGA-II algorithm running as serial code on the main CPU core, with each individual evaluated as a CUDA kernel running on the GPU. The process begins by sending the entire dataset to be evaluated, along with a corresponding list of the locations of target anomalies, into the device memory of the GPU; as this data remains static it needs to be transferred only once. The algorithm then creates an initial population, with each genotype decoded to the relevant set of RDA parameters and passed to the individual GPU cores. Each individual is the assessed in parallel, return two integer values to the NSGA-II algorithm corresponding to the number of detected anomalies and the number of false-positive detections.

The test GPU is a GeForce GTX 460 card, which features Compute Capability 2.1 for CUDA code and a total of 336 CUDA cores, divided across 7 multiprocessors. As a desktop GPU card, it is penalised when performing double precision mathematics, so single precision operations were used throughout. Minor internal differences were observed in the relevant vectors between the CUDA code and the CPU-based C code that can be attributed to the lack of IEEE-754 precision in certain operations in CUDA code, however these were minor enough to have no effect on the final scores [4]. The authors acknowledge that at present such a GPU is unlikely to be suited to direct deployment on a robotic device due to its power consumption, however its is likely that within a few product generations the thermal design power (TDP) of an equivalently powered card will be comparable to that of a current mobile CPU platform [3].

To assess the performance of the CUDA implementation, a batch of 100 runs of the algorithm were run with 8-parameters, matching the tests conducted initially in Section 4. These runs were allowed to run for a total of 1,000 generations, with the Pareto-optimal fronts also extracted after 50 and 250 generations to compare directly with the CPU-bound results and also at the end of the run. Population sizes of 48, 336 and 1,344 were chosen for the GPU runs, to test the effectiveness at different population sizes relative to the number of available CUDA cores on the given card. As the entire data-set could fit entirely within the GPU memory, with only a minimal amount of data passed back to the CPU code each generation (the two respective scores from each individual), a vast speed-up was observed over the previous disc-access based CPU optimisation model.

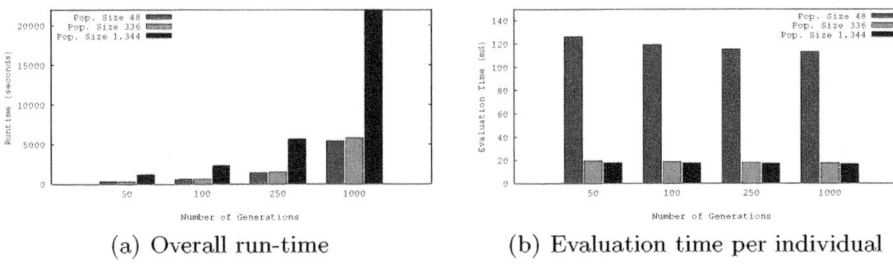

(a) Overall run-time   (b) Evaluation time per individual

Fig. 6. The run-time results for the CUDA implementation of the RDA optimisation algorithm

As can be seen in Figure 6, a significant amount of the overall running time can be attributed to the initial transfer of data, given the significant increase in the relative compute times per individual when the results over 50 generations are compared to those for 1000 generations. In addition, a population size of 336 comes at very little penalty over the population size of 48 in terms of per-generation time, due to the number of available cores on the GPU. Scaling beyond 336 brought little benefits in the compute time per individual.

6   Conclusion

The RDA has proven to be an effective algorithm at detecting anomalies within spectral data obtained from mass-spectrometry devices. However, the process of tuning the RDA parameters to values suited to providing a desired trade-off between correct detections and false-positive detections is a skilled and laborious process. A genetic algorithm based on the NSGA-II algorithm has shown promising results in allowing this process to be automated, however it requires a sizable reference data set and consequentially a lengthy run-time to produce the required results when run using conventional CPU. Fortunately, the nature of the task suits itself well to adopting the parallel processing that is cheaply afforded by GPGPU processors.

A CUDA implementation of the RDA in has been created, which has demonstrated a vast improvement in the runtime of the GA, allowing optimisation of parameter sets in much shorted time-frames than would be achievable on conventional processors. Furthermore, this implementation opens up many potential future avenues of research through allowing multiple instances of the RDA to be run in parallel using different parameter sets. GPUs now offer theoretical computing performance which vastly exceeds that of conventional CPUs, with significant growth in terms of FLOPS combined with reductions in power consumption with each generation, and a more rapid product release cycle than is found in CPUs; as such it is an area which should provide an extensive opportunity for exploitation and research within the AIS field and beyond.

Acknowledgments. This work is funded Defence Science and Technology Laboratory (DSTL), contract number 1000032154. The PTRMS data has been provided by Ionicon Analytik.

References

1. Apostolico, A., Galil, Z.: Pattern matching algorithms. Oxford University Press, Oxford (1997)
2. Bell, S., Nazarov, E., Wang, Y.F., Rodriguez, J.E., Eiceman, G.A.: Neural Network Recognition of Chemical Class Information in Mobility Spectra Obtained at High Temperatures. Analytic Chemistry 72, 1192–1198 (2000)
3. Collange, S., Defour, D., Tisserand, A.: Power Consumption of GPUs from a Software Perspective. In: Allen, G., Nabrzyski, J., Seidel, E., van Albada, G.D., Dongarra, J., Sloot, P.M.A. (eds.) ICCS 2009. LNCS, vol. 5544, pp. 914–923. Springer, Heidelberg (2009)
4. CUDA C Programming Guide Version 3.1.1. NVIDIA (2010), http://developer.download.nvidia.com/compute/cuda/3_2_prod/toolkit/docs/CUDA_C_Programming_Guide.pdf
5. Deb, K., et al.: A fast and elitest multiobjective genetic algorithm: NSGA-II. IEEE Transactions on Evolutionary Computation 6, 182–197 (2002)
6. Eiceman, G., Karpas, Z.: Ion Mobility Spectrometry, 2nd edn. CRC Press, Boca Raton (2004)
7. Gazit, I., Terkel, J.: Explosives detection by sniffer dogs following strenuous physical activity. Applied Animal Behaviour Science 81, 149–161 (2003)
8. International Conference on Artificial Immune Systems (ICARIS), Competitions (DSTL: Anomaly Detection in Mass Spectra) (2010), http://www.artificial-immune-systems.org/icaris/2010/competition.html
9. Nickolls, J., Buck, I., Garland, M., Skadron, K.: Scalable Parallel Programming with CUDA. Queue ACM 6(2), 40–53 (2008)
10. Owens, N.D.L., Greensted, A., Timmis, J., Tyrrell, A.: T Cell Receptor Signalling Inspired Kernel Density Estimation and Anomaly Detection. In: Andrews, P.S., Timmis, J., Owens, N.D.L., Aickelin, U., Hart, E., Hone, A., Tyrrell, A.M. (eds.) ICARIS 2009. LNCS, vol. 5666, pp. 122–135. Springer, Heidelberg (2009)
11. Owens, N.D.L., Timmis, J., Greensted, A., Tyrrell, A.: Elucidation of T Cell Signalling Models. Journal of Theoretical Biology 262(3), 452–470 (2010)
12. Owens, N.D.L., Greensted, A., Timmis, J., Tyrrell, A.: T Cell Receptor Signalling Inspired Kernel Density Estimation and Anomaly Detection. Accepted for publication in the Journal of Theoretical Computer Science (2011)
13. Owens, N.D.L.: From Biology to Algorithms. PhD Thesis. University of York. Department of Electronics (2010)
14. Owens, N.D.L., et al.: Robot Mounted Chemical Detection. Submitted to IEEE Transactions on Systems, Man and Cybernetics, Part C (2011)
15. Zupan, J., Gasteiger, J.: Neural networks: A new method for solving chemical problems or just a passing phase? Analytica. Chimica. Acta. 248, 1–30 (1991)

An Engineering-Informed Modelling Approach to AIS

Emma Hart and Despina Davoudani

Edinburgh Napier University, Edinburgh, Scotland, UK
{e.hart,d.davoudani}@napier.ac.uk

Abstract. A recent shift in thinking in Artificial Immune Systems (AIS) advocates developing a greater understanding of the underlying biological systems that serve as inspiration for engineering such systems by developing abstract computational models of the immune system in order to better understand the natural biology. We propose a refinement to existing frameworks which requires development of such models to be driven by the engineering problem being considered; the constraints of the engineered system must inform not only the model development, but also its validation. Using a case-study, we present a methodology which enables an abstract model of dendritic-cell trafficking to be developed with the purpose of building a self-organising wireless sensor network for temperature monitoring and maintenance. The methodology enables the development of a model which is consistent with the application constraints from the outset and can be validated in terms of the functional requirements of the application. Although the result models are not likely to be biologically faithful, they enable the engineer to better exploit the underlying metaphor, ultimately leading to reduced development time of the engineered system.

1   Introduction

The field of Artificial Immune Systems (AIS) has derived inspiration from many different elements of the natural immune system in order to develop engineered systems that operate in environments with constraints similar to those faced by the immune system [1]. Encouraged perhaps by views such as that of Timmis *et al* [2] that suggest rapid development in AIS is being hindered by both the lack of theoretical foundation and the lack of challenging application areas, a shift in focus has been apparent in the literature over recent years. On the one hand, we see the use of immune-inspired algorithms arising in increasingly more complex application areas, e.g swarm robotics [3] and wireless sensor networks [4]. Such applications embody the principles laid down in [5] which attempted to define the characteristics of applications which could properly benefit from the use of immune-inspiration. Simultaneously, significantly more research in AIS is under-pinned by the use of modelling techniques (both computational and mathematical) which provide theoretical foundations for algorithms, and proper immunological grounding. We propose that this shift towards theoretical

P. Liò, G. Nicosia, and T. Stibor (Eds.): ICARIS 2011, LNCS 6825, pp. 240–253, 2011.

development is necessary to drive innovations and development in future complex applications. In this paper, we examine the role that modelling can play in informing the development of a complex engineered system through the use of a case-study. The chosen study examines the creation of an immune-inspired prototype for controlling a *specknet* [6] — a particular type of ad-hoc wireless network which enables programmable computational networks to be constructed from thousands of miniature devices which sense, process and store information.

We consider the use of one particular aspect of immunology in association with specknets, that of dendritic-cell trafficking, and use an agent-based modelling approach to bridge the gap between the two complex systems. Specifically, we draw on a study which concerns mapping the data-collection and monitoring functionality of dendritic cells into an application which monitors and controls the environment inside a building. Although modelling as a tool has been used extensively by immunologists in efforts to either explain experimental data or to suggest novel lines of experimentation, our approach approach differs in that we specifically seek to understand how immune-inspired algorithms might be used within a complex engineered environment through the model. We deliberately make no attempt to produce an immunologically meaningful model that could be expected to provide insights to biologists (an approach also advocated by [7]). Instead, we propose that the model fulfills the following roles:

- it captures the high-level functionality of the biological system *and* the constraints of the engineered system
- it enables exploration of a range of state-of-the-art mechanisms from the biological literature, which may often be conflicting
- it enables validation of the functionality of the model according to metrics or measures appropriate to the engineered system

Through the use of a case-study, we show how a model can be developed with the above in mind. The proposed methodology is generically applicable to other domains propose a methodology and successfully bridges the gap between complex domains.; the results suggest that modelling is a useful exercise in tacking complex engineering problems, even if it leads to models which are biologically unfaithful.

2   On Immunology, Engineering and Modelling

Cohen [8] notes that there are three categories of people pursuing research which relates computing and immunology:

1. those of the *literal* school that build systems in silico to try and do what the actual immune system does (e.g. build computer security systems that discriminate between self and non-self),
2. those of the *metaphorical* school that look for inspiration from the immune system and build computational systems with the immune system in mind, and
3. those who aim to understand immunity through the development of computer and mathematical models.

This work is rooted in the second category, in that our goal is to build engineered systems. In line with this, we take a brief look at the literature which advocates the use of modelling to facilitate achieving this goal.

One of the seminal papers responsible for advocating a swing towards a theoretical approach to AIS was published by Stepney *et al* in [9], in which a Conceptual Framework for AIS development was presented. The framework suggests a three-phase process which begins with biology; in Phase 1, the underlying biology system which is being used for inspiration is probed, utilising biological observations and experiments to provide a partial view of the biological system. Phase 2 concerns the development of two types of model: firstly, abstract models of the biology are built from which analytical computational frameworks developed which can be analysed and validated and provide a set of *design principles*. In Phase 3, the principles are used to construct bio-inspired algorithms applicable to non-biological domains.

While following such a process undoubtedly leads to a greater understanding of the immunology on the part of the computer scientist, to date, there remain few algorithms in the literature which credit their derivation to following this framework. A few notable exceptions exist. Owens *et al* [10,11] refer to biological literature in Phase 1 of the framework, then show how models of T-cell receptor signalling, developed and validated in Phase 2, can be used to derive a Kernel Density Estimation method for anomaly detection. Andrews [12] evaluates the framework itself in his PhD, first examining immunological literature for inspiration, then building models of a receptor degeneracy which inspire the creation of a pattern classification algorithm. [13] begin with Phase 2 and develop a model of self-assertion in the immune system and analyse the model properties in depth. They suggest that the model can be transferred to data-mining applications, although they fall short of actually deriving an algorithm, i.e. Phase 3. Work by [14] is also worth mentioning — they present a lineage of work on the Dendritic Cell Algorithm (DCA) which resulted from very close interactions with lab-based immunologists. In fact, early versions of the algorithm even derived values for numeric parameters from results observed in the laboratory.[1] In this work, a modelling phase did not occur; the jump was made directly from Phase 1 to algorithm development in Phase 3.

However, it remains clear that there are some issue with the framework as originally proposed. Firstly, little guidance is given as to how to usefully follow the framework, as noted by [12] who proposes that *an approach would be to bias the route through the Conceptual Framework by having an application in mind*. Secondly, it seems clear that the computational and abstracted models which are formulated in Phase 2 may be inconsistent with engineering requirements of an application. This point is taken up by Timmis *et al* in an approach dubbed *immuno-engineering* [15], which proposes a mechanism for the abstraction, adaptation and application of immune principles to engineering, taking into account the differences between articial systems and biological systems. This could for

---

[1] Note, however, that in subsequent refinements of the algorithm much of the immunological detail has been removed.

example account for the different numbers, kinds, and rates of signals that need to be monitored and processed; the different kinds of decisions that need to be made; the different effectors available to support and implement those decisions; and the different constraints of embodiment, either physically or virtually engineered. We are unaware however of any cited examples of this approach being followed.

We therefore propose a modification to the Conceptual Framework in which the engineering requirements of the application in question are explicitly identified before Phase 1 and Phase 2 are undertaken. With engineering functionality and constraints clearly identified, the immunology literature or immunology expert can be consulted; an abstract model of the immunology can be developed at an appropriate level; this can be than translated into computational model which is consistent with the engineering constraints. The resulting translation and validation process may result in models which necessitate the introduction of mechanisms inconsistent with the immunological system. Further, the modelling process may further illuminate aspects of the desired functionality that are not appropriate to derived from biological metaphors.

An obvious question arises of how such a model can be validated given that it is no longer appropriate to calibrate it against experimental immunological data. We propose that the validation process shifts to validating *functionality* rather than either mechanistic detail or the ability to replicate experimental results. We propose instead a shift in focus to achieving similar functionality in the two systems. In this respect, modelling can be viewed as explorative, rather than restrictive, with no requirement for models to be biologically plausible.

3   The Application Domain: SpeckNets

This section provides a brief overview of specks in order to illustrate the complexity of the engineering environment under consideration. Details of the engineering aspects of specks, including technical specifications, are discussed in [6]. A detailed motivation of the use of a dendritic cell (DC) analogy is given in [4]. For the purpose of the paper, it is sufficient to focus on the constraints imposed by this complex engineering system, rather than focus on the implementation details.

Specknets are *large scale* — they can consist of thousands of nodes. As they are designed to be sprayed into an environment, they necessarily have an *ad-hoc topology*. Minimal battery power means communication is *limited in both range and in terms of power* as sending and receiving messages is extremely energy draining. The use of on-board energy saving mechanisms means that the nodes *cannot be guaranteed to be functioning* at any moment time. Finally, lack of a central control system forces the network to operate in a *decentralised* and *asynchronous fashion*.

4   Scoping the Model by Consideration of Engineering

Consider an application in which specks sprayed onto the walls of a large build-ing monitor temperature in their local area. Individual radiators can be remotely switched on and off to control temperature in a local area and the goal is to maintain a constant ambient temperature in the building. From an engineer-ing perspective, we require a system which is capable of *monitoring* the envi-ronment and *effecting decisions*. Control must be *de-centralised* and there is a desire to *minimise communication overhead* in order to save power. Turning to immunology for inspiration, the role played by dendritic-cell trafficking mecha-nisms appears a plausible metaphor for meeting these requirements: these cells serve as *sentinels* of the immune system, acting as scouts which both monitor an environment and prime the adaptive immune system by presenting it with the information regarding how and where to mount a response.

A possible mapping between the two systems is to enable radio signals to function as dendritic cells; signals propagating around the network can sample data from specks and return collected information to specks designated as 'lymph nodes'. The lymph specks evaluate returned data and modulate the temperature as required. At this level of abstraction, the mapping is straightforward. However, when one looks in detail at the immunological literature describing mechanisms which enable trafficking of dendritic cells it becomes clear that the processes are both complex and incompletely understood. In particular, the number of actors is immense, and furthermore, the literature is ambiguous regarding the conditions under which cells are triggered to migrate to lymph nodes (the reader is referred to [16] for an overview).

Given the engineering constraints of the application in terms of minimising power and overhead, it is clear that a model which utilises all the actors present in the biological system will fail. Therefore, in line with the views of Forrest [1], it is necessary to abstract the immune functionality and capture generic properties, rather than intricate detail. In order to do this, it is necessary to clearly articulate the high-level *functionality* of the immune system which map to the engineered requirements:

- Dendritic cells as *scouts*: mobile cells circulate through an environment sam-pling signals from it.
- Dendritic cells as *reporters*: DCs return to lymph nodes to present a snapshot of the information collected in the tissue on maturation.
- *Routing* via chemical gradients: chemokine gradients are used to route DCs back to lymph node and to direct T cells back to infected sites.
- System *stabilisation*: T cells are released from lymph-nodes if determining a response is required, and are able to participate in reactions which ultimately eliminate infection at local sites.

Note that this is in contrast to the majority of work inspired by DCs in AIS which focuses on the differentiation capabilities of these cells in response to rela-tive amounts of predefined types of signal collected and therefore their function as *classifiers*. Instead, our emphasis is on the ability of DCs to function as *scouts* and *reporters*. The model is not concerned with the details of how the decision to either tolerate or react to the information returned by DCs is arrived at; this is a property of the adaptive immune system, and is the subject of ongoing research and a further model. It is, however, useful in this model to investigate a crucial property of the response, that it can be directed back to an infected site (stabilisation), assuming a decision to respond had been made as this functionality also relates to DC trafficking.

5   An Engineering Constrained Immunological Model

A high-level description of an *immunological* model of dendritic-cell trafficking which can be analysed and validated in order to determine whether it achieves the required *functionality* can be summarised as follows: a constant size population of immature DCs circulates at random through the tissue. Spontaneous infections randomly arise in the tissue which release danger signals. Naïve DCs differentiate into mature DCs if the amount of danger signal collected from the tissue exceeds a threshold. Immature DCs die naturally on reaching the end of a predefined lifespan. Lymph nodes are found at random locations within the tissue, each of which is surrounded by a cytokine gradient which attracts mature DCs. Mature DCs reaching a lymph node cause the lymph to release T cells; these circulate at random until they are attracted by a cytokine gradient which surrounds an infection. T cells passing through an infected site reduce the amount of infection at that site until the infection is cleared.

5.1   Validation of the Model

Validation of the model must confirm that the high-level properties defined in section 4, emerge from the model. This contrasts to the majority of work in biological modelling where validation involves comparing the model to experimentally observed results to determine its correctness. According to the engineering application, the validation may be quantitative or qualitative, depending on whether appropriate metrics can be defined.

In this case, the properties listed in section 4 can be measured by the metrics defined in table 1 : these quantities can be extracted from the simulation. Note in some cases the measured quantity is a proxy from another measure. For example, we monitor the *reporting* ability of DCs by directly measuring the number of T cells produced in the system, as T cells are only produced in response to returning DCs.

5.2   Model Implementation

We have chosen to model DC trafficking using an agent-based model (ABM). Bonabeau [17] discusses in depth the advantages of agent-based models which can be summarised as: *(i) they capture emergent phenomena; (ii) they provide*

Table 1. The table shows quantitative measures which can be used to give an indication of whether the system is exhibiting the desired characteristics

Property	Description	Measure
Scouting	Tissue is adequately sampled	Tissue coverage
Reporting	Mature DCs return to lymph nodes	(1) size of T-cell population (2) no. DCs reaching lymph
Routing	DCs directed back to lymph T cells directed to infected sites	(1) no. DCs at lymph (2) infection level
Stabilisation	t-cells effect a reaction	infection level

a natural description of a system; and (iii) they are flexible. More specifically, Forrest and Beauchemin [1] have discussed in depth the effectiveness of applying Agent-Based Modelling techniques (ABM) to immunology. The particular environment adopted is NetLogo [18], due to both its popularity in the community and ease of use.

5.3   Assumptions and Simplifications from an Engineering Perspective

Evaluation of the biological literature to determine what to model must be guided by engineering rather immunological considerations. Further assumptions and simplifications will be necessary in the model implementation — it is vital that the implementation must respect engineering constraints from the outset. In this case, we consider the following aspects:

Production of dendritic cells: Dendritic cells originate in the bone marrow from where they are circulated through the tissue. This is simplified in the immunological model by generating DCs at random locations throughout the tissue, corresponding to generation of radio signals by individual specks in the engineering system.

Trafficking of immature DCs: Mobilisation of dendritic cells into lymphatic vessels is generally assumed to require maturation (either semi or full). However, evidence that immature DCs also gather in the lymph nodes is slowly accumulating, suggesting that, for example, immature Langerhans cells also traffic to lymph nodes [19]. According to Janeway [20], tissue DCs reaching the end of their life-span in body tissues without having been activated by infection can also travel via the lymphatics to local lymphoid tissue where they induce tolerance. The former approach corresponds to returning "pre-classified" information to the lymph, the latter to returning all collected information. Both mechanisms are plausible from the engineering perspective, we implement both trafficking scenarios in the model.

Simplification of cytokine network: Rather than modelling the large numbers of cytokines and chemokines which are known to orchestrate dendritic cell trafficking, we use a single class of cytokine agents as a proxy for those cytokines expressed by mature DCs which attract them back to lymph nodes, and another single class of cytokine agent to represent cytokines which direct T cells to infected sites within the body. Reducing the numbers, and by implication, volume, of cells trafficking around the system will clearly be of utmost importance in the engineered system.

Placement of lymph nodes: In the body, the secondary lymphoid organs are strategically placed near major organs and important sites. As specific placement of individual specks is unlikely to be feasible in distributed specknets which may consists of thousands of specks, we model a random distribution of lymph nodes in the environment.

Lymph nodes: A lymph node consists of an outermost cortex and inner medulla, the cortex being divided mainly into lymphoid follicles, paracortical (T-cell) areas and germinal centres. We simplify this to a single compartment within which all interactions between cells occur. Again, this simplification is driven by engineering requirements; lymph nodes are represented by individual specks in the network and will undertake processing of all received messages.

Lack of lymphatic vessels: Cells are physically directed to lymph nodes via a system of lymphatic vessels in the natural immune system. Such a physical system cannot be created in a specknet in which messages travel by radio broadcast and cannot be constrained to certain pathways. Therefore, we replace physical lymphatic vessels in the model with cytokine gradients emanating from lymph nodes which serve to direct cells back to the lymph.

Antigens are not explicitly modelled: The focus of the model is to understand how dendritic cell trafficking can be used to collect information from a system, and return that information to a location where collaborative decision making takes place based on all returned information. Therefore, we are not explicitly concerned with modelling responses to specific antigen initiated by T cells finding their cognate antigen in the lymph.[2] Furthermore, in specknet applications, antigen collected will be specific to the particular application. Therefore, we do not model collection of antigen explicitly.

Lack of specificity of T cells: Activated T cells exhibit particular cytokine profiles depending on the information they received in the lymph node from mature DCs. As the inclusion of T cells in the model only serves to illustrate that a response can be directed back to a specific site, one class of T-cell agent is modelled which is assumed to invoke the correct response at any site.[3]

A snapshot of the model running is shown in figure 1.

6 Analysis of the Model from an Engineering Perspective

According to the validation criteria listed above, the model was run using various scenarios and appropriate measures gathered. Due to space limitations, we do not present results from the model here. Instead, we present an analysis of how the processes implemented in the model contribute to the functional behaviour of the system, while considering the likelihood of transferring these behaviours

---

[2] The learning process taking place in the lymph should be the focus of a separate model.

[3] The implications of this are discussed later in the paper.

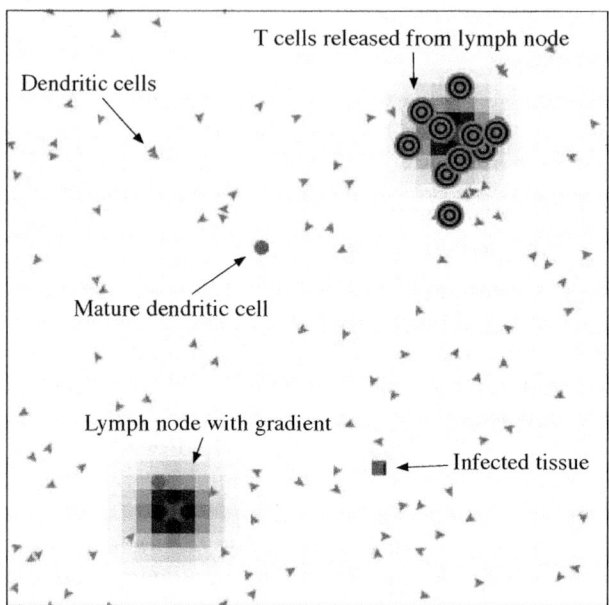

Fig. 1. A snapshot of the model running showing lymph nodes, infections and agents (dendritic cells, mature dendritic cells and T cells)

to the engineered system. The analysis requires the model to be iterated — this must be undertaken in a manner driven by the engineering constraints of the system, rather than a drive to replicate biology, bearing in mind the functional requirements.

6.1   Dendritic Cell Generation

Immunological theory is clear that DCs are generated from bone marrow — this is replicated in the model and results show that it achieves the desired functionality of providing scouts. Note however that this is localised control mechanism; each tissue node releases DCs independently of each of the other nodes. In the context of specknets, this potentially has unwanted consequences — flooding of the network leading to loss of messages can occur through each node behaving independently of others. This could be ameliorated by incorporating a global mechanism to control the release of DCs across the entire system, however, this is antithetical to the vision of specknets which are self-organising and autonomous. Therefore, a balance should be found between local and global control: we propose to delegate control of DC generation to the lymph nodes in the engineered model. Although implausible from a biological perspective, this facilitates a method of controlling the number of DCs (radio messages) by allowing each lymph node to be responsible for when messages are sent out to scout the network.[4] The balance between local and global control can be altered by changing the number of lymph nodes . Although this has obvious implications in the expected coverage of the environment - areas close to lymph nodes are likely to be more frequently visited by DCs, the metrics can be used to quantify the effect on functionality. The model is therefore updated accordingly results are shown in figure 2. Although functionality is preserved in terms of reporting ability and stabilisation, the time to clear increases when DCs are generated from the lymph nodes.

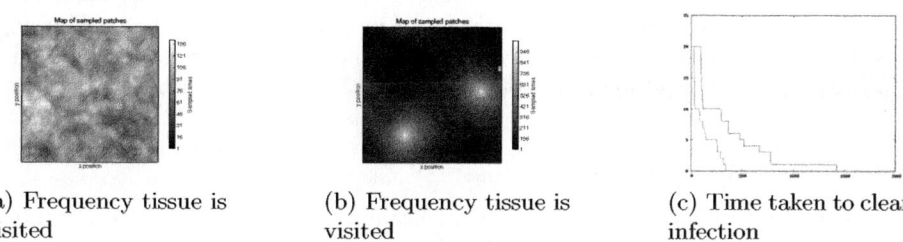

(a) Frequency tissue is visited

(b) Frequency tissue is visited

(c) Time taken to clear infection

Fig. 2. Figure (a) and (b) contrast the frequency with which tissue patches are visited under tissue generation of DCs (a) and lymph-node DC generation regimes (b) (lighter = more frequent). Figure (c) contrasts the rate of clearance of infection under each scheme (left-hand line is tissue-generation method).

Generating DCs from lymph nodes limits the initial exploratory behaviour of immature DCs to areas surrounding the lymph nodes, as clearly shown in figure 2. As well as affecting clearance time, the resulting pattern of communication can potentially be problematic in specknets: nodes visited more frequently have increased overhead in terms of message sending which can deplete energy resources to the extreme in which nodes die. This potentially leave the lymph nodes isolated from the rest of the network. On the other hand, the pattern illustrated in figure 2(a) reveals a more even distribution of the communication load across the network. The suitability of each method will be ultimately be dictated by the requirements of the application; exploring the impact of approaches both within and beyond the bounds of biological plausibility using the model is however of of value.

6.2   Trafficking of Immature Dendritic Cells

Although the immunological literature is ambivalent regarding the trafficking of *immature* DCs back to the lymph nodes, it is useful to examine the options from an engineering perspective. In an engineering context, collection of data, i.e routing messages around the network is costly in terms of energy. Discarding data

---

[4] Note that this has the potential side-effect in the worst case scenario of introducing *multiple local SPOF (Single Point of Failure)* into the system due to failed lymph specks.

by mimicking cell death 'because it occurs in the immune system' is therefore particularly wasteful. Routing 'healthy' data back to the lymph nodes clearly has an associated cost, but this is likely to be outweighed by the increased volume of data the classification algorithm implemented at the lymph node receives. Arrival of messages denoting healthy network states enables the learning algorithm to build a more accurate picture of the network.

Validation of this hypothesis is beyond the scope of this paper as it involves the *learning and classification* part of the algorithm derived from adaptive immunology, and not programmed as part of this model. However, this process provides an explicit link between the innate and adaptive parts of the system, therefore requires consideration during the innate modelling phase. The engineering constraints are used to evaluate mechanisms from the immunological literature for potential inclusion in the model.

6.3   Routing via Gradients

Dendritic cell trafficking in the natural immune systems occurs as a result of physical and chemical means: a physical network of conduits transport immune cells to lymph nodes through the tissue; cytokines and other chemicals recruit immune cells to the site of infection and promote healing of any damaged tissue following the removal of pathogens. As the former mechanism relies on a physical routing system which cannot be implemented in a WSN, any immune-inspiration for routing in the speck system must be gained from the chemical gradient based method.

The WSN literature already contains many examples of gradient-based routing techniques which have been optimised in term of minimising energy usage and thereby maximising lifespan of a WSN (e.g. [21,22]). It is therefore clear from the outset that these can be used directly within the application without further recourse to immunology. While these techniques differ in exact implementation detail, they essentially have common ingredients: a cost associated with each node; a mechanism for setting up the costs (gradient); an optional mechanism which periodically refreshes costs. Although the model is unlikely to offer any further improvements on existing routing mechanisms, it does however offer an opportunity to investigate potential behaviours which may emerge when using gradient based routing.

Routing to Lymph. Specknets typically have a static topology, with certain nodes within the network designated as lymph nodes. All lymph nodes perform identical processing. While it is preferable for a scouting message to return to the nearest lymph, it is acceptable for a message to be received by any lymph node. These requirements map exactly to typical situations in any WSN network, and therefore, the model adds no further insight; a routing mechanism can be selected directly from engineering literature.

Routing of T-cells to infected sites. Infections (synonomous with an *incident* in a network) occur at random locations. This requires a new gradient to be set up by returning scouting messsages each time an infection is encountered. Depending on the application two situations may arise: if all "infections" are identical, any lymph node can send out t-cells to counter the infection. If different types of infections occur however, appropriate t-cells must be routed to a specific infected site, rather than any infected site.

In initial simulations, all infected sites diffuse the *same* chemical to attract t-cells from a lymph node, in recognition of the complexity and energy cost associated with maintaining multiple gradient types within a specknet. Simulations showed that although t-cells are routed to infected sites, they can arrive at *any* infected site as the gradient is non-specifc. The problem is exacerbated the further an infection is from the lymph nodes (recall the lymphs are randomly placed). *Stabilisation* of the network will therefore depend whether the application incurs homogeneous or heterogeneous infections. In the latter case, stabilisation would only occur if multiple gradients were maintained. Given the additional overhead this would require, it appears prudent to look to engineering rather than immunology at this point to solve a potential problem. The engineer is free to increase the number of lymph nodes — this simple modification would increase the probability of a message from a lymph node arriving at the closest infected site due to closer proximity.

An alternative approach would be to depart once again from the immunology. The functionality of lymph nodes could be modified, allowing them to take on a dual role as centres where information can be accumulated and classified, but also as *effectors* which can take actions based on that information. In this case, the need for implementing messages which function as T-cells is completely removed and the problem eliminated.

The model has therefore highlighted some possible consequences of using gradient based routing mechanisms in terms of the required functionality of the system, illuminating aspects of the model in which immunology can provide the required inspiration, and those in which engineering techniques are more appropriate.

7   Conclusion

In line with current thinking in the domain of AIS, we have developed a model of a complex immunological mechanism in order to derive a prototype for ultimately monitoring the state of a complex engineered environment, a specknet. From the outset, the model was developed with engineering constraints in mind. Immunological mechanisms were selected for inclusion in the model according to engineering constraints, and the model was validated in terms of functionality, rather than against immunological data. Although this process is likely to yield a biologically unfaithful model, it is of considerable help in the development of the engineered systems. In particular:

- It provides a mechanism for defining the correct level of abstraction of the biological system such that high-level properties of interest are conserved using minimal complexity.

- It is able to illuminate aspects of the model which cannot be transferred to an engineered system for practical reasons.
- It provides an environment in which modifications can be made to the model in light of engineering constraints, and tested to ensure that the model retains similar emergent properties.
- It facilitates the study of the computational aspects of the engineered model in an environment free from complex engineering constraints.

The necessity to produce models which represent computational abstractions of the immune system was identified by Stepney *et al* in the design of the Conceptual Framework. It was further elaborated by Timmis *et al* when proposing Immuno-Engineering, which takes into account differences between engineered and biological system. This paper however makes explicit the requirement to consider engineering constraints from the outset when following a modelling process if a successful result is to be achieved: we propose that the conceptual framework be modified to reflect this. Rather than simply biasing a route through the framework with *an application in mind* as suggested in [12], we show through the case-study that the framework can be of great benefit when the engineering requirements have been explicitly defined before the process begins. Bonabeau [23] recognised *the freedom of the engineer to adapt models in a manner limited only by one's imagination and the available technology*. As advances in technology lead to ever more complex engineered systems, an informed approach to modelling will enable the AIS engineer to develop truly novel algorithms, pushing the boundaries of the current state-of-the-art.

References

1. Forrest, S., Beauchemin, C.: Computer Immunology. Immunol. Rev. 216(1), 176–197 (2007)
2. Timmis, J.: Artificial immune systems: Today and tomorow. Natural Computing 6(1), 1–18 (2007)
3. Lau, H., Bate, I., Timmis, J.: An immuno-engineering approach for anomaly detection in swarm robotics. In: Andrews, P.S., Timmis, J., Owens, N.D.L., Aickelin, U., Hart, E., Hone, A., Tyrrell, A.M. (eds.) ICARIS 2009. LNCS, vol. 5666, pp. 136–150. Springer, Heidelberg (2009)
4. Davoudani, D., Hart, E., Paechter, B.: Computing the state of specknets: Further analysis of an innate immune-inspired model. In: Bentley, P.J., Lee, D., Jung, S. (eds.) ICARIS 2008. LNCS, vol. 5132, pp. 95–106. Springer, Heidelberg (2008)
5. Hart, E., Timmis, J.: Application areas of AIS: The past, the present and the future. Applied Soft Computing 8(1), 191–201 (2008)
6. Arvind, D., Wong, K.: Speckled computing: Disruptive technology for networked information appliances. In: Proceedings of the IEEE International Symposium on Consumer Electronics (ISCE 2004), pp. 219–223 (2004)
7. Ismail, A., Timmis, J.: Aggregation of swarms for fault tolerance in swarm robotics. In: UK Workshop on Computational Intelligence (2009)
8. Cohen, I.: Real and artificial immune systems: computing the state of the body. Nature Reviews Immunology 07, 569–574 (2007)

9. Stepney, S., Smith, R., Timmis, J., Tyrrell, A., Neal, M., Hone, A.: Conceptual frameworks for artificial immune systems. Int. J. Unconventional Computing 1(3), 315–338 (2006)
10. Owens, N.D., Timmis, J., Greensted, A., Tyrrell, A.: Elucidation of t cell signalling models. Journal of Theoretical Biology 262(3), 452–470 (2010)
11. Owens, N., Greensted, A., Timmis, J., Tyrrell, A.: T cell receptor signalling inspired kernel density estimation and anomaly detection. In: Andrews, P.S., Timmis, J., Owens, N.D.L., Aickelin, U., Hart, E., Hone, A., Tyrrell, A.M. (eds.) ICARIS 2009. LNCS, vol. 5666, pp. 122–135. Springer, Heidelberg (2009)
12. Andrews, P.: An Investigation of a Methodology for the Development of Artifical Immune Systenms: A Case Study in Immune Receptor Degeneracy. PhD thesis, University of York (2008)
13. Dilger, W., Strangfeld, S.: Properties of the Bersini experiment on self-assertion. In: Cattolico, M. (ed.) GECCO, pp. 95–102. ACM, New York (2006)
14. Greensmith, J., Aickelin, U., Tedesco, G.: Information fusion for anomaly detection with the dendritic cell algorithm. Information Fusion 11(1), 21–34 (2010)
15. Timmis, J., Hart, E., Hone, A., Neal, M., Robins, A., Stepney, S., Tyrrell, A.: Immuno-engineering. In: Biologically-Inspired Collaborative Computing, vol. 268, pp. 3–17. Springer, Boston (2008)
16. Randolph, G.: Dendritic-cell trafficking to lymph nodes through lymphatic vessels. Nature Reviews Immunology 5(8), 617–628 (2005)
17. Bonabeau, E.: Agent-based modeling: Methods and techniques for simulating human systems. PNAS: Proceedings of the National Academemy of Sciences of the United States of America 99(suppl.3), 7280–7287 (2002)
18. Willensky, U.: Netlogo. Center for Connected Learning and Computer-Based Modeling. Northwestern University, Evanston, IL (1999), http://ccl.northwestern.edu/netlogo
19. Randolph, G.: Is maturation required for langerhans cell migration? J. Exp. Med. 196(4), 413–416 (2002)
20. Janeway, C.A., Paul, T.: Immunobiology: The Immune System in Health and Disease, 3rd edn. Garland Publishing, New York (1997)
21. Ye, N.F., Chen, F.Y.A.: A scalable solution to minimum cost forwarding in large sensor. In: Computer Communications and Networks, pp. 304–309 (2001)
22. Faruque, J., Psounis, K., Helmy, A.: Analysis of gradient-based routing protocols in sensor networks. In: Distributed Computing in Sensor Systems: First IEEE International Conference, pp. 258–275. Springer, Heidelberg (2005)
23. Bonabeau, E., Dorigo, M., Theraulaz, G.: Swarm Intelligence: From Natural to Artificial Systems. Oxford University Press, Oxford (1999)

Collective Self-detection Scheme for Adaptive Error Detection in a Foraging Swarm of Robots

HuiKeng Lau[1,3], Jon Timmis[1,2], and Iain Bate[1]

[1] Department of Computer Science, University of York
[2] Department of Electronics, University of York,
Heslington, YO10 5DD, UK
[3] School of Engineering and IT, Universiti Malaysia Sabah,
88999 Kota Kinabalu, Sabah, Malaysia
{hklau,iain.bate,jtimmis}@cs.york.ac.uk

Abstract. In this paper we present a collective detection scheme using receptor density algorithm to self-detect certain types of failure in swarm robotic systems. Key to any fault-tolerant system, is its ability to be robust to failure and have appropriate mechanisms to cope with a variety of such failures. In this work we present an error detection scheme based on T-cell signalling in which robots in a swarm collaborate by exchanging information with respect to performance on a given task, and self-detect errors within an individual. While this study is focused on deployment in a swarm robotic context, it is possible that our approach could possibly be generalized to a wider variety of multi-agent systems.

Keywords: swarm robotics, error detection, receptor density algorithm, collective detection scheme, self-detection.

1 Introduction

Swarm robotic systems (SRS) refer to systems with a large number of simple and physically homogeneous robots interacting with each other and the environment to achieve certain tasks [3]. In order to allow a swarm of robots to perform its task over extended periods of time, the swarm needs to be tolerant to failures that can occur within the swarm. Distributed autonomous systems, such as SRS, are susceptible to failure, and as recently shown by [11] the assumption that SRS are immune to such issues is not necessarily the case. In this paper, we focus on producing a fault-tolerant swarm of robots, but rather than having a central point of control for the identification of errors within the swarm, the swarm itself is responsible for the detection. Therefore the swarm collectively self-monitors and identifies errors within the swarm, which in principle would allow for a greater degree of fault tolerance.

Implicit redundancy and explicit error detection-and-recovery are two ways to address fault tolerance in swarm robotics. With redundancy, uncompleted tasks by a failed agent is taken over by a redundant agent in the system. This approach has typically been preferable as it is straightforward to implement [11]. It works

P. Liò, G. Nicosia, and T. Stibor (Eds.): ICARIS 2011, LNCS 6825, pp. 254–267, 2011.

well when a minimal number of *healthy* robots are still available to complete a given task and also that failures are independent, i.e., faulty robots do not have undesirable effects on the overall swarm. However, these conditions do not always hold. Winfield and Nembrini [11] showed that a few failing robots can significantly affect the overall swarm and should (if possible) be repaired. Initial work into such a self-repairing approach has been outlined in [10], but assumes that an effective error detection system is in place. To activate any recovery measure, we need to first detect the error and identify the faults. This is the second approach to achieve a fault-tolerant system. These two approaches do not have to be used in isolation but rather are used together to complement each other for an improved overall performance.

With respect to error detection in swarm robotics, limited work is available especially when dealing with dynamically changing environmental conditions. There are many challenges in developing an error detection system in swarm robotics. First we require an accurate detection of errors, second we require an adaptive and low resource solution due to potential limitations of the hardware platform. Third, a quick response time coupled with robustness in detection are desirable, it is no use to detect an error in a time frame that makes it impossible to do any form of recovery or response.

In this work, we make use of an immune-inspired solution that has many of the properties we require for a detection system: it is lightweight in terms of computational overhead, it is adaptive and superior in performance to more traditional statistical approaches (such as quartile- and T-test based algorithms). We employ a T-cell signaling inspired algorithm called the Receptor Density Algorithm (RDA) [7] as part of a collective self-detection scheme and in this paper, we analyze the approach with respect to accuracy, adaptivity, responsiveness,and robustness in detection.

The rest of the paper is structured as follows. Section 2 briefly describes error detection in swarm robotics and the use of RDA as an error detection method. Section 3 provides details on the experimental set up. The results and discussions are presented in Section 4 and conclusions in Section 5.

2   Background and Related Work

2.1   Error Detection in Swarm Robotics

SRS are subject to anomalies due to reasons such as faulty hardware components, design errors, or deliberate sabotage [11]. To ensure dependability, these faults need to be dealt with to avoid more faults and errors. The error detection-and-recovery involves a 3-stage process: error detection, fault diagnosis, and recovery. Error detection examines the system's behaviour for errors. If an error has been detected, fault diagnosis is activated to identify the faults followed by corresponding recovery measures.

In swarm robotics, the work on error detection is limited. However, in robotics in general, neural networks and its variations have been used to detect faults in the joints of the robotic manipulator [9], wheels of a Robuter [8], and *treels* (combined tracks and wheels) [1]. These techniques work very well with the system behaviour being non-dynamic, i.e., not affected by the changes in the operational environment. Otherwise, re-training is required. This is undesirable as prior knowledge of changes might not be available. With SRS normally deployed in a dynamic environment, it is crucial for the detection to be adaptive. This is the focus of our work.

Mokhtar et al. [5] implemented a dendritic cell inspired error detection in a resource limited micro-controller as part of an integrated homeostatic system in SYMBRION project[1]. Their focus is on single individual detection utilizing only individual's own sensor data, i.e., standalone detection. The drawback with standalone detection is that a change in the behaviour of a robot could be caused either by faults or the external effects, e.g., change in the environment. Our work with collective detection scheme takes advantage of local interactions among individuals to exchange information for self-detection of errors. By cross-referencing one robot's behaviour with others, a more accurate detection can be achieved (Fig. 1). In Fig. 1, robot R1 exchanges its data with other robots within its communication range namely robot R2, R3 and R5. Note that the neighbourhood at different time instance varies as the robots move around in the environment.

2.2   Receptor Density Algorithm

Robots in SRS are typically simple with limited communication ability, processing and memory. For example, the e-puck robot is equipped with 64 MHz CPU with 16 MIPS peak processing power, 4kB RAM and 144kB flash memory [6]. Therefore, the error detection mechanism has to be lightweight and statistical methods such as the RDA offer a potential solution.

Owens et al. introduced the RDA in [7] an algorithm developed through the study of T Cell receptors' signaling mechanisms in the immune system. By extracting features of these receptors, a mapping was made onto kernel density estimation, a technique from statistical machine learning. Assuming the RDA is on R1 in Fig 1, it works as follows (illustrated in Fig. 2):

Step 1: Training
   1. Calculate total stimulation $S(x)$ on each receptor x by input x_i from nb robots in a communication range of a robot (Fig. 2(a)). For R1 at T7, nb = 3, n = 4, and considering only variable a as input, $x_1 = {}^{R2}a_7$, $x_2 = {}^{R3}a_7$, and $x_3 = {}^{R5}a_7$.

$$S(x) = \sum_{i=1}^{nb} \frac{1}{n \times h} K_s\left(\frac{x - x_i}{h}\right) \qquad (1)$$

where $K_s(x)$ is the kernel, h is the kernel width, and n is total number of robots in a robot's communication range including itself.

---

[1] SYMBRION - Symbiotic Evolutionary Robot Organisms project
  (http://www.symbrion.eu)

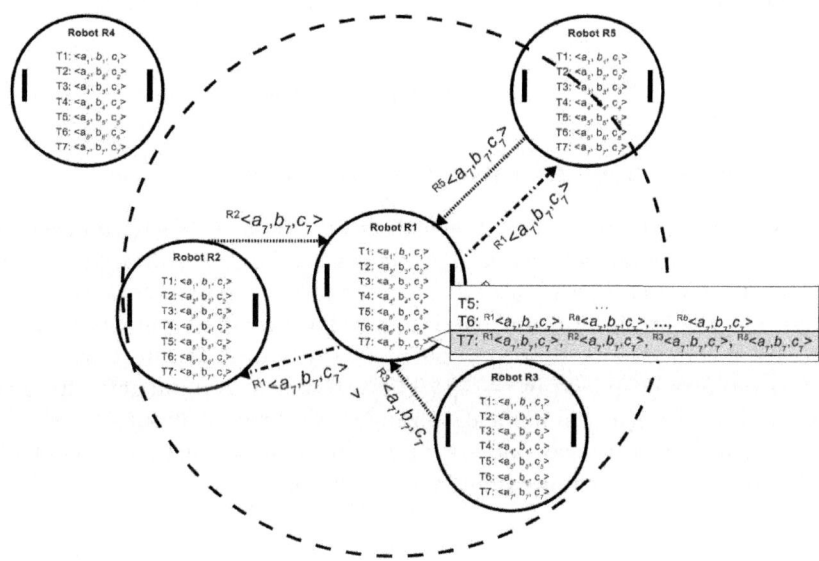

Fig. 1. Collective self-detection with exchanges of data between robots. The communication range of robot R1 is indicated by a dotted circle, and periodically R1 communicates (exchange data) with other robots within this range as indicated by dotted arrows. Rx <a_t, b_t, c_t > is the data vector for robot Rx at time t. At current time T7, R1 exchanges data with robot R2, R3, and R5 and thus has input data from four robots (including itself) as highlighted in the diagram.

2. Calculate negative feedback $neg(x)$ for each receptor x (Fig. 2(b)).

$$neg(x) = \begin{cases} S(x) - \beta, & \text{if } S(x) \geq \beta \\ 0, & \text{otherwise} \end{cases} \quad (2)$$

where β is the base negative barrier.

Step 2: Testing

1. Set the receptor position $r_p(x)=0$ for all receptors.
2. Set receptor length l to the maximum height of the stimulation kernel K_s scaled by n and h, $l = \frac{1}{n \times h(\sqrt{2\pi})}$.
3. Calculate updated receptor position $r_p^*(x)$ with input v ($^{R1}a_7$) from the robot (Fig. 2(c)).

$$r_p^*(x) = b \times S(x) + gb \times K_s(\frac{x - v}{h}) - \alpha \times neg(x) \quad (3)$$

where b is receptor position's decay rate, gb is current input stimulation rate,

α is negative feedback's stimulation rate.

4. Classify v:

$$v = \begin{cases} Normal, & \text{if } r_p^*(x) < l \\ Anomaly, & otherwise \end{cases} \tag{4}$$

Step 3: Repeat 1 and 2 for every control cycle

An receptor x is a point in the kernel density estimate. We normalized these points to fall within an interval of expected values for each variable of interest. For instance, if we choose to use 20 receptors to represent the kernel density estimate and the minimum and maximum value for input data is 0 and 100. By equally spacing the receptors to fall between 0 and 100, we have receptors from 0 to 100 evenly spaced by $\frac{100-0}{20-1}$. The variable x_i is input data from other robots that are within a communication range from a robot running the detection algorithm. Base negative feedback β, b, gb, and α is a constant to control the level of stimulation and suppression on each receptor.

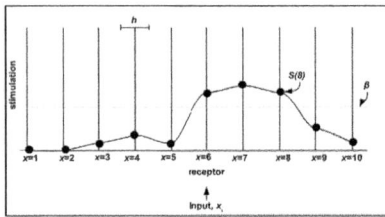

(a) calculate stimulation from input

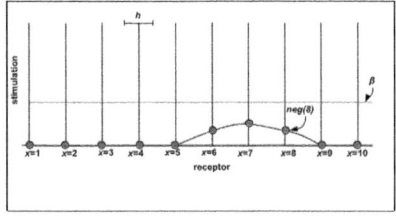

(b) calculate negative feedback

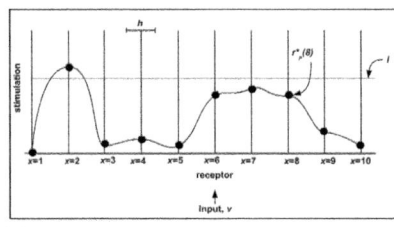

(c) calculate updated receptor position

Fig. 2. An illustration on using the RDA for error detection in a foraging SRS. (a) Calculate the stimulation level of each receptor from input data of neighbouring robots of a communication range. (b) If the stimulation level of a receptor is higher than the base negative barrier β, negative feedback is generated. (c) The stimulation level (receptor position) is updated when input from current robot is added. If any resulting receptor position is higher than a maximum stimulation level (receptor length) l, an error is detected, as seen at receptor $x=2$.

3   Experimental Setting

3.1   Simulation Setting

The foraging SRS is simulated with Player/Stage[2] [4]. Ten robots are placed within a 10-metre x 10-metre bounded octagonal shaped arena with a circular base at the centre. The task of the robots is to continuously search for, collect, and deposit objects at the base, this is a typical foraging task used in SRS. New objects are added to the arena at a rate referred to as the object placement rate (OPR) with OPR=0.10 in a non-dynamic environment.

A simulation begins with 100 initial objects placed randomly in the arena with a maximum of 200 objects at any time instance to avoid overcrowding. At time 5000s, a fault is injected to one robot and the fault persists until the end of simulation. Each simulation lasts for 20000s and this is further split into a smaller interval called a control cycle of 250s. Thus, there are $20000/250 = 80$ control cycles in each simulation. A control cycle of a smaller length is possible and it is very much dependent on the specific task and input data. We chose 250s to reduce the amount of data to process and to smooth irregularities that might otherwise exist in one of the input data, i.e., number of objects collected. At each control cycle, robots exchange their behavioural data with others in a communication range. The data consists of the number of objects collected (V1), energy used (V2), and distance travelled (V3). We recorded the data[3] as comma separated variable (CSV) files and analyzed them off-line so that the same data can be used for further analysis, fair comparisons with other methods and parameters tuning. Each scenario is repeated 20 runs.

For the RDA, the initial setting was obtained from manual inspections: number of receptor = 20, β=0.01, b=0.1, gb=1.1, α=1, the interval for V1=[0,8], V2=[0,300], V3=[0,40], and the kernel is Gaussian kernel with kernel width h_{v1}=1, h_{v2}=12, and h_{v3}=3. We discuss the tuning process of these parameters in section 4.2.

3.2   Modes of Failure

Component faults on a robot can be due to wear-and-tear, power loss or damaged circuitry connections. These faults can occur either instantaneously or gradually, and can be either complete failure or partial failure. We simulate three failure modes on the robot wheels: complete failure (P_{CP}), partial failure (P_{PT}), and gradual failure (P_{GR}). P_{CP} and P_{PT} occur instantaneously while P_{GR} is gradual.

With P_{CP}, robot wheels stop responding completely by moving in circles and are unable to move to target objects. With P_{PT}, the wheels suffer a sudden failure and the speed is reduced instantaneously to x meter/s from normal speed of 0.15 meter/s, while with P_{GR} the robot moves with gradually reducing speed by y meter/s per second. These faults are highly possible due to power loss

---

[2] Player 2.1 and a modified version of stage 2.1.0 from
http://www.brl.uwe.ac.uk/projects/swarm/index.html

[3] Data online at http://sites.google.com/site/researchmaterialshkl/data

or damaged circuitry connections. Unless specified otherwise, P_{PT} is simulated with an instantaneous motor speed reduction to 0.045 meter/s while P_{GR} with a gradual speed reduction of 100×10^{-5} meter/s². These values are appropriate as they range from the easier to detect complete failure to more difficult gradual failure that are still feasible to detect.

3.3 Dynamic Environment

We simulate scenarios in which the concentration (or the availability) of target objects change with time. Three conditions for our SRS: non-dynamic (CST), varying object placement rate (V_{OPR}), and varying object distribution (V_{ODS}). In CST, the OPR is fixed at 0.1 with homogeneous object distribution. In V_{OPR}, the OPR in the arena changes between 0.1 and 0.025, and in V_{ODS} the spatial distribution of objects in the arena is biased between top right and bottom left regions in the arena. Dynamic scenarios are simulated with a 2-cycle configuration in which dynamic changes occur at control cycle 20-40 and 60-80.

3.4 Performance Metrics

The performance of detection is evaluated based on the false positive rate (FP), the responsiveness (Latency), and true positive rate (TP). The Latency is time elapsed from the moment of fault injection until the moment of detection. For our problem, we are not only interested whether an error is detected but also how fast it can be detected. This is to prevent faulty robots being a cause of further disruptions to the rest of the swarm. Note that the Latency is also dependent on the control cycle length, a smaller control cycle may results in faster respond.

Given,
$N(pos)$ = Number of positives,
$N(tpos)$ = Number of true positives,
$N(neg)$ = Number of negatives,
$N(fpos)$ = Number of false positives,
T_{pd} = Fault detection time (in control cycle),
T_{ft} = Fault injection time (in control cycle),

Then, $\text{FP} = \frac{N(fpos)}{N(neg)}$, and $\text{Latency} = T_{pd} - T_{ft}$, $\text{TP} = \frac{N(tpos)}{N(pos)}$.

4   Results and Discussion

4.1 Performance

Boxplots of the FP from the 20 evaluation runs are shown in Fig. 3(a). In each box, the centre line is the median, the upper edge is the third quartile, and the lower edge is the first quartile. The whiskers extend to cover data points within 1.5 times interquartile range. Outliers are plotted individually. In the figure, the results are plotted according to the operational environment with the first 3

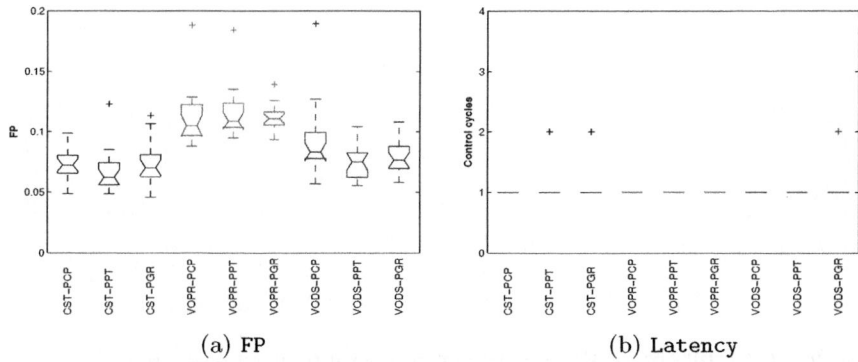

(a) FP   (b) Latency

Fig. 3. Boxplots of the FP and Latency for collective self-detection of errors with the RDA

boxplots for CST followed by V_{OPR}, and finally V_{ODS}. The median FP is approximately 0.1 in all scenarios. Two important observations on the results. Firstly, the collective scheme with RDA produces a low FP. Secondly, the FP is consistent across all scenarios including those in dynamic environments. This shows that the proposed method is adaptive to environmental changes. Otherwise, the FP would be much higher (≥ 0.5) in both V_{OPR} and V_{ODS}. We also note that in every trial, the error was detected (TP=1).

The results for Latency are shown in Fig. 3(b). The median response time is 1 control cycle for all scenarios. Since an evaluation is at every control cycle, this response is immediate. Similarly, the consistency in the Latency for all scenarios signify the ability to adapt accordingly.

We compared the results of proposed method using the RDA with two other detection algorithms based on quartiles and T-test. Results for quartile-based algorithm in Fig. 4 and T-test in Fig. 5. The RDA outperforms the other methods with a lower FP and a lower and more consistent Latency. These results are very encouraging. They indicate that through collective detection scheme with the RDA, an error within a robot can be self-detected within a short time even under dynamic environments. These results provide motivation to investigate other aspects such as fine-tuning the system (section 4.2) and the robustness of detection (section 4.3).

4.2   Parameter Tuning

We adopted the hill-climbing method in tuning the RDA's parameters. A chosen starting value is gradually increased or decreased by a small constant amount to observe its effect on the performance metrics. One parameter is tuned at a time, and a found optimal value is then used for subsequent tuning of other parameters.

Fig. 6 shows results for the tuning of V1's kernel width (h_{v1}) with a starting value of 0.0 and an increment of 0.2. The results of FP and Latency are plotted

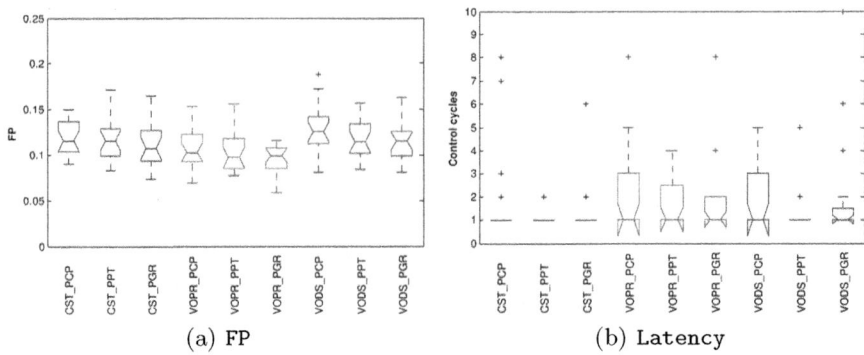

(a) FP   (b) Latency

Fig. 4. Results of (a) FP and (b) Latency with quartile-based detection

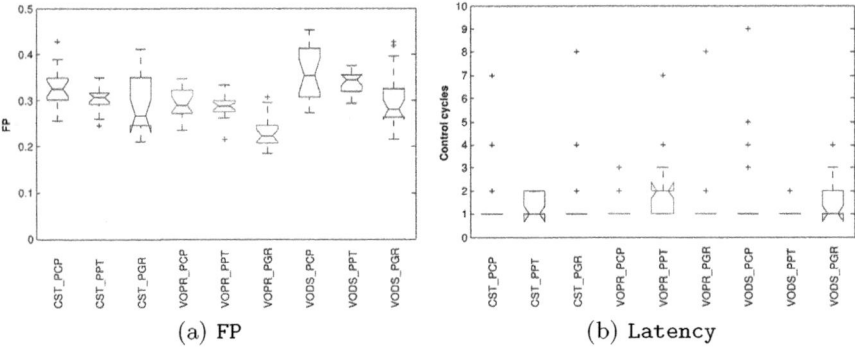

(a) FP   (b) Latency

Fig. 5. Results of the (a) FP and (b) Latency with T-test based detection

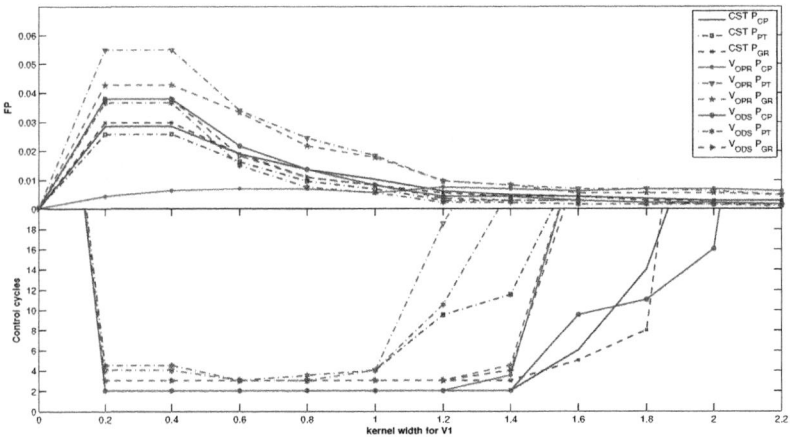

Fig. 6. Graphs of the median FP and Latency with different values of h_{v1}

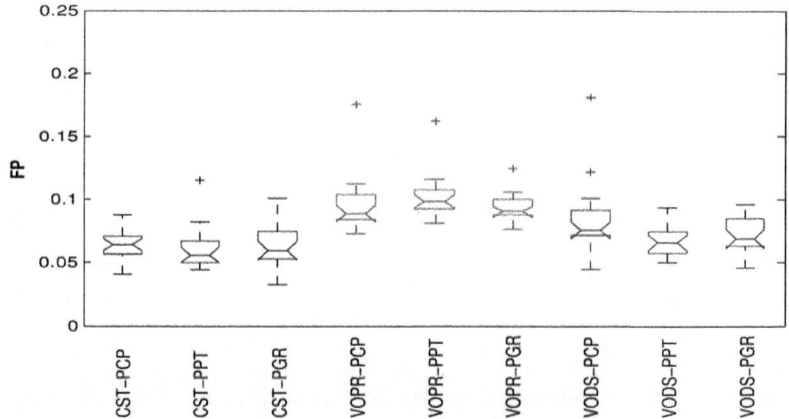

Fig. 7. Boxplots of the FP in detecting injected faults with the tuned RDA

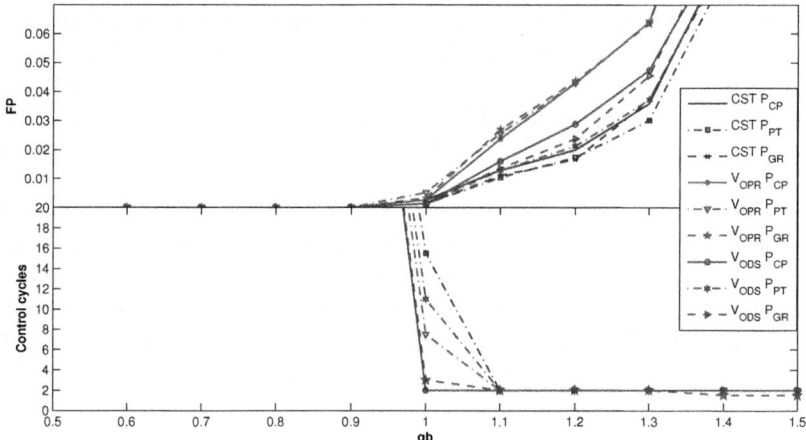

Fig. 8. Graphs for the median FP and Latency with different values of gb

side-by-side to show the effect of different h_{v1} on the performance. On the top figure, a sharp drop of FP is seen at $h_{v1}=0.4$ until $h_{v1}=1.2$ where the decrease became more subtle. On the bottom figure, a small drop in Latency is seen at $h_{v1}=0.4$ until $h_{v1}=0.6$ where it starts to rise. At $h_{v1}=1.0$, the latency rises sharply with P_{PT} errors and eventually followed by P_{CP} and P_{GR} at $h_{v1}=1.4$. Here, a suitable value for h_{v1} can be selected depending on the preference of the performance metrics. For example, if a requirement of FP$\leq$0.04 and Latency$\leq$5 is given, h_{v1} within the range of 0.6 and 1.0 can be used.

By analyzing the results for each RDA parameter through hill-climbing, we have found a set of optimal value for our problem with $h_{v1}=1.0$, $h_{v2}=12$, $h_{v3}=2.5$, $b=0.02$, $gb=1.1$, $\alpha=1.7$. FP results in Fig. 7 with these values showed that a lower FP is obtained in all scenarios compared to initial results in Fig. 3(a), significantly

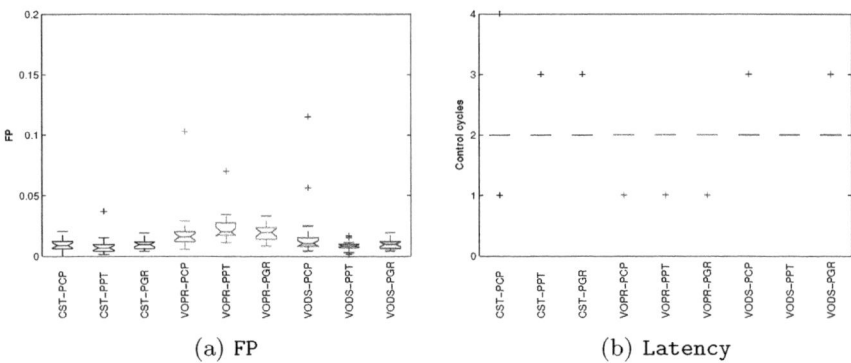

(a) FP   (b) Latency

Fig. 9. Boxplots of the FP and Latency detecting injected faults with a size 2 detection window

better in V_{OPR}. The results for the median Latency and TP, on the other hand, are exactly the same (as in Fig. 3(b)) and are thus omitted here. These results show that through parameter tuning, the performance can be improved.

From the same tuning exercise, we found some interesting observations. For example, the parameter b and α has no obvious effect on the latency of detection, i.e., irrespective of what value of b and α, the Latency remained constant at 2. For these parameters, the selection for the optimal value is based solely on the FP results.

For parameter gb, its influence on Latency appears to be one-sided (Fig.8). From the figure, the Latency changes drastically as the value of gb approaching 1.1. Beyond that point it remained constant and unchanged irrespective of the value of gb. This is an interesting observation but can be explained as the role of gb is to control the amount of stimulation from test data point. Higher stimulation pushes the receptor position $r_p^*(x)$ beyond receptor length l and thus an earlier detection. However, note that an earlier detection does not mean a positive detection.

In order to further reduce the FP, we implemented a similar mechanism as in [2] by increasing the size of detection window (DW) from 1 to 2. This means that a positive detection requires a detection for two consecutive control cycles. We call this RDA-DW2. The results (Fig. 9(a)) showed that a significantly lower FP is produced. A bigger DW helps in reducing false alarms because a sudden and drastic change in behaviour that last only one control cycle will be ignored. On the contrary, by increasing the size of DW also meant that a longer response time is involved. The Latency is directly related to the size of DW, Latency $\geq$ DW. With DW=2, the median Latency also increased to 2 control cycles (Fig. 9(b)).

4.3   On Robustness

We view the robustness of an error detection method from 2 perspectives: scalability in implementation and scalability in detection. Our implementation of

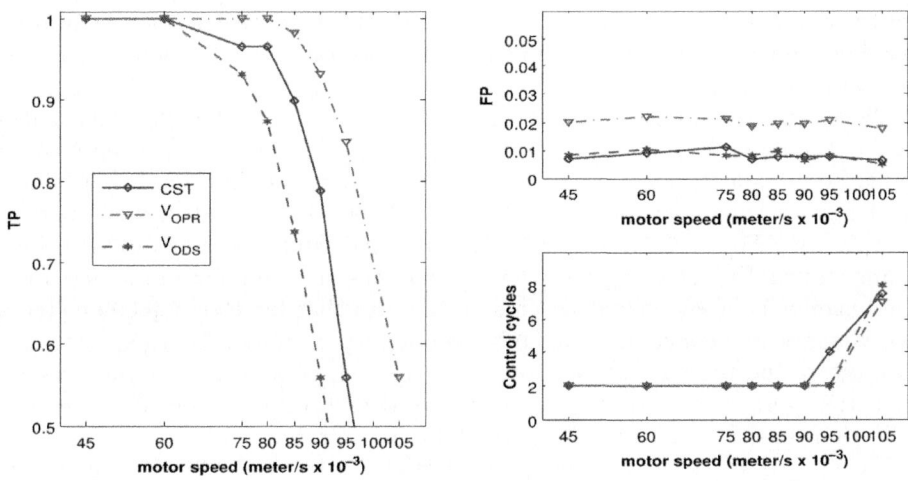

Fig. 10. The graphs of the median TP, FP and Latency in detecting various magnitudes of P_{PT}

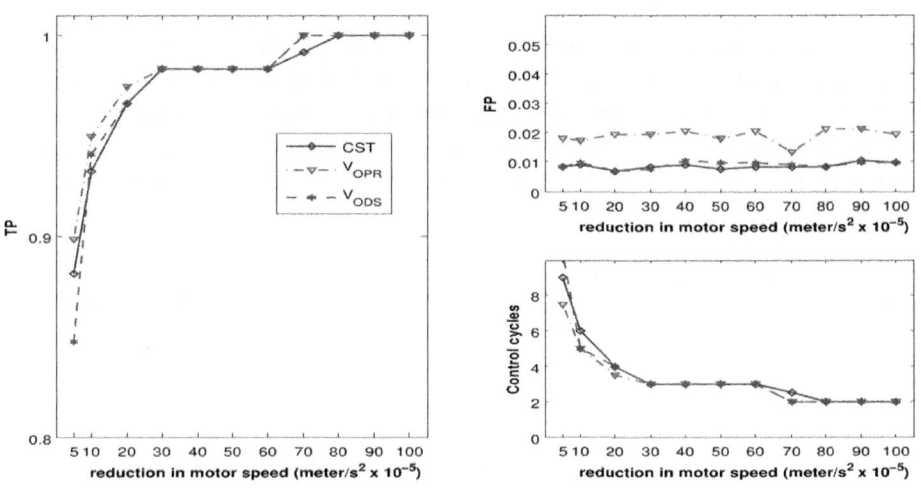

Fig. 11. The graphs of the median TP, FP and Latency in detecting various magnitudes of P_{GR}

the RDA-DW2 is on every robot and thus it is distributed and should scale to a larger swarm. To be aware of the magnitudes of faults detectable with our implementation, we conducted further experiments by injecting P_{PT} and P_{GR} with a range of magnitudes. If such a range can be established, we can then be aware of the detection capability of our implementation for informed decision for recovery actions.

We tested P_{PT} with different magnitudes: 0.105, 0.095, 0.090, 0.085, 0.080, 0.075, 0.060 and 0.045 meter/s. With P_{PT}, a bigger value signifies a more subtle fault. Results for the median FP and median Latency are shown in Fig. 10. From the figure, the median Latency is 2 for $P_{PT} \leq 0.090$ meter/s and starts to increase sharply with $P_{PT} > 0.090$ meter/s. On the other hand, the median FP does not change much. From the results, we know that the critical point of an increase in the Latency is at P_{PT}=0.090 meter/s. This mean that for $P_{PT} > 0.090$ meter/s, the changes in behaviour of a faulty robot is too subtle, for this algorithm, to indicate the presence of an error. If so desired, re-tuning of parameters can be carried out to increase the sensitivity of detection. However, an increase in detection sensitivity also increases the false alarm rate.

For P_{GR}, we tested P_{GR} with magnitudes from 5×10^{-5} to 100×10^{-5} meter/s^2. The interpretation of the magnitudes for P_{GR} is the direct opposite with P_{PT}. With P_{GR}, a smaller value signifies a more subtle fault. Results (Fig. 11) shows four trends in the latency of detection: $P_{GR} < 30 \times 10^{-5}$ meter/s^2 (T1), 30×10^{-5} meter/s$^2 \leq P_{GR} \leq 50 \times 10^{-5}$ meter/s^2 (T2) , 50×10^{-5} meter/s$^2 \leq P_{GR} < 80 \times 10^{-5}$ meter/s^2 (T3), and $P_{GR} \geq 80 \times 10^{-5}$ meter/s^2 (T4). The median latency for T2 and T4 is constant with the Latency=3 in T2 and Latency=2 in T4. An increase is seen in the median Latency at T1 and T3. The increase in T3 is gradual and much smaller compared to T1. If we consider T2, T3, and T4 to be an acceptable Latency, then the critical point at which to expect a drastic increase in the Latency is at P_{GR}=30×10^{-5} meter/s^2. This mean that with $P_{GR} < 30 \times 10^{-5}$ meter/s^2, the fault is too subtle and only apparent after a while.

With these results, we have established the range of magnitudes of P_{PT} and P_{GR} that can be effectively detected by collective RDA-DW2. These findings provide us evidence that the proposed method with RDA is robust in detection.

5   Conclusions

In this paper, we presented an error detection approach with collective self-detection scheme of errors using an immune-inspired algorithm, the RDA in the context of a foraging SRS. Results show that our approach is able to produce an accurate detection with a low rate false alarms and adaptive to dynamic environments. To date, no approach (to our knowledge) has been proposed for this specific problem in the context of SRS. We have also shown the tuning of the RDA's parameters for optimal performance. To assess the limitations of our approach, we investigated the detection capability and established the critical points that is useful for subsequent recovery measures.

References

1. Christensen, A.L., O'Grady, R., Birattari, M., Dorigo, M.: Automatic Synthesis of Fault Detection Modules for Mobile Robots. In: Proc. 2nd NASA/ESA Conf. Adaptive Hardware and Systems, pp. 693–700. IEEE Computer Society Press, Los Alamitos (2007)
2. Christensen, A.L., O'Grady, R., Birattari, M., Dorigo, M.: Exogenous fault detection in a collective robotic task. In: Almeida e Costa, F., Rocha, L.M., Costa, E., Harvey, I., Coutinho, A. (eds.) ECAL 2007. LNCS (LNAI), vol. 4648, pp. 555–564. Springer, Heidelberg (2007)
3. Şahin, E.: Swarm Robotics: From Sources of Inspiration to Domains of Application. In: Şahin, E., Spears, W.M. (eds.) Swarm Robotics 2004. LNCS, vol. 3342, pp. 10–20. Springer, Heidelberg (2005)
4. Gerkey, B., Vaughan, R.T., Howard, A.: The player/stage project: Tools for multi-robot and distributed sensor systems. In: Proc. 11th International Conf. Advanced Robotics, pp. 317–323 (2003)
5. Mokhtar, M., Timmis, J., Tyrrell, A., Bi, R.: In: Proc. Congress on Evolutionary Computation, pp. 2055–2062. IEEE Press, New York (2009)
6. Mondada, F., Bonani, M., Raemy, X., Pugh, J., Cianci, C., Klaptocz, A., Magnenat, S., Zufferey, J.-C., Floreano, D., Martinoli, A.: The e-puck, a Robot Designed for Education in Engineering. In: Proc. 9th Conf. Autonomous Robot Systems and Competitions, pp. 59–65 (2009)
7. Owens, N.D.L., Greensted, A., Timmis, J., Tyrrell, A.: T cell receptor signalling inspired kernel density estimation and anomaly detection. In: Andrews, P.S., Timmis, J., Owens, N.D.L., Aickelin, U., Hart, E., Hone, A., Tyrrell, A.M. (eds.) ICARIS 2009. LNCS, vol. 5666, pp. 122–135. Springer, Heidelberg (2009)
8. Skoundrianos, E.N., Tzafestas, S.G.: Finding fault-fault diagnosis on the wheels of a mobile robot using local model neural networks. IEEE Robotics and Automation Magazine, 83–90 (2004)
9. Terra, M.H., Tinos, R.: Fault Detection and Isolation in Robotic Manipulators via Neural Networks   A Comparison Among Three Architectures for Residual Analysis. Journal of Robotic Systems 18(7), 357–374
10. Timmis, J., Tyrrell, A., Mokhtar, M., Ismail, A., Owens, N., Bi, R.: An artificial immune system for robot organisms. In: Levi, P., Kernback, S. (eds.) Symbiotic Multi-Robot Organisms: Reliability, Adaptability and Evolution, pp. 268–288. Springer, Heidelberg (2010)
11. Winfield, A.F.T., Nembrini, J.: Safety in Numbers Fault Tolerance in Robot Swarms. International Journal on Modelling Identification and Control 1(1), 30–37 (2006)

Principles and Methods of Artificial Immune System Vaccination of Learning Systems

Waseem Ahmad and Ajit Narayanan

School of Computing and Mathematical Sciences
Auckland University of Technology (AUT), Auckland, New Zealand
{waseem.ahmad,ajit.narayanan}@aut.ac.nz

Abstract. Our body has evolved a complex system to combat viruses and other pathogens. Computing researchers have started paying increasing attention to natural immune systems because of their ability to learn how to distinguish between pathogens and non-pathogens using immunoglobulins, antibodies and memory cells. There are now several artificial immune system algorithms for learning inspired by the human natural immune system. Once the body gains immunity to a specific disease it generally remains free from it almost for life. One way to build such immunity is through vaccination. Vaccination is a process of stimulating the immune system by using a weaker infectious agent or extracting proteins from an infectious agent. A vaccine typically activates an immune response in the form of generation of antibodies, which are cloned and hyper-mutated to bind to antigens (fragments) of pathogens. The main aim of this paper is to explore the effectiveness of artificial vaccination of learning systems, where memory cells and their antibodies are introduced into the learning process to evaluate performance. Artificial neural networks are used to model the learning process and an artificial immune system to synthesize the vaccination material for injecting into the learning process. Two other phenomena of natural immune systems, namely, immune-suppression and auto-immune disease, are also explored and discussed in terms of hyper mutation of antibodies.

Keywords: Artificial immune system, Artificial neural network, Memory cells, Antibodies, Hyper mutation, Supervised learning.

1 Introduction

Artificial Immune System (AIS) is a relatively new computing paradigm inspired by the Natural Immune System (NIS). The human body has evolved complex methods for fighting infections, including viruses and other pathogens, without apparently any central coordination or control. Natural immune systems are a feature of multi-cellular organisms and have taken millions of years to evolve into their current state in the human body, where it can not only distinguish harmful cells from cells which are harmless to the body but also identify those cells that were initially recognized as harmless but subsequently become harmful due to infections or mutation. AIS covers a range of computing techniques in artificial intelligence (AI) and machine learning that adopt concepts from NIS and can be broadly classified as nature inspired computing,

P. Liò, G. Nicosia, and T. Stibor (Eds.): ICARIS 2011, LNCS 6825, pp. 268–281, 2011.

similar to other biologically-inspired techniques such as evolutionary/genetic algorithms [1, 2], artificial neural networks [3] and swarm intelligence [4]. AIS has been successfully applied in a number of areas ranging from clustering/classification [5-8], optimization [9], anomaly detection [10], computer security [11] and robotics [12].

The main motivation of researchers for using the natural immune system as their inspiration is due to its self-evolving, self-organizing and self-sustaining capabilities. The immune system can deal with previously unseen pathogens and viruses based on existing knowledge and can also trigger much faster responses to already seen pathogens (if in the future same pathogen attacks again) because of the immune memory attained by the NIS during the previous attack.   Some of the main characteristics of AIS described by Dasgupta [13] are recognition, diversity, memory, self regulation, learning, dynamic protection and probabilistic detection.

There are two main parts to a natural immune system: innate and adaptive. The innate immune system, we have at birth and remain fairly constant through our life span. On the other hand, the adaptive immune system evolves as it encounters new viruses and pathogens. One method of learning in an NIS (adaptive immune system) is vaccination, where inactive or weakened forms of the pathogens are introduced into the NIS to stimulate a defensive response without leading to the disease [14]. Vaccines lead to the production of antibodies so that the NIS is primed should the strong version of the pathogen be encountered. Vaccines are categorized by composition and formulation (how they are derived, how they are used and how their effects are mediated). For example, the tetanus vaccine is produced from the toxic chemicals (antigens) extracted from the tetanus pathogen, as are vaccines for hepatitis B and diphtheria [14].

Memory cells and the antibodies they produce are therefore important parts of the adaptive immune system. Memory cells encourage specialization by keeping track of already encountered pathogens and, if the same pathogen attacks the body in the future, the presence of memory cells can trigger a faster response to eliminate these pathogens by producing the relevant antibodies. Once released by memory cells, antibodies circulate in the body and help recognize and eliminate similar pathogens by binding to pathogenic antigens. Even as memory cells proliferate to produce antibodies, the paratope of the antibodies (that is, the sequence of amino acids that binds to the epitope on an antigen) can mutate with high frequency so that they may be able to form a better binding with the antigens. This mutation, called hyper mutation, is commonly used in AIS clustering/classification approaches to find improved solutions on the assumption that pathogens/antigens are data samples and antibodies and their cells are classes or clusters. But despite the importance of hyper mutation in AIS, there is relatively little understanding of its behavior or of how to use it most effectively in learning. This paper explores immune-suppression and auto-immune disease in the context of hyper mutation within AIS. Immune-suppression refers to reduced activation of the immune response, whereas auto-immune disease signifies an over-activated immune response of the body [14]. One of the most significant potential benefits of using memory cells in AIS is their data reduction/generalization capability. The objective of data reduction is to simplify the representation of the data while keeping the core information of the original data intact. This paper will demonstrate that memory cells obtained using an AIS algorithm can also provide effective data reduction capabilities.

Hart and Timmis [15] proposed that AISs be incorporated with other biologically inspired techniques, such as neural networks, swarm algorithms and genetic algorithms, to realize their full potential. The aim of this paper is to bring together two existing strands of research, namely, Artificial Immune System (AIS) and Artificial Neural Networks (ANNs) to form a new hybrid architecture, where the AIS is embedded with the ANN to help the ANN learn through memory cells and hyper mutated antibodies. Learning capabilities, highly specialized cells, diversity and memory are some of common features of both systems [16]. ANNs are inspired by the way a human brain works at the level of neurons. ANNs are very well established in the fields of classification and machine learning in general [3, 17].

The task of any classifier (in supervised learning) is not only to build up a model that can produce minimum classification errors on training data but also, and more importantly, to generate a model that can classify unseen and future patterns efficiently and accurately, i.e. a model that generalizes to unseen data. Typically, a k-fold technique is used to assess generalization capabilities of a classification algorithm. On the other hand, AISs are known to possess the characteristics of recognizing future patterns through their computational equivalent of paratopes and hyper mutation. The main objective of this paper is to demonstrate that vaccination of ANNs through memory cells and antibodies does not reduce the ANN's learning capability and in some cases can improve on it.

2 Background to Artificial Immune System

AIS and immunoinformatics more generally refer to computational paradigms inspired by natural immune systems [18-22]. As noted earlier, the main idea in AIS algorithms is to represent data samples as antigens and clusters as antibodies or B-cells. One of the earliest AIS algorithms for unsupervised clustering was proposed by De Castro and Zuben [8], Artificial Immune Network (aiNet). It utilizes the concepts of memory cells, clonal selection and hyper mutation. This is a two stage clustering algorithm. In stage 1, a number of memory cells are generated from the original data and then in stage 2 minimum spanning trees (MST) are used to obtain the number of clusters in the data. Another AIS clustering algorithm, inspired by the humoral mediated response triggered by adaptive immune system, is HAIS   [7], which involves an iterative process where antigens are presented to the algorithm randomly and then compared against existing memory cells and/or antibodies. A distinguishing feature of HAIS is that a clear distinction is made between Igs, antibodies and B-cells to separate the different biological and therefore computational functions they perform at the microbiological level.

The main work in AIS supervised learning algorithm is proposed by Watkins *et al* [6], which uses the concept of artificial recognition balls (ARBs), resource limitation, memory cell, hyper-mutation. Their artificial immune recognition system (AIRS) adopts a single shot approach so that learning patterns are allocated to the closest matching ARB in the pool of ARBs, followed by a competitive stage where the ARBs either survive or die depending on their fitness with regard to capturing antigens of the right class. Resources are re-allocated throughout the ARBs depending on which ARBs survive or die. The final output of this algorithm is in the form of memory cells, which adopt a k-nearest neighbor (KNN) method for determining the class of test samples.

While memory cells are used in the algorithm, there are some differences in their functionality in comparison to their natural counterparts. In NISs, once the memory cell is generated by B cells, it stays in the body for a long time, but in AIRS memory cells can be replaced by more affine or more active memory cells. Also, affinity maturation and the effect of mounting a faster response to already seen pathogens could be more fully utilized. HAIS [23] is another AIS based classifier for supervised learning and is inspired by the humoral mediated response triggered by adaptive immune system [7]. HAIS uses core immune system concepts such as memory cells, plasma cells, Igs, antibodies and B-cells as well as parameters such as negative clonal selection and affinity thresholds. In particular, HAIS uses local and global similarity based measures based on affinity thresholds to avoid over-fitting or under-fitting of data. More details about HAIS for supervised learning can be found in the next section.

3   HAIS Supervised Learning Algorithm

As noted above, the HAIS supervised learning algorithm is based on the humoral mediated immune response triggered by the adaptive immune system. B cells, Igs, antibodies, hyper mutation, memory cells, affinity maturation and negative clonal selection are the main components of this algorithm. Each B cell is considered as a class, antigens as fragments (either partial or complete) of data instances and memory cells constitute information extracted from already seen pathogens. The algorithm starts with generating as many B cells as classes in the data by choosing, at random, one data sample from each class. The B cell Ig receptors are set to the attribute values for that data sample, an initial plasma cell is generated that releases antibodies that replicate the Ig with varying degrees of mutation, and a memory cell is formed that displays the Ig on its surface. The HAIS algorithm for supervised learning then follows a three layered approach for classifying all the other data samples, picked at random one at a time without replacement. When a pathogen (data instance) enters into the AIS system, it is brought into the respective B cell. At the first layer pathogen is compared against existing memory cells. If a match is found, B cell will capture the pathogens, but if first layer can't trap pathogen, then it is exposed to the population of antibodies of that particular B cell, if any of the antibodies trap pathogen, the B cell will capture the pathogens and perform certain actions such as generation of memory cell and antibodies, affinity maturation process for stimulated antibody. If even this layer cannot trap pathogen, then in the final layer, the closest antibody is mutated until required affinity maturation is achieved which subsequently result in generation of plasma cell (further generate memory cell and antibodies). The comparison between pathogen and Igs/antibodies is performed using normalized Euclidean distance. Two affinity threshold measures are presented, namely, local and global affinity threshold (AT). Local AT calculates a varying measure for each class based on its own distribution of data instances, whereas global AT find a global AT measure which is used for all classes (B cells). Two different mutation rates, namely, hyper mutation and local mutation, are used. Hyper mutation is used to generate new antibodies whereas local mutation is used for affinity maturation. Negative clonal selection is performed within the population of B cells of each class, meaning removal of antibodies that are too similar to each others. This 'present-and-match' process of pathogen presentation continues until the pool of data is empty. More details regarding HAIS supervised learning algorithm can be found in [23].

4 Proposed Hybrid Method

The hybrid method proposed in this paper is based on Artificial Immune System (AISs) and Artificial Neural Network (ANNs). The ANN is used to determine whether the introduction of memory cells at a suitable stage of learning (a form of vaccination) aids or hinders the learning process. AIS algorithms are known to possess data reduction capabilities through memory cells. Memory cells are considered to be a subset of original data or, in this case, proteins extracted from pathogens (referred to as acellular vaccines). But there is currently very little understanding of how effective the memory cells are for reducing the data (i.e. for generalizing to important structural properties of the data) while at the same time preserving critical class information. The HAIS algorithm [23] proposed for supervised learning is used to extract memory cells from the data and then those memory cells are used to generate antibodies with different mutation rates, which can be seen as various level of activated immune response. In this paper, mutation rate of antibodies varies from 5 to 40 percent depending on the dataset. Negative clonal selection is performed while generating antibodies to keep diversity and population size in control. The ANN is used to model the effectiveness of the memory cells/antibodies, hence the hybrid architecture. The ANN here is our virtual learning organism that is going to be experimented on, and the HAIS is a subpart of the ANN to produce the vaccination material. A simple back propagation and logistic activation function based ANN is used for the experiments. JavaNNS (a version of SNNS) [24] is used to implement the ANN.

Our hypotheses in this paper are that: (a) training an ANN with only memory cells prior to exposure to the data leads to effective learning (i.e. memory cells as data reduction are effective); and (b) effective learning of pathogens and the classes to which they belong can be achieved by using vaccination. The vaccination experiment itself has two conditions: (C1) there is no prior immune system in the ANN, and (C2) there is a prior immune system in the ANN (Fig. 1). The first condition is achieved by

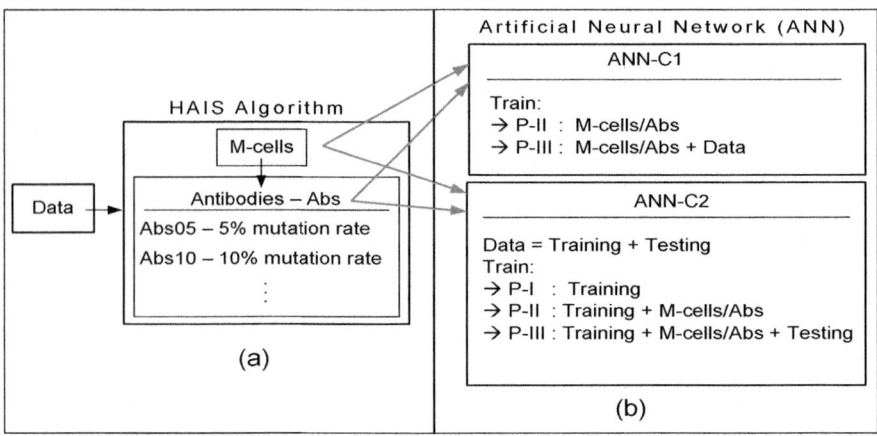

Fig. 1. Snapshot of hybrid architecture proposed in this paper using HAIS and ANN

using all the data to train ANN after exposure to the vaccine (i.e. no test phase), and the second by separating the full data into training and testing data and initially training the ANN on training data only prior to checking generalization capabilities. Vaccines (memory cells) in C1 are extracted from whole data whereas in C2, are extracted from test data. The method can be explained in three phases, as follow:

Initial phase (P-I): Train ANN on Training data if primary immune system exists, or skip this phase.

Vaccination phase (P-II): Use vaccination (memory cells or antibodies) as well as training data to train the ANN.

Pathogen exposition phase (P-III): Once the ANN has converged during the vaccination phase, expose original pathogens (or testing data) to the ANN.

5   Experimental Results

One simulated dataset and two well known datasets (Iris and Wisconsin breast cancer) are used. Both these datasets are available from the machine learning repository at UCI [25]. The simulated dataset is used to test whether the proposed method can find perfect classification when both classes are linearly separable. The main purpose of this paper is not to compare results against existing state of the art techniques, but only to demonstrate that memory cells and the information they contain can be exported to other techniques (in this case, ANNs) to produce models that are more robust and generalized than using those techniques alone.   The ANN architecture for the simulated dataset was 2x(6x10)x1 (two input nodes, a hidden layer of 60 nodes configured 6 by 10, and one output node), for the iris data 4x(3x10)x3 and for the breast cancer data 30x(4x15)x1.

5.1 Simulated Data

The simulated data has two distinct classes with only two features and consists of 153 instances. The 2-D projection of simulated data can be seen in the Fig. 1 (Right). Under C1 (no primary immune system), all the data is considered as pathogens and memory cells are extracted from the full data. 34 memory cells were produced using HAIS: 16 are from class one and 18 from class two, resulting in 78% reduction. The memory cells are introduced into a 'bare' ANN and the ANN run until convergence (3000 iterations) to approximately zero error. The original data is then introduced into the trained ANN as shown in Fig. 2. The ANN's error momentarily goes higher and then converges to zero error (error sum of square - ESS). This experiment indicates that memory cells extracted from the HAIS are accurate representation of the data in reduced form for supervised learning. In other words, the structural properties of the data are kept intact in memory cells.

Vaccination consists of introducing the discovered memory cells (34). But the main purpose of any vaccine is to trigger production of antibodies (secondary response). The role of secondary response is evaluated in the following experiments using the same simulated data. The memory cells generated in the above experiment are used to generate antibodies with different mutation rates ranging from 5 to 40 percent (condition C1 above). Separate ANNs are then trained using these antibodies that have

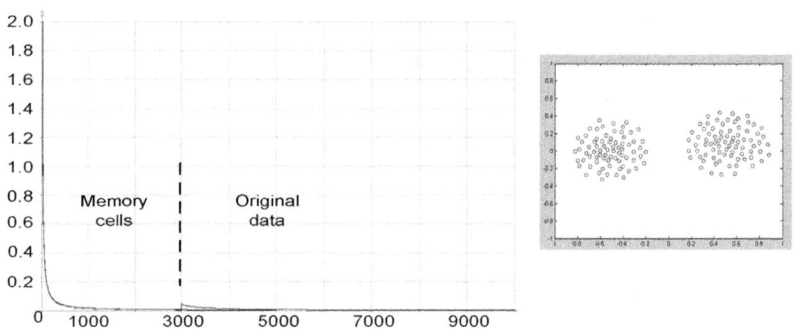

Fig. 2. Left: ESS curve, where X-axis represents Learning cycles (iterations) and Y-axis are ESS obtained for simulated data. Right: The original projection of two class data

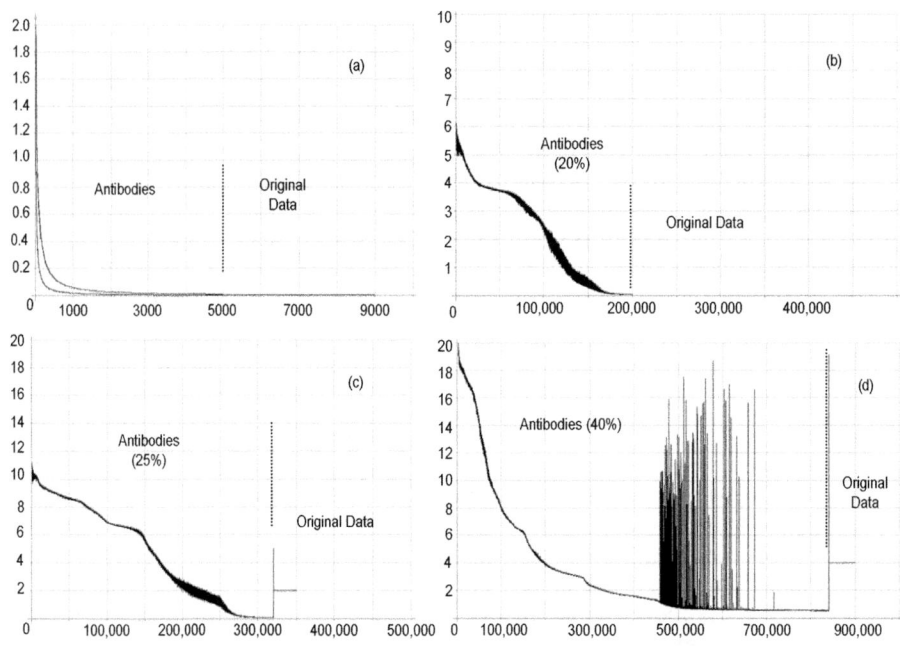

Fig. 3. (a) Antibodies with 5 and 10 percent mutation rate prior to exposure to full data (b) Antibodies with 20% mutation rate, (c) antibodies with 25% mutation rate and finally (d) antibodies with 40% mutation rate

been generated with different mutation rates and, just as before, after ANN convergence the original data is introduced to the trained ANN. The purpose of these experiments is to observe the learning and generalization capabilities of immune response triggered by vaccination. In Figure 3a, when mutation of 5 and 10 percent of antibodies is used, the ANN took 5000 iteration to converge and when original data is introduced, the ANN stays stabilized and the ESS stayed at zero (condition C1). The same behavior can be seen in Fig. 3b, where 20 percent mutation is used to generate antibodies. An interesting behavior started to emerge in Fig. 3c, where 25% mutation rate is used to generate antibodies. Once the ANN converges to zeros after 320,000 iterations, on exposure to the original data the ANN error curve goes higher and then stabilized at SSE of 2. Exactly the same behavior can be seen while using 40% mutation rate (Fig. 3d). In this case the final error on the original data stabilizes at 4. These experimental results with mutation rates of 25 and 40 percent suggest over-generalization of antibodies. Also, as the rate of mutation increases, the ANN needed more iterations to converge. This is because the antibodies started to overlap in feature space, leading to more time (iterations) to converge to minimum error due to reduction in linear separability, and over-generalization of data leading to increased classification error.

The above sets of experiments were repeated 10 times for each mutation rate and the overall averages are reported in Table 1. For antibodies with mutation rate of 5, 10 and 20 percent, the ANN always finds zero error on the original data.

Table 1. 10 run of antibodies using different mutation rates on simulated data

Index	1	2	3	4	5	6	7	8	9	10	Avg.	Min.	Max.
Abs 5%	0	0	0	0	0	0	0	0	0	0	0	0	0
Abs 10%	0	0	0	0	0	0	0	0	0	0	0	0	0
Abs 20%	0	0	0	0	0	0	0	0	0	0	0	0	0
Abs 25%	3	1	1	1	3	1	0	1	1	3	1.5	0	3
Abs 40%	4	2	0	2	4	3	2	1	3	4	2.5	0	4

5.2 Iris Data

The iris data has three classes consisting of 50 instances each. The dataset has four features (Sepal Length, Sepal Width, Petal Length and Petal Width) and three classes (Setosa, Versicolor and Virginica). The HAIS supervised learning algorithm produced 66 memory cells (56% data reduction). The ANN by itself produced 2 errors (Fig. 4 Left). But when memory cells are used to train the ANN it converges to zero error, and when original data is introduced the error curve converges at 2 errors (Fig. 4). The ANN in both cases (original data, and memory cells + original data) converges to exactly same error, which indicates that data reduction in the form of memory cells has not affected the ANN detrimentally, even when errors exist.

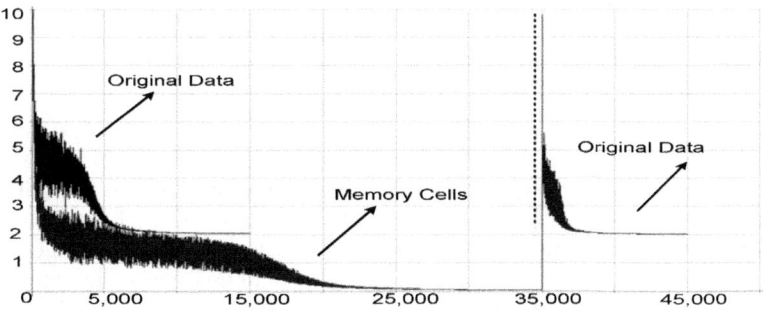

Fig. 4. Learning curve of both original data and memory cells + original data

When the experiment is repeated using antibodies with different mutation rates (ranges from 5 to 20 percent), the antibodies with 5% mutation rate converge to zero error (Fig. 5a), but once the original data is introduced into the trained ANN (C1), the error curve goes higher and subsequently converges to 2 errors (which is same as original data with or without memory cells). An interesting behavior emerged when antibodies mutation rate of 10% is set and the ANN is trained (Fig. 5b). The training error goes higher from zero to 10 in comparison with 5% mutation rate. But when original data is introduced the error rapidly converges to zero. This suggests that when the ANN is trained on 10% mutated antibodies, due to the diverse population of antibodies the ANN converges at higher error (meaning over-generalization of data), which is then corrected on exposure to the full dataset. Figure 5c shows the results with 15% mutation rate, where the ANN with antibodies converges to training error of over 50 (70,000 iterations), but when the original data is introduced it produced few errors. The same behavior can be seen when 20% mutation rate (Fig. 5d).

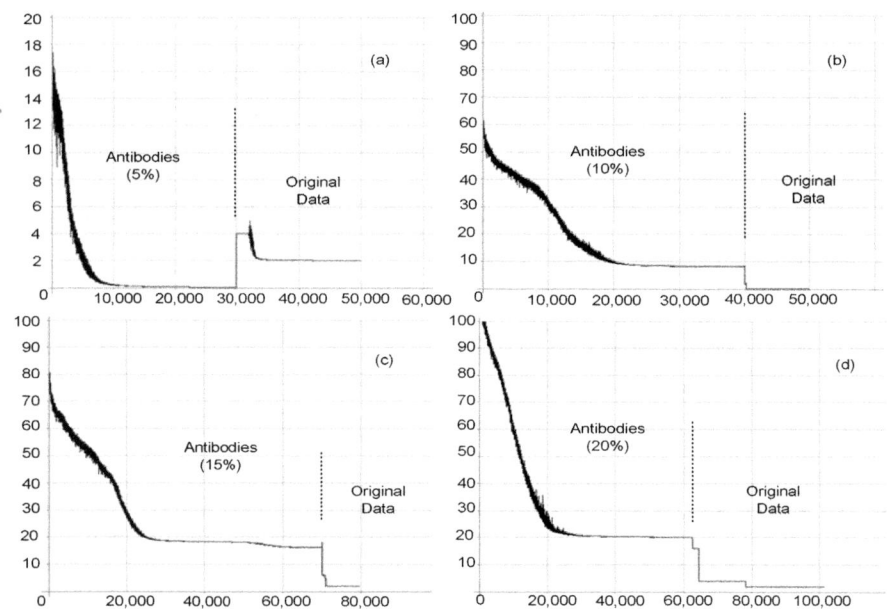

Fig. 5. Training ANN with Antibodies with different mutation rates, and then introducing original data

The whole process of obtaining memory cells for data reduction followed by generation of antibodies for vaccination using different mutation rates demonstrates some important characteristics of the generalization capabilities of memory cells/antibodies. Low mutation rate leads to less generalization of the data and hence under-fitting of the desired model. High mutation rates lead to higher generalization of the data, but when mutation is too high, the obtained antibodies tends to over-generalize, resulting in over-fitting of the final model. In Fig. 5, it can be noticed that with 5% mutation rate the final error stayed the same (ESS of 2) and with 10%

mutation the final error on the original data drops to zero. But if mutation rate keeps increasing, the error increases again. This behavior of under-generalization and over-generalization of data in relation to under-fitting and over-fitting of models can also be explained in term of immunology. Immune-suppression refers to under-activation of the immune response and auto-immune disease refers to over-activation of immune response. The generation of antibodies with different mutation rates represents various level of activation of the immune response. Lower mutation means under-activation of immune response or immune-suppression, higher mutation means over-activation of immune response or auto-immune disease.

The above experiment on the iris data were run 10 times for each mutation rate (Table 2). The 5 percent mutation rate produced 2 errors in all 10 runs, whereas 10% mutation produced zeros error on 9 occasions and only once 2 errors. 15% mutation produced zero error 6 out of 10 times, whereas 20% mutation produced only one run of zero error.

Table 2. 10 run of antibodies using different mutation rates on Iris data

Index	1	2	3	4	5	6	7	8	9	10	Avg.	Min.	Max.
Abs 5%	2	2	2	2	2	2	2	2	2	2	2	2	2
Abs 10%	0	0	0	0	2	0	0	0	0	0	0.2	0	2
Abs 15%	0	0	2	0	0	0	2	4	2	0	1.0	0	4
Abs 20%	4	4	2	6	4	0	4	4	2	6	3.6	2	6

For the following C2 experiments, the original iris data is divided into two groups, namely, training data and testing data (75 instances each), randomly selected. The training data is used to generate the primary immune system, and this experiment will consist of three phases. In P-I, the primary immune system is generated running the ANN on training data. P-II will use both training and testing (or memory cells) to train the ANN and finally P-III will only train on test data. Figure 6a shows what happens for a non-vaccinated ANN, three sub-conditions: training data, followed by training + testing data and finally test data. The ANN converges to zero for the training data, but when both training and testing data are used, the error curve converges to 2, and finally when only testing data is used, the ANN stayed at 2 errors without any oscillation. Figure 6b shows what happens when memory cells are used

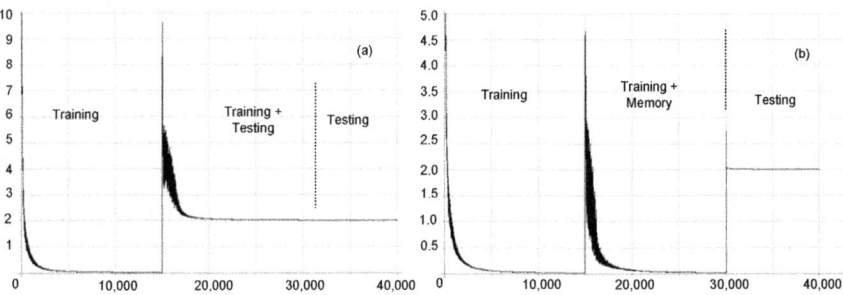

Fig. 6. (a) Training and testing data are used (b) Memory cells are used instead of training data in P-II to train the ANN

along with training data in P-II, where the ANN converges to zero error. But once test data is introduced, the error converges to 2 as well.

The same experiment is conducted by replacing memory cells with antibodies with different mutation rates. The final results can be seen in Fig. 7. Antibodies with 5% mutation rate produce 2 error on test data, whereas antibodies with 10% mutation rate has been able to find zero errors on test data. The error increased with antibodies with 15 and 20 percent mutation rates.

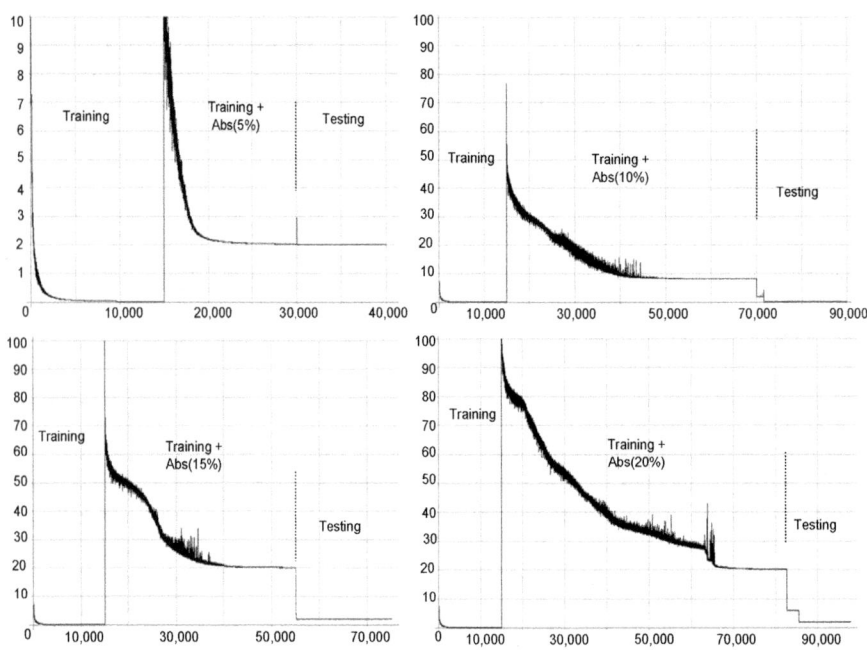

Fig. 7. Training data is used in to train ANN in P-I, Antibodies with different mutation rates are used along with training data in P-II and finally testing data is introduced in P-III

5.3 Breast Cancer Data

The Breast Cancer dataset has 569 instances with 30 features and 2 classes, namely, benign and malignant. Class benign has 357 instances and class malignant 212 instances. The breast cancer data is divided into 369 training and 200 test instances. The test error of 3 is recorded when non-vaccinated ANN comprises of training data (P-I), training + testing data (P-II) and testing data (P-III) are used (Fig. 8a). The same test error of 3 is obtained when vaccinated ANN with combination of Training data + Memory cells are used in P-II (Fig. 8b).

The same experiment is conducted as before, with antibodies introduced with different mutation rates in P-II along with training data. Antibodies with 5% mutation rate produced 3 errors (average) on test data, whereas 10% mutation resulted in 1.6 errors (average). Antibodies with 15% and 20% mutations produced 1 and 2 average errors, respectively, on testing data (Table 3). The results of all 10 runs with different mutation rates can be seen in Table 3, which indicates that the best mutation rate for antibodies is 15% and any other mutation rate above or below results in more errors.

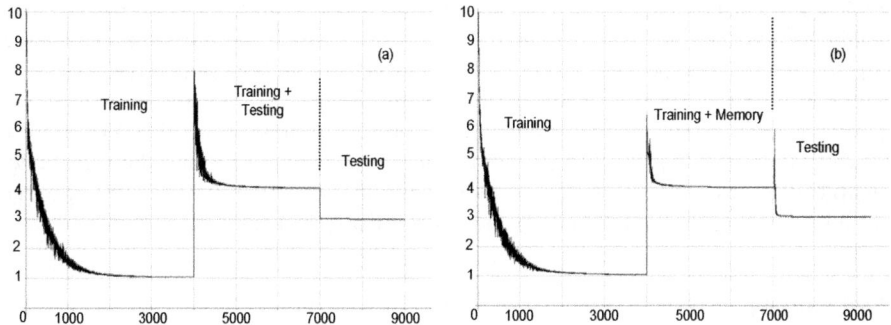

Fig. 8. (a) Training and testing data used in P-II (b) Training and memory cells are used in P-II

Table 3. 10 run of antibodies using different mutation rates for Breast cancer data

Index	1	2	3	4	5	6	7	8	9	10	Avg.	Min.	Max.
Abs 5%	3	3	3	3	3	3	3	3	3	3	3.0	3	3
Abs 10%	1	1	3	3	1	1	3	1	1	1	1.6	1	3
Abs 15%	1	1	1	1	1	1	1	1	1	1	1.0	1	1
Abs 20%	2	2	2	2	2	2	2	2	2	2	2.0	2	2

6 Conclusion

AIS can contribute novelty in at least two ways: data reduction/generalization through memory cells and vaccination through antibodies derived from memory cells, with varying rates of hyper mutation. The aim of this paper has been to explore these potential claims for novelty through a systematic series of experiments using an ANN as the 'virtual learning organism' in which a particular AIS algorithm – the HAIS algorithm for supervised learning – is embedded to result in novel hybrid architecture. We have shown by experiments that activation of immune response can be explained through mutation rates by which antibodies are generated. If the mutation rate is too low, antibodies can't adapt to the full range of pathogens in their scope and will suffer from under-generalization in terms of memory cells. On the other hand, if mutation is too high, the immune response is over-activated and antibodies started to overlap in feature space, resulting in over-generalization of data. In this paper we have proposed that under-generalization and over-generalization of data can be seen in immunological terms as immune-suppression and auto-immune disease. It is also observed during the experiments that the learning capabilities deteriorated when mutation rate is too high. Memory cells are an essential part of any AIS algorithm; in our experiments we have shown that memory cells possess excellent data summarization/reduction capabilities for fitting the data. Memory cells prime the ANN in such an efficient manner that when the real data (pathogens) attack the ANN, it is well prepared to handle those pathogens. The main focus of this paper was to integrate two nature inspired techniques, ANNs and AIS in a novel hybrid architecture, where the ANN is the virtual learning organism and the AIS is the embedded immune system engine that both primes and, for the most part, vaccinates the ANN against possible future attack by pathogens. The ANN is currently passive: it only learns what the AIS primes it for or vaccinates it against. The next stage of work is to allow the ANN to feed back the results of its learning to the AIS to fine-tune the immune system further, thereby directing the AIS to find even better solutions when confronted by hard-to-categorize samples. Also, the AIS algorithm used in this paper is supervised. Future work will consist of using the unsupervised version of HAIS [7] to generate memory cells that can then be used for supervised learning to check for data reduction and vaccination purposes.

References

1. Meng, L., Wu, Q.H., Yong, Z.Z.: A Faster Genetic Clustering Algorithm. In: Oates, M.J., Lanzi, P.L., Li, Y., Cagnoni, S., Corne, D.W., Fogarty, T.C., Poli, R., Smith, G.D. (eds.) EvoIASP 2000, EvoWorkshops 2000, EvoFlight 2000, EvoSCONDI 2000, EvoSTIM 2000, EvoTEL 2000, and EvoROB/EvoRobot 2000. LNCS, vol. 1803, pp. 22–33. Springer, Heidelberg (2000)
2. Tseng, L., Yang, S.: A genetic clustering algorithm for data with non-spherical-shape clusters. Pattern Recognition 33, 1251–1259 (2000)
3. Hsu, K., Gupta, H.V., Sorooshian, S.: Artificial Neural Network Modeling of the Rainfall-Runoff Process. Water Resources Research 31(10), 2517–2530 (1995)
4. Marinakis, Y., Marinaki, M., Matsatsinis, N.: A Stochastic nature inspired metaheuristic for clustering analysis. Int. J. Business Intelligence and Data Mining 3, 30–44 (2008)
5. Timmis, J., Neal, M., Hunt, J.: An artificial immune system for data analysis. Biosystems 55(1-3), 143–150 (2000)
6. Watkins, A., Timmis, J., Boggess, L.: Artificial Immune Recognition System (AIRS): An Immune-Inspired Supervised Learning Algorithm. Genetic Programming and Evolvable Machines 5(3), 291 (2004)
7. Ahmad, W., Narayanan, A.: Humoral-mediated Clustering. In: Proceedings of the IEEE 5th International Conference on Bio-Inspired Computing: Theories and Applications (BIC-TA 2010), pp. 1471–1481 (2010)
8. de Castro, L.N., Zuben, F.J.V.: aiNet: An Artificial Immune Network for Data Analysis. Data Mining: A Heuristic Approach 1, 231–260 (2002)
9. Khaled, A., Abdul-Kader, H.M., Ismail, N.A.: Artificial Immune Clonal Selection Algorithm: A Comparative Study of CLONALG, opt-IA and BCA with Numerical Optimization Problems. International Journal of Computer Science and Network Security 10(4), 24–30 (2010)
10. Ayara, M., Timmis, J., de Lemos, R., Forrest, S.: Immunising automated teller machines. In: Jacob, C., Pilat, M.L., Bentley, P.J., Timmis, J.I. (eds.) ICARIS 2005. LNCS, vol. 3627, pp. 404–417. Springer, Heidelberg (2005)
11. Harmer, P.K., Williams, P.D., Gunsch, G.H., Lamont, G.B.: An artificial immune system architecture for computer security applications. IEEE Transactions on Evolutionary Computation 6(3), 252–280 (2002)
12. Whitbrook, A.M., Aickelin, U., Garibaldi, J.M.: Idiotypic Immune Networks in Mobile Robot Control. IEEE Transactions on Systems, Man, and Cybernetics - Part B: CYBERNETICS 37(6), 1581–1598 (2007)
13. Dasgupta, D.: Artificial Immune Systems and Their Applications. Springer, Berlin (1999)

14. How Vaccines Work, NPI Reference Guide on Vaccines and Vaccine Safety pp. 5-8,
    `http://www.path.org/vaccineresources/files/`
    `How_Vaccines_Work.pdf`
15. Hart, E., Timmis, J.: Application area of AIS: The Past, The Present and the Future. Applied Soft Computing 8(1) (2008)
16. Castro, L.N. de., Zuben, F.J.V.: Artificial Immune Systems: Part I - Basic Theory and Applications. Technical Report - RT DCA 01/99 (1999),
    `http://eva.evannai.inf.uc3m.es/docencia/doctorado/cib/`
    `documentacion/OverviewIS.pdf`
17. Heskes, T.: Self-organizing maps, vector quantization, and mixture modelling. IEEE Transactions on Neural Networks 12(6), 1299–1305 (2001)
18. Forrest, S., Hofmeyer, S.: Immunology as information processing. In: Segel, L., Cohen, I. (eds.) Design Principles for Immune System and Other Distributed Autonomous Systems, p. 361. Oxford University Press, Oxford (2000)
19. Hunt, J.E., Cook, D.E.: Learning using an artificial immune system. Journal of Network and Computer Applications 19, 189–212 (1996)
20. Timmis, J., Knight, T.: An Immmunological Approach to Data Mining. In: Proceedings IEEE International Conference on Data Mining, vol. 1, pp. 297–304 (2001)
21. Castro, L.N.de., Zuben, J.: The Clonal Selection Algorithm with Engineering Applications. In: Workshop Proceedings of GECCO, Workshop on Artificial Immune Systems and Their Applications, Las Vegas, pp. 36–37 (2000)
22. Dasgupta, D., Gonzalez, F.: Artificial immune system (AIS) research in the last five years. In: Proceedings of the Congress on Evolutionary Computation, p. 123 (2003)
23. Ahmad, W., Narayanan, A.: Humoral Artificial Immune System (HAIS) For Supervised Learning. In: Proceedings of NaBIC2010 IEEE World Congress on Nature and Biologically Inspired Computing, pp. 37–44 (2010)
24. Fischer, I., Hennecke, F., Bannes, C., Zell, A.: Java Neural Network Simulator - JavaNNS. University of Tubingen,
    `http://www.ra.cs.uni-tuebingen.de/software/JavaNNS/`
25. UCI Machine Learning Repository, `http://archive.ics.uci.edu/ml/`

Immune System Inspired Reliable Query Dissemination in Wireless Sensor Networks

Rui Teng, Kenji Leibnitz, and Bing Zhang

National Institute of Information and Communications Technology, Japan
{teng,leibnitz,zhang}@nict.go.jp

Abstract. Wireless sensor networks collect data from sensor nodes according to each query from users. These query messages are disseminated from the sink node in a multihop manner into the network. However, packet losses may result in the failure of sensor nodes correctly receiving the query message and timely reporting the requested data. In this paper, we propose an immune system inspired approach to locally discover and recover from losses of query messages at sensor nodes. The proposed approach enables high success rate of query messages delivery by utilizing local clusters of "loss detectors" around each sensor node, which cooperate in a distributed and scalable manner to recognize and recover from losses of query messages, similar to antibodies in an immune system.

Keywords: Sensor networks, data query losses, local discovery and recovery, immune system.

1 Introduction

Wireless sensor networks (WSN) consist of a large number of small nodes with sensing, computation and wireless communication capabilities. Such networks of sensor nodes enable distributed sensing and processing of natural phenomena applied to areas such as environmental or healthcare monitoring. In a sensor network, a sink node requests data from the sensor nodes by sending queries to them. A query typically consists of a data-centric operation instead of conventional address-centric operations as used in current communication network protocols [1,2]. For example, a query might be *"what is the temperature in the geographical region X?"* or *"what is the humidity in region Y?"* rather than *"what is the humidity level at node A?"*, cf. Fig. 1. Nodes with data matching to the query interest will report this information back to the sink node.

However, a query packet may not successfully reach the corresponding sensor nodes that should reply to the query, either due to packet loss in the wireless propagation or sensor nodes being temporarily unavailable. This in turn results in the failure of sensor nodes to report their data information correctly to the sink. Since the query does not identify an individual destination node, query loss would lead to the losses of data sources, which might cause a wrong evaluation of the situation of the monitoring region with respect to the query.

P. Liò, G. Nicosia, and T. Stibor (Eds.): ICARIS 2011, LNCS 6825, pp. 282–293, 2011.

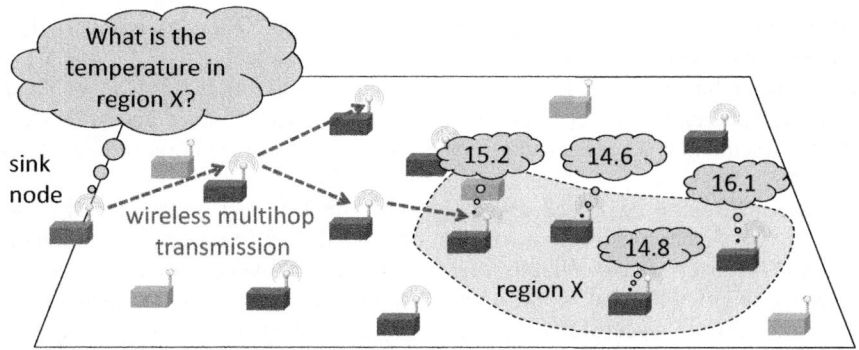

Fig. 1. Data-centric query in sensor networks

Our objective is to design a reliable query dissemination system for sensor networks with the target of successful data collection from corresponding sensor nodes. We attempt to design a query dissemination approach that is tolerant to the loss of query packets with local discovery and capable of recovering from query packet and data source losses. To achieve this goal, we present an immune system inspired scheme for reliable data query dissemination in sensor networks. The proposed approach discovers query losses in a local and event-driven manner. Furthermore, it locally recovers from query loss and eliminates the need for rebroadcasting the query to the entire network, leading to small recovery delay and high energy-efficiency.

The rest of this paper is organized as follows. Section 2 introduces related works. Section 3 describes the inspirations from immune systems. Section 4 presents the proposed approach of local discovery and recovery of query losses. Section 5 provides the analytical evaluations of the proposed approach and Section 6 concludes this paper.

2 Related Work

The immune system (IS) is a natural mechanism that defends the human body from invading pathogens. In the past, immune inspired algorithms have been proposed to improve computer network security and communication reliability.

In [3], an immune system model was proposed in application to computer security maintenance. When there is an intrusion of a computer virus, the computer detects the virus in a similar way to the immune system. The goal is to efficiently detect and eliminate the invading virus in a distributed manner. The approach uses the negative selection algorithm to provide antibodies and this procedure applies string matching to detect intruders. The proposed approach highly reduces the traffic overhead for security maintenance.

An immune system based distributed node and rate selection (DNRS) approach was proposed in [4]. Based on the mechanism of B-cell stimulation in natural immune systems, DNRS selects the most appropriate sensor nodes that report the samples of observed events. Based on the immune network principles, DNRS locally selects the appropriate frequencies of sensing reports at sensor nodes.

In [5], a reliable query approach was proposed with the goal of having an efficient discovery and recovery of query packets. The approach lets a sensor node that finds a query packet loss send out a NACK message to the sink. The sink recovers this loss by delivering the query message to the node again. To detect a loss of a query packet, sensor nodes adopt the NACK mechanism based on utilizing a query sequence at the sink node. This approach assumes that all nodes are synchronized and all nodes hear each query sequence. These assumptions cause a practical limitation of their proposed approach.

Directed diffusion discussed about the basic operation of data queries in sensor networks [6]. A naming mechanism for query and sensing data is presented. The proposed approach finds reliable routes for data delivery based on the routes' confidence degrees. In that work, query broadcast is assumed to be ideal, i.e., each sensor node always successfully receives every query message from the sink node.

There are approaches that have been proposed to enable the sensor to sink reliability, such as Event-to-Sink Reliable Transport (ESRP) [7] and Pump Slowly Fetch Quickly (PSFQ) [8] in sensor networks. However, most of these approaches focused on the reliable data delivery from sensor to sink in sensor networks, and the broadcast of data queries was generally assumed to be successfully performed or not discussed.

Many approaches of local route recovery have been proposed in mobile ad hoc networks [9], [10]. A basic idea of local route recovery is utilizing alternative relay nodes to build a new connection to the destination. However, these approaches are especially proposed for the end–to-end uncast routing, which does not requires specific detection processes for a route failure, since a node can know that it encounters a route failure when it can not be deliver a packet to the next hop node in its routing table.

3   Inspirations from Immune Systems

In this section, we formulate the problem of detecting and recovering from query message losses in a sensor network. Our approach is inspired by immune systems, so we also briefly summarize the essential features of artificial immune systems and introduce the insights gained from them to solve the considered problem.

3.1   Problem Formulation

A sensor network operates in a data-centric way in which the queries do not need to identify an individual destination node. As shown in Fig. 2, in order to collect sensing data, the sink node disseminates a query that describes the data of interest, e.g., temperature or humidity, to the network. Upon receiving a query message that matches their data, the corresponding sensors reply to this query. A sink node is not concerned with knowing which node should reply or whether sensor nodes have received the query. This will cause an essential transport problem that the sink node will not detect sensing source loss in the network. For example, in Fig. 2 the nodes A, B, C, D and E should reply to a query of brightness data, but nodes A and B have not received the query due to loss or node failure. In this case, the sink node will not know that sensor nodes A and B are data sources for this query. In the case that A and B have critical and unique data that are essential to this query, this will lead to an incorrect judgment and decision at the sink node.

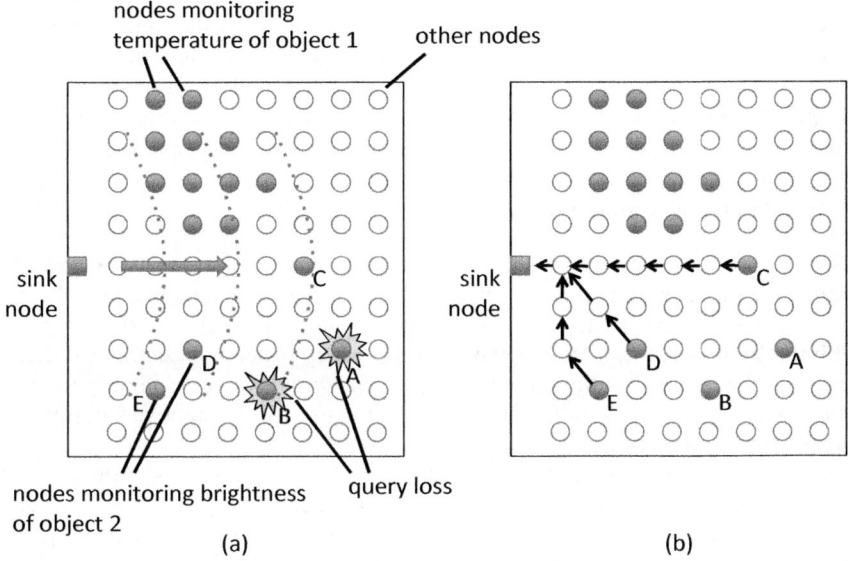

Fig. 2. (a) Data query and (b) data collection in WSN

Due to the large number of queries from various users and the large size of sensor networks, it is difficult to adopt conventional reliable broadcast schemes with high complexity. Furthermore, packet losses caused by temporary failures of sensor nodes cannot be solved by any reliable broadcast method.

3.2 Artificial Immune Systems

The natural immune system is a complex adaptive system that protects the (body) organism from invading pathogens. *Artificial immune systems* (AIS) are algorithms and systems that use the human immune system as inspiration by mimicking the behavior and properties of immunological cells.

AIS consist of two major procedures: pathogen detection and pathogen elimination. All these are performed in a distributed and localized manner. Pathogen detection operates by distinguishing "self" and "non-self" in the immune system and it uses immune system detectors, such as lymphocyte cells including B-cells and T-cells, for this task. The generation of immune detectors in AIS can be realized by, for example, utilizing negative selection, which generates the immune detectors as a random process and compares with "self" samples. Those candidates that match the samples are eliminated and others are left as detectors.

In the pathogen detection, a "non-self" cell is detected if an immune detector finds a matched cell (molecule), [11], [12]. Once pathogens are detected, the immune system eliminates them in different ways. The appropriate type of defense mechanism is performed depending on the harmfulness of "non-self" cells. Pathogen elimination copes with the problem of choosing the right receptors for the particular kind of pathogen to be eliminated [11]. The cells that eliminate the pathogen are called *effectors*. For example, the activated B-cell will produce antibodies that have a Y shaped structure, where the arm of the Y is variable and can bind to the pathogens.

In the adaptive immune system, the successful detections are memorized allowing an accelerated response the next time the pathogen is found. A single B-cell can clone multiple B-cells and is stimulated to produce more and more antibodies by cloning IS cells that have receptors matching the pathogens before they are spreading in the body.

3.3 Insights from Immune Systems

AIS bring together the notions of local discovery of irregular situations and adaptive elimination of pathogen invasion and give rise to several insights into the reliable query broadcast. At first, the generation of immune cells to detect pathogens highlights an efficient model of local fault discovery instead of centralized discovery. Secondly, the pathogen elimination approach in immune system highlights a change of activation that dynamically increases the possibility of pathogen elimination by increasing the number of cells.

In the query dissemination in sensor networks, a query loss should be locally discovered in order to achieve small traffic overhead and delay for loss recovery. Furthermore, sensor nodes should cooperatively and reliably recover from query loss. By following these insights from IS, we now propose a localized query loss discovery and recovery approach to solve query loss problems in sensor networks. In the proposed approach, the query losses in the sensor network are regarded as pathogens, since they cause the failure of successful query dissemination at sensor nodes and cause irregular situations in data collection.

In analogy to the immune system, the proposed approach enables a local detection of "pathogens", the decision of whether to "remove a pathogen" and a local recovery process. In response to the query losses, the detectors are selected around each sensor node to locally detect the query loss. The local detection of a query message loss is realized by utilizing the wireless broadcast feature. The decision of "removing" a query loss with recovery is realized by utilizing a distributed name resolution mechanism among sensor nodes. Recovery packets correspond to the antibodies to let the sensor nodes that encounter query losses correctly obtain the query message and report their sensing data.

4 Local Discovery and Recovery of Query Losses

We now propose our immune system inspired method for local discovery and recovery of query losses in sensor networks. In particular, this section presents the mechanisms required for detector cluster formation, query address resolution, and query loss recovery.

4.1 Local Query Loss Detection

Similar to the idea of the detector model in AIS [11], [12], each sensor node in the network is provided with collective loss detectors that are made of a cluster of local neighbor nodes. The cluster is termed *detector cluster* and the sensor node being monitored in the cluster center is termed the *object node*. The clustering algorithm is shown in Table 1.

Table 1.

Detector Cluster Formation (DCF) Algorithm

Input: Node ID, attributes, the scope (T) of random start time
Output: Detector cluster
1. **begin**
2. t = current time
3. $T_0 = t$
4. Randomly select a cluster broadcast time $T_{start} = T_0 + Rand (0 - T)$
5. **if** $(t = T_{start})$ **then**
    a. Perform 1-hop cluster invitation broadcast with (node ID, location, attributes)
    b. Set the number of cluster invitation broadcasts = 1
    c. **wait** (); // a randomly selected duration, e.g. 10 times of around of one-hop packet delivery and reply
6. **end if**
7. **while** (the number of replied nodes > threshold_reply) **and** (the number of cluster invitation broadcasts < threshold_invitation) **do**
    a. Perform 1-hop cluster invitation broadcast with (node ID, location, attributes)
    b. Increase the number of cluster invitation broadcasts
    c. **wait** ()
8. **end while**
9. Perform 1-hop confirmation broadcast with (Node ID, cluster size)
10. **end**

An object node invites its one-hop neighbor node to perform the role of loss detector by broadcasting an invitation message. The broadcast is initiated at a random time to prevent collisions of clustering operations at other object nodes. The nodes that receive the invitation message send a reply to accept being a detector.

The invitation message includes node ID, location, and sensing attributes of the object sensor nodes. This message lets neighbor detectors have the information for correlating between a query and the object node. If there are not enough nodes to perform the role of detectors, the object node will initiate the invitation again until there are sufficient detectors or the number of query broadcasts is large enough.

The detectors of an object node recognize the loss of a query at the object node that should respond to the query. This is realized by a distributed query resolution mechanism at each node. The query loss is detected based on the judgment of following two conditions:

(a) A detector detects that the query is associated with the object node that it is monitoring.

(b) The object node does not respond to the query. This information is known to the detector by receiving or overhearing the wireless transmission of the object node.

When the above two conditions (a) and (b) are satisfied, a query loss is detected.

4.2 Localized Query-Address Resolution

The basic function of Query-Address Resolution (QAR) is in some way analogous to that of "pathogen harmfulness" judgment. It enables each detector node in sensor networks to make a correct decision of whether to "remove" a query loss by initiating a query loss discovery. QAR resolves the query at each individual sensor node to the corresponding addresses of sensor nodes. QAR lets each loss detector judge whether a query is correlated with the object node of a detector. Each node registers its ID, location and attributes, such as temperature and humidity, to its detectors. A query message can be resolved to the corresponding sensor addresses by the QAR.

An example of the information maintained at QAR of a node is illustrated in Table 2, where nodes 16, 18, and 19 register their ID, location and attributes to a loss detector. Upon receiving a query message "*what is the temperature in the region* [20,70]×[30,80]*?*", the detector is able to judge that node with ID 16 in the resolution table should give a response. The detector will initiate a loss recovery if it detects that the node ID 16, rather than other nodes, has not replied to the query.

Table 2. Query to address resolution table at a loss detector

ID	Attribute	Location
16	Temperature	[23,76]
18	Humidity	[67,58]
19	Brightness	[53,99]

4.3 Localized Query Loss Recovery

Loss elimination is a local process to recover from query loss at a node. Compared with the conventional centralized approach, the local recovery has very low overhead and is able to perform a fast recovery. The basic concept is similar to utilizing a growing number of IS cells and the recovery procedure is a dynamic collaborative operation. It increases recovery efficiency and avoids recovery collisions among detectors with a growing reaction to the query loss.

As shown in Fig. 3(a), the proposed approach adopts a growing recovery operation to cope with the instability of detectors such as X, Y, etc. When a query loss is found at node A, the detectors (nodes W, X, Y, Z) operate in a sequential manner with a time division based delivery. For example, the first time slot is for detector W to send to node A the recovery packet that is cached at W and has not arrived at node A, see arrow (1) in Fig. 3. Due to the wireless broadcast, if node A responds to the recovery packet by delivering sensing data to the sink (arrow (2)), the detectors W, X, Y, and Z will overhear this sensing data packet. If the detector node X has not received the response from node A, it will send the query message to A (arrow (3)). With regard to the same query, other receptors operate following if there are no responses from A until the last detector in turn (node Z) initiates its recovery operation, see Fig. 3(b).

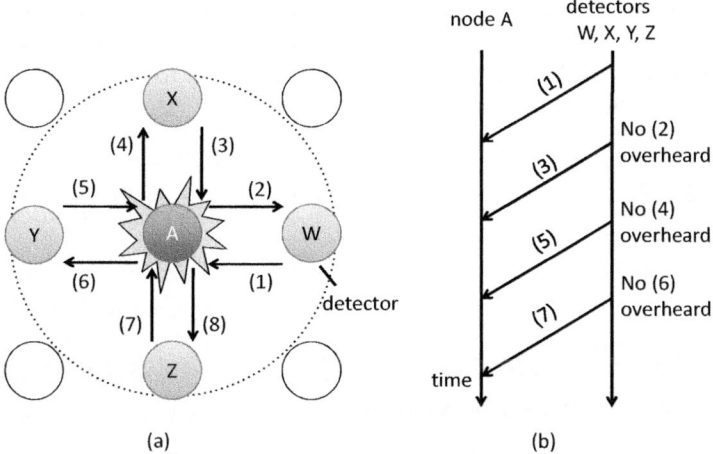

Fig. 3. (a) A detector cluster; (b) recovery of query packet loss

5   Analytical Evaluation

In this section, we provide a simple analysis of the impact of the proposed approach on the improvement of discovery and recovery of query losses with regard to successful query delivery rate and scope of detection/recovery.

Since other related methods all focus on slightly different aspects than our method or do not consider query losses, we compare our proposal with the centralized management of query loss at the sink node, which collects a list of replied data for a query and checks the loss of packets, assuming the sink node is able to resolve each query to the corresponding sensors.

5.1   Successful Query Delivery Probability

Let p denote the probability of a query loss at a sensor node in the query dissemination. The successful query delivery probability at a sensor node is $S_1 = 1 - p$ and in case of utilizing the local query loss detectors, the successful query delivery probability at a sensor node is $S_2 = 1 - p^{n+1}$, where n is the average number of loss detectors for an object node.

Therefore, the ratio of successful queries in the conventional approach to the local detector based approach is as shown in Equation. (1).

$$R_{success} = \frac{S_2}{S_1} = \frac{1 - p^{n+1}}{1 - p} \tag{1}$$

Figure 4 illustrates the impact of utilizing loss detectors on the successful query delivery by varying the probability of a query loss. The proposed approach keeps a successful delivery probability that is at least equal or higher than that without utilizing the query detectors. For example, in case that the number of loss detectors of a sensor node is $n = 4$, the success rate of the proposed approach is maintained above 70% when the loss probability $p < 0.8$ and the ratio is up to 3 times to the approach without utilizing the loss detectors.

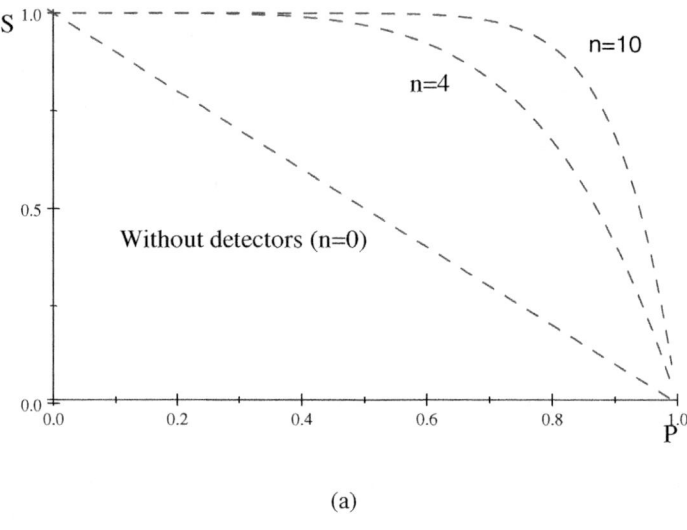

(a)

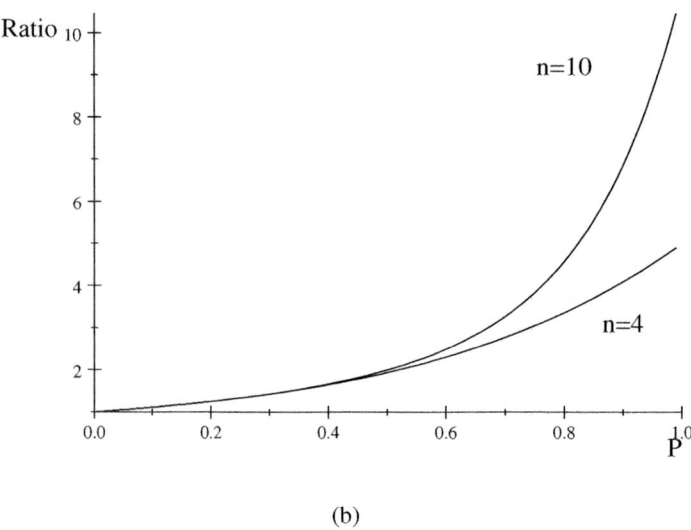

(b)

Fig. 4. (a) Successful query delivery probability and (b) the ratio of successful queries (S2/S1)

5.2 Scalability of Loss Discovery

The scope of loss discovery in the rebroadcast-based approach is the whole network with N nodes. On the other hand, the proposed approach requires only n one-hop neighbor nodes for query loss discovery and recovery. Therefore, the ratio of query loss discovery in the conventional approach to the one with local detectors is as in Eqn. (2).

$$R_{scope} = \frac{n}{N} \tag{2}$$

Equation (2) can be interpreted as follows. For every query loss in the standard flooding method, all N nodes need to be involved in the rebroadcast process. On the other hand, when using local detectors, the scope of rebroadcasts is limited to only the n neighboring nodes at the node where the query was lost. Since we usually have $N \gg n$, our approach can significantly limit the traffic overhead caused by rebroadcast messages and scales linearly with the number of neighbors per node.

5.3 The Route Length of Recovery (RLR)

In the conventional approaches of localized recovery of query loss, the sink node plays a central role to recover from failure of receiving query packets at a sensor node. In [5], the retransmission of the query packet to a sensor node that lost the query message can be localized by using unicast from sink to a sensor node, assuming that every query is disseminated to all sensor nodes in the network and each sensor node knows the route to the sensor sink.

We compare the sink based recovery approach with the proposed approach by analyzing the route length of recovery (RLR), which is defined as the minimum route length (in hops) that is taken in the recovery operation. RLR reflects the effectiveness of localization in the query loss recovery. In the calculation of route length, we assume the link between two nodes in the sensor network is bi-directional.

As shown in Equation (3), in the proposed recovery, the RLR L_{IS} consists of one hop for loss notification and retransmission of recovery packet. While in the conventional sink based approach, the RLR $L_{Sink-based}$, as shown in Equation (4) includes the number of hops $R(sink, i)$ from sink to a sensor node i for loss notification, and the same number of hops from the sink to the sensor for the retransmission of recovery packet.

$$L_{IS} = 1 \tag{3}$$

$$L_{Sink-based} = 2R(sink, i) \tag{4}$$

The Fig. 5 illustrates the overall differences of RLR with varying the route length from sink to the sensor where query loss occurs. The RLR of sink-based recovery grows linearly with the distance of the sink to where the loss occurs, while our proposed method is independent of the location of the loss.

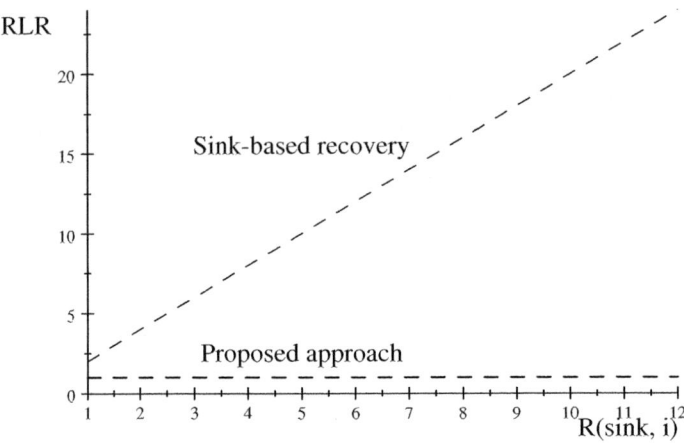

Fig. 5. The route length of recovery

6 Conclusion

Avoiding query message losses at sensor nodes is an essential issue for sensor networks to successfully collect and report sensing data in an accurate and timely manner. This paper introduces a simple yet effective immune system inspired approach for the local discovery and recovery of query losses in sensor networks. The proposed approach is inspired by the notion of local discovery of unusual situations and adaptive elimination of pathogen invasions in the immune system. Our approach constructs a cluster of loss detectors for each sensor node and each detector attempts to detect query loss by query resolution. Detectors cooperate with each other to locally recover from query losses. The proposed approach is scalable, energy-efficient and operates in a fully distributed manner.

In the future, we wish to perform more detailed evaluations of our proposal through theoretical analysis, simulation, and experiments in actual sensor nodes to highlight the benefits of applying AIS based query loss recovery in sensor networks.

References

1. Krishnamachari, B., Estrin, D., Wicker, S.: Modeling data centric routing in wireless sensor networks. In: Proc. of IEEE INFOCOM, pp. 1–11. IEEE, New York (2002)
2. Teng, R., Zhang, B.: On-demand information retrieval in sensor networks with localised query and energy-balanced data collection. Sensors 11, 341–361 (2011)
3. Harmer, P.K., Williams, P.D., Gunsch, G.H., Lamont, G.B.: An artificial immune system architecture for computer security applications. IEEE Transactions on Evolutionary Computation. 6, 252–280 (2002)
4. Atakan, B., Akan, O.B.: Immune system based distributed node and rate selection in wireless sensor networks. In: Proc. of BIONETICS, Cavalese, Italy (2006)

5. Nurcan, T., Wang, W.: Distributed coordination of sensors for end-to-end reliable event and query delivery. In: Proc. of IEEE WCNC, Hong Kong, pp. 2986–2991 (2007)
6. Intanagonwiwat, C., Govindan, R., Estrin, D., Heidemann, J., Silva, F.: Directed diffusion for wireless sensor networking. ACM/IEEE Transactions on Networking 11, 2–16 (2002)
7. Akan, O.B., Akyildiz, I.F.: Event-to-Sink Reliable Transport in Wireless Sensor Networks. IEEE/ACM Transactions on Networking 13, 1003–1016 (2005)
8. Wan, C.Y., Campbell, A.T., Krishnamurthy, L.: Pump-Slowly, Fetch-Quickly (PSFQ): A Reliable Transport Protocol for Sensor Networks. IEEE Journal on Selected Areas in Communications 23, 862–872 (2005)
9. Jeon, J., Lee, K., Kim, C.: Fast route recovery scheme for Mobile Ad Hoc Networks. In: Proc. of International Conference on Information Networking (ICOIN), Kuala Lumpur, Malaysia, pp. 419–423 (2011)
10. Sarma, N., Nandi, S., Tripathi, R.: Enhancing Route Recovery for QAODV Routing in Mobile Ad Hoc Networks. In: Proc. of International Symposium on Parallel Architectures, Algorithms, and Networks (I-SPAN), Sydney, Australia, pp. 39–44 (2008)
11. Hofmeyr, S.A., Forrest, S.: Architecture for an artificial immune system. Evolutionary Computation Journal 8, 443–473 (2000)
12. Dipankar, D.: Advances in artificial immune systems. IEEE Computational Intelligence Magazine 1, 40–49 (2006)

Fault Detection in Analog Circuits Using a Fuzzy Dendritic Cell Algorithm

Jorge L.M. Amaral

Dept. of Electronics and Telecommunications Engineering,
Rio de Janeiro State University, 20550-013 Rio de Janeiro, RJ, Brazil
{jamaral}@uerj.br

Abstract. This work presents the early stages of the development of a fault detection system based on the Dendritic Cell Algorithm. The system is designed to detect parametric faults in linear time invariant circuits. The safe signal is related to the mean square error between the PAA representations of the impulse responses of the circuit under test and the golden circuit. The danger signal is related to the variation of that error. Instead of using a weighted sum with fixed weights, a fuzzy inference system (FIS) is used, since it is easier to define linguistic rules to infer the combination of the signals than to find appropriate weight values.

Keywords: Fault Detection, Dendritic Cell Algorithm, Analog Circuits.

1 Introduction

The development of test strategies for detecting and diagnosing faults in analog and mixed-signal circuits is a very challenging task that has encouraged a good amount of research, due to the increasing number of applications that use analog and mixed-signal integrated circuits and the high cost of testing this kind of circuits. Several domains such as telecommunications, multimedia and biomedical applications, need good overall performance in high frequency, low noise and low power applications that can only be achieved using analog and mixed-signal integrated circuits. Thus, a strategy to detect and diagnose faults in these circuits is very important [1]. In the past, an integrated circuit was just one component in a system, but today the integrated circuit itself is the whole system (SoC – system on a chip). This level of integration has generated difficult problems in the test and design of this kind of circuit. There are many factors that increase the difficulties such as: the lack of good fault models, lack of controllability and observability, lack of an industrial standard analog design for testability (DFT) methodology, and raising the importance of the timing-related faults [2]. As a result, test strategies for detecting and diagnosing faults is still severely dependent on engineers' expertise on the knowledge they have about the system's operational characteristics [3]. As a result, fault detection and identification is still an interactive and time-consuming process. A survey of research [4] in the area shows that, in the last decades, a good amount of research on fault diagnosis has concentrated on the development of tools to make the task of fault diagnosing easier. Although there have been several important developments, these

P. Liò, G. Nicosia, and T. Stibor (Eds.): ICARIS 2011, LNCS 6825, pp. 294–307, 2011.
© Springer-Verlag Berlin Heidelberg 2011

new technologies have not been widely accepted. This should motivate the researchers to look for other paradigms and to develop new strategies for fault diagnosis.

Artificial immune systems [5] take their inspiration from the operation of the human immune system to create novel solutions to problem solving. The first algorithms have been presented as implementations of artificial immune systems are: the immune network, the Clonal Selection Algorithm and the Negative Selection Algorithm [5], [6], [7]. The Negative Selection algorithm has a potential application in fault detection. This algorithm uses the property of the immune systems in distinguish any foreign cells (non-self) from the body's own cell [5]. This characteristic can be used to discriminate normal systems patterns form abnormal ones, providing a fault detection mechanism. It is important to identify situations where this characteristic could be advantageous [8]: (I) when the normal behavior of a system is defined by a set of complicated patterns, where it is very difficult to obtain their relations. In this case, it may be easier to look at the abnormal patterns instead of the normal ones; (II) there are systems where the number of possible abnormal patterns is much larger than the normal ones. Since the training of a fault detection system with a large number of fault situations becomes unpractical, it is advisable to first detect any abnormal behavior and after try to identify its cause. The results presented in the literature posed lots of questions regarding the application of Negative Selection Algorithms to fault (anomaly) detection [9], [10], [11]. Recently, a new paradigm, the Dendritic Cell Algorithm (DCA) [12], was developed based on the Danger Theory [13] has become a popular an immune inspired approach to solve for solving anomaly detection problems [14]. This work presents the early stages of the development of a fault detection system based on the Dendritic Cell Algorithm. It is designed to detect parametric faults in linear time invariant circuits. From the circuit's impulse response, a safe and a danger signal is generated. The safe signal is related to the mean square error between the PAA representations [15] of the circuit under test and the golden circuit. The danger signal is related to the variation of error. Instead of using a weighted sum with fixed weights, a fuzzy inference system (FIS) is used, since it is easier to define linguistic rules to infer the combination of the signals than to find appropriate fixed weight values.

The material in this paper is arranged in the following order. In section 2 Challenges in analog circuit fault detection are briefly reviewed. In section 3 Immune inspired approaches to fault detection are briefly reviewed. In section 4 the proposed fault detection system using a DCA and a Fuzzy inference system is described. The results obtained for fault detection in a Sallen-Key bandpass filter are discussed in section 5. Finally, section 6 concludes this work.

2   Challenges in Analog Circuit Fault Detection

The fault detection in analog circuits is a difficult task. There are many factors that increase the difficult in testing these circuits such as: the difficult of measure currents without breaking the connections [16], the lack of good fault models, lack of controllability and observability, lack of an industrial standard analog design for testability (DFT) methodology, and raising the importance of the timing-related faults [2]. Other factors can be found in [17]. First, the authors point out that analog systems sometimes present non-linear effects, noise and have parameters values that can suffer a wide variation, thus deterministic methods are often ineffective; second, the statistical distribution of faults is usually not known with enough precision to make use of probabilistic methods and third, the conventional automatic test equipment (ATE) does not have enough storage capacity and computation capability to deal with the increasing complex of today´s analog circuits. In Fani et al. [18], the authors argue that classical methods require computationally intensive calculations if parameter identification is applied or a large number of simulations if a fault dictionary method is used. They also point out that one of the main problems in the analog testing is the presence of undetectable faults. This can happen due to circuit topology and limited number of test points. It is also important to define if the application requires on-line fault detection or an off-line diagnostic. In the case of on-line fault detection, the procedures cannot be computationally intensive nor can use other input signals to enhance the fault observability, unless there is an integrated BIST module.

A survey of research [4] in the area shows that, in the last decades, a good amount of research on fault diagnosis has concentrated on the development of tools to make the task of fault diagnosing easier. Some of strategies mentioned in the survey were: Rule based systems, Fault trees, Model Based approaches and Machine learning approaches (Case Base Reasoning, Fuzzy Logic and Neural Networks). Although there have been several important developments, these new technologies have not been widely accepted. The use of computation intelligent techniques is usually based on model building or in the use of classifiers. The success in model based approaches is closed related to the accuracy and in the quality of the model. In a complex system, a mathematical model is hard to build. The classifiers look for specific fault patterns and they become vulnerable when they have to deal with fault patterns that were not used to train the classifier. To overcome this problem, use of one-class classifier is promising solution [19], but it hasn't been much explored.

3   AIS Applied to Fault Detection

3.1   Negative Selection

The Negative Selection Algorithm (NSA) [7] was one of the first attempts in applying an immune inspired algorithm to anomaly (fault) detection. The work developed by Forest et al, stimulated different implementations of this algorithm using the binary and real value representations [20], [21], [22], [23].

Although, the Negative Selection Algorithms were continuously been improved, the applicability of these algorithms were always questioned. In Stibor et al. [10], it was shown that the V-Detector algorithm presented a poor performance in KDD 1999 dataset when compared with others statistical anomaly detection algorithms such as Parzen Windows and one class support vector machine. In another paper, Hart & Timmis [9] pointed out that until that moment; the results presented in the literature did not clear indicate that the Negative Selection Algorithms have anything to offer. Some of the criticisms regarding the V-Detectors were questioned in [24]. Stibor

&Timmis [11] presented other results pointing out problems in the V-Detector algorithm and the superiority of one class SVM in a digit recognition problem. Freitas & Timmis [25] claimed that the problems found in the Negative Selection Algorithm were not in the metaphor itself, but in the way that it was used. In order to be useful, the NSA should be combined with more adaptive process. In order to overcome the problems presented by the Negative Selection Algorithm, the researchers started to look to other metaphors such as Danger Theory [13], which allowed the development of the Dendritic Cell Algorithm [12], [26].

3.2 Dendritic Cell Algorithm

The Dendritic Cell Algorithm (DCA) is inspired in the mechanisms used by the innate immune system to control the maturity of the dendritic cells. They are responsible to look for any antigen that maybe responsible for damage in the tissue [26]. The maturity levels of the dendritic cells are immature, semi-mature and mature, and they are determined based on the concentration and potency of the signals that the dendritic cells are exposed to [27]. There are three types of signals: PAMP, safe and danger. The PAMP signals are known to be pathogenic. The safe signals are released in the apoptosis (controlled cell death), while the danger signals are released in the event of a necrotic cell death, as a result of a cell damage caused by infection or exposure to extreme conditions [26]. From the immature state, the dendritic cells can become semi-mature due to expose to safe signals. In this case they promote an anti-inflammatory response (tolerance cytokines), otherwise if they become mature, meaning that they received a higher concentration of danger signals, generating a pro-inflammatory response (reactive cytokines).

In this original implementation [12], [26], Dendritic Cell Algorithm is a population based algorithm that initially composed of immature cells. For every antigen presented, there were sampled a number of cells of the pool. For each one of the sampled dendritic cells, there is an update of the signal concentration, to calculate the concentration of the output cytokines and an update of the total concentration of each output cytokines. If the total concentration reaches a certain level, the cell migrates and does not come back to the pool. Each cell that migrates is considered mature or semi-mature depending on the cytokines concentration levels. The antigens presented can be classified as malignant of benign based on the number of mature and semi-mature dendritic cells there were presented to.

As stated in [28], most of the works that applied DCA were related to computer security, but there are also applications in wireless sensor networks, robotics and scheduling of processes. Also, the authors pointed out that the initial implementations of DCA used a large number of parameters that were difficult to set, leaving the algorithm open to criticisms. Two variations of DCA that simplify the original DCA are: deterministic DCA (dDCA) [28] and the Modified Dendritic Cell Algorithm (mDCA) [27]. The mDCA was applied to on-line error detection in robotic systems. It uses a fixed number of cells and a fixed maturation threshold in order to simplify the implementation in a resource limited embedded system. The cells are related to the robot sensors. The PAMP signal is related to the difference between the sensor's current value and its neighboring sensor' value; the Safe and Danger signal is related to changes in sensor values. An indication of the sensor state (OC) is calculated using (1).

$$OC = \frac{w_p * C_P + w_S * C_S + w_D * C_D}{w_p + w_S + w_D} \tag{1}$$

C_P, C_S and C_D correspond to the concentration of PAMP, Safe and Danger signals, respectively. The weigths w_P, w_S and w_D have fixed values and they are also related to their respective signals. A threshold is applied to OC signal and a danger count is calculated over a time window. When the danger count is at 100% during the time window, the sensor is considered anomalous and it is not used in the calculation of the speed and turning rate of the robot [27].

4 Proposed Method

In the Figure 1, it can be seen the framework used for fault detection. Depending on the circuit complexity, this structure could be implemented in a BIST or in ATE system. In the center of the picture, one can see a linear time invariant (LTI) circuit. It presents M inputs and N observable nodes (outputs). It is possible to define a matrix H(M,N), where each element $h_{i,j}$ represents the transfer function between the input i and the output j.

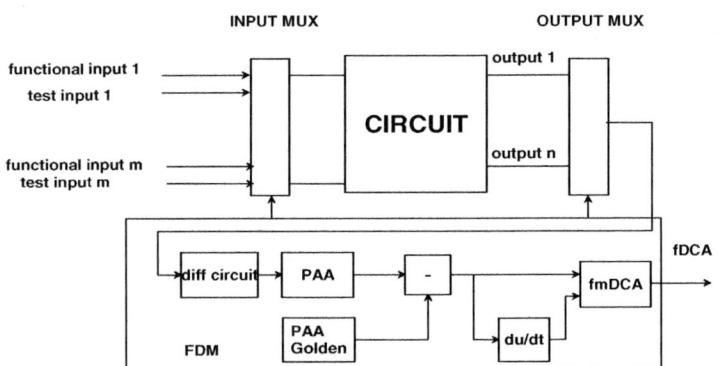

Fig. 1. Framework for fault detection

The parameters presented in each transfer function depend on the value of the components of the circuit and their allowed tolerances. So it is possible to obtain the matrix H$_{\text{golden}}$(M,N), where that parameters in each transfer function is defined by the nominal value of the components. A functional test is performed in the circuit by the Fault Detection Module (FDM). This module is responsible to provide the selection inputs for both multiplexers to put the circuit in test mode and to select the desired input-output pair. The adopted approach uses the Impulse Response (IR), which is closed related to the transfer function of the circuit. It can be used to characterize dynamic behavior of any linear, time invariant (LTI) system or circuit. As a result, it provides functional information about the circuit and it can be used to implicitly infer the performance parameters instead of directly measuring them. Due to this characteristic there is a significant advantage in using IR for testing linear analog components because fault modeling of analog circuits is a complex problem. Several methods are available for obtaining the IR of a LTI system. These include impulse and step response tests, sinusoidal oscillation tests, deconvolution based frequency domain techniques, and cross-correlation methods [29]. In the proposed test methodology, the circuit under test (CUT) is stimulated by a step input signal (test input). Then, the step response of the CUT is applied to the differentiation circuit, which generates the impulse response of CUT. The presence of a defect or variations in circuit and/or device parameters may cause the impulse response of a CUT to be altered from the impulse response of a reference circuit (golden circuit). So, the fault detection system must have a means of quantifying how different two IR waveforms are in terms of their shape characteristics [29]. The differentiation circuit (diff circuit) plays an important role in the acquisition of the impulse response. It can be implemented as digital filter or it can be implemented as analog circuit. It provides the appropriate differential function in the desired frequency range, attenuate high frequency noise, and limit the gain to avoid no linear operation.

Once the CUT´s impulse response is available, we proceed to the generation of the signals that will be used the dendritic cell algorithm. First, we perform a Piecewise Aggregate Approximation (PAA) [15]. This is a dimension reduction technique that is simple to understand and implement. It is also allows different distance measures and it is competitive with more sophisticated transformations, such as Singular Value Decomposition (SVD), Discrete Fourier transform (DFT), and the Discrete Wavelets Transform (DWT), for the task of time series indexing [15]. A time series (signal) $X = x_1, ..., x_n$ can be represented in a space N, $N \le n$, by $\overline{X} = \overline{x}_1, ..., \overline{x}_N$, where each element can be calculated by the following (2).

$$\overline{x}_i = \frac{N}{n} \sum_{j=\frac{n}{N}(i-1)+1}^{\frac{n}{N}i} x_j \tag{2}$$

The equation simply states that a time series is divided in N windows and the mean value represents all the points in the window. The parameter N can be chosen considering a plot reconstruction error versus N for a database of time series one wants to represent.

The safe signal can be obtained by comparing the PAA representation of the CUT (circuit under test) impulse response (PAA_CUT) and the one obtained from the golden circuit - circuit with nominal component values (PAA_Golden). The safe signal is related to the mean square error (mse) calculated between PAA_Golden and PAA_CUT. If the error is big it means that the safe signal must be low. The danger signal is related to the variation of error between tests. If the variation of the error starts to increase, it can be a warning that the value of the circuits components are changing due aging, environmental condition or poor manufacturing process.

The dendritic cell algorithm used here is very similar to mDCA [27]. First, it presents a fixed number of Dendritic Cells (DC) that corresponds to the observable nodes of the circuit. Second, it also provides an output signal OC that is generated from the combination of the signals (only danger and safe signals are used), third a threshold is applied to OC signal and forth a danger count is calculated over a time window.

The main difference between the mDCA and this work is that the *OC* signal is generated by fuzzy inference system (FIS), instead of the weight sum with fixed weights. As it was pointed out in [30], the weights in DCA are derived using biologically motivated arguments and not inferred by a learning algorithm. A fuzzy inference system (FIS) provides another way to find the appropriate signal combination using the experience and intuition of the designer. It is easier to define linguistic rules to infer the combination of the signals than to try to find appropriate fixed weight values for a specific application. Figure 2 shows the fuzzy sets used to describe the FIS. From left to right, one can see the fuzzy sets that represent the error, variation of error (derror) and the output signal *OC*. Table 1 provides the rules used to calculate the *OC* signal. Rule 1 state that if the error is ZERO and derror is NEG then *OC* is LOW. It means that if the error is ZERO, so the PAA representation of the impulse response is very close to the one that the golden circuit has, so it represents a safe condition. Also the variation of error is NEG. This indicates that the error is decreasing from the last observation, so this situation is not dangerous. That is why the output (*OC*) is considered LOW, indicating that the circuit is in normal operation. The other rules can be described in a similar manner.

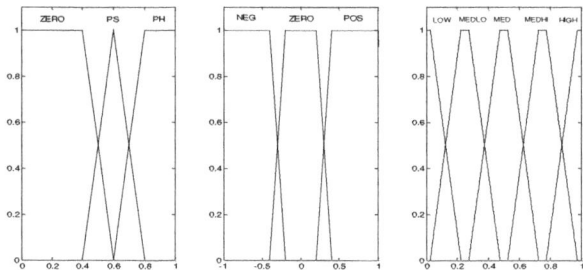

Fig. 2. Fuzzy Sets for the FIS

Table 1. Rules for the Fuzzy Inference System (FIS)

ERROR\DERROR	NEG	ZERO	POS
ZERO	LOW	LOW	MEDLO
PS	MEDLO	MEDLO	MEDI
PH	MEDHI	MEDHI	HIGH

5 Case Study

In order to evaluate the first stages of development of proposed method to detect parametric faults in analog circuits, two experiments were made. The circuit under test is Sallen Key bandpass represented by its transfer function. This circuit present low sensitivity, i.e, it presents a low degree of variation of its performance from nominal, due to changes in the value of the components constituting the circuit. Also it has been used in several publications [31], [32]. Figure 3 shows a picture of the circuit.

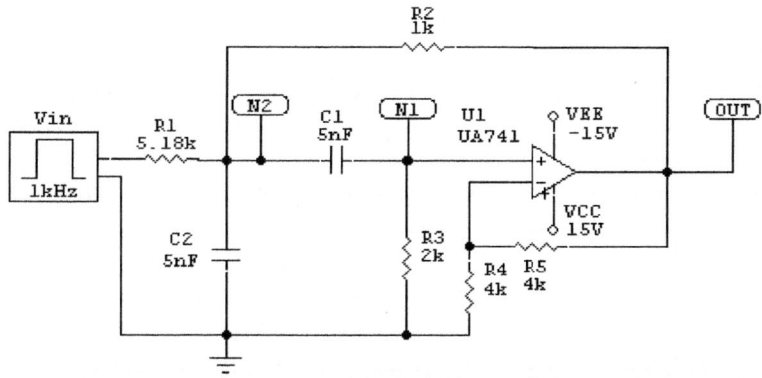

Fig. 3. Sallen Key Bandpass circuit

In the first case study, the value of the resistor R1 is linearly altered from R1 = 259 Ω to R1= 10101 Ω and the other components are within the specified tolerance (1%). The objective is to simulate a component value drift and evaluate the capability of the proposed method (Fuzzy mDCA) to detect this kind of parametric fault. The performance of the Fuzzy mDCA is compared with a fault detection performed by Bode analysis and with one class classifier called support vector data description (SVDD) [33]. First, a large number of circuits (1000) with components values within tolerance were generated to represent the circuit in normal operation. Then, Bode diagram frequency responses of those normal circuits were obtained. These bode responses are then used to create an upper and lower bounds that discriminate normal behavior in the frequency domain. This set of normal circuits is also used to generate impulse responses. These responses will be represented using PAA and the resulting set is used to train the one class classifier SVDD [33] implemented in Matlab$^{\copyright}$ toolbox written by David Tax. SVDD was trained with 1% of rejection. The choice the number of segments (N=32) in the PAA representation was done analyzing the mean square reconstruction error of normal impulse responses as a function of N, as it is shown the Figure 4.

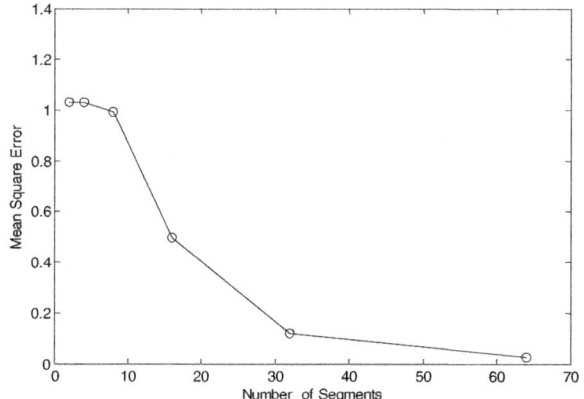

Fig. 4. Reconstruction Error versus number of segments (N)

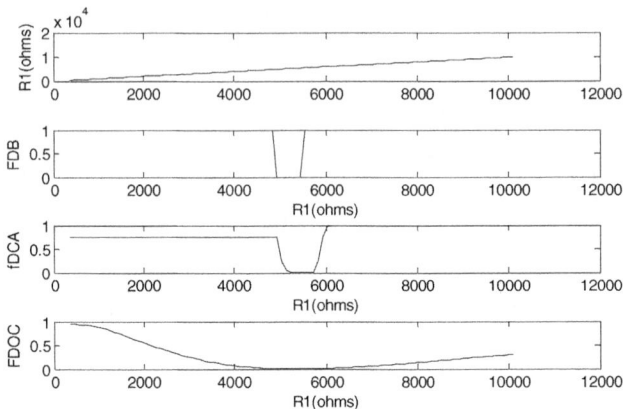

Fig. 5. Results of the First Case Study

As the R1 value varies, a new circuit is obtained and the PAA representation of its impulse response compared to the PAA representation of the golden circuit, calculating the mean square error. The error (which is related to a safe condition) and its variation (which is related with a danger condition) are normalized and presented as input to the FIS (see Section 4), which generates the output signal (*OC*). For this experiment, time window was equal to 1, meaning that the *OC* signal represents the circuit's state, and it is used as a fault index. As it was said before, the purpose of the experiment is to verify if the fuzzy mDCA is capable of detecting the parametric fault caused by the drift in the component value. It is expected that the fault indexes generated by fuzzy mDCA, Bode Analysis and SVDD will be close to zero when R1 is considered to be close to its normal range. This behavior is shown in Figure 5. In Figure 5a, it can be seen the linear variation on R1 value. Figure 5b, shows the results when Bode responses bounds are used. Figure 5c shows the results for the fuzzy mDCA and 5d for the one class classifier SVDD. In all cases, the fault indexes were close to zero, when the R1 is close to its normal range (5128,2 Ω - 5231,8 Ω, for 1% tolerance). However, the fault indexes indicate different normal ranges for R1. The Bode analysis (FDB) considered that the circuit was operating in normal conditions when R1 is in the range 4931.5 Ω to 5428.5 Ω. Both Fuzzy mDCA (fmDCA) and SVDD presented a wider range. In this particular experiment, Fuzzy mDCA normal range was 5030.9 Ω to 5826.2 Ω using a 0.5 threshold. For SVDD, the range was 4931.5 Ω to 5826.2 Ω. SVDD presented a much smoother behavior that Fuzzy mDCA and looking at its output it is possible to verify that the circuit is changing. If the same threshold value was used the SVDD would have a poor performance, so the chosen threshold was 0.01. Figure 6 shows the Bode plots for this experiment. Rlf and Ruf are the Bode plots for the lower and upper bounds of the normal range of R1 value for Fuzzy mDCA and Rls and Rus represent the same bounds for SVDD. One can see that the Bode plots generated, using the lower and upper bounds of normal range, are very close to the ones considered normal. It is important because the normal ranges were defined using a procedure totally developed in the time domain (impulse responses) and the results are very close to the ones found using procedures in the frequency domain, which are more complex to implement. The wider normal range found by Fuzzy mDCA and SVDD has two reasons: The first one is related to the low sensitivity the circuit presents in relation to R1. It means that the circuit will work properly even if the R1 value is outside of the tolerance limits. The second reason can be seen in Figure 7. It shows the impulse responses (zoom) and the PAA representation for the lower and upper bound of the range. The impulse responses are closer and harder to distinguish than the Bode plots. It means that although impulses response requires less calculation than the Bode plots, they present less power in separating the normal behavior, contributing to wider the normal range found by Fuzzy mDCA and SVDD. The Table 2 shows the mean and the standard deviation of the lower and upper bounds in 30 repetitions of the same experiment. Both SVDD and Fuzzy mDCA presented similar results. Considering that R1 has 100 values linearly distributed of the full range, which represent 99.4 Ω steps, the standard deviation corresponds to approximately 2 steps to the lower bounds and 3 steps to the upper bound.

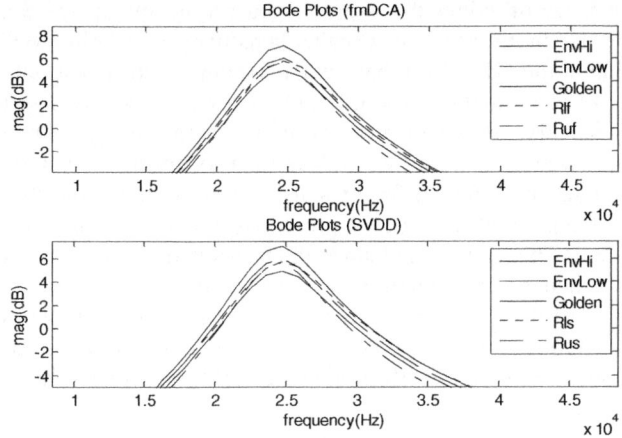

Fig. 6. Bode Plots

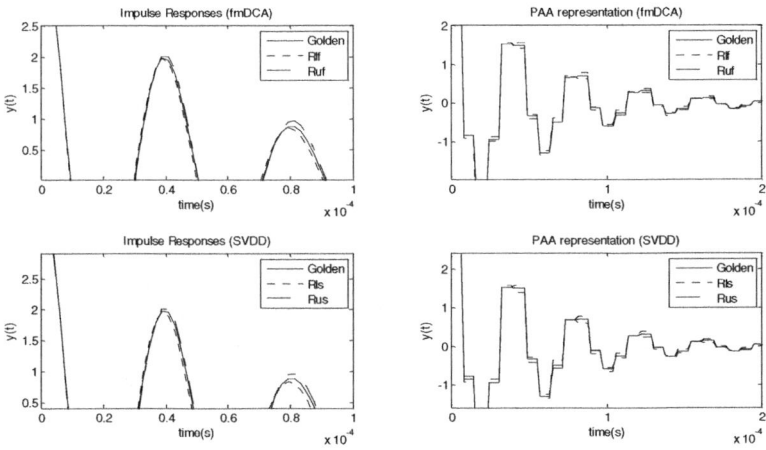

Fig. 7. Impulse Responses and PAA representation

Table 2. Mean and standard deviation for lower and upper bounds

R1 Value (Ω)	fmDCA	SVDD
Lower bound	4798.7 ±209.1	4709.7±191
Upper bound	5428.5± 257.8	5489±273.9

In the second case study, the value of the capacitor C1 is linearly altered from C1 = 0.25 nF to C1= 9.75 nF and the other components are within the specified tolerance (1%). There were used 200 values. The Figure 8 shows the performance of Fuzzy mDCA applied in all circuit nodes, Node 1 (N1), Node 2 (N2) and the output (OUT) (see Figure 3). Node 1 and the output present the same shape of the fDCA index. This is expected because the voltage signal in the output is equal to the voltage in Node 1 multiplied by a gain given by the op amp U1, R4 and R5. In this particular experiment, the range of values that were considered normal is 4.928 nF to 5.024 nF. This means that the circuit presents a higher sensitivity in relation to C1. This can be observed looking at the C1 values that were considered faulty just outside the normal range, C_{before} = 4.881 nF and C_{after} = 5.072 nF. They present a variation of only 2.4% and 1.4%, respectively. It is worth to mention that the Fuzzy mDCA in the output presents a higher value for higher C1 values than to lower C1 values. It can also be seen that the nodes presents different sensitivities to the fault. In this particular experiment, the Output and the Node 1 presented a higher sensitivity to the variation of C1 than Node 2. This is expected since the transfer function between the input and the Node 2 is a better representation of the circuit. Table 3 shows the mean and standard variation of the upper and lower bounds of the normal range found by Fuzzy mDCA in the Output and in the Node 2 over 30 repetitions of the experiments. The results in the nodes were similar. Both indicate that the normal value on average area within the tolerance (1%).

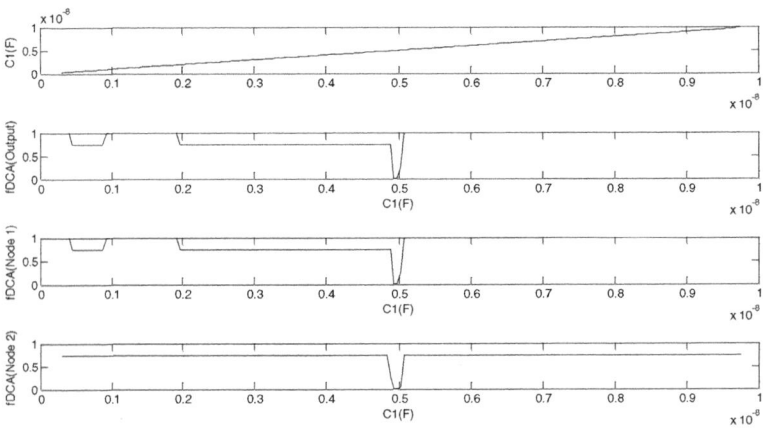

Fig. 8. Results of Second Case Study

Table 3. Mean and standard deviation for lower and upper bounds for the second case study

C1 Value (nF)	fmDCA (Output)	fmDCA (Node2)
Lower bound	4.938 ±0.045	4.926±0.048
Upper bound	5.038±0.043	5.048±0.043

5 Conclusions

This work presented the initial stages of the development of a fault detection system based on the Dendritic Cell Algorithm (Fuzzy mDCA). The system is designed to detect parametric faults in a linear time invariant circuit. The safe signal is related to the mean square error between the PAA representations of the impulse responses of the circuit under test and the golden circuit. The danger signal is related to the variation of that error. Instead of using a weighted sum with fixed weights, a fuzzy inference system (FIS) is used, since it is easier to define linguistic rules to infer the combination of the signals than to find appropriate fixed weight values. In the first case study presented, the performance of the system was found to be competitive to the one presented by SVDD. In the second case study, it was shown that Fuzzy mDCA can be easily applied to all observable nodes in the circuit. This is helpful because a fault can be more easily detected depending on its effect in the observable nodes. The system can be implemented resource constrained embedded system as BIST module (with the multiplex) or in ATE system. It requires a small amount of storage for the PAA representation of the impulse response of the golden circuit; the Fuzzy inference system can be implemented with low resources, even in 8 bit microcontrollers and the differentiator circuit can be implemented with analog components or as a digital filter. The next steps in the development of the system will deal with more extensive experimentation with other circuits and in the evaluation of the effects of the time window and the threshold values in the performance of the system. Also, the system will be tested with other input test signals to address the possibility of using this system in the fault detection of non linear circuits.

References

[1] Albustani, H.: Modeling Methods for Testability Analysis of Analog Integrated Circuits Based on Pole-Zero Analysis. Ph.D Thesis, Universität Duisburg-Essen, p.182 (2004)
[2] Claasen, T.A.C.M.: System on a Chip: Changing IC Design Today and in the Future. IEEE, Micro 23(3), 20–26 (2003)
[3] Conca, P., Nicosia, G., Stracquadanio, G., Timmis, J.: Nominal-Yield-Area Tradeoff in Automatic Synthesis of Analog Circuits: A Genetic Programming Approach using Immune-Inspired Operators. In: 2009 NASA/ESA Conference on Adaptive Hardware and Systems, pp. 399–404 (2009)
[4] Fenton, W.G., McGinnity, T.M., Maguire, L.P.: Fault diagnosis of electronic systems using intelligent techniques: a review. IEEE, Transactions on Systems, Man and Cybernetics – Part C 31(3), 269–281 (2001)

[5] Castro, L.N., Timmis, J.: Artificial Immune System: A New Computational Intelligence Approach. Springer, Heidelberg (2002)

[6] Dasgupta, D., Ji, Z., González, F.: Artificial Immune System (AIS) Research in the Last Five Years. In: Proceedings of the International Conference on Evolutionary Computation, Australia (December 8-12,2003)

[7] Forrest, S., Perelson, A.S., Allen, L., Cherukuri, R.: Self-Nonself Discrimination in a Computer. In: Proc. IEEE Symposium on Research in Security and Privacy, Oakland, USA, May 16-18, 1994, pp. 202–212 (1994)

[8] Martins, J.F., Costa Branco, P.J., Dente, J.A.: Fault detection using immune-based systems and formal language algorithms. In: Proc. 39th IEEE Conference on Decision and Control Sidney, Australia, vol. 3, pp. 2633–2638 (2000)

[9] Hart, E., Timmis, J.I.: Application areas of AIS: The past, the present and the future. In: Jacob, C., Pilat, M.L., Bentley, P.J., Timmis, J.I. (eds.) ICARIS 2005. LNCS, vol. 3627, pp. 483–497. Springer, Heidelberg (2005)

[10] Stibor, T., Timmis, J.I., Eckert, C.: A comparative study of real-valued negative selection to statistical anomaly detection techniques. In: Jacob, C., Pilat, M.L., Bentley, P.J., Timmis, J.I. (eds.) ICARIS 2005. LNCS, vol. 3627, pp. 262–275. Springer, Heidelberg (2005)

[11] Stibor, T., Timmis, J.: Comments on real-valued negative selection vs. real-valued positive selection and one-class SVM. In: Stibor, T., Timmis, J. (eds.) IEEE, Congress on Evolutionary Computation, pp. 3727–3734. IEEE, Los Alamitos (2007)

[12] Greensmith, J.: The Dendritic Cell Algorithm. PhD thesis, The University of Nottingham, Computer Science, Jubilee Campus, Wollaton Road, Nottingham, NG8 1BB (2007)

[13] Matzinger, P.: Tolerance, danger, and the extended family. Annual Review of Immunology 12(1), 991–1045 (1994)

[14] Stibor, T., Oates, R., Kendall, G., Garibaldi, J.M.: Geometrical insights into the dendritic cell algorithm. In: Proceedings of the 11th Annual conference on Genetic and evolutionary computation (GECCO 2009), pp. 1275–1282. ACM Press, New York (2009)

[15] Keogh, E., Chakrabarti, K., Pazzani, M., Mehrotra, S.: Dimensionality Reduction for Fast Similarity Search in Large Time Series Databases. Knowledge and Information Systems 3(3), 263–286 (2000)

[16] Bandler, J.W., Salama, A.E.: Fault Diagnosis in Analog Circuits. Proc. IEEE 73(8), 1235–1279 (1985)

[17] Mustapha, S., Bozena, K.: Analog Circuit Fault Diagnosis Based on Sensitivity Computation and Functional Testing. IEEE Des. Test 9(1), 30–39 (1992)

[18] Fani, A., Giua, A., Marchesi, M., Montisci, A.: A Neural Network Diagnosis Approach for Analog Circuits. Applied Intelligence 11(2), 169–186 (1999)

[19] Yi, Z., Xueye, W., Haifeng, J.: One-class classifier based on SBT for analog circuit fault diagnosis. Measurement 41(4), 263–2241 (2008) ISSN 0263-2241

[20] Gonzalez, F., Dasgupta, D., Kozma, R.: Combining negative selection and classification techniques for anomaly detection. In: Proc. Congress on Evolutionary Computation, Hawaii, pp. 705–710 (2002)

[21] Ji, Z., Dasgupta, D.: Real-valued negative selection algorithm with variable-sized detectors. In: Deb, K., et al. (eds.) GECCO 2004. LNCS, vol. 3102, pp. 287–298. Springer, Heidelberg (2004)

[22] Amaral, J.L.M., Amaral, J.F.M., Tanscheit, R.: An Immune Fault Detection System for Analog Circuits with Automatic Detector Generation. IEEE Congress on Evolutionary Computation, 2966–2972 (2006)

[23] Amaral, J.L.M., Amaral, J.F.M., Tanscheit, R.: Real-valued negative selection algorithm with a quasi-monte carlo genetic detector generation. In: de Castro, L.N., Von Zuben, F.J., Knidel, H. (eds.) ICARIS 2007. LNCS, vol. 4628, pp. 156–167. Springer, Heidelberg (2007)

[24] Ji, Z., e Dasgupta, D.: Applicability issues of the real-valued negative selection algorithms. In: Proceedings of Genetic and Evolutionary Computation Conference (GECCO), pp. 111–118. ACM Press, New York (2006)

[25] Freitas, A.A., Timmis, J.: Revisiting the Foundations of Artificial Immune Systems for Data Mining. IEEE, Transactions on Evolutionary Computation 11(4) (2007)

[26] Greensmith, J., Aickelin, U., Cayzer, S.: Introducing Dendritic Cells as a Novel Immune-Inspired Algorithm for Anomaly Detection. In: Jacob, C., Pilat, M.L., Bentley, P.J., Timmis, J.I. (eds.) ICARIS 2005. LNCS, vol. 3627, pp. 153–167. Springer, Heidelberg (2005)

[27] Mokhtar, M., Bi, R., Timmis, J., Tyrrell, A.M.: A modified Dendritic Cell Algorithm for on-line error detection in robotic systems. IEEE, Congress on Evolutionary Computation, 2055–2062 (2009)

[28] Greensmith, J., Aickelin, U.: The Deterministic Dendritic Cell Algorithm. In: Bentley, P.J., Lee, D., Jung, S. (eds.) ICARIS 2008. LNCS, vol. 5132, pp. 291–302. Springer, Heidelberg (2008)

[29] Singh, A., Patel, C., Plusquellic, J.: On-chip impulse response generation for analog and mixed-signal testing. In: Proc. IEEE International Test Conference, Charlotte, NC, pp. 262–270 (2004)

[30] Stibor, T.: On Aspects of Machine Learning and the Benefits to the AIS Community, http://www.sec.in.tum.de/~stibor (accessed on March 2011)

[31] Spina, R., Upadhyaya, S.: Linear circuit fault diagnosis using neuromorphic analyzers. IEEE, Transactions on Circuits and Systems II 44(3), 188–196 (1997)

[32] Aminian, M., Aminian, F.: Neural-network based analog-circuit fault-diagnosis using wavelet transform as preprocessor. IEEE,Transactions on Systems, Man and Cybernetics 47(2), 151–156 (2000)

[33] Tax, D.M.J., Duin, R.P.W.: Support vector domain description. Pattern Recognition Letters 20(11-13), 1191–1199 (2000)

A Memetic Immunological Algorithm for Resource Allocation Problem

Jole Costanza, Vincenzo Cutello, and Mario Pavone

Department of Mathematics and Computer Science
University of Catania
V.le A. Doria 6 – 95125 Catania, Italy
{costanza,cutello,mpavone}@dmi.unict.it

Abstract. In this research work, we present a combination of a memetic algorithm and an immunological algorithm that we call Memetic Immunological Algorithm – MIA. This algorithm has been designed to tackle the *resource allocation problem on a communication network*. The aim of the problem is to supply all resource requested on a communication network with minimal costs and using a fixed number of providers, everyone with a limited resource quantity to be supplied. The scheduling of several resource allocations is a classical combinatorial problem that finds many applications in real-world problems. MIA incorporates two deterministic approaches: (1) a local search operator, which is based on the exploration of the neighbourhood; and (2) a deterministic approach for the assignment scheme based on the *Depth First Search* (DFS) algorithm. The results show that the usage of a local search procedure and mainly the DFS algorithm is an effective and efficient approach to better exploring the complex search space of the problem. To evaluate the performances of MIA we have used 28 different instances. The obtained results suggest that MIA is an effective optimization algorithm in terms of the quality of the solution produced and of the computational effort.

Keywords: Immunological algorithms, memetic algorithms, combinatorial optimization, scheduling resources allocation problem, resource allocation problem, scheduling problems.

1 Introduction

In this work we present an immunological algorithm based on a deterministic approach that involves the *Depth First Search* (DFS) algorithm, and ad-hoc local search strategy to tackle a combinatorial optimization task, the *Resource Allocation* problem [12,2,13], whose main goal is to satisfy the resource allocation requests from several items with minimal efforts. Any request can be satisfied by only one provider, which however has limited resources. Resource allocation problem on a communication network is a classical combinatorial optimization problem, which finds many applications in real-world problems, such as fuel

P. Liò, G. Nicosia, and T. Stibor (Eds.): ICARIS 2011, LNCS 6825, pp. 308–320, 2011.
© Springer-Verlag Berlin Heidelberg 2011

distribution problem, drugs distribution in hospitals, postal services distribution, and distribution networks in general.

In many NP-hard problems, the goal is *to pack* items into a set of *containers*, without exceeding the capacities of each individual container. These kinds of problems are simply refereed as *multi-container packing problem* (MCPP) [15], and a typical example is the classical *bin packing problem* (BPP). In general, for these kinds of problems, two types of containers are considered [11]: (1) with *capacity*, i.e. the sum of the weights of the items cannot exceed a given capacity; (2) with *quota*, i.e. the sum of the weights of the items must be at least as large as the quota. Resource allocation problem asks to satisfy with minimal costs all resource allocation requests received from several items using a given fixed number of providers, each one based on a limited *capacity*, i.e. maximal quantity to be supplied. How to schedule the resource distribution depends on several aspects: how many quantities have been required in the overall; how many providers are available; how much is the capacity of each available provider; the traffic on communication network; and many other conditions that influence either communication network or the quantity of available resource. Moreover, the problem is also subject to several constrains: any provider is able to supply a limited quantity of resource; the number of providers is given and fixed; the sum of resource quantity of a subset of items satisfied by a provider cannot exceed its own capacity. Thus, to face this problem is required optimizing several objectives, which are subject to various constraints: maximize the number of resource satisfied; maximize the number of items served; minimize the path from one item to other in the network; minimize the costs on each path in the communication network. Resource allocation on a communication network can be seen as a problem very similar to the *Vehicle Routing Problem*(VRP), and primarily with its variant called *Capacitated Vehicle Routing Problem* (CVRP) [17]. VRP represents the class of problems in which a fixed number of vehicles must visit a set of customers, or cities, through a set of routes. The goal of VRP is to satisfy any customer request, everyone with a known demand, minimizing the costs on the routes, and respecting some constraints, such as: (i) each customer can be visited once and at most by one vehicle, and (ii) each vehicle starts, and ends to the depot. CVRP is the more studied member of the family, where capacity restrictions are imposed for the vehicles.

2   The Problem

The problem of resource allocation on a communication network can be formulated as follows: let be $G = (V, E)$ a graph, where the node $v \in V$ represents an item, and the set E represents the paths on the network. We assume that $|V| = n$ and $|E| = m$. For any node v is assigned a weight $q(v) \geq 0$ $(q : V \to \mathbb{R})$, which indicates the resource required by the item v; also for any edge $e \in E$ is assigned a weight $c(e) > 0$ $(c : E \to \mathbb{R})$, which represents the cost on the segment e. Given a set of providers, $R = \{1, \ldots, h\}$, such that $|R| < |V|$. To each provider $r \in R$ is assigned a limited resource capacity, i.e. a maximal resource quantity that can be supplied by r: $b(r) > 0$ with $b : R \rightarrow \mathbb{R}$. We note that the sum of all weights of items is greater than the maximal capacity allowed, $\left(\sum_{v \in V} q(v) > max_{r \in R} \{b(r)\} \right)$, and that $min_{v \in V} \{q(v)\} \leq min_{r \in R} \{b(r)\} \leq max_{v \in V} \{q(v)\} \leq max_{r \in R} \{b(r)\}$.

The goal of this combinatorial optimization task is to assign h providers over n items such that: (1) the number of satisfied items is maximal, i.e. all resource allocated required have been supplied; (2) each provider must supply resources to all those items that are as topologically near as possible in the communication network; finally (3) the sum of the weights of items supplied by provider r must be not greater than the capacity of r itself. This definition is equivalent to partitioning the set V in h subsets, such that their union is V, and their intersection is the empty set. A proper way to face this problem could be to tackle it as a multi-objective problem; however, in this research work we have tackled the problem using a *single-objective function*:

$$f(\boldsymbol{x}) = \frac{C_{tot}(\boldsymbol{x})}{\sum_{r \in R} |V_r|} \times \left[1 + \left(|V| - \sum_{r \in R} |V_r| \right)^{\beta} \right] \qquad (1)$$

where V_r is the set of all items that have been supplied by the provider r; β is a constant, and represents a penalty factor that gives priority to solutions able to satisfy all resources required; and $C_{tot}(\boldsymbol{x})$ is the total cost produced by the given solution $\boldsymbol{x}$ on the communication network $G = (V, E)$, and it is given by

$$C_{tot}(\boldsymbol{x}) = \sum_{r=1}^{|R|} \left(\sum_{j=1}^{|V_r|} q(x_{rj}) + \sum_{j=1}^{|E_r|} c(e_{rj}) \right)$$

where E_r is the subset of all edges visited by the provider r, and e_{rj} is the edge connecting $(x_{r(j-i)}, x_{rj})$.

To understand what are the parameters that affect the output, we performed the *Morris method* [14] on a graph with 256 vertices, and 32640 edges (*queen16_16.col* – see section 4). The Morris method is a sensitivity analysis useful to understand the effects of a parameter with respect to all others, which vary simultaneously. Figure 1 shows the sensitivity analysis carried out for our objective function (equation 1). Inspecting this figure is possible to see how the vertices {36, 115, 139, 152, 172, 234} seem to be the most important, since they affect more on the objective function than the remaining vertices, whereas nodes 118, 101, and 182 are the less influential ones.

3   The Memetic Immunological Algorithm

MIA is based on clonal selection principle whose own main features are cloning, hypermutation, and aging operators. As in the classical clonal selection algorithms, the antigen (Ag) represents the problem to tackle, that is the communication network $G = (V, E)$, whilst the B cells are a population of candidate

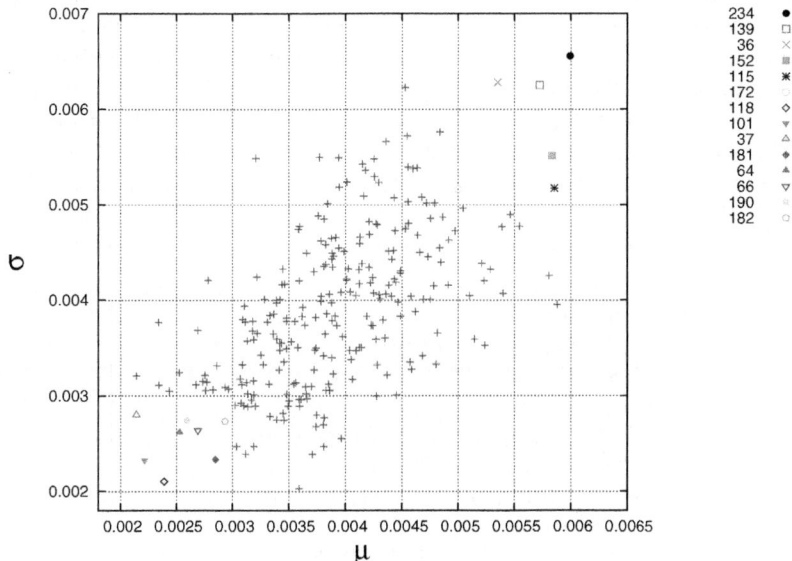

Fig. 1. Normalized μ and σ of Sensitivity analysis using the Morris method. A high value of μ indicates a parameter with an important overall influence on the output. A high value of σ indicates a parameter involved in interaction with other parameters or whose effect is nonlinear.

solutions, defined hence as strings of integers (vertices). B cells are represented as a permutation of vertices from which the algorithm starts the visiting process in order to assign the items to providers. With $P^{(t)}$ we denote a population of d individuals of length $\ell = |V|$. The first population is created randomly by a uniform distribution, which represents a subset of the space of solutions.

MIA incorporates the *static cloning operator*, that clones all B cells *dup* times producing an intermediate population $P^{(clo)}$. Afterwards, each cloned B cell is subject to the hypermutation operator, which mutates any clones M times without an explicit usage of mutation probability. In this work, the number M of mutations is inversely proportional to the fitness function, albeit there exists several approaches (e.g. ones proposed in [6]). Let $e^{-\rho\hat{f}}$ the *mutation rate*, where ρ is an input parameter, and $\hat{f}$ is the fitness function normalized in the range $[0,1]$, then the number of mutations M on a given candidate solution x is given as $M(x) = \lfloor (\alpha \times \ell) + 1 \rfloor$, with ℓ the length of x. At least one mutation is guaranteed on any B cell, which happens exactly when the candidate solution is very close to the optimal one. Thus, for any B cell the hypermutation operator chooses randomly M times two vertices u and v, and then swaps them. At the end of the hypermutation process, we have a new population that is denoted by $P^{(hyp)}$. To normalized the fitness function in the range $[0,1]$, as proposed in [9], MIA uses the best current fitness value decreased of an *user-defined threshold* Θ; this is necessary because *a priori* is not known any kind of information about global optima. As proposed in [10,6,7], also MIA is based on the particular scheme that when an hypermutated B cell improves the value of the fitness (called *constructive mutations*), then it will be considered to have age equal to 0. Using this scheme, we give an equal opportunity to each new B cell to effectively explore the given landscape. To improve the quality of the solution, MIA incorporates an heuristic local search based on the exploration of the neighbourhood, where the neighbours are explored through the swapping of the vertices. This operator is applied to the best B cell of $P^{(hyp)}$, producing a new population $P^{(LS)}$.

Table 1. Pseudo-code of *Memetic Immune Algorithm – MIA*

$\textbf{MIA}(d, dup, \tau_B, \rho)$
  $P^{(0)} \leftarrow$ Init_Population(d)
  Evaluate_Fitness($P^{(0)}$)
  $t \leftarrow 1$
  while ($\neg Termination\_Condition()$)**do**
    $P^{(clo)} \leftarrow$ Cloning ($P^{(t)}, dup$)
    $P^{(hyp)} \leftarrow$ Hypermutation($P^{(clo)}, \rho$)
    Evaluate_Fitness($P^{(hyp)}$);
    $P^{(LS)} \leftarrow$ LocalSearch($P^{(hyp)}[best]$)
    Evaluate_Fitness($P^{(LS)}$);
    Static_Aging($P^{(t)}, P^{(hyp)}, P^{(LS)}, \tau_B$);
    $P^{(t+1)} \leftarrow (\mu + \lambda)$-Selection($P_a^{(t)}, P_a^{(hyp)}, P_a^{(LS)}$);
    $t \leftarrow t + 1$;
  end_while

After the perturbation operators, all old B cells inside the populations $P^{(t)}$, $P^{(hyp)}$, and $P^{(LS)}$ are eliminated using the *static aging operator*. The parameter τ_B in input indicates the maximum number of generations, that allows to each B cell to remain into own population; when a B cell is $\tau_B + 1$ old it is erased from the own population independently from its fitness value. Each B cell is allowed to remain into the population for a fixed number of generations; an exception is made only for the B cell with the current best fitness value (*elitist static aging operator*). The strength of this operator is to produce a high diversity into the current population, and avoid premature convergences. After the aging operator, follows the $(\mu+\lambda)$-*Selection operator*, which generates the new population $P^{(t+1)}$; it selects the best d survivors B cells from the populations $P^{(t)}$, $P^{(hyp)}$, and $P^{(LS)}$. If only ($d_A < d$) B cells are survived, then it creates randomly ($d - d_A$) new B cells (*Birth phase*).

In table 1 we report the pseudo-code of the memetic immunological algorithm, where *Termination_Condition()* is a Boolean function, which returns true if the maximum number of generations, or the maximum number of fitness function evaluations allowed, is reached; false otherwise. Instead, *Evaluate_Fitness()* computes the fitness function value of each B cell using the equation 1.

Local Search. The used approach for the design of the local search was taken from [7,5], and it relies on the definition of neighbourhood, where neighbours are generated through the swapping of the vertices. One B cell y is said a neighbour of a B cell x if it can be obtained from x by swapping two of its elements. Since swapping all pairs of vertices is time consuming, we have used a reduced neighbourhood by a radius R_{LS}, as proposed in [5,8]: in each B cell, all vertices were swapped only with their R_{LS} nearest neighbours, to the left and to the right. Taking into account the large size of the neighbourhood the local search procedure is applied only on the best hypermutated B cell (i.e., the best of $P^{(hyp)}$). If a single swap between two vertices reduces the fitness function value, then the new mutated B cell is added into the new population $P^{(LS)}$; otherwise it is not taken into account, and hence erased. The process continues until the whole neighbourhood with radius R_{LS} will be explored. To avoid the problem to study

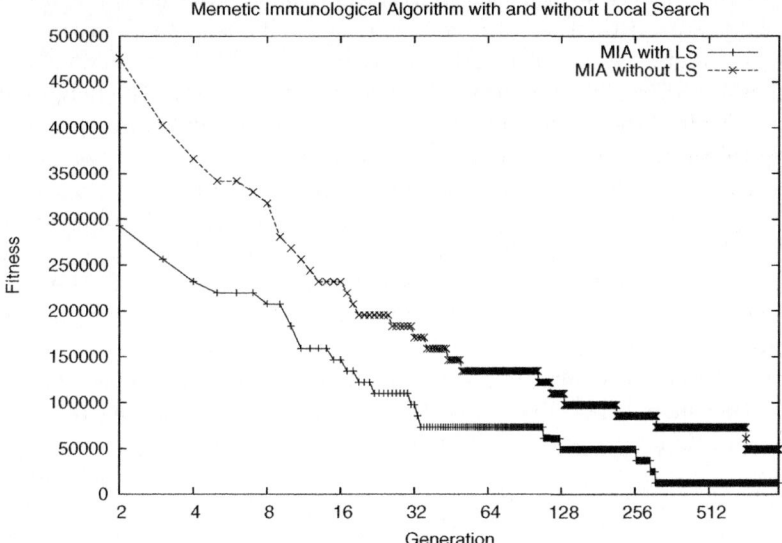

Fig. 2. Convergence process of MIA with and without local search (LS)

which is the best tuning for R_{LS} radius we assign a random value in the range $[1, (|V| - 1)]$, using a uniform distribution. In this way it is guaranteed to swap at least two vertices. Figure 2 shows the convergence process of the best fitness values with and without the local search procedure. The experiment was made on a graph with 82 vertices (planar topology), and fixing the minimal values for the parameters: $d = 100$, $dup = 1$, $\tau_B = 5$, $\rho = 5.5$ and $MaxGen = 1000$. This figure shows how the local search procedure ease the convergence towards better solutions.

Heuristics for the assignment scheme. How to assign a provider to one item or vice versa is a central point in the design of the algorithm. Since any provider has a limited resource capacity, choosing one vertex rather than an other can determine the satisfiability of all received requests, or only some of them. Let $x = \{x_1, \ldots, x_n\}$ a generic B cell; $R = \{r_1, \ldots, r_h\}$ the set of the providers; and $b(r_i)$ the capacity of the *ith* provider, with $i \in [1, h]$. A provider r_i is randomly chosen to be assigned to the first x_1 vertex of the permutation $\boldsymbol{x}$, and afterwards decreasing the capacity of r_i, i.e. $b_{(curr)}(r_i) = b_{(prev)}(r_i) - q(x_1)$. For all remaining vertices x_j, with $j = (2, \ldots, \ell = |V|)$, is possible to distinguish the following three cases:

1. if exists a vertex $v \in V$ adjacent to x_j, and a provider $r \in R$ assigned to v (i.e. r supplies v) such that $\sum_{v \in V_r} q(v) + q(x_j) \leq b(r)$, where V_r is the subset of the vertices already assigned to r, then the provider r is assigned to supply x_j. If there exist two or more vertices adjacent to x_j, with assigned different providers suitable to satisfy x_j, then the one with higher available capacity will be assigned to x_j;

2. for all vertices $v \in V$ adjacent to x_j, either there exists no $r \in R$ assigned to v, or if there exists, it is not able to satisfy x_j. Thus, if there are one or more free providers, i.e. not yet assigned, then one of these is randomly chosen, and assigned to x_j; otherwise a deep search is made into the neighbourhood of x_j. If after the search, at least one available provider was found, this is assigned to x_j, otherwise the vertex will be labelled *"not satisfied"*. Of course, case 2 occurs only if the first step failed. In this work, as search model, was used the classical *"depth first search"* algorithm (DFS) [4], but reduced of a radius $R_{(DFS)}$: is fixed a limit $R_{(DFS)} < |V|$ to the depth of the search into the neighbourhood. The aim of this reduced DFS is to satisfy the request of the vertex x_j trough an available provider not too far from it, in such way to generate homogeneous groups. If, by the reduced DFS we found two or more suitable providers then the nearest one is assigned to the vertex x_j. In the experiments described in section 4, $R_{(DFS)}$ was fixed as 15% of $|V|$. We call this kind of approach *"random + dfs assignment"*.

3. There exists no provider able to satisfy the given vertex (when cases 1 and 2 fail): i.e. for all $r \in R$, $\sum_{v \in V_r} q(v) + q(x_j) > b(r)$, where V_r is the subset of the vertices assigned to r. In this case the vertex will be labelled *"not satisfied"*.

After any assignment, the capacity of each chosen provider r is decreased: $b_{curr}(r) = b_{prev}(r) - q(x_j)$.

It is possible to derive an algorithmic variant of the *"random + dfs assignment"*, which occurs in the case 2: before randomly choosing a free provider to be assigned, this variant checks if there exist an available provider inside the nearest neighbourhood. This is done applying the reduced DFS algorithm, with radius $R_{(DFS)}$ equal to 5% of $|V|$. We call this variant as *"dfs² assignment"*. This new scheme guarantees the design of homogeneous groups, that is, all providers will supply only items close to each other.

Figure 3 shows the comparisons of the best fitness values obtained by the two described heuristics. These curves were obtained on a graph with 82 vertices, and using the following parameters: $d = 100$, $dup = 2$, $\tau_B = 15$, $\rho = 5.5$, and $MaxGen = 1000$. The figure shows how $dfs²$ allows to MIA a better convergence towards high quality solutions, lower costs and better compactness of the groups. The inset plot shows for both approaches the success rate of the DFS over the

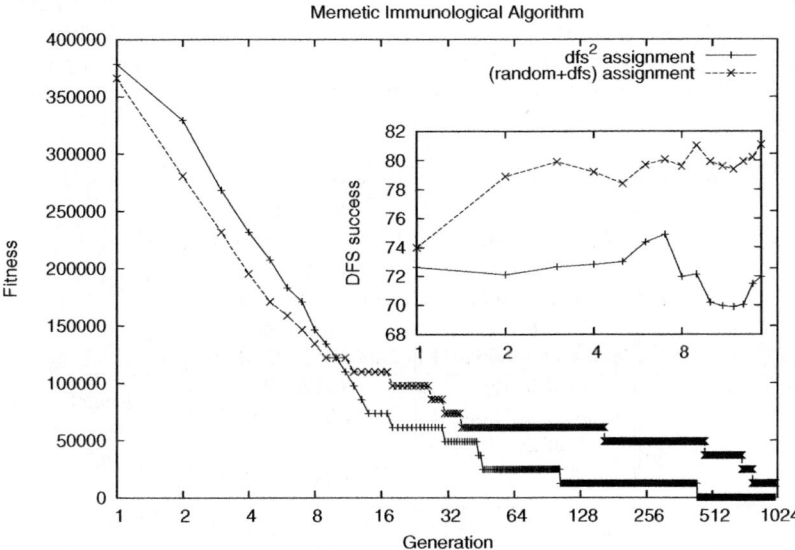

Fig. 3. Convergence process of the best fitness function values for "*random + dfs assignment*" and "*dfs² assignment*" heuristics. The inset plot shows the success rate of the DFS.

best run. Obviously, as we expected, the curves of $random + dfs$ are higher than dfs^2, since it obtains poor solutions, and therefore it needs more calls to the DFS with long radius: more calls generate a higher success rate. However, the overall percentages of the DFS successes, averaged with their own calls, computed over 10 independent runs, is higher in dfs^2 (73.08%) than in $random + dfs$ (66.28%). This means that our optimization strategy, which is to reduce the search of an available provider in a nearest neighbourhood, is efficient in order to design very compact groups. In table 2 is showed the comparison between the two approaches, varying the parameters on a graph with 82 vertices (a planar graph). This instance, has been used to evaluate the performances of MIA in terms of fitness value, and the ability to develop homogeneous groups. The table shows the best fitness values, the mean and the standard deviation. Last column, Δ, of the table indicates the differences of the two approaches with respect the best fitness values. In bold face is highlighted the best fitness values for each pairs of parameters. The results have been obtained with $d = 100$, $\rho = 2$, $MaxGen = 100$, and 10 independent runs. The number of the providers h is equal to 6, using the same capacity for all h providers. Given all weights on the vertices, we can consider $\Lambda = \frac{\sum_{i=1}^{n} q(x_i)}{h}$ as lower bound to determine in average how much should be the capacity of each provider to satisfy all request. This lower bound is not necessarily the optimal capacity value. In this work, the averaged capacity is the lower bound Λ increased by 0.2%. Inspecting the results in the table, dfs^2 is suitable to find better solutions and more homogeneous groups.

Table 2. dfs^2 vs. $random + dfs$. For each experiment we report the best fitness value, the mean and the standard deviation. Last column, Δ, indicates the difference of the best fitness function values. For these experiments has been used the graph with $|V| = 82$. In bold face is highlighted the best fitness value for each pairs of parameter dup and τ_B.

dup τ_B		dfs^2	$random + dfs$	Δ
1	5	**236.28**	12422.63	−12186.35
		2675.12 ± 4877.68	19742.75 ± 8091.68	
	20	**236.04**	12428.42	−12192.38
		1455.39 ± 3658.04	20963.34 ± 10967.25	
	∞	**228.84**	12439.09	−12210.25
		1453.59 ± 3662.04	20967.5 ± 5583.16	
5	5	**235.37**	12443.66	−12208.29
		7555.31 ± 5969.99	17314.52 ± 5965.55	
	20	**232.38**	12425.92	−12193.54
		232.93 ± 1.1	17305.04 ± 8091.91	
	∞	**244.33**	12418.84	−12174.51
		13647.11 ± 6563.78	23396.64 ± 16768.86	
10	5	245.00	**226.83**	+18.17
		245.00 ± 0.0	24616.53 ± 21121.18	
	20	**225.19**	227.32	−2.13
		5106.2 ± 14638.93	227.32 ± 0.0	
	∞	**230.49**	12427.99	−12197.5
		1452.14 ± 3663.05	18526.56 ± 6098.57	

We note that high values of mean and standard deviation (tables 2 and 3) are due to β penalty parameter of the objective function (eq. 1); when a solution is not able to satisfy all items required then the objective function returns high values. Thus, high values of mean and standard deviation indicate that the algorithm is not able to satisfy all required in all runs. In all experiments $\beta = 5$.

4   Results

To evaluate the performance of MIA algorithm we have used two different metrics: (1) MIA is able to obtain good approximated solutions using the capacity of the providers as small as possible, and (2) the homogeneity in the assignment of the providers to the vertices, i.e., to avoid that a provider has to supply two vertices placed in opposite sites from a topological point of view. For the experiments, we used a graph with 82 vertices and planar topology. Afterward, to extend our test bed we have tested MIA on several graphs, taken by the *dimacs colouring benchmark* [1]. Once experimentally proved that dfs^2 has better performances than $random + dfs$ with respect to the costs and the homogeneity of the solutions (see table 2), all results presented in this section have been obtained using the dfs^2 heuristic.

Table 3. Best solution, mean of the best solutions, and standard deviation (σ) obtained on the graph with 82 vertices, varying the parameters dup, and τ_B. For this class of experiments was fixed $d = 100$, $MaxGen = 100$, and each test was made 10 independently runs. Moreover, we have fixed $\rho = 4$ for all trucks with same capacity, and $\rho = 5.5$ with different capacity values. The shown results were obtained fixing either the same capacity for all used trucks (the lower bound Λ increased by 0.2%), than with different capacity values.

		using same capacity			using different capacity		
dup	τ_B	best	mean	σ	best	mean	σ
	5	229.45	231.42	1.28	36830.49	53902.77	23894.93
1	20	232.81	233.15	0.68	36845.67	36845.67	0.004
	∞	228.05	2670.81	4884.66 49017.31	57563.87	17294.56	
	5	226.22	5116.51	9750.32	36830.98	38051.81	3662.52
5	20	235.00	5112.00	9754.00	36828.41	36835.69	4.29
	∞	244.64	11213.28	10125.65	**12436.16**	**14877.58**	**7314.36**
	5	229.15	2686.72	4874.28	24639.02	40491.00	17291.04
10	20	**220.92**	**6323.55**	**6102.63**	36825.49	41707.80	5979.59
	∞	229.82	7547.70	9759.12	24635.98	42929.53	23299.84

In table 3 we report the results obtained by MIA using for all providers either the same maximum quantity of resources to be supplied, or different capacities. These experiments have been made varying the parameters $dup = \{1, 5, 10\}$, and $\tau_B = \{5, 20, \infty\}$, and a population size constant ($d = 100$), $\rho = 4$ for the experiments where all resources have the same capacity, and $\rho = 5.5$ for all experiments with different capacity values. Moreover, the maximum number of generations was fixed to 100, and each test has been averaged over 10 independent runs. Inspecting the results obtained using the same capacity, is possible to see that, although the best solution is obtained with high values of dup parameter ($dup = 10$), in general the best performances have been obtained using small values of the dup parameter. If we use different capacities, instead, $dup = 5$ seems to be the adequate setting.

To simulate a real world application, we have considered the graph as road network, where each weight has been randomly generated in the range $[200, 10000]$ for the vertices, while for the edges in the range $[5, 180]$. Moreover, we have used a small number of providers in order to better simulate a real application. Since in the real world case is likely that not all items require resource allocation, i.e. someone can have weight null, the random generator assigns each weight on vertices with a probability $P = 0.5$.

To understand the real exploration and exploitation capabilities of MIA we have compared MIA with a classical Genetic Algorithm (GA) and a deterministic algorithm based on locally optima choice strategy. For this deterministic algorithm we present three different versions: (1) starting from the vertex V_1 the naive method proceeds sequentially ($V_1, V_2, ..., V_n$). We labelled this version as *naive*; (2) starting from a random vertex V_k, this method proceeds as follow

Table 4. MIA vs. GA and three different versions of a deterministic algorithm. These experiments have been made using *dimacs graph colouring instances* as test bed [1], being one of the most popular in literature. For each instance is showed the number of items satisfied (Γ), and relative best cost found. The experiments have been performed for 30 independent runs. We point out that if one of the algorithms is not able to satisfy all requested of the items, the relative costs have been not included in the table ($-$).

				MIA		$naive$		DBO		DPB		GA	
instance	$\|V\|$	$\|E\|$	h	Γ	best	Γ	best	Γ	best	Γ	best	Γ	best
$DSJC125.1.col$	125	1472	4	125	**1018.06**	124	$-$	123	$-$	124	$-$	125	1056.5
$DSJC125.5.col$	125	7782	4	125	**977.92**	123	$-$	123	$-$	124	$-$	125	1010.92
$DSJC125.9.col$	125	13922	4	125	**978.532**	124	$-$	124	$-$	125	1167	125	1034.34
$queen6\_6.col$	36	580	3	36	**1106.46**	35	$-$	35	$-$	35	$-$	36	1131.4
$queen7\_7.col$	49	952	3	49	**1252.84**	48	$-$	48	$-$	49	1304.76	49	1274.53
$queen8\_8.col$	64	1456	3	64	**1276.75**	63	$-$	63	$-$	64	1309.96	64	1298.4
$queen8\_12.col$	96	2736	4	96	**1133.69**	94	$-$	95	$-$	96	1148.92	96	1146.2
$queen9\_9.col$	81	2112	4	81	**1146.1**	80	$-$	80	$-$	80	$-$	81	1161.33
$queen10\_10.col$	100	2940	4	100	**1157.4**	99	$-$	99	$-$	100	1198.01	100	1182.73
$queen11\_11.col$	121	3960	4	121	**1082**	120	$-$	119	$-$	121	1127.98	121	1105.54
$queen12\_12.col$	144	5192	5	144	**1252.47**	143	$-$	143	$-$	144	1296.76	144	1271.63
$queen13\_13.col$	169	6656	5	169	**1282.47**	168	$-$	168	$-$	169	1313.1	169	1297.33
$queen14\_14.col$	196	8372	5	196	**1283.31**	195	$-$	195	$-$	196	1307.6	196	1294.6
$queen15\_15.col$	225	10360	6	225	**1103.09**	224	$-$	224	$-$	225	1126.5	225	1111.21
$queen16\_16.col$	256	12640	6	256	**1326.89**	255	$-$	255	$-$	256	1345.1	256	1335
$miles500.col$	128	2340	4	128	**1141.23**	127	$-$	127	$-$	128	1168.028	128	16833
$miles750.col$	128	4226	4	128	**1110.67**	127	$-$	127	$-$	128	1150	128	1153.65
$miles1000.col$	128	6432	4	128	**1105.77**	126	$-$	127	$-$	128	1143.3	128	1137
$miles1500.col$	128	10396	4	128	**1096.96**	127	$-$	127	$-$	128	1130.4	128	1128.61
$myciel5.col$	47	236	3	47	**1246.87**	46	$-$	46	$-$	47	1280	47	1266.3
$myciel6.col$	95	755	4	95	**1140.14**	94	$-$	94	$-$	95	1147.7	95	1149.1
$myciel7.col$	191	2360	5	191	**1180.82**	190	$-$	190	$-$	191	1194.6	191	1193.7
$david.col$	87	812	4	87	**1076.67**	86	$-$	86	$-$	n.a.	$-$	87	1114.6
$games120.col$	120	1276	4	120	**1279.02**	120	1301	119	$-$	120	1292	120	1350
$anna.col$	138	986	5	138	**984.129**	138	$-$	138	$-$	n.a.	$-$	138	44505.3

$(V_k, V_{k+1}, ..., V_n, V_1, ..., V_{k-1})$. We call this second version as DBO; (3) the last method performs the optimal locally selection based on a permutation of the vertices (DBP). Table 4 presents the results obtained on this new benchmark. The table indicates the number of items satisfied (Γ) for each algorithm, and relative best cost found. For these experiments, it has been used the following parameters $d = 100$, $dup = 15$, and $\tau_B = 15$. For GA, instead, we have used the best tuning of parameters obtained after several experiments: $pop\_size = 100$, $P_c = 1.0$, and $P_m = 0.3$. Moreover, in all experiments we have used as stop criterion a maximum number of fitness function evaluations $T_{max} = 5 \times 10^4$ for all graphs with $|V| < 100$, and $T_{max} = 5 \times 10^5$ otherwise. Finally, 30 independent runs have been performed for each instance. MIA is able to satisfy all requests received, with respect deterministic algorithms. MIA and GA have been able to satisfy all request received on different dimensions of the problem (from 36 to 256 vertices). However, comparing MIA and GA is possible to see how the proposed algorithm is able to find better costs in all tested instances, which means that MIA is able to produce more compact groups from a topologically point of view. In the table 4, if one of the algorithms has not been able to satisfy all requested, the relative costs have been not included in the table (labelled as $-$), because the fitness value produced is high due to the penalty factor β (equation 1).

5 Conclusion

From the shown results, the reduced DFS produces good solutions in term of quality and homogeneity of assignments. The designed approach seems to be very promising. Currently, our research is primarily directed, (1) on the study of the best tuning of the DFS (i.e., the radius R_{DFS}); (2) design a good refinement operator, such to improve the convergence speed of MIA; (3) and finally take into account the dynamical environment where the weights either on the vertices and on the edges may change during the time.

All results have been obtained using as capacity, the lower bound Λ increased by 0.2%, i.e. as small as possible, to properly understand the search ability of MIA. The proposed algorithm has been compared with standard GAs and with three different versions of a deterministic algorithm. MIA outperforms the compared algorithms; MIA satisfies always all the requests, as opposed to compared algorithms, which fail on several instances.

References

1. Graph Colouring Instances, http://mat.gsia.cmu.edu/COLOR/instances.html
2. Bretthauer, K., Shetty, B.: The nonlinear resource allocation problem. Operations Research 43(4), 670–683 (1995)
3. Coffman, E.G., Garey, M.R., Johnson, D.S.: Approximation Algorithms for Bin Packing: A Survey. In: Hochbaum, D. (ed.) Approximation Algorithms for NP-Hard Problems, pp. 46–93. PWS Publishing, Boston (1997)
4. Cormen, T.H., Leiserson, C.E., Rivest, R.L., Stein, C.: Introduction to Algorithms. MIT Press, Cambridge (2001)
5. Cutello, V., Nicosia, G., Pavone, M.: A Hybrid Immune Algorithm with Information Gain for the Graph Colouring Problem. In: Cantú-Paz, E., Foster, J.A., Deb, K., Davis, L., Roy, R., O'Reilly, U.-M., Beyer, H.-G., Kendall, G., Wilson, S.W., Harman, M., Wegener, J., Dasgupta, D., Potter, M.A., Schultz, A., Dowsland, K.A., Jonoska, N., Miller, J., Standish, R.K. (eds.) GECCO 2003. LNCS, vol. 2723, pp. 171–182. Springer, Heidelberg (2003)
6. Cutello, V., Nicosia, G., Pavone, M.: Exploring the capability of immune algorithms: a characterization of hypermutation operators. In: Nicosia, G., Cutello, V., Bentley, P.J., Timmis, J. (eds.) ICARIS 2004. LNCS, vol. 3239, pp. 263–276. Springer, Heidelberg (2004)
7. Cutello, V., Nicosia, G., Pavone, M.: An Immune Algorithm with Hyper-Macromutations for the Dill's 2D Hydrophobic - Hydrophilic Model. In: Proc. of Congress on Evolutionary Computation (CEC 2004), vol. 1, pp. 1074–1080. IEEE Press, Los Alamitos (2004)

8. Cutello, V., Nicosia, G., Pavone, M.: An immune algorithm with stochastic aging and kullback entropy for the chromatic number problem. Journal of Combinatorial Optimization 14(1), 9–33 (2007)
9. Cutello, V., Nicosia, G., Pavone, M., Narzisi, G.: Real Coded Clonal Selection Algorithm for Unconstrained Global Numerical Optimization using a Hybrid Inversely Proportional Hypermutation Operator. In: SAC 2006, vol. 2, pp. 950–954 (2006)
10. Cutello, V., Nicosia, G., Pavone, M., Timmis, J.: An Immune Algorithm for Protein Structure Prediction on Lattice Models. IEEE Transaction on Evolutionary Computation 11(1), 101–117 (2007)
11. Fukunaga, A.S., Korf, R.E.: Bin completion algorithms for multicontainer packing, knapsack, and covering problems. Journal of Artificial Intelligence Research 28, 393–429 (2007)
12. Ibaraki, T., Katoh, N.: Resource Allocation Problems – Algorithmic Approaches. MIT Press, Cambridge (1988)
13. Lin, X., Johansson, M., Boyd, S.P.: Simultaneous routing and resource allocation via dual decomposition. IEEE Transactions on Communications 52(7), 1136–1144 (2004)
14. Morris, M.D.: Factorial sampling plans for preliminary computational experiments. Technometrics 33(2), 161–174 (1991)
15. Raidl, G.R., Kodydek, G.: Genetic Algorithms for the Multiple Container Packing Problem. In: Eiben, A.E., Bäck, T., Schoenauer, M., Schwefel, H.-P. (eds.) PPSN 1998. LNCS, vol. 1498, pp. 875–884. Springer, Heidelberg (1998)
16. Ralphs, T.K., Kopman, L., Pulleyblank, W.R., Trotter, L.E.: On the Capacitated Vehicle Routing Problem. Mathematical Programming 94, 343–359 (2003)
17. Toth, P., Vigo, D.: The Vehicle Routing Problem. SIAM Monographs on Discrete Mathematics and Applications (2002)

Artificial Immune System Based on Clonal Selection and Game Theory Principles for Multiobjective Optimization

Pawel Jarosz[1] and Tadeusz Burczyñski[1,2]

[1] Cracow University of Technology, Institute of Computer Science,
Warszawska 24, 31-155 Cracow, Poland
pjarosz@pk.edu.pl
[2] Silesian University of Technology,
Department for Strength of Materials and Computational Mechanics,
18A Konarskiego str., 44-100 Gliwice, Poland
tb@polsl.pl

Abstract. In order to make decisions in multi-criteria environments there is a need to find solutions with compromises. They are compromises for all criteria and create a set of solutions named the Pareto frontier. Based on these possibilities the decision maker can choose the best solution by looking at the current preferences. This paper is dedicated to methods of finding solutions in multi-criteria environments using Artificial Immune System and game theory, and coupling both approaches to create a new intelligent hybrid system of decision making.

1 Introduction

Multi-criteria decision making is a sophisticated process of finding a solution in an environment with several objectives. Most of problems, which occur in the real life, consist of several objectives which should be taken into account. Solving such problems is a challenging task and has been deeply investigated. Despite this, however, the solutions used in real applications often use simple methods. A market's requirements lead to situations in which solutions accepted by decision makers are not really the optimal solutions. There are two reasons for such situations. First, the simple algorithms are easy to understand and implement. However, they have several disadvantages especially in terms of solutions feasibility and determining local optima. On the other hand, algorithms which do not have these disadvantages are very time consuming, providing the second reason for simple methods. The big challenge faced by scientists is how to create effective algorithms which will lead to optimal solutions. That is why there are several attempts to implement biologically inspired algorithms, which succeed solving single-objective problems.

Because of totally different definitions of optimality and different kinds of expected results (not only one global optimum, but the set of compromise solutions) transferring these bio-inspired algorithms to multi-objective cases is not

P. Liò, G. Nicosia, and T. Stibor (Eds.): ICARIS 2011, LNCS 6825, pp. 321–333, 2011.

so easy. Furthermore of currently available methods are fully acceptable by real life customers. Still, there is a need for new approaches, to reduce the amount of computation time and to create better solutions.

For a few years a new population-based approach named an Artificial Immune System for solving different problems has been presented. There were many proposals of using these algorithms for optimization. This approach was also adopted for solving multiobjective optimization. First such an algorithm was presented in 2002 by Coello Coello and Cruz Cortez [1]. Later on several concepts based on immunology were presented in [2] [3] [4]. On the other hand a new interesting approach based on connection the Nash theory and evolutionary algorithms in multiobjective optimization have appeared ([5]).

2   Multi-criteria Decision Making and Multiobjective Optimization

The multi-criteria decision making, which is analyzed in this work, is one of the most interesting kinds of optimization, while also being the most difficult one. The basic terms should be introduced in here, to start the further discussion.

The most important elements while defining the multiobjective problem are the goals, criteria or just objective functions.

Objectives are written as $f_1(x), f_2(x), ..., f_k(x)$, where k is number of criteria in the problem. The space, where the values of objectives are analyzed is called the fitness space or the objective space.

The vector of decision variables can be stated as x

$$x = [x_1, x_2, x_3..., x_n] \tag{1}$$

where n is the number of decision variables which are sought. A set of equality and non-equality constraints is imposed on decision variables:

$$g_i(x) <= 0, i = 1, .., m; h_i(x) = 0, i = 1, ..., p \tag{2}$$

m is the number of non-equality constraints, and p is the number of equality constraints. It is important to ensure that $p < n$. Otherwise, the problem has zero degrees of freedom, and it becomes impossible to find an equilibrium.

Two spaces are defined for such a problem problem:

- n-dimensional space of solutions, where each dimension is assigned to each element of the x vector.
- k-dimensional space of fitness values, where each dimension is assigned to one of the objectives.

Each point in the solution space has one corresponding point in the objective space.

As the effect of making a decision in a multi-criteria environment, a choice of one final solution should be made. To make a final decision, using the knowledge and experience of a decision maker is crucial. The methods are divided to different categories, based on how the decision maker's knowledge is utilized [6].

2.1   Multiobjective Optimization

The role of the decision maker is very important in solving multicriteria problems. Not all of the processes can by automated. The majority of researchers' work using the computational intelligence is applied to Posteriori methods, particularly for finding the set of the Pareto-optimal solutions what is the goal of the multiobjective optimization and the following discussion concerns itself with the problem of finding the set of optimal solutions for many objectives [7].

Theoretically, there can be a situation in which a solution exists as the global optimum for all criteria. This is not considered in here, though, because the problem of multiobjective optimization makes sense when the criteria stay in conflict which each other. The solutions desired in multiobjective problems are the compromises between criteria, solutions which are deemed the best, after taking into account all criteria. Such solutions are named the Pareto optima - the optimal solutions in the sense of Pareto. The Pareto optimal solution can be defined as follows:

Definition 1. *The solution x which belongs to Ω is the optimal solution in the Pareto sense if, and only if, there does not exist x' belonging to Ω, for which vector $v = F(x')$ dominates vector $u = F(x)$. The concept of the Pareto optimality is considered to be whole solution space for the problem. In other words, vector x is the optimal Pareto solution when there does not exist any other feasible vector x', for which one of the functions has lower value at the same time not increasing values of other criteria (for minimization problem).*

A very important concept while investigating the multiobjective optimization is the domination, which appeared in the previous definition.

Definition 2. *Vector $u = (u_1, ..., u_k)$ dominates another vector $v = (v_1, ..., v_k)$ if, and only if when u is partly lower than v, i.e for each i $u_i \leq v_i$ and there exists i for which $u_i < v_i$.*

The goal of multiobjective optimization is to search the set of the Pareto-optimal solutions. This set should satisfy two goals: to be as close as possible to the real Pareto frontier and to be uniformly distributed.

To summarize, multiobjective optimization is a process of searching the set of Pareto-optimal solutions. This is a step towards the multi-criteria decision making, where there is only one final solution as an effect.

2.2   Evaluation of the Results

The great challenge is to evaluate a set of solutions found by a particular method. It is strictly connected with metrics which are used for algorithms evaluation. One of the found set of solutions features, is their distribution over the Pareto front. It is expected that they will be equally spaced and the front representation is smooth and uniform. The metric which define such a goal is named *Spacing* and was proposed by Schott in [8]. Mathematically, it can be defined as follows:

$$S = \sqrt{\frac{1}{N_{known} - 1} \sum_{i=1}^{N_{known}} (\overline{d_i} - d_i)^2} \tag{3}$$

where

$$d_i = min_j \sum_{k=1}^{m} \left| f_k^i(x) - f_k^j(x) \right| \tag{4}$$

and $\overline{d}$ is the mean value of all d_i. The another criteria which should be taken into account, when evaluating found optimal set of solutions, is the closeness to true Pareto front. Van Veldhuizen and Lamont in [9] have proposed a metric named *Generational Distance* which definition looks as follows:

$$GD = \frac{1}{N_{known}} \sqrt{\sum_{i=1}^{N_{known}} d_i{}^2} \tag{5}$$

There exists also other metrics for example discreet metrics *Error Ratio* which counts a number of solutions which belong to the true Pareto front. We decided to use two presented metrics as the most often used ones, and representing the features which should have the found Pareto front.

3   Evolutionary Algorithms

Evolutionary algorithms are methods which are based on evolution of species. These algorithms are described quite well in literature, so here is just a short presentation [7].

An evolutionary algorithm operates on the population. At the beginning, the population is randomly generated. Each element of the population named individual, is encoded as a solution of the solved problem. Each individual corresponds to a biological genotype, which is composed of chromosomes.

The population becomes subject to several evolutionary operators to generate individuals with better fitness. The first operator is a selection. The goal of the selection is to promote good solutions, and to remove the bad ones. Different kinds of selection methods exist, the most popular one is the roulette wheel selection (proportional fitness). Other methods are based on tournaments between individuals or on rankings of solutions. The second operator is a crossover. The goal of the crossover is to exchange the genetic code between individuals. The last operator, a mutation, introduces wild cards into the evolution. Genes are mutated with the low probability. The evolutionary algorithms with several variations, but still based on the presented general schema, have been applied to solve several problems with one criterion: linear and nonlinear programming, problems with constraints or combinatorial problems.

Attempts to apply evolutionary algorithms to solving multiobjective optimization have appeared since the 1980s. A few of the most well known approaches are described in the following paragraphs.

Non-dominated Sorting Genetic Algorithm (NSGA and NSGA 2). The NSGA algorithm was proposed by N.Srinivans and K.Deb in [10]. It is a modification of a rank assignment mechanism proposed by Goldberg [11]. In the NSGA algorithm several layers of the non-dominated solutions exist. In the first step, all non-dominated solutions are found in a population. Fixed fitness values are assigned to them. In the next step, these solutions are ignored and a new layer of non-dominated solutions is created. Another fixed fitness value is assigned to each of the solutions. This mechanism is continued till some fitness values have been assigned to all solutions. After this procedure, the first layer of solutions should have the maximum value of fitness, and the successive levels significantly less. Based on these fitness values the proportional selection is performed. This algorithm evaluated relatively well, but it was not very effective.

An improved version of the algorithm, NSGA 2, was proposed by Deb et al. in [12]. The changes concerning evaluation of solutions as well as a crowding mechanism were introduced. For each solution the crowding parameter is calculated and has an influence on selection.

Strength Pareto Evolutionary Algorithm (SPEA and SPEA 2). The SPEA algorithm proposed by Zitzler and Thiele [13] uses an external population to store previously found non-dominated solutions. At each generation, the non-dominated solutions are copied to the external set. For each solution in the external set the strength is calculated. Strength in this algorithm is similar to rank in the MOGA algorithm. The fitness of a solution in the current population is calculated based on the strengths of all external non-dominated solutions which dominates it. A pruning method is applied to avoid increase the size of the external population too excessively. SPEA 2 introduces some changes in the algorithm, such as a change in the calculation of strength, and the introduction of a density estimator to keep the external set to an appropriate size.

4   Artificial Immune Systems

The natural immune system is mainly built from lymphocytes and its main goal is to protect organism against pathogens (infectious foreign elements). A lymphocyte has about 10^5 receptors. A receptor is an antibody molecule embedded in the membrane of a cell. These antibodies are specific for antigens. By binding to these antibodies, with additional signals from accessory cells (e.g. T-helper cell), an antigen stimulates a B-cell to divide and mature into a non-dividing antibody secreting plasma cells. During the process of cell division clones are generated. T-cells play a central role in the regulation of the B-cell behavior. The rate of cloning a cell is proportional to the affinity to an antigen - the best cells replicate the most. Clones come under a somatic hypermutation - a mutation rate is much higher than in the case of the normal mutation. To create best-fitted antibodies such an intensive mutation is realized. Clones with the low affinity to antigens are removed - clones with high affinity become plasma (memory) cells [14]. In immunology there is a known mechanism of reducing ability of lymphocytes to produce new antibodies, known as the suppression.

Artificial Immune Systems appeared in the 1990s as a new area in Computational Intelligence. Based on immune system concepts, researchers tried to generate new possibilities to solve different problems. The three most developed mechanisms were: immune networks, the clonal selection and the negative selection.

The immune network is based on an idea that all B-cells are connected together to cooperate in order to recognize antigens. Cells stimulate and suppress each other to stabilize the network.

In the clonal selection optimization fitness functions correspond to the affinities of antibodies to antigens. Antibodies are solutions to problems collected in a population. Like in the real immune system, antibodies are cloned. The number of clones is proportional to an antibody's affinity to antigen (its value of the fitness function) and clones undergo the hypermutation. This ideas are extended with the suppression. Such a algorithm was described by Wierzchon in [14].

The negative selection is based on the assumption that the goal of the immune system is to learn how to categorize cells as self or non-self. The system has an ability of reacting to unknown antigens while at the same time not reacting to self cells [15].

The clonal selection algorithm is based on basic immune response mechanisms. It is interesting that the metaphor of action of these algorithms can be useful for solving optimization problems. As the optimization problem one can imagine the maximal match of B cells to antigens. In an immune system, cells are cloned and mutated in order to maximize the affinity. The main concept of the algorithm is as follows: the population of B cells is created (the potential solution of the optimization problem), these cells are linked with antigens and the affinity is calculated (the fitness of the optimized problem), and the cells are cloned and undergo somatic hypermutation (the solutions of the problem are cloned and mutated). From all clones of the cell, only the best stay in the population. Next, cells come under the suppresion mechanism, i.e. the removal of useless cells.

5   Game Theory

The Game Theory is a branch of mathematics applied to different sciences: economics, sociology, politics as well as engineering. The goal of the game theory is to describe the strategic situations, where parties try to make a decision based on others behavior. Games can be divided into two groups: cooperative and non-cooperative. The cooperative game is when the players should build compromises to get maximum payoff. The cooperation between the players is allowed in such games. The biggest payoff of all players can be gained only by cooperation between them. On the other hand, in non-cooperative games there is no possibility of cooperation and the communication between the players is not allowed.

The most popular applications of the game theory is to find an equilibrium in games. Is such an equilibrium the player has a strategy which is the best in the current situation. One of the most important theorem in the game theory is the Nash equilibrium, defined by the J.F. Nash in 1951 [5]. Imagine there is G players playing the same game. Each player optimize its strategy following his payoff function and it is given that all other players' strategies are fixed (optimized for themselves). If there are no player which can improve his strategy, it means that players' strategies are Nash strategies and there are in the Nash equilibrium.

Taking into account the properties of the cooperative games and Nash equilibrium it can be stated, that these concepts are similar to problems with many objectives.

6   Description of the IMmune GAme Theory MultiObective (IMGAMO) Algorithm

The metaphor of the game theory and immunology is used to solve the problems of multiobjective optimization [16]. Each player has its own objective (a payoff function in the Nash equilibrium). The Nash strategy for a particular player is the optimum solution for this player's problem remembering that other players also play their best strategies. The solution of the optimized problem consists of several parameters, each of which is assigned to one of the players. Each player optimizes only its parameters (its strategy) taking the rest of them as constant. The rest of the parameters are set by taking the best solutions the from other players. Solutions from all players should establish the solution of the problem. Then all players use the immune algorithm to optimize their objectives. The general idea of the algorithm is presented in Figure 1.

The most important assumptions to the IMGAMO algorithm are as follows:

- each player has its own fitness function (payoff function),
- each player has assigned the part of parameters of the solution (strategy of this player) (this is changed at each iteration),
- the rest of parameters are set as constants and taken from the best solutions from the other players (this is done at each iteration),
- all solutions are coded with real values,
- the result of the algorithm (the determined Pareto frontier) is stored in the result_population,
- each player optimize uses the immune algorithm to optimize its objective (each player has its own population).

The clonal selection is an element of the algorithm which is based on the Nash equilibrium. Each player searches for optimal values of his parameters to receive maximum payoff, taking other players' best parameters values as constants. During the clonal selection the solutions which are best take into account all criteria searched and they approach the Pareto frontier. The goal of the suppression is to diversify the solutions in populations. The Pareto frontier must fulfill two conditions. The first is to be as close as possible to the real frontier, for which clonal selection is used. Second it should be regularly distributed on this frontier. This is the task of the supression. During the suppression each players' solution is tried to be added to external archive (result population). If in the result_population the analyzed solution dominate other ones - it is added and

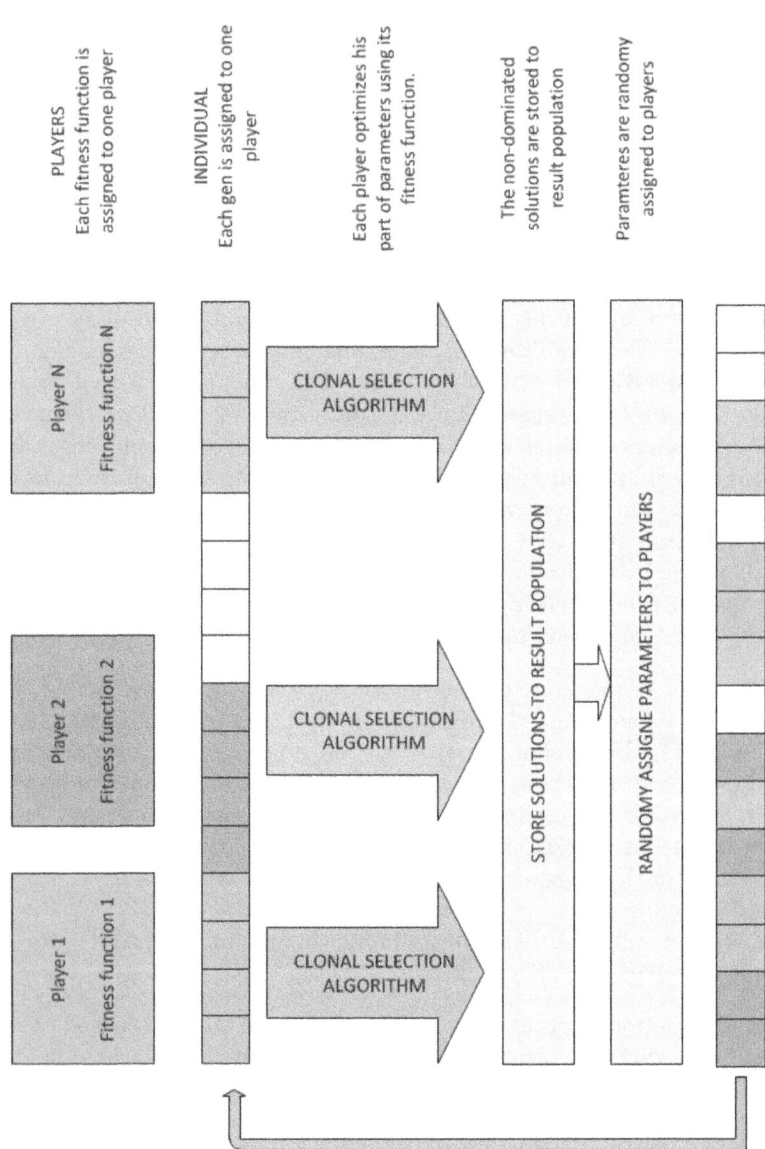

Fig. 1. General schema of Immune Game Theory Multi Objective algorithm

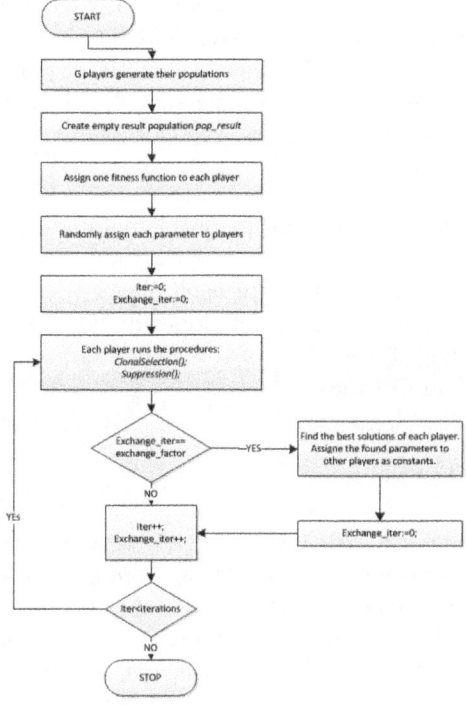

Fig. 2. IMGAMO algorithm

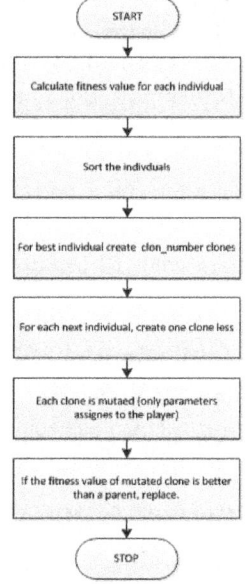

Fig. 3. Clonal selction algorithm

dominated solutions are removed. Additionally if the solution does not dominate any others but it is nondominated - it also is added to the external archive. There is parameter d_{sup} - suppression distance - which is responsible for avoiding the grouping the solutions in one point of the space. The solution is not added to the result_population of the distance to the closest one is smaller than d_{sup}.

Parameters of the algorithm:

- G - number of fitness functions in problem (number of players and their populations),
- pop_size - size of the population for each player,
- $clon\_number$ - maximum number of clones in clonal selection,
- $iterations$ - number of iterations of the algorithm,
- d_sup - suppression distance.

7   Numerical Tests

Several tests for problems with two objective were presented in [16] and [17]. The conclusions were promising - algorithm were competitive with other state of the art methods. In this article the results obtained by IMGAMO algorithm in three problems with more than two objectives are presented. The results are compared with NSGA2 and SPEA2 algorithms. For each problem the results are compared using two metrics: spacing and generational distance. All three algorithms are tested for three, four and five objective versions of problems. All results are presented in Fig. 4.

The parameters of the algorithms were configured to run the same number of function evaluations (100,000). The parameters for IMGAMO were: pop_size=25, clon_number=25, iterations=200, d_sup=0.05. The parameters for SPEA2 and NSGA2 were: pop_size=100, iterations=500, mutation probability=0.1, recombination probability=0.17.

7.1   The DTLZ1 Problem

This is a multi-objective problem with 12 parameters proposed by Deb [12].

$$\text{Minimize} F = (f_1(x), f_2(x), f_3(x)) \qquad (6)$$
$$f_1(x) = 0.5 \cdot x_1 \cdot x_2 \cdot x_3 \cdot x_4 \cdot (1 + g(x))$$
$$f_2(x) = 0.5 \cdot x_1 \cdot x_2 \cdot x_3 \cdot (1 - x_4) \cdot (1 + g(x))$$
$$f_3(x) = 0.5 \cdot x_1 \cdot x_2 \cdot \cdot (1 - x_3)(1 + g(x))$$
$$f_4(x) = 0.5 \cdot x_1 \cdot (1 - x_2) \cdot (1 + g(x))$$
$$f_5(x) = 0.5 \cdot (1 - x_1)(1 + g(x))$$
$$g(x) = 100 \cdot (10 + \sum_{i=3}^{n} (x_i - 0.5)^2 - cos(20\pi(x_i - 0.5)))$$

where

$0 \leq x_i \leq 1$ and $n = 12$

The difficulty provided by this problem is the convergence to the Pareto-optimal hyper-plane. The search space contains many local optimal frontiers. For 3 objective problem three algorithms approached the Pareto front - the IMGAMO's results were best. For the 4 and 5 objective problems only IMGAMO algorithm gave satisfactory results.

7.2   The DTLZ2 Problem

This is the another multi -objective problem with 12 parameters proposed by Deb [12].

$$\text{Minimize} F = (f_1(x), f_2(x), f_3(x)) \qquad (7)$$
$$f_1(x) = cos(x_1 \cdot \pi/2) \cdot cos(x_2 \cdot \pi/2) \cdot cos(x_3 \cdot \pi/2) \cdot cos(x_4 \cdot \pi/2) \cdot (1 + g(x))$$
$$f_2(x) = cos(x_1 \cdot \pi/2) \cdot cos(x_2 \cdot \pi/2) \cdot cos(x_3 \cdot \pi/2) \cdot sin(x_4 \cdot \pi/2) \cdot (1 + g(x))$$
$$f_3(x) = cos(x_1 \cdot \pi/2) \cdot cos(x_2 \cdot \pi/2) \cdot sin(x_3 \cdot \pi/2) \cdot (1 + g(x))$$
$$f_4(x) = cos(x_1 \cdot \pi/2) \cdot sin(x_2 \cdot \pi/2) \cdot (1 + g(x))$$
$$f_5(x) = sin(x_1 \cdot \pi/2) \cdot (1 + g(x))$$
$$g(x) = \sum_{i=3}^{n} (x_i - 0.5)^2$$

where

$0 \leq x_i \leq 1$ and $n = 12$

In this problem, all three algorithms approached the front. For 3 and 4 objective problems the algorithms were quite competitive. For 5 objective problem the IMGAMO gave best results.

7.3   The DTLZ4 Problem

This is the another multi-objective problem with 12 parameters proposed by Deb [12].

$$\text{Minimize} F = (f_1(x), f_2(x), f_3(x)) \qquad (8)$$
$$f_1(x) = cos(x_1^{100} \cdot \pi/2) \cdot cos(x_2^{100} \cdot \pi/2) \cdot cos(x_3^{100} \cdot \pi/2) \cdot cos(x_4^{100} \cdot \pi/2) \cdot (1 + g(x))$$
$$f_2(x) = cos(x_1^{100} \cdot \pi/2) \cdot cos(x_2^{100} \cdot \pi/2) \cdot cos(x_3^{100} \cdot \pi/2) \cdot sin(x_4^{100} \cdot \pi/2) \cdot (1 + g(x))$$
$$f_3(x) = cos(x_1^{100} \cdot \pi/2) \cdot cos(x_2^{100} \cdot \pi/2) \cdot sin(x_3^{100} \cdot \pi/2) \cdot (1 + g(x))$$
$$f_4(x) = cos(x_1^{100} \cdot \pi/2) \cdot sin(x_2^{100} \cdot \pi/2) \cdot (1 + g(x))$$
$$f_5(x) = sin(x_1^{100} \cdot \pi/2) \cdot (1 + g(x))$$
$$g(x) = \sum_{i=3}^{n} (x_i - 0.5)^2$$

where

$0 \leq x_i \leq 1$ and $n = 12$

For this problem with 3 objectives all algorithms approached the front. For the 4 and 5 objectives problems IMGAMO behave best.

DTLZ1		SPEA2		NSGA2		IMGAMO	
		Avg	Std.Dev	Avg.	Std.Dev	Avg.	Std.Dev
3 obj							
	GD	0,42	0,24	1,8	0,5	0,07	0,06
	S	0,03	0,02	0,44	0,05	0,02	0,01
4 obj							
	GD	146,01	10,03	99,19	20	0,47	0,14
	S	8,26	1,59	8,55	2,88	0,02	0,01
5 obj							
	GD	574,56	17,45	551	15,56	0,26	0,15
	S	41	2	27	2	0,03	0,01

DTLZ2		SPEA2		NSGA2		IMGAMO	
		Avg	Std.Dev	Avg.	Std.Dev	Avg.	Std.Dev
3 obj							
	GD	0,03	0,01	0,04	0,01	0,05	0,02
	S	0,03	0,01	0,4	0,01	0,03	0,01
4 obj							
	GD	0,27	0,04	0,67	0,13	0,24	0,05
	S	0,06	0,01	0,06	0,01	0,07	0,01
5 obj							
	GD	4,46	0,07	4,61	0,87	0,44	0,08
	S	0,09	0,01	0,12	0,01	0,12	0,02

DTLZ4		SPEA2		NSGA2		IMGAMO	
		Avg	Std.Dev	Avg.	Std.Dev	Avg.	Std.Dev
3 obj							
	GD	0,18	0,11	0,03	0,01	0,03	0,02
	S	0,02	0,01	0,15	0,02	0,11	0,02
4 obj							
	GD	1,44	0,21	1,69	0,11	0,31	0,04
	S	0,06	0,01	0,3	0,1	0,32	0,11
5 obj							
	GD	4,71	0,23	4,77	0,33	1,22	0,02
	S	0,17	0,02	0,3	0,1	0,85	0,15

Fig. 4. Results obtained by the SPEA2, NSGA2 and IMAGMO algorithms

8   Conclusions

The Artificial Immune System for solving multiobjective optimization problems was presented in this paper. The novel idea of coupling ideas from Artificial Immune Systems and the Game Theory was adopted to solve problems with many objectives. The IMGAMO (IMmune GAme theory MultiObjective) algorithm was described and the results of tests on traditional problems with three, four and five objectives were presented. The results of the algorithm behavior were compared with the state-of-the-art evolutionary algorithms: NSGA2 and SPEA2.

Looking at the results it can be stated that for 3-objective problems algorithms are competitive and lead to well results. When the 4 and 5 objective problems are considered the weakness of NSGA2 and SPEA2 algorithm appear. For these problems IMGAMO algorithm had no problem with approaching the front.

Based on these tests it can be concluded that coupling the Artificial Immune System concept with Game Theory principles can lead to new algorithms which are more scalable.

Acknowledgments

This work was supported by the Polish Ministry of Science and Higher Education under grant No. N N519 405437.

References

1. Coello, C.A., Cortés, N.C.: Solving multiobjective optimization problems using an artificial immune system. Genetic Programming and Evolvable Machines 6(2), 163–190 (2005)
2. Gong, M., Jiao, L., Du, H., Bo, L.: Multiobjective immune algorithm with non-dominated neighbor-based selection. Evol. Comput. 16(2), 225–255 (2008)
3. Gao, J., Wang, J.: Wbmoais: A novel artificial immune system for multiobjective optimization. Comput. Oper. Res. 37(1), 50–61 (2010)
4. Luh, G.C., Chueh, C.H., Liu, W.W.: MOIA: Multi-Objective Immune Algorithm. Engineering Optimization 35(2), 143–164 (2003)
5. Sefrioui, M., Periaux, J.: Nash genetic algorithms: Examples and applications. In: Proceedings of the 2000 Congress on Evolutionary Computation CEC 2000, pp. 509–516. IEEE Press, USA (2000)
6. Lam Thu Bui, S.A.: An introduction to multi-objective optimizatio. Multi-Objective Optimization in Computational Intelligence: Theory and Practice, 1–19 (2008)
7. Coello, C.A.C., Lamont, G.B., Veldhuizen, D.A.V.: Evolutionary Algorithms for Solving Multi-Objective Problems (Genetic and Evolutionary Computation). Springer- Verlag, New York Inc., Secaucus (2006)
8. Schott, J.R.: Fault Tolerant Design Using Single and Multicriteria Genetic Algorithm Optimization. Master's thesis, Department of Aeronautics and Astronautics, Massachusetts Institute of Technology, Cambridge, Massachusetts (May 1995)
9. Van Veldhuizen, D., Lamont, G.: On measuring multiobjective evolutionary algorithm performance. In: Proceedings of the 2000 Congress on Evolutionary Computation, vol. 1, pp. 204–211 (2000)
10. Srinivas, N., Deb, K.: Muiltiobjective optimization using nondominated sorting in genetic algorithms. Evol. Comput. 2, 221–248 (1994)
11. Goldberg, D.E.: Genetic Algorithms in Search, Optimization and Machine Learning, 1st edn. Addison-Wesley Longman Publishing Co., Inc., Boston (1989)
12. Deb, K., Agrawal, S., Pratap, A., Meyarivan, T.: A fast elitist non-dominated sorting genetic algorithm for multi-objective optimisation: Nsga-ii. In: Deb, K., Rudolph, G., Lutton, E., Merelo, J.J., Schoenauer, M., Schwefel, H.-P., Yao, X. (eds.) PPSN 2000. LNCS, vol. 1917, pp. 849–858. Springer, Heidelberg (2000)
13. Zitzler, E., Thiele, L.: Multiobjective evolutionary algorithms: A Comparative Case Study and the Strength Pareto Approach (1999)
14. Wierzchon, S.T.: Function optimization by the immune metaphor. Task Quarterly 6 (2002)
15. Dasgupta, D.: Advances in artificial immune systems. IEEE Computational Intelligence Magazine 1(4), 40–49 (2006)
16. Jarosz, P., Burczyski, T.: Coupling of immune algorithms and game theory in multiobjective optimization. Artifical Intelligence and Soft Computing, 500–507 (2010)
17. Jarosz, P., Burczyski, T.: Solving multiobjective optimization methods using an immune metaphor and the game theory. In: Proceedings of Invers Problems, Design and Optimization Syposium, Joao Pessoa (August 2010)

Tunable Immune Detectors for Behaviour-Based Network Intrusion Detection

Mário Antunes[1,2] and Manuel E. Correia[2]

[1] School of Technology and Management, Polytechnic Institute of Leiria, Portugal
mario.antunes@ipleiria.pt
[2] Center for Research in Advanced Computing Systems (CRACS-INESC LA),
Faculty of Science, University of Porto, Portugal
mcc@dcc.fc.up.pt

Abstract. Computer networks are highly dynamic environments in which the meaning of normal and anomalous behaviours can drift considerably throughout time. Behaviour-based Network Intrusion Detection System (NIDS) have thus to cope with the temporal normality drift intrinsic on computer networks, by tuning adaptively its level of response, in order to be able to distinguish harmful from harmless network traffic flows. In this paper we put forward the intrinsic Tunable Activation Threshold (TAT) theory ability to adaptively tolerate normal drifting network traffic flows. This is embodied on the TAT-NIDS, a TAT-based Artificial Immune System (AIS) we have developed for network intrusion detection. We describe the generic AIS framework we have developed to assemble TAT-NIDS and present the results obtained thus far on processing real network traffic data sets. We also compare the performance obtained by TAT-NIDS with the well known and widely deployed signature-based `snort` network intrusion detection system.

Keywords: Artificial Immune System, Tunable Activation Threshold, Network Intrusion Detection, Anomaly Detection.

1   Introduction

The vertebrate Immune System (IS) [1] can be seen as acting as a highly sophisticated *anomaly detector*, since it is able to mount an immune response to foreign microorganisms (pathogens), like bacteria and virus, that suspiciously may be the cause of an ongoing intrusion (anomaly). The IS has also the ability to simultaneously *tolerate* harmless inoffensive pathogens, thus preventing the initiation of an otherwise immune reaction. These observable behaviours occur continuously during each individual lifetime, and are manifested by the body interaction with a highly dynamic environment, where it is constantly being exposed to *new and unseen* external pathogens that can mutate rather rapidly and unexpectedly. Under this environment, the individual body is constantly tuning its levels of adaptation to new stimulus, naturally promoted by the dynamic surroundings where *new* forms of previously unseen *normal* behaviours start being gradually *tolerated* by the IS. These cognitive capabilities can also

P. Liò, G. Nicosia, and T. Stibor (Eds.): ICARIS 2011, LNCS 6825, pp. 334–347, 2011.

be observed by the now well accepted idea that the IS is *trained* to recognise each body composition during embryo life and then adapts to the physiological and environmental changes as each individual matures, ages and interacts with the environment where he lives. Moreover, this *learning* process is at the same time *evolutionary* and *adaptive*, allowing each individual to have his IS gradually adapted, at each given moment.

Artificial Immune Systems (AIS) [2, 3] have been an intensive bubbling area of research, particularly in the development and deployment of adaptive behaviour-based Network Intrusion Detection System (NIDS) [4]. The research done so far has been falling mainly within two theoretical immunological tenets, namely *negative selection* and *danger theory* [4, 5].

In this paper we present an AIS for anomaly detection based on another less explored immunological theory, which is Tunable Activation Thresholds (TAT) dynamics applied to T-cells [6, 7]. We describe TAT immunological model and its underlying information processing capabilities for developing innovative network intrusion detection systems. We also present results obtained with real world data sets. Moreover, in [8] we proposed an exploratory proposal of TAT-NIDS, where we reported some preliminary results obtained with two data sets with a very small subset of attacks. Although TAT dynamics has already been employed by other AIS [9, 10], its application on dynamic anomaly detection environments, like computer network intrusion detection, has not yet been sufficiently evaluated.

The theory behind TAT dynamics for T-cells tries to grasp why self tolerance solely based on a deletional process is not able to explain the presence of mature auto-reactive lymphocytes in normal healthy individuals that may cause autoimmune diseases. Interestingly, those auto-reactive lymphocytes circulate in healthy individuals and are prevented from mounting an harmful immune response against its own body tissues. Moreover, the accuracy on how the IS tolerates harmless self and non-self antigens and, at the same time, mount an immune response to the harmful non-self, must be related to its cells' adaptive tuning capabilities, according to their iterations with the environment [1, 6, 7].

In what follows, in Section 2 we present a model for tuning detectors activation thresholds, inspired on the TAT model. We then proceed to Section 3 where we describe the generic TAT-based AIS framework (TAT-AIS) we have developed, which is the main building block behind the TAT-NIDS we present and evaluate in this paper. In Section 4 we evaluate TAT-NIDS with real network traffic data sets and we compare the performance obtained with that of the signatures-based snort NIDS [11]. Finally, in Section 5 we discuss the main results obtained thus far and propose some directions for future work.

2   TAT Model

The TAT-based AIS framework we have developed for anomaly detection is based on the tunable immune detector thresholds theory postulated by Grossman [6] and further explored by Carneiro's TAT mathematical modelling of these thresholds on individual T-cells [7]. In TAT the activation process is controlled by the activity of two specific enzymes that respond to antigenic signalling (S) delivered by an Antigen Presenting Cell (APC): *Kinase* (K) phosphorilates molecules that "excite" the cell and; *Phosphatase* (P) that dephosphorilates them, returning the cell to a "de-excitation" state. It is also assumed that the *T-cell activation* is a switch-type response that requires that K supersedes P, at least transiently. At each given moment in time, T-cells interact with the peptides presented by each APC and receive a stimulus that depends on the *affinity* between its receptor and the peptide ligand, causing the cell to adapt by increasing or decreasing its activation threshold. Moreover, foreign antigens will cause a very fast increase in the cells excitation level, whereas tissue-specific self-ligands will induce a much slower increase excitation level. Accordingly, since the de-excitation levels are kept above the excitation ones, it is possible to maintain tolerance to self for extended periods of time.

T-cells react differently to the signals they receive from each APC, by *adjusting* its activation threshold proportionally to the received signals. So, within this model, each T-cell has its own level of responsiveness and tuning, updated according to the history of intracellular interactions between itself and each APC. This means that different T-cells with different antigen-specificity end up having very different activation thresholds as they are exposed to different stimuli.

The T-cell is stimulated with a stimulus S that leads to a linear increase of both K and P, but their maximum value is limited by a turnover limit, determined by τK and τP. This means that, for the same signal, K increases faster than P (with slopes ϕK and ϕP), but if the signal persists P will eventually supersede K and hence reach a higher plateau. Similarly, during signal absence, K returns to the basal level at a faster rate than P. This mechanism allow each T-cell to become regulated according to received signal from each APC and consequently to adjust dynamically its levels of activations and inaction for a particular antigen. For TAT-AIS we have made the following assumptions:

- Both K and P are exposed to the same stimulus S.
- P's basal value (P_0) is higher than K's (K_0).
- S_0 is the initial value for S.
- P's turnover rate (τP) is higher than K's (τK).
- K's slope (ϕK) is higher than P's (ϕP).

We have however made the rather pragmatic deliberate choice of deriving K_0, P_0, τK and ϕP from other variables. This reduces the number of cell simulator parameters thus simplifying the run parameter set optimisation process and dramatically decreasing the overall processing time without compromising the effectiveness of the TAT-AIS general framework. Overall, the simplifications made to the original TAT model can be described as follows:

- We assumed that the initial values for K and P (K_0 and P_0) are calculated as a function of their corresponding turnover limits (τK and τP) and S_0, according to the following: $K_0 = S_0 \cdot \tau K \quad P_0 = S_0 \cdot \tau P$.
- We fixed τP and obtained $\tau K = \tau \cdot \tau P$, with $\tau = \frac{\tau K}{\tau P}$.
- We also fixed ϕK and calculated $\phi P = \phi \cdot \phi K$, with $\phi = \frac{\phi P}{\phi K}$.
- The speed of response is given by a constant value, t.

Assuming $\{P_0, K_0\}$ as the basal values, in each iteration i, the values for K and P are given by the following Equations 1 and 2:

$$K_i = \begin{cases} \min((S + S_0) \cdot \tau K, K_{i-1} + \phi K \cdot t); & \text{if } (S + S_0) \cdot \tau K > K_{i-1} \\ \max((S + S_0) \cdot \tau K, K_{i-1} - \phi K \cdot t); & otherwise \end{cases} \quad (1)$$

$$P_i = \begin{cases} \min((S + S_0) \cdot \tau P, P_{i-1} + \phi P \cdot t); & \text{if } (S + S_0) \cdot \tau P > P_{i-1} \\ \max((S + S_0) \cdot \tau P, P_{i-1} - \phi P \cdot t); & otherwise \end{cases} \quad (2)$$

For this simple set-up, the higher the value of P relative to K, the more difficult it is to activate the T-cell. Under these conditions, those T-cells that receive continuous or sufficiently frequent antigenic signals from an APC become unresponsive and those that rarely bind with a peptide remain highly sensitive for further reactivation [7].

In order to strengthen the exposure to more recent temporal events, the cell stimulus S is calculated as a function of the affinity between T-cell Receptor (TCR) and the peptides ligand that exists in the *APC lifespan*. By this reason, for each T-cell, S reflects not only the signal sent by the bound peptides in the current APC, but also by all the others that were presented by the APCs *recently* processed and whose lifetime has not yet expired.

It is also widely accepted from Biology that an immunological response to an APC is usually not initiated by a single activated cell, being instead initiated by a *committee* of activated cells that happen to be within the neighbourhood of the antigen [1, 6]. We incorporated this immunological concept into TAT-AIS by triggering an immune response only if the ratio between the amount of activated and bound cells exceeds a calculated dynamic *committee threshold* (denoted Ct).

In each APC processing, Ct is dynamically adjusted over time according to the classification made by the system, in the following way. It starts with a predefined value and during the training phase, for each processed APC, Ct is adjusted according to a classification feedback made by the system. In this phase, Ct is supervised and its adjustment reflects the correctness of each classification, by comparing the APC tag with the classification result. During the testing phase, the classification process is unsupervised and Ct increases in the presence of an immune response and decreases otherwise.

3   TAT-AIS Framework

The general TAT-AIS framework we have developed is depicted in Figure 1 [12]. A considerable effort has been made to keep it as much faithful as possible to the TAT immunological model described in Section 2. The TAT-AIS framework is conceptually composed by four main building blocks: data sets preprocessing, a parameters set choice procedure, a TAT dynamics processing simulator for T-cells and, finally, a performance evaluation and analysis module [12]. The initial

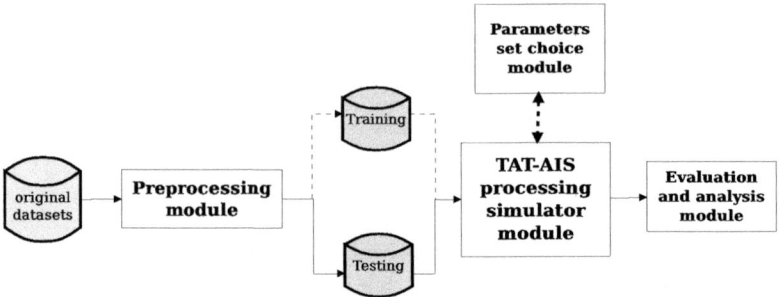

Fig. 1. Generic TAT-AIS framework building blocks

preprocessing module convert the original raw application data into a generic and pre-defined format expected by the TAT-AIS processing simulator (Section 3.1). The output produced by this module consists on two separated data sets: one for training and another one for performance evaluation (testing).

The core of the TAT-AIS framework is its cell simulator. It corresponds to an artificial T-cell dynamics simulator that implements the TAT processing functions advocated by the adopted model (Section 2). The simulator processes the training and testing data sets against an artificial T-cells repertoire. The result of each APC processing is its classification, whether it is part of a normal or anomalous behaviour, and is reported by the evaluation module for further results analysis. The parameters set choice module consists on an optimiser that finds a suitable conjugated optimised TAT parameter set for a specific training problem domain data set (e.g. network intrusion detection), which is then used by TAT-AIS simulator to process other data sets of the same problem domain.

3.1 Data Format and Representation

The most relevant immunological players involved in the TAT model and suitable to be represented in the TAT-AIS framework are peptide ligands, TCR and APC. From an information processing point of view both peptide ligands and TCR can be seen as *patterns*, represented by streams of characters, binding to each other in accordance with some affinity measure function. On the same light an APC can be seen as a list of characters strings (peptides) representing a behaviour. They are sequentially ordered and are being labelled as positive (ALERT) and negative (NORMAL) examples for evaluation purposes. The generic format adopted for TAT-AIS processing and evaluation is similar to the one depicted in Figure 2. Each data set is comprised by APCs that represent a timely ordered set of events

METADATA				LIST OF PEPTIDES				
apc:	<ID>:	...	<LABEL>:	<Additional Information>:	Peptide 1	Peptide 2	Peptide 3	...	Peptide n

Fig. 2. Generic format of an APC processed by TAT-AIS simulator

and the corresponding observed patterns. Each APC corresponds to a character stream that ends with a CRLF character control sequence and is composed by two distinct parts: the *metadata* and the *list of peptides*. The former starts with the string apc and the APC identifier, followed by a list of context-dependent related information separated by the character ":". The latter represents the core of each APC and is composed by a list of strings (peptides) separated by a white space.

3.2   Run Parameters Set Discovery and Choice

From the equations 1 and 2 (Section 2) one may conclude that TAT dynamics depends on a pre-defined simulator parameter set. In order to simplify and accelerate the parameters set discovery procedure, we managed to reduce the cell simulator parameters to a minimal set composed of $\phi = \frac{\phi P}{\phi K}$, $\tau = \frac{\tau K}{\tau P}$ and t (Section 2). We must reinforce here that our main focus was on finding a suitable parameter set on which we could satisfactorily evaluate TAT dynamics and test the TAT-AIS processing capabilities, on very specific problem domains, even if the found and used simulator parameters are most certainly not the best possible for a specific training data set.

We have therefore incorporated a parameter set discovery and optimisation strategy based on the Latin Hypercube (LHC) [13] sampling method. LHC sampling is a statistical method to generate a distribution of plausible collections of parameter values from a multidimensional distribution. In the context of statistical sampling, a square grid containing sample positions is a Latin square if there is only one sample in each row and each column. A Latin hypercube is the generalisation of this concept to an arbitrary number of dimensions [13]. When sampling a function of N variables, the range of each variable is divided into M equally probable intervals that satisfy the LHC requirements.

3.3   APC Processing Algorithm

The processing of each APC presented to the TAT-AIS system is described in Algorithm 1. Regarding the classification decision rule, we have defined it as a function of the amount of both activated and bound T-cells. If its ratio exceeds the threshold Ct, then an alarm is raised and the APC is probably related with an anomaly. Concerning the distance measure, it was defined as a function of the maximal length of the sub-strings common to both the peptide and the TCR strings. We have also implemented a cell apoptosis mechanism where the cell death consists on removing from the repertoire those detectors that are not stimulated within a certain period of time and thus have K and P reach their basal values (K_0 and P_0).

4   Experimental Evaluation and Results

In this Section we survey the general methodology employed for our experiments. We start by describing the data sets employed, followed by their preprocessing for

---

Algorithm 1. Algorithm applied by TAT-AIS to process each APC

---

1 **Input:** L_{tcell} = N strings over the alphabet Σ of fixed length (T-cells)
2 **Input:** L_{pep} = N strings over the alphabet Σ of fixed length (peptides)
3 **Input:** At = Affinity Threshold
4 **Input:** Ct = Actual committee Threshold
5 **Output**: Classification of the APC: `NORMAL` or `ALERT`
6 $T_{bind} = ()$ /* List of bound detectors */
7 $T_{active} = ()$ /* List of activated detectors */
8 **forall the** $tcell$ in L_{tcell} **do**
9 $\quad$ $S = 0$ /* Reset signal sent by the APC to each T-cell */
10 $\quad$ **forall the** $UNIQUE(peptide)$ in L_{pep} **do**
11 $\quad\quad$ $a = DISTANCE(peptide, tcell)$
12 $\quad\quad$ $c = COUNT(peptide)$ /* `peptide` count in the APC lifespan */
13 $\quad\quad$ **if** $a >= At$ **then**
14 $\quad\quad\quad$ $S+ = c \cdot a$
15 $\quad\quad\quad$ $ADD(T_{bind}, tcell)$
16 $\quad\quad$ **end**
17 $\quad\quad$ **else**
18 $\quad\quad\quad$ $ADD(L_{tcell}, peptide, S_0, CS_0)$
19 $\quad\quad\quad$ $S+ = c$
20 $\quad\quad\quad$ $ADD(T_{bind}, peptide)$
21 $\quad\quad$ **end**
22 $\quad$ **end**
23 $\quad$ $UpdateTCell(tcell, S)$ /* Equations 1 and 2 (Section 2) */
24 **end**
25 **forall the** $tcell$ in T_{bind} **do**
26 $\quad$ **if** $K >= P$ **then**
27 $\quad\quad$ $ADD(T_{active}, tcell)$
28 $\quad$ **end**
29 **end**
30 $Status = NORMAL$
31 **if** $\dfrac{size(T_{active})}{size(T_{bind})} > Ct$ **then**
32 $\quad$ $Status = ALERT$
33 **end**
34 $ReportStatus(Status)$
35 $UpdateCt(Status)$
36 $CellDeath(L_{tcell})$

TAT-AIS. We then proceed to the process employed for the simulator parameter set optimisation. Finally, we present the anomaly detection results thus obtained with TAT-NIDS.

4.1 Methodology for Experiments

In the TAT-AIS framework, system processing is divided into two distinct parts. To each part corresponds a specific data set of the same problem domain: one is used for training and the other is used for evaluation. The training data set is further sub-divided into two distinct parts: *validation* and *calibration*, which are processed separately. In the validation phase the system creates in run time a new T-cell if no one in the repertoire was able to bind with the presented peptides. In the calibration phase the system is presented with a set of APCs whose artificial peptides correspond to both normal behaviour and *known* anomalous activity. In this phase the system is executed with different simulator parameter sets, following a LHC search procedure in order to calibrate the system into a the best possible performance. The calibration phase ends with the system containing two different groups of T-cells in its repertoire. One group has T-cells that have been continuously exposed to peptides representative of normal behaviours. These T-cells are in a quiescent state with their value for P higher than K. The other group corresponds to those T-cells that were transiently activated in the presence of unknown and highly concentrated peptides and are therefore possibly related to some kind of anomalous activity. The calibration or training phase is followed by the testing phase, where TAT-AIS is now confronted with a data set belonging to the same problem domain, but containing peptide patterns corresponding to known and unknown normal and abnormal behaviours. The main reason behind the introduction of anomalies in the training phase is to better guide the parameter set selector module in finding a parameters set that not only minimises the rate of false positives, but can also achieve a low rate for false negatives for the data set it has been trained to recognise. Otherwise, the parameters obtained are very likely to be too permissive and inefficient to be able to achieve a reasonable degree of accuracy during the testing phase.

4.2 Data Sets Analysis

To conduct a meaningful experimental evaluation of the TAT-NIDS we have employed real network traffic samples for normal behaviour, corresponding to network packets collected from an active local network with different users. The network traffic samples of intrusions comprise data sets of pre-selected malicious activities collected from a catalogue of network attacks. In order to overcome the documented limitations of the popular and well known DARPA KDD-CUP data set [14, 15], we took advantage of the vast catalogue of documented attack samples produced and made available by Massicotte *et al.* [16]. This massive catalogue has been produced by employing a virtual architecture, comprised by a series of heterogeneous networked virtual machines, to collect the network packets produced by the launch of a subset of well known network attack scenarios within the virtual network. The packets produced were fully captured and saved into the PCAP format.

The data sets corresponding to normal behaviour were collected during a period of about one hour for *training* and four hours for *testing* in a busy local computer network. During the whole period we have also monitored the network with the snort NIDS [11] to make sure that no alarm has been raised and the captured packets correspond to what can be considered benign network activities. For our experiments we have concentrated our efforts on network

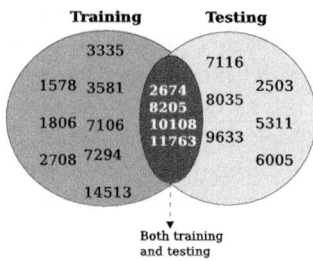

Fig. 3. Distribution of the attacks samples (BID) used in each data set

attack samples that target diverse network services running on various versions of `Windows` and then tested each one of these with `snort` NIDS. From the selected sample set, comprised of 57 different attacks, 41 have been incorporated into the data sets employed to train (calibrate) TAT-NIDS. The remaining 16 samples have been confirmed to be `snort` NIDS false negatives, and have, because of this, been included into the testing data sets. For our experiments we have used all the variations for each one of these particular attacks samples, available at the Massicotte's public database. Figure 3 depicts the *Bugtrack ID* (BID) (`www.securityfocus.com`) of each attack used for training and testing. It clearly distinguishes those BID used only in one processing cycle from those that were used both for training and testing, but with slight variations. Each one of the vulnerabilities identified by BID {2674,8205,10108,11763} corresponds to more than one attack sample due to different execution parameters. For these attacks in particular, `snort` NIDS was unable to detect all of their sample variations and this fact motivated us to train TAT-NIDS with the variations of the attack that have been detected by `snort` NIDS and to include the other samples into the testing data sets, in order to see if TAT-NIDS was able to detect them and therefore to perform better than `snort` NIDS, at least for these cases.

4.3   Data Set Preprocessing

The data sets used for the conducted experiments were preprocessed into the general TAT-AIS format, described in Section 3.1. Figure 4 depicts the data set preprocessing methodology adopted for network packets and implemented in TAT-NIDS. To better evaluate TAT-NIDS detection accuracy and be able to compare it with `snort` NIDS on the same data sets, the overall preprocessing procedure has been sub-divided into five main steps. The first consists in randomly picking which attack samples are to be part of the data set. Then, in step two, and for each one of the selected attack samples, we pick a random relative start time and then interleave, in a consistent temporal order its corresponding network packets into a `PCAP` file that already contains regular validated normal traffic. In step three all the `PCAP` packet payloads are converted into a `base64` encoded stream, which allows for an easier and more consistent representation of non-printable characters. This stream of chars is then partitioned into a temporal sequence of peptides of fixed length (l).

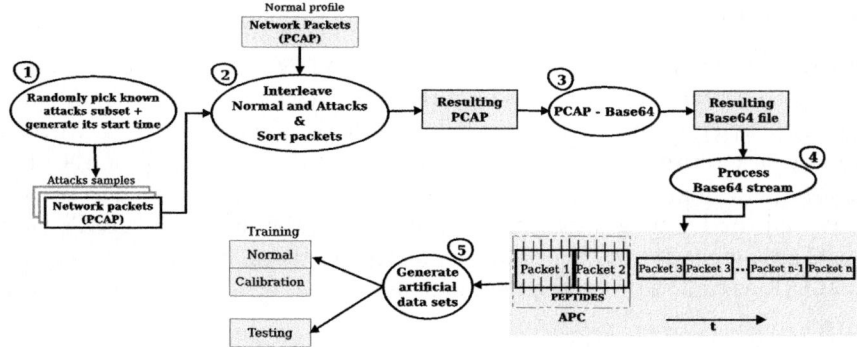

Fig. 4. Data sets preprocessing module for network packets

In step four we partition the temporal sequence of peptides into a sequence of APCs where each one has a maximum duration (fixed to 5 seconds in our experiments) which are then orderly queued into the data sets.

Each APC contains a base64 encoded char stream, ending with a CRLF character control sequence and is composed by two distinct parts: a metadata header followed by the list of peptides that resulted from breaking the base64 stream into a set of fixed size strings. The metadata stores additional information that is used for further report analysis, like the APC start and end time stamp. For the APCs labelled as ALERT the metadata also includes information related to the corresponding malware BID.

4.4 Parameters Set Optimisation

The training data sets are processed against different parameter sets in order to obtain the higger detection performance. We have used the LHC search methodology to discover candidate values for τ, ϕ and t. The parameter Ct is also updated during run time according to the classification feedback, with the other parameters remaining fixed for the rest of each processing cycle.

For each of the 10 runs, we have processed 10 training data sets using different parameters sets. The parameters combinations is described as follows:

- τ, ϕ and t: values suggested by the LHC sampling generator.
- Ct: initial value of 0.05, updated linearly by a fixed value of 0.005.
- APC lifespan (number of APC): $LS = \{5, 10\}$
- Affinity threshold, between $[0, 1]$: $At = \{0.25, 0.5\}$
- Peptide length (string length): $l = \{4, 8, 12\}$

The best average performance results in processing the 10 training data sets for accuracy (A) and $F1$ score were obtained with the following fixed parameters: $l = 8$, $LS = 5$ and $a = 0.5$. The corresponding parameters set that were obtained by the LHC optimisation procedure, was the following: $\phi = 0.8140914$, $\tau = 0.8189538$ and $t = 10.93574$.

4.5   Results

In these experiments we have observed that TAT-NIDS was able to cope with new unseen patterns by distinguishing them between those corresponding to self network activity from others included in APCs related to ongoing intrusions. Table 1 characterises the distribution of APCs per data set, stressing the amount of known and unknown attacks that were randomly introduced into each data set. For all the training data sets the table shows the number of APCs labelled with ALERT, while for testing data sets it depicts those labelled both as NORMAL and ALERT, as well as its corresponding number of attacks. For example, the data

Table 1. APC data set distribution

#	APC Training Alerts	Testing Normal	Testing Alerts	Events Attacks Known	Events Attacks New	#	APC Training Alerts	Testing Normal	Testing Alerts	Events Attacks Known	Events Attacks New
1	66	1931	127	9	4	6	64	1561	951	7	5
2	63	1928	118	9	8	7	72	1773	426	11	10
3	62	1975	48	4	3	8	68	1585	913	4	5
4	64	1948	78	8	4	9	64	1982	41	6	5
5	67	1932	92	10	6	10	60	1968	64	11	6

set 1 has 66 APC labelled as ALERT in the training data set. For testing it has 1931 APCs representative of normal network behaviour and 127 corresponding to unknown anomalies. These 127 APC contain 13 attacks, 9 of which first appeared during the training phase while the remaining 4 are completely new or variations.

Table 2 presents the performance results obtained on processing the 10 testing data sets with the run parameters set obtained during the training phase.

By analysing Table 2 it is possible to compare the amount of attacks detected for each data set. For example in data set 1, from the 9 known attacks (see Table 1) 7 were successfully detected by TAT-NIDS. Regarding those new and previously unseen attacks, from the 4 included in this data set, TAT-NIDS was able to detect 3. On the other side, snort was only able to detect 9 attacks to which it has a valid signature. The remaining columns of Table 2 show the performance attained by TAT-NIDS for each data set, particularly the amount of false positives, the accuracy, and the rates of true negatives and false positives. However, the negative examples are in greater number than positive ones, which justifies the high accuracy results observed. It is also worth noting that some attacks are longer than the APC duration time (fixed to 2 seconds) and therefore may fill more than one APC. However, from a monitoring point of view and for performance calculation purposes, a true positive event (network intrusion) only needs to have one of its APC correctly classified. By the same reason, a false positive event corresponds to a chunk of one or more *contiguous APC* that has been incorrectly classified by the system as an intrusion.

Table 2. Comparative analysis of TAT-NIDS and snort processing

#	TP events			TP rate		Performance (tat)			
	Known	New	snort	tat	snort	FP rate	FP(apc)	Acc.	TN rate
1	7	3	9	0.77	0.69	0.05	106	0.94	0.95
2	6	6	9	0.71	0.53	0.06	109	0.94	0.94
3	4	1	4	0.71	0.57	0.05	97	0.95	0.95
4	8	2	8	0.83	0.63	0.05	102	0.95	0.95
5	3	5	10	0.5	0.62	0.05	96	0.95	0.95
6	4	4	7	0.67	0.58	0.05	77	0.95	0.95
7	6	3	11	0.43	0.52	0.05	93	0.94	0.95
8	2	2	4	0.44	0.44	0.05	85	0.94	0.95
9	3	1	6	0.36	0.55	0.06	112	0.94	0.94
10	9	2	11	0.65	0.65	0.05	102	0.95	0.95
Mean	-	-	-	0.62	0.58	-	-	0.94	0.95
St.Dev.	-	-	-	0.16	0.07	-	-	0.005	0.004

5   Conclusions

In this paper we have presented a generic AIS framework (TAT-AIS) based on
the TAT immunological theory for the temporal adaptation of the immune T-
cells activation thresholds. We have used this framework to build a behaviour-
based NIDS (TAT-NIDS). Our experiments demonstrate that TAT-NIDS can
effectively distinguish normal from anomalous network traffic, sometimes even
outperforming snort NIDS, solely based on its initial training and on the subsequent interactions with the environment. We have shown that TAT-AIS and
particularly TAT-NIDS, possesses the following main strengths:

- The automatic adjustment of individual T-cells activation thresholds based
  on the system input dynamic activity is a direct consequence of what happens
  within computer networks and other highly complex system. Each network
  is unique and contains traffic generated by different users, each with different
  usage profiles in the presence of highly sporadic and very specific attacks.
  Therefore an effective network intrusion detector should be based on highly
  specific and dynamic detectors to that particular computer network. This is
  precisely what is promoted and achieved with the TAT-AIS framework.
- The activation of an individual detector is an automatic process, simply
  based on the kinetics between the signal intensity it receives and the activation threshold.
- the TAT operation tunes the activation threshold of T-cells in the repertoire in a temporal and adaptive way. This means that those T-cells bound
  recurrently with normal patterns are prevented from being activated.
- the decision of raising an alarm during APC processing is made by the conju-
  gation of two distinct adaptive and evolutionary processes: the intrinsic TAT
  dynamics that regulates the T-cell activation threshold and the committee

decision threshold feedback adaptation. Both mechanisms allow the system to evolve into temporal drifting states in which the normal is constantly being re-tolerated and the abnormal state re-identified throughout time.

- recurrent signals are usually related to normal activity, while abnormal activities are exceptional events that happen sporadically. This is a general assumption that is adequate to make in the context of computer networks.

We have observed that our system was not only capable of tolerating new unseen normal traffic (*self tolerance*) but also and at the same time, capable of detecting unseen anomalous network activity.

By directly comparing TAT-NIDS with snort NIDS, using the same network traffic data sets, we may identify some circumstances where it can be advantageous to also rely on TAT-NIDS for network intrusion detection. During our experiments we have discovered that the current set of available signatures for snort NIDS was unable to cover all the variations that may occur, even for already known attacks. However, by taking advantage of its intrinsic evolutionary features, TAT-NIDS was able to detect some of the attacks that were being treated as false negatives by snort NIDS.

Interestingly, we have also observed that some attacks were not detected by snort NIDS even when there was supposed to exist a signature covering it. This is a major concern because it demonstrates that a snort NIDS signature for an attack sometimes does not cover all the possible variation of parameters that an attack may have. We have also observed that some alarms were raised for legitimate and benign network traffic, thus producing nefarious false positives events. This was to be expected but it also constitutes a good indication that an hybrid system based on an ensemble of both TAT-NIDS and snort NIDS may outperform the overall classification of network traffic obtained by each one individually. This could be achieved for example with the deployment of TAT-NIDS as a plug-in for the snort NIDS.

We have also obtained some promising results by using TAT-AIS in a hybrid ensemble committee, together with Support Vector Machine (SVM) based machine learning systems. These preliminary good results have been obtained with the Reuters-21578 data set for text classification [17].

From what has been mentioned above, we are very confident that the TAT-AIS framework intrinsic adaptive and temporal drifting features could improve upon the normal/abnormal discrimination functions, implemented by other state of the art behaviour-based systems. This is mainly due to its temporal drifting adaptation, resilience and tolerance, which, in the studied domain, derived from the TAT-NIDS continuous sampling and processing of network traffic.

References

1. Cohen, I.: Tending Adam's Garden: evolving the cognitive immune self. Academic Press, San Diego (2000)
2. Castro, L., Timmis, J.: Artificial Immune Systems: A New Computational Intelligence Approach. Springer, Heidelberg (2002)

3. Flower, D., Timmis, J.: In silico immunology. Springer, Heidelberg (2007)
4. Kim, J., Bentley, P., Aickelin, U., Greensmith, J., Tedesco, G., Twycross, J.: Immune system approaches to intrusion detection - a review. Journal of Natural Computing 6(4), 413–466 (2007)
5. Dasgupta, D., Yu, S., Nino, F.: Recent Advances in AIS: Models and Applications. J. Applied Soft. Computing 11, 1574–1587 (2010)
6. Grossman, Z., Paul, W.: Adaptive cellular interactions in the immune system: The tunable activation threshold and the significance of subthreshold responses. National Academy of Sciences 89(21), 10365–10369 (1992)
7. Carneiro, J., Paixão, T., Milutinovic, D., Sousa, J., Leon, K., Gardner, R., Faro, J.: Immunological self-tolerance: Lessons from mathematical modeling. Journal of Computational and Applied Mathematics 184(1), 77–100 (2005)
8. Antunes, M., Correia, M.: TAT-NIDS: an immune-based anomaly detection architecture for network intrusion detection. In: Proceedings of IWPACBB, Advances in Intelligent and Soft. Computing, vol. 49, pp. 60–67 (2008)
9. Andrews, P., Timmis, J.: Tunable Detectors for Artificial Immune Systems: From Model to Algorithm. Bioinformatics for Immunomics (Ed. Springer) 3, 103–127 (2010)
10. Andrews, P.S., Timmis, J.: Adaptable lymphocytes for artificial immune systems. In: Bentley, P.J., Lee, D., Jung, S. (eds.) ICARIS 2008. LNCS, vol. 5132, pp. 376–386. Springer, Heidelberg (2008)
11. Caswell, B., Beale, J.: Snort Intrusion Detection and Prevention Toolkit. Syngress Press (2007)
12. Antunes, M., Correia, M.: Self tolerance by tuning t-cell activation: an artificial immune system for anomaly detection. In: LNICST, Springer, Heidelberg (2010)
13. Helton, J., Davis, F.: Latin hypercube sampling and the propagation of uncertainty in analyses of complex systems. Reliability Engineering and System Safety 81(1), 23–69 (2003)
14. Lippmann, R., Haines, J., Fried, D., Korba, J., Das, K.: The 1999 DARPA off-line intrusion detection evaluation. Computer Networks 34, 579–595 (2000)
15. McHugh, J.: Testing intrusion detection systems: A critique of the 1998 and 1999 DARPA intrusion detection system evaluations as performed by Lincoln Laboratory. ACM Transactions on Information and System Security 3(4), 262–294 (2000)
16. Massicotte, F., Gagnon, F., Labiche, Y., Briand, L., Couture, M.: Automatic evaluation of intrusion detection systems. In: Proceedings of ACSAC, pp. 361–370. IEEE, Los Alamitos (2006)
17. Antunes, M., Silva, C., Ribeiro, B., Correia, M.: A hybrid ais-svm ensemble approach for text classification. In: Dobnikar, A., Lotrič, U., Šter, B. (eds.) ICANNGA 2011, Part II. LNCS, vol. 6594, pp. 342–352. Springer, Heidelberg (2011)

Population-Based Artificial Immune System Clustering Algorithm

Waseem Ahmad and Ajit Narayanan

School of Computing and Mathematical Sciences
Auckland University of Technology (AUT), Auckland, New Zealand
{waseem.ahmad,ajit.narayanan}@aut.ac.nz

Abstract. Artificial immune systems inspired by humoral-mediated immunity use hyper mutation to simulate the way that natural immune systems refine their B cells and antibodies in response to pathogens in a process called affinity maturation. Such hyper mutation is typically performed on individual computational antibodies and B cells, and has been shown to be successful in a variety of machine learning tasks, including supervised and unsupervised learning. This paper proposes a population-based approach to affinity maturation in the problem domain of clustering. Previous work in humoral-mediated immune systems (HAIS), while using concepts of immunoglobulins, antibodies and B cells, has not investigated the use of population-based evolutionary approaches to evolving better antibodies with successively greater affinities to pathogens. The population-based approach described here is a two step algorithm, where the number of clusters is obtained in the first step using HAIS and then in step two a population-based approach is used to further enhance the cluster quality. Convergence in the fitness of populations is achieved through transferring memory cells from one generation to another. The experiments are performed on benchmarked real world datasets and demonstrate the feasibility of the proposed approach. Additional results also show the effectiveness of the crossover operator at the population level. The outcome is an artificial immune system approach to clustering that uses both mutation within antibodies and crossover between members of B cells to achieve effective clustering.

Keywords: Adaptive immune system, Clustering, Mutation, Crossover, Cluster validation.

1 Introduction

The main purpose of cluster analysis is to discover patterns in data samples and separate those samples into groups in such a way that each group has maximum within-group similarity and, ideally, maximum between-group dissimilarity. Clustering is 'unsupervised learning' in that metrics for estimating similarity and dissimilarity are not dependent on an objective top-level measure of which group or cluster a sample should belong to. Nature inspired computing researchers have noted the similarities between unsupervised learning and decentralized, bottom-up processes

P. Liò, G. Nicosia, and T. Stibor (Eds.): ICARIS 2011, LNCS 6825, pp. 348–360, 2011.
© Springer-Verlag Berlin Heidelberg 2011

in nature, with many nature inspired clustering algorithms proposed over the years based on genetic algorithms, ant colony optimization and particle swarm optimization [1-4]. Such approaches typically derive their inspirations from macro-level biological phenomena, i.e. at the level of individual organisms (ants, particles) or populations of individuals (genetic algorithms). As our understanding of nature grows, researchers have started to focus their attention on much deeper natural processes for designing and developing new computational algorithms. One such example is natural immune system, where micro-level interactions between antibodies and antigens lead to the macro-level property of an organism remaining alive by distinguishing between pathogens (which must be reacted to) and self (which must not be reacted to), with no macro-level or micro-level executive control, as far as we are aware. The main reason for choosing the immune system as the main focus of inspiration for clustering is due to the fact that immune system knowledge is growing very rapidly, as is the knowledge about its self-organizing, self-evolving and self-sustaining capabilities and also its ability to distinguish between self and non-self. Some of the principles of immune system, such as mutation and fitness thresholds, are also shared by other biologically inspired computational methods, such as genetic algorithm, genetic programming and evolutionary computing in general.

Clustering techniques can mainly be categorized into two sub-groups, namely, partitional and hierarchical methods. In partitional methods, samples are allocated to groups based on some proximity measure, such as closeness to centroids. This is in contrast to hierarchical methods, where each sample is considered a group and then groups merged depending on their proximity to each other (bottom-up), or all samples are considered as forming one group which is then divided into subgroups (top-down). Humoral mediated clustering algorithm (HAIS) [5] is also an example of a partitional AIS method which is inspired by humoral mediated response triggered in natural immune system. It is a stochastic algorithm, so different runs of this algorithm using the same parameters can produce different clustering results. Previously reported results of HAIS algorithm indicate that its average performance in terms of clustering solutions is no worse than classical k-means clustering algorithm. Clustering results obtained by HAIS are largely dependent on the order of data presentation. Given a dataset of   objects, there are   ways the data can be presented to HAIS. This stochastic indeterminacy is typically addressed in two ways. The first way is to fix the pathogen presentation order, which means that the final model is acknowledged to be just one possible model out of all the models that can exist. A second way is to accept different presentation orders of data and construct a number of models that, by and large, return the same result. The main motivation of our proposed work is to demonstrate that stable and better clustering solutions on HAIS can be found when incorporated with evolutionary approach.

Hart and Timmis [6] proposed that immune system must be embodied, since natural systems do not work in isolation, with suggestions for integrating AIS with other natural inspired approaches such as neural networks, swarm algorithms and genetic algorithms to find out the true potential of immune system based algorithms. However, the way that such integration should occur, taking into account the problem domain, was left open. In the experiments to be described below, we attempt to improve the performance of HAIS algorithm by integrating micro-level processes of cluster formation with macro-level processes of allocation of samples to clusters, where the micro-level consists of initial humoral mediated cluster formation and the macro-level of genetic algorithms that optimize allocation of samples to clusters. A two-step algorithm is proposed, where in the first step initial data partitioning and the appropriate numbers of clusters are obtained using the HAIS algorithm, and in the second step those obtained groupings are optimized in terms of data allocation using an evolutionary approach. The convergence in population of solutions is obtained by incremental transfer of memory cells (knowledge acquired through interaction with pathogens) from one generation to another.

The idea of hybridizing AIS algorithms with evolutionary approaches is not new [7-9]. Potter *et al.* uses the co-evolutionary approach to evolve a population of antibodies for concept learning [7]. Ahmadi and Maleki [8] use the similar approach to evolve AIS for network security applications. In separate research, Louis and McDonnell [10] incorporated genetic algorithm with case based memory (of past knowledge) to obtain better performance and fast convergence on problems such as combinational circuit design, asset allocation and job shop scheduling. The approach is called CIGAR, which periodically injects previously solved problems into GA's population (random population). In our proposed population-based HAIS approach, we integrate concepts of [7, 8] with [10] in a novel way, where memory cells are used for reinforcement learning and GA for adaptability. The aim is to combine the advantages of both paradigms so that (a) HAIS acquires knowledge through interaction with antigens, which are stored in the form of memory cells for faster convergence; and (b) the GA provides enhanced search capability and adaptation [10].

In the population-based HAIS approach below, the evolved immune system of each individual is tested against some evaluation criteria (environmental factor/s) and only the fittest and best individuals (solutions) are carried forward to the next generation, with all remaining individuals are discarded. Reinforcement learning is performed at both micro and macro levels. Rank selection is adopted as the selection strategy: copying the best individuals into the next generation for the purpose of preserving the best solutions obtained so far ('survival of the fittest'). An external clustering validation criterion is used to evaluate the fitness of each individual in the population. The aim of this paper is not to compare the results with existing state of the art clustering techniques, but to demonstrate that micro-biological nature inspired models such as HAIS can be incorporated with macro-biological processes at the population level to develop novel nature inspired clustering algorithms.

2   Background to Artificial Immune System

Artificial immune systems (AIS) and immunoinformatics refer to computational paradigms inspired by natural immune systems [11-14]. There are several AIS algorithms in the domain of optimization, supervised learning and unsupervised clustering [5, 14-16]. The main idea in these algorithms is to represent data samples as antigens and clusters as antibodies or B-cells. The main work in AIS supervised learning is the Artificial Immune Recognition System (AIRS) by Watkins and Timmis [15]. One of the earliest AIS algorithms for unsupervised clustering was proposed by De Castro and Zuben [17], Artificial Immune network (aiNet). It utilizes the concepts of memory cells and clonal selection and hyper mutation. This is a two stage clustering algorithm. In the first step, a number of memory cells are generated from the original data and then in stage 2 minimum spanning trees (MST) are used to obtain the number of clusters in the data.

CLONALG [14] is mainly based on the immunology concept of clonal selection. This algorithm was originally designed for pattern recognition and engineering optimization purposes but it can also be extended to clustering. This algorithm uses many immune system concepts such as antigens, antibodies, somatic hyper-mutation and clonal selection of matching antibodies. This algorithm has three variant in the literature which use different clonal selection techniques. The comparative analysis of all three variants can be found in [18]. An AIS clustering algorithm is proposed by Younsi and Wang [16], which is also similar to CLONALG. The immune system inspired clonal selection process is replaced with random generation of new B-cells (clusters). It is a two phase algorithm. Recognition of antigens is performed in the first phase, and then memory cells produce by the first phase are used to find clusters in the data by building an inter-connected network of memory cells.

The HAIS clustering algorithm used here is inspired by the humoral mediated response triggered by adaptive immune system [5]. It is an iterative process where antigens are presented to the algorithm randomly and then compared against existing memory cells and/or antibodies. A distinguishing feature of HAIS is that a clear distinction is made between Igs, antibodies and B-cells to separate the different biological, and therefore computational, functions they perform at the micro level. More detail about this algorithm will be presented in next section.

3 Humoral-Mediated Clustering Algorithm (HAIS)

The inspiration of the HAIS algorithm is based on the humoral immune response triggered in natural immune system. B-cells, antigens, memory cells, antibodies, affinity threshold are the main components of this algorithm. The algorithm starts with 10% of data instances and considers each instance as an individual B-cell. B-cells are clusters for storing data and these B-cells generate memory cells (a 'synopsis' of data so far captured) as well as antibodies. An antibody is an array of values, one for each attribute present in the data. Samples are captured or trapped by the antibody that is closest in value to their attributes (subject to a threshold of proximity). Two types of antibodies are produced: one is generated by B-cells (b-Abs) while others are generated by memory cells (m-Abs). The similarity between an antigen (Ag) and antibodies (Abs) is calculated by the pair-wise square normalized Euclidean distance. The mapping of artificial immune system expressions to classical clustering concepts is stated in Table 1.

The HAIS algorithm works mainly in three layers, as shown in Fig. 1. At the first layer, m-Abs' (memory cell antibodies) try to capture Ags. If the capture is successful (subject to satisfying the proximity threshold), the stimulated m-Ab brings the Ag to its respective B-cell. If not, the Ag goes to the second layer, where it is compared against existing b-Abs (B cell antibodies). If an Ag is captured at this level, the stimulated b-Ab will bring the Ag to its respective B-cell, which holds on to it until the end of the cycle. Moreover, after capture the B-cell produces a memory cell which further generates an m-Ab, which is an exact copy of the captured Ag. B-cells also produce mutated b-Abs', which are non-identical copies of the captured Ag to allow the B-cell to capture other Ags that have similar but not identical attribute values. If even this layer fails to capture the Ag, a new B-cell is generated just for this particular Ag which will generate b-Abs. After each successful capture of an Ag, similarities between B-cells are calculated using a between-cluster metric and, if the similarity between two B-cells is greater than the network measure threshold (NT), both B-cells form an inter-connected cluster (cluster mergence).

Table 1. Mapping of AIS to classical clustering concepts

NIS Expressions	Clustering Concepts
Antigens	Samples
B cells	Clusters
Antibodies	Mutated copies of captured samples
Interaction between antibodies and Antigens	Pair-wised comparison
Mutation	Creation of diverse population of solutions
Memory Cells	Tracks already known patterns
Affinity threshold	Similarity criterion

This is an iterative algorithm: at the end of each iteration, B-cells are evaluated and less stimulated B-cells (small clusters) are removed and their Ags are released, based on a threshold criterion called DT. Surviving B-cells update their centroids according to the samples captured. All the antibodies generated by B-cells or memory cells are also released, whereas some M percent of memory cells near to the centroid of B-cells are carried to the next cycle. All the parameters (AT, NT and DT) are updated before the start of the next cycle. This whole process is repeated until there is no change in the number of surviving B-cells for two consecutive cycles. Two important parameters used in this HAIS algorithm are affinity measure threshold (AT) and network measure threshold (NT). The AT parameter is used to capture similar antigens whereas NT is used to merge B-cells that are close to each other. The algorithm starts with the same value for AT and NT. The parameter NT decreases whereas AT increases with iterations. At the end of each cycle parameters AT and NT are updated. More details about these parameters can found in [5, 19].

4   Population-Based HAIS Algorithm and its Explanation

A descriptive overview of the proposed algorithm is provided here and a full explanation follows the algorithm.

1. Initial population of clustering solutions is obtained from HAIS (initial populations of clusters and their antibodies)
2. Generate new population (of clustering solutions) by exposing individual clustering solutions to random order of pathogens

3. Next population := existing population + new population
4. Generate off-springs (of clustering solutions) by performing crossover on Next population
5. Evaluate and select H% of clustering solutions
6. Go back to Step 2 until termination condition

The main difference between the standard HAIS algorithm and the population-based HAIS algorithm described above is that mutation of antibodies by B-cells after successful capture of an antigen is now complemented by crossover involving the population of clustering solutions formed at the first step. The subsequent steps (Steps 2-6) constitute optimization of the initial clustering solutions. After Step 1 the number of clusters stays constant (although clustering solutions can evolve through mutation of their antibodies) and only the membership of samples (antigens) changes. Layer three of the original HAIS algorithm [5, 19] is now revised to take into account the two-phase approach (Fig. 1). If an antigen within a clustering solution cannot be trapped at the first two levels, instead of generating a new B-cell (cluster) the antigen is put back into the pool for re-selection later. This revision to the original HAIS algorithm ensures that the number of clusters is kept constant within each solution after the initial cluster formation stage at Step 1.

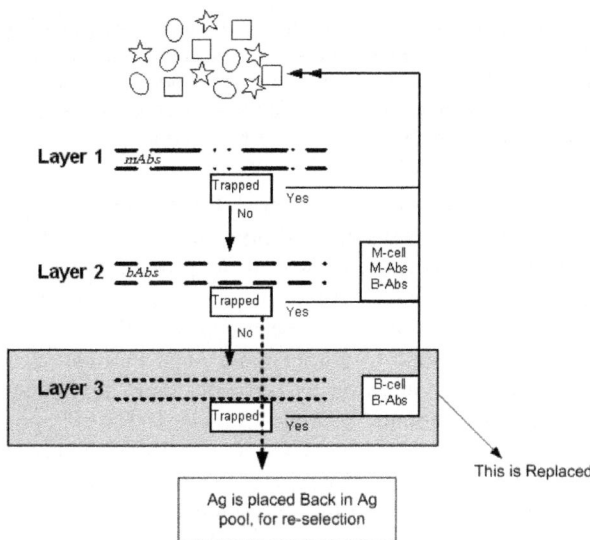

Fig. 1. An overview of three-layered HAIS algorithm, and also revised layer 3

At the start of each generation during the second phase of the algorithm, a new population of clustering solutions is generated through random order of pathogen exposure (step 2) and crossover (step 4). The population in the start of new generation carries B-cells position (centroids) and selected memory cells from the last generation. At the end of each generation all Ags' are set free for fresh random selection. Two cluster solutions are randomly chosen as parents for crossover.

A subset of clusters within each solution (B- cell) is selected randomly and swapped between the two selected parents to generate two new off-spring clustering solutions through single-point crossover (Fig. 2). The selection strategy which follows crossover is rank selection. The population of clustering solutions at any stage consists of (1) the best clustering solutions found in last generation, (2) the population of clustering solutions generated by random order of antigens' exposure and (3) off-spring clustering solutions generated by crossover. The H% of best solutions are selected for the next generation from the existing population of solutions. The termination condition is user-defined and, in the experiments below, is fixed at 12 generations.

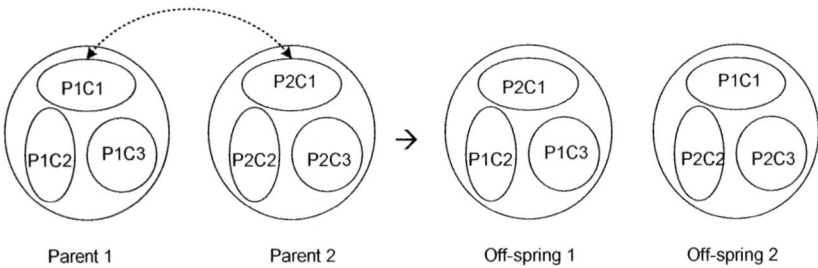

| Parent 1 | Parent 2 | Off-spring 1 | Off-spring 2 |

Fig. 2. Single Point crossover between two parents producing two off-spring. Parent 1 and Parent 2 (P1 and P2) are two randomly chosen clustering solutions, consisting of three clusters C1-C3. Shown here is P2's C1 swapped with P1's C1 to produce two new clustering solutions as off-spring. All antigens, memory cells and antibodies attached to a cluster involved in crossover are also transferred to the offspring clustering solution.

Nature inspired algorithms are characterized by reinforcement learning. For example, genetic algorithms (GAs) select chromosomes for the next generation from the whole population of parents and off-spring to provide the best opportunity for evolving globally best solutions. Ants in ant colony optimization perform reinforcement by attaching pheromone to the travelled path; so that more frequently used paths have more pheromone to attract more ants. Particle swarm optimization algorithms have reinforcement learning by directing their movements through local and global best solutions found so far. Standard HAIS approach performs reinforcement learning through transfer of memory cells from one generation to the next. In this paper, an incremental reinforcement learning technique is used, where the number of memory cells transferred to the next generation increases as the number of generations increases. In the experiments below, 10% incremental transfer of memory cells is used, which means that in the first generation 10% of memory cells are transferred to next generation and in second generation 20% memory cells will be transferred and so on. This is a form of transfer of knowledge from a previous generation to the next generation. Once the transfer of memory cells reaches 100%, there will be no further change in antigen allocation to B-cells, which helps in achieving convergence. The last two generations in Figure 3, for example, show that the algorithm finds local optimum solutions with no changes in value of fitness function. One advantage of such an approach is that not only the population of best selected individual converges but also the whole population of solutions converges as well. With the introduction of crossover and rank selection as the selection mechanism for clustering solutions, a second form of reinforcement learning is now also introduced into HAIS. In the original HAIS algorithm no antibodies (b-Abs) are transferred to the next generation, and this also applies here. But in this revised algorithm, before the start of generating new population, new antibodies are generated based on existing memory cells in the system (transferred from the previous generation) to provide a 'memory' of data already encountered.

Cluster validity is evaluated through a fitness function. Several cluster validity measures have been proposed [20-22]. Cluster validity techniques can be classified into three groups: external criteria, internal criteria and relative criteria [21]. External criteria are used to compare the clustering results with predefined partitions or class labels. Rand index, Jaccard coefficient and Fowlkes-Mallows index [23] are examples of external cluster validity criteria. Internal criteria only consider the information within data to produce some quantitative measure about obtained clusters. Davies-Bouldin index, Dun index, silhouette index and SD validity index [20, 24] are examples of internal cluster validity criteria. With relative criteria, clustering solutions obtained by the same algorithm using different parameters are compared with each others to find optimal clustering. In this paper, the number of clustering errors founds by each individual clustering solution against true class labels will be used to evaluate the clustering solutions (external criteria).

5   Experimental Results

The experiments are conducted on datasets with varying size and clusters. Five real world datasets namely Iris, Wine, Thyroid, Breast Cancer diagnostic and Breast Cancer Wisconsin original are used to show the effectiveness of the proposed algorithm. All these datasets are available at UCI repository [25]. The HAIS algorithm is dependent on three parameters: α, β and γ [5, 19]. The parameter α is a scalar value which controls the tightness of boundaries among the clusters whereas β and γ helps AT parameter to converge. β and γ are set at 0.25 and 0.75, respectively, in the experiments below. Mutation rate for evolving antibodies of 5.0% is used for Iris, Wine and Breast Cancer datasets, and 10.0% mutation rate is used for Thyroid and Breast Cancer Wisconsin datasets. The termination condition is set to be at 12 generations, since this was found adequate to lead to convergence across all the datasets. The initial population is set at 10 (i.e. the number of runs of the standard HAIS algorithm). Population size (clustering solutions) of 100 is set with subsequently another 100 off-spring generated through crossover. At the end of each generation the 10 best clustering solutions are selected and carried to the next generation.

The Iris data has three classes consisting of 50 instances each. The dataset has four features (Sepal Length, Sepal Width, Petal Length and Petal Width) and three classes (Setosa, Versicolor and Virginica). The algorithm starts with an initial population of 10 clustering solutions which has an average error of 21.90 instances (Fig. 3), index zero along x-axis represent initial population of solutions and 1 to 12 represent 12 generations. The average error among best selected individuals at the end of first generation decreases to 6.4, with more gradual decrease in error subsequently. The

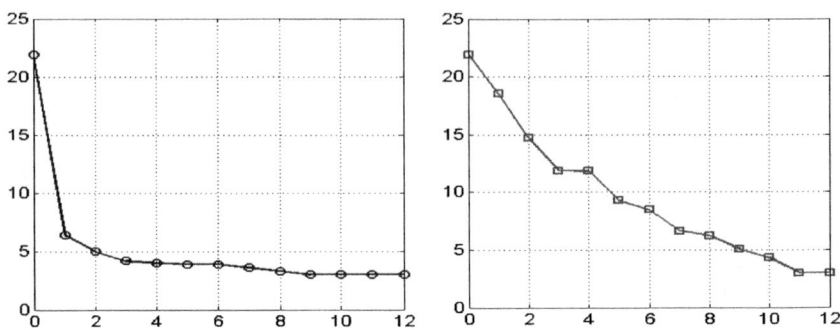

Fig. 3. Average number of errors (y-axis) obtained at the end of each generation (x-axis), Left: Average number of errors obtained for best selected individuals at the end of each generation. Right: Average number of errors obtained for whole population for each generation.

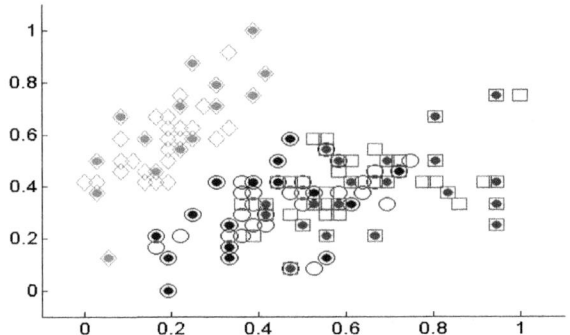

Fig. 4. 2-D projection of iris data using feature 1 and 2. Three clusters are shown with different colors and shapes. Memory cells are represented with solid marks.

error curve decreases until the 9th generation and then stabilizes at 3. The same trend can be observed in the average error curve of the whole population (Fig. 3 Right). The convergence on the whole population of clustering solution is more slow and steady than best solution. The slow convergence on whole population of solutions depicts exploration of search space to find better clustering solutions.

The 2-D projection of Iris data can be seen in Fig. 4, with different colors and shapes representing different clusters and solid marks within those shapes showing memory cells generated. This is a projection of one of the clustering solution obtained at the end of the algorithm. 51 memory cells are used to store 150 instances, which represents 66.0% data reduction.

For comparison, the standard HAIS algorithm is run 50 times using Iris data and the results (clustering errors) show oscillation between good and poor clustering results. The average outcome of these 50 runs is 16.46 errors. The best error obtained is 7, and the worst error is 27. The population-based HAIS (Fig. 3) has found better clustering solutions than standard HAIS.

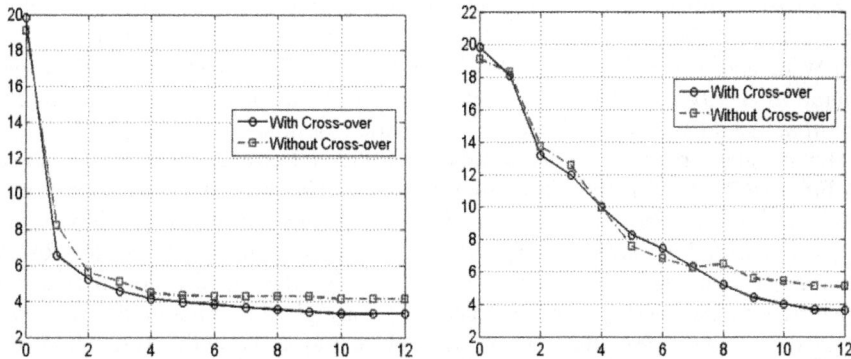

Fig. 5. Average number of errors (y-axis) obtained at the end of each generation (x-axis). Left: Average number of errors obtained for the best selected individuals at the end of each generation, with and without crossover. Right: Average number of errors obtained for the whole population for each generation, with and without the crossover operator.

Table 2. results on best population obtained using population-based HAIS, with and without cross-over operator, for 10 runs

Index	Min.	Max.	Avg.
With cross-over	3	4	3.267
Without cross-over	3.7	5	4.147

Crossover is performed on randomly selected individuals. If no crossover is introduced, the population-based approach can be regarded as simple hill-climbing. An experiment was conducted on the Iris data to justify the use of crossover. The experiment was run 15 times with and without crossover and the average results are shown in Fig. 5. It can be seen that both curves (best population curve and whole population curve) show the same convergence behavior, but the algorithm with crossover has found better solutions in terms of fewer clustering errors. It can also be seen from the figure 5 (Right) that the convergence curve of population based HAIS approach with cross-over is smoother than without cross-over. The minimum, maximum and average results obtained by running this algorithm over 15 runs can be seen in Table 2.

Wine data has 13 features and 3 clusters with a total of 178 instances. All three clusters vary in size. The Breast Cancer wisconsin (diagnostic) dataset has 569 instances with 30 features and 2 classes, namely benign and malignant. Class benign has 357 instances and class malignant 212 instances. Thyroids dataset contains 215 instances, five attributes and three classes. Breast Cancer Wisconsin (original) has 699 instances with 16 missing values, and these instances are removed. It has 10 features including class labels (benign and malignant).

The average error over best population selected at the end of each generation is shown in the Fig. 6 (Left) for four datasets (Wine, Thyroid, Breast Cancer and Breast Cancer Wisconsin). All error curves show the same convergence behavior, starting from a high number of errors and gradually converging to some stable local optimum. For the Breast Cancer Wisconsin data, convergence is after the 9th generation; for both Wine and Thyroid data the 10th generation; and for Breast Cancer data the 11th generation. It appears that as the number of features and instances increases, the algorithm takes more generations to settle on local optima.

The average error over whole population at the end of each generation is shown in the Fig. 6 (Right) for the same four datasets. The population error curves also converge as the number of generations increases. This convergence behavior in both the best selected population and the whole population is due to reinforcement incremental learning of memory cells. That is, the number of memory cells transferred to the next generation increases through the generations to provide a cumulative reward for the system through exploration and exploitation of the environment. The final local optima obtained by the algorithm are dependent on population size and incremental learning through transfer of memory cells. The experiments have also shown that sometimes the best population and whole population do not converge to the same error, due to differences in population size as well as presence of cross-over operator. The population-based HAIS algorithm is run for 10 times on above mentioned datasets, and results in terms of minimum, maximum and average errors achieved are shown in Table 3.

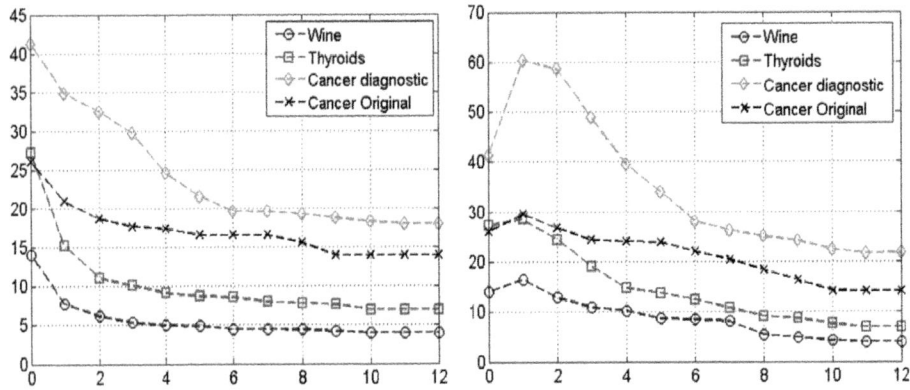

Fig. 6. Average number of errors obtained (y-axis) in each generation (x-axis) for Wine, Thyroid, Breast Cancer and Breast Cancer Wisconsin datasets. Left: Average number of errors obtained for best selected individuals at the end of each generation. Right: Average number of errors obtained for whole population for each generation.

Table 3. Average results over 10 runs using population-based HAIS algorithm on benchmark real world dataset

Index	Min.	Max.	Avg.
Iris	3	4	3.2
Wine	3	5	4.0
Thyroids	6	9	7.2
Breast cancer (diagnostic)	16	21	18.2
Breast cancer (original)	13	16	14.1

6 Conclusion

The main focus of this paper was to integrate micro-level processes of an artificial immune system with macro-level process of a population-based approach. The experimental results show that HAIS can benefit from a population-based approach to result in better clustering outcomes. That is, crossover can help find better clustering solutions than simple mutation of antibodies for the databases used in the experiments here. In the population based HAIS algorithm, reinforcement learning is implemented at both micro and macro levels to aid exploitation and exploration of the search space with incremental reward. Selecting only the fittest (best) individuals forms a basis for macro-level reinforcement learning and incremental reinforcement learning is performed at micro-level by selecting only the most affine memory cells. Also, it has been shown that the population-based approach is not sensitive to data presentation order. That is, the number of errors across runs is stabilized through transfer of the best solutions (memory cells) to the next generation as a result of the rank selection strategy adopted. Finally, while 12 generations were sufficient for convergence in our chosen datasets, other datasets may require more generations.

In summary, we have shown that antigen presentation order can vary in AIS models and that integrating micro level AIS processes with macro-level genetic algorithms can lead to a benefit that the AIS by itself cannot achieve. Future work will deal with investigating the relationship between hyper mutation and crossover to determine closer coupling of micro (hyper mutation) and macro (crossover) level processes in the context of reinforcement learning. In particular, the relationship between different mutations rates and their effects on optimal allocation of samples to cluster through crossover will need detailed analysis. Finally, further work is required to evaluate different population sizes in relation to data size, crossover strategies and number of generations for convergence.

References

1. Marinakis, Y., Marinaki, M., Matsatsinis, N.: A Stochastic nature inspired metaheuristic for clustering analysis. Int. J. Business Intelligence and Data Mining 3, 30–44 (2008)
2. Kao, Y., Cheng, K.: An ACO-based clustering algorithm, vol. 4150, pp. 340–347. Springer, Heidelberg (2006)
3. Premalatha, K., Natarajan, A.M.: A New Approach for Data Clustering Based on PSO with Local Search. Computer and Information Science 1(4), 139–145 (2008)
4. Sheikh, R.H., Jaiswal, A.N., Raghuwanshi, N.M.: Genetic Algorithm Based Clustering: A Survey. In: First International sConference on Emerging Trends in Engineering and Technology, pp. 314–319 (2008)
5. Ahmad, W., Narayanan, A.: Humoral-mediated Clustering. In: Proceedings of the IEEE 5th International Conference on Bio-Inspired Computing: Theories and Applications (BIC-TA 2010), pp. 1471–1481 (2010)
6. Hart, E., Timmis, J.: Application area of AIS: The Past, The Present and the Future. Applied Soft. Computing 8(1) (2008)
7. Potter, M.A., DeJong, K.A.: The co-evolution of antibodies for concept learning. In: Fifth International Conference on Parallel Problem Solving From Nature, pp. 530–539 (1998)

8. Ahmadi, M.R., Maleki, D.: A co-evolutionary immune system framework in a grid environment for enterprise network security. In: SSI, pp. 1136–1143 (2006)
9. Hajela, P., Yoo, J., Lee, J.: Ga Based Simulation Of Immune Networks Applications In Structural Optimization. Engineering Optimization 29(1), 131–149 (1997)
10. Louis, S.J., McDonnell, J.: Learning with case-injected genetic algorithms. IEEE Transactions on Evolutionary Computation 8(4), 316–328 (2004)
11. Forrest, S., Hofmeyer, S.: Immunology as information processing. In: Segel, L., Cohen, I. (eds.) Design Principles for Immune System and Other Distributed Autonomous Systems, p. 361. Oxford University Press, Oxford (2000)
12. Hunt, J.E., Cook, D.E.: Learning using an artificial immune system. Journal of Network and Computer Applications 19, 189–212 (1996)
13. Timmis, J., Knight, T.: An Immmunological Approach to Data Mining. In: Proceedings of IEEE International Conference on Data Mining, vol. 1, pp. 297–304 (2001)
14. Castro, L.N.De., Zuben, J.: The Clonal Selection Algorithm with Engineering Applications. In: Workshop Proceedings of GECCO, Workshop on Artificial Immune Systems and Their Applications, Las Vegas, pp. 36–37 (2000)
15. Watkins, A., Timmis, J., Boggess, L.: Artificial Immune Recognition System (AIRS): An Immune-Inspired Supervised Learning Algorithm. Genetic Programming and Evolvable Machines 5(3), 291 (2004)
16. Younsi, R., Wang, W.: A New Artificial Immune System Algorithm for Clustering. Lecture Notes in Computer Science, p. 58 (2004)
17. Castro, L.N.D., Zuben, F.J.V.: AiNet: An Artificial Immune Network for Data Analysis. Data Mining: A Heuristic Approach 1, 231–260 (2002)
18. Khaled, A., Abdul-Kader, H.M., Ismail, N.A.: Artificial Immune Clonal Selection Algorithm: A Comparative Study of CLONALG, opt-IA and BCA with Numerical Optimization Problems. International Journal of Computer Science and Network Security 10(4), 24–30 (2010)
19. Ahmad, W., Narayanan, A.: Outlier Detection using Humoral-mediated Clustering (HAIS). In: Proceedings of NaBIC 2010 (IEEE World Congress on Nature and Biologically Inspired Computing), pp. 45–52 (2010)
20. Halkidi, M., Batistakis, Y., Vazirgiannis, M.: On Clustering Validation Techniques. Journal of Intelligent Information Systems 17, 107–145 (2001)
21. Halkidi, M., Batistakis, Y., Vazirgiannis, M.: Cluster validity methods: part I. SIGMOD Record 31(2), 40–45 (2002)
22. Halkidi, M., Batistakis, Y., Vazirgiannis, M.: Cluster validity methods: part II. SIGMOD Record 31(3), 19–27 (2002)
23. Tan, P.N., Steinbach, M., Kumar, V.: Cluster Analysis: basic concepts and algorithms: Introduction to Data Mining, pp. 487–568. Addison-Wesley, Reading (2006)
24. Bezdek, J.C., Pal, N.R.: Some New Indexes of Cluster Validity. IEEE Transactions on Systems, Man, and Cybernetics - Part B: Cybernetics 28, 301–315 (1998)
25. UCI Machine Learning Repository, http://archive.ics.uci.edu/ml/

Clonal Selection Algorithm for Classification

Anurag Sharma and Dharmendra Sharma

Faculty of Information Sciences and Engineering
University of Canberra, ACT, Australia
{Anurag.Sharma,Dharmendra.Sharma}@canberra.edu.au

Abstract. Clonal selection principle based CLONALG is one of the most popular artificial immune system (AIS) models. It has been proposed to perform pattern matching and optimization task but has not been applied for classification tasks. Some work has been reported that accommodates CLONALG for classification but generally they do not perform well. This paper proposes an approach for classification using CLONALG with competitive results in terms of classification accuracy, compared to other AIS models and evolutionary algorithms tested on the same benchmark data sets. We named our algorithm CLONAX.

Keywords: CLONALG, clonal selection principle, artificial immune system, pattern matching, optimization, classification, evolutionary algorithms, CLONAX.

1 Introduction

Artificial immune system is an emerging field of study in the field of computational intelligence. There has been increasing interest in the development of computational models inspired by several immunological principles [6]. Much of the early work in the development of artificial immune systems (AIS) was carried out using genetic and evolutionary computation techniques [10]. Genetic algorithms and artificial immune systems are both variations of evolutionary algorithms but the main distinction between them is the manner how the population evolves. In genetic algorithms the population is evolved using crossover and mutation. However in the AIS, reproduction is asexual where each child produced by a cell is an exact copy of its parent. Both algorithms use mutation to alter the progeny of the cells to maintain diversity in the population [18].

Currently, three immunological principles are primarily used for artificial immune systems [6], [7]. These are briefly explained below:

1.1 Immune Network Theory

In this proposed hypothesis by [19] which states that immune system maintains an idiotypic network of interconnected B cells for antigen recognition. These cells both stimulate and suppress each other in certain ways that lead to the stabilization of the network. The model was known as Artificial Immune Network (AIN) [15] which was later updated and called AINE [23].

P. Liò, G. Nicosia, and T. Stibor (Eds.): ICARIS 2011, LNCS 6825, pp. 361–370, 2011.

1.2 Negative Selection Mechanism

As the immune system differentiates between self and non-self cells a model was created to simulate this mechanism artificially in [9]. The most natural domain to apply this technique was computer security mainly intrusion detection [14] [20].

1.3 Clonal Selection Principle

The Clonal Selection Principle describes the basic features of an immune response to an antigenic stimulus. It establishes the idea that only those cells that recognize the antigen proliferate, thus being selected against those that do not. CLONALG [5] is a well known model based on the clonal selection and affinity maturation principle which is similar to mutation-based evolutionary algorithms. Survival of fittest concept of evolutionary algorithm also applies here. CLONALG algorithm has been proposed to apply some basic principles of clonal selection principle that can lead to a very efficient solutions for pattern matching and optimization problems. This algorithm which has become perhaps the most popular in the field of AIS, was originally called CSA in [8] but later it was renamed to CLONALG (CLONal selection ALGorithm) [5].

As AIS is still emerging area of research so providing a new classification algorithm that is based on clonal selection principle shows the capability of AIS in solving wide area of problem domains. There has been more focus on CLONALG because of its simplicity in simulating the clonal selection behavior of immune system efficiently but so far it does not provide a model for classification task. Some work has been done in accommodating CLONALG for classification purpose so we are proposing an alternative approach using modified CLONALG that shows promising results in classification of some benchmark datasets.

The paper is organized as follows: Section 2 reviews AIS used in classification tasks. Section 3 briefly describes CLONALG algorithm and its usage in classification. Section 4 describes our proposed algorithm CLONAX based on clonal selection principle and how it is operated in training and testing phases of data classification. Section 5 evaluates the classification accuracy of CLONAX with other evolutionary and AIS algorithms. Section 6 discusses the output generated by CLONAX algorithm and section 7 concludes the paper.

2 Review of Artificial Immune System and Classification

Research into AIS has led to the development of many of different algorithms, including a variety of clonal selection, immune network and negative selection algorithms. All of these methods seek to utilize the dynamic learning mechanisms of the immune system and apply this power to real world problems [18]. Many computational models have been developed inspired by these immunological principles to solve problems like fraud detection, network security, data analysis, clustering, optimization, data mining etc [6].

There are few classification algorithms derived from the concept of AIS like CLONCLAS [18], CSCA [17], AIRS [24] and Immunos [4] which are providing promising results for many engineering problems. We will be using some of these algorithms to do comparative analysis with CLONAX algorithm. As described earlier that CLONALG solves pattern matching and optimization problems efficiently by simulating clonal selection analogy gracefully. This shows its potential in applying this algorithm in some other tasks as classification. The next section describes how CLONALG can be incorporated to solve classification task.

3 CLONALG for Classification

CLONALG has been proposed for pattern recognition but not been applied to classification problems [5], [18], [17]. The closest application of CLONALG is CLONCLAS that has been tested on binary character recognition problem [18]. Jennifer A. White in [18] has suggested that CLONALG can be transformed into classification algorithm. The emphasis was on enabling the evolution of "generalist memory cells" that represent the common features of the example set for each individual pattern class. Evolutional process promotes the proliferation of these generalized cells. This provides the useful starting point for classification process through CLONALG. Here antigen is exposed to the antibodies one at a time then classification is performed by always selecting the best matching antibody.

As CLONALG algorithm was proposed for pattern recognition and optimization purpose, its augmented version called CLONCLAS developed by [18] to be used for classification takes the advantage of the temporary knowledge gained through the cloning and affinity maturation process and carry forward them to next generations. This technique was not tested on classification problems but only on the binary pattern recognition dataset used in [5]. Jason Brownlee in [17] has incorporated some basic changes in the naive CLONALG to use it for classification task by always selecting the best matching antibody for a given antigen if it belongs to the same antigen's class. However, it generally doesn't perform well so later he has proposed Clonal Selection Classifier Algorithm (CSCA) which aims to maximize classification accuracy and minimize misclassification accuracy. CSCA is also based on clonal selection principle.

The main aspect of CLONALG algorithm is to produce memory cells that are best suited to capture given antigens. The CLONALG for pattern recognition described in [5] is as follows:

CONALG is composed of two repertoires: a set of antibodies and a set of antigens. A repertoire of antibodies Ab is randomly generated which is composed of two subsets Ab_m (memory repertoire of size m) and Ab_r (remaining repertoire of size r). The memory repertoire is the output of this algorithm.

```
1) FOR predetermined number of generations
2)      Release Antigen: Select an antigen Ag_i from the
        repertoire Ag and present it to Ab repertoire.
3)      Affinity: Determine the affinity (attraction) of
        antigen Ag_i with each member of Ab repertoire.
4)      Clone antibodies: Select the n highest affinity
        antibodies and generate a number of clones for
        each  antibody independently and in proportion
```

        to their antigenic affinity, generating a repertoire of C_i clones.

5)   *Affinity maturation*: The repertoire C_i goes through affinity maturation process. Affinity maturation is simply mutation of the clone population C_i inversely proportional to their affinity.

6)   *Affinity*: Now determine the affinity of these matured clones and select the one with the highest affinity to be a candidate to enter the set of memory antibodies Ab_m.

7)   *Update memory*: If the above candidate clone has its affinity greater than its respective memory Ab, then this candidate clone cell will replace this memory Ab.

8)   *Update Antibody repertoire*: Finally replace d lowest affinity antibodies from the repertoire of Ab_r with new randomly generated individuals.

9) End FOR loop

CLONAX algorithm is a simple modification in CLONALG algorithm that impresses its performance on classification tasks. Our algorithm evolves generalized memory cells that have least or no misclassification during training session. We use k Nearest Neighbor (KNN) concept by finding a memory cell that represents a region of same classes clustered together in a training set and are far away from other class(es).

4 Proposed Classification Algorithm CLONAX

We have proposed our algorithm that produces the generalized memory cells that represent a "common structure" of antigens after evolving many generations through clonal selection scheme. It has been named CLONAX (CLONal selection Algorithm for ClaSSification) as it is a variation of CLONAG that performs classification task only. Classification task involve separating different classes based on Euclidean distance and density. The idea of k Nearest Neighbor (KNN) technique has been adopted where the main purpose is to evolve generalized memory cells that are able to capture (detect) many of the similar structure of antigens as shown in Fig. 1.

For a classification task Ag repertoire represents training data and Ab_m repertoire represents trained output i.e. generalized memory cells. The size of memory cells is predefined and repertoire of memory cells are preassigned to the classes in the proportion to the classes available in the training data set.

Suppose $Ab_c \subset Ab_m$ where, $c \in \{classes\ in\ training\ set\}$ where total class size is CT i.e Ab_c is a subset of antibody repertoire Ab_m that belongs to class c only and $TD_c \subset \{Training\ Data\}$ where data belongs to class c only. so the size of subset Ab_c can be given by:

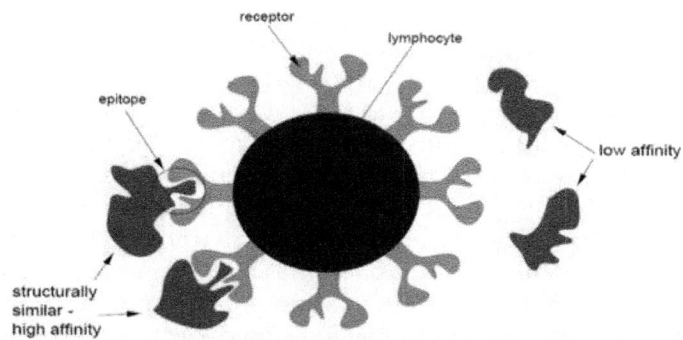

Fig. 1. Binding between lymphocyte (memory cell) with structurally similar high affinity antigens - [13]

$$|Ab_c| = \frac{|TD_c|}{\sum_{c=1}^{CT}|TD_c|} \times |Ab_m| .$$ (1)

After assigning the classes to memory repertoire, classification task begins with training phase which produces "generalized memory cells" at the end that are later fed into testing phase. The details are given below:

4.1 Training Phase

Preprocess the memory cells by randomly initializing them and labeling them to the classes according to eq.1. The labels are never changed throughout the cloning process.

```
1) FOR predetermined number of generations
2)      Release Antigen: Select an antigen Ag_i from the
        repertoire Ag and determine its class c, then
        present it to repertoire Ab_r and Ab_c(only those
        memory cells of Ab_m repertoire that are
        labeled with the same class c).
3)      Affinity: Determine the affinity (attraction) of
        antigen Ag_i with each member of Ab_r and Ab_c
        repertoire.
4)      Clone antibodies: Select the n highest affinity
        antibodies and generate a number of clones for
        each antibody independently and in proportion to
        their antigenic affinity, generating a
        repertoire of C_i clones.
5)      Affinity maturation: The repertoire C_i goes
        through affinity maturation process. Affinity
        maturation is simply mutation of the clone
```

population C_i inversely proportional to their affinity.

6) *Select clones*: Instead of picking just one cloned cell for candidate memory cell that has the highest affinity with Ag_i, select k highest affinity clones with Ag_i to promote local search that ensures not so good individual initially at step 6 may later produce better results when generality of memory cells with other antigens are considered as explained in step 7 and 8.

7) *Average Affinity*: These k highest affinity cloned antibodies are now further evaluated by replacing their affinities with average affinity of p nearest antigens that are of the same class of Ag_i. This process will ensure that these k cloned cells are generalized cells which attract antigens of similar structure as shown in Fig.1.

8) *Filter Noise*: These selected k cloned cells go through filtering process to eliminate/reduce the possibility of noise in the data. If any of these cloned cells' average affinity calculated above is lower than at least two antigens of different class(es)then the cloned cell is no longer the candidate for memory cell, however If only one antigen of any different class has higher affinity with any of the k cloned cell then this higher affinity antigen cell is considered noise and it is removed from the training data set.

9) *Update Memory*: If the highest affinity clone among k filtered clones is higher than the minimum affinity value of the same class of existing memory repertoire Ab_c then it replaces the minimum affinity memory cell of Ab_c.

10) *Update Antibody repertoire*: finally replace d lowest affinity antibodies from the repertoire of Ab_r with new randomly generated individuals.

11) End FOR loop.

The memory cells can provide generalization of training data set. The value of parameter p should be carefully chosen as very large value can give too "generalized" memory cell and very small value can give very "specialized" memory cell. A memory cell preserves the key features of a class and thus reacts strongly to those features if present in a new example. The algorithm also tries to filter out noise in the data implicitly in step 8 in search for best generalized memory cell. The testing phase is described below:

4.2 Testing Phase

There are two ways to treat the testing data after a testing data (or antigens) is introduced to the repertoire of generalized memory cells.

1. Select the memory cell with the highest affinity towards the data instance (antigen). The classification of this antigen is labeled as the class of highest affinity memory cell. If memory cells of different classes have same highest affinity value then the data instance remains unclassified.
2. Use the concept of K nearest neighbor (KNN) technique and determine the affinities of entire memory cells towards the given data instance (antigen). The K highest-affinity memory cells get to vote on the class. The majority determines the type of the class and in the case of tie the data instance cannot be classified. We used first approach for our experiment.

5 Experiment

We have used some benchmark biomedical problems from UCI library [11] to test the classification accuracy of CLONALG algorithm with other classification algorithm used in the field of evolutionary algorithms (EA) and artificial immune system (AIS). We split our data randomly into 80% training and 20% testing and then an average of 5 successive runs is taken into account for each problem to compare the classification accuracy of algorithms. The results are discussed below:

Table 2 shows the results of classification accuracy of EAs taken from [22] where the tested algorithms were: (1) reinforcement learning based Michigan style XCS [3], (2) supervised learning based Michigan style UCS [2], (3) Pittsburgh style GAssist [1], (4) Ant Colony Optimization (ACO) inspired cAnt-Miner [21], (5) genetic fuzzy iterative learner SLAVE [12], and (6) genetic fuzzy classifier Ishibuchi [16]. Table 1 shows the parameter settings for the same benchmark problems solved by our CLONAX algorithm in the experiment. Table 3 shows the test results of various AIS classification algorithms obtained through *Weka* 3.4.11 [17] implementation.

Table 1. Parameter Settings and Results for CLONAX for Classification

Dataset	Gen	Memory cell size (m)	Remaining cells (r)	Replaceable antibody size (d)	best (n) antibodies picked for cloning	Best (k) picked to candidate memory cell	clones make for	Max antigens per memory cell (p)	Average results of 5 test runs (%)	Individual best (%)
Breast Cancer Diagnostic	8	120	0.1xm	0.5xr	20	10		5	93.4±2.2	95.6
Haberman's Survival	8	70	0.1Xm	0.5Xr	20	10		5	73.8±6.6	80.3
Liver Disorder	16	60	0.1xm	0	30	10		8	68.1±5.8	73.9
New-Thyroid	8	60	0.1xm	0.5xr	10	10		6	90.7±7.0	97.7
Pima-Indian-Diabetes	8	100	0.1xm	0.5xr	20	10		8,10	74.4±5.6	79.9

Table 2. Classification Accuracy of some Evolutionary Algorithms

Datasets	XCS	UCS	GAssist	cAnt-Miner	SLAVE	Ishibuchi	CLONAX
Breast Cancer Diagnostic	93.7%	92.4%	95.4%	93.2%	91.6%	92.1%	93.4±2.2
Haberman's Survival	74.2%	74.2%	70.0%	71.5%	73.2%	73.2%	73.8±6.6
Liver Disorder	63.3%	67.3%	61.2%	65.%	58.5%	58.3%	68.1±5.8
New Thyroid	94.9%	92.6%	92.2%	90.2%	91.2%	86.2%	90.7±7.0
Pima Indian Diabetes	73.7%	74.8%	72.2%	75.0%	72.7%	68.6%	74.4±5.6

Table 3. Classification Accuracy for AIS Algorithms

Datasets	CLONALG	CSCA	AIR1	AIRS2	AIRS PARALLEL	Immunos1	immunos2	immuno99	CLONAX
Breast Cancer Diagnostic	71.9%	72.8%	90.3%	95.6	93.0%	71.0%	65.8%	57.9%	93.4±2.2
Haberman's Survival	70.9%	74.1%	54.8%	64.5%	71.0%	80.6%	79.0%	79.0%	73.8±6.6
Liver Disorder	69.6%	66.7%	55.1%	55.1%	52.2%	53.6%	62.3%	50.7%	68.1±5.8
New Thyroid	93.0%	95.3%	93.0%	93.0%	93.0%	90.7%	65.1%	86.0%	90.7±7.0
Pima Indian Diabetes	74.7%	76%	73.4%	70.8%	75.3	73.4%	68.2%	66.2%	74.4±5.6

6   Discussion

Results for classification accuracy produced by our CLONAX algorithm are looking promising. It has not been proved to be overall best for all of the data sets tested but it is showing consistent results and performing really well in each of the data sets. For example as CSCA and CLONALG fails to perform well for Breast Cancer Diagnostic and perform well for other datasets, but our CLONAX performs equally well in all the tested datasets and produced competitive results. If only the best individual test results are taken into account rather than average test results then clearly our CLONAX outperforms the results of all other algorithms.

The major change introduced in CLONAX from CLONALG is that the memory cells are valued for their generalization, using a form of k-nearest-neighbor measure to assess them. Generalization comes together with the cost of noise checking/filtering process in each generation.

The computational complexity of naïve CLONALG for pattern matching algorithm is $O(M(N + N_c + N_cL))$ or simply $O(M(N + N_cL))$ where M is antigen size i.e. size of training data, N is size of antibodies including memory cells and remaining cells, n is antibody size selected for cloning in each generation, N_c is total cloned cells generated from n selected antibodies, and L is the length of antibody/antigen bit string. Calculating affinity and sorting N antibodies is performed in $O(N)$ time for each antigen and mutating N_c clones takes $O(N_cL)$ time [5]. Due to addition of local search and generality of memory cells the computational complexity for our algorithm is increased to $O(MN + MN_cL + kM^2 + kM^2)$ or simply $O(MN + MN_cL + kM^2)$.

The first kM^2 component is contributed from the local search by recalculating affinity of k antibodies by sorting all antigens of C_i classes to select best p antigens in step 6 and 7. The total of M antigens can be divided into $[C_1 + C_2 + \cdots + C_i + \cdots + C_{CT}]$ classes of antigens where CT is the total classes in antigen set Ag. So kC_i antigens are sorted for every antigen introduced to the system which can be expressed as:

$$[kC_1.C_1 + kC_2.C_2 + \cdots + kC_{CT}.C_{CT}] < kM^2$$

The second kM^2 component is introduced from step 8 to reduce the noise by filtering k clones to see if there is a better affinity with other class of antigens. For each antigen, the k cloned cells are compared with $(M - C_i)$ antigens to check for noise in the worst case. So for all M antigens the computation cost is:

$$[k(M - C_1).C_1 + k(M - C_2).C_2 + \cdots + k(M - C_{CT}).C_{CT}] < kM^2$$

The variable k is in the range of $[1, N)$. Generally, $N = round(\alpha.M)$ where $\alpha < 1$ and the constant value $k \ll M$, so the complexity of our algorithm can be rewritten as $O(M^2 + MN_cL)$ which is same as the complexity of naïve CLONALG for pattern matching.

7 Conclusion

This paper has introduced a new variation of CLONALG model CLONAX, to perform a classification task which has produced promising and consistent results on all tested benchmark datasets that shows its potential to classify data effectively and efficiently. It shows that algorithms based on clonal selection principle can help in looking the classification problems from other dimensions through evolution of the individuals to represent the data distribution of given datasets with only few generalized memory cells. The immediate future direction is to automate the parameter *maximum antigen per memory cell (p)* which highly depends on data distribution but currently set manually. The high variation of results in the same datasets is another concern for this algorithm.

References

1. Bacardit, J., Garrell, J.M.: Bloat control and generalization pressure using the minimum description length principle for a pittsburgh approach learning classifier system. In: Proceedings of the 2003-2005 International Conference on Learning Classifier Systems, pp. 59–79. Springer, Heidelberg (2007)
2. Bernadó-Mansilla, E., Garrell-Guiu, J.M.: Accuracy-Based Learning Classifier Systems: Models, Analysis and Applications to Classification Tasks. Evolutionary Computation 11(3), 209–238 (2003)
3. Butz, M.V., et al.: Toward a theory of generalization and learning in XCS. IEEE Transactions on Evolutionary Computation 8(1), 28–46 (2004)
4. Carter, J.H.: The Immune System as a Model for Pattern Recognition and Classification. Journal of the American Medical Informatics Association 7(1), 28–41 (2000)
5. de Castro, L.N., Von Zuben, F.J.: Learning and optimization using the clonal selection principle. IEEE Transactions on Evolutionary Computation 6(3), 239–251 (2002)

6. Dasgupta, D.: Advances in artificial immune systems. IEEE Computational Intelligence Magazine 1(4), 40–49 (2006)
7. Dasgupta, D., et al.: Artificial immune system (AIS) research in the last five years. In: The 2003 Congress on Evolutionary Computation, CEC 2003, vol. 1, pp. 123–130 (2003)
8. De Castro, L.N., Von Zuben, F.J.: The Clonal Selection Algorithm with Engineering Applications. In: GECCO 2002 - Workshop Proceedings, pp. 36–37 (2000)
9. Forrest, S., et al.: Self-nonself discrimination in a computer. In: Proceedings of IEEE Computer Society Symposium on Research in Security and Privacy, pp. 202–212 (1994)
10. Forrest, S., et al.: Using genetic algorithms to explore pattern recognition in the immune system. Evol. Comput. 1, 191–211 (1993)
11. Frank, A., Asuncion, A.: UCI Machine Learning Repository. University of California, Irvine, School of Information and Computer Sciences (2010)
12. Gonzblez, A., Perez, R.: SLAVE: a genetic learning system based on an iterative approach. IEEE Transactions on Fuzzy Systems 7(2), 176–191 (1999)
13. Hofmeyr, S.A.: An immunological model of distributed detection and its application to computer security. The University of New Mexico (1999)
14. Hofmeyr, S., Forrest, S.: Immunity by Design: An Artificial Immune System (1999)
15. Hunt, J., et al.: Jisys: Development of an Artificial Immune System for real world applications. In: Artificial Immune Systems and their Applications, pp. 157–186. Springer, Heidelberg (1998)
16. Ishibuchi, H., et al.: Performance evaluation of fuzzy classifier systems for multidimensional pattern classification problems. IEEE Transactions on Systems, Man, and Cybernetics, Part B: Cybernetics, 29(5), 601–618 (1999)
17. Brownlee, J.: Clonal selection theory & CLONALG - The Clonal selection classification algorithm (CSCA). Swinburne University of Technology (2005)
18. White, J.A., Garrett, S.M.: Improved Pattern Recognition with Artificial Clonal Selection? In: Timmis, J., Bentley, P.J., Hart, E. (eds.) ICARIS 2003. LNCS, vol. 2787, pp. 181–193. Springer, Heidelberg (2003)
19. Jerne, N.K.: Towards a network theory of the immune system. Ann. Immunol (Paris) 125C(1-2), 373–389 (1974)
20. Ma, W., Tran, D., Sharma, D.: Negative selection with antigen feedback in intrusion detection. In: Bentley, P.J., Lee, D., Jung, S. (eds.) ICARIS 2008. LNCS, vol. 5132, pp. 200–209. Springer, Heidelberg (2008)
21. Otero, F.E.B., Freitas, A.A., Johnson, C.G.: cAnt-Miner: An Ant Colony Classification Algorithm to Cope with Continuous Attributes. In: Dorigo, M., Birattari, M., Blum, C., Clerc, M., Stützle, T., Winfield, A.F.T. (eds.) ANTS 2008. LNCS, vol. 5217, pp. 48–59. Springer, Heidelberg (2008)
22. Tanwani, A.K., Farooq, M.: Performance evaluation of evolutionary algorithms in classification of biomedical datasets. In: Proceedings of the 11th Annual Conference Companion on Genetic and Evolutionary Computation Conference: Late Breaking Papers, pp. 2617–2624 (2009)
23. Timmis, J., et al.: An Artificial Immune System for Data Analysis. Biosystems 55(1/3), 143–150 (2000)
24. Watkins, A., et al.: Artificial Immune Recognition System (AIRS): An Immune-Inspired Supervised Learning Algorithm. Genetic Programming and Evolvable Machines 5(3), 291–317 (2004)

Towards a Mapping of Modern AIS and LCS

Larry Bull

Department of Computer Science & Creative Technologies,
University of the West of England, Bristol BS16 1QY, U.K.
Larry.Bull@uwe.ac.uk

Abstract. For many years correlations between aspects of Artificial Immune Systems (AIS) and Learning Classifier Systems (LCS) have been highlighted. However, neither field appears to have benefitted from such work not least since the differences between the two approaches have far outweighed the similarities. More recently, a form of LCS has been presented for unsupervised learning which, with hindsight, may be viewed as a form of AIS. This paper aims to bring the aforementioned LCS to the attention of the AIS community with the aim of serving as a catalyst for the sharing of ideas and mechanisms between the two fields to mutual benefit.

1 Introduction

Twenty five years ago, Farmer et al. [16] took a dynamical systems view of Artificial Immune Systems (AIS), a network form in particular, and Learning Classifier Systems (LCS) [20] as a means by which to compare them. Perhaps due to the relative immaturity of both fields, the results were not particularly enlightening beyond motivating further exploration of AIS as a form of machine learning. Later, Farmer [15] produced a "Rosetta Stone for connectionism" in which a network-based view was taken of a variety of bio-inspired techniques to highlight similarities and differences. Again, AIS and LCS were included, although the direct comparison was extremely brief and somewhat unenlightening. Since then vague similarities between the two general approaches have periodically been noted, e.g., [23][18][32], but the fields have developed independently. Recently, a form of LCS has been presented for unsupervised learning (YCSC) [27] which can in hindsight be viewed as a type of clonal AIS and therefore with the potential to form a meaningful bridge between the two fields. This paper begins by briefly putting YCSC in the context of LCS before presenting a simple executable model and showing its performance as an approach to clustering. Finally, some future directions for bringing ideas and techniques from the fields of LCS and AIS together are discussed.

Holland's LCS was initially presented as a form of reinforcement learner wherein a Genetic Algorithm (GA) [19] was used to evolve generalisations over the state-action space in the form of traditional production system rules. In the original implementation, termed Cognitive System 1 (CS-1) [22], the fitness of rules was based on their ability to predict the reinforcement received by their use. That is, fitness for reproduction was primarily based upon the accuracy of rules' predicted reward for a given state-action pair since over-prediction resulted in penalization. The

P. Liò, G. Nicosia, and T. Stibor (Eds.): ICARIS 2011, LNCS 6825, pp. 371–382, 2011.

GA was periodically used in niches of rules with the same action. Moreover, to encourage rules to evolve which accurately aggregate as many states together as possible for a given action, the replacement strategy for the GA used rule age, a counter of the time since the rule had last matched an input. Thus more frequently used rules, which were accurate, were more likely to be selected for reproduction and less likely to be replaced. However, probably due to the GA needing to be run in a priori defined action niches, i.e., one niche per action, the fitness scheme for rules was immediately altered to one based on accumulated reward and included fitness sharing – the canonical form which was used for over a decade after (e.g., see [21]). Unfortunately, effective fitness sharing within such LCS is difficult to establish (e.g., see [9]) and interest in them waned. It is this general form of LCS which has been used in almost all previous comparisons between AIS and LCS.

In 1995 Stewart Wilson revisited the concept of an accuracy-based fitness scheme and presented the eXtended Classifier System (XCS) [33]. This form of LCS was shown to learn a number of benchmark tasks optimally and to produce maximally general rules in the process, i.e., to evolve optimally large, accurate aggregations of a given state-action space. Thereafter the field of LCS blossomed, with many successful applications to real-world problems being reported (e.g., see [4]), together with a growing theoretical basis (e.g., see [6]). Despite being originally presented as a reinforcement learner, both supervised [1] and unsupervised [27] learning variants have also been developed, with data mining the largest area of application of modern LCS (e.g., see [8]). As noted above, the latter form of LCS may be viewed as a form of clonal selection AIS and so is now discussed in detail.

2   YCSC: Clustering with LCS Gives a Type of AIS

Clustering is an important unsupervised classification technique where a set of data are grouped into clusters in such a way that data in the same cluster are similar in some sense and data in different clusters are dissimilar in the same sense. For this it is necessary to first define a measure of similarity which will establish a rule for assigning data to the domain of a particular cluster centre. One such measure of similarity may be the Euclidean distance D between two data x and y defined by $D=||x\text{-}y||$. Typically in data clustering there is no one perfect clustering solution of a dataset, but algorithms that seek to minimize the cluster spread, i.e., the family of centre-based clustering algorithms, are the most widely used (e.g., see [37] for an overview). Typically, each has their own mathematical objective function which defines how well a given clustering solution fits a given dataset. In this paper comparison is made to the most well-known of such approaches, the k-means algorithm. As a measure of the quality of each clustering solution the total of the k-means objective function is used:

$$o(X,C) = \sum_{i=1}^{n} \min_{j \in \{1...k\}} \| x_i - c_j \|^2 \tag{1}$$

Define a d-dimensional set of n data points $X = \{x_1, ..., x_n\}$ as the data to be clustered and k centers $C = \{c_1, ..., c_k\}$ as the clustering solution. However most clustering algorithms require the user to provide the number of clusters (k), and the user in general has no idea about the number of clusters (e.g., see [29]). Hence this typically results in the need to make several clustering trials with different values for k where k = 2 to k_{max} = square-root of n (data points) and select the best clustering among the partitioning with different number of clusters. The commonly applied Davies-Bouldin [12] validity index is used as a guideline to the underlying number of clusters here. Evolutionary algorithms (e.g., [31]) and AIS (e.g., [2]) have been used for clustering, of course. It has been suggested that modern accuracy-based LCS are well-suited to the clustering problem due to their generalization capabilities (e.g., see [28] for an overview).

YCS [5] is a simple LCS derived from XCS [33] and has been used to present a simple form for clustering - termed YCSC. YCSC is a Learning Classifier System without internal memory, where the rulebase consists of a number (N) of rules. Associated with each rule is a scalar which indicates the average error (ε) in the rule's matching process and an estimate of the average size of the niches (match sets - see below) in which that rule participates (σ). The initial random population of rules have their parameters somewhat arbitrarily set to 10.

On receipt of an input data, the rulebase is scanned, and any rule whose condition matches the message at each position is tagged as a member of the current match set [M]. The rule representation here is the Centre-Spread encoding (see [26] for discussions). A condition consists of interval predicates of the form $\{\{c_1, s_1\}, \ldots \{c_d, s_d\}\}$, where c is the interval's range centre from [0.0,1.0] and s is the "spread" from that centre from the range $(0.0, s_0]$ and d is a number of dimensions. Each interval predicates' upper and lower bounds are calculated as follows: $[c_i - s_i, c_i + s_i]$. If an interval predicate goes outside the problem space bounds, it is truncated. A rule matches an input x with attributes x_i if and only if $c_i - s_i \leq x_i < c_i + s_i$ for all x_i. Hence affinity is bounded in LCS over a learned interval.

Learning in YCSC consists of updating the matching error ε which is derived from the Euclidean distance with respect to the input x and c in the condition of each member of the current [M] using the Widrow-Hoff delta rule with learning rate β:

$$\varepsilon_j \leftarrow \varepsilon_j + \beta(((\sum_{l=1}^{d}(x_l - c_{lj})^2))^{1/2} - \varepsilon_j)$$ (2)

That is, error is a weighted running average of affinity. It can be noted that Forrest et al. [17] use a vaguely similar scheme. Next, the niche size estimate is updated:

$$\sigma_j \leftarrow \sigma_j + \beta(|[M]| - \sigma_j)$$ (3)

YCSC employs two discovery mechanisms, a niche GA and a covering operator. The general niche GA technique was introduced by Booker [3], who based the trigger on a number of factors including the reward prediction "consistency" of the rules in a given [M], to improve the performance of LCS. XCS uses a time-based mechanism under which each rule maintains a time-stamp of the last system cycle upon which it was consider by the GA. The GA is applied within the current niche when the average number of system cycles since the last GA in the set is over a threshold θ_{GA}. If this condition is met, the GA time-stamp of each rule in the niche is set to the current system time, two parents are chosen according to their fitness using standard roulette-wheel selection, and their offspring are potentially crossed and mutated, before being inserted into the rulebase. This mechanism is used here within match sets, as in the original XCS algorithm [33], which was subsequently changed to work in action sets to aid generalization per action [10].

The GA uses roulette wheel selection to determine two parent rules based on the inverse of their error:

$$f_i = \frac{1}{\varepsilon^v + 1} \tag{4}$$

Thus the use of selection within niches of co-active rules is akin to the clonal selection scheme used in CLONALG [13] and others.

Offspring are produced via mutation (probability μ) where, after [34], an allele is mutated by adding an amount + or - $rand(m_0)$, where m_0 is a fixed real, rand picks a real number uniform randomly from $(0.0, m_0]$, and the sign is chosen uniform randomly. Crossover (probability χ, two-point) can occur between any two alleles, i.e., within an interval predicate as well as between predicates, inheriting the parents' parameter values or their average if crossover is invoked. Replacement of existing members of the rulebase uses roulette wheel selection based on estimated niche size. If no rules match on a given time step, then a covering operator is used which creates a rule with its condition centre on the input value and the spread with a range of $rand(s_0)$, which then replaces an existing member of the rulebase in the same way as the GA. Whilst not biologically realistic, such an operator has proven a useful engineering solution. Hence, in contrast to most AIS, YCSC typically uses recombination and attempts to balance a finite population resource over the problem space through replacement. It can be noted that Forrest et al. [17] used recombination but maintained replacement based on affinity, the latter also true in CLONALG.

Recently, Butz et al. [11] have proposed a number of interacting "pressures" within XCS. Their "set pressure" considers the more frequent reproduction opportunities of more general rules in multiple niches. Opposing the set pressure is the pressure due to fitness since it represses the reproduction of inaccurate rules. Thus to produce an effective, i.e., general but appropriately accurate, solution an accuracy-based LCS using a niche GA with global replacement should have these two pressures balanced through the setting of the associated parameters. This is akin to the ideas in CS-1 but XCS greatly improves upon them. As will be shown, the same mechanisms can be used within YCSC to identify clusters within a given dataset; the set pressure encourages the evolution of rules which cover many data points and the fitness pressure acts as a limit upon the separation of such data points, i.e., the error.

A simple executable model can be used to demonstrate this point.

3   A Simple Model of YCSC

The evolutionary algorithm in YCSC is a steady-state GA. A simple steady-state GA without genetic operators can be expressed in the form:

$$n(j, t+1) = n(j, t) + n(j, t) S(j, t) - n(j, t) R(j, t) \qquad (5)$$

where $n(j, t)$ refers to the number of individuals of type j in the population at time t, $S(j, t)$ refers to their probability of reproductive selection and $R(j, t)$ to their probability of deletion. Roulette-wheel selection is used, i.e., $S(j, t) = f(j, t)/f(J, t)$, where $f(j, t)$ is the fitness of individuals of type j and $f(J, t)$ is the total population (J) fitness. Replacement is proportional to niche size as described above.

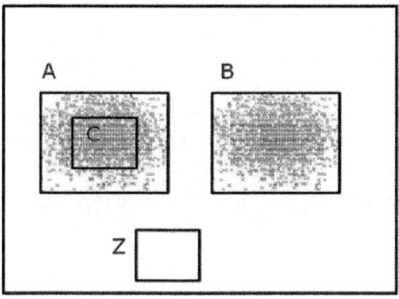

Fig. 1. The stylized clustering scenario envisaged for the simple model

Figure 1 shows the simple 2D clustering scenario used. As can be seen, two clusters exist and four rule types. Two rules, A and B, each represent the maximally general descriptors for one of the clusters (average ε=0.01), whereas rule C is over-specific to the first cluster (average ε=0.005), and rule Z does not match any data points. The rulebase is of size N=400 and the initial proportions of each of the four rules in the population are equal ($N/4$), and $v = 1$ and β=0.2. It is assumed that data points from both clusters are presented with equal frequency and that the GA fires once every two presentation cycles (i.e., θ_{GA}=1). The rules' parameters are updated according to Equations 2 and 3 on each such cycle, with an addition made to Equation 4. Bull [5] presented simple models of the GA working within LCS, examining the difference in fitness pressure between system types. The reproductive bias inherent in more general rules was approximated very simply for such executable models through increasing the fitness of the more general rule by a given factor. The same approach can be used within the simple difference equation model presented here by altering Equation 4:

$$f_j = \pi_j \left(1 / (\varepsilon_j^v + 1) \right) \qquad (6)$$

where π_j is the proportion of all possible action sets in which the rule participates. Thus for the problem in Figure 1, rules A and B containing maximal generalizations over the clusters have $\pi_j = 1/2$, whereas for the specific rule C $\pi_j = 1/4$.

Figure 2 shows the effects of this approximation of YCSC modelled on the task in Figure 1. As can be seen, the accurate generalizations of the two clusters are the most numerous, with the fraction of the other two rules diminishing. That is, the system is converging upon the maximally general solution to the problem, as expected.

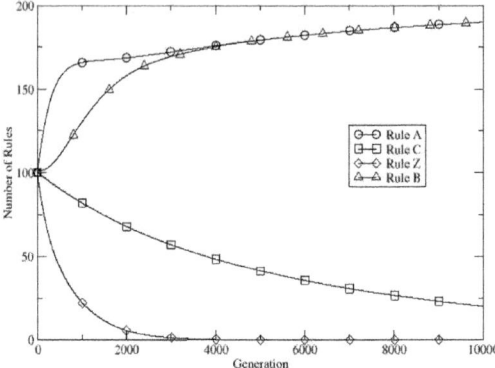

Fig. 2. The emerging proportions of rule types in the simple model

4 Performance

In this section YCSC as described above is used on two synthetic datasets, as previously reported in [27]. The first dataset is well-separated as shown in Fig 3(a). A randomly generated synthetic dataset is used. This dataset has $k = 25$ true clusters arranged in a 5x5 grid in $d = 2$ dimension. Each cluster is generated from 400 data points using a Gaussian distribution with a standard deviation of 0.02, for a total of $n = 10,000$ datum. The second dataset is not well-separated as shown in Fig 3(b). It is generated in the same way as the first dataset except the clusters are not centred on that of their given cell in the grid.

The parameters used were: $N=800$, $\beta=0.2$, $v=5$, $\chi=0.8$, $\mu=0.04$, $\theta_{GA}=12$, $s_0=0.03$, $m_0=0.006$. All results presented are the average of ten runs. Learning trials consisted of 200,000 presentations of a randomly sampled data point.

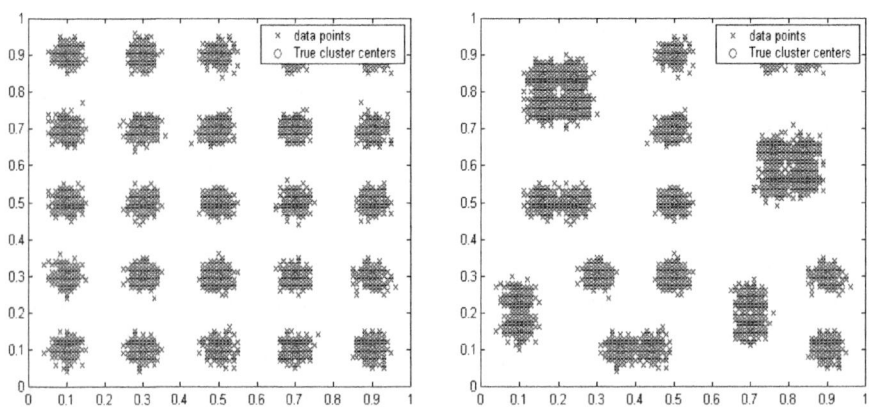

Fig. 3. The well-separated (a) and less-separated (b) data sets used

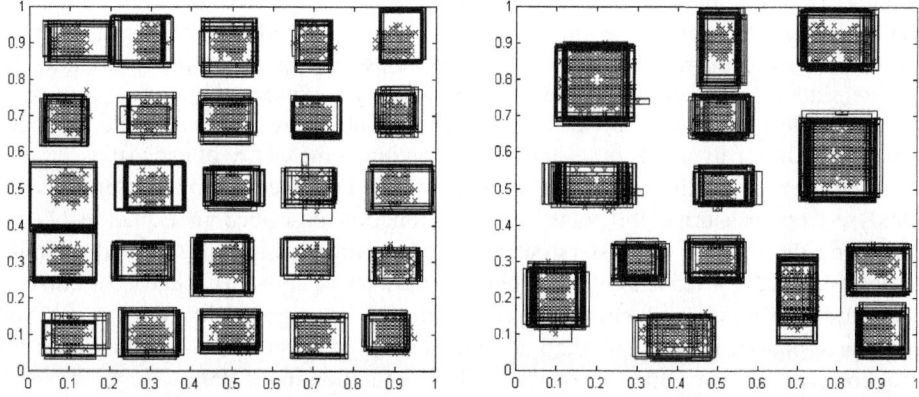

Fig. 4. Typical solutions for the well-separated (a) and less-separated (b) data sets

Figure 4 shows a typical example solution produced by YCSC on both data sets. That is, the region of the 2D input space covered by each rule in the final rule-base is plotted along with the data. As can be seen, in the well-separated case the system roughly identifies all 25 clusters whereas in the less-separated case contiguous clusters are covered by the same rules.

As expected, solutions contain many overlapping rules around each cluster. For knowledge extraction purposes, LCS use methods by which to identify the maximally general solution from within the population. The next section presents a rule compaction algorithm which enables identification of the underlying clusters.

5   Rule Compaction

Wilson [35] introduced a rule compaction algorithm for XCS to aid knowledge discovery during classification problems (others have been presented since, e.g., [36]). A compaction algorithm for clustering has subsequently been developed [27]:

Step 1: Delete the useless rules: The useless rules are identified and then deleted from the ruleset in the population based on their coverage. Low coverage means that a rule matches a small fraction (20%) of the average coverage.

Step 2: Find the required rules from numerosity: The population $[P]_{N[deleted]}$ is sorted according to the numerosity of the rules and delete the rules that have lower numerosity, less than 2. Then $[P]_M$ $(M < N)$ is formed by selecting the minimum sequential set of rules that covers all data.

Step 3: Find the required rules from average error : The population $[P]_M$ is sorted according to the average error of the rules. Then $[P]_P$ $(P < M)$ is formed by selecting the minimum sequential set of rules that covers all data.

Step 4: Remove redundant rules: This step is an iterative process. On each cycle it selects the rule in $[P]_P$ that maximum number of match set. This rule is removed into the final ruleset $[P]_F$ and the data that it covers deleted from the dataset. The process continues until the dataset is empty.

Figure 5 shows the final set $[P]_F$ for both the full solutions shown in Figure 4. YCSC's identification of the clusters is now clear. Under the (simplistic) assumption of non-overlapping regions as described by rules in $[P]_F$ it is easy to identify the clusters after compaction and the bounded affinity representation makes rule scope clear. In the case where no rules subsequently match new data we could of course identify a cluster by using the distance between it and the centre of each rule.

The average quality of the clustering solutions produced during the ten runs was analysed by measuring the total objective function described in Equation (1) and checking the number of clusters defined. The average quality on the well-separated dataset is 8.12 +/- 0.54 and the number of clusters is 25 +/- 0. That is, it correctly identifies the number of clusters every time. The average quality on the not well-separated dataset is 24.50 +/- 0.56 and the number of clusters is 14 +/- 0. Hence it is not correct every time due to the lack of clear separation in the data.

For comparison, the k-means algorithm was applied to the datasets. The k-means algorithm (assigned with the known k=25 clusters) averaged over 10 runs gives a quality of 32.42 +/- 9.49 and 21.07 +/- 5.25 on the well-separated and less-separated datasets respectively. The low quality of solutions in the well-separated case is due to the choice of the initial centres; k-means is well-known for becoming less reliable as the number of underlying clusters increases. For estimating the number of clusters we ran, for 10 times each, different k (2 to 30) with different random initializations. To select the best clustering with different numbers of clusters, the Davies-Bouldin validity index is shown in Figure 6. The result on well-separated dataset has a lower negative peak at 23 clusters and the less-separated dataset has a lower negative peak at 14 clusters. That is, it is not correct on both datasets, for the same reason as noted above regarding quality. Thus YCSC performs as well or better than k-means whilst also identifying the number of clusters during learning.

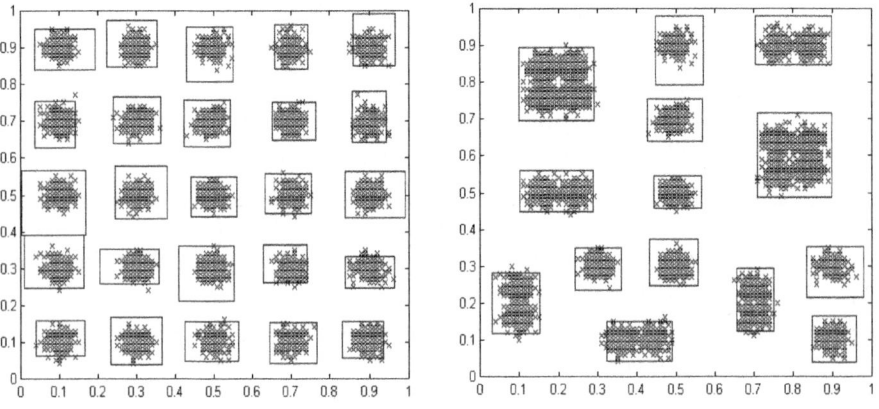

Fig. 5. Showing the effects of the rule compaction on the typical solutions shown in Figure 4 for the well-separated (a) and less-separated (b) data sets

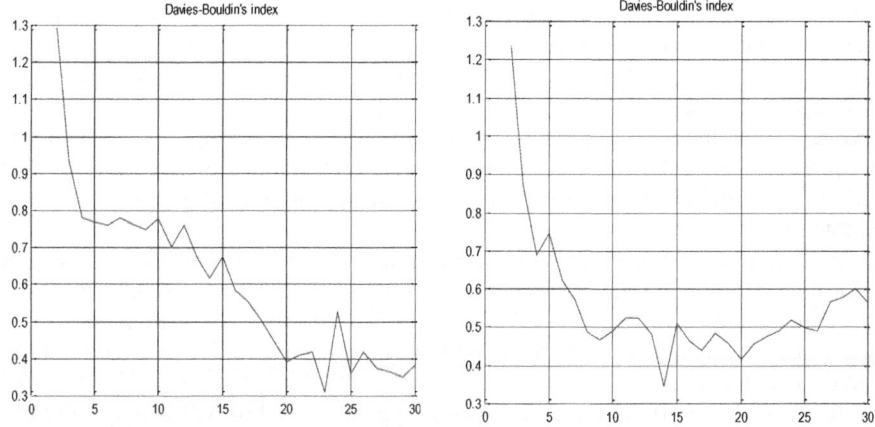

Fig. 6. *K*-means algorithm performance using the Davies-Bouldin index for the well-separated (a) and less-separated (b) data sets

6 Conclusions

For 25 years analogies have been drawn between AIS and LCS with varying degrees of success. This paper has highlighted how a simple form of modern LCS designed for unsupervised learning can also be viewed as a form of AIS, a clonal selection algorithm in particular. The motivation for this being to encourage the cross-fertilization of mechanisms between what are now two relatively mature fields.

The LCS/AIS commonality, known as YCSC, includes a formally understood mechanism by which to encourage maximally general solutions over an input space. Although, it should be noted that a direct version for unsupervised learning does not currently exist – but experimental results such as those above indicate assuming an extrapolation is sensible. The process uses a time-triggered GA within sets of co-active rules, controlled by parameter θ_{GA}. The maintenance of niches within clonal selection algorithms relies upon the evolutionary search occurring on every antigen presentation, as used in [13], or after a random sample s of antigens, as used in [17] (see [25] for formal analysis). Whilst beyond the scope of this paper, future work will explore the use of a controllable rate of expansion and maturation within CLONALG (and others) and compare performance with YCSC, with benefit to AIS expected.

Within the same formal understanding of generalization in LCS is the concept of a fitness pressure balancing the pressure for generalization. A number of affinity schemes and subsequent selection procedures have been reported with AIS. Within YCSC the fitness pressure is controlled by a simple power scaling of the raw affinity. A development of YCSC to include other aspects of XCS, termed XCSC [28], included a mechanism more akin to those used in artificial immune networks: XCS adjusts affinities relative to the affinities of the rules within the current active-set. Hence rules essentially increase or decrease the level of activation of other co-active rules. Results with XCSC improve those of YCSC, especially on the less-separated data set above (quality 6.71 +/- 0.14 and the number of clusters is 25 +/- 0, not shown). Again, the fitness mechanisms of LCS would appear to offer potential benefits to the related clonal selection AIS algorithms and networks. It can also be noted that an adaptive affinity threshold added further benefits in XCSC much like the result reported in [2] with an AIS.

More recent theoretical considerations of LCS have highlighted the similarities between their niched rule-sets and ensemble or mixture-of-expert systems widely used in machine learning (see [14]). This viewpoint may therefore also provide insights into AIS.

Conversely, whilst reinforcement learning LCS have struggled to use rules which perform only internal, i.e., cognitive-like, functions effectively (e.g., see [24] for historical discussions), AIS networks appear able to do this to some extent, e.g., [30]. Future LCS work in areas such as non-Markov domains could almost certainly learn from these algorithms.

The affinity proportional rate of mutation typically used in AIS is not used in LCS. Given their basis in traditional evolutionary algorithms, variable mutation rates through parameter self-adaptation have been used (e.g., [7]) but, again, closer links may open new avenues to improve performance.

There are many other fertile areas of cross-fertilization, such as the many representation schemes used in LCS, but perhaps more generally, the recognition and understanding of underlying similarities between algorithms inspired by immune and neural systems, e.g., see [38] for a new theory of neural Darwinism which has been implemented as an LCS, may result in the creation of artificial systems which can capture the useful properties of both coherently thereby improving performance in complex domains. The aim of this paper is to provoke such considerations.

Acknowledgement

The experimental results in Sections 4 and 5 were produced in collaboration with Kreangsak Tammee during a sabbatical visit to the author's group.

References

1. Bernado-Mansilla, E., Garrell, J.: Accuracy-based Learning Classifier Systems: Models, Analysis and Applications to Classification Tasks. Evolutionary Computation 11(3), 209–238 (2003)
2. Bezerra, G., Barra, T., de Castro, L.: Von Zuben Adaptive Radius Immune Algorithm for Data Clustering. In: Pilat, C., et al. (eds.) Proceedings of the 4th International Conference on Artificial Immune Systems, pp. 290–303. Springer, Heidelberg (2005)
3. Booker, L.B.: Triggered Rule Discovery in Classifier Systems. In: Schaffer, J.D. (ed.) Proceeding of the Third International Conference on Genetic Algorithms, pp. 265–274. Morgan Kaufmann, San Francisco (1989)
4. Bull, L. (ed.): Applications of Learning Classifier Systems. Springer, Heidelberg (2004)
5. Bull, L.: Two Simple Learning Classifier Systems. In: Bull, L., Kovacs, T. (eds.) Foundations of Learning Classifier Systems, pp. 63–90. Springer, Heidelberg (2005)
6. Bull, L., Kovacs, T.: Foundations of Learning Classifier Systems. Springer, Heidelberg (2005)

7. Bull, L., Hurst, J., Tomlinson, A.: Self-Adaptive Mutation in Classifier System Controllers. In: Meyer, J.-A., Berthoz, A., Floreano, D., Roitblatt, H., Wilson, S.W. (eds.) From Animals to Animats 6 - The Sixth International Conference on the Simulation of Adaptive Behaviour, pp. 460–468. MIT Press, Cambridge (2000)

8. Bull, L., Bernado-Mansilla, E., Holmes, J. (eds.): Learning Classifier Systems in Data Mining. Springer, Heidelberg (2008)

9. Bull, L., Hurst, J.: ZCS Redux. Evolutionary Computation 10(2), 185–205 (2002)

10. Butz, M., Wilson, S.: An algorithmic description of XCS. In: Lanzi, P.L., Stolzmann, W., Wilson, S.W. (eds.) Advances in Learning Classifier Systems: Proceedings of the Third International Workshop, pp. 211–230. Springer, Heidelberg (2001)

11. Butz, M., Kovacs, T., Lanzi, P.-L., Wilson, S.W.: Toward a Theory of Generalization and Learning in XCS. IEEE Transactions on Evolutionary Computation 8(1), 28–46 (2004)

12. Davies, D.L., Bouldin, D.W.: A Cluster Separation Measure. IEEE Trans. On Pattern Analysis and Machine Intelligence PAMI-1(2), 224–227 (1979)

13. De Castro, L., Von Zuben, F.: Learning and Optimization using the Clonal Selection Principle. IEEE Transactions on Evolutionary Computation 6(3), 239–251 (2002)

14. Drugowitsch, J.: Design and Analysis of Learning Classifier Systems. Springer, Heidelberg (2008)

15. Farmer, J.D.: A Rosetta Stone for Connectionism. Physica D 42, 153–187 (1990)

16. Farmer, J.D., Packard, N., Perelson, A.: The Immune System, Adaptation and Machine Learning. Physica D 22, 187–204 (1986)

17. Forrest, S., Javornik, B., Smith, R.E., Perelson, A.: Using Genetic Algorithms to Explore Pattern Recognition in the Immune System. Evolutionary Computation 1(3), 191–211 (1993)

18. Hofmeyr, S., Forrest, S.: Architecture for an Artificial Immune System. Evolutionary Computation 8(4), 443–473 (2000)

19. Holland, J.: Adaptation in Natural and Artificial Systems. Univ. Michigan Press (1975)

20. Holland, J.: Adaptation. In: Rosen, R., Snell, F.M. (eds.) Progress in Theoretical Biology, vol. 4, pp. 313–329. Academic Press, London (1976)

21. Holland, J.H.: Escaping Brittleness. In: Michalski, R.S., Carbonell, J.G., Mitchell, T.M. (eds.) Machine Learning: An Artificial Intelligence Approach, vol. 2, pp. 48–78. Morgan Kaufmann, San Francisco (1986)

22. Holland, J.H., Reitman, J.S.: Cognitive Systems based on Adaptive Algorithms. In: Waterman, D.A., Hayes-Roth, F. (eds.) Pattern Directed Inference Systems, pp. 313–329. Academic Press, London (1978)

23. Hunt, J., Cooke, D.: Learning using an Artificial Immune System. Network and Computer Applications 19, 189–212 (1986)

24. Smith, R.E.: Memory Exploitation in Learning Classifier Systems. Evolutionary Computation 2(3), 19–36 (1994)

25. Smith, R.E., Forrest, S., Perelson, A.: Population Diversity in an Immune System Model: Implications for Genetic Search. In: Whitley, D. (ed.) Foundations of Genetic Algorithms, vol. 2, pp. 153–166. Morgan Kaufmann, San Francisco (1993)

26. Stone, C., Bull, L.: For Real! XCS with Continuous-Valued Inputs. Evolutionary Computation 11(3), 299–336 (2003)

27. Tammee, K., Bull, L., Pinngern, O.: A Learning Classifier System Approach to Clustering. In: Proceedings of the Sixth International Conference on Intelligent System Design and Application, pp. 621–626. IEEE Press, Los Alamitos (2006)

28. Tammee, K., Bull, L., Pinngern, O.: Towards Clustering with Learning Classifier Systems. In: Bull, L., Bernado-Mansilla, E., Holmes, J. (eds.) Learning Classifier Systems in Data Mining, pp. 191–204. Springer, Heidelberg (2008)
29. Tibshirani, R., Walther, G., Hastie, T.: Estimating the Number of Clusters in a Dataset Via the Gap Statistic. Journal of the Royal Statistical Society, B B 63, 411–423 (2000)
30. Timmis, J., Neal, M.: A Resource Limited Artificial Immune System for Data Analysis. Knowledge Based Systems 14(3-4), 121–130 (2001)
31. Tseng, L.Y., Yang, S.B.: A Genetic Approach to the Automatic Clustering Problem. Pattern Recognition 34, 415–424 (2001)
32. Vargas, P., de Castro, L., Von Zuben, F.: Mapping Artificial Immune Systems into Learning Classifier Systems. In: Lanzi, P.-L., Stolzmann, W., Wilson, S.W. (eds.) Advances in Learning Classifier Systems, pp. 187–230. Springer, Heidelberg (2003)
33. Wilson, S.W.: Classifier Fitness Based on Accuracy. Evolutionary Computation 3(2), 149–177 (1995)
34. Wilson, S.W.: Get real! XCS with continuous-valued inputs. In: Lanzi, P.L., Stolzmann, W., Wilson, S.W. (eds.) Learning Classifier Systems. From Foundations to Applications, pp. 209–219. Springer, Heidelberg (2000)
35. Wilson, S.: Compact Rulesets from XCSI. In: Lanzi, Stolzmann, Wilson (eds.) Proceedings of the 4th International Workshop on Learning Classifier Systems, pp. 197–210. Springer, Heidelberg (2002)
36. Wyatt, D., Bull, L., Parmee, I.: Building Compact Rulesets for Describing Continuous-Valued Problem Spaces Using a Learning Classifier System. In: Parmee, I. (ed.) Adaptive Computing in Design and Manufacture VI, pp. 235–248. Springer, Heidelberg (2004)
37. Xu, R., Wunsch, D.: Clustering. IEEE Press, Los Alamitos (2009)

Towards an Artificial Immune System for Online Fraud Detection

Rentian Huang, Hissam Tawfik, and Atulya Nagar

Faculty of Business and Computer Sciences, Liverpool Hope University, Liverpool,
United Kingdom
{Huangr,Tawfikh,Nagara}@hope.ac.uk

Abstract. Fraud is one of the largest growing problems experienced by many organizations as well as affecting the general public. Over the past decade the use of global communications and the Internet for conducting business has increased in popularity, which has been facing the fraud threat. This paper proposes an immune inspired adaptive online fraud detection system to counter this threat. This proposed system has two layers: the innate layer that implements the idea of Dendritic Cell Analogy (DCA), and the adaptive layer that implements the Dynamic Clonal Selection Algorithm (DCSA) and the Receptor Density Algorithm (RDA). The experimental results demonstrate that our proposed hybrid approach combining innate and adaptive layers of immune system achieves the highest detection rate and the lowest false alarm rate compared with the DCA, DCSA, and RDA algorithms for Video-on-Demand system.

Keywords: Fraud Detection; Receptor Density Algorithm, Dynamic Clonal Selection Algorithm, and Dendritic Cells Analogy.

1 Introduction

While E-commerce provides people with convenience, and offers businesses with opportunities, it also brings companies and users security risks, which can lead to fraud for consumers and E-commerce merchants [1]. Due to the exponential increasing of threat from cyber attacks, E-commerce organizations start to recognize the importance of information security. The theft and misuse of online identity has become a major concern for online service providers. Such identity theft and misuse not only victimize consumers but also have a negatively impact on companies and financial institutions. Thus, the increase in the number of identity theft cases require that online service providers pay more attention to detect and prevent access to malicious sources, in order to minimize financial loss and protect legitimate customers [2].

To counter such threats, many companies providing online services record information about all the requests and replies between the user and the server. Each entry of log is automatically generated by the server. Different servers have different log formats. These kinds of data provide plenty of information to analyze using various data mining techniques for specific purposes and applications. Currently, in many companies, monitoring and investigation of fraud usage based on logs requires

P. Liò, G. Nicosia, and T. Stibor (Eds.): ICARIS 2011, LNCS 6825, pp. 383–394, 2011.

significant human effort. Thus, a great amount of time and money need to be invested to handle the enormous amount of log data. In addition, analysis of log data is not usually done on real-time basis, which implies that there is a window of vulnerability. To improve this situation, an automated mechanism is desirable, which can help identify suspicious requests that need greater scrutiny by human specialists.

In this paper, we develop an immune-inspired system based on a hybrid approach, which can dynamically update the knowledge obtained from the previous process, and adapt itself to the changing environment to perform online fraud detection tasks. The rest of the paper is structured as follows. The next section introduces the related work in the problem domain. Section 3 describes the implementation of our Artificial Immune System for online fraud detection. Section 4 describes the case study and discusses the results produced by the proposed hybrid system. The final section presents the concluding remarks and future work.

2   Related Work

Artificial immune systems (AIS) represent an important strategy inspired by biological systems. There is significant growth in the applications of immune system models in various domains and across many fields such as computer security [3, 4, 5], optimization [6, 7], robotics [8], fault detection [9] etc. But for fraud detection, there are only few attempts in this area.

Tuo et al. (2002) proposed a case-based genetic Artificial Immune System for Fraud Detection (AISFD), it is a self-adapted system designed for credit card fraud detection, but it's only the framework and did not test the proposed system [10].

Huang et al. (2009) introduced an AIS based on Dendritic Cells Algorithm, and apply it to detect the online break-in fraud for an online video on demand system. The result not only suggests the algorithm is applicable to fraud detection, also shown better performance when compared with another immunology based algorithm which is negative selection. They also improved the performance for the video on demand system by using hybrid algorithms from both innate and adaptive layers with or without other type of classification methodology [11, 12].

Gadi et al. (2008) has demonstrated the AIS algorithm outperforms other traditional techniques for credit card fraud detection which the data are highly imbalanced [13]. Another work done by Brabazon et al (2010) also demonstrated artificial immune technique can be used for online credit card fraud prevention. In their paper, they investigate the effectiveness of AIS for credit card fraud detection. The results suggest AIS algorithm have potential for inclusion in fraud detection system [14].

In the fraud detection research area, developing new fraud detection framework and fraud detection methods are made difficult by the fact that the exchange of ideas in the fraud detection field is severely limited. Describing fraud detection techniques in the public domain is not logical as it gives fraudsters the information they require to evade detection. Further, due to security issues, literature regarding the techniques and frameworks of fraud detection is limited and generally not made available to the public as the data is sensitive, often containing financial detail of banking customers, and so, experimental results, and real world data is also kept private from academic researchers. In the next section, our proposed AIS based architecture for online fraud detection will be described in detail.

3   An Immune Inspired System for Online Fraud Detection

The natural immune system can be conceptually divided as innate and adaptive immune system. The innate immune system is the second line of defense. It protects the body against common bacteria, worms and some viruses, and clears it from debris. It also interacts with the adaptive immune system, signaling the infections or the presence of damage and activating the appropriate immune system.

The adaptive immune system learns about invaders and tunes its detection mechanisms in order to provide an effective response even against previously unknown pathogens. It provides an effective protection against viruses even after they enter the body cells. It adapts to newly encountered viruses and memorizes them for more efficient and fast detection in the future.

Our proposed fraud detection for online services model draws inspiration from both the innate and adaptive portions of the natural immune system. Figure 1 outlines the proposed framework of our system which is inspired by the work done by Jon Timmis et al. [15].

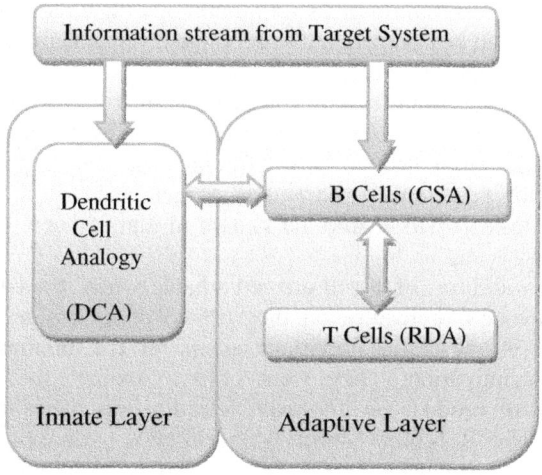

Fig. 1. System architecture

3.1   Innate Layer

In the innate layer of our system, we use dendritic cell analogy (DCA) of the innate immune system to correlate disparate data streams in the form of antigen and signals and to label groups of identical antigen as normal or anomalous.

The idea of DCA is to correlate disparate data-streams in the form of antigen and signals and label groups of identical antigens as normal or anomalous [4]. In user levels, the selected attributes still need to be categorized into three different signals including Pathogen Associated Molecular Patterns (PAMP), Danger, and Safe signal. The output of $O(t)$ from Equation (1) is the output value calculates from three different signals provide by a user at a time, the output will then compare $O(t)$ to the threshold value T to provide the value of $D(t)$.

$$O(t) = \frac{(W_P * P(t)) + (W_S * S(t)) + (W_D * D(t))}{|W_P| + |W_S| + |W_D|} \tag{1}$$

Where W_P, W_S, W_D are weights of PAMP, Danger, Safe signals respectively.

$$D(t) = \begin{cases} 0 & O(t) < T \\ 1 & O(t) \geq T \end{cases} \tag{2}$$

In order to add the temporal aspect, a time window from (t-w) to w is applied to describe the danger of the input in a certain time.

$$InnateO = \frac{1}{\omega + 1} \sum_{t=0}^{\omega} D(t - \omega) \tag{3}$$

3.2 Adaptive Layer

In the adaptive layer, we introduce two immunology inspired algorithms which borrows the idea from two key players in the adaptive layer of natural immune system which is B-cells and T-cells.

The clonal selection algorithm borrows heavily from it but not exact copy of its immune behavior of B-cells [16]. Here, we implemented the dynamic clonal selection algorithm (DCSA) for fraud detection will define and maintain a population of self-detectors; the detector represents a particular normal state of a user when they perform a particular task. It will enable the system to identify new fraud that it may not have seen before.

The discrimination abilities of T cell are remarkable when it need to discriminate between self and non-self molecules on the surface of an antigen-presenting cell (APC) [17]. T Cells is one of the important agents for the immune system; it can perform 2-class discrimination. They were able to extract the features of the generalized receptor to produce an anomaly detection algorithm similar to kernel density estimation. The Receptor Density Algorithm is proposed by Owens was inspired by the signaling mechanisms of T Cells can apply for anomaly detection with dynamic data [18].

3.2.1 Receptor Density Algorithm

For the target system, attributes will be selected as inputs and each input will provide a real input as $x_1, x_2 .... x_n \in x = \mathfrak{R}^n$ at the time of $t_1, t_2 .... t_n \in \mathfrak{R}^+$. We will create many receptor distributed in the input space, each of them will have its own position at x at the time of t. The receptor can be presented as $r_p^t(x)$ and its negative feedback can be also written as $r_n^t(x)$.

  1) First, we need to do the initialization for the RDA; it includes the initialization for each receptor and its negative feedback. For each user at time t, calculate the summarized stimulation of each receptor over a sample size of n:

$$r_p^t(x) = \sum_{i=1}^{n} \frac{1}{nh} K_s(\frac{x - x_i}{h}) \tag{4}$$

where $K_s(x)$ is the kernel function. If we choose Gaussian kernel function, it can be defined as follow:

$$K(\frac{x - x_i}{h}) = \frac{1}{\sqrt{2\pi}} e^{\frac{(x-x_i)^2}{-2h^2}} \tag{5}$$

The negative feedback can also be calculated for each receptor:

$$r_n^t(x) = \begin{cases} r_p^t(x) - \beta, & \text{if } (r_p^t(x) \geq \beta \\ 0 & \text{otherwise} \end{cases} \tag{6}$$

Where β called base negative barrier.

2) After the initialization stage of the RDA, the new data of the user can pass to the RDA for classification. The classification is done by compare the updated position of $r_p^t(x)$ and the receptor length l. The length of l can be defined by the number of samples n and kernel width h:

$$l = \frac{1}{nh\sqrt{2\pi}} \tag{7}$$

And the new position of the $r_p^t(x)$ is calculated using equation below for a given test point v:

$$r_p^t(x) = b * r_p^{t-1}(x) + gb * K_s(\frac{x - v}{h}) - \alpha * r_n^{t-1}(x) \tag{8}$$

Where b is the receptor position's decay rate, gb is current input stimulation rate, and α is negative feedback's stimulation.

If the receptor length l is larger than the updated $r_p^t(x)$ at the test point v; the test point v will be classified as normal. Otherwise it will be classified as anomaly.

3) After each new test data been processed and classified, the negative feedback $r_n^t(x)$ need to be updated before classify the next test data:

$$r_n^t(x) = d * r_p^{t-1}(x) + g * H(r_p^{t-1} - \beta), \quad H(x) = \begin{cases} 0, (x < 0) \\ 1, (x > 0) \end{cases} \tag{9}$$

Where d is the negative feedback decay rate, and g is the negative feedback stimulation rate.

4) Repeat step 2 and 3 until all the data had been processed.

3.2.2 Dynamic Clonal Selection Algorithm

The Dynamic Clonal Selection Algorithm for fraud detection will define and maintain a population of self-detectors; the detector represents a particular normal state of a user when they perform a particular task. Through dynamic clonal selection, detector will be cloned and mutate to create more updated self-detector which will be slightly different from the previous one. It will enable the system to identify new fraud that it may not have seen before.

The new coming data will present to the DCSA as antigen consists of values which describe the behavior of the user. Based on the values, antigens will be classified into different task groups. Different possible combinations of the inputs can help the system to detect anomaly and generate rule for mutations, which only allow the system to generate new self-detector in the way the system allows.

In the beginning, all users will share a gene library which consists of different task groups' recorded the normal behavior [19]. After the gene library established, the new coming data will present itself to the self detectors, if the affinity with the best match self detector is less than a threshold. The data will go through cloning and mutation and selection process; new self detectors are generated and may save into its memory cells. When the new data do not match any of the self detectors, it can turn to get help from the gene. If the new data is classified as normal, then new self detectors will be generated, and old ones with weak affinity will be removed in order to keep the size of memory cells constant. Figure 2 describes the detail of the algorithm.

Input: Antigens have 7 outputs of system; affinity threshold (ϕ)

Output: M=memory cell, data is anomaly or not.
Begin perform on-line
    For each user
        Find best match ($affinity_H$) from M

        Find best match ($gene_H$) in same task group

          If $affinity_H < \phi$
            Antigen is normal
          Elseif $affinity_H > \phi$ & $gene_H < \phi$
            Antigen is normal
            New self is detected
            Create a new self detectors
          Else Anomaly is found
        Clone and mutate randomly selected self detectors in M
        Replace them with the low affinity one
    End
Until forever

Fig. 2. Dynamic Clonal Selection Algorithm

4   Experimental Setup and Results Analysis

The experiments and results analysis use the same target system as Huang et al. (2010). Figure 3 is the flowchart of the whole system [12]. The user can login to the

User   Target System   AIS Engines   Risk Score

LOG EVENT
MANAGEMENT

Fig. 3. AIS based fraud detection system

```
0: 20010210T10:23:48,
1: 20010214T20:46:03,
2: 20010210T17:10:23,194.24.6.106 1,Login
3: 20010211T22:35:06,194.24.6.106 ,0,Orders
4: 20010214T20:22:46,194.24.6.106 ,1,Orders
5: 20010214T20:22:50,194.24.6.106, Delivery
6: 20010214T20:22:46,194.24.6.106, Billing
```

```
20010206T23:59:27,93090,6840055110
20010207T23:59:27,104290,7560062310
20010208T23:59:27,111490,7560069510
20010209T23:59:27,144410,11340081440
```

Fig. 4. Data record file format   **Fig. 5.** Router daily logs file format

application server, browse the video database and order a movie. When the user provides correct identity and billing information to the server, the application server will generate an authentication ticket for the user. The Video-on-Demand server then starts delivering the chosen movie after verifying of the ticket. The details of data generation can be found in [20].

Two useful information files are extracted from the raw logs produced by the system. As shown in Figure 4, data record file will start with Event Index 0 and 1 will indicate the set-top-box states (0 is off, 1 is on), Index larger than 1 is the event activities during this session which can be successful login or not, successful order or not, billing and delivery. Further information also includes event date, time, and IP address from the user. The second file (Figure 5) called router daily logs, which contains one line per day for the information of the date, time, user IP address, uploaded bytes and downloaded bytes.

The potential attributes extract from the raw log, event data and sum of events over 24 hours are as follow:

1.   Sum of failed login attempts
2.   Sum of successful login attempts
3.   Sum of failed movie order
4.   Sum of successful movie orders
5.   Sum of movie delivery notifications
6.   Sum of billing notifications
7.   Ratio between uploaded & downloaded (bytes)

The Video-on-Demand system will produce these 7 attributes for each user every day. The simulation will last for 7 months which contain 600 normal users and 100 break-in fraudsters. These users will be randomly selected and generate two data sets which will have 200 normal users and 33 break-in fraudsters in data set 1, and the rest in data set 2. Before our proposed algorithm performs online, the system will require offline initializations and parameters setting. The data set 1 is used for this purpose. The data set 2 will be used for performance evaluation.

4.1 Experimental Setup

For innate layer, a time window is applied to describe the danger of the input in a certain time. Empirically, the time window size is set as 3 which mean two previous data are required to calculate the danger level of the current data. The parameters in the Equation 1 are set as: $W_P = 2, W_S = 1, W_D = 1$. The threshold value in the Equation (2) is derived from the data set 1 by calculating the mean and standard deviation of the output based on Equation (1). Threshold is 8 which equal to three time value of standard deviation above the mean.

For RDA in adaptive layer, the initialization for each receptor and its negative feedback require calculating the summarized stimulation of each receptor over a sample size of n. The kernel function $K_s(x)$ is Gaussian kernel. The size of n and the parameters of RDA also defined empirically. The value of n=3, β =0.5, b =0.02, gb =0.5, α =1.2, d =0.03, g=2.1, h =0.4, and l =1. The size of the receptor is 100.

For simplicity and consistency, the sample size for memory cell initialization in DCSA also set as 3. The 7 inputs will be normalized within a range of 0 to 1, based on maximum values derived in data set 1. Each antigen produced 5 antibodies which mean after initialization, each user will have 15 antibodies. These remaining antigens also generated 5 antibodies each. The Euclidean distance threshold ϕ is 0.2. The maximum population for each user is 30. The multiplying factor for cloning is 5, and the mutation rate is 0.25. Apart from it, DCSA also require to establish a Gene library from data set 1 which includes samples from 200 normal over 5 days.

The newly collected data for each user will process their own data; compared with the threshold T. *InnateO* will indicate the number of time $O(t)$ less than the threshold T in the time window of 3. The output could be 0.33, 0.37, and 1. If the value less or equal to 0.33, it indicates there is no fraud behavior occurring in the process. Otherwise, it's fraud behavior.

In adaptive layer, RDA will classify the new coming data into normal or abnormal dynamically. By combining the results of innate layer and RDA result of adaptive layer, the systems will have the ability to classify the user into different categories as shown in Table 1. There will be 4 different combination of output provide by them. The rules based decision will determine whether the transaction of the user should be accepted, rejected or suspended for further analysis.

Table 1. Decision rules for DCA & RDA

DCA	RDA	Decision
Normal	Normal	Accept
Normal	Anomaly	Suspend
Danger	Normal	Suspend
Danger	Anomaly	Reject

Table 2. Decision rules for suspended cases

Suspended Cases	DCSA	Decision
Normal/Anomaly	Normal	Accept
Normal/Anomaly	Fraud	Reject
Danger/Normal	Normal	Accept
Danger/Normal	Fraud	Reject

The dynamic clonal selection is used under the situations when innate layer and RDA cannot make a decision. The final decision for the suspended cases is showed in Table 2.

4.2 Results Analysis

In this section, the performance of our hybrid algorithmic approach for break-in fraud detection will be compared with the results achieved by only using DCA, RDA, and DCSA as individual algorithms.

The factors used to define the parameters for algorithms are the detection rate (DR) and false alarm rate (FA), which can be calculated from true positive (TP), false positive (FP) true negative (TN), and false negative (FN) in Equation (1) and (2).

$$DR = \frac{TP}{TP + FN} \tag{10}$$

$$FA = \frac{FP}{FP + TN} \tag{11}$$

4.2.1 User Classification

First, the performance of the proposed algorithms will be addressed on whether they successfully classify the 67 fraud users and 400 normal users into the correct groups in the defined time periods. In order to determine whether the good solution is found, the baseline performance has to be defined. In our case, the baseline for TP and FP is set to 0.8 and 0.1. Which means to successfully classify a user, 80% of the fraud behaviors has to be detected, and the normal behaviors misclassify as fraud behaviors has to be less than 10%. Table 3 has concluded different classification methods results based on different testing time periods (one week, two weeks, and four weeks). The DR and FA in Table 4 can be calculated based on the results provided by Table 3.

Table 3. Training and testing results for different approaches (User level)

Method	TP			TN			FP			FN		
	One	Two	Four	One	Two	Four	One	Two	Four	One	Two	Four
DCA	45	48	48	357	359	359	43	41	41	22	19	19
RDA	44	46	52	355	358	360	45	42	40	23	21	15
DCSA	43	47	53	350	354	356	50	46	44	24	20	14
Hybrid	48	52	60	342	362	365	38	38	35	19	15	7

Table 4. Detection Rate and False Alarm Rate for different approaches (User level)

Method	DR%			FA%		
	One	Two	Four	One	Two	Four
DCA	67	71	71	10.70	10.25	10.25
RDA	66	69	78	11.25	10.50	10.00
DCSA	64	70	79	12.50	11.50	11.00
Hybrid	71	77	89	9.50	9.50	8.75

As shown in Table 3 and 4, there is a difference between the results in all approaches that is when the testing period increase, the detection rate increase as well. Since some fraudster did not start their behaviors yet. In this case, the longer period provided higher detection rates and lower false alarm rates. Tables also showed that, three different immunology inspired algorithm can be used as an efficient and reliable technique to take break-in fraud in an online environment. Our proposed methods of combing innate and adaptive later of immune system demonstrate the hybrid approach has the highest detection rate, and lowest false alarm rate when compared with the results achieved by only using them as individual algorithms.

4.2.2 Data Classification

The 267 users which produced more than 56000 samples during 7 months will be used to test the performance of the proposed system. The results are shown in Table 5.

Table 5. Detection Rate and False Alarm Rate for different approaches (data level)

Method	DR%	FA%
DCA	69	14
RDA	82	12
DCSA	80	18
Hybrid	90	8

In the Table 5, both RDA and DCSA achieved more than 80 % detection rate; and the false alarm rate around 16%. But for DCA, it only produced an average of approximately 69% in detection rate and 14% for false alarm rate. Overall, the results achieved by RDA and DCSA individual already exhibited better performance, with more than 10% higher in detection rate compared with DCA. Our hybrid algorithm demonstrates improvements over the innate layer, RDA, and DCSA. It shows a significantly better positive predictive value of fraud detection than what is achieved by three single approaches when applied on the same data. The results calculated by equation (10) and (11) show that the hybrid approach has a higher detection rate at 90% with far lower false alarm rate at 8%.

5 Conclusions

This paper has developed a novel online immunology-inspired system for the detection of fraudulent e-commerce transactions This proposed system has two layers: the innate layer that implements the idea of Dendritic Cell Analogy (DCA), and the adaptive layer that implements the Dynamic Clonal Selection Algorithm (DCSA) and the Receptor Density Algorithm (RDA).

Existing offline systems in the literature could not apply for online fraud detects system. Since it needs to be adaptive and evolve over time. It should also be a dynamic detection model that continually learns from examples seen to keep automatically adjusting their parameters and their values to match the latest patterns of them. The proposed approach in this paper helps e-commerce to better understand the issues and plan the activities involved in a systemic approach to counter E-fraud. This approach focuses on logging data since many systems have logging for the purpose of accounting.

The experimental results demonstrate that our proposed hybrid approach combining innate and adaptive layers of immune system achieves the highest detection rate and the lowest false alarm rate compared with the DCA, DCSA, and RDA algorithms for Video-on-Demand system.

In the future, we will further investigate the application of the proposed system for online credit card fraud detection. Sensitivity analysis is another important issue we intend to investigate since the AIS based algorithms have to define and understand the effects of a large number of parameters and stochastic elements on the system.

References

1. Satti, M.M., Gamer, B.J., Nagrial, M.H.: Information security standard for E businesses. In: Proc. 8th Intl. Conf. on Commun. System, vol. 2, pp. 641–645 (2008)
2. Mashima, D., Ahamad, M.: Using Identity Credential Usage Logs to Detect Anomalous Service Accesses. DIM, Chicago (2009)
3. Williams, P.D., Anchor, K.P., Bebo, J.L., Gunsch, G.H., Lamont, G.D.: CDIS: Towards a Computer Immune System for Detecting Network Intrusions. In: Lee, W., Mé, L., Wespi, A. (eds.) RAID 2001. LNCS, vol. 2212, pp. 117–133. Springer, Heidelberg (2001)
4. Greensmith, J., Twycross, J., Aickelin, U.: Dendritic cells for anomaly detection. In: Harper, R., Rauterberg, M., Combetto, M. (eds.) ICEC 2006. LNCS, vol. 4161, pp. 664–671. Springer, Heidelberg (2006)
5. Hofmeyr, S.A., Forrest, S.: Architecture for an artificial immune system. Evolutionary Computation 7(1), 45–68 (2000)
6. Cortés, P., García, J.M., Onieva, L., Muñuzuri, J., Guadix, J.: Viral System to Solve Optimization Problems: An Immune-Inspired Computational Intelligence Approach. In: Bentley, P.J., Lee, D., Jung, S. (eds.) ICARIS 2008. LNCS, vol. 5132, pp. 83–94. Springer, Heidelberg (2008)
7. Castro, P.A.D., Zuben, F.J.Von.: Mobais: a Bayesian Artificial Immune System for Multi-Objective Optimization. In: Bentley, P.J., Lee, D., Jung, S. (eds.) ICARIS 2008. LNCS, vol. 5132, pp. 49–59. Springer, Heidelberg (2008)
8. Oates, R., Greensmith, J., Aickelin, U., Garibaldi, J., Kendall, G.: The application of a dendritic cell algorithm to a robotic classifier. In: de Castro, L.N., Von Zuben, F.J., Knidel, H. (eds.) ICARIS 2007. LNCS, vol. 4628, pp. 204–215. Springer, Heidelberg (2007)
9. Qiang, C., Xiangpin, L., Chuang, X.: A Model for Detection and Diagnosis of Fault Based on Artificial Immune Theory. Journal of Southern Institute of Memallurgy 126(3) (2005)

10. Tuo, J., Ren, S., Liu, W., Li, X., Li, B., Lei, L.: Artificial Immune System for Fraud Detection. In: proceeding of IEEE International Conference on Systems, Man and Cybernetics, pp. 1407–1411 (2004)
11. Huang, R., Tawfik, H., NagaRentian, A.: Artificial Dendritic Cells Algorithm for Online Break-in Fraud Detection. In: Proceeding of International Conference on Developments in eSystems Engineering, Abu Dhabi, UAE, pp. 181–189 (2009)
12. Huang, R., Tawfik, H., Nagar, A.: Electronic Fraud Detection for Video-on-Demand System Using Hybrid Immunology-Inspired Algorithms. In: Proceeding of The 9th International Conference on Artificial Immune Systems, Edinburgh, UK, pp. 290–303 (2010)
13. Gadi, M.F.A., Wang, X., do Lago, A.P.: Credit Card Fraud Detection with Artificial Immune System. In: Bentley, P.J., Lee, D., Jung, S. (eds.) ICARIS 2008. LNCS, vol. 5132, pp. 119–131. Springer, Heidelberg (2008)
14. Brabazon, A., Cahill, J., Keenan, P., Walsh, D.: Identifying online credit card fraud using artificial immune systems. In: Yang, H.S., Malaka, R., Hoshino, J., Han, J.H. (eds.) ICEC 2010. LNCS, vol. 6243. Springer, Heidelberg (2010)
15. Timmis, J., Tyrrell, A., Mokhtar, M., Ismail, A.R., owen, N., Bi, R.: An Artificial Immune System for Robot Organisms. Adaptive Control Mechanisms, 279–302 (2010)
16. De Castro, L.N., Von Zuben, F.J.: The clonal selection algorithm with engineering applications. In: Proceedings of GECCO 2000. Workshop on Artificial Immune Systems and Their Applications. 36–37 (2000)
17. Yu, S., Dasgupta, D.: Conserved Self Pattern Recognition Algorithm. In: Bentley, P.J., Lee, D., Jung, S. (eds.) ICARIS 2008. LNCS, vol. 5132, pp. 279–290. Springer, Heidelberg (2008)
18. Owens, N., Greensted, A., Timmis, J., Tyrrell, A.: T cell receptor signalling inspired kernel density estimation and anomaly detection. In: Andrews, P.S., Timmis, J., Owens, N.D.L., Aickelin, U., Hart, E., Hone, A., Tyrrell, A.M. (eds.) ICARIS 2009. LNCS, vol. 5666, pp. 122–135. Springer, Heidelberg (2009)
19. Secker.,Freitas, A., Timmis, J.: AISEC: An Artificial Immune System for Email Classification. In: Proceedings of the Congress on Evolutionary Computation, vol. 2003, pp. 131–139. IEEE, Canberra (2005)
20. Lundin, E., Kvarnström, H., Jonsson, E.: A synthetic fraud data generation methodology. In: Deng, R.H., Qing, S., Bao, F., Zhou, J. (eds.) ICICS 2002. LNCS, vol. 2513, pp. 265–277. Springer, Heidelberg (2002)

Immune Approach for Neuro-Fuzzy Systems Learning Using Multiantibody Model

Nikolay Korablev and Irina Sorokina

Kharkiv National University of Radioelectronics,
Computer Engineering Department,
Lenin av., 14, 61166, Kharkiv, Ukraine
{korablev,i.sorokina}@kture.kharkov.ua

Abstract. In this work we propose an immune approach for learning neuro-fuzzy systems, namely Adaptive-Network-based Fuzzy Inference System (ANFIS). ANFIS is proved to be universal approximator of nonlinear functions. But in case of great number of input variables ANFIS structure grows essentially and the dimensionality of learning task becomes a problem. Existing methods of ANFIS learning allow only to identify parameters of ANFIS without modifying its structure. We propose an immune approach for ANFIS learning based on clonal selection and immune network theories. It allows not only to identify ANFIS parameters but also to reduce number of neurons in hidden layers of ANFIS. These tasks are performed simultaneously using the model of adaptive multiantibody.

Keywords: artificial immune system, multiantibody, clonal selection, immune network, neuro-fuzzy system, ANFIS.

1 Introduction

Nowadays methods of intellectual information processing in the uncertainty conditions have gained an increased scientific and practical interest. Fuzzy models are among such methods. They allow to describe processes with the help of natural language and linguistic variables using human understandable mechanism of fuzzy logic inference. That is why fuzzy models are widely used to solve identification, recognition, decision support problems. However fuzzy models have some disadvantages. The most important one is that databases are created by experts and it leads to some subjectivity. To overcome this problem adaptive neuro-fuzzy systems were created. They allow to identify parameters of the model using experimental data. One of the most popular neuro-fuzzy systems is Adaptive Neuro-Fuzzy inference system (ANFIS) created by Robert Jang [7]. ANFIS is a universal approximator because of using neural network units and ANFIS provides good logic inference because of using fuzzy logic. But it has the problem of dimensionality in case of big number of input variables. Existing methods of ANFIS learning, namely gradient, hybrid gradient methods [7] are intended to identify parameters of neurons in hidden layers but they say nothing about changing the structure of ANFIS.

P. Liò, G. Nicosia, and T. Stibor (Eds.): ICARIS 2011, LNCS 6825, pp. 395–405, 2011.

We propose the immune approach that allows not only to identify all the parameters of ANFIS but to find the optimal structure of ANFIS as well. This approach allows to reduce the number of neurons in the hidden layers of ANFIS using artificial immune systems.

AIS is a relatively novel computational paradigm that was originated from attempts to model and apply immunological principles to problem solving in a wide range of areas such as optimization, data analysis, computer security etc [1, 2, 8].

In this work, we investigate the use of artificial immune system based on clonal selection theory to adjust parameters of ANFIS. We also propose the model of multiantibody in order to change structure of ANFIS together with the immune network theory.

The remaining of the paper is as follows. ANFIS structure is briefly described in section 2. Section 3 presents immune approach for ANFIS learning. First the parametrical identification of ANFIS is given. Then the model of multiantibody is presented to perform both parametrical and structural approach to ANFIS learning. Experimental results are presented and discussed in section 4. Finally, section 5 concludes the paper.

2   ANFIS Structure

ANFIS [7] is a multi-layer feed forward network in which each node performs a particular function on incoming signals.

Consider the fuzzy inference system with n inputs and 1 output. The number of membership functions assigned to each input variable is m. The rule base contains m^n fuzzy if-then rules of Takagi-Sugeno type:

$$R_i : IF \;\; x_i \; is \; A_{i1} \; AND \; ... \; AND \; x_j \; is \; A_{ij} \; AND \; ... \; AND \; x_n \; is \; A_{in},$$
$$THEN \;\; y = k_{i1}x_1 + ... + k_{ij}x_j + ... + k_{in}x_n + k_{i0}, \;\; i = 1,...,n. \tag{1}$$

The corresponding ANFIS architecture according to [7] is shown on the fig. 1.

Neurons of the 1st layer calculate membership functions $\mu_{Aij}(x_i)$ using the Gaussian function:

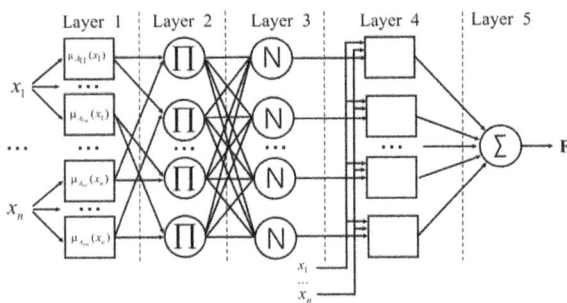

Fig. 1. Structure of ANFIS

$$\mu(x) = \exp\left[-\left(\frac{x-c}{\sigma}\right)^2\right], \tag{2}$$

where $\{c, \sigma\}$ is the parameter set.

Neurons of the 2nd layer multiply the incoming signals:

$$w_i = \prod_{j=1}^{m} \mu_{Aij}(x_i), \ i = \overline{1, m^n}. \tag{3}$$

Neurons of the 3rd layer calculate the ratio of the i-th rule's firing strength to the sum of all rules' firing strength:

$$\overline{w}_i = w_i / \sum_{i=1}^{m^n} w_i, \ i = \overline{1, m^n}. \tag{4}$$

4th layer neurons compute the node function:

$$\overline{w}_i f_i = \overline{w}_i (k_{i0} + k_{i1}x_1 + k_{i2}x_2 + \ldots + k_{in}x_n), \ i = \overline{1, m^n}, \tag{5}$$

which performs Takagi-Sugeno fuzzy reasoning method.

The only neuron of the fifth layer computes the overall output as the summation of all incoming signals:

$$F = \sum \overline{w}_i f_i, \ i = \overline{1, m^n}. \tag{6}$$

The first and the fourth layers of ANFIS are adaptive. The first layer contains parameters of Gaussian function and the fourth layer contains parameters of Takagi-Sugeno fuzzy rules to be identified.

Existing methods of ANFIS learning are based on classic methods of neural networks learning:

– stochastic methods. Such methods take a lot of training steps;
– gradient methods, namely least squares methods, Kalman filter, Newton method, Levenberg-Marquardt algorithm, backpropagation method etc. Gradient methods to identify parameters of ANFIS are generally slow and likely to become trapped in local minima.

One of the most effective methods of ANFIS learning is hybrid gradient learning rule which combines the gradient method and the least squares estimate to identify parameters [7].

Existing methods of ANFIS learning have computational complexity and have mathematical demands to criterion functions. These methods do not allow to modify the structure of the network (rule base in fuzzy inference system). That is why we propose artificial immune system to identify parameters and structure of ANFIS.

3 Immune Approach for ANFIS Learning

3.1 Parametrical Identification of ANFIS

First we consider only the task of ANFIS parameters identification using artificial immune system [6].

The proposed immune approach identifies parameters of ANFIS adaptive layers, namely membership functions parameters (1st layer neurons) and fuzzy rules parameters (4th layer), in order to minimize the deviation of expected and real output of the network.

The population of antigens Ag $=\{Ag_1,...,Ag_M\}$ in the immune system is represented by learning patterns while the population of antibodies Ab=$\{Ab_1,...,Ab_N\}$ represents possible vectors of ANFIS parameters. All the parameters to identify are coded in one antibody (fig.2). Such approach allows to identify all the ANFIS parameters simultaneously. The real-valued coding is used.

$$c_{11},...,c_{1m},...,c_{n1},...,c_{nm};\sigma_{11},...,\sigma_{1m},...,\sigma_{n1},...,\sigma_{nm} \quad \big| \quad k_{10},...,k_{1n} \quad \big| \cdot \cdot \big| \quad k_{q0},...,k_{qn}$$

Fig. 2. Structure of the antibody

Affinity of an antibody with an antigen is calculated as the root mean squared error:

$$Aff = \sqrt{\frac{1}{M}\sum_{r=1}^{M}\left[F_{ANFIS}\left(X_r,P\right)-y_r\right]^2} \quad , \tag{7}$$

where P is a vector of ANFIS parameters coded in the antibody;

X_r is an input pattern;

$F_{ANFIS}\left(X_r,P\right)$ is an output of ANFIS initialized with parameters P and X_r as an input pattern;

y_r is an expected output of the net;

M is the size of the learning sample.

Producing of antibodies in the immune system is based on the clonal selection theory [2, 4, 5]. According to this theory those antibodies that recognize an antigen start proliferating. A number of clones is generated and clones suffer mutation proportional to their affinity with antigens.

The algorithm may be described by following steps:

1. Generate the population of antibodies Ab ;
2. Initialize ANFIS with parameters decoded from the antibody Ab_i
3. Calculate affinity of antibody Ab_i with the population of antigens Ag by presenting them to ANFIS.
4. Select n best antibodies to clone N times.
5. Clone, form the population of clones C .
6. Mutate clones in population C , form the population $C*$.
7. Calculate affinity of clones in population $C*$ with the population of antigens Ag .
8. Edit population of antibodies Ab by replacing antibodies with their improved clones.
9. Replace d worst antibodies with the newly generated ones in the population of antibodies Ab .
10. If the stopping condition was not met return to step 2.
11. End.

The result of the algorithm is the antibody with the best affinity.

Such approach allows to identify only parameters of ANFIS without considering its structure.

3.2 Parametrical and Structural Identification

To solve the task of parametrical and structural identification we present the model of multiantibody, which helps to identify structure of ANFIS by removing redundant neurons from the network.

The immune approach for ANFIS learning now is based not only on the clonal selection theory but also on the immune network theory [2, 3]. According to the immune network theory the important feature of the immune system is that it varies dynamically and the immune response is based not only on the interaction of antibodies and antigens but also on the interaction between antibodies.

According to our immune approach all the parameters of ANFIS are coded in the adaptive multiantibody $mAb_i = \{ab_0, ab_1, ab_2, ..., ab_{L-1}\}$, $i = \overline{1, N}$, where L – is the length of $mAbi$ vector; N – is the size of the multiantibody population.

Multiantibody is a structured vector (fig.3). Its length is not fixed.

Each multiantibody of the population consists of the whole set of parameters to identify, which are divided into two separate parts: part 1 with parameters of membership functions and part 2 with parameters of Takagi-Sugeno fuzzy rules.

$c_{11},...,c_{1m},...,c_{n1},...,c_{nm}; \sigma_{11},...,\sigma_{1m},...,\sigma_{n1},...,\sigma_{nm}$	$k_{10},...,k_{1n}$	$\cdots$	$k_{q0},...,k_{qn}$
Ab_0	Ab_1	$\cdots$	Ab_q
part 1	part 2		
Multiantibody			

Fig. 3. Structure of the multiantibody

On the fig.3 c_{ij}, σ_{ij} , $i = \overline{1,n};$ $j = \overline{1,m}$ – are parameters of the Gauss membership function for n input variables with m terms each; $k_{i0},,...k_{in}$, $i = \overline{1,q};$ – are parameters of q fuzzy rules.

Part 1 of the multiantibody consists of the only antibody Ab_0 , its length is fixed because the number of membership functions for input variables is constant.

Part 2 of the multiantibody consists of q separate antibodies $Ab_1, Ab_2,...,Ab_q$, each representing parameters $k_{i0},,...k_{in}$, $i = \overline{1,q}$ for one fuzzy rule. Part 2 is adaptive and general number of antibodies in this part varies performing the structural identification and reducing the number of neurons in the hidden layers of the network. Such structurization helps to raise the efficiency of the algorithm because each part of the multiantibody corresponds to different aspects of the solution and immune operators are applied to different parts of the multiantibody separately.

Cloning and mutation are performed to both parts of multiantibody, while suppression of antibodies concerns only part 2 of the multiantibody. The antibody-antibody affinity is calculated for all the antibodies of the part 2 and if it overrides the suppression threshold the corresponding antibody is deleted from the multiantibody. Affinity between two antibodies is calculated as follows:

$$Aff_{Ab-Ab} = \|Ab_1 - Ab_2\| = \sqrt{\sum_{j=0}^{n}(k_{1j} - k_{2j})^2} \ . \tag{8}$$

Suppression of antibodies inside part 2 of the multiantibody leads to removing of neurons in hidden layers 2-4 of the network. This corresponds to deleting redundant fuzzy inference rules.

The initial population of multiantibodies is generated randomly. The real-valued coding is used which helps to raise the accuracy and to reduce the complexity.

Using the immune network theory provides the interaction of antibodies and performs the suppression, thus reducing the redundancy of fuzzy rules.

Batch learning is used and the values of identified parameters are changed only after all the learning patterns are given. Thus the affinity of the multiantibody is calculated with the whole population of antigens.

Our immune approach can be described by the following steps:

1. Generate the population of multiantibodies mAb ;
2. Initialize ANFIS with parameters decoded from the multiantibody mAb_i ;
3. Calculate affinity of multiantibody mAb_i with the population of antigens by presenting them to the ANFIS;
4. Select n best multiantibodies to clone N times;
5. Clone, form the population of clones C ;
6. Mutate clones in population C , form the population $C*$;
7. Calculate affinity of clones in population $C*$ with the population of antigens Ag ;
8. Edit population of multiantibodies by replacing multiantibodies with their improved clones.
9. Calculate antibody-antibody affinity for antibodies from part 2 of the multiantibody mAb_i , suppress those antibodies whose affinity overrides the suppression threshold.
10. Replace d worst multiantibodies with the newly generated ones in the population of multiantibodies mAb .
11. If the stopping condition was not met return to step 2.
12. End.

Multiantibody with the best affinity in the population is the solution. It contains all the identified parameters of ANFIS. Number of antibodies left in part 2 of the multiantibody corresponds to the number of neurons in hidden layers of ANFIS. Thus parametrical and structural identification of ANFIS is performed.

4   Experimental Results

This section provides the simulation results of ANFIS with batch learning using the proposed immune approach and the model of multiantibody.

In order to evaluate the performance of the proposed immune approach for ANFIS learning it was applied to modeling test functions.

Table 1. Test functions

	Test function	Range of definition
1	$F_1(x_1,x_2) = x_1{}^2 + x_2{}^2$	$x_1, x_2 \in [-3;3]$
2	$F_2(x_1,x_2) = 3(1-x_1)^2 \exp(-x_1^2 - (x_2+1)^2) -$ $-10\left(\dfrac{x_1}{5} - x_1^3 - x_2^5\right)\exp(-x_1^2 - x_2^2) - \dfrac{1}{3}\exp(-(x_1+1)^2 - x_2^2)$	$x_1, x_2 \in [-3;3]$
3	$F_3(x_1,x_2) = \dfrac{\sin(x_1)}{x1} + \dfrac{\sin(x_2)}{x_2}$	$x_1, x_2 \in [-10;10]$
4	$F_4(x_1,x_2,x_3) = (1 + x_{1,0.5} + x_{2-1} + x_{3-1.5})^2$	$x_1, x_2, x_3 \in [1;6]$

For each test function the learning sample $\left(x_1^{(k)}, x_2^{(k)}, ..., x_n^{(k)}, y^{(k)}\right)$ is obtained from the grid points of the definition range. The size of learning sample is taken according to the number of parameters to identify in ANFIS. The number of parameters varies according to the number of membership functions associated with input variables of test functions.

The number of membership functions, the number of parameters to identify and the size of learning sample are given in Table 2.

The initial (maximum) number of rules for each case is given in Table 3.

Test functions F_3, F_4 are used in [7] to train ANFIS using hybrid gradient method.

According to [7] the size of learning samples for functions F_3, F_4 is 121 and 216.

Immune approach for parametrical and structural identification is applied to train ANFIS.

Parameters of immune algorithm are obtained experimentally from the perspective of precision and computational efficiency:

Population size	15
Number of multiantibodies to clone	7
Minimal number of clones	10
Maximal number of clones	20
Minimal mutation rate	0.3
Maximal mutation rate	0.7
Number of multiantibodies to replace	1
Suppression threshold	0.005
Maximal number of generations	15000
Affinity threshold	0.001

The number of clones for each multiantibody is determined using affinity proportionate mechanism described in [8].

Mutation mechanism is based on [8, 9] and is performed as follows. The mutation rate is taken from the range $[R_{mut\_min}; R_{mut\_max}]$, where R_{mut_min} and R_{mut_max} are minimal and maximal mutation rates. For each mutation operation the mutation rate is calculated as follows:

$$R_{mut}(mAb_i) = \beta * R_{mut\_max} + (1-\beta) * R_{mut\_min}, \tag{9}$$

$$\beta = \frac{Aff(mAb_i) - Aff_{best}}{Aff_{worst} - Aff_{best}}, \tag{10}$$

where $Aff(mAb_i)$ is the affinity of the multiantibody mAb_i; Aff_{best}, Aff_{worst} are the best and the worst affinities in the current generation.

To determine the parameters of multiantibody that suffer mutation we randomly generate the probability vector $p(mAbi) = \langle p_1, p_2, ..., p_L \rangle$ from the range $[0;1]$ according to the uniform distribution. Here p_j is the probability of j-th multiantibody parameter mutation. Parameters of multiantibody with $p_j < R_{mut\_max}$ suffer mutation.

Mutation of chosen parameters is performed using Gaussian noise [9], e.g. by adding to the current parameter value the random variable with normal distribution and zero mathematical expectation:

$$mab_{i+1} = mab_i + N(0, \sigma_i), \tag{11}$$

where σ_i is the dispersion of the random value N, which is associated with each parameter mab_i of the multiantibody.

We use σ_i as a mutation step and adopt it according to the affinity of the multiantibody:

$$\sigma_{i+1} = \sigma_i \frac{Aff(mAb_i) - Aff_{best}}{Aff_{worst} - Aff_{best}}. \tag{12}$$

Thus the mutation parameters are adjusted according to the affinity of each multiantibody.

The stopping criterion of the algorithm is the predefined affinity threshold or if it is not reached the predefined number of generations.

Results of parametrical adaptation are shown in Table 2. Table 3 gives results of structural adaptation (reducing the number of fuzzy rules and the number of neurons in hidden layers 2-4 correspondingly). Results are the average of ten runs.

Table 2. Results of parametrical identification

Number of membership functions	Number of parameters to identify	Size of learning sample	RMSE			
			F_1	F_2	F_3	F_4
2	20	121	-	-	-	0.010
3	39	121	0.065	0.157	-	-
4	64	216	-	-	0.008	-
5	95	289	0.008	0.012	-	-
7	175	400	0.006	0.010	-	-

Table 3. Results of structural identification

Number of membership functions	Maximal number of fuzzy rules	F_1	F_2	F_3	F_4
2	8	-	-	-	7
3	9	8	8	-	-
4	16	-	-	15	-
5	25	22	24	-	-
7	49	42	45	-	-

From Table 2 we can see that the more membership functions are used to describe the input variable the higher accuracy we obtain. And the proposed immune approach to learn ANFIS is able to give good results on big number of parameters to identify.

Reducing the number of neurons in hidden layers leads to reducing the number of parameters to identify and thus allows to reduce the computation time.

The comparison of the proposed immune approach to train ANFIS and existing methods are given in Table 4.

In Table 4: L – number of parameters to identify, M — size of the learning sample. Last three rows are taken from [7].

The given comparison shows the efficiency of the proposed immune approach for ANFIS learning.

Table 5 gives computing time for ANFIS learning using proposed immune approach (test function F_1, 2 membership functions, 20 parameters to identify). Results are obtained for single algorithm running (5000 generations). From table we see that computing time increases almost linearly with increasing of number of parameters to identify.

Table 4. Comparison of existing methods for ANFIS learning

	F_1, 5 MF L=95, M=289	F_2, 5 MF L=95, M=289	F_3, 4 MF L=64, M=216	F_4, 2 MF		
	RMSE	RMSE	RMSE	L	M	RMSE
Immune approach	0.008	0.012	0.008	20	121	0.010
Backpropagation	0.012	0.088	0.093	20	121	0.150
Hybrid gradient method	0.001	0.019	0.020	20	121	0.021
Levenberg-Marquardt Algorithm	0.017	0.012	0.156	20	121	0.185
Genetic algorithm	0.021	0.98	0.120	20	121	0.148
GMDH model [7]				-	20	4.7
Fuzzy Model 1 [7]				22	20	1.5
Fuzzy Model 2 [7]				32	20	0.59

Table 5. Computing time (INTEL Core 2 Quad Q6600)

Number of membership functions	2	3	4	5	7
Number of parameters to identify	20	39	64	95	175
Computing time, s	225	415	700	1120	1900

Table 6. Results of using parallel computing

Processor	Number of cores	Computing time, s
INTEL Celeron 430	1	583
INTEL Core 2 Duo E8400	2	334
INTEL Core 2 Quad Q6600	4	250

To increase performance of the immune algorithm we propose to use OpenMP technology. OpenMP is effective in case of big number of cycles and splittable data arrays. In the proposed immune approach the affinity of each multiantibody is calculated on every generation irrespective of all the other multiantibodies. To calculate affinity it is necessary to create ANFIS with parameters decoded from the multiantibody. Using OpenMP technology these tasks are done in parallel. Results of running immune algorithms on processors with different number of cores are shown in Table 6 (test function F_4, 2 membership functions, 20 parameters to identify). Results are obtained for 5000 generations. We can see that parallel computing allows to reduce computing time essentially.

5 Conclusions

This work proposed an immune approach for ANFIS learning. Our approach is based on clonal selection and immune network theories. Additionally a multiantibody model is implemented to perform simultaneous identification of parameters and structure of ANFIS.

Experiments on test functions with different number of input variables and associated membership functions have demonstrated that the proposed immune approach performs good results in ANFIS learning. Computation time is estimated for ANFIS learning procedures with different number of identified parameters and the OpenMP technology was proposed to perform parallel computing.

References

1. Dasgupta, D. (ed.): Artificial Immune Systems and Their Applications. Springer, Heidelberg (1999)
2. Timmis, J.I., Knight, T., De Castro, L.N., Hart, E.: An Overview of Artificial Immune Systems. In: Computation in Cells and Tissues: Perspectives and Tools for Thought. Natural Computation Series, pp. 51–86. Springer, Heidelberg (2004)

3. De Castro, L.N., Von Zuben, F.J.: AiNet: An Artificial Immune Network for Data Analysis. In: Abbass, H.A., Sarker, R.A., Newton, C.S. (eds.) Data Mining: A Heuristic Approach, ch. XII pp. 231–259. Idea Group Publishing, USA (2001)
4. De Castro, L.N., Von Zuben, F.J.: Learning and optimization using the clonal selection principle. IEEE Trans. Evolut. Comput. 6(3), 239–251 (2002)
5. De Castro, L.N., Von Zuben, F.J.: The Clonal Selection Algorithm with Engineering Applications. In: Proceedings of GECCO 2000, Workshop on Artificial Immune Systems and Their Applications, pp. 36–37 (2000)
6. Korablyov, N.M., Ovcharenko, I.V.: Adaptation of fuzzy inference models using artificial immune systems. In: 3-rd International Conference Advanced Computer Systems and Networks: Design and Application, Lviv, pp. 89–91 (2007)
7. Jang, J.-S.R.: ANFIS: Adaptive-Network-Based Fuzzy Inference System. IEEE Trans. Systems & Cybernetics 23, 665–685 (1993)
8. Castro, P.A.D., Coelho, G.P., Caetano, M.F., Von Zuben, F.J.: Designing Ensembles of Fuzzy Classification Systems: An Immune-Inspired Approach. In: Jacob, C., Pilat, M.L., Bentley, P.J., Timmis, J.I. (eds.) ICARIS 2005. LNCS, vol. 3627, pp. 469–482. Springer, Heidelberg (2005)
9. Sebag, M., Schoenauer, M., Ravise, C.: Inductive Learning of Mutation Step-Size in Evolutionary Parameter Optimization. In: Angeline, P.J., McDonnell, J.R., Reynolds, R.G., Eberhart, R. (eds.) EP 1997. LNCS, vol. 1213, pp. 247–261. Springer, Heidelberg (1997)

The Danger Theory Applied to Vegetal Image Pattern Classification

Esma Bendiab and Mohamed Khirreddine Kholladi

MISC Laboratory, Department of Computer Science, University of Constantine, 25017, Algeria
Bendiab_e@yahoo.fr, Kholladi@yahoo.com

Abstract. Artificial Immune Systems (AIS) are a type of intelligent algorithm inspired by the principles and processes of the human immune system. Despite the successful implementation of different AIS, the validity of the paradigm "self non self" have lifted many questions. The Danger theory was an alternative to this paradigm. If we involve its principles, the AIS are being applied as a classifier. However, image classification offers new prospects and challenges to data mining and knowledge extraction. It is an important tool and a descriptive task seeking to identify homogeneous groups of objects based on the values of their attributes. In this paper, we describe our initial framework in which the danger theory was apprehended by the Dendritic cells algorithm is applied to vegetal image classification. The approach classifies pixel in vegetal or soil class. Experimental results are very encouraging and show the feasibility and effectiveness of the proposed approach.

Keywords: Artificial Immune Systems (AIS), Danger Theory (DT), Dendritic Cell Algorithm (DCA), Image Classification.

1 Introduction

Artificial immune systems (AIS) are new metaphor, inspired by the human defence mechanism. It provides protection from invading entities such as bacteria and regulates numerous bodily functions. These systems are massively distributed and parallel, highly adaptive and reactive systems, evolutionary where learning is native.
AIS can be defined [1] as the composition of intelligent methodologies, inspired by the natural immune system for the resolution of real world problems.

Many merits are at the basis of AIS use. Since natural mechanisms, such as: recognition, identification, intruders' elimination, which allow the human body to reach its immunity, suggest new ideas for: models recognition, machine learning, communication, adaptation, memorization, auto organization and distributed controls.

Whereas, AIS have successful applications which are quoted in literature [1-3]; the self non self paradigm, which performs discriminatory process by tolerating self entities and reacting to foreign ones, was much criticized for many reasons, which will be described in section 2. Therefore, a controversial alternative way to this paradigm was proposed: the danger theory [4].

P. Liò, G. Nicosia, and T. Stibor (Eds.): ICARIS 2011, LNCS 6825, pp. 406–418, 2011.

The danger theory offers new perspectives and ideas to AISs [4-6]. It stipulates that the immune system react to danger and not to foreign entities. In this context, it is a matter of distinguishing non self but harmless from self but harmful invaders, termed: antigen.

If the labels self and non self were to be replaced by interesting and non interesting data, a distinction would prove beneficial. In this case, the AIS are being applied as a classifier [5].

Besides, image classification, including supervised and unsupervised approaches, was at all times a powerful tool used in the analysis of the numerical image processing, in particular for interpretation purposes [7]. Supervised classification procedures require a human analyst to provide training areas, which form a group of pixels with known class label, so as to assemble groups of similar pixels into the correct classes. In comparison, unsupervised classification proceeds with only minimal input. An unsupervised classification divides all pixels within an image into a corresponding class pixel by pixel. Typically, the only input an unsupervised classification needs is the number of scene classes [8, 9].

In recent years, many advanced classification approaches, such as: artificial neural networks, fuzzy-sets, and expert systems, have been widely applied on image classification. Researches focus on the bio-inspired and Meta heuristic ones [7], in order to discover more novel, more efficient or just unusual new techniques, intended for determining their flaws. Mainly, image classification presents new challenges to data mining and knowledge extraction.

Moreover, one important issue emerging strongly in agriculture is related to the identification of green plants. So, some types of action can be carried out to improve their qualities in terms of: esthetic, growth or water deficit. Also the identification of textures belonging to the soil could be useful to know some variables, such as humidity, smoothness or many others. This implies that the images to be processed contain textures of two main types to be identified: green plants and soil.

This paper proposes a new approach for classifying these main textures. The Dendritic cell algorithm from danger theory is applied on two class classification of vegetation cover in vegetal images in order to classify pixels in "vegetal" or "soil" class. This makes an interesting contribution which provides information about quality criteria indicators which direct experts' decision concerning the quality of plants. Some works have been proposed in this way, we can mention [10, 11]. In the first, the authors proposed a classification approach based on pixels segmentation using an artificial neural network. While in the second work, the authors expose a classification approach of scenes containing vegetation (Forsythia) and soil by hierarchical analysis of bi-dimensional histograms. In both works, the authors use colorimetric spaces to achieve the classification task.

The rest of the paper is organized as follows. Section 2 contains relevant background information and motivation regarding the danger theory. Section 3 describes the Dendritic Cell Algorithm. In section 4, we describe the classification problem. This is followed by Sections 5, presenting formalized description of the DCA and its implementation as a classifier to vegetal images. This is followed by experimentations. Section 6 includes a sensitivity analysis of a parameters selection. The paper ends with a conclusion and future works.

2 The Danger Theory

The main goal of the immune system is to protect our bodies from invading entities, called: antigens, which cause damage and diseases.

At the outset, the traditional immune theory considers that the protection was done by distinguishing self and non self inside the body and by eliminating the non self.

Incompetent to explain certain phenomena, the discriminating paradigm in the immune system presents many gaps, such [4]:

-   There is no immune reaction to foreign bacteria in the guts or to the food which we eat although both of them are foreign entities.
-   The system does not govern to body changes, thus self changes as well.
-   whereas, there are certain auto immune processes which are harmful like some diseases and certain types of tumours that are fought by the immune system (both attacks against self) and successful transplants.

So, a new field in AIS emerges baptized: The danger theory, which offers an alternative to self non self discrimination approach. The danger theory stipulates that the natural immune response is done in reaction to a danger not to a foreign entity. In the sense, that the immune system is activated upon the receipt of molecular signals, which indicate damage or stress to the body, rather than pattern matching in the self non self paradigm. Furthermore, the immune response is done in reaction to signals during the intrusion and not by the intrusion itself.

These signals can be mainly of two natures [4, 5]: safe and danger signal. The first indicates that the data to be processed, which represent antigen in the nature, was collected under normal circumstances. While the second signifies potentially anomalous data. The danger theory is a theory for natural immune system that has been adapted to AIS. It can be apprehended by: the Dendritic Cells Algorithm (DCA), which will be presented in the following section.

3 The Dendritic Cell Algorithm

The Dendritic Cell Algorithm (DCA) is a bio-inspired algorithm. It was introduced by Greensmith and al [6] [12] and has demonstrated potential as a classifier for static machine learning data [12,13], as a simple port scan detector under both off-line conditions and in real time experiments [13-20]. The DCA accomplished the task of classification per correlation, fusion of data and filtering [19, 20].

Initial implementations of the DCA have provided promising classification accuracy results on a number of benchmark datasets. However, the basic DCA uses several stochastic variables which make its systematic analysis and functionality understanding very difficult. In order to overcome those problems, a DCA improvement was proposed [21]: the dDCA (deterministic DCA). In this paper, we focus on the new version. Its pseudo code can be found in [21].

The dDCA is based population algorithm in which each agent of the system is represented by a virtual cell, which carries out the signal processing and antigen sampling components. Its inputs take two forms, antigens and signals. The first, are elements which act as a description of items within the problem domain which will be classified. While the second are a set dedicated to monitor some informative data features. This set can be on two kinds: 'safe' and 'danger' signal. At each iteration t, the dDCA inputs consist of the values of the safe signal St, the danger signal Dt and antigens At. The dDCA proceeds on three steps as follows:

1. **Initialization**

    The DC population and algorithm parameters are initialized and initial data are collected.

2. **Signal Processing and Update phase**

All antigens are presented to the DC population so that each DC agent samples only one antigen and proceeds to signal processing. At each step, each single cell$i$ calculates two separate cumulative sums, called $CSMi$ and Ki, and it places them in its own storage data structure. The first is an intermediate signal; named after the biological term "co-stimulatory molecule; it is a measure of the magnitude of the input signal. While the second is the interim context output value. The values CSM and K can be given by eq.(1) and (2) respectively :

$$CSM = St + Dt \qquad (1)$$

$$K = Dt \quad 2St \qquad (2)$$

This process is repeated until all presented antigens have been assigned to the population. At each iteration, incoming antigens undergo the same process. All DCs will process the signals and update their values $CSMi$ and Ki. If the antigens number is greater than the DC number only a fraction of the DCs will sample additional antigens.

The DCi updates and cumulates the values $CSMi$ and Ki until a migration threshold Mi is reached. Once the $CSMi$ is greater than the migration threshold Mi, the cell presents its temporary output Ki as an output entity $Kout$. For all antigens sampled by DCi during its lifetime, they are labeled as normal if $Kout < 0$ and anomalous if $Kout > 0$.

After recording results, the values of $CSMi$ and Ki are reset to zero. All sampled antigens are also cleared. DCi then continues to sample signals and collects antigens, as it was mentioned before, until stopping criterion is met.

3 Aggregation phase

At the end, at the aggregation step, the nature of the response is determined by measuring the number of cells that are fully mature. In the original DCA, antigens analysis and data context evaluation are done by calculating the mature context antigen value (MCAV) average. A representation of completely mature cells can be done. An abnormal MCAV is closer to the value 1. This value of the $MCAV$ is then thresholded to achieve the final binary classification of normal or anomalous. The $K\alpha$ metric, an alternative metric to the $MCAV$, was proposed with the dDCA in [21]. The $K\alpha$ uses the average of all output values $Kout$ as the metric for each antigen type, instead of thresholding them to zero into binary tags.

4   Image Classification

Image classification is the process of recognizing natural groupings or clusters in an image, based on some similarity measures [9]. Distance measurement is generally used for evaluating similarities between patterns. In particular the problem is stated as follows: given N objects, allocate each object to one of K clusters and minimize the sum of squared Euclidean distances between each object and the centre of the cluster belonging to every such allocated object. The clustering problem minimizing Eq. 3 is described as in [9]:

$$f(w,z) = \sum_{i=1}^{N} \sum_{j=1}^{K} wij \, \|xi - zj\|^2 \tag{3}$$

Where K is the number of clusters, N the number of patterns, $x_i(i = 1, \ldots, N)$ the location of the ith pattern and $zj(j = 1, \ldots, K)$ is the center of the jth cluster, to be found by Eq. 4:

$$z_i = \frac{1}{N_j} \sum_{i=1}^{N} w_{ij} x_i \tag{4}$$

Where N_j is the number of patterns in the jth cluster, w_{ij} the association weight of pattern x_i with cluster j, which will be either 1 or 0 (if pattern i is allocated to cluster j; w_{ij} is 1, otherwise 0).

The clustering process, separating the objects into groups (classes), is realized by unsupervised or supervised learning. An unsupervised classification divides all pixels within an image into a corresponding class pixel by pixel. Typically, the only input an unsupervised classification needs is the number of scene classes.

In this paper, the objective is to merge into two classes (vegetation and soil) the pixels that present similar colorimetric and textural characteristics in colour images, in an unsupervised way.

5   The Application of the DCA to Image Classification

An approach based on artificial immune system must describe two aspects:

1.   The projection and models advocating of immune elements in the real world problem.

2.   The use of the appropriate immune algorithm or an approach to solve the problem.

These two aspects are presented in following sections.

5.1   Immune Representation Using the DCA

For sake of clarity, before describing the immune representation, we must depict the features space. In this paper, we consider colour and texture features. They can be defined as follows:

5.1.1 The Feature Space
1. Colour features
Colour moment is a compact representation of the colour feature to characterize a colour image. It has been shown that most of the colour distribution information is captured by the three low-order moments. The first order moment (μ_c) captures the mean colour, the second order moment (σ_c) captures the standard deviation, and the third order moment captures the skewness (θ_c) of colour. These three low-order moments (μ_c, σ_c, θ_c) are extracted from each of the three colour planes (R G B), using the mathematical formulation in table.1.

2. Texture features based on the co-occurrence matrix
In statistical approaches, the textures are described by statistical measures. One commonly applied and referenced method is the co occurrence method [22]. In the co occurrence method, the relative frequencies of gray level pairs of pixels at certain relative displacements are computed and stored in a matrix, the co occurrence matrix P. For G gray levels in the image, P will be of size $G*G$. If G is large, the number of pixel pairs contributing to each element, p_{ij}, in P will be low and the statistical significance poor. Four features that are commonly used, are selected. There are the Entropy (Ent), Energy (Ene) Contrast (Cont) and Homogeneity (Hom). They are given in table 1.

Table 1. Representation of colour and texture features

	Features	Formula
Colour Moments	The first order moment (μc)	$\mu_c = \frac{1}{MN}\sum_{i=1}^{M}\sum_{j=1}^{N} p_{ij}^c$
	The second order moment (σc)	$\sigma_c = \left[\frac{1}{MN}\sum_{i=1}^{M}\sum_{j=1}^{N}\left(p_{ij}^c - i_c\right)^2\right]^{1/2}$
	The third order moment (θc)	$\theta_c = \left[\frac{1}{MN}\sum_{i=1}^{M}\sum_{j=1}^{N}\left(p_{ij}^c - i_c\right)^3\right]^{1/3}$
Texture Features	Entropy	$Ent = -\sum_i \sum_j c(i,j)\log(c(i,j))$
	Energy	$Ene = \sum_i \sum_j c^2(i,j)$
	Contrast	$Cont = \sum_i \sum_j (i-j)^2 c(i,j)$
	Homogeneity	$Hom = \sum_i \sum_j \frac{c(i,j)}{1+|i-j|}$

5.1.2 Immune Elements Modelling
We describe the different elements used by the DCA for image classification:

➤ **Antigens:** In AIS, antigens symbolize the problem to be resolved. In our approach, antigens are pixels set to be classified into one of the two classes: vegetal or soil class. We consider features on a pixel neighbourhood. The pixel context is described by colour and texture features on its neighbourhood.

Both antigens and the features of classes are represented as vectors as the schematically representation shown in Fig. 1.

μ_{cR}	μ_{cG}	μ_{cB}	σ_{cR}	σ_{cG}	σ_{cB}	θ_{cR}	θ_{cG}	θ_{cB}	Ent	Ene	Cont	Hom

Fig. 1. Immune antigen and features classes from colour and texture features. (μc_R , μc_G, μc_B) The red, green and blue colour moment of the first order. (σc_R, σc_G, σc_B) The red, green and blue colour moment of the second order. (θc_R, θc_G, θc_B)The red, green and blue colour moment of the third order. Ent, Ene, Cont and Hom represent respectively the texture characteristics: entropy energy, contrast and homogeneity.

➤ **Signals:** Signals input correspond to the information set about the concerned class. In this context, we suggest that:

1. Danger signal: denote Euclidian distance between a vegetal class features and pixels neighbourhood features.

2. Safe signal: denote Euclidian distance between a soil class features and pixel neighbourhood features.
   The two signals can be given by D_{danger} and D_{safe} as described in Eq. 5 and 6.

$$\text{Danger signal} = D_{danger} = \sqrt{\sum(vegetal - Pixel(i,j))^2} \qquad (5)$$

$$\text{Safe signal} = D_{safe} = \sqrt{\sum(Soil - Pixel(i,j))^2} \qquad (6)$$

5.2 Outline of the Proposed Approach

In this section, we describe the proposed approach in the context of image classification. The approach operates as follows:

1. **Initialization** setting various parameters:
   1.1 Antigens collection: for each pixel having the coordinate (x,y) from an image, we calculate colour and texture features on its neighbourhood.
   1.2 Signals input construction: firstly, we consider image containing only plants vegetation, chosen randomly. We proceed to features extraction and we calculate its colour and texture features. Secondly, we consider soil image and we proceed in the same way. Then, we calculate, D_{danger} and D_{safe}, as given in Eq.5 and 6, in order to construct the danger and the safe signals respectively.

2. Signal Processing and Update phase

2.1 Data Update: we collect pixels with neighbourhood for the antigen set collection. Also, we choose randomly an image from the vegetal library and one from the soil library. Then, we assess the danger D_{danger} and the safe signal D_{safe}, as given in Eq.5 and 6. Both streams are presented to the dDCA. (This process is repeated until the number of pixel present at each time i, is assigned to the DC population).

2.2 Cells cycle: The DC population is presented by a matrix, in which rows correspond to cells. Each row-cell i has a maturation mark $CSMi$ and a temporary output Ki.

2.2.1 For each cell i, we evaluate the maturation mark $CSMi$ as follows:

$$CSMi = D_{danger}\, t + D_{safe}\, t$$

2.2.2 We calculate the cumulatively output signal Ki of the cell i .

$$Ki = D_{danger}\, t \quad 2\, D_{safe}\, t$$

2.2.3 Steps 2.1 and 2.2 are repeated, Once ($CSMi > Mi$), the cell :

- prints a pixel context: $Kout$.

- Is removed from the sampling population.

- Its contents is reset after being logged for the aggregation stage,

- Finally, the cell is returned to the sampling population.

These cycling 2.1 and 2.2 of DCs continue until the stopping condition is met. In our case the same image is represented until the iteration number is met.

3 Aggregation phase

In this phase, we analyse the pixel and we evaluate its context. In this work, we consider the *MCAV* metric (the Mature Context Antigen Value) only, as it generates a more intuitive output score. We calculate the mean mature context pixel value (MCAV: The total fraction of mature DCs presenting said pixel is divided by the total amount of times that the pixel was presented. So, semi mature context indicates that collected pixel is part of vegetal class. While, mature context signifies that the collected pixel is part of soil class.

6 Results and Discussion

One possible strategy for image segmentation is pixels classification. In this context, we propose an image clustering method by appealing to pixels classification.

In our approach, the classifier needs more information about classes in order to give a significant indication about the pixel context. So, we have used a set of images labelled as green plants and others as soil ones. This collection of 60 images composes the library of vegetal images. The samples typically include: green plants images or soil ones, with varying lighting conditions. The collection and the image to be classified are presented during the run time in order to form signals inputs

Obtaining two classes, vegetation and soil, depends significantly on a number of parameters. Some parameters depend directly on the nature of the considered images and their contents and some others depend on the algorithm use.

If we focus on the first kind, we can quote: the characteristic space, the image dimension and the pixel neighbourhood. Some clarifications can be given as follows:

For each pixel, the neighbourhood (Ng) is taken into account. Therefore, we evaluate not only the colour moment of chromatic components within a window size of (7x7) pixels, centred on the pixel of interest, but also the texture information. So, by considering the three colour moments of the RGB space (we obtain 9 elements) and the four texture characteristics of the neighbourhood, each antigen vector has the dimension E = 13 (see fig.1). We used a collection of 150 different vegetal images of dimension 80*80. Some samples are presented in Table. 2.

Concerning the algorithm parameters, we can mention: the cell number, the iteration number and the migration threshold. Hereby, we have considered 100 cells and 100 iterations for one image. The maturation mark is evaluated by $CSMi$. Ideally, for vegetal pixels $CSMi = D1 + D2 = D2$ and for soil pixels $CSMi = D1 + D2 = D1$.

Table 2. Samples of images used in tests

Image 01	Image 02	Image 03	Image 04
Image 05	Image 06	Image 07	Image 08
Image 09	Image 10	Image 11	Image 12
Image 13	Image 14	Image 15	Image 16

To achieve a single step classification, a migration threshold Mi is introduced. So, it takes care of pixels in the overlapping regions containing vegetal and soil pixels. The migration threshold Mi is fixed to one of the input signals. In the sense that if $CSMi$ tends toward one of the two signals, this is implies that one of them tends to zero. So, we can conclude that the pixel has more chance to belong to the one approaching zero.

In order to evaluate the pixel membership to one of two classes, we assess the metric $MCAV$. Each pixel is given a $MCAV$ coefficient value which can be compared with a threshold. Once a threshold is applied, it is then possible to classify the pixel as either 'vegetal' or 'soil'. Therefore the relevant rates of true and false positives can be shown. Especially since the same image is presented at all iterations. To test our system we have used images of different canopy. Their pixels will be the antigen input of the dDCA. The result of the clustering can be shown in Fig 2.

(a)   (b)

Fig. 2. Example of vegetal image: (a) RGB image and (b) image segmented in two classes

We evaluate the performance of the proposed approach in terms of sensitivity, specificity and overall accuracy. Sensitivity, true positive fraction, is the probability that a test is positive, that is to say, the given pixel is part of a vegetal class. Specificity, true negative fraction, is the probability that a test is negative, which means, the given pixel is a part of soil class. Overall accuracy is the probability that a test is correctly performed. The three indices are defined respectively as in (Eq. 7, 8 and 9):

$$Sensitivity = \frac{TP}{TP + FN};$$ (7)

$$Specificity = \frac{TN}{TN + FP}$$ (8)

$$Accuracy = \frac{TP + TN}{TP + TN + FN + FP}$$ (9)

Where: TP, FP, TN, and FN refer respectively to: true positive, false positive, true negative and false negative. Those values are derived from a confusion matrix. The true positive (TP) represents the number of vegetal pixels correctly classified as vegetal pixels while false positive (FP) represents the number of non-vegetal pixels incorrectly classified as vegetal pixels. The true negative (TN) represents the number of non vegetal pixels correctly classified as non vegetal pixels while false negative (FN) represents the number of vegetal pixels incorrectly classified as non vegetal pixels.

Some classification rates, by applying the dDCA to vegetal classification assessed from Table 2 are shown in Table 3.

Also, we have tested the influence of the pixel neighbourhood size and the features of the two spaces on the approach quality in the manner of [10]. The outcome of the influence showed that the pixel neighbourhood Ng of (7×7) provides a lower overall error in both spaces tested. However, we can note that the use of the textural features have decreased again the overall error. This explains our parameters and features spaces choice. The results can be shown in table 4.

Table 3. Qualitative analysis of the proposed approach

Images	Sensitivity	Specificity	Accuracy (%)
Image 1	0,98	0,98	94,03
Image 2	0,94	0,95	93,01
Image 3	0,97	0,96	91,66
Image 4	0,85	0,93	85,08
Image 5	0,90	0,89	89,03
Image 6	0,96	0,95	90,11
Image 7	0,92	0,90	92,15
Image 8	0,97	0,97	93,22
Image 9	0,84	0,89	92,28
Image 10	0,82	0,92	75,12
Image 11	0,93	0,89	90,02
Image 12	0,82	0,88	92,22
Image 13	0,93	0,94	91,23
Image 14	0,90	0,92	93,06
Image 15	0,91	0,88	89,35
Image 16	0,88	0,89	83,02
	Overall Accuracy	89,66 %	

We have compared the dDCA with another clustering algorithm: multilayer perceptron (*MLP*). The algorithms were applied to the same datasets. Their prototypes were also developed in the same language Matlab 9 and executed on the same PC (Pentium 4, 2.3-GHz, Ram 2GB). To make a reasonable comparison between the two algorithms, it was necessary to consider the same features and the same chromatic space. In the experiments, the two algorithms have been compared according to the specificity, the sensitivity and the overall error. The results can be seen in table 5.

Table 4. The Influence of the neighbourhood and the features space on the classification quality

Features Space	Ng	Sensitivity (%)	Specificity (%)	Global Error (%)
RGB colour moments	3×3	90,25	90,45	5,56
	7×7	92,37	93,36	1,98
RGB colour moments + Texture features	3×3	91,38	92,58	2,56
	7×7	96,25	95,54	1,46

Table 5. Results of the comparison of the dDCA and MLP applied to the image clustering

The Approach	Sensitivity (%)	Specificity (%)	Global Error (%)
dDCA	94,25	94,54	1,03
MLP	95,44	95,61	0,8

We can conclude from the results presented above that the system gave encouraging results for both classes vegetal and soil inputs. The use of texture and colour features enhanced the performance of our system and gave recognition accuracy of 90 % in the generalization test.

7 Conclusion and Future Work

In this paper, we have proposed a classification approach based on the danger theory from artificial immune systems to two classes classification. The approach needs some knowledge about the context of data to be classified. It aims to classify pixel representations as: vegetal or soil class.

The proposed approach is applied on covered vegetation images. Besides the use of colours features; we also made use of texture information, which made it robust against noisy pixels. Hence the overall accuracy was increased. We have presented our preliminary results obtained in this way. We are pretty confident about its feasibility.

In future work, we will further investigate the potential influence of other parameters and we will use alternative information signals to measure the correlation, the representations space and the image chromatic space. Moreover, we will apply the proposed method to other classification problems, object recognition, particularly to larger data and other types of knowledge discovery problems.

References

1. Dasgupta, D. (ed.): Artificial Immune Systems and their applications. Springer, Heidelberg (1999)
2. De Castro, L., Timmis, J. (eds.): Artificial Immune Systems: A New Computational Approach, September 2002. Springer, London (2002)
3. Hart, E., Timmis, J.: Application Areas of AIS: The Past, The Present and The Future. In: Jacob, C., Pilat, M.L., Bentley, P.J., Timmis, J.I. (eds.) ICARIS 2005. LNCS, vol. 3627, pp. 483–497. Springer, Heidelberg (2005)

4. Aickelin, U., Bentley, P.J., Cayzer, S., Kim, J., McLeod, J.: Danger theory: The link between AIS and IDS? In: Timmis, J., Bentley, P.J., Hart, E. (eds.) ICARIS 2003. LNCS, vol. 2787, pp. 147–155. Springer, Heidelberg (2003)
5. Aickelin, U., Cayzer, S.: The danger theory and its application to artificial immune systems. In: The 1th International Conference on Artificial Immune Systems (ICARIS 2002), Canterbury, UK, pp. 141–148 (2002), The 1th International Conference on Artificial Immune Systems (ICARIS 2002)
6. Greensmith, J.: The Dendritic Cell Algorith. PhD thesis, School of Computer Science. University of Nottingham (2007)
7. Mitra Tinkuacharya, S. (ed.): Data Mining, Multimedia, Soft Computing and Bioinformatics. John Wiley & Sons, Chichester (2003)
8. Lu, D., Weng, Q.: A survey of image classification methods and techniques for improving classification performance. International Journal of Remote Sensing 28(5) (2007)
9. Berkhin, P.: Survey of clustering data mining techniques. Technical Report, Accrue Software, San Jose, California (2002)
10. Foucher, P., Revollon, P., Vigouroux, B.: Segmentation d'images en couleurs par réseau de neurones: Application au domaine végétal, Actes du Congrées francophone de Vision par Ordinateur (ORASIS), Cahors, France, pp. 309–317 (2001)
11. Clement, A., Vigouroux, B.: Unsupervised segmentation of scenes containing vegetation (Forsythia) and soil by hierarchical analysis of bi-dimensional histograms. Pattern Recognition Letters 24, 1951–1957 (2003)
12. Greensmith, J., Aickelin, U., Cayzer, S.: Introducing Dendritic Cells as a Novel Immune-Inspired Algorithm for Anomaly Detection. In: Jacob, C., Pilat, M.L., Bentley, P.J., Timmis, J.I. (eds.) ICARIS 2005. LNCS, vol. 3627, pp. 153–167. Springer, Heidelberg (2005)
13. Oates, R., Greensmith, J., Aickelin, U., Garibaldi, J., Kendall, G.: The Application of a Dendritic Cell Algorithm to a Robotic Classifier. In: Bersini, H., Carneiro, J. (eds.) ICARIS 2006. LNCS, vol. 4163, pp. 204–215. Springer, Heidelberg (2006)
14. Greensmith, J., Twycross, J., Aickelin, U.: Dendritic Cells for Anomaly Detection. In: IEEE World Congress on Computational Intelligence, Vancouver, Canada, pp. 664–671 (2006)
15. Greensmith, J., Aickelin, U., Twycross, J.: Articulation and clarification of the dendritic cell algorithm. In: Bersini, H., Carneiro, J. (eds.) ICARIS 2006. LNCS, vol. 4163, pp. 404–417. Springer, Heidelberg (2006)
16. Aickelin, U., Greensmith, J., Twycross, J.: Immune System Approaches to Intrusion Detection – A Review. In: Nicosia, G., Cutello, V., Bentley, P.J., Timmis, J. (eds.) ICARIS 2004. LNCS, vol. 3239, pp. 316–329. Springer, Heidelberg (2004)
17. Greensmith, J., Twycross, J., Aickelin, U.: Dendritic cells for anomaly detection. In: IEEE Congress on Evolutionary Computation (2006)
18. Greensmith, J., Aickelin, U., Feyereisl, J.: The DCA-SOMe comparison: A comparative study between two biologically-inspired algorithms. Evolutionary Intelligence: Special Issue on Artificial Immune Systems. accepted for publication (2008)
19. Hoffman, K.: all: Danger theory and collaborative filtering in MANETs. Springer, Heidelberg (2008)
20. Greensmith, J., Aickelin, U., Tedesco, G.: Information Fusion for Anomaly Detection with the Dendritic Cell Algorithm. Journal Information Fusion 11(1) (2010)
21. Greensmith, J., Aickelin, U.: The deterministic dendritic cell algorithm. In: Bentley, P.J., Lee, D., Jung, S. (eds.) ICARIS 2008. LNCS, vol. 5132, pp. 291–302. Springer, Heidelberg (2008)
22. Haralick, R.M., Shanmugam, K., Dinstein, I.: Textural Features for Image Classification. IEEE Transactions on Systems, Man, and Cybernetics 3, 610–621 (1973)

Further Exploration of the Fuzzy Dendritic Cell Method

Zeineb Chelly and Zied Elouedi

LARODEC, Université de Tunis,
Institut Supérieur de Gestion de Tunis,
41 Avenue de la liberté, cité Bouchoucha, 2000 Le Bardo,
Tunisia
zeinebchelly@yahoo.fr, zied.elouedi@gmx.fr

Abstract. A new immune-inspired model of the fuzzy dendritic cell method is proposed in this paper. Our model is based on the function of dendritic cells within the framework of fuzzy set theory and fuzzy c-means clustering. Our purpose is to use fuzzy set theory to smooth the crisp separation between DCs' contexts (semi-mature and mature) since we can neither identify a clear boundary between them nor quantify exactly what is meant by "semi-mature" or "mature". In addition, we aim at generating automatically the extents and midpoints of the membership functions which describe the variables of the model using fuzzy c-means clustering. Hence, we can avoid negative influence on the results when an ordinary user introduces such parameters. Simulations on binary classification databases show that by alleviating the crisp separation between the two contexts and generating automatically the extents of the membership functions, our method produces more accurate results.

Keywords: artificial immune systems, dendritic cells, fuzzy set theory, fuzzy c-means clustering.

1 Introduction

The Dendritic Cell Algorithm (DCA) is an immune inspired algorithm developed by Greensmith in [1]. The DCA which is an abstract model of dendritic cells (DCs) behavior is applied to a wide range of applications. It is also used as a classifier for a static machine learning data set [2], where it was shown that the algorithm can process data classification. Nevertheless, the DCA suffers from some shortcomings as it is sensitive to the data order [3]. Such a drawback is the result of an environment characterized by a crisp separation between normality (semi-mature) and abnormality (mature). If the difference value between these two DCs' context is small, then the context of the DC will be hard to be defined. Thus, it could change the decision of the context affectation. Not considering this case, has a negative effect on classification accuracy when the class of data instances changes over time. Hence, in [4], a first work named the Fuzzy Dendritic Cell Method (FDCM) was developed to solve this issue. FDCM is based on the

P. Liò, G. Nicosia, and T. Stibor (Eds.): ICARIS 2011, LNCS 6825, pp. 419–432, 2011.

fact of smoothing the mentioned crisp separation between the DCs' contexts, since we can neither identify a clear boundary between them nor quantify exactly what is meant by "semi-mature" or "mature". This was handled by the use of fuzzy set theory since it offers the possibility to the systems to deal with the ambiguity that can be found in the definition of a concept or the meaning of a word. However, FDCM suffers from some limitations. In fact, the parameters of the system specifically the extents and midpoints of the membership functions which describe the variables of the system were defined by an ordinary user. Such a drawback influences negatively the results since the user is not an expert in the field. Thus, in this paper, we propose to develop a modified fuzzy dendritic cell method, where we generate automatically the parameters of the system. This can avoid false and uncertain values given by the ordinary user.

In this paper, our new classification technique is based on natural dendritic cells within the framework of fuzzy set theory and adopts the fuzzy c-means clustering approach in order to generate automatically the parameters of the system. In fact, fuzzy c-means (FCM) which is a popular data clustering technique has shown its effectiveness when applied in situations where little prior knowledge exists [5]. An important element in FCM is how to determine the similarity between two objects, so that clusters can be formed from objects with a high similarity to each other. Commonly, distance functions, such as the Manhattan and Euclidian distance functions, are used to determine similarity. A distance function yields a higher value for pairs of objects that are less (or more) similar to one another. Hence, it is important to determine the right distance function which is the most appropriate for the data in hand. Thus, we present our new modified fuzzy dendritic cell method on two versions; each one utilizes a different distance function applied to FCM. The first one uses FCM with the Euclidian distance and the other uses the Manhattan distance. The purpose of our contribution in this work is to improve the classification accuracy. In addition, we aim to show that our method does not depend on the class transitions neither demand any intervention from the user to determine the parameters of the system. Indeed, we try to determine the right distance function which will be the most appropriate to use with the fuzzy clustering method.

This paper is structured as follows: in Section 2, we introduce in brief the fuzzy set theory framework, basics of the fuzzy c-means clustering technique are presented in Section 3, the dendritic cell algorithm will be presented in Section 4. Section 5 describes our modified fuzzy dendritic cell method in detail including its two versions, the experimental setup and results are given in Section 6.

2   Fuzzy Set Theory

Fuzzy set theory was introduced by Zadeh in [6]. It is a mathematical theory that offers the possibility to the systems to deal with the ambiguity that can be found in the definition of a concept or the meaning of a word [7]. Imprecise terms such as "semi-mature" or "mature" can be called fuzziness. Fuzzy sets were introduced as an extension of the classical set theory where a fuzzy set is a set without a clearly defined boundary. It permits the gradual evaluation of the membership of elements in a set; this is supported by the use of "membership functions". Fuzzy sets are based on linguistic variables [8]. A linguistic variable is defined as a linguistic term to represent a concept or a variable of a problem in inaccurate manner such as "low", "medium", "high", etc. The set of values that a linguistic variable can take is called the "term set". Each term set constitutes a fuzzy set in the "universe of discourse" which contains all elements that can come into consideration. A fuzzy set A is defined as follows:

$$A = \{x, \mu_A(x) | x \in X\} \ . \tag{1}$$

where X denotes the universe of discourse and its elements are denoted by x. $\mu_A(x)$ is called the membership function of x in A. The membership function maps each element of X to a membership value between 0 and 1. The membership function μ_A - by which a fuzzy set A is defined - has the form:

$$\mu_A : X \to [0,1] \ . \tag{2}$$

where [0, 1] is the interval of real numbers from 0 to 1, inclusive. The membership function $\mu_A(x)$ quantifies the grade of membership of the elements x to the fundamental set X. An element mapping to the value 0 means that the member is not included in the given set, 1 describes a fully included member. Values strictly between 0 and 1 characterize the fuzzy members. Fuzzy sets are also based on a set of fuzzy rules with C hypotheses (classes) and n attributes. These rules can be written as [9]:

$$R_j : \ \text{if } x_1 \text{ is } A_1^j \dots \text{ and } x_n \text{ is } A_n^j \text{ then Class } C_j, \quad j = 1, \dots, N \ . \tag{3}$$

where x = $(x_1; \dots; x_n)$ is an n-dimensional pattern vector (observations); A_1^i is an antecedent linguistic value such as "low" or "medium" (i=1, ...,n); C_j is a consequent class and N is the number of fuzzy IF..THEN rules. The antecedent part of each rule is specified by a combination of linguistic values, produced by the partitions of the universe of discourse into a set of linguistic terms. In order to draw conclusions from a rule base, we need a mechanism that can produce an output from a collection of IF-THEN rules. This is done using the "compositional rule of inference" which evaluates all the rules and determines their truth values. There are many methods dealing with the inference process such as "Mamdani"[10], "Sum-Prod"[11], etc. Since different fuzzy rules might have different conclusions, all rules should be considered. Thus, fuzzy set theory allows the fact of combining all fuzzy conclusions obtained by the inference process into a single conclusion by a process called "composition" given by (4):

$$\mu_C = max[min(\mu_{X_1}), min(\mu_{X_2}), \dots, min(\mu_{X_N})] \ . \tag{4}$$

where X_i are the observations and μ_C is the single conclusion. From the composition process, a fuzzy value is obtained. This value has to be converted into a crisp value. This mechanism is called the "defuzzification". There are many defuzzification methods such as the maximum method [12] and the centroid method [13] given by the following equation:

$$\frac{\sum_{i=1}^{N} \mu_{(i)} * output(i)}{\sum_{i=1}^{N} \mu_{(i)}} \,. \tag{5}$$

where $\mu_{(i)}$ is the truth value of the result membership function for rule i, output(i) is the value (for rule i) where the result membership function is maximum over the output variable fuzzy set range and N is the number of rules.

3   Fuzzy C-Means Clustering

Earlier clustering methods are based on dividing, in a crisp manner, the data into groups (clusters) in such a way that similar data objects belong to the same cluster and dissimilar data objects to different clusters. However, in real applications there is often no sharp boundary between clusters. Hence, fuzzy clustering is better suited for the data.

Fuzzy c-means (FCM), introduced by Bezdek in [14], is a data clustering technique wherein each data point belongs to a cluster to some degree that is specified by a membership grade. Membership degrees between 0 and 1 are used in fuzzy clustering instead of crisp assignments of the data to clusters. The fact of using FCM allows building a fuzzy inference system by creating membership functions to represent the fuzzy qualities of each cluster. This is because FCM provides a list of cluster centers and several membership grades for each data point. Hence, an automatic generation of the extents and midpoints of membership functions which describe any system's variables could be determined.

Fuzzy c-means algorithm works by assigning membership to each data point corresponding to each cluster center on the basis of distance between the cluster center and the data point. The nearer the data to the cluster center the more its membership towards the particular cluster center. Clearly, the summation of the membership of each data point should be equal to 1. After each iteration, membership and cluster centers are updated according to (6) and (7) [14]:

$$\mu_{ij} = \frac{1}{\sum_{k=1}^{c} \left(\dfrac{d_{ij}}{d_{ik}}\right)^{(2/m-1)}} \,. \tag{6}$$

$$v_j = \frac{\sum_{i=1}^{n} \mu_{ij}^m x_i}{\sum_{i=1}^{n} \mu_{ij}^m} \,. \tag{7}$$

Where n is the number of data points, c denotes the number of fuzzy clusters, μ_{ij} represents the membership of ith data to j^{th} cluster center, v_j represents the jth cluster center, and d_{ij} represents the distance function between datum x_i and the jth cluster center. The parameter m is the fuzziness index; $m \in [1, \infty[$. The fuzzy c-means algorithm main objective is to minimize the following equation:

$$J(U,V) = \sum_{i=1}^{n} \sum_{j=1}^{c} (\mu_{ij})^m d_{ij}^2 \,. \tag{8}$$

The algorithmic steps for fuzzy c-means clustering are the following [14]:

1- Initialize $U = [\mu_{ij}]$ matrix, $U^{(0)}$;
2- At k-Step: calculate the centers vectors $v_i(k) = [v_i]$ with U^k;
3- Update $U^{(k)}$, $U^{(k+1)}$;
4- Repeat step (2) and (3) until the minimum J value is achieved or $\| U^{k+1} - U^k \| < \varepsilon$.

Where k is the iteration step, ε is the termination criterion between $[0, 1]$, U is the fuzzy membership matrix and J is the objective function. FCM's output is a list of cluster centers and several membership grades for each data point.

4   The Dendritic Cell Algorithm

The dendritic cell algorithm was first introduced in [2] and it is based on the behavior of natural dendritic cells. Before describing the function of the algorithm, we introduce in brief the biological principles used in the DCA.

4.1   Introducing Dendritic Cells

Dendritic cells, types of antigen-presenting cells, are sensitive to the concentration of signals (PAMPs, danger, safe) received from their neighborhood. Thus, resulting in three different maturity levels. Immature DCs (iDCs) are the initial maturation state of a DC. Their differentiation depends on the combination of the various signals received leading to a full or partial maturation state. Under the reception of safe signals (SS), iDCs migrate to the semi-mature state (smDCs) and they cause antigens tolerance. iDCs migrate to the mature state (mDCs) if they are more exposed to danger signals (DS) and to pathogenic associated molecular patterns (PAMPs) than safe signals. They present the collected antigens in a dangerous context.

4.2   Abstract View of the Dendritic Cell Algorithm

The DCA introduced in [2] is capable of adhering several signals and antigen to fix the context of each object (DC). The input signals of the system are pre-categorized as "PAMP", "danger" and "safe". In biology, PAMPs definitely indicate an anomalous situation. Danger signals are indicators of abnormality but with lower value of confidence than PAMPs signals. Safe signals are indicators of normality generating a tolerance to the collected antigen. These signals are processed by the algorithm in order to get three output signals: costimulation signal (Csm), semi-mature signal (Semi) and mature signal (Mat).

A migration threshold is incorporated into the DCA in order to determine the lifespan of a DC. As soon as the Csm exceeds the migration threshold; the DC ceases to sample signals and antigens. The DCs differentiation direction is determined by the comparison between cumulative Semi and cumulative Mat. If the cumulative Semi is greater than the cumulative Mat, then the DC goes to semi-mature context (context=0), which implies that the antigen data was collected under normal conditions. Otherwise, it goes to mature context (context=1), signifying a potentially anomalous data item. The nature of the response is determined by measuring the number of DCs that are fully mature and is represented by the value: MCAV (the mature context antigen value). The MCAV is used to assess the degree of anomaly of a given antigen. The closer the MCAV is to 1, the greater the probability that the antigen is anomalous. By applying thresholds at various levels, analysis can be performed to assess the anomaly detection capabilities of the algorithm. Those antigens whose MCAV are greater than the anomalous threshold are classified into the anomalous category, while the others are classified into the normal category.

5   The Modified Fuzzy Dendritic Cell Method

According to [3], the DCA suffers from some shortcomings as it is sensitive to the data order. Once the context changes multiple times in a quick succession (data are randomized between the classes), the DCA gives bad classification results. This is due to an environment characterized by a crisp evaluation in its context assessment phase. This problem was partially solved in [4] by proposing a fuzzy dendritic cell method (FDCM).

FDCM is based on the idea of smoothing the crisp separation between the two contexts resulting in the achievement of better classification results. Nevertheless, these good results were only noticed in case of disordered contexts. Thus, FDCM presents some limitations. In fact, FDCM involves ordinary users in the determination of the system parameters specifically in the determination of the extents and midpoints of the membership functions which describe the variables of the system. Hence, it influences negatively the classification results. In this new modified fuzzy dendritic cell method (MFDCM), the fuzzy process consists in the definition of a new model of FDCM taking into account the fact of alleviating the crisp assessment task as well as generating automatically the extents and midpoints of the systems' parameters. Figure 1 shows the fuzzy procedure which is composed of five main steps.

5.1   Fuzzy System Inputs-Output Variables

In order to describe each context of each object, we use linguistic variables. Two inputs (one for each context) and one output are defined. The semi-mature context and the mature context denoted respectively C_s and C_m are considered as the input variables to the fuzzy system.

The final state "maturity" of a DC (object), S_{mat}, is chosen as the output variable. All the system's inputs and output are defined using fuzzy set theory [4].

$$C_s = \{\mu_{C_s}(c_{s_j})/c_{s_j} \in X_{C_s}\} \ . \tag{9}$$

$$C_m = \{\mu_{C_m}(c_{m_j})/c_{m_j} \in X_{C_m}\} \ . \tag{10}$$

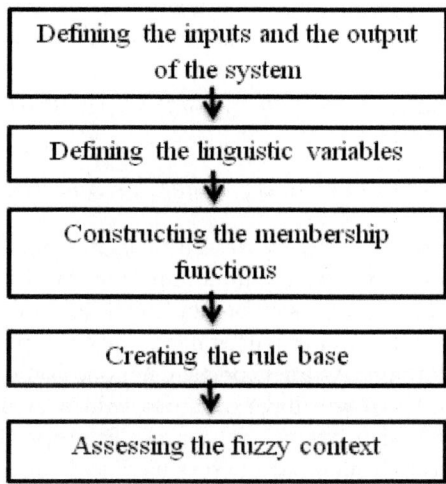

Fig. 1. Five steps of the fuzzy process

$$S_{mat} = \{S_{mat}(s_{mat_j})/s_{mat_j} \in X_{S_{mat}}\} \ . \tag{11}$$

where c_{s_j}, c_{m_j} and s_{mat_j} are, respectively, the elements of the discrete universe of discourse X_{C_s}, X_{C_m} and $X_{S_{mat}}$. μ_{C_s}, μ_{C_m} and $\mu_{S_{mat}}$ are, respectively, the corresponding membership functions.

5.2   Linguistic Variables

As mentioned previously, the basic tools of fuzzy set theory are linguistic variables. The term set $T(S_{mat})$ interpreting S_{mat} which is a linguistic variable that constitutes the final state of maturity of a DC, could be:

$$T(S_{mat}) = \{Semi - mature, Mature\} \ . \tag{12}$$

Each term in $T(S_{mat})$ is characterized by a fuzzy subset in a universe of discourse $X_{S_{mat}}$. Semi-mature might be interpreted as an object (data instance) collected under safe circumstances, reflecting a normal behavior and Mature as an object collected under dangerous circumstances, reflecting an anomalous behavior. Similarly, the input variables C_s and C_m are interpreted as linguistic variables with:

$$T(Q) = \{Low, Medium, High\} \ . \tag{13}$$

where $Q = C_s$ and C_m respectively.

5.3   Fuzzy and Membership Functions Construction

In order to specify the range of each linguistic variable, we have run the DCA and we have recorded both semi-mature and mature values which reflect the (Semi) and (Mat) outputs generated by the DCA. Then, we picked up the minimum and maximum values of each of the two generated values to fix the borders of the range. The range of the output variable is determined as follows[4]:

$$min(range(S_{mat})) = min(min(range[C_m]), min(range[C_s])) \ . \qquad (14)$$

$$max(range(S_{mat})) = max(max(range[C_m]), max(range[C_s])) \ . \qquad (15)$$

Once the range of the output S_{mat} is determined, it seems important now to fix the extents and midpoints of each membership function. In [4], these parameters were determined by an ordinary user. In fact, involving ordinary users or experts to determine these parameters influences negatively the results since the user is not an expert in the domain. As for experts, each one could propose his/her own parameters. As a result, we will have different values, which could give rise to some confusion about which ones are the most appropriate to our system. To overcome these limitations, such parameters have to be automatically generated by the system. Hence, our choice can be focused on the use of the fuzzy c-means clustering algorithm detailed in Section 3. To the recorded list of (Mat) and (Semi) values, we apply FCM. It helps to build a fuzzy inference system by creating membership functions to represent the fuzzy qualities of each cluster. Each cluster reflects a membership function. The number of clusters is relative to the number of the membership functions of each variable (inputs and output). The output of this phase is a list of cluster centers and several membership grades for each data point (object). Thus, the extents and midpoints of the membership functions which describe the system's variables are automatically determined.

An important point in FCM is how to determine the similarity between two objects, so that clusters can be formed from objects with a high similarity to each other. The most straightforward way of computing distances between objects in a multi-dimensional space (the recorded list of Mat and Semi values) is to compute the Manhattan or Euclidean distance. These distances are the best descriptors of similarity for our case. A distance function yields a higher value for pairs of objects that are less (or more) similar to one another. Hence, it is important to determine the right distance function which is the most appropriate for the data in hand. We therefore present our new modified fuzzy dendritic cell classification method on two versions; each one utilizes a different distance function applied to the FCM. The first one uses fuzzy c-means clustering with the Euclidian distance (MFDCM-Euc) and the other uses fuzzy c-means clustering with the Manhattan distance (MFDCM-Man).

MFDCM-Euc. As stated previously, the choice of the similarity metric in FCM is important since it influences the belongings of data to each cluster. MFDCM-Euc is based on the Euclidian distance applied to the FCM where the distance function d_{ij} is defined as follows:

$$d_{ij} = \sqrt{|x_{i1} - v_{j1}|^2 + |x_{i2} - v_{j2}|^2 + \ldots + |x_{ip} - v_{jp}|^2} \ . \qquad (16)$$

MFDCM-Man. The motivation of MFDCM-Man is the use of the Manhattan distance in the FCM instead of the Euclidian distance. The Manhattan distance is defined as follows:

$$d_{ij} = |x_{i1} - v_{j1}| + |x_{i2} - v_{j2}| + \ldots + |x_{ip} - v_{jp}| \ . \tag{17}$$

In the empirical tests, we will show which version is the best for our MFDCM.

5.4 The Fuzzy Rule Sets Description

A knowledge base, comprising rules, is built to support the fuzzy inference. The different rules of the fuzzy system are extracted from the information reflecting the effect of each input signal on the state of a dendritic cell which is the following:

- Safe signals: in increase in value is a probable indicator of normality. High values of the safe signal can cancel out the effects of both PAMPs and DS.
- Danger signals: in increase in value is a probable indicator of damage, but there is less certainty than with a PAMP signal.
- PAMPs: in increase in value is a definite indicator of anomaly.
- Inflammation: has the effect of amplifying the other three categories of input signals, but is not sufficient to cause any effect on DCs when used in isolation.

From the list above, we can generate the following set of rules where all the mentioned signals are taken into account implicitly in the fuzzy system [4].

1. If (C_m is Low) and (C_s is Low) then (S_{mat} is Mature)
2. If (C_m is Low) and (C_s is Medium) then (S_{mat} is Semi-mature)
3. If (C_m is Low) and (C_s is High) then (S_{mat} is Semi-mature)
4. If (C_m is Medium) and (C_s is Low) then (S_{mat} is Mature)
5. If (C_m is Medium) and (C_s is Medium) then (S_{mat} is Semi-mature)
6. If (C_m is Medium) and (C_s is High) then (S_{mat} is Semi-mature)
7. If (C_m is High) and (C_s is Low) then (S_{mat} is Mature)
8. If (C_m is High) and (C_s is Medium) then (S_{mat} is Mature)
9. If (C_m is High) and (C_s is High) then (S_{mat} is Mature)

Let us consider Rule (2) as an example: if the C_m input is set to its first membership function "Low" and the second input C_s to its second membership function "Medium", then the "Semi-mature" context of the output S_{mat} is assigned. This could be explained by the effect of the high values of SS (which lead to the semi-mature context) that cancel out the effects of both PAMPs and DS (which lead to the mature context). The same reasoning is affected to the rest of the rules.

5.5 The Fuzzy Context Assessment

Our MFDCM is based on the "Mamdani" composition method and the "centroid" defuzzification mechanism seen in Section 2. Once the inputs are fuzzified and the output (centroid value) is generated, the cell context has to be fixed by comparing the output value to the middle of the S_{mat} range. In fact, if the centroid value generated is greater than the middle of the output range then the final context of the object is "Mature" indicating that the collected antigen may be anomalous; else the antigen collected is likely to be normal[4].

6   Experiments

6.1   Experimental Setup

We have developed our programs in Matlab V7.1 for the evaluation of our MFD-CMs versions: MFDCM-Euc and MFDCM-Man. Different experiments are performed using two-class data sets from [15] described in Table 1.

Table 1. Description of databases

Database	Ref	♯ instances	♯ attributes
Mammographic Mass	MM	961	6
Pima Indians Diabetes	PID	768	8
Blood Transfusion Service Center	BTSC	748	5
Wisconsin Breast Cancer	WBC	700	9
Haberman's Survival	HS	306	4
SPECTF Heart	SPECTF	267	44

Data items with the largest standard deviation form the DS. To generate concentrations for SS and PAMPs, the attribute with the next greatest standard deviation is chosen. In spite of incorporating inflammation signals into the model, they are not used in our experiments, as no obvious mapping is available. Antigen is represented in its simplest form as the identification number of a data item within the database. All featured parameters are derived from empirical immunological data.

In [3] it was shown that the DCA is sensitive to the data order. Hence, when the class of data instances changes multiple times (data randomized between classes); the DCA produces bad classification results unlike when applied to an ordered data set (all class 1 items followed by all class 2 items). Trying to handle this limitation, FDCM gave better results but only in case of disordered contexts (items not ordered between the two classes) [4]. Hence, with our new MFDCM, our experimentations are based on randomizing the data more and more between the classes and to notice the effect of this randomization on our new MFDCM. We try to show that the performance of our MFDCM does neither depend on such transitions nor on ordered data sets contrary to the DCA and FDCM.

In the different experimentations realized, the order of the data items varies according to experiments. Experiment 1 uses all class 1 items followed by all class 2 items. The rest of the experiments uses data from class 1 and class 2 that is randomized once, then 20 times, then 60, 70, 90, 120, 140, 160, 200, and finally 300 times successively. Each experiment is performed 20 times. The fact of increasing the number of randomization (R) from one experiment to another lead to a database randomized more between the two classes, so to successive transitions (class of data instances changes multiple times). We also have to mention that randomizing the data n times is based on checking each time that the database at iteration n + 1 is more randomized than the database generated in the previous iteration n as well as more randomized then all the previous iterations (n-1, n-2, n-3, etc.). Hence we obtain a database where the class of data instances changes multiple times in a quick succession. Each run samples each data item 10 times, giving 9610, 7680, 7480, 7000, 3060 and 2670 antigen presentations per run for all the mentioned data sets. To perform anomaly detection, a threshold which is automatically generated from the data must be applied to the MCAVs (defined in Section 4.2). The distribution of data between class one and class two is used and reflects the potential danger rate. The calculation displayed in Equation 18 shows this process. In this equation, an is the number of anomalous data items, tn is the total number of data items and at is the derived anomaly threshold.

$$at = \frac{an}{tn} \ . \tag{18}$$

Items exceeding the threshold are classified as class 2, with lower valued antigen labeled as class 1. As for the parameters of the FCM algorithm, the fuzziness parameter was chosen m=2.

In order to measure the performance of our MFDCM, we have based our evaluation on accuracy. In fact, the accuracy of a classification method is determined by measuring the number of instances it, correctly, classifies among the total number of testing instances presented to the classifier. Hence, we will use the Percent of Correct Classification (PCC) as a principal evaluation criteria:

$$PCC = \frac{\text{number of well classified instances}}{\text{total number of classified instances}} * 100 \ . \tag{19}$$

6.2   Results and Discussion

Let us remind that the aim of our method is to improve the classification accuracy in the case of contexts' change as well as in ordered data sets. Hence, in this Section, we try to show the effectiveness of our MFDCM as well as to select the best clustering distance supported by the fuzzy c-means algorithm. For that, we will compare the two MFDCM's versions: MFDCM-Euc and MFDCM-Man, and the one giving better results will be compared to the DCA which is the non-fuzzy case and FDCM.

Results for MFDCM-Euc and MFDCM-Man. So far, in this paper, we have introduced two versions of our MFDCM: MFDCM-Euc applying FCM with the Euclidian distance and MFDCM-Man applying FCM with the Manhattan distance. Table 2 presents a comparison between these two techniques in terms of Percent of Correct Classification (PCC). From Table 2, we conclude that results provided by our MFDCM-Euc are notably better than the ones provided by MFDCM-Man, in all databases.

For instance, by applying the MFDCM-Euc to the SPECTF Heart database and with the variation of the different values of R, the PCC varies from 98,5% to 99,62%. Whereas, with MFDCM-Man, the PCC varies from 79,4% to 87,26%. Furthermore, MFDCM-Euc gives better results when the SPECTF Heart data

Table 2. Experimental measures PCC (%) (E1=Experiment 1, R=Randomized)

Database	Method	E1	R1	R20	R60	R70	R90	R120	R140	R160	R200	R300
MM	MFDCM-Euc	99,89	96,67	99,58	99,37	96,67	98,43	96,98	99,37	97,08	98,85	98,12
	MFDCM-Man	96,77	93,23	93,13	93,86	91,57	96,14	97,6	92,61	85,43	96,04	94,69
PID	MFDCM-Euc	97,52	98,69	99,86	99,86	98,04	99,86	96,35	98,43	97,13	96,61	98,95
	MFDCM-Man	80,07	68,75	74,47	82,68	70,05	95,83	73,04	92,96	66,01	84,63	93,09
BTSC	MFDCM-Euc	99,59	98,66	98,39	97,86	98,66	97,32	97,45	98,12	99,06	97,32	99,73
	MFDCM-Man	76,2	97,32	76,2	76,2	76,2	76,2	76,2	76,2	77,27	76,2	76,2
WBC	MFDCM-Euc	98,28	98,14	97,28	97,57	98,57	99,85	98,85	99,42	98,57	98,57	99,71
	MFDCM-Man	66,42	93,57	65,71	92,42	95,14	98,28	92,28	92	58,14	78,85	55,85
HS	MFDCM-Euc	99,67	97,05	99,34	99,01	98,69	97,71	99,34	98,36	98,69	98,03	98,36
	MFDCM-Man	81,69	92,48	96,73	96,4	97,38	91,5	95,75	96,07	92,15	94,44	94,44
SPECTF	MFDCM-Euc	99,62	98,5	98,5	98,5	98,87	99,25	98,5	99,62	99,25	99,62	98,87
	MFDCM-Man	96,66	84,26	81,61	81,27	81,27	87,26	81,64	79,4	79,4	79,77	79,77

set is ordered (E1), the PCC reaches a value of 99,62%. However, with MFDCM-Man, the PCC takes a value of 96,66%.

From the obtained results, we notice that when the context changes multiple times in a quick succession as well as in case of an ordered database (E1), it is more appropriate to apply MFDCM-Euc than the MFDCM-Man since the former produces more accurate results in terms of classification accuracy. Thus, in what follows, we continue our experimentation analysis with MFDCM-Euc.

Results for MFDCM-Euc, FDCM and DCA. Previous examinations with DCA, in [2], show that the misclassifications occur exclusively at the transition boundaries. Hence, DCA makes more mistakes when the context changes multiple times in a quick succession (different values of R) unlike when the data is ordered between the classes. This problem was partially solved, in [4], with FDCM via the new fuzzy context assessment phase. However, FDCM gives bad results in case of ordered contexts, which could be explained by involving the ordinary user in the determination of the system's parameters. To handle the drawbacks of DCA and FDCM, we developed our MFDCM-Euc which is based on generating automatically the parameters of the fuzzy inference system. Our new MFDCM-Euc gives better classification results in both ordered and disordered contexts when compared to the DCA and FDCM. This is confirmed by the results presented in Table 3.

From Table 3, it is clearly noticed that our MFDCM-Euc has given good results in terms of PCC. In fact, by randomizing the data between classes (increasing the value of R), the PCCs of our MFDCM-Euc are better than those given by DCA and FDCM. This remark also includes the case of an ordered database (E1). For instance, by applying our MFDCM-Euc to the Haberman's Survival (HS) database and with the variation of the different values of R, the PCC varies from 97,05% to 99,34%. In case of an ordered database, the PCC reaches a value of 99,67%. Whereas, when applying the DCA to the same database and with

Table 3. Experimental measures PCC (%) (E1=Experiment 1, R=Randomized)

Database	Method	E1	R1	R20	R60	R70	R90	R120	R140	R160	R200	R300
	DCA	98,43	62,85	62,85	62,85	62,85	62,85	62,85	62,85	62,85	62,85	62,85
MM	FDCM	62,85	97,19	95,63	96,67	94,48	97,5	96,15	95,42	97,09	96,77	96,36
	MFDCM-Euc	99,89	96,67	99,58	99,37	96,67	98,43	96,98	99,37	97,08	98,85	98,12
	DCA	96,35	98,82	96,48	94,14	98,56	95,31	96,35	96,61	96,35	96,22	96,09
PID	FDCM	98,05	96,87	97	96,48	97,79	95,83	96,74	98,31	96,22	95,57	97
	MFDCM-Euc	97,52	98,69	99,86	99,86	98,04	99,86	96,35	98,43	97,13	96,61	98,95
	DCA	91,71	93,31	91,44	93,98	90,1	91,57	93,18	92,24	91,71	91,57	91,44
BTSC	FDCM	48,66	48,52	98,53	96,8	95,45	96,25	96,25	98,26	98,4	94,92	97,33
	MFDCM-Euc	99,59	98,66	98,39	97,86	98,66	97,32	97,45	98,12	99,06	97,32	99,73
	DCA	99,42	91	89,71	91,14	90,42	90,71	89,71	90,71	91	90,85	90,57
WBC	FDCM	98	97,57	98,57	99,57	96,57	97,57	99,28	97,57	97,14	97,14	99
	MFDCM-Euc	98,28	98,14	97,28	97,57	98,57	99,85	98,85	99,42	98,57	98,57	99,71
	DCA	83	17,32	17,32	17,64	16,99	17,32	16,99	16,99	17,64	16,66	16,66
HS	FDCM	29	82,35	92,15	90,85	82,02	93,8	92,48	92,15	89,54	92,15	91,83
	MFDCM-Euc	99,67	97,05	99,34	99,01	98,69	97,71	99,34	98,36	98,69	98,03	98,36
	DCA	93,63	91,76	91,01	91,76	91,38	92,13	91,38	90,63	90,63	89,13	88,01
SPECTF	FDCM	79,4	79,4	92,5	94,38	95,13	94,75	93,63	94,75	94,75	94,75	94,38
	MFDCM-Euc	99,62	98,5	98,5	98,5	98,87	99,25	98,5	99,62	99,25	99,62	98,87

the variation of R values, the PCC varies from 16,66% to 17,64% and in case of an ordered contexts it takes a value of 83%. This high value is explained by the appropriate use of this algorithm only in cases of ordered databases. From these results, we can conclude that our MFDCM-Euc produces better classification results than DCA in both cases: ordered and disordered contexts. Indeed, by applying the FDCM to the same database, the PCC varies from 82,02% to 93,8% with the variation of the different values of R and in case of an ordered contexts it takes a value of 29%. This low value is explained by the use of arbitrary midpoints and extents for the system's membership functions. Again, we can easily remark that MFDCM-Euc generates better results than those of the FDCM with the variation of the different values of R as well as in case of an ordered database.

7   Conclusion and Future Works

In this paper, we have developed a modified version of the standard fuzzy dendritic cell method. Our method aims at smoothing more the crisp separation between the two contexts and generating automatically the parameters of the system leading to better results in terms of classification accuracy. As future work, we intend to further explore this new instantiation of our MFDCM by the use of the type-2 fuzzy set theory.

References

1. Greensmith, J.: The Dendritic Cell Algorithm. PhD Thesis, University of Nottingham (2007)
2. Greensmith, J., Aickelin, U., Cayzer, S.: Introducing dendritic cells as a novel immune-inspired algorithm for anomaly detection. In: Jacob, C., Pilat, M.L., Bentley, P.J., Timmis, J.I. (eds.) ICARIS 2005. LNCS, vol. 3627, pp. 153–167. Springer, Heidelberg (2005)
3. Aickelin, U., Greensmith, J.: The Deterministic Dendritic Cell Algorithm. In: 7th International Conference on Artificial Immune Systems, Phuket, hailand, pp. 291–302 (2008)
4. Chelly, Z., Elouedi, Z.: FDCM: A fuzzy dendritic cell method. In: Hart, E., McEwan, C., Timmis, J., Hone, A. (eds.) ICARIS 2010. LNCS, vol. 6209, pp. 102–115. Springer, Heidelberg (2010)
5. Basbuska, R.: Fuzzy modeling for control. Kluwer Academic Publishers, Boston (1998)
6. Zadeh, L.: Fuzzy Sets. Information and Control 8, 338–353 (1965)
7. Zimmermann, J.: Fuzzy Set Theory and Its Applications. European Journal of Operational Research 1, 227–228 (1996)
8. Zadeh, L.: The Concept of a Linguistic Variable and its Application to Approximate Reasoning I. Information Sciences 8, 199–251 (1975)
9. Ishibuchi, H., Nakashima, T.: Effect of rule weights in fuzzy rule-based classification systems. IEEE Transactions on Fuzzy Systems 9, 506–515 (2001)
10. Mamdani, H., Assilian, S.: An experiment in linguistic synthesis with a fuzzy logic controller. International Journal of Man-Machine Studies 7, 1–13 (1975)
11. Mizumoto, M.: Fuzzy controls by product-sum gravity-method. Fuzzy Sets and Systems, c1.1–c1.4 (1990)
12. Lee, C.: Fuzzy logic in control systems: Fuzzy logic controller - Parts 1 and 2. IEEE Transactions on Systems, Man and Cybernetics 2, 404–435 (1990)
13. Broekhoven, E., Baets, D.: Fast and accurate center of gravity defuzzification of fuzzy system outputs defined on trapezoidal fuzzy partitions. Fuzzy Sets and Systems 157, 904–918 (2006)
14. Bezdek, J.: Pattern Recognition with Fuzzy Objective Function Algorithms. Plenum Press, New York (1981)
15. UCI machine learning repository, http://archive.ics.uci.edu

Author Index